Management
Information Systems

Moving Business Forward

Fourth Edition

KELLY RAINER

BRAD PRINCE

HUGH WATSON

with contributions by
Alina M. Chircu, Bentley University
Marco Marabelli, Bentley University

WILEY

VICE PRESIDENT AND DIRECTOR	George Hoffman
DIRECTOR	Veronica Visentin
EXECUTIVE EDITOR	Darren Lalonde
ASSISTANT DEVELOPMENT EDITOR	Emma Townsend-Merino
SENIOR CONTENT MANAGER	Dorothy Sinclair
SENIOR PRODUCTION EDITOR	Jane Lee Kaddu
SENIOR MARKETING MANAGER	Chris DeJohn
ASSOCIATE PRODUCT DESIGNER	Wendy Ashenberg
SENIOR DESIGNER	Maureen Eide
SENIOR PHOTO EDITOR	Billy Ray
COVER DESIGNER	Maureen Eide
PRODUCTION MANAGEMENT SERVICES	Thomson Digital
COVER CREDIT	Aleksandarvelasevic © Getty Images

This book was set in Source Sans Pro 9.5/12.5 by Thomson Digital and printed and bound by CPI Group (UK) Ltd, Croydon, CR0 4YY.

This book is printed on acid free paper.

Founded in 1807, John Wiley & Sons, Inc., has been a valued source of knowledge and understanding for more than 200 years, helping people around the world meet their needs and fulfill their aspirations. Our company is built on a foundation of principles that include responsibility to the communities we serve and where we live and work. In 2008, we launched a Corporate Citizenship Initiative, a global effort to address the environmental, social, economic, and ethical challenges we face in our business. Among the issues we are addressing are carbon impact, paper specifications and procurement, ethical conduct within our business and among our vendors, and community and charitable support. For more information, please visit our Web site: www.wiley.com/go/citizenship.

ISBN-13: 978-1-119-58861-0

The inside back cover will contain printing identification and country of origin if omitted from this page. In addition, if the ISBN on the back cover differs from the ISBN on this page, the one on the back cover is correct.

Library of Congress Cataloging-in-Publication Data
Names: Rainer, R. Kelly, Jr., 1949-
Title: Management information systems / R. Kelly Rainer, Jr., Brad Prince, Hugh Watson.
Description: Fourth edition. | Hoboken, NJ : John Wiley & Sons, Inc., 2017. | Includes bibliographical references and index.
Identifiers: LCCN 2016034800 (print) | LCCN 2016035388 (ebook) | ISBN 9781119588610 (paperback : acid-free paper) | ISBN 9781118890431 (pdf) | ISBN 9781119321095 (epub)
Subjects: LCSH: Management information systems.
Classification: LCC HD30.213 .R35 2017 (print) | LCC HD30.213 (ebook) | DDC 658.4/038011--dc23
LC record available at https://lccn.loc.gov/2016034800

10 9 8 7 6 5 4 3 2 1

Dear Student,

Why are you here? We are not asking you a philosophical question—that is a different course. We are asking, "Why are you about to spend an entire term learning about information systems? Why are you—an accounting major, or a marketing or management major—being required to study this topic?" You may be asking, "What's in IT for me?" The short answer is that "IT's About Business," and the longer answer is the goal of this book.

Information systems are making the world a very small place and are contributing to rapidly increasing global competition. As a result, organizations are constantly trying to find ways to gain a competitive advantage—by achieving operational excellence, developing new products and services, developing new business models, providing superb customer service, improving decision making, and so on. It should be obvious, then, that an introductory course in information systems is critically important for success in your chosen career.

Rapid advances in information systems mean that, as business students, change will be the only constant you will encounter in today's dynamic digital business environment. We wrote this book for business students of all majors who will soon become business professionals. We have three goals in mind:

1. To help you be immediately successful when you join your organization

2. To help you understand the importance of information systems for individuals, organizations, and society as a whole

3. To enable you to become informed users of your organization's information systems

To accomplish these goals, we have tried to provide the essential, relevant knowledge that you need to understand to effectively use information systems in your careers.

The way we propose to do this is by keeping you *actively involved* in the material. Every section of the chapters has an activity that asks you to do something beyond just reading the textbook that will help you see why the content is useful for your future business career.

We hope you will enjoy this active approach and successfully complete the course with a richer understanding of what's in IT for you.

KELLY RAINER, BRAD PRINCE, AND HUGH WATSON

To The Instructor

Dear Instructor,

We are like you. All of us who teach the introductory course in information systems realize that it is difficult for students to understand the importance and relevance of the topics in the course. As a result, students often memorize the content just before the exam, and then forget it as soon as the exam is over. We all want to engage students at a much deeper level. We know that the best way to accomplish this objective is through *hands-on active learning,* leading to *increased student engagement* in our course content.

Accordingly, active learning and student engagement are key principles of our new book. We recognize the need to actively involve students in problem solving, creative thinking, and capitalizing on opportunities. Every section of every chapter includes extensive hands-on exercises, activities, and mini-cases. End-of-chapter material also includes exercises that require students to use software application tools. Through these activities, we enable students to understand how to *do* something with the concepts they learn, such as meet business goals using information systems, configure products, and use spreadsheets and databases to facilitate problem solving.

The preface on the next page further outlines the goals, features, and support material provided with our new text. We hope you will enjoy teaching with this approach!

KELLY RAINER, BRAD PRINCE, AND HUGH WATSON

Preface

Chapter Organization

Each chapter contains the following elements:

- **Chapter Outline:** Lists the major concepts covered in each chapter.
- **Learning Objectives:** Provide an overview of the key learning goals that students should achieve after reading the chapter.
- **Chapter-Opening Case:** A short case that focuses on a small or start-up company that is using information systems to solve a business problem. Cases in introductory information systems textbooks typically involve very large organizations. In contrast, our chapter-opening cases demonstrate that small and start-up companies also have business problems that they address using information systems. Students will see that small firms usually have to be quite creative in building and implementing IS solutions, because they do not have MIS departments or large budgets. These small-business cases also add an entrepreneurial flavor to each chapter for students who are planning to start their own businesses.
- **Apply the Concept Activities:** This book's unique pedagogical structure is designed to keep students actively engaged with the course material. Reading material in each chapter subsection is immediately followed by an "Apply the Concept" activity that is directly related to a chapter objective. These activities include links to online videos and articles and other hands-on activities that require students to immediately apply what they have learned. Via WileyPLUS, instructors can assign a section of text along with an Apply the Concept activity. Each Apply the Concept has the following elements:
  - Background (places the activity in the context of relevant reading material)
  - Activity (a hands-on activity that students carry out)
  - Deliverable (various tasks for students to complete as they perform the activity)
- **IT's About Business:** Short cases that demonstrate real-world applications of IT to business. Each case is accompanied by questions relating the case to concepts covered in the chapter. Icons relate these boxes to the specific functional areas.
- **IT's Personal:** Sprinkled throughout the chapters, these short vignettes explain the relevance of MIS concepts to students' daily lives.
- **Before You Go On:** End-of-section reviews prompt students to pause and test their understanding of concepts before moving on to the next section.

- **Examples:** Interspersed throughout the text, these highlight the use (and misuse) of information systems by real-world organizations, thereby illustrating the concepts discussed in the chapter.
- **What's in IT for Me?:** A unique end-of-chapter summary that demonstrates the relevance of each key chapter topic to different functional areas, including accounting, finance, marketing, production/operations management, human resources management, and management information systems. This cross-functional focus makes the book accessible for students from any major.
- **Summary:** Keyed to the Learning Objectives listed at the beginning of the chapter, the summary enables students to review major concepts covered.
- **Discussion Questions and Problem-Solving Activities:** Provide practice through active learning. These exercises are hands-on opportunities to apply the concepts discussed in the chapter.
- **Collaboration Exercises:** Team exercises that require students to take on different functional roles and collaborate to solve business problems using Google Drive. These exercises allow students to get first-hand experience solving business problems using Cloud-based tools while also experiencing an authentic business team dynamic.
- **Closing Cases:** Each chapter concludes with two cases about business problems faced by actual companies and how they used IS to solve those issues. The cases are broken down into three parts: a description of the problem, an overview of the IS solution implemented, and a presentation of the results of the implementation. Each case is followed by discussion questions, so that students can further explore the concepts presented in the case.
- **Spreadsheet Activity:** Every chapter includes a hands-on spreadsheet project that requires students to practice their Excel skills within the context of the chapter material. WileyPLUS Learning Space includes an Excel Lab Manual for students who need introductory coverage or review.
- **Database Activity:** Every chapter includes a hands-on database project that requires students to practice their Access skills while using concepts learned in the chapter. WileyPLUS Learning Space includes an Access Lab Manual for students who need introductory coverage or review.
- **Internship Activity:** Every chapter includes an Internship Activity which presents a business problem found in one of four recurring industries (healthcare, banking, manufacturing, and retail.) STUDENTS are directed to various software demos that provide useful tools for addressing the business problem. Then the students must act as interns and apply

the concepts they learned in the chapter to provide a solution to the business problem.

- **Glossary:** A study tool that highlights vocabulary within the chapters and facilitates studying.

Key Features

Student Engagement As discussed in the note addressed to instructors at the beginning of this preface, one of the chief goals of this text is to engage students at a level beyond recognition of key terms. We believe the best way to achieve this goal is through hands-on, active learning that will lead to increased student engagement with the course and its content.

Accordingly, every section of every chapter provides resources that actively involve students in problem solving, creative thinking, and capitalizing on opportunities. Every chapter includes extensive hands-on exercises, activities, and mini-cases, including exercises that require students to solve business problems using Excel and Access.

Cross-Functional Approach We emphasize the importance of information systems by calling attention in every chapter to how that chapter's topic relates to each business major. Icons guide students to relevant issues for their specific functional area—accounting (ACC), fi nance (FIN), marketing (MKT), production operations management (POM), human resources management (HRM), and management information systems (MIS). Chapters conclude with a detailed summary (entitled "What's in IT for Me?") of how key concepts in the chapter relate to each functional area.

ACCT **FIN** **MKT** **POM** **HRM** **MIS**

Diversified and Unique Examples from Different Industries Extensive use of vivid examples from large corporations, small businesses, and government and not-for-profit organizations enlivens the concepts from the chapter. Th e examples illustrate everything from the capabilities of information systems, to their cost and justification and the innovative ways that corporations are using IS in their operations. Small businesses have been included in recognition of the fact that many students will work for small-to mid-sized companies, and some will even start their own small business. In fact, some students may already be working at local businesses, and the concepts they are learning in class can be readily observed or put into practice in their part-time jobs. Each chapter constantly highlights the integral connection between business and IS. This connection is especially evident in the chapter-opening and closing cases, the "IT's About Business" boxes, and the highlighted examples.

Successes and Failures Many textbooks present examples of the successful implementation of information systems, and our book is no exception. However, we go one step beyond by also providing numerous examples of IS failures, in the context of lessons that can be learned from such failures. Misuse of information systems can be very expensive.

Global Focus An understanding of global competition, partnerships, and trading is essential to success in a modern business environment. Therefore, we provide a broad selection of international cases and examples. We discuss the role of information systems in facilitating export and import, the management of international companies, and electronic trading around the globe.

Innovation and Creativity In today's rapidly changing business environment, creativity and innovation are necessary for a business to operate effectively and profitably. Throughout our book, we demonstrate how information systems facilitate these processes.

Focus on Ethics With corporate scandals appearing in the headlines almost daily, ethics and ethical questions have come to the forefront of business people's minds. In addition to devoting an entire chapter to ethics and privacy (Chapter 6), we have included examples and cases throughout the text that focus on business ethics.

A Guide to Icons in This Book

As you read this book, you will notice a variety of icons interspersed throughout the chapters.

These icons highlight material relating to different functional areas. MIS concepts are relevant to all business careers, not just careers in IT. The functional area icons help students of different majors quickly pick out concepts and examples of particular relevance to them. Below is a quick reference of these icons.

ACCT **For the Accounting Major** highlights content relevant to the functional area of accounting.

FIN **For the Finance Major** highlights content relevant to the functional area of finance.

MKT **For the Marketing Major** highlights content relevant to the functional area of marketing.

POM **For the Production/Operations Management Major** highlights content relevant to the functional area of production/operations management.

HRM **For the Human Resources Major** highlights content relevant to the functional area of human resources.

MIS **For the MIS Major** highlights content relevant to the functional area of MIS.

What's New in the Fourth Edition?

Content changes include:

- Chapter 5: Completely rewritten chapter on Business Analytics. Chapter provides a visual overview of the Analytics process (Figure 5.3), and extensive coverage of descriptive analytics, predictive analytics, and prescriptive analytics.
- Plug IT In 5: Completely rewritten Plug IT In on Artificial Intelligence. This Plug In differentiates between weak AI and strong AI and then addresses AI technologies such as expert systems, machine learning, deep learning, and neural networks. The Plug In continues with a discussion of AI applications, including machine vision, natural language processing, robotics, speech recognition, and intelligent agents.
- Chapter 3 contains expanded coverage of Big Data.
- Plug IT In 1 provides expanded coverage of business processes.
- All new or updated IT's About Business, chapter-opening and closing cases, and examples.
- Pedagogical changes include:
  - Revised and streamlined "Apply the Concept" activities now relate directly to chapter objectives.
  - New "Internship Activities" replace the Ruby's Club activities from previous editions. Each Internship Activity includes a software demo that requires students to apply new tools to business problems.
  - Revised "Collaboration Exercises" now each require use of Google Drive.
  - Revised and streamlined database and spreadsheet exercises for every chapter. These include references to lessons in the WileyPLUS lab manual for students who need instruction or review.

Online Resources

www.wiley.com/college/rainer

Our book also facilitates the teaching of an Introduction to Information Systems course by providing extensive support materials for instructors and students. Visit www.wiley.com/college/rainer to access the Student and Instructor Companion Sites.

Instructor's Manual The *Instructor's Manual* includes a chapter overview, teaching tips and strategies, answers to all end-of-chapter questions, supplemental mini-cases with essay questions and answers, and experiential exercises that relate to particular topics. It also includes answers and solutions to all spreadsheet and database activities, along with a guide to teaching these exercises, and links to the separate Excel and Access starter and solutions files.

Test Bank The test bank is a comprehensive resource for test questions. Each chapter contains multiple choice, true/false, short answer, and essay questions. In addition, each chapter includes "Apply Your Knowledge" questions that require more creative thought to answer. Each multiple choice and true/false question is labeled to indicate its level of difficulty: easy, medium, or hard.

The test bank is available for use in Respondus' easy-to-use software. Respondus® is a powerful tool for creating and managing exams that can be printed or published directly to Blackboard, WebCT, Desire2Learn, eCollege, ANGEL, and other learning systems. For more information on Respondus® and the Respondus Test Bank Network, please visit www.respondus.com.

Reading Quizzes These multiple choice conceptual questions can be used by instructors to evaluate a student's understanding of the reading. They are available in Respondus, the WileyPLUS course, and the Book Companion Site.

PowerPoint Presentations The *PowerPoint Presentations* consist of a series of slides for each chapter. The slides are designed around each chapter's content, incorporating key points from the chapter and chapter illustrations as appropriate, as well as real-life examples from the Web.

Image Library All textbook figures are available for download from the Web site. These figures can easily be added to PowerPoint presentations.

Weekly Updates (http://wileyinformationsystemsupdates.com)
Weekly updates, harvested from around the Internet by David Firth of the University of Montana, provide you with the latest IT news and issues. These are posted every Monday morning throughout the year at http://wileyinformationsystemsupdates.com/. They include links to current articles and videos as well as discussion questions to assign or use in class.

OfficeGrader Office Grader™ is an Access-Based VBA Macro that enables automatic grading of Office assignments. The macros compare Office files and grade them against a master file. OfficeGrader™ is available for Word, Access, Excel, and PowerPoint for Office 2010 and 2013. For more information, contact your Wiley sales representative or visit http://www.wiley.com/college/sc/office2013/officegrader.html.

WileyPLUS Learning Space

WileyPLUS Learning Space is an easy way for students to learn, collaborate, and grow. With WileyPLUS Learning Space, students create a personalized study plan, assess progress along the way, and make deeper connections as they interact with the course material and each other. Through a combination of dynamic course materials and visual reports, this collaborative learning environment gives you and your students immediate insight into strengths and problem areas in order to act on what's most important.

- This online teaching and learning environment integrates the entire digital textbook with the most effective instructor and student resources to accommodate every learning style.
- Students achieve concept mastery in a rich, structured environment that is available 24/7.
- Instructors personalize and manage their course more effectively with assessment, assignments, grade tracking, and more. You can even add your own materials to your Wiley-PLUS course
- With WileyPLUS Learning Space you can identify students who are falling behind and intervene accordingly, without having to wait for them to come to office hours.
- WileyPLUS Learning Space can complement the textbook or replace the printed textbook altogether.

WileyPLUS Learning Space for Rainer MIS 3e includes the following resources to support teaching and learning:

- New author lecture videos for every section of every chapter will facilitate switch to "flipped classrooms" and/or will provide additional learning support for students.
- Orion, an adaptive, personal learning experience that helps students highlight their strengths and problems areas and navigate through their studies to get optimal results in the most efficient amount of time. (See more information below.).
- Group chat function facilitates student discussion about activities and cases.
- Complete eText allows searching across all chapters, note-taking, highlighting, and the ability to copy and paste or print key sections.
- Lab Manual for Microsoft Office 2010 and Office 2013.
- Automatically graded practice questions
- Vocabulary flash cards and quizzes
- Library of additional "IT's About Business" cases.

For more information and a demo, visit here: http://www .wiley.com/college/sc/wpls/

ORION Included in WileyPLUS Learning Space, ORION helps gauge students' strengths and weaknesses so that instructors can tailor instruction accordingly. Instructor reports track aggregate and individual student proficiency at the objective or chapter level, to show exactly where students excel as well as the areas that need reinforcement.

Based on cognitive science, WileyPLUS with ORION is a personalized, adaptive learning experience that helps students build proficiency on topics while using their study time most effectively.

For more information and a demo, visit here: http://www .wiley.com/college/sc/ oriondemo/.

WILEY Flex

In addition to WileyPLUS Learning Space, Wiley provides a wide variety of printed and electronic formats that provide many choices to your students at a wide range of price points. Contact your Wiley sales representative for more details on any of the below.

Wiley E-Text Powered by VitalSource Wiley E-Texts are complete digital versions of the text that help students study more efficiently. Students can access content online and offline on their desktops, laptops, and mobile devices; search across the entire book content, take notes and highlight, and copy and paste or print key sections.

Wiley Binder Version A three-hole-punched, loose-leaf version allows students to carry only the content they need, insert class notes and hand-outs, and keep all materials in one place.

Wiley Custom This group's services allows you to adapt existing Wiley content and combine text materials, incorporate and publish your own materials, and collaborate with Wiley's team to ensure your satisfaction.

Wiley Custom Select Wiley Custom Select allows you to build your own course materials using selected chapters of any Wiley text and your own material if desired. For more information, visit http:// customselect.wiley.com.

Acknowledgments

Creating, developing, and producing a text for the introduction to information systems course is a formidable undertaking. Along the way, we were fortunate to receive continuous evaluation, criticism, and direction from many colleagues who regularly teach this course.

Special thanks to the following contributors: Ken Corley for designing the PowerPoint slides, Jennifer Gerow for writing test bank questions,

Bob Gehling for working on the Instructor's Manual, and Carole Hollingsworth for designing Wiley PLUS activities.

Special thanks to contributors Dawna Dewire, Joan Lumpkin, Kevin Lertwachara, Roy DeJoie, and Kala Seal for working on the original Apply the Concept activities that appeared in prior editions. Thanks also to Efrem Mallach for creating the original database activities in the prior editions. Many thanks also to Alina M. Chircu and Marco Marabelli of Bentley University for developing new material that enhances our coverage of business processes and ERP. We are grateful for the dedication and creativity of all these contributors in helping us craft this new text.

We would like to thank the Wiley team: Darren Lalonde, Executive Editor; Emma Townsend-Merino, Assistant Development Editor; Wendy Ashenberg, Associate Product Designer; and Chris DeJohn, Senior Marketing Manager. We also thank the Content Management team, including Dorothy Sinclair, Content Manager; Jane Lee Kaddu, Senior Production Editor; and Abhishek Sarkari of Thomson Digital. And thanks to Maureen Eide, Senior Designer; and Billy Ray, Senior Photo Editor. We would also like to thank Robert Weiss for his skillful and thorough editing of the manuscript.

Finally, we would like to acknowledge the contributions made by the individuals listed below who participated in focus groups, telesessions, surveys, chapter walkthroughs, class tests, user feedback surveys, and reviews.

KELLY RAINER
BRAD PRINCE
HUGH WATSON

Monica Adya, *Marquette University*
Lawrence Andrew, *Western Illinois University, Macomb*
Orakwue (Bay) Arinze, *Drexel University*
Laura Atkins, *James Madison University*
Nick Ball, *Brigham Young University*
Nicholas Barnes, *Nicholls College*
Susan Barzottini, *Manchester Community College*
Kristi Berg, *Minot State University*
Andy Borchers, *Lipscomb University*
David Bouchard, *Metropolitan State University*
Dave Bourgeois, *Biola University*
Mari Buche, *Michigan Tech University*
Richard Burkhard, *San Jose State University*
Ashley Bush, *Florida State University*
Frank Canovatchel, *Champlain College*
Donald Carpenter, *Mesa State College*
Teuta Cata, *Northern Kentucky University*
Wendy Ceccucci, *Quinnipiac University*
Amita Chin, *Virginia Commonwealth University*
Susan Chinn, *University of Southern ME, Portland*
Richard Christensen, *Metropolitan State University*
Dmitriy Chulkov, *Indiana University Kokomo*
Phillip Coleman, *Western Kentucky University*
Emilio Collar, *Western CT State University*
Daniel Connolly, *University of Denver*
Lee Cornell, *Minnesota State University, Mankato*
David Croasdell, *University of Nevada, Reno*
Jakov Crnkovic, *University at Albany, SUNY*
Reet Cronk, *Harding University*
Marcia Daley, *Clark, Atlanta*
Donald Danner, *San Francisco State University*
Roy DeJoie, *Purdue University*
Dawna Dewire, *Babson College*
Kevin Duffy, *Wright State University*
Lauren Eder, *Rider University*
Sean Eom, *Southeast Missouri State University*
Ahmed Eshra, *St. John's University*

Roger Finnegan, *Metropolitan State University*
Thomas Fischer, *Metropolitan State University*
Jerry Flatto, *University of Indianapolis*
Jonathan Frankel, *University of Massachusetts, Boston*
Judith Gebauer, *University of North Carolina, Wilmington*
Jennifer Gerow, *Virginia Military Institute*
Matt Graham, *University of Maine*
Katie Gray, *University of Texas, Austin*
Penelope (Sue) Greenberg, *Widener University*
Naveen Gudigantala, *University of Portland*
Saurabh Gupta, *University of North Florida*
Bernard Han, *Western Michigan University*
Hyo-Joo Han, *Georgia Southern College*
John Hagle, *Texas State Technical College*
Peter Haried, *University of Wisconsin, LaCrosse*
Ranida Harris, *Indiana University Southeast*
Roslin Hauck, *Illinois State University*
Bernd Haupt, *Penn State University*
Jun He, *University of Michigan, Dearborn*
Richard Herschel, *St. Joseph's University*
Bogdan Hoanca, *University of Alaska*
Mary Carole Hollingsworth, *Georgia Perimeter College, Clarkston Campus*
Terri Holly, *Indian River State College*
Derrick Huang, *Florida Atlantic University*
Maggie Hutchison, *Flagler College*
Mark Hwang, *Central Michigan University*
Lynn Isvik, *Upper Iowa University, Fayette*
Curtis Izen, *Baruch College, City University of New York*
Radhika Jain, *Baruch College, City University of New York*
Arpan Jani, *University of Wisconsin, River Falls*
Jonathan Jelen, *St. John's University*
Hong Jiang, *Benedict College*
Nenad Jukic, *Loyola University*
Elene Kent, *Capital University*
Stephen Klein, *Ramapo College*
Brian Kovar, *Kansas State University*
Subodha Kumar, *Texas A&M*
Diane Lending, *James Madison University*
Kevin Lertwachara, *Cal Poly San Luis Obispo*
Terry Letsche, *Wartburg College*
Victor Lipe, *Trident Tech*
Chuck Litecky, *Southern Illinois University, Carbondale*
Joan Lumpkin, *Wright State University*
Nicole Lytle, *Cal State, San Bernardino*
George Mangalaraj, *Western Illinois University*
Parand Mansouri-Rad, *University of Texas, El Paso*
Michael Martel, *Ohio University*
Nancy Martin, *Southern Illinois University, Carbondale*
Richard McMahon, *University of Houston, Downtown*
Tony McRae, *Collin College*
Vishal Midha, *University of Texas, Pan American*
Esmail Mohebbi, *University West Florida*
Luvai Motiwalla, *University Mass Online*
Mahdi Nasereddin, *Penn State, Berks*
Sandra K. Newton, *Sonoma State University*
Ann O'Brien, *University of Wisconsin, Madison*
Sungjune Park, *University of North Carolina, Charlotte*
Yang Park, *Georgia Southwestern State University*
Alan Peace, *West Virginia University*
Jacqueline Pike, *Duquesne University*

Tony Pittarese, *East Tennessee State University*
Jennifer Pitts, *Columbus State University*
Richard Platt, *University of West Florida*
Larisa Preiser, *Cal Poly Pomona*
Michelle Ramim, *Nova Southeastern University*
Alison Rampersad, *Lynn University*
Ralph Reilly, *University of Hartford*
Wes Rhea, *Kennesaw State University*
Julio Rivera, *University of Alabama, Birmingham*
Thomas Roberts, *William Patterson University*
Cynthia Ruppel, *Nova Southeastern University*
James Ryan, *Troy University*
Russell Sabadosa, *Manchester Community College*
Jim Samuel, *Baruch College, City University of New York*
Tom Sandman, *Cal State, Sacramento*
Kala Seal, *Loyola Marymount*
Tod Sedbrook, *University of Northern Colorado*
Elaine Seeman, *East Carolina University*
Richard Segall, *Arkansas State University*
Lee Sellers, *Eastern Oregon University—Mt. Hood Metro Center*
Judy Ann Serwatka, *Purdue University, North Central*
John Seydel, *Arkansas State University*
Jollean Sinclaire, *Arkansas State University*
Vivek Shah, *Texas State University, San Marcos*
Mehrdad Sharbaf, *Loyola Marymount University*
Suengjae Shin, *Mississippi State University, Meridian*
Todd Stabenow, *Hawkeye Community College*

Jo Lynne Stalnaker, *University of Wyoming*
Cynthia Stone, *Indiana University*
Nathan Stout, *University of Oklahoma*
Yi Sun, *Cal State, San Marcos*
Winston Tellis, *Fairfield University*
Doug Francis Tuggle, *Chapman University*
Wendy Urban, *Temple University*
Darlene de Vida, *Lower Columbia College*
James Villars, *Metropolitan State University*
Padmal Vitharana, *Syracuse University*
Haibo Wang, *Texas A&M International University*
Hong Wang, *North Carolina A&T State University*
June Wei, *University of West Florida*
Melody White, *University of North Texas*
Rosemary Wild, *Cal Poly San Luis Obispo*
Tom Wilder, *Cal State, Chico*
Karen Williams, *University of Texas, San Antonio*
Marie Wright, *Western Connecticut State University*
Yaquan Xu, *Virginia State University*
Benjamin Yeo, *Loyola Marymount University*
Bee Yew, *Fayetteville State University*
Jigish Zaveri, *Morgan State University*
Grace Zhang, *Augusta State University*
Wei Zhang, *University of Massachusetts, Boston*
Zuopeng Zhang, *SUNY, Plattsburgh*
Fan Zhao, *Florida Gulf Coast University*
Robert Zwick, *Yeshiva University*

Brief Contents

Contents

Plug IT In 6   Project Management   477

Plug IT In 7   Protecting Your Information Assets   488

Management Information Systems

Fourth Edition

STOCK4B-RF/Getty Images

CHAPTER 1

Introduction to Information Systems

CHAPTER OUTLINE

LEARNING OBJECTIVES

1.1 Identify the reasons why being an informed user of information systems is important in today's world.

1.2 Describe the various types of computer-based information systems in an organization.

1.3 Discuss ways in which information technology can affect managers and nonmanagerial workers.

1.4 Identify positive and negative societal effects of the increased use of information technology.

Opening Case

MKT FanDuel

POM Founded in 2009, FanDuel (www.fanduel.com) operates a Web-based fantasy sports game. It is the largest company in the daily fantasy sports business. In May 2016, FanDuel was legal in 39 states, taking advantage of an exclusion in the 2006 Unlawful Internet Gambling Enforcement Act. This statute bans credit card issuers and banks from working with poker and sports-betting Web sites, effectively preventing U.S. customers from participating in those industries.

The law, however, exempts fantasy sports because they are considered a game of skill, not luck. To maintain legal status, the operator of a fantasy sports business must follow four rules: (1) publish prize amounts before the games begin, (2) make prize amounts independent of the number of players in the game, (3) level the playing field by allowing anyone in a league to draft any player they want, and (4) disregard point spreads and game scores.

FanDuel delivers simple and fast fantasy betting. After paying an entry fee, players become eligible to win daily cash payouts based on the statistical performance of athletes in games played that day. Traditional fantasy sports often frustrate players because the experience lasts for an entire season. If a player drafts a bad team, then he or she is stuck with that team for several months. In addition, serious fantasy league players analyze large amounts of statistics, roster changes, and injury reports. Many casual players do not have time for such analyses. In contrast to these leagues, FanDuel allows customers to play for just a day, a weekend, or a week.

FanDuel lets players participate for free or bet up to $5000 to draft a team of players in the National Football League (NFL), the National Basketball Association (NBA), Major League Baseball (MLB), and the National Hockey League (NHL), plus college football and basketball. Players can compete head-to-head against another individual or in a league with up to 125,000 teams. The winner is the one with the best player statistics, which translate into fantasy points. FanDuel takes an average of 9 percent of each prize.

MIS By May 2016, FanDuel claimed more than 1 million customers and operated in 39 states. However, the company was not yet profitable. It has to spend millions of dollars on computing power from Amazon Web Services to manage, as only one example, the increase in Web traffic just before Sunday's NFL kickoff. At that time, FanDuel must manage 150,000 simultaneous users, who make 250,000 roster changes per hour. The company also provides 15 million live scoring updates per minute during games, meaning that it must manage 6 terabytes of network traffic during game day. (A terabyte equals 1 trillion bytes.)

Professional sports have noted that FanDuel, with its easy-to-use app, appeals to young and mobile sports fans. Further, these fans have money at stake, so they are more inclined to watch games on television than they otherwise would be. An increase in viewers leads to an increase in advertising rates for the teams. In fact, in 2015 FanDuel signed multiyear sponsorship agreements with 15 NFL teams. These deals generally include stadium signage, radio and digital advertising, and other promotions. Interestingly, the NBA owns an equity stake in FanDuel.

Despite continued success, daily fantasy sports companies face a substantive problem. They can operate only as long as the federal government allows them to do so. The government could close the fantasy loophole in the 2006 statute at any time.

Significantly, the federal law does not give daily fantasy sports businesses immunity from state laws. In October 2015, New York Attorney General Eric Schneiderman launched an inquiry into FanDuel and its chief rival DraftKings. Shortly thereafter, he ruled that the two companies were operating illegally and issued a cease and desist order, ordering the two companies to stop taking bets in New York State.

FanDuel, which is based in New York, said that it would check the locations of its users to ensure that they submitted entries from states where it is permitted to do so. Users who attempt to circumvent this decision could see their accounts terminated and FanDuel refuse to pay out any winnings.

On the other hand, DraftKings, which is based in Massachusetts, sent an e-mail to its New York customers assuring them that they could continue submitting entries. DraftKings told its New York customer that their right to play in New York will remain unchanged unless a New York court decides otherwise.

Interestingly, in the spring of 2016, FanDuel suspended contests on college sports in all states as part of a negotiation with the National Collegiate Athletic Association.

And the bottom line? The legal battle continues.

Sources: Compiled from D. Purdum, "DraftKings, FanDuel to Stop Offering College Fantasy Games," *ESPN.com*, March 31, 2016; M. Brown, "FanDuel Lays Off Workers as Legal Pressure Mounts," *Forbes*, January 20, 2016; R. Axon, "Facing Threat from N.Y. Attorney General, FanDuel Suspends Entries in State," *USA Today*, November 17, 2015; L. Baker, "FanDuel, DraftKings Vow to Fight New York's Halt on Bets," *Reuters*, November 12, 2015; D. Alba, "DraftKings and FanDuel Scandal Is a Cautionary Startup Tale," *Wired*, October 9, 2015; D. Roberts, "Are DraftKings and FanDuel Legal?" *Fortune*, September 24, 2015; K. Wagner, "DraftKings and FanDuel Are Battling over Your Favorite Teams," *www.recode.net*, July 17, 2015; R. Sandomir, "FanDuel and DraftKings, Leaders in Daily Fantasy Sports, Are Quickly Gaining Clout," *The New York Times*, July 13, 2015; S. Rodriguez, "Yahoo Enters World of Daily Fantasy Sports, Takes on DraftKings and FanDuel," *International Business Times*, July 8, 2015; B. Schrotenboer, "FanDuel Signs Deals with 15 NFL Teams, Escalating Daily Fantasy Integration," *USA Today*, April 21, 2015; D. Primack, "DraftKings and FanDuel Close in on Massive New Investments," *Fortune*, April 6, 2015; S. Ramachandran and Am Sharma, "Disney to Invest $250 Million in Fantasy Site DraftKings," *The Wall Street Journal*, April 3, 2015; M. Kosoff, "Fantasy Sports Startup FanDuel May Soon Be Worth $1 Billion," *Business Insider*, February 18, 2015; D. Heitner, "DraftKings Reports $304 Million on Entry Fees in 2014," *Forbes*, January 22, 2015; S. Bertoni, "Fantasy Sports, Real Money," *Forbes*, January 19, 2015; B. Schrotenboer, "Fantasy Sports Debate: Gambling or Not Gambling?" *USA Today*, January 12, 2015; "The FanDuel Scam," *The Daily Roto*, December 19, 2014; D. Heitner, "Fantasy Sports Service, FanDuel, Secures $11 Million Investment; Includes Money from Comcast Ventures," *Forbes*, January 30, 2013; www.fanduel.com, www.draftkings.com, accessed July 17, 2015.

Questions

1. Describe how information technology is essential to FanDuel's operations.

2. Discuss the nontechnological problems that FanDuel faces.

3. Describe FanDuel's information technology infrastructure. Now discuss possible technological problems that FanDuel might face.

Introduction

Before we proceed, we need to define information technology and information systems. **Information technology (IT)** refers to any computer-based tool that people use to work with information and to support the information and information-processing needs of an organization. An **information system (IS)** collects, processes, stores, analyzes, and disseminates information for a specific purpose.

IT has far-reaching effects on individuals, organizations, and our planet. Although this text is largely devoted to the many ways in which IT has transformed modern organizations, you will also learn about the significant impacts of IT on individuals and societies, the global economy, and our physical environment. In addition, IT is making our world smaller, enabling more and more people to communicate, collaborate, and compete, thereby leveling the competitive playing field.

When you graduate, you either will start your own business or you will work for an organization, whether it is public sector, private sector, for-profit, or not-for-profit. Your organization will have to survive and compete in an environment that has been radically transformed by information technology. This environment is global, massively interconnected, intensely competitive, 24/7/365, real-time, rapidly changing, and information-intensive. To compete successfully, your organization must use IT effectively.

As you read this chapter and this text, keep in mind that the information technologies you will learn about are important to businesses of all sizes. No matter what area of business you major in, what industry you work for, or the size of your company, you will benefit from learning about IT. Who knows? Maybe you will use the tools you learn about in this class to make your great idea a reality by becoming an entrepreneur and starting your own business! In fact, as you see in the chapter opening case and in chapter closing case 2, you can use information technology to help you start your own business.

The modern environment is intensely competitive not only for your organization, but for you as well. You must compete with human talent from around the world. Therefore, you will also have to make effective use of IT.

Accordingly, this chapter begins with a discussion of why you should become knowledgeable about IT. It also distinguishes among data, information, and knowledge, and it differentiates computer-based information systems from application programs. Finally, it considers the impacts of information systems on organizations and on society in general.

1.1 | Why Should I Study Information Systems?

You are part of the most connected generation in history: You have grown up online; you are, quite literally, never out of touch; you use more information technologies (in the form of digital devices), for more tasks, and are bombarded with more information, than any generation in history. The *MIT Technology Review* refers to you as *Homo conexus*. Information technologies are so deeply embedded in your lives that your daily routines would be almost unrecognizable to a college student just 20 years ago.

Essentially, you practice continuous computing, surrounded by a movable information network. This network is created by constant cooperation between the digital devices you carry (for example, laptops, tablets, and smartphones); the wired and wireless networks that you access as you move about; and Web-based tools for finding information and communicating and collaborating with other people. Your network enables you to pull information about virtually anything from anywhere, at any time, and to push your own ideas back to the Web, from wherever you are, via a mobile device. Think of everything you do online, often with your smart phone: register for classes; take classes (and not just at your university); access class syllabi, information, PowerPoints, and lectures; research class papers and presentations; conduct banking; pay your bills; research, shop, and buy products from companies or other people; sell your "stuff"; search for, and apply for, jobs; make your travel reservations (hotel, airline, rental car); create your own blog and post your own podcasts and videocasts to it; design your own page on Facebook; make and upload videos to YouTube; take, edit, and print your own digital photographs; "burn" your own custom-music CDs and DVDs; use RSS feeds to create your personal electronic newspaper; text and tweet your friends and family throughout your day; send Snaps; and many other activities. (*Note:* If any of these terms are unfamiliar to you, don't worry. You will learn about everything mentioned here in detail later in this text.)

The Informed User—You!

So, the question is: Why you should learn about information systems and information technologies? After all, you can comfortably use a computer (or other electronic devices) to perform many activities, you have been surfing the Web for years, and you feel confident that you can manage any IT application that your organization's MIS department installs.

The answer lies in you becoming an **informed user**; that is, a person knowledgeable about information systems and information technology. There are several reasons why you should be an informed user.

MIS

In general, informed users tend to get more value from whatever technologies they use. You will enjoy many benefits from being an informed user of IT, including:

- You will benefit more from your organization's IT applications because you will understand what is "behind" those applications (see Figure 1.1). That is, what you see on your computer screen is brought to you by your MIS department, who are operating "behind" your screen.

- You will be in a position to enhance the quality of your organization's IT applications with your input.

- Even as a new graduate, you will quickly be in a position to recommend—and perhaps help select—the IT applications that your organization will use.

- Being an informed user will keep you abreast of both new information technologies and rapid developments in existing technologies. Remaining "on top of things" will help you to anticipate the impacts that "new and improved" technologies will have on your organization and to make recommendations on the adoption and use of these technologies.

- You will understand how using IT can improve your organization's performance and teamwork as well as your own productivity.

- If you have ideas of becoming an entrepreneur, then being an informed user will help you use IT when you start your own business.

Going further, managing the IS function within an organization is no longer the exclusive responsibility of the IS department. Rather, users now play key roles in every step of this process. The overall objective in this text is to provide you with the necessary information to contribute immediately to managing the IS function in your organization. In short, the goal is to help you become a very informed user!

IT Offers Career Opportunities

MIS

Because IT is vital to the operation of modern businesses, it offers many employment opportunities. The demand for traditional IT staff—programmers, business analysts, systems analysts, and designers—is substantial. In addition, many well-paid jobs exist in areas such as the Internet and electronic commerce (e-commerce), mobile commerce (m-commerce), network security, telecommunications, and multimedia design.

FIGURE 1.1 IT skills open many doors because IT is so widely used.

USERS | MIS

© Slawomir Fajer/iStockphoto

The IS field includes the people in various organizations who design and build information systems, the people who use those systems, and the people responsible for managing those systems. At the top of the list is the chief information officer (CIO).

The CIO is the executive who is in charge of the IS function. In most modern organizations, the CIO works with the chief executive officer (CEO), the chief financial officer (CFO), and other senior executives. Therefore, he or she actively participates in the organization's strategic planning process. In today's digital environment, the IS function has become increasingly strategic within organizations. As a result, although most CIOs still rise from the IS department, a growing number are coming up through the ranks in the business units (e.g., marketing, finance). Regardless of your major, you could become the CIO of your organization one day. This is another reason to be an informed user of information systems!

Table 1.1 provides a list of IT jobs, along with a description of each one. For further details about careers in IT, see www.computerworld.com/careertopics/careers and www.monster.com.

Career opportunities in IS are strong and are projected to remain strong over the next ten years. In fact, the *U.S. News & World Report* listed its "25 best jobs of 2015," *Money* listed its "best jobs in America for 2015," and *Forbes* listed its "10 best jobs" for 2015. Let's take a look at these rankings. (Note that the rankings differ because the magazines used different criteria in their

TABLE 1.1 Information Technology Jobs

Position	Job Description
Chief Information Officer	Highest-ranking IS manager; responsible for all strategic planning in the organization
IS Director	Manages all systems throughout the organization and the day-to-day operations of the entire IS organization
Information Center Manager	Manages IS services such as help desks, hot lines, training, and consulting
Applications Development Manager	Coordinates and manages new systems development projects
Project Manager	Manages a particular new systems development project
Systems Manager	Manages a particular existing system
Operations Manager	Supervises the day-to-day operations of the data and/or computer center
Programming Manager	Coordinates all applications programming efforts
Systems Analyst	Interfaces between users and programmers; determines information requirements and technical specifications for new applications
Business Analyst	Focuses on designing solutions for business problems; interfaces closely with users to demonstrate how IT can be used innovatively
Systems Programmer	Creates the computer code for developing new systems software or maintaining existing systems software
Applications Programmer	Creates the computer code for developing new applications or maintaining existing applications
Emerging Technologies Manager	Forecasts technology trends; evaluates and experiments with new technologies
Network Manager	Coordinates and manages the organization's voice and data networks
Database Administrator	Manages the organization's databases and oversees the use of database-management software
Auditing or Computer Security Manager	Oversees the ethical and legal use of information systems
Webmaster	Manages the organization'sWeb site
Web Designer	Creates Web sites and pages

research.) As you can see, jobs suited for MIS majors rank extremely high in all three lists. The magazines with their job rankings are as follows:

U.S. News & World Report (out of 25)

#3 Software Developer

#7 Computer System Analyst

#8 Information Security Analyst

#11 Web Developer

#21 IT Manager

Money

#1 Software Architect

#2 Video Game Designer

#8 Database Developer

#9 Information Assurance (Security) Analyst

#11 Clinical Applications Specialist (IT in healthcare)

#14 User Experience Designer

#17 IT Program Manager

Forbes (out of 10)

#8 Software Engineer

#10 Computer Systems Analyst

Not only do IS careers offer strong job growth, but the pay is excellent as well. The Bureau of Labor Statistics, an agency within the Department of Labor that is responsible for tracking and analyzing trends relating to the labor market, notes that the median salary in 2015 for "computer and information systems managers" was approximately $130,000, and predicted that the profession would grow by an average of 15 percent per year through 2022.

Managing Information Resources

Managing information systems in modern organizations is a difficult, complex task. Several factors contribute to this complexity. First, information systems have enormous strategic value to organizations. Firms rely on them so heavily that, in some cases, when these systems are not working (even for a short time), the firm cannot function. (This situation is called "being hostage to information systems.") Second, information systems are very expensive to acquire, operate, and maintain.

A third factor contributing to the difficulty in managing information systems is the evolution of the management information systems (MIS) function within the organization. When businesses first began to use computers in the early 1950s, the MIS department "owned" the only computing resource in the organization, the mainframe. At that time, end users did not interact directly with the mainframe.

In contrast, in the modern organization, computers are located in all departments, and almost all employees use computers in their work. This situation, known as *end user computing*, has led to a partnership between the MIS department and the end users. The MIS department now acts as more of a consultant to end users, viewing them as customers. In fact, the main function of the MIS department is to use IT to solve end users' business problems.

As a result of these developments, the responsibility for managing information resources is now divided between the MIS department and the end users. This arrangement raises several important questions: Which resources are managed by whom? What is the role of the MIS department, its structure, and its place within the organization? What is the appropriate relationship between the MIS department and the end users? Regardless of who is doing what, it is essential that the MIS department and the end users work in close cooperation.

There is no standard way to divide responsibility for developing and maintaining information resources between the MIS department and the end users. Instead, that division depends on several factors: the size and nature of the organization, the amount and type of IT resources, the organization's attitudes toward computing, the attitudes of top management toward computing, the maturity level of the technology, the amount and nature of outsourced IT work, and even the countries in which the company operates. Generally speaking, the MIS department is responsible for corporate-level and shared resources, and the end users are responsible for departmental resources. Table 1.2 identifies both the traditional functions and various new, consultative functions of the MIS department.

TABLE 1.2   The Changing Role of the Information Systems Department

Traditional Functions of the MIS Department

Managing systems development and systems project management

- As an end user, you will have critical input into the systems development process. You will learn about systems development in Chapter 13.

Managing computer operations, including the computer center

Staffing, training, and developing IS skills

Providing technical services

Infrastructure planning, development, and control

- As an end user, you will provide critical input about the IS infrastructure needs of your department.

New (Consultative) Functions of the MIS Department

Initiating and designing specific strategic information systems

- As an end user, your information needs will often mandate the development of new strategic information systems.

You will decide which strategic systems you need (because you know your business needs better than the MIS department does), and you will provide input into developing these systems.

Incorporating the Internet and electronic commerce into the business

- As an end user, you will be primarily responsible for effectively using the Internet and electronic commerce in your business. You will work with the MIS department to accomplish this task.

Managing system integration including the Internet, intranets, and extranets

- As an end user, your business needs will determine how you want to use the Internet, your corporate intranets, and extranets to accomplish your goals. You will be primarily responsible for advising the MIS department on the most effective use of the Internet, your corporate intranets, and extranets.

Educating the non-MIS managers about IT

- Your department will be primarily responsible for advising the MIS department on how best to educate and train your employees about IT.

Educating the MIS staff about the business

- Communication between the MIS department and the business units is a two-way street. You will be responsible for educating the MIS staff on your business, its needs, and its goals.

Partnering with business-unit executives

- Essentially, you will be in a partnership with the MIS department. You will be responsible for seeing that this partnership is one "between equals" and ensuring its success.

(Continued)

Managing outsourcing

- Outsourcing is driven by business needs. Therefore, the outsourcing decision resides largely with the business units (i.e., with you). The MIS department, working closely with you, will advise you on technical issues such as communications bandwidth, security, as well as other issues.

Proactively using business and technical knowledge to seed innovative ideas about IT

- Your business needs often will drive innovative ideas about how to effectively use information systems to accomplish your goals. The best way to bring these innovative uses of IS to life is to partner closely with your MIS department. Such close partnerships have amazing synergies!

Creating business alliances with business partners

- The needs of your business unit will drive these alliances, typically along your supply chain. Again, your MIS department will act as your advisor on various issues, including hardware and software compatibility, implementing extranets, communications, and security.

So, where do the end users come in? Take a close look at Table 1.2. Under the traditional MIS functions, you will see two functions for which you provide vital input: managing systems development and infrastructure planning. Under the consultative MIS functions, in contrast, you exercise the primary responsibility for each function, while the MIS department acts as your advisor.

Before you go on...

1. Rate yourself as an informed user. (Be honest; this isn't a test!)
2. Explain the benefits of being an informed user of information systems.
3. Discuss the various career opportunities offered in the IT field.

Apply the Concept 1.1

LEARNING OBJECTIVE 1.1 Identify the reasons why being an informed user of information systems is important in today's world.

STEP 1: Background (Here is what you are learning.)

Section 1.1 discussed how businesses are utilizing modern technologies to become more productive by connecting to their customers, suppliers, partners, and other parties. Those connections, however, do not exist simply to support the businesses. Do you realize how connected *you* are? Computers and information systems have become an essential feature of our everyday lives. Most of you have a cell phone within reach and have looked at it within the past 5 minutes. No longer is a phone just a phone; rather, it is your connection to family, friends, shopping, driving directions, entertainment (games, movies, music, etc.), and much more.

When you embark on your career, you likely will have to interface with information systems to post transactions and search for or record information. Accomplishing these tasks will require you to

work effectively with computers, regardless of the industry you find yourself employed in.

STEP 2: Activity (Here is what you do.)

Visit the Web sites of three local businesses: a bank, a dentist, and a retail shop. Examine their information to see if you can determine what types of information systems they use to support their operations. It is likely that you will find some similarities and differences among the three. Also, see if they have any open positions. If they do, what technical skills do these positions require? Summarize your findings in a paragraph or two.

STEP 3: Assignment (Here is what you turn in.)

Based on your research, identify five reasons why it is important for you to be an informed user of information technology. Reference your summarized findings to support your reasoning. Submit this list to your instructor, but also keep it in mind. You have just looked into the real world (your local world, in fact) and identified a reason for taking this course!

1.2 Overview of Computer-Based Information Systems

Organizations refer to their management information systems functional area by several names, including the MIS Department, the Information Systems (IS) Department, the Information Technology (IT) Department, and the Information Services Department. Regardless of the name, however, this functional area deals with the planning for—and the development, management, and use of—information technology tools to help people perform all the tasks related to information processing and management. Recall that information technology relates to any computer-based tool that people use to work with information and to support the information and information-processing needs of an organization.

As previously stated, an information system collects, processes, stores, analyzes, and disseminates information for a specific purpose. The purpose of information systems has been defined as getting the right information to the right people, at the right time, in the right amount, and in the right format. Because information systems are intended to supply useful information, we need to differentiate between information and two closely related terms: data and knowledge (see Figure 1.2).

Data items refer to an elementary description of things, events, activities, and transactions that are recorded, classified, and stored but are not organized to convey any specific meaning. Data items can be numbers, letters, figures, sounds, and images. Examples of data items are collections of numbers (e.g., 3.11, 2.96, 3.95, 1.99, 2.08) and characters (e.g., B, A, C, A, B, D, F, C).

Information refers to data that have been organized so that they have meaning and value to the recipient. For example, a grade point average (GPA) by itself is data, but a student's name coupled with his or her GPA is information. The recipient interprets the meaning and draws

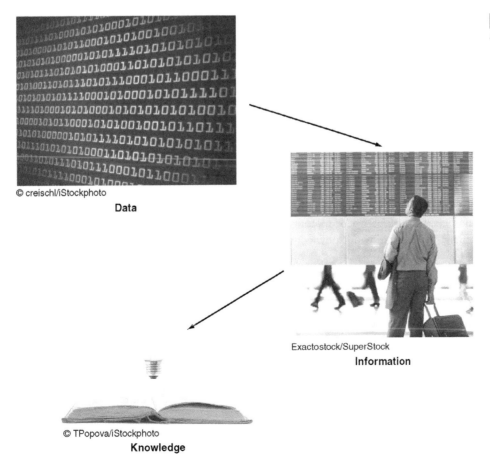

© creischl/iStockphoto
Data

Exactostock/SuperStock
Information

© TPopova/iStockphoto
Knowledge

FIGURE 1.2 Data, Information, and Knowledge

conclusions and implications from the information. Consider the examples of data provided in the preceding paragraph. Within the context of a university, the numbers could be grade point averages, and the letters could be grades in an Introduction to MIS class.

Knowledge consists of data and/or information that have been organized and processed to convey understanding, experience, accumulated learning, and expertise as they apply to a current business problem. For example, suppose that a company recruiting at your school has found over time that students with grade point averages over 3.0 have experienced the greatest success in its management program. Based on this accumulated knowledge, that company may decide to interview only those students with GPAs over 3.0. This example presents an example of knowledge because the company utilizes information—GPAs—to address a business problem—hiring successful employees. As you can see from this example, organizational knowledge, which reflects the experience and expertise of many people, has great value to all employees.

Consider this example:

Data	Information	Knowledge
[No context]	[University context]	
3.16	3.16 + John Jones = GPA	* Job prospects
2.92	2.92 + Sue Smith = GPA	* Graduate school prospects
1.39	1.39 + Kyle Owens = GPA	* Scholarship prospects
3.95	3.95 + Tom Elias = GPA	

Data	Information	Knowledge
[No context]	[Professional baseball pitcher context]	
3.16	3.16 + Ken Rice = ERA	
2.92	2.92 + Ed Dyas = ERA	* Keep pitcher, trade pitcher, or send pitcher to minor leagues
1.39	1.39 + Hugh Carr = ERA	* Salary/contract negotiations
3.95	3.95 + Nick Ford = ERA	

GPA = Grade point average (higher is better)

ERA = Earned run average (lower is better); ERA is the number of runs per nine innings that a pitcher surrenders.

You see that the same data items, with no context, can mean entirely different things in different contexts.

Now that you have a clearer understanding of data, information, and knowledge, let's shift our focus to computer-based information systems. As you have seen, these systems process data into information and knowledge that you can use.

A **computer-based information system (CBIS)** is an information system that uses computer technology to perform some or all of its intended tasks. Although not all information systems are computerized, today most are. For this reason the term "information system" is typically used synonymously with "computer-based information system." The basic components of computer-based information systems are listed below. The first four are called **information technology components**. **Figure 1.3** illustrates how these four components interact to form a CBIS.

- **Hardware** consists of devices such as the processor, monitor, keyboard, and printer. Together, these devices accept, process, and display data and information.

- **Software** is a program or collection of programs that enable the hardware to process data.

- A **database** is a collection of related files or tables containing data.

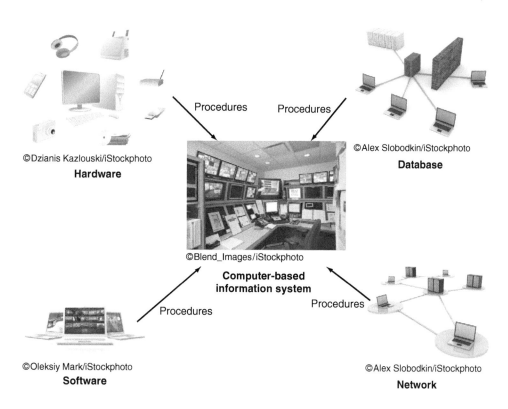

©Dzianis Kazlouski/iStockphoto
Hardware

©Alex Slobodkin/iStockphoto
Database

©Blend_Images/iStockphoto
**Computer-based
information system**

©Oleksiy Mark/iStockphoto
Software

©Alex Slobodkin/iStockphoto
Network

Procedures   Procedures

Procedures   Procedures

FIGURE 1.3 It takes technology (hardware, software, databases, and networks) with appropriate procedures to make a CBIS useful for people.

- A network is a connecting system (wireline or wireless) that permits different computers to share resources.
- Procedures are the instructions for combining the above components to process information and generate the desired output.
- People use the hardware and software, interface with it, or utilize its output.

Figure 1.4 illustrates how these components are integrated to form the wide variety of information systems found within an organization. Starting at the bottom of the figure, you see that the IT components of hardware, software, networks (wireline and wireless), and databases

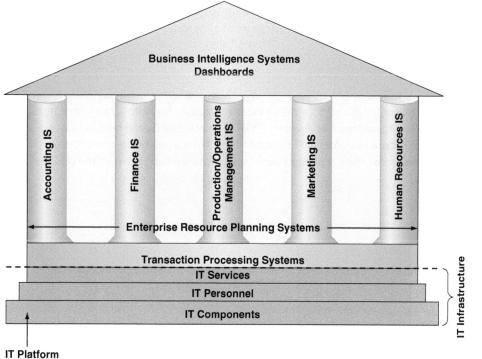

FIGURE 1.4 Information technology inside your organization.

form the **information technology platform**. IT personnel use these components to develop information systems, oversee security and risk, and manage data. These activities cumulatively are called **information technology services**. The IT components plus IT services comprise the organization's **information technology infrastructure**. At the top of the pyramid are the various organizational information systems.

Computer-based information systems have many capabilities. **Table 1.3** summarizes the most important ones.

Information systems perform these various tasks via a wide spectrum of applications. An **application** (or **app**) is a computer program designed to support a specific task or business process. (A synonymous term is **application program**.) Each functional area or department within a business organization uses dozens of application programs. For instance, the human resources department sometimes uses one application for screening job applicants and another for monitoring employee turnover. The collection of application programs in a single department is usually referred to as a **departmental information system** (also known as a **functional area information system**). For example, the collection of application programs in the human resources area is called the **human resources information system (HRIS)**. There are collections of application programs—that is, departmental information systems—in the other functional areas as well, such as accounting, finance, marketing, and production/operations.

Types of Computer-Based Information Systems

Modern organizations employ many different types of information systems. Figure 1.4 illustrates the different types of information systems that function *within* a single organization, and **Figure 1.5** shows the different types of information systems that function *among* multiple organizations. You will study transaction processing systems, management information systems, and enterprise resource planning systems in Chapter 11. You will learn about customer relationship management (CRM) systems in Chapter 12 and supply chain management (SCM) systems in Chapter 13.

In the next section you will learn about the numerous and diverse types of information systems employed by modern organizations. You will also read about the types of support these systems provide.

Breadth of Support of Information Systems. Certain information systems support parts of organizations, others support entire organizations, and still others support groups of organizations. This section addresses all of these systems.

Recall that each department or functional area within an organization has its own collection of application programs, or information systems. These **functional area information systems (FAISs)** are supporting pillars for the information systems located at the top of Figure 1.4, namely, business intelligence systems and dashboards. As the name suggests, each FAIS supports a particular functional area within the organization. Examples are accounting IS, finance IS, production/operations management (POM) IS, marketing IS, and human resources IS.

ACCT
FIN

Consider these examples of IT systems in the various functional areas of an organization. In finance and accounting, managers use IT systems to forecast revenues and business activity,

TABLE 1.3	Major Capabilities of Information Systems

Perform high-speed, high-volume numerical computations.

Provide fast, accurate communication and collaboration within and among organizations.

Store huge amounts of information in an easy-to-access, yet small space.

Allow quick and inexpensive access to vast amounts of information, worldwide.

Analyze and interpret vast amounts of data quickly and efficiently.

Automate both semiautomatic business processes and manual tasks.

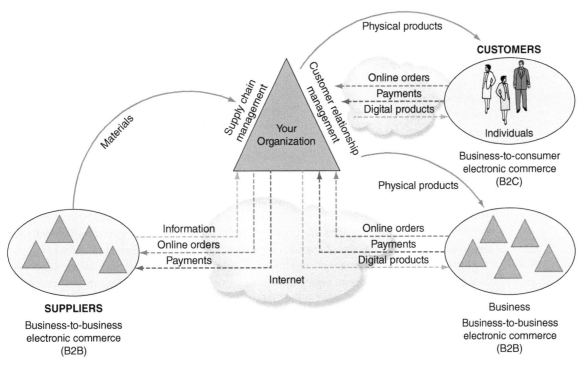

FIGURE 1.5 Information systems that function among multiple organizations.

to determine the best sources and uses of funds, and to perform audits to ensure that the organization is fundamentally sound and that all financial reports and documents are accurate.

In sales and marketing, managers use information technology to perform the following functions:

- *Product analysis:* Developing new goods and services.
- *Site analysis:* Determining the best location for production and distribution facilities.
- *Promotion analysis:* Identifying the best advertising channels.
- *Price analysis:* Setting product prices to obtain the highest total revenues.

Marketing managers also use IT to manage their relationships with their customers. In *manufacturing*, managers use IT to process customer orders, develop production schedules, control inventory levels, and monitor product quality. They also use IT to design and manufacture products. These processes are called *computer-assisted design (CAD)* and *computer-assisted manufacturing (CAM)*.

Managers in *human resources* use IT to manage the recruiting process, analyze and screen job applicants, and hire new employees. They also employ IT to help employees manage their careers, to administer performance tests to employees, and to monitor employee productivity. Finally, they rely on IT to manage compensation and benefits packages.

Two information systems that support the entire organization, enterprise resource planning systems and transaction processing systems, are designed to correct a lack of communication among the functional area ISs. For this reason Figure 1.4 shows ERP systems spanning the FAISs. ERP systems were an important innovation because the various functional area ISs were often developed as standalone systems and did not communicate effectively (if at all) with one another. ERP systems resolve this problem by tightly integrating the functional area ISs via a common database. In doing so, they enhance communications among the functional areas of an organization. For this reason, experts credit ERP systems with greatly increasing organizational productivity.

A transaction processing system (TPS) supports the monitoring, collection, storage, and processing of data from the organization's basic business transactions, each of which generates data. When you are checking out at Walmart, for example, a transaction occurs each time the cashier swipes an item across the bar code reader. Significantly, within an organization, different functions or departments can define a transaction differently. In accounting, for example, a transaction is anything that changes a firm's chart of accounts. The information system definition of a transaction is broader: A transaction is anything that changes the firm's database. The chart of accounts is only part of the firm's database. Consider a scenario in which a student transfers from one section of an Introduction to MIS course to another section. This move would be a transaction to the university's information system, but not to the university's accounting department (the tuition would not change).

The TPS collects data continuously, typically in *real time*—that is, as soon as the data are generated—and it provides the input data for the corporate databases. TPSs are considered critical to the success of any enterprise because they support core operations. Significantly, nearly all ERP systems are also TPSs, but not all TPSs are ERP systems. In fact, modern ERP systems incorporate many functions that previously were handled by the organization's functional area information systems. You study both TPSs and ERP systems in detail in Chapter 11.

ERP systems and TPSs function primarily within a single organization. Information systems that connect two or more organizations are referred to as **interorganizational information tion systems (IOSs)**. IOSs support many interorganizational operations, of which *supply chain management* is the best known. An organization's **supply chain** is the flow of materials, information, money, and services from suppliers of raw materials through factories and warehouses to the end customers.

Note that the supply chain in Figure 1.5 shows physical flows, information flows, and financial flows. Digitizable products are those that can be represented in electronic form, such as music and software. Information flows, financial flows, and digitizable products go through the Internet, whereas physical products are shipped. For example, when you order a computer from www.dell.com, your information goes to Dell via the Internet. When your transaction is completed (that is, your credit card is approved and your order is processed), Dell ships your computer to you. (We discuss supply chains in more detail in Chapter 13.)

Electronic commerce (e-commerce) systems are another type of interorganizational information system. These systems enable organizations to conduct transactions, called business-to-business (B2B) electronic commerce, and customers to conduct transactions with businesses, called business-to-consumer (B2C) electronic commerce. E-commerce systems typically are Internet-based. Figure 1.5 illustrates B2B and B2C electronic commerce. Electronic commerce systems are so important that we discuss them in detail in Chapter 7, with additional examples interspersed throughout the text. IT's About Business 1.1 shows how information systems have enabled two roadside assistance companies to grow rapidly via e-commerce.

IT's About Business 1.1

Disrupting the Roadside Assistance Industry

Roadside assistance is a $10-billion industry in the United States, encompassing a range of services including accidents, dead batteries, flat tires, towing services, tire services, fuel services, and locksmith services. Today, the industry faces disruption from technology companies that are replacing call centers with algorithms that dispatch the nearest vehicle to help a driver who is locked out of his car or to winch a car out of a ditch. These companies provide an on-demand alternative to paying for insurance plans that drivers might not use or to having to call a tow company without knowing how much it charges.

Two of these companies, Urgent.ly (http://urgent.ly) and Honk (www.honkforhelp.com), offer flat rates, promise quick response times, and provide maps in their apps that display the location of the company vehicle, with real-time updates. The companies do not charge annual membership fees, unlike the American Automobile Association (AAA; www.aaa.com).

Customers are not limited to particular tow-truck operators. The companies call the closest service vehicle to the customer, which can arrive in less than half the time and cost up to half the amounts charged by industry competitors. A basic roadside service costs $49. Before users click for service, they are informed in advance of the total fee, which they pay via credit card.

These app-based roadside assistance services also benefit tow-truck drivers, most of whom work as independents or for small operators. The traditional towing industry relies on receiving bookings from a central dispatcher, such as the AAA. Those drivers get an average of $23 per call, even though customers are typically charged $200. Drivers for Urgent.ly and Honk earn nearly double the traditional fee, mostly because these services don't need call centers. These drivers can also complete more calls in a day because the apps use algorithms for dispatching and the drivers use GPS-enabled smartphones.

Drivers for Urgent.ly and Honk work as contractors, not employees, using the apps to find customers. The services only work with established towing companies, which must have their own business licenses and insurance, so that they are covered in the event of accidents or other mishaps. The drivers must also add Urgent.ly and Honk to their insurance policies and get extra insurance for general liability. The apps check out towing companies' customer reviews before signing them on to the services.

Urgent.ly and Honk face intense competition from both the AAA and car manufacturers that offer roadside assistance. Well-known examples are General Motors' OnStar (www.onstar.com), BMW, Volvo, Lexus, Acura, Mazda, Audi, and Ferrari. The AAA, a nonprofit organization, is a federation of 43 motor clubs dispersed throughout the United States. The organization responds to more than 30 million calls per year. Members typically receive travel discounts or other membership perks. In addition, the AAA offers members four free tows per year.

Each AAA motor club can customize its offerings. For example, in late 2014, the Mid-Atlantic club launched RescueMeNow (www.rescuemenow.co), a Web-based on-demand service for nonmembers, which comes with a follow-up contract enticing users to join the organization.

The AAA does not disclose how much its towing-service contractors are paid. However, tow-truck operators state that the amount is about $25 per call. One towing-service company owner claimed he makes about $75 if the same call comes through his Urgent.ly app. Like Uber, both startups take about 25 percent of the total cost, and the driver keeps the rest.

How intense is the competition between the established organizations and the disrupters? Honk maintains that it received a number of call-and-cancel orders in 2014 that it traced to AAA employees. An AAA spokesperson acknowledged that the organization does "mystery shop" to determine how the comparable services compare.

Sources: Compiled from A. Goodwin, "Urgent.ly Is Like Uber for Roadside Assistance," *CNET*, June 11, 2015; J. Biggs, "Urgent.ly Is Uber for When Your Ride Breaks Down," *TechCrunch*, February 14, 2015; "Honk for Help: The Roadside Assistance Startup," *Insurance Zebra*, February, 12 2015; R. Rudnansky, "Roadside Assistance Apps Challenging AAA," *Travel Pulse*, December 11, 2014; K. Owram, "Watch Out, CAA: New Roadside Assistance Apps Seeking to 'Revolutionize' Towing Industry," *Financial Post*, December 9, 2014; C. Elliott, "Have Roadside Assistance Apps Replaced AAA?" *Outside*, December 4, 2014; K. Steinmetz, "There's an App for the Next Time Your Car Breaks Down," *Time*, December 1, 2014; M. Carney, "Forget AAA: Honk Is a Nationwide On-Demand Towing Platform Fueled by Technology," *Pando*, November 19, 2014; R. Gray, "Honk Is a New App that Offers Help on the Highway," *Fox News*, November 19, 2014; http://urgent.ly, www.honkforhelp.com, accessed July 19, 2015.

Questions

1. Discuss how information technology enables the business models of the Urgent.ly and Honk apps.
2. Describe the advantages and disadvantages of Urgent.ly and Honk for customers and for tow-truck operators.
3. Would you use Urgent.ly or Honk? Why or why not?
4. If you were the CEO of AAA, how would you compete with Urgent.ly and Honk? Provide specific examples in your answer.

Support for Organizational Employees. So far, you have concentrated on information systems that support specific functional areas and operations. Now you will learn about information systems that typically support particular employees within the organization.

Clerical workers, who support managers at all levels of the organization, include bookkeepers, secretaries, electronic file clerks, and insurance claim processors. *Lower-level managers* handle the day-to-day operations of the organization, making routine decisions such as assigning tasks to employees and placing purchase orders. *Middle managers* make tactical decisions, which deal with activities such as short-term planning, organizing, and control.

Knowledge workers are professional employees such as financial and marketing analysts, engineers, lawyers, and accountants. All knowledge workers are experts in a particular subject area. They create information and knowledge, which they integrate into the business. Knowledge workers, in turn, act as advisors to middle managers and executives. Finally, *executives* make decisions that deal with situations that can significantly change the manner in which business is done. Examples of executive decisions are introducing a new product line, acquiring other businesses, and relocating operations to a foreign country.

Office automation systems (OASs) typically support the clerical staff, lower and middle managers, and knowledge workers. These employees use OASs to develop documents (word processing and desktop publishing software), schedule resources (electronic calendars), and communicate (e-mail, voice mail, videoconferencing, and groupware).

Functional area information systems summarize data and prepare reports, primarily for middle managers, but sometimes for lower-level managers as well. Because these reports typically concern a specific functional area, report generators (RPGs) are an important type of functional area IS.

Business intelligence (BI) systems provide computer-based support for complex, non-routine decisions, primarily for middle managers and knowledge workers. (They also support lower-level managers, but to a lesser extent.) These systems are typically used with a data warehouse, and they enable users to perform their own data analysis. You learn about BI systems in Chapter 5.

Expert systems (ES) attempt to duplicate the work of human experts by applying reasoning capabilities, knowledge, and expertise within a specific domain. They have become valuable in many application areas, primarily but not exclusively areas involving decision making. For example, navigation systems use rules to select routes, but we do not typically think of these systems as expert systems. Significantly, expert systems can operate as standalone systems or be embedded in other applications. We examine ESs in greater detail in Plug IT In 5.

Dashboards (also called **digital dashboards**) are a special form of IS that support all managers of the organization. They provide rapid access to timely information and direct access to structured information in the form of reports. Dashboards that are tailored to the information needs of executives are called *executive dashboards*. Chapter 5 provides a thorough discussion of dashboards.

Table 1.4 provides an overview of the different types of information systems used by organizations.

TABLE 1.4   Types of Organizational Information Systems

Type of System	Function	Example
Functional area IS	Supports the activities within specific functional area.	System for processing payroll
Transaction processing system	Processes transaction data from terminal	Walmart checkout point-of-sale business events
Enterprise resource planning	Integrates all functional areas of the organization.	Oracle, SAP system
Office automation system	Supports daily work activities of individuals and groups.	Microsoft® Office
Management information system	Produces reports summarized from transaction data, usually in one functional area.	Report on total sales for each customer
Decision support system	Provides access to data and analysis tools.	"What-if" analysis of changes in budget
Expert system	Mimics human expert in a particular area and makes decisions.	Credit card approval analysis
Executive dashboard	Presents structured, summarized information about aspects of business important to executives.	Status of sales by product
Supply chain management system	Manages flows of products, services, and information among organizations.	Walmart Retail Link system connecting suppliers to Walmart
Electronic commerce system	Enables transactions among organizations and between organizations and customers.	www.dell.com

Before you go on...

1. What is a computer-based information system?

2. Describe the components of computer-based information systems.

3. What is an application program?

4. Explain how information systems provide support for knowledge workers.

5. As we move up the organization's hierarchy from clerical workers to executives, how does the type of support provided by information systems change?

Apply the Concept 1.2

LEARNING OBJECTIVE 1.2 Classify the activities supported by various types of computer-based information systems in an organization.

STEP 1: Background

Section 1.2 discussed the various functional areas in which you most likely will be employed and the different IS that support them. It should be no surprise that these are the majors you can choose from in most colleges of business. The four major functional areas are marketing/sales, finance/accounting, manufacturing, and human resources. Often, these areas will use the same database and networks within a company, but they will use them to support their specific needs. This activity will help you develop a solid understanding of the role of IS within the different functional areas.

STEP 2: Activity

Review the section material that describes the major functions of the four major functional areas. Then, review the basic functions of the following types of information systems: transaction processing, management information, and decision support.

After you have acquired a solid understanding of the functional areas and information systems that support them, you are ready to move forward with the activity!

STEP 3: Assignment

Create a table like the one shown below, and classify the activities supported by various types of computer-based information systems. To assist you, we have prefilled one item in each type of system. After you complete your chart, submit it to your professor.

	Transaction Processing	Management Information System	Decision Support System
Marketing/ Sales	Enter Sales Data		
Accounting/ Finance			
Human Resources			Comply with EEOC
Manufacturing		Inventory Reporting	

1.3 | How Does IT Impact Organizations?

Throughout this text you will encounter numerous examples of how IT affects various types of organizations, which will give you an idea just how important IT actually is to organizations. In fact, for the vast majority of organizations, if their information systems fail, they cease operations until the problems are found and fixed. Consider these examples:

- In July 2015, United Airlines flights were grounded worldwide for about two hours due to a computer problem in the airline's reservation system. United canceled 61 flights and another 1,162 flights were delayed.
- Also in July 2015, the New York Stock Exchange suspended trading for almost four hours due to a software upgrade.

This section provides an overview of the impact of IT on modern organizations. As you read this section you will learn how IT will affect you as well.

IT Impacts Entire Industries

As of mid-2015, the technology required to transform industries through software had been developed and integrated and could be delivered globally. In addition, software tools and Internet-based services enabled companies in many industries to launch new software-powered startups without investing in new infrastructure or training new employees. For example, in 2000, operating a basic Internet application cost businesses approximately $150,000 per month. In mid-2015, operating that same application in Amazon's cloud (we discuss cloud computing in detail in Plug IT In 4) cost less than $1,000 per month.

In essence, software is impacting every industry, and every organization must prepare for these impacts. Let's examine a few examples of software disruption across several industries. Many of these examples focus on two scenarios: (1) industries where software disrupted the previous market-leading companies and (2) industries where a new company (or companies) used software to achieve a competitive advantage.

The Book Industry. What is the largest book publisher and bookseller in the United States today? Would it surprise you to learn that the answer is Amazon, a software company? Amazon's core capability is its software engine, which can sell virtually anything online without building or maintaining any retail stores. Now, even books themselves have become software products, known as electronic (or digital) books, or eBooks. (In mid- 2015, electronic books were gaining in popularity, but approximately 80 percent of book sales were still for print books.)

- Consider the Borders bookstore chain. In 2001, Borders agreed to hand over its online business to Amazon because Borders was convinced that online book sales were nonstrategic and unimportant. Ten years later, Borders filed for bankruptcy.

The Music Industry. Total U.S. album sales peaked at 785 million in 2000, which was the year after Napster was created. (Recall that Napster allowed anyone with a computer and a reasonably fast Web connection to download and trade music for free.) From 2000 to 2015, the major music labels (companies) worked diligently to eliminate illegal downloading and sharing, but album sales continued to decline. The result was that the music labels earned about $8 billion less in annual retail sales in 2015 than they did in 2000. In addition, prior to 1999 six major music labels dominated the industry. By 2015, a series of mergers had created the "Big Three" music labels: Warner Music Group (www.wmg.com), Universal Music (www.universal-music.com), and Sony (www.sonymusic.com).

These large changes in the music industry were due to the emergence of digital music streaming technologies over the Internet. Two digital-streaming business models emerged: Internet radio companies such as Pandora (www.pandora.com) that allow subscribers to passively listen to music that is customized for their tastes and interactive companies such as Spotify (www.spotify.com) and Apple's iTunes (www.apple.com/itunes) that allow users to pick songs. Internet radio companies can operate under a government-mandated license that dictates how much they have to pay. In contrast, interactive companies must make deals with labels and music publishers in order to license music for legal use in the United States.

Responding to these disruptions, the Big Three music labels have been buying stakes in digital entertainment startups, such as established streaming services Spotify (www.spotify.com) and Rdio (www.rdio.com). The labels buy stakes very cheaply, and then often give themselves the right to buy larger amounts at deep discounts to market at a later date. The labels have purchased parts of startups such as choose-your-own-adventure music video seller Interlude (https://interlude.fm), song-recognition company Shazam (www.shazam.com), and SoundCloud (https://soundcloud.com). Industry analysts estimate that the three labels have amassed positions in digital music startups valued at some $3 billion.

The Video Industry. Blockbuster—which rented and sold videos and ancillary products through its chain of stores—was the industry leader until it was disrupted by a software company, Netflix (www.netflix.com). In mid-2015, Netflix had the largest subscriber base of any video service with millions of subscribers. Meanwhile, Blockbuster declared bankruptcy in February 2011 and was acquired by satellite television provider Dish Network (www.dish.com) a month later.

MIS

The Software Industry. Incumbent software companies such as Oracle and Microsoft are increasingly threatened by software-as-a-service (SaaS) products (e.g., Salesforce.com) and Android, an open-source operating system developed by the Open Handset Alliance (www.openhandsetalliance.com). (We discuss operating systems in Plug IT In 2 and SaaS in Plug IT In 4.)

The Videogame Industry. Today, the fastest growing entertainment companies are videogame makers—again, software. Examples are: Zynga (www.zynga.com), the creator of Farm-Ville; Rovio (www.rovio.com), the maker of Angry Birds; and Minecraft (www.minecraft.net), now owned by Microsoft (www.microsoft.com).

The Photography Industry. This industry was disrupted by software years ago. Today it is virtually impossible to buy a mobile phone that does not include a software-powered camera. In addition, people can upload photos automatically to the Internet for permanent archiving and global sharing. Leading photography companies include Shutterfly (www.shutterfly.com), Snapfish (www.snapfish.com), Flickr (www.flickr.com), and Instagram (www.instagram.com). Meanwhile, the longtime market leader, Kodak—whose name was almost synonymous with cameras—declared bankruptcy in January 2012.

The Marketing Industry. Today's largest direct marketing companies include Facebook (www.facebook.com), Google (www.google.com), and Foursquare (www.foursquare.com). All of these companies are using software to disrupt the retail marketing industry.

`MKT`

The Recruiting Industry. LinkedIn (www.linkedin.com) is disrupting the traditional job recruiting industry. For the first time, employees and job searchers can maintain their resumes on a publicly accessible Web site that interested parties can search in real time.

`HRM`

The Financial Services Industry. Software has transformed the financial services industry. Practically every financial transaction (for example, buying and selling stocks) is now performed by software. Also, many of the leading innovators in financial services are software companies. For example, Square (https://squareup.com) allows anyone to accept credit card payments with a mobile phone.

`FIN`

The Motion Picture Industry. The process of making feature-length computer-generated films has become incredibly IT intensive. Studios require state-of-the-art information technologies, including massive numbers of servers, sophisticated software, and an enormous amount of storage (all described in Plug IT In 2).

Consider DreamWorks Animation (www.dreamworksanimation.com), a motion picture studio that creates animated feature films, television programs, and online virtual worlds. For a single motion picture, the studio manages more than 500,000 files and 300 terabytes (a terabyte is 1 trillion bytes) of data, and it uses about 80 million central processing unit (CPU; described in Plug IT In 2) hours. As DreamWorks executives state, "In reality, our product is data that looks like a movie. We are a digital manufacturing company."

Software is also disrupting industries that operate primarily in the physical world. Consider these examples:

- **The Automobile Industry:** In modern cars, software is responsible for running the engines; controlling safety features; entertaining passengers; guiding drivers to their destinations; and connecting the car to mobile, satellite, and GPS networks. Other software functions in modern cars include Wi-Fi receivers, which turn your car into a mobile hot spot; software, which helps maximize fuel efficiency; and ultrasonic sensors, which enable some models to parallel-park automatically.

The next step is to network all vehicles together, a necessary step toward the next major breakthrough: self-driving or driverless cars. The creation of software-powered driverless cars is already being undertaken at Google as well as at several major car companies, and interestingly, Apple.

- **The Agriculture Industry:** Agriculture is increasingly powered by software, including satellite analysis of soils linked to per-acre seed selection software algorithms. In addition, precision agriculture makes use of automated, driverless tractors controlled by global positioning systems and software. (Precision agriculture is based on observing, measuring, and responding to inter- and intra-field variability.)
- **National Defense:** Even national defense is increasingly software based. The modern combat soldier is embedded in a web of software that provides intelligence, communications, logistics, and weapons guidance. Software-powered drone aircraft launch airstrikes without placing human pilots at risk. Intelligence agencies perform large-scale data mining with software to uncover and track potential terrorist plots.

- **The Fashion Industry:** Women have long "borrowed" special-occasion dresses from department stores, buying them and then returning them after wearing them for one evening. Now, Rent the Runway (www.renttherunway.com) has redefined the fashion business, making expensive clothing available to more women than ever before. The firm is also disrupting traditional physical retailers. After all, why buy a dress when you can rent one for a very low price? Some department stores feel so threatened by Rent the Runway that they have reportedly told vendors that they will remove floor merchandise if it ever shows up on that company's Web site.

- **Education:** College graduates owe approximately $1 trillion in student debt, a crippling burden for many recent graduates. Consider UniversityNow (www.unow.com), founded to make college more accessible to working adults by offering online, self-paced degrees. Two key characteristics distinguish UniversityNow from an increasing number of rivals: (1) very low fees (as little as $2,600, which includes tuition and books for as many courses as students can complete in one year) and (2) fully accredited degrees, from an associate's degree to an M.B.A.

- **The Legal Profession:** Today, electronic discovery (e-discovery) software applications can analyze documents in a fraction of the time that human lawyers would take, at a fraction of the cost. For example, Blackstone Discovery (www.blackstonediscovery.com) helped one company analyze 1.5 million documents for less than $100,000. That company estimated that the process would have cost $1.5 million had it been performed by lawyers.

IT Reduces the Number of Middle Managers

IT makes managers more productive, and it increases the number of employees who can report to a single manager. Thus, IT ultimately decreases the number of managers and experts. It is reasonable to assume, therefore, that in coming years organizations will have fewer managerial levels and fewer staff and line managers. If this trend materializes, promotional opportunities will decrease, making promotions much more competitive. Bottom line: Pay attention in school!

IT Changes the Manager's Job

One of the most important tasks of managers is making decisions. A major consequence of IT has been to change the manner in which managers make their decisions. In this way, IT ultimately has changed managers' jobs.

IT often provides managers with near-real-time information, meaning that managers have less time to make decisions, making their jobs even more stressful. Fortunately, IT also provides many tools—for example, business analytics applications such as dashboards, search engines, and intranets—to help managers handle the volumes of information they must deal with on an ongoing basis.

So far in this section, we have been focusing on managers in general. Now, let's focus on you. Due to advances in IT, you will increasingly supervise employees and teams who are geographically dispersed. Employees can work from anywhere at any time, and teams can consist of employees who are literally dispersed throughout the world. Information technologies such as telepresence systems (discussed in Chapter 4) can help you manage these employees even though you do not often see them face-to-face. For these employees, electronic or "remote" supervision will become the norm. Remote supervision places greater emphasis on completed work and less emphasis on personal contacts and office politics. You will have to reassure your employees that they are valued members of the organization, thereby diminishing any feelings they might have of being isolated and "out of the loop."

Will IT Eliminate Jobs?

One major concern of every employee, part-time or full-time, is job security. Relentless cost-cutting measures in modern organizations often lead to large-scale layoffs. Put simply, organizations are responding to today's highly competitive environment by doing more with less. Regardless of your position, then, you consistently will have to add value to your organization and to make certain that your superiors are aware of this value.

Many companies have responded to difficult economic times, increased global competition, demands for customization, and increased consumer sophistication by increasing their investments in IT. In fact, as computers continue to advance in terms of intelligence and capabilities, the competitive advantage of replacing people with machines is increasing rapidly. This process frequently leads to layoffs. At the same time, however, IT creates entirely new categories of jobs, such as electronic medical record keeping and nanotechnology.

IT Impacts Employees at Work

Many people have experienced a loss of identity because of computerization. They feel like "just another number" because computers reduce or eliminate the human element present in noncomputerized systems.

The Internet threatens to exert an even more isolating influence than have computers and television. Encouraging people to work and shop from their living rooms could produce some unfortunate psychological effects, such as depression and loneliness.

IT Impacts Employees' Health and Safety. Although computers and information systems are generally regarded as agents of "progress," they can adversely affect individuals' health and safety. To illustrate this point, we consider two issues associated with IT: job stress and long-term use of the keyboard. `HRM`

An increase in an employee's workload and/or responsibilities can trigger *job stress*. Although computerization has benefited organizations by increasing productivity, it also has created an ever-expanding workload for some employees. Some workers feel overwhelmed and have become increasingly anxious about their job performance. These feelings of stress and anxiety can actually diminish rather than improve workers' productivity while jeopardizing their physical and mental health. Management can help alleviate these problems by providing training, redistributing the workload among workers, and hiring more workers.

On a more specific level, the long-term use of keyboards can lead to *repetitive strain injuries* such as backaches and muscle tension in the wrists and fingers. *Carpal tunnel syndrome* is a particularly painful form of repetitive strain injury that affects the wrists and hands.

Designers are aware of the potential problems associated with the prolonged use of computers. To address these problems, they continually attempt to design a better computing environment. The science of designing machines and work settings that minimize injury and illness is called ergonomics. The goal of ergonomics is to create an environment that is safe, well lit, and comfortable. Examples of ergonomically designed products are antiglare screens that alleviate problems of fatigued or damaged eyesight and chairs that contour the human body to decrease backaches. Figure 1.6 displays some sample ergonomic products.

IT Provides Opportunities for People with Disabilities. Computers can create new employment opportunities for people with disabilities by integrating speech-recognition and vision-recognition capabilities. For example, individuals who cannot type can use a voice-operated keyboard, and individuals who cannot travel can work at home.

Going further, adaptive equipment for computers enables people with disabilities to perform tasks they normally would not be able to do. For example, the Web and graphical user interfaces (GUIs; e.g., Windows) can be difficult for people with impaired vision to use. To address this problem, manufacturers have added audible screen tips and voice interfaces, which essentially restore the functionality of computers to the way it was before GUIs become standard.

Other devices help improve the quality of life in more mundane, but useful, ways for people with disabilities. Examples are a two-way writing telephone, a robotic page turner, a hair brusher, and a hospital-bedside video trip to the zoo or the museum. Several organizations specialize in IT designed for people with disabilities.

FIGURE 1.6 Ergonomic products protect computer users.

Media Bakery

Media Bakery

Media Bakery

Media Bakery

Before you go on...

1. Why should employees in all functional areas become knowledgeable about IT?
2. Describe how IT might change the manager's job.
3. Discuss several ways in which IT impacts employees at work.

Apply the Concept 1.3

LEARNING OBJECTIVE 1.3 Discuss ways in which information technology can affect managers and nonmanagerial workers.

STEP 1: Background

Section 1.3 demonstrated that the essential reason businesses use information systems is to add value to their daily activities. In fact, IS have radically transformed the nature of both managerial and nonmanagerial work. Managers employ IT to instantly track information that previously was available only in monthly reports. Support staff can view calendars and schedules for all employees and can schedule meetings more easily. Sales representatives can view current product information while visiting with clients. This list does not even scratch the surface of the countless ways technology has added value to modern businesses.

STEP 2: Activity

Consider the restaurant industry. You have probably visited some "old school" restaurants where your order is written down on a piece of paper and never entered into a computer system for preparation. You have most likely also been to a very modern restaurant where you enter your own order with a tablet, smartphone, or other piece of equipment. Visit http://www.wiley.com/go/rainer/MIS4e/applytheconcept and watch the two videos about using the restaurant table as the menu and ordering stem.

STEP 3: Assignment

Imagine that you are a manager in each type of restaurant. How does working without technology impact how you do your job? How does adding the technology change your performance? Based on your thoughts from Step 2, imagine that you are explaining to your friend the ways that restaurants could benefit from IT. Prepare a paragraph or two that will discuss the ways that the traditional job of a restaurant manager and other employees has been changed by IT.

1.4

Importance of Information Systems to Society

This section explains in greater detail why IT is important to society as a whole. Other examples of the impact of IT on society appear throughout the text. IT's About Business 1.2 illustrates how IT is impacting one society—Cuba—in its entirety.

IT's About Business 1.2

Information Technology Has the Potential for "Revolutionizing" Cuba

In recent years, Cuba's private sector has been undergoing a huge transformation. Hundreds of thousands of Cubans have obtained licenses to operate small businesses, but only in a limited set of service categories such as restaurants, hair salons, and translation services. Despite the limitations, by the end of 2014, the number of licensed entrepreneurs—called *cuentapropistas* in Cuba; roughly translated as "those who are on their own"—rose to more than 471,000.

Unfortunately, the vast majority of these entrepreneurs do not use the Internet because they do not have access to it. In fact, experts estimate that only about 5 percent of Cuba's citizens have even periodic Internet access. As of mid-2015, only the "elite" had easy Internet access, and only 5 percent of Cubans could access the Internet from home. The public can visit cybercafés that are sanctioned by the government. However, it costs more than $5 per hour to access sites outside the country. To put this in perspective, the average Cuban earns $20 a month. Another barrier to Internet access is that visitors to cybercafés must sign agreements that their Internet use will not harm "public security."

As we discuss below, Cuba is a country of memory sticks and human middlemen, physically sent to conduct what in the developed world are frictionless digital transactions. In Cuba, smartphones are common, but they do not have data connections. Further, there is no legal way to send or receive payments using credit cards or PayPal.

Young, highly motivated Cuban entrepreneurs, the country's millennials, are circumventing these enormous hindrances by using digital technologies in different ways. Let's consider four examples: Revolico, AlaMesa, El Paquete Semanal, and Vistar.

MKT *Revolico* (www.revolico.com). Black markets have been commonplace in Cuba for many years, but it was difficult for buyers and sellers to find each other. In December 2007, a young Cuban anonymously created Revolico, a Web site for classified ads that quickly became the Craigslist of Cuba.

Three months after the site's launch, the government blocked it. Revolico got around the blocks by changing the Web address for its servers and e-mailing personalized URLs to its users. The back-and-forth between Revolico and the government continues as of this writing (July 2015). Despite these tensions, however, Revolico has become part of the daily life of many Cubans.

By July 2015, Revolico had approximately 8 million page views per month and 25,000 new listings daily. About half of its traffic came from outside Cuba—most of it from south Florida, which houses a large Cuban population—where the site makes some money selling ads. In Cuba, Revolico has no legal standing. The site charges for premium listings, which it promotes. Associates of Revolico collect payment for those listings unofficially, in cash.

MKT *AlaMesa* (www.alamesacuba.com). AlaMesa is a Web site and Android app that promotes Cuban culinary culture (think Yelp and OpenTable). Going door-to-door, AlaMesa staff members check out restaurants, examine their menus, and, if the restaurants agree, list them on the Web site and app. More than 600 restaurants in nine Cuban provinces have agreed to be listed. Roughly 30 percent of these restaurants pay, in cash, to be promoted on the site and app. Foreigners planning a trip to Cuba can download the app while at home. In Cuba, devoted fans spread the app by physically passing memory sticks to one another.

El Paquete Semanal. El Paquete Semanal ("the weekly package") is the "Internet-in-a-box" for a nonconnected country. More precisely, it is the Internet on a portable hard drive. El Paquete is a large digital collection of recent movies, TV shows, magazines, apps, software updates, and other digital content made available to Cubans. It is copied and distributed on portable hard drives to 100 people, who then distribute it to 1,000 people, and so on. El Paquete is delivered through an informal network of human "mules" who travel in public buses to every corner of the island. Most customers get the drive at home, where they exchange it for last week's drive. Customers pay more for more recent material and they pay based on the amount of material they receive.

Vistar (www.vistarmagazine.com). In 2013, the Cuban government's Office of Periodicals and Publications turned down a young Cuban's application to start an online magazine focusing on Cuba's youth culture. The young man decided to publish the magazine anyway, without identifying the magazine's creators. The first issue of *Vistar* came out in March 2014. It contained excellent photography and articles on food, music, ballet, art, and celebrities. By July 2015, *Vistar* had published sixteen monthly issues and even listed the magazine's staff on the masthead. Significantly, the government has not yet officially objected.

Although *Vistar*'s readers have not been harassed by the government, they have to deal with their country's lack of connectivity. As a result, they access the magazine by sharing memory sticks and hard drives. The magazine's staff support themselves through advertising. This process is noteworthy because advertising that is not linked to the government has been almost nonexistent for 50 years. *Vistar*, which now publishes in English as well as Spanish, has more than 100,000 downloads, with 60 percent of them originating outside Cuba.

Cuba's relations with the United States are improving, following President Obama's decision in December 2014 to begin normalizing relations between the two countries. Under the proposal, Cuban citizens could enjoy much improved access to communications technology. However, the Internet is still strictly controlled under the Raúl Castro regime, and there are economic barriers as well as political ones, so it's not certain whether and when Cubans will have inexpensive and open Internet access.

And the bottom line? Cuban citizens continue their entrepreneurial activities, not knowing whether the government will shut them down. Meanwhile, in June 2015, the Cuban government announced it would sanction 35 Wi-Fi hotspots around the country, which Cubans can access for $2 per hour. Cubans wryly note that this is "good news, bad news." The good news is that the government is allowing any Wi-Fi hotspots at all. The bad news is that most Cubans still cannot afford to use them.

Sources: Compiled from A. Popescu, "Cuban Web Entrepreneur Endures a Murky Status," *MIT Technology Review*, October 6, 2015; I. Lakshmanan, "Where the Internet Revolution Is Waiting to Happen," *Bloomberg BusinessWeek*, September 1420, 2015; M. Helft, "Cuba's Tech Revolutionaries," *Forbes*, July 21, 2015; J. Hamre, "Cuba, an Internet Laggard, Opens Wi-Fi Hotspots across Country," *Reuters*, July 2, 2015; V. Burnett, "Cuba Offers Its Citizens Better Access to Internet," *The New York Times*, June 18, 2015; "Cuba to Expand Internet Access to Battle Country's Dire Lack of Connectivity," *Associated Press*, June 18, 2015; D. Renwick and B. Lee, "U.S.-Cuba Relations," *Council on Foreign Relations*, May 29, 2015; S. Marshall, "This Is What It's Like Using the Internet in Cuba," *ABC News*, March 31, 2015; N. Young, "Cuba's Underground Alternative to the Internet," *www.cbc.ca*, January 25, 2015; T. Johnson, "No Internet in Cuba? For Some, Offline Link to World Arrives Weekly," *McClatchyDC*, January 9, 2015; D. Talbot, "Cuba's Internet Revolution Faces Economic and Political Realities," *MIT Technology Review*, December 21, 2014; S. Fernandes and A. Halkin, "Do Cubans Really Want U.S.-Style Internet Freedom?" *nacla.org*, December 20, 2014; P. Baker, "U.S. to Restore Full Relations with Cuba, Erasing a Last Trace of Cold War Hostility," *The New York Times*, December 17, 2014.

Questions

1. Describe the "work-arounds" that Cuban entrepreneurs must perform to use digital technologies in the four examples discussed in this case.

2. Discuss how free, open access to high-speed Internet connections would transform the operations of each of the four examples.

3. Why would the Cuban government limit access to the Internet? Provide specific examples in your answer.

IT Affects Our Quality of Life

IT has significant implications for our quality of life. The workplace can be expanded from the traditional 9-to-5 job at a central location to 24 hours a day at any location. IT can provide employees with flexibility that can significantly improve the quality of leisure time, even if it doesn't increase the total amount of leisure time.

From the opposite perspective, however, IT also can place employees on "constant call," which means they are never truly away from the office, even when they are on vacation. In fact, surveys reveal that the majority of respondents take their laptops and smartphones on their vacations, and 100 percent took their cell phones. Going further, the majority of respondents did some work while vacationing, and almost all of them checked their e-mail regularly.

The Robot Revolution Is Here Now

Once restricted largely to science fiction movies, robots that can perform practical tasks are becoming more common. Around the world, quasi-autonomous devices have become increasingly common on factory floors, in hospital corridors, and in farm fields. Let's look at two examples: Baxter and drones.

Baxter Baxter is a new kind of industrial robot by Rethink Robotics (www.rethinkrobotics.com) that sells for $25,000. Humans share a workspace with Baxter, making it an excellent example of a social, collaborative robot. Baxter works right out of the box and can be integrated into a factory's workflow in about one hour. Another benefit of Baxter is that other factory workers can train it.

In November 2014 Rethink Robotics announced its new Robot Positioning System for Baxter. This system enables Baxter to adapt to changing, real-world environments, such as tables and benches being moved. The new system highlights a huge advantage for companies that acquire Baxter. Because so much of Baxter's capabilities are contained in its software, when the robot is upgraded it tends to *increase in value*.

However, Baxter does raise the question of the future of low-skilled labor in the United States: How fast will Baxter replace these workers, and what will they do after they are replaced?

Drones   A *drone* is an unmanned aerial vehicle (UAV) that either is controlled by pilots from the ground or autonomously follows a preprogrammed mission. Commercial drones are used for a wide variety of business purposes, in contrast to drones used by hobbyists for recreational purposes. Let's examine five industries that are currently employing drones.

Sensors on drones, coupled with data analytics (see Chapter 12), are extending *precision agriculture* beyond simply monitoring crops. Drones help farmers increase crop yields by optimizing the fertilizer mix for different parts of a field down to the square meter. They similarly help winemakers increase yields by precisely controlling drip irrigation down to the individual vine.

On large-scale *construction* sites, envisioning the overall "picture" presents a major challenge for contractors. Drones enable project managers from construction giants such as Bechtel (www.bechtel.com) and DPR (www.dpr.com) to monitor progress and supply stockpiles on a real-time basis.

The *energy* industry uses drones for applications beyond monitoring and inspecting pipelines. In Alaska, BP (www.bp.com) uses drones to monitor its gravel-extraction operations to comply with environmental guidelines. ConocoPhillips (www.conocophillips.com) and Chevron (www.chevron.com) use drones in the Arctic to help search for new sources of oil. First Solar (www.firstsolar.com) uses drones to inspect for faulty solar panels.

Large *mining* companies such as Rio Tinto (www.riotinto.com) are reducing risk to their workers by using drones to detect potential landslides and to inspect safety infrastructure, as well as to more accurately monitor how much mineral their workers are extracting.

American *film and television* studios, such as 20th Century Fox (www.foxmovies.com) and Warner Bros (www.warnerbros.com), have been using drones in their overseas productions because they were allowed to do so by foreign governments. When the FAA allowed them to use drones in U.S. airspace, these studios began to move their operations back to the United States.

It probably will be a long time before we see robots making decisions by themselves, handling unfamiliar situations, and interacting with people. Nevertheless, robots are extremely helpful in various environments, particularly those that are repetitive, harsh, or dangerous to humans.

Improvements in Healthcare

IT has brought about major improvements in healthcare delivery. Medical personnel use IT to make better and faster diagnoses and to monitor critically ill patients more accurately. IT also has streamlined the process of researching and developing new drugs. Expert systems now help doctors diagnose diseases, and machine vision is enhancing the work of radiologists. Surgeons use virtual reality to plan complex surgeries. They also employ surgical robots to perform long-distance surgery. Finally, doctors discuss complex medical cases via videoconferencing. New computer simulations recreate the sense of touch, allowing doctors-in-training to perform virtual procedures without risking harm to an actual patient.

Information technology can be applied to improve the efficiency and effectiveness of healthcare. In IT's About Business 1.3 you will see how Apricot Forest is using information technology to improve healthcare in China.

IT's About Business 1.3

MIS Apricot Forest Helps China's Physicians

In China, entry-level doctors earn about as much as taxi drivers—roughly $500 a month. Most work in state-operated hospitals and see up to 60 patients per day. Not only are their caseloads potentially overwhelming, but doctors also face violence from patients. In 2012, each Chinese hospital experienced an average of 27 patient assaults of healthcare providers. In some cases, they beat, stabbed, or even killed doctors who didn't meet their expectations.

Needless to say, there was an opportunity for technology to help Chinese physicians manage their caseload and work environment. Essentially, such tools must provide China's physicians with more data—about patients, their records, and their illnesses—as well as easier access to those data. Further, the tools must allow physicians and their patients to communicate seamlessly.

Apricot Forest (http://www.xingshulin.com) is a Beijing-based startup company that developed three apps to help Chinese physicians. The main app is MedClip, the Swiss army knife of applications. It allows doctors to take photos of patient records, dictate notes, and store and organize patient charts. It links up with the popular Chinese messaging system Weixin ("WeChat") to send reminders and health information to patients. Doctors can also consult with each other regarding more challenging cases. Apricot Forest's second medical app, e-Pocket, is a database that doctors can refer to with information on drug formulations and specialized calculators. Medical Journals, the third app, gives doctors access to articles in medical journals. The company notes that all these apps allow doctors to make house calls, accessing patient and other information at the touch of a button.

With China's doctors earning so little money, how does Apricot Forest get revenues? It goes beyond the app sales for other revenue streams. For example, it charges drug companies for advertisements inside the apps. It earns a commission on the books and other publications purchased through the e-Pocket and Medical Journals apps. The company plans to charge patients for using MedClip to contact their doctors, which is difficult under the existing health care system. Doctors would benefit from keeping their phone numbers private and controlling the amount of contact with patients. Another potential moneymaker from the apps is to aggregate and analyze the data that doctors upload to MedClip and sell reports to companies that make medical products.

And the results? By early 2015, roughly 1 in 4 of China's 2.5 million physicians were using at least one of Apricot Forest's apps.

Sources: Compiled from "The Healthcare System and Medical Device Market in China," *PR Newswire,* February 17, 2015; "Most Innovative Companies 2015," *FastCompany,* March 2015; L. Qi and L. Burkitt, "Falling through the Cracks of China's Health-Care System," *The Wall Street Journal*, January 4, 2015; S. Shankar, "Hospital Attack in Northern China's Beidaihe Town Kills 7 People, Including 6 Nurses," *International Business Times,* November 20, 2014; C. Beam, "Under the Knife," *The New Yorker,* August 25, 2014; E. Rauhala, "Why China's Doctors Are Getting Beaten Up," *Time,* March 7, 2014; P. Bischoff, "Apricot Forest Wants to Streamline Your Hospital Visits," *TechinAsia,* June 6, 2013; www.xingshulin.com, accessed February 25, 2015.

Questions

1. Explain how Apricot Forest's apps will help improve the relationship between physicians and patients in China.

2. Explain how Apricot Forest's apps will help improve overall healthcare in China.

3. Discuss potential disadvantages of Apricot Forest's apps to patients.

4. Discuss potential disadvantages of Apricot Forest's apps to physicians.

Among the thousands of other healthcare applications, administrative systems are critically important. These systems perform functions ranging from detecting insurance fraud, to creating nursing schedules, to financial and marketing management.

The Internet contains vast amounts of useful medical information (see www.webmd.com, for example). Despite the fact that this information exists on the Internet, physicians caution against self-diagnosis. They maintain that people should use diagnostic information obtained from Google and medical Web sites such as WebMD (www.webmd.com) only to ask questions of their physicians.

Before you go on...

1. What are some of the quality-of-life improvements made possible by IT? Has IT had any negative effects on our quality of life? If so, explain, and provide examples.

2. Describe the robotic revolution, and consider its implications for humans.

3. Explain how IT has improved healthcare practices.

Apply the Concept 1.4

LEARNING OBJECTIVE 1.4 Identify positive and negative societal effects of the increased use of information technology.

STEP 1: Background

As you have just read, the increased use of IS has had a significant impact on society. Section 1.4 focused on three areas—quality of life improvements, robotics, and healthcare—to spark your interest in the ways our lives are being touched. Unfortunately, the technologies that provide quality-of-life improvements can also create economic and political problems. For example, robots that make production more streamlined also eliminate jobs. Similarly, healthcare improvements raise concerns regarding shared data and privacy violations.

STEP 2: Activity

Conduct a Web search for "technology and work/life balance." Look for programs, articles, research, suggestions, and other materials that help you understand the positive and negative effects of the increased use of information technologies.

STEP 3: Assignment

Create a table that identifies the positive and negative effects for the following areas: quality of life, robotics, healthcare, and work/life balance. Set your table up as in the example below, and submit it to your instructor.

	Positive	Negative
Quality of Life		
Robotics		
Healthcare		
Work/Life Balance		

What's in IT for me?

In Section 1.2, we discussed how IT supports each of the functional areas of the organization. Here we examine the MIS function.

MIS For the MIS Major

The MIS function directly supports all other functional areas in an organization. That is, the MIS function is responsible for providing the information that each functional area needs in order to make decisions. The overall objective of MIS personnel is to help users improve performance and solve business problems using IT. To accomplish this objective, MIS personnel must understand both the information requirements and the technology associated with each functional area. Given their position, however, they must think "business needs" first and "technology" second.

Summary

1. **Identify the reasons why being an informed user of information systems is important in today's world.**

The benefits of being an informed user of IT include the following:

- You will benefit more from your organization's IT applications because you will understand what is "behind" those applications.
- You will be able to provide input into your organization's IT applications, thus improving the quality of those applications.
- You will quickly be in a position to recommend, or participate in the selection of IT applications that your organization will use.
- You will be able to keep up with rapid developments in existing information technologies, as well as the introduction of new technologies.
- You will understand the potential impacts that "new and improved" technologies will have on your organization and therefore will be qualified to make recommendations concerning their adoption and use.
- You will play a key role in managing the information systems in your organization.
- You will be in a position to use IT if you decide to start your own business.

2. **Describe the various types of computer-based information systems in an organization.**
- Transaction processing systems (TPS) support the monitoring, collection, storage, and processing of data from the organization's basic business transactions, each of which generates data.
- Functional area information systems (FAISs) support a particular functional area within the organization.
- Interorganizational information systems (IOSs) support many interorganizational operations, of which supply chain management is the best known.
- Enterprise resource planning (ERP) systems correct a lack of communication among the FAISs by tightly integrating the functional area ISs via a common database.
- Electronic commerce (e-commerce) systems enable organizations to conduct transactions with other organizations (called

- business-to-business (B2B) electronic commerce), and with customers (called business-to-consumer (B2C) electronic commerce).

- Office automation systems (OASs) typically support the clerical staff, lower and middle managers, and knowledge workers, by enabling them to develop documents (word processing and desktop publishing software), schedule resources (electronic calendars), and communicate (e-mail, voice mail, videoconferencing, and groupware).

- Business intelligence (BI) systems provide computer-based support for complex, nonroutine decisions, primarily for middle managers and knowledge workers.

- Expert systems (ESs) attempt to duplicate the work of human experts by applying reasoning capabilities, knowledge, and expertise within a specific domain.

3. **Discuss ways in which information technology can affect managers and nonmanagerial workers.**

Potential IT impacts on managers:

- IT may reduce the number of middle managers;

- IT will provide managers with real-time or near real-time information, meaning that managers will have less time to make decisions;

- IT will increase the likelihood that managers will have to supervise geographically dispersed employees and teams.

- Potential IT impacts on nonmanagerial workers:

- IT may eliminate jobs;

- IT may cause employees to experience a loss of identity;

- IT can cause job stress and physical problems, such as repetitive stress injury.

4. **List positive and negative societal effects of the increased use of information technology.**

Positive societal effects:

- IT can provide opportunities for people with disabilities;

- IT can provide people with flexibility in their work (e.g., work from anywhere, anytime);

- Robots will take over mundane chores;

- T will enable improvements in healthcare.

Negative societal effects:

- IT can cause health problems for individuals;

- IT can place employees on constant call;

- IT can potentially misinform patients about their health problems.

Chapter Glossary

application (or app) A computer program designed to support a specific task or business process.

business intelligence (BI) systems Provide computer-based support for complex, nonroutine decisions, primarily for middle managers and knowledge workers.

computer-based information system (CBIS) An information system that uses computer technology to perform some or all of its intended tasks.

dashboards A special form of IS that support all managers of the organization by providing rapid access to timely information and direct access to structured information in the form of reports.

data items An elementary description of things, events, activities, and transactions that are recorded, classified, and stored but are not organized to convey any specific meaning.

database A collection of related files or tables containing data.

electronic commerce (e-commerce) systems A type of interorganizational information system that enables organizations to conduct transactions, called business-to-business (B2B) electronic commerce, and customers to conduct transactions with businesses, called business-to-consumer (B2C) electronic commerce.

enterprise resource planning (ERP) systems Information systems that correct a lack of communication among the functional area ISs by tightly integrating the functional area ISs via a common database.

ergonomics The science of adapting machines and work environments to people; focuses on creating an environment that is safe, well lit, and comfortable.

expert systems (ES) Attempt to duplicate the work of human experts by applying reasoning capabilities, knowledge, and expertise within a specific domain.

functional area information systems (FAISs) ISs that support a particular functional area within the organization.

hardware A device such as a processor, monitor, keyboard, or printer. Together, these devices accept, process, and display data and information.

information Data that have been organized so that they have meaning and value to the recipient.

information system (IS) Collects, processes, stores, analyzes, and disseminates information for a specific purpose.

information technology (IT) Relates to any computer-based tool that people use to work with information and support the information and information-processing needs of an organization.

information technology components Hardware, software, databases, and networks.

information technology infrastructure IT components plus IT services.

information technology platform Formed by the IT components of hardware, software, networks (wireline and wireless), and databases.

information technology services IT personnel use IT components to perform these IT services: develop information systems, oversee security and risk, and manage data.

informed user A person knowledgeable about information systems and information technology.

interorganizational information systems (IOSs) Information systems that connect two or more organizations.

knowledge Data and/or information that have been organized and processed to convey understanding, experience, accumulated learning, and expertise as they apply to a current problem or activity.

knowledge workers Professional employees such as financial and marketing analysts, engineers, lawyers, and accountants, who are experts in a particular subject area and create information and knowledge, which they integrate into the business.

network A connecting system (wireline or wireless) that permits different computers to share resources.

procedures The set of instructions for combining hardware, software, database, and network components in order to process information and generate the desired output.

software A program or collection of programs that enable the hardware to process data.

supply chain The flow of materials, information, money, and services from suppliers of raw materials through factories and warehouses to the end customers.

transaction processing system (TPS) Supports the monitoring, collection, storage, and processing of data from the organization's basic business transactions, each of which generates data.

Discussion Questions

1. Describe a business that you would like to start. Discuss how information technology could: (a) help you find and research an idea for a business, (b) help you formulate your business plan, and (c) help you finance your business.

2. Your university wants to recruit high-quality high school students from your state. Provide examples of (a) the data that your recruiters would gather in this process, (b) the information that your recruiters would process from these data, and (c) the types of knowledge that your recruiters would infer from this information.

3. Can the terms data, information, and knowledge have different meanings for different people? Support your answer with examples.

4. Information technology makes it possible to "never be out of touch." Discuss the pros and cons of always being available to your employers and clients (regardless of where you are or what you are doing).

5. Robots have the positive impact of being able to relieve humans from working in dangerous conditions. What are some negative impacts of robots in the workplace?

6. Is it possible to endanger yourself by accessing too much medical information on the Web? Why or why not? Support your answer.

7. Describe other potential impacts of IT on societies as a whole.

8. What are the major reasons why it is important for employees in all functional areas to become familiar with IT?

9. Given that information technology is impacting every industry, what does this mean for a company's employees? Provide specific examples to support your answer.

10. Given that information technology is impacting every industry, what does this mean for students attending a college of business? Provide specific examples to support your answer.

11. Is the vast amount of medical information on the Web a good thing? Answer from the standpoint of a patient and from the standpoint of a physician.

Problem-Solving Activities

1. Visit some Web sites that offer employment opportunities in IT. Prominent examples are: www.dice.com, www.monster.com, www.collegerecruiter.com, www.careerbuilder.com, www.jobcentral.com, www.job .com, www.career.com, www.simplyhired.com, and www.truecareers .com. Compare the IT salaries to salaries offered to accountants, marketing personnel, financial personnel, operations personnel, and human resources personnel. For other information on IT salaries, check *Computerworld*'s annual salary survey.

2. Enter the Web site of UPS (www.ups.com).

   a. Find out what information is available to customers before they send a package.

   b. Find out about the "package tracking" system.

   c. Compute the cost of delivering a 10" × 20" × 15" box, weighing 40 pounds, from your hometown to Long Beach, California (or to Lansing, Michigan, if you live in or near Long Beach). Compare the fastest delivery against the least cost. How long did this process take? Look into the business services offered by UPS. How do they make this process easier when you are a business customer?

3. Surf the Internet for information about the Department of Homeland Security (DHS). Examine the available information, and comment on the role of information technologies in the department.

4. Access www.irobot.com, and investigate the company's Education and Research Robots. Surf the Web for other companies that manufacture robots, and compare their products with those of iRobot.

Closing Case 1

POM The United States Postal Service Utilizes Information Technology to Modernize

The Problems

Every American is a customer of the United States Postal Service (USPS; www.usps.gov), an agency that delivers 158 billion pieces of mail per year. Despite its importance to U.S. citizens, however, the agency faces multiple challenges, including:

- Electronic mail has contributed to a decrease in the volume of first-class (or stamped) mail. This decrease has led to a decline in USPS revenue.

- Another cause of declining revenues is competition from private delivery companies like FedEx (www.fedex.com) and UPS (www.ups.com). These businesses are taking customers away from USPS's package delivery service while sometimes relying on the agency for last-mile delivery. Last-mile delivery is the final and typically most expensive leg of a delivery route.

- Other companies are also developing services that could disrupt the USPS's parcel delivery service. For example, Matternet (http://mttr.net), Amazon (Amazon Prime Air), and Google (Project Wing) have developed unmanned aerial vehicles, or drones, that can deliver packages and letters.

- Transportation has long been the essential skill at the USPS. Nevertheless, the agency has approximately 160,000 delivery vehicles that are 20 years old and need to be replaced.

- In contrast to transportation skills, digital technology has *not* been an essential skill at the USPS. One major example that illustrates this problem occurred in November 2014, when the USPS became a victim of a cyberattack that threatened to put the names, addresses, and social security numbers of 800,000 of its employees at risk.

Further, USPS efforts to utilize cloud computing to reduce costs have raised concerns. In September 2014, the USPS inspector general (IG) criticized the agency for not properly controlling applications in its cloud environment with regard to information accessibility and data security.

The USPS has long recognized these problems, and it has tried to introduce cost-saving measures. However, even though the agency is part of the executive branch of the federal government, Congress has enormous power over it. (The USPS is not funded by taxpayers.) Specifically, Congress has rejected proposals to eliminate Saturday delivery of first-class mail, and it has prevented the USPS from consolidating little-used post offices in rural areas. These moves would have helped the agency reduce costs. Congress has also required the USPS to make regular payments into its future retirees' health benefits, a mandate that imposed financial burdens on the agency.

The USPS also has massive amounts of data on every piece of mail exchanged among millions of Americans as well as the companies that sell to them. However, the agency must meet the privacy statutes that apply to federal agencies. As a result, the agency cannot sell its data to businesses to help them better target consumers and therefore increase sales revenues.

And the result of these numerous and diverse problems? Despite taking measures to reduce costs, such as closing processing centers and reducing employee working hours, 2015 was the USPS's ninth consecutive year of losses.

A Variety of Solutions

To address these problems, the USPS is implementing a variety of solutions. The agency is redesigning its mail-tracking system to encode as much information as possible on its letter and parcel bar codes with its Intelligent Mail bar code (IMB) system. The IMB uses automatic scanning devices and sorting equipment to scan bar codes to capture billions of data points and transmit them to a central database. Data range from the type of mail being delivered to a parcel's final destination. The IMB enables the agency's postal processing facilities to operate more efficiently.

In addition to supporting this real-time responsiveness, the USPS is also using data to enhance mail delivery. Accurately tracking how mail moves around the country, from the moment a delivery vehicle arrives at a dock to the second a letter reaches a delivery point, provides the agency with massive amounts of data. Data analytics enables the USPS to develop *dynamic routing*—the use of sophisticated algorithms to map out the most efficient and cost-effective mail delivery routes.

In addition, mobile computing is driving innovation at the USPS. The agency has been replacing letter carriers' cellphones with mobile delivery devices (MDDs). These handheld devices access multiple wireless networks to track parcels in real time. In addition, the MDDs provide the USPS with location data from its delivery vehicles. This process helps the agency to ensure its employees' safety, predict delivery times, and pick up urgent materials from its customers.

In the fall of 2014, the agency introduced an augmented reality technology designed to convert standard print ads into interactive experiences. The system enables consumers to use a free Android or iOS app to view digital presentations when they scan special icons that marketers attach to advertising brochures sent through the mail.

In November 2013, Amazon entered into an arrangement with the USPS to deliver packages on Sundays in select cities. The partnership created an opportunity for the USPS to establish a stronger foothold in the growing package-delivery market. Consequently, its package revenue increased 12 percent from 2012 to 2014.

In response to the Inspector General's criticisms regarding cloud applications, the USPS is utilizing the Federal Cloud Credential Exchange. The exchange is a cloud-based clearing service that acts as a hub for validating the digital credentials of people who want access to online government services. As a result, the Exchange also provides a high level of security for USPS applications running in the cloud.

And the largest missed opportunity for a possible solution? If federal privacy guidelines allowed the practice, the USPS could use the IMB to help retailers and catalog companies create successful marketing campaigns. Consider a retailer that receives an e-mail or a text message alert from the USPS that a particular customer has just received the company's catalog. The retailer could immediately e-mail the customer a digital coupon or a promotional offer in an effort to drive sales and enhance the overall customer experience.

The Results

The CIO of the USPS notes that information technology has become a core function within the agency. That is, IT is no longer a cost center. Instead, it adds essential value to the organization. However, the success or failure of these diverse initiatives remains to be seen. That is, can the USPS stop losing so much money each year, or at least slow the hemorrhage?

Sources: Compiled from D. Leonard, "From: Postmaster General; To: Amazon," *Bloomberg BusinessWeek*, August 3-9, 2015; S. Tracy, "Autonomous Vehicles Will Replace Taxi Drivers, but That's Just the Beginning," *Huffington Post*, June 12, 2015; "Intelligent Mail Barcode for Mailpieces," *United States Postal Service*, May 4, 2015; S. Edelstein, "U.S.P.S. 'Long Life' Vehicles Last 25 Years, But Age Shows Now," *Green Car Reports*, February 17, 2015; J. Williams, "Heading into 2015, USPS Looks to Tech to Reshape Model," *fedscoop*, December 31, 2014; C. Waxer, "Digital SOS: How Technology Can Save the USPS," *Computerworld*, December 8, 2014; C. Waxer, "Modernizing the Mail," *Computerworld*, December, 2014; J. Williams, "USPS Cloud Systems Don't Comply with Established Standards, OIG Says," *fedscoop*, September 10, 2014; M. Ashley, "Why Amazon Locker Is Better Than Home Delivery," *TechHive*, July 28, 2014; "U.S. Postal Service Parcel Delivery Lockers," *Office of Inspector General, United States Postal Service*; December 2013; J. Edgar, "How Technology Is Changing the USPS," *The Wall Street Journal*, October 10, 2013; W. Jackson, "USPS Set to Put Federal ID System to the Test," *GCN.com*, August 22, 2013; www.usps.gov, accessed July 14, 2015.

Questions

1. Provide specific examples of how information technology is negatively impacting the USPS.

2. Provide specific examples of how information technology is positively impacting the USPS.

3. Describe how information technology both positively and negatively impacts your university.

4. Is it possible to generalize and describe information technology as a "two-edged" sword for all organizations? Why or why not?

Closing Case 2

POM New Delivery Services Use Information Technology

The Problem

Webvan, an online grocery business that went bankrupt in 2001, is considered to be the largest dotcom failure in history. The company's business model was to deliver products to customers' homes within 30 minutes of a time they chose.

Today, busy consumers are increasingly looking for the convenience of having many items delivered on demand, with food being the largest category. In fact, despite the well-known failure of Webvan, many same-day, third-party delivery providers are emerging to compete in the $70 billion delivery business. Delivery services are an excellent strategy for small businesses to differentiate themselves from their competitors and to compete with giant online retailers.

Delivery service providers include some of the largest firms in technology and retail, as well as specialized startups. The major challenge facing these companies is how to deliver groceries and other items door-to-door without incurring unmanageable costs.

A Variety of Rapid Delivery-Service Solutions

These companies use information technology such as apps on GPS-enabled smartphones to bypass the need for warehouses and delivery fleets in their attempt to serve customers who are willing to pay a bit extra to have things done quickly. In addition, these companies often do not hire their workers. Rather, they use independent contractors who are willing to forgo benefits packages (e.g., health insurance, 401 K plans) for jobs they can perform whenever they want to.

The delivery services differ from more established grocery delivery companies such as FreshDirect (www.freshdirect.com), Peapod (www.peapod.com), and AmazonFresh (https://fresh.amazon.com) because they do not actually sell groceries directly to you. Instead, you select what you want online or via an app and choose a delivery time. The service then sends a contractor to the store to pick up your order and deliver it to your door. Let's take a look at some of these services.

Instacart. Instacart (www.instacart.com) delivers items from chains such as Safeway, Whole Foods, and Costco as well as local markets. Instacart has no physical infrastructure. In fact, the company consists of two grocery-delivery smartphone apps.

Customers place orders using Instacart's Web site or mobile app. A separate app, used by more than 4,000 personal shoppers whom Instacart has hired across 15 cities, guides the shoppers to stores from which they buy goods. The app actually identifies the aisle and the shelf where an item is located. The goal is to deliver orders within one hour of the order being placed.

Personal shoppers fill several orders at once as they go from store to store. The app suggests the optimal driving route to a customer's home, taking into account weather, traffic, sporting events, and local construction. Instacart charges a premium based on the size of each purchase. The company also offers a $99-per-year membership that waives the delivery fee for orders greater than $35.

Postmates. Postmates (https://postmates.com) works like this: The company's 13,000 couriers receive orders on their smartphones. For example, a customer wants 18 pounds of crushed ice, and Postmates offers the courier $4.80 to pick up the ice and deliver it. When the courier accepts the job, his phone guides him to the grocery store and then to the customer.

The majority of deliveries made by Postmates are hot meals. The company analyzes data such as food-preparation times to become more effective at *stacking*—as their couriers drop off one order, their next pickup is already assigned and being prepared.

Although roughly 80 percent of Postmates' orders are prepared food, the company is expanding to deliver other commodities; for example, healthcare and beauty products. In addition, in mid-2015 the company reached a deal with Apple to deliver MacBooks and other products the same day that customers purchase them online.

Uber. In 2015, Uber (www.uber.com) launched a meal-delivery service, called UberEats, in New York and Chicago. The items on UberEats come from a range of local restaurants, with the offerings changing every day. The option to order from UberEats shows up on the Uber app only when a user is in an area that is covered.

Sidecar. Sidecar (www.side.cr) is leveraging people who are already on the road. The app, which allows people to pay for rides in other people's cars, requires all users to enter in a destination before they get a ride, In February 2015, Sidecar announced that it was going to begin using those data to combine ride sharing with delivery. Doubling up means more money for both Sidecar and the driver.

GrubHub/Seamless. GrubHub/Seamless (www.grubhub.com) is a leading provider of digital ordering services, with 35,000 restaurant partners. The app allows customers to browse menus, place orders, and pay for delivery online or via a mobile app. In 2015, the company acquired delivery providers Restaurants on the Run and DiningIn. These acquisitions enable GrubHub/Seamless to own the "last mile" of delivery and become a one-stop shop for food, from ordering to delivery.

Ola Cabs. Ola Cabs (Ola; https://www.olacabs.com) provides different types of cab service in India. Customers can reserve a cab through a Web browser or a mobile app. The company commands about 60 percent of the market share in India. In 2015, Ola launched a grocery delivery service, Ola Store, that offers customers a choice of 12,000 products across 13 categories, including fruits, vegetables, eggs, dairy, frozen goods, and baby items.

The Results

These companies do experience challenges. To begin with, the workforce that is essential to this business model may present a problem. That is, their labor costs will probably rise. In addition, several on-demand companies are being sued for classifying their couriers as independent contractors rather than as employees to avoid providing them with benefits packages. In June 2015, California's labor commissioner ruled that a driver for Uber should be classified as a company employee.

Another challenge is that convenience can be expensive because delivery charges can vary greatly. For example, Instacart offers flat rates, where Postmates' fees depend on the distance of the delivery. Besides delivery costs, Instacart charges a premium for items from some of the stores it delivers from. Another downside is that shoppers may miss out on using coupons or browsing for cheaper alternatives in the store. Also, the orders do not always go according to plan. For example, if an item is sold out, then the delivery person has to call the customer for instructions on what to do.

Perhaps the most serious challenge in the delivery market is competition from many large, established companies that offer delivery services. Consider these examples:

- Amazon (www.amazon.com) is considering a crowdsourced (see Chapter 4) delivery solution that uses individuals to deliver packages and existing retailers to store them, all powered by a mobile app.

- Walmart (www.walmart.com), which generates half of its business from food, is testing the online grocery concept.

- Safeway grocery stores (https://shop.safeway.com) offers its "fresh to your door" delivery service.

- Starbucks (www.starbucks.com) offers a delivery service.

With the intense competition in the delivery services market, it is too early to predict any results. However, the companies discussed in this case are receiving large amounts of venture capital funding.

Sources: Compiled from J. Russell, "India's Ola Takes a Leaf Out of Uber's Book with New Grocery-Delivery Service," *Tech Crunch*, July 21, 2015; L. Rao, "Instacart Is Asking Its Customers to Do Something New," *Fortune*, June 26, 2015; K. Kokalitcheva, "Why On-Demand Delivery Startup Postmates Really Raised $80 Million," *Fortune*, June 25, 2015; M. Kosoff, "$2 Billion Grocery Delivery Startup Instacart Is Reclassifying Some of Its Workers as Employees," *Business Insider*, June 22, 2015; G. Bensinger, "Amazon's Next Delivery Drone: You," *The Wall Street Journal*, June 16, 2015; L. Heller, "Amazon's Uber-Like Delivery Service Could Be Coming Soon," *Forbes*, June 16, 2015; A. Connolly, "Amazon Considers Copying Postmates with New Crowdsourced Delivery Service," *The Next Web*, June 16, 2015; P. Vasan, "Tech Giants Serving Up Real Competition for FreshDirect," *CNBC*, June 12, 2015; J. Pinsker, "What Does the On-Demand Workforce Look Like?" *The Atlantic*, May 20, 2015; L. Jennings, "New Services Disrupt Restaurant Delivery Landscape," *Nation's Restaurant News*, May 18, 2015; K. Taylor, "We Tested Chipotle and McDonald's New Delivery Services. Here's What Happened," *Entrepreneur*, May 6, 2015; R. Tepper, "Watch Out Seamless: New Delivery Services Are Invading Your Turf," *Yahoo*, May 1, 2015; A. Stevenson, "Death to Amazon? Postmates' Boost to Small Business," *CNBC*, April 29, 2015; P. Sawers, "Uber Launches a Curated Meal-Delivery Service in New York and Chicago," *Venture Beat*, April 28, 2015; K. Steinmetz, "Go Fetch," *Time*, March 16, 2015; B. Solomon, "America's Most Promising Company: Instacart, the $2 Billion Grocery App," *Forbes*, January 21, 2015; D. Matthews, "Watch Out, Seamless and GrubHub – Amazon Is Coming for You," *Fast Company*, December 3, 2014; K. Spors, "What Starbucks' New Delivery Service Means for Local Businesses," *American Express*, November 3, 2014; J. Mangalindan, "Shop Till You're on Top," *Fortune*, October 27, 2014; J. Bercovici, "The Same-Day War," *Forbes*, May 5, 2014.

Questions

1. Describe the information technology used and developed by the entrepreneurs who founded Instacart, Postmates, GrubHub/Seamless, Uber, Sidecar, and Ola Cabs. What is the impact of these technologies on the costs of starting a business?

2. What are the advantages and disadvantages of being an independent contractor for a company?

3. Would you consider a job as a courier for one of these companies? Why or why not?

CHAPTER 2

© Maartje van Caspel/iStockphoto

Organizational Strategy, Competitive Advantage, and Information Systems

CHAPTER OUTLINE

2.1 Business Pressures, Organizational Responses, and Information Technology Support

2.2 Competitive Advantage and Strategic Information Systems

LEARNING OBJECTIVES

2.1 Identify effective IT responses to different kinds of business pressures.

2.2 Describe the strategies that organizations typically adopt to counter Porter's five competitive forces.

Opening Case

 Disney Animation Develops Software to Make Big Hero 6

At Disney Animation (www.disneyanimation.com), technology is essential. The Disney animated motion picture *Big Hero 6* centers on a robot (Baymax) and a robotics prodigy (Hiro) who form a superhero group and take on a villain in the futuristic city of San Fransokyo. This city, a mash-up of San Francisco and Tokyo, is located on a large bay and has many skyscrapers and flashing neon lights.

MIS The hero of *Big Hero 6* is not necessarily Baymax, but, rather, the artists and software engineers who developed the technology behind this hit motion picture. This animated film is the first ever produced with Hyperion, a software package created by Disney that simulates the behavior of light. That is, the software attempts to create light the way we actually see it in the real world. The software must mimic the many obstacles the sun's rays encounter in our atmosphere and then diffuse the light the same way natural light does.

The software, which took two years and 200 million computing hours to develop, is what provides *Big Hero 6* with its cinematic imagery and depth. Until Disney developed Hyperion, the company had never been able to use light in such a way. For example, the software gives Baymax a transparent glow by allowing light to bounce around inside him.

Before Hyperion, the process of simulating light was tedious, because each ray of light's trajectory had to be individually tracked. A single frame of animation could contain several light sources, and each ray of light could bounce off multiple surfaces, making the calculation of those individual pathways computationally intensive.

Disney engineers spent so much time creating Hyperion because they were simulating 10 billion rays of light bouncing around in each scene. Hyperion provides a softness, a depth to shadows, and lifelike highlights in every scene.

Disney needed huge amounts of processing power to produce the film. Three Disney server farms in Los Angeles and one in San Francisco were connected to create a supercomputer of 4,600 servers that contained 55,000 central processing units (CPUs). (We describe server farms in Plug IT In 4 and supercomputers and CPUs in Plug IT In 2.) Coda, an automated information management system, integrated the information being processed from the four server farms. Because Disney artists could utilize such a huge amount of computational power to process the images, they could see their work the next morning.

Animated films typically take about four years to produce, and the Disney team was writing the Hyperion software and using it on *Big Hero 6* at the same time. One Disney software engineer explained, "The process was just like building a car while you were driving it."

And the result of using the Hyperion software? *Big Hero 6* cost $165 million to produce. By July 2015, the film had generated more than $600 million in box office ticket sales worldwide. *Big Hero 6* also won an Oscar for Best Animated Feature Film. Disney used Hyperion in its movie *Zootopia*, which the studio released in March 2016.

Sources: Compiled from R. Conli and A. Hendrickson, "The Secrets Behind Disney's Latest Oscar-Winning Animation," *Creative Blog*, February 24, 2015; D. Miller, "Software Behind 'Big Hero 6' Pushes Envelope on Computer Animation," *The Los Angeles Times*, February 20, 2015; K. Costello, "Innovative Light Technology, Algorithmic Swarms, and an Inflatable Robot – Big Hero 6 Has It All!" *Dogo News*, December 4, 2014; T. Hammond, "Disney Animation Team Pushes Technical Boundaries with Big Hero 6," *TechRepublic*, November 28, 2014; S. Karlin, "The Monster Supercomputing Achievement that Lights Up Disney's 'Big Hero 6'," *Fast Company*, November 28, 2014; J. Volpe, "Disney Rendered Its New Animated on a 55,000 – Core Supercomputer," *Endgadget*, October 18, 2014; S. Ford, "Disney Creates New Digital Animation Process for 'Big Hero 6'," *Orlando Sentinel*, October 20, 2014; M. Seymour, "Disney's New Production Renderer 'Hyperion'— Yes, Disney!" *fxguide*, October 13, 2014; www.disneyanimation.com, accessed July 24, 2015.

Questions

1. Is Hyperion a strategic information system for Disney Animation? Why or why not? Provide specific examples to support your answer.

2. Will Hyperion provide a sustainable competitive advantage for Disney Animation? Why or why not?

3. Look ahead in this chapter. Which one of Porter's strategies for competitive advantage is Disney pursuing? Explain your answer.

Introduction

Organizations operate in the incredible complexity of the modern high-tech world. As a result, they are subject to a myriad of business pressures. Information systems are critically important in helping organizations respond to business pressures and in supporting organizations' global strategies. As you study this chapter, you will see that any information system can be *strategic*, meaning that it can provide a competitive advantage if it is used properly. The chapter opening case, as well as all the other cases in this chapter, illustrate how information technology (IT) can provide competitive advantage to organizations.

Competitive advantage refers to any assets that provide an organization with an edge against its competitors in some measure such as cost, quality, or speed. A competitive advantage helps an organization to control a market and to accrue larger-than-average profits. Significantly, both strategy and competitive advantage take many forms.

Although there are many companies that use technology in more expensive ways, an entrepreneurial spirit coupled with a solid understanding of what IT can do for you will provide competitive advantages to entrepreneurs just as it does for Wall Street CIOs. As you study this chapter, think of the small businesses in your area that are utilizing popular technologies in interesting and novel ways. Have any of them found an innovative use for Twitter? Facebook? Amazon? PayPal? If not, then can you think of any businesses that would benefit from employing these technologies?

This chapter is important for you for several reasons. First, the business pressures we address in the chapter will affect your organization. Just as important, however, they also will affect *you*. Therefore, you must understand how information systems can help you—and eventually your organization—respond to these pressures.

In addition, acquiring competitive advantage is essential for your organization's survival. Many organizations achieve competitive advantage through the efforts of their employees. Therefore, becoming knowledgeable about strategy and how information systems affect strategy and competitive position will help you throughout your career.

This chapter encourages you to become familiar with your organization's strategy, mission, and goals and to understand its business problems and how it makes (or loses) money. It will help you understand how information technology contributes to organizational strategy. Further, you likely will become a member of business/IT committees that decide (among many other things) how to use existing technologies more effectively and whether to adopt new ones. After studying this chapter, you will be able to make immediate contributions in these committees when you join your organizations.

In this chapter, you will see how information systems enable organizations to respond to business pressures. Next, you will learn how information systems help organizations gain competitive advantages in the marketplace.

2.1 | Business Pressures, Organizational Responses, and Information Technology Support

Modern organizations compete in a challenging environment. To remain competitive, they must react rapidly to problems and opportunities that arise from extremely dynamic conditions. In this section, you examine some of the major pressures confronting modern organizations and the strategies that organizations employ to respond to these pressures.

Business Pressures

The **business environment** is the combination of social, legal, economic, physical, and political factors in which businesses conduct their operations. Significant changes in any of these factors are likely to create business pressures on organizations. Organizations typically respond to these pressures with activities supported by IT. **Figure 2.1** illustrates the relationships among business pressures, organizational performance and responses, and IT support. You will learn about three major types of business pressures: market, technology, and societal pressures.

Market Pressures. Market pressures are generated by the global economy, intense competition, the changing nature of the workforce, and powerful customers. Let's look more closely at each of these factors.

Globalization. **Globalization** is the integration and interdependence of economic, social, cultural, and ecological facets of life, made possible by rapid advances in information technology. Today, individuals around the world are able to connect, compute, communicate, collaborate, and compete everywhere and anywhere, anytime and all the time; to access limitless amounts of information, services, and entertainment; to exchange knowledge; and to produce and sell goods and services. People and organizations can now operate without regard to geography, time, distance, or even language barriers. The bottom line? Globalization is markedly increasing competition.

These observations highlight the importance of market pressures for you. Simply put, you and the organizations you join will be competing with people and organizations from all over a flat world.

Let's consider some examples of globalization:

- Multinational corporations operate on a global scale, with offices and branches located worldwide.
- Many automobile manufacturers use parts from other countries, such as a car being assembled in the United States with parts coming from Japan, Germany, or Korea.

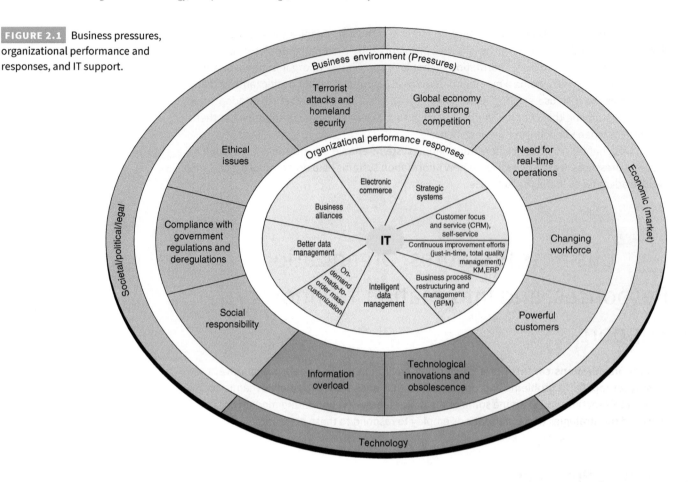

FIGURE 2.1 Business pressures, organizational performance and responses, and IT support.

- The World Trade Organization (WTO; www.wto.org) supervises international trade.
- Regional agreements such as the North American Free Trade Agreement (NAFTA), which includes the United States, Canada, and Mexico, have contributed to increased world trade and increased competition.
- The European Union is an economic and political union of 28 countries that are located primarily in Europe.
- The rise of India and China as economic powerhouses has increased global competition.

One important pressure that businesses in a global market must contend with is the cost of labor, which varies widely among countries. In general, labor costs are higher in developed countries such as the United States and Japan than in developing countries such as Bangladesh and El Salvador. Also, developed countries usually offer greater benefits, such as healthcare, to employees, driving the cost of doing business even higher. Therefore, many labor-intensive industries have moved their operations to countries with low labor costs. IT has made such moves much easier to implement.

However, manufacturing overseas is no longer the bargain it once was, and manufacturing in the United States is no longer as expensive. For example, manufacturing wages in China have more than doubled between 2002 and 2015, and they continue to rise. Meanwhile, the value of China's currency has steadily risen.

HRM **The Changing Nature of the Workforce.** The workforce, particularly in developed countries, is becoming more diversified. Increasing numbers of women, single parents, minorities, and persons with disabilities are now employed in all types of positions. IT is easing the integration of these employees into the traditional workforce. IT is also enabling people to work from home, which can be a major benefit for parents with young children and for people confronted with mobility and/or transportation issues.

Powerful Customers. Consumer sophistication and expectations increase as customers become more knowledgeable about the products and services they acquire. Customers can use the Internet to find detailed information about products and services, to compare prices, and to purchase items at electronic auctions.

Organizations recognize the importance of customers and they have increased their efforts to acquire and retain them. Modern firms strive to learn as much as possible about their customers to better anticipate and address their needs. This process, called *customer intimacy*, is an important component of *customer relationship management* (CRM), an organization-wide effort toward maximizing the customer experience. You will learn about CRM in Chapter 12.

Technology Pressures. The second category of business pressures consists of those pressures related to technology. Two major technology-related pressures are technological innovation and information overload.

Technological Innovation and Obsolescence. New and improved technologies rapidly create or support substitutes for products, alternative service options, and superb quality. As a result, today's state-of-the-art products may be obsolete tomorrow. For example, how fast are new versions of your smartphone being released? How quickly are electronic versions of books, magazines, and newspapers replacing traditional hard copy versions? These changes force businesses to keep up with consumer demands.

Consider the rapid technological innovation of the Apple iPad (www.apple.com/ipad):

- Apple released the first iPad in April 2010 and sold three million devices in just 80 days.
- Apple released the iPad 2 on March 11, 2011, only 11 months later.
- Apple released the iPad 3 on March 7, 2012.
- Apple released its fourth-generation iPad on November 2, 2012, along with the iPad mini.
- On November 1, 2013, Apple released the fifth generation of its iPad, called the iPad Air.
- On November 12, 2013, Apple released its iPad Mini 2 with Retina Display.
- In October 2014, Apple released the iPad Air 2 and the iPad Mini 3.
- In September 2015, Apple announced the iPad Pro.

One manifestation of technological innovation is "bring your own device (BYOD)." BYOD refers to the policy of permitting employees to bring personally owned mobile devices (laptops, tablet computers, and smartphones) to the workplace and to use those devices to connect to the corporate network as well as for personal use as well. The academic version of BYOD involves students' utilizing personally owned devices in educational settings to connect to their school's network.

The rapid increase in BYOD represents a huge challenge for IT departments. Not only has IT lost the ability to fully control and manage these devices, but employees are now demanding that they be able to conduct company business from multiple personal devices.

The good news is that BYOD has increased worker productivity and satisfaction. In fact, some employees with BYOD privileges actually work longer hours with no additional pay.

The bad news is security concerns. Many companies with BYOD policies have experienced an increase in malware (malicious software, discussed in Chapter 7). Further, there is an increased risk of losing sensitive, proprietary information. Such information might not be securely stored on a personal, mobile device, which can be lost or stolen.

Information Overload. The amount of information available on the Internet doubles approximately every year, and much of it is free. The Internet and other telecommunications networks are bringing a flood of information to managers. To make decisions effectively and efficiently, managers must be able to access, navigate, and utilize these vast stores of data, information, and knowledge. Information technologies, such as search engines (discussed in Chapter 4) and data mining (Chapter 5), provide valuable support in these efforts.

Societal/Political/Legal Pressures. The third category of business pressures includes social responsibility, government regulation/deregulation, spending for social programs, spending to protect against terrorism, and ethics. This section will explain how all of these elements affect modern businesses. We start with social responsibility.

Social Responsibility. Social issues that affect businesses and individuals range from the state of the physical environment, to company and individual philanthropy, to education. Some corporations and individuals are willing to spend time and/or money to address various social problems. These efforts are known as organizational social responsibility or individual social responsibility.

One critical social problem is the state of the physical environment. A growing IT initiative, called *green IT*, addresses some of the most pressing environmental concerns. IT is instrumental in organizational efforts to "go green" in three areas:

1. *Facilities design and management.* Organizations are creating more environmentally sustainable work environments. Many organizations are pursuing Leadership in Energy and Environmental Design (LEED) certification from the U.S. Green Building Council, a nonprofit group that promotes the construction of environmentally friendly buildings. One impact of this development is that IT professionals are expected to help create green facilities.

2. *Carbon management.* As companies try to reduce their carbon footprints, they are turning to IT executives to develop the systems needed to monitor carbon throughout the organization and its supply chain, which can be global in scope. Therefore, IT employees need to become knowledgeable about embedded carbon and how to measure it in the company's products and processes.

3. *International and U.S. environmental laws.* IT executives must deal with federal and state laws and international regulations that impact everything from the IT products they buy, to how they dispose of them, to their company's carbon footprint.

Continuing our discussion of social responsibility, social problems all over the world may be addressed through corporate and individual philanthropy. In some cases, questions arise as to what percentage of contributions actually goes to the intended causes and recipients and what percentage goes to the charity's overhead. Another problem that concerns contributors is that they often exert little influence over the selection of projects their contributions will support. The Internet can help address these concerns and facilitate generosity and connection. Consider the following examples:

- *PatientsLikeMe* (www.patientslikeme.com), or any of the thousands of message boards dedicated to infertility, cancer, and various other ailments. People use these sites and message boards to obtain information about healthcare decisions based on volunteered information, while also receiving much-needed emotional support from strangers.

- *Collaborative Consumption* (www.collaborativeconsumption.com): This Web site is an online hub for discussions about the growing business of sharing, resale, reuse, and barter (with many links to Web sites engaged in these practices).

- *Kiva* (www.kiva.org): Kiva is a nonprofit enterprise that provides a link between lenders in developed countries and entrepreneurs in developing countries. Users pledge interest-free loans rather than tax-deductible donations. Kiva directs 100 percent of the loans to borrowers.

- *DonorsChoose* (www.donorschoose.org): DonorsChoose is an education-oriented Web site that functions entirely within the United States. Users make donations rather than loans. The Web site addresses the huge problem of underfunded public schools.

Still another social problem that affects modern business is the digital divide. The digital divide refers to the wide gap between those individuals who have access to information and communications technology and those who do not. This gap exists both within and among countries.

Many government and international organizations are trying to close the digital divide. As technologies develop and become less expensive, the speed at which the gap can be closed will accelerate. On the other hand, the rapid pace of technological development can make it more difficult for groups with few resources to keep up with more affluent groups.

One well-known project to narrow the divide is the One Laptop per Child (OLPC) project (http://one.laptop.org). OLPC is a nonprofit association dedicated to developing a very inexpensive laptop—a technology that aims to revolutionize how the world can educate its children. In early 2015, the price of OLPC's laptop remains approximately $200. We should note however, that this price includes educational software loaded on the laptop.

IT's About Business 2.1 examines the role that IT plays in two important social issues: (1) social responsibility in the form of protecting the environment and (2) narrowing the digital divide.

IT's About Business 2.1

Using Information Technology for Social Good

Stopping illegal logging. According to a 2014 study by Interpol (www.interpol.int), an organization that encourages cooperation among law enforcement agencies in different countries, illegal logging is pervasive, accounting for between 50 and 90 percent of all trees harvested. According to the World Wildlife Fund (WWW; www.worldwildlife.org), illegal logging is particularly serious in the Amazon and Congo Basins, but it is widespread all over the world.

Going further, these activities contribute to a multibillion-dollar black market for wood, reducing world timber prices by about 15 percent. The World Bank estimates that illegal logging costs the global industry $10 billion every year.

These illegal logging activities reduce the size of the world's rainforests by 5 to 10 percent every 10 years, causing a biodiversity crisis. Moreover, about 17 percent of greenhouse gas emissions are caused by illegal logging.

One organization that is hoping to halt illegal logging is a San Francisco-based nonprofit known as the Rainforest Connection (https://rfcx.org). Volunteers put solar panels on old smartphones and place them high in the trees in the middle of a rainforest. The phones can pick up the sound of chainsaws cutting down a tree within one square mile, and emit data to rangers patrolling the forest, who can quickly stop the loggers. Just one phone can save enough trees to stop 15,000 tons of carbon from entering the atmosphere.

MIS   **The Infoladies of Bangladesh.** Just 3 percent of people in Bangladesh have regular Internet connections. Most people who want to use the Internet are in rural villages. To provide regular access to villagers, the nonprofit organization Dnet (http://dnet.org.bd) set up the Infoladies project (http://infolady.com.bd). Armed with a laptop and other digital equipment, a group of

50 young women cycle to the villages to make computers, tablets, smartphones, and digital cameras available to all. The Infoladies also bring a glucometer so that villagers can monitor their blood sugar levels. Farmers can also research information on crops and farming methods. The most popular request is for villagers to communicate with male relatives via Skype. Many of these men work in the Middle East. Dnet also lends women $650 so they can buy their own equipment to have an Infoladies franchise. Each franchisee earns an average of $90 per month for offering these digital services, more than what most farmers in Bangladesh earn.

Sources: Compiled from "Start-Up Creates Devices from Old Cell Phones to Tackle Illegal Logging and Poaching," *We Are Anonymous*, July 28, 2015; J. Prentice-Dunn, "How Technology Can Help Stop Illegal Logging," *Sierra Club*, July 6, 2015; J. Szczepanska, "Infoladies of Bangladesh," *OpenIDEO*, April 15, 2015; "Bangladesh's Travelling Infoladies: A Rural Revolution," *Philanthropy Age*, January 25, 2015; J. Hance, "Daring Activists Use High-Tech to Track Illegal Logging Trucks in the Brazilian Amazon," *MongaBay*, October 15, 2014; S. Chowdhury, "'Infoladies' Bring Change in Rural Bangladesh," *Aljazeera*, August 28, 2014; L. Gilpin, "How Recycled Solar Powered Phones Could Save Rainforests and Change How the Tech Industry Tackles Climate Change," *TechRepublic*, August 8, 2014; G. Akash, "The Infoladies of Bangladesh," *Bloomberg BusinessWeek*, July 3, 2014; http://infolady.com.bd; https://rfcx.org, accessed July 26, 2015.

Questions

1. Describe how the Infoladies are a strategic information system for the country of Bangladesh. Provide specific examples to support your answer.

2. Discuss how the Rainforest Connection's use of smartphones is a strategic information system for our planet. Provide specific examples to support your answer.

Compliance with Government Regulations. Another major source of business pressures is government regulations regarding health, safety, environmental protection, and equal opportunity. Businesses tend to view government regulations as expensive constraints on their activities. In general, government deregulation intensifies competition.

In the wake of 9/11 and numerous corporate scandals, the U.S. government passed many new laws, including the Sarbanes–Oxley Act, the USA PATRIOT Act, the Gramm–Leach–Bliley Act, and the Health Insurance Portability and Accountability Act (HIPAA). Organizations must be in compliance with the regulations contained in these statutes. The process of becoming and remaining compliant is expensive and time consuming. In almost all cases, organizations rely on IT support to provide the necessary controls and information for compliance.

Protection Against Terrorist Attacks. Since September 11, 2001, organizations have been under increased pressure to protect themselves against terrorist attacks. In addition, employees who are in the military reserves have been called up for active duty, creating personnel problems. Information technology can help protect businesses by providing security systems and possibly identifying patterns of behavior associated with terrorist activities, including cyberattacks (discussed in Chapter 7). For a good example of a firm that provides this protection, see Palantir (www.palantir.com).

An example of protection against terrorism is the Department of Homeland Security's (DHS) Office of Biometric Identity Management (OBIM) program. (We discuss biometrics in Chapter 7.) OBIM is a network of biometric screening systems, such as fingerprint and iris and retina scanners, that ties into government databases and watch lists to check the identities of millions of people entering the United States. The system is now operational in more than 300 locations, including major international ports of entry by air, sea, and land.

Ethical Issues. Ethics relates to general standards of right and wrong. Information ethics relates specifically to standards of right and wrong in information processing practices. Ethical issues are very important because, if handled poorly, they can damage an organization's image and destroy its employees' morale. The use of IT raises many ethical issues, ranging from monitoring e-mail to invading the privacy of millions of customers whose data are stored in private and public databases. Chapter 6 covers ethical issues in detail.

Clearly, then, the pressures on organizations are increasing, and organizations must be prepared to take responsive actions if they are to succeed. You will learn about these organizational responses in the next section.

Organizational Responses

Organizations are responding to the various pressures just discussed by implementing IT such as strategic systems, customer focus, make-to-order and mass customization, and e-business. This section explores each of these responses.

Strategic Systems. Strategic systems provide organizations with advantages that enable them to increase their market share and/or profits, to better negotiate with suppliers, and to prevent competitors from entering their markets. IT's About Business 2.2 provides another example of how strategically important information systems can be by examining technology improvements in airports and airlines.

IT's About Business 2.2

POM **Innovative Technologies for Airlines and Airports**

Airlines and airports are producing innovative tools in ground and air operations, with the idea of making the flying experience more convenient and enjoyable. Technology is also improving customer service, allowing staff to spend more time with passengers needing help.

Airports are deploying multifunction kiosks in many areas, allowing passengers to serve themselves without agents' help. Passengers can use these kiosks to weigh and tag their luggage without the assistance of an agent and drop them off at a baggage drop-off. At other kiosks, customers can do things such as rebook a cancelled flight. If they need help, passengers can ask an agent who is stationed near the kiosks.

Some airport gates have kiosks that provide do-it-yourself boarding, speeding up the process. Passengers scan their boarding passes and can head directly to their seats.

Many international airports allow passengers to serve themselves at Customs, scanning their passports at an automated kiosk and answering questions on the touch screen. These kiosks speed up the process of going through Customs.

Dallas/Fort Worth International Airport is rolling out "digital way finders"—touch screens allowing passengers to find restrooms, restaurants, and other amenities—by 2018.

It's not just passengers who are benefiting from self-serve technology—many airports are equipping staff with the means to improve productivity. For example, many airports have given staff iPads so they can inspect stores, take photos of any issues, such as a full trash can, and report the issue to the store management to take immediate action. In the not-too-distant future, passengers may be able to use their smartphones in the terminal to order food and gifts.

Walkbase (www.walkbase.com) developed the tools for managing the flow of people through Helsinki airport. The company is taking advantage of the fact that up to 70 percent of airport visitors leave the Wi-Fi turned on their smartphones. Walkbase's dozens of sensors in the airport track the movements of these passengers, without gathering any of their personal data. The sensors track passenger flows throughout the entire terminal, from the car parks to departure gates.

The Walkbase technology aims to improve the flying experience by alleviating bottlenecks in passenger flow, such as in certain shopping areas or at the security gate. The system allows stores and services in the airport to send marketing notifications and offer to passengers' smartphones.

Airports regularly face the problem of lost bags. Airports such as Hong Kong International Airport are using radio frequency identification (RFID) technology (discussed in Chapter 10) to track where bags are and where they should go. Helping alleviate a common source of passenger frustration, the RFID tags allow fliers to find out in real time where their bags are, thanks to Bluetooth and other mobile technologies.

MIS Another burgeoning airport technology is iris scanners. It's used at London's Gatwick Airport to help speed up the check-in and boarding processes. At check-in, passengers scan their irises and then do it again at the gate, to ensure they made their flight. Gatwick contends that this technology has decreased wait times.

In another use of a biometric system (discussed in Chapter 7), French company Thales (www.thalesgroup.com) has developed technology that scans passengers' facial features for identification purposes. The system takes a photo of the passenger's face and iris and shares that with computers around the airport. When the passenger gets to Immigration, a machine can confirm their identity. When the passenger receives their boarding pass at check-in, a photo of their face is encrypted on the pass, which is scanned at the gate to confirm their identity.

MIS Safran (www.safran-group.com) has developed software to analyze the large amount of data being collected on more than 100 million passengers. The software analyzes passenger records, looking for more than 300 warning signs of behavior that could indicate a problem passenger. The software also compares passenger data against Interpol and other police databases in case any passengers are flagged as potential terrorists or organized criminals.

The popular Google Glass device is helping customer service agents at Edinburgh Airport in Scotland provide better services to passengers, such as real-time flight information and foreign-language translations. The device allows the agents to display the information hands-free while they communicate with the Internet via voice commands or take pictures by winking.

Delta Airlines' 20,000 flight attendants are equipped on-board with mobile devices that allow them to read their on-board manual, sell meals, find out information about minors traveling alone, and help passengers who didn't receive their requested upgrade.

The mobile devices can also be used in maintenance operations. For example, the flight crew can use the device on board to take a picture of a broken armrest or luggage compartment door and send it to maintenance. Mechanics can then be ready to meet the plane with the proper parts when it lands.

Sources: Compiled from C. Weissman, "These Are the Insane New Technologies Airports Are Using to Learn Everything about You," *Business Insider*, June 19, 2015; E. Randolph, "Robot Border Guards among New Airport Tech at Paris Air Show," *phys.org*, June 19, 2015; K. Moskvitch, "The New Tech Changing Airport Security," *BBC News*, May 19, 2015; A. Chardy, "Miami Airport: Apps, Kiosks, Shorten Wait Times at Immigration Control", *Miami Herald*, May 9, 2015; "SFO: Airport Unveils New Automated Passport Kiosk," *San Jose Mercury News*, April 23, 2015; B. Peterson, "Do Self-Service Kiosks at Airport Customer Actually Save Time?" *Condé Nast Traveler*, April 3, 2015; G. Korte, "U.S. Airports Will Automate Customs to Speed Passengers," *USA Today*, February 13, 2015; M. Leibovitz, "Flight Attendants, Prepare for Takeoff (and Wi-Fi Tech Support)," *Innovation Insights*, January 5, 2015; "Edinburgh Airport First in Scotland to Use Google Glass to Enhance Its Passenger Experience," *Airport Business*, October 8, 2014; Y. Hammett, "New Tampa Airport Kiosks Speed International Visitors through Customs," *Tampa Tribune*, August 19, 2014; "A Global First – Helsinki Airport's New Technology to Develop the Travel Experience," *Finavia*, July 30, 2014; C. Jones, "Airlines, Airports Improve Technology for Passengers," *USA Today*, April 14, 2014.

Questions

1. Look ahead to Porter's five strategies for competitive advantage. Provide an example of a technology discussed in this case that supports each of Porter's strategies.

2. Propose additional applications that airports and airlines might develop that could create a competitive advantage in the marketplace.

3. Are the technologies discussed in this case examples of strategic information systems? Why or why not?

Customer Focus. Organizational attempts to provide superb customer service can make the difference between attracting and retaining customers versus losing them to competitors. Numerous IT tools and business processes have been designed to keep customers happy. (Recall that a *business process* is a collection of related activities that produce a product or a service of value to the organization, its business partners, and/or its customers.) Consider Amazon, for example. When you visit Amazon's Web site any time after your first visit, the site welcomes you back by name and it presents you with information about items that you might like, based on your previous purchases. In another example, Dell guides you through the process of purchasing a computer by providing information and choices that help you make an informed buying decision.

MKT

Make-to-Order and Mass Customization. Make-to-order is a strategy of producing customized (made to individual specifications) products and services. The business problem is how to manufacture customized goods efficiently and at a reasonably low cost. Part of the solution is to change manufacturing processes from mass production to mass customization. In mass production, a company produces a large quantity of identical items. An early example of mass production was Henry Ford's Model T, where buyers could pick any color—as long as it was black.

Ford's policy of offering a single product for all of its customers eventually gave way to *consumer segmentation*, in which companies provided standard specifications for different consumer groups, or segments. Clothes manufacturers, for example, designed their products in different sizes and colors to appeal to different customers. The next step was *configured mass customization*, in which companies offer features that allow each shopper to customize his or her product or service with a range of components. Examples are ordering a car, a computer, or a smartphone, where the customer can specify which features he or she wants.

In the current strategy, known as mass customization, a company produces a large quantity of items, but it customizes them to match the needs and preferences of individual customers. Mass customization is essentially an attempt to perform make-to-order on a large scale. Examples include:

- NikeID (www.nikeid.com): Allows customers to design their footwear.
- M&M candies: My M&Ms (www.mymms.com) allows customers to add photos, art, and messages to candy.
- Dell (www.dell.com) and HP (www.hp.com): Allow customers to exactly specify the computer that they want.

It's About Business 2.3 provides another example of mass customization, the problem of "fit" in online shopping for clothes.

IT's About Business 2.3

 The "Fit" Problem When Shopping
POM **for Clothes Online**

Online shopping for the latest fashions is convenient for customers, but they cannot try on the clothes. Not being able to determine actual fit is a problem because in the fashion world, size varies from brand to brand, so even when an online retailer provides clothing measurements, it is not necessarily an accurate indication of how a garment will actually fit. Fashion industry analysts claim this situation is deliberate: If a customer knows that Levi's jeans, for example, are going to fit, then he or she will generally purchase that brand. Going further, there is not much agreement across brands about what a specific size is, leading to customer frustration.

Even if sizes were standard, there would still be a fit problem. Specifically, consider the different types of clothing fabrics—some are more "stretchy" than others. Two pieces of clothing of the same size could be made from different fabrics and therefore fit differently.

The lack of virtual dressing rooms contributes to the high rates of return (20 to 40 percent) and shopping cart abandonment (50 percent) in online fashion shopping. Online retailer Zappos has set the industry standard on returns, pioneering no-cost shipping and handling for returns. No-cost shipping for returns raised customer satisfaction to new levels and stimulated online retail purchasing, reducing barriers to shoppers being reluctant to buy something they couldn't try on. However, the policy costs online retailers a great deal of money.

As a result of these return costs, several startup companies are addressing the fit problem. These companies believe that if customers' clothes fit better, then they will be more satisfied and less likely to return the items. Let's consider several of these companies.

Virtusize (www.virtusize.com) asks the user to provide the measurements of a favorite dress shirt or pair of jeans for an online comparison. The measurements are used to create reference garments so that, when customers are shopping online, they can layer a silhouette of the garment they are interested in buying over the silhouette of the garment they already own.

Clothes Horse (acquired in December 2014 by fits.me; http://fits.me) has developed data-driven software that takes data from both consumers (body type, favorite brands, fit preferences) and clothing manufacturers. The result is a third-party database of actual fit data—chest, waist, hips, sleeves—for every garment and every brand in the company's database, which it then uses to make a recommendation to a customer regarding fit. The software also contains proprietary algorithms that take variables such as type of fabric into account.

LoveThatFit (http://beta.lovethatfit.com) allows consumers to upload a full body image taken in tightly fitting clothing. The startup uses proprietary algorithms to address the fit problem. It even adjusts for tilt and distortion in the picture, while accurately identifying the points of fit on the customer's body. The Web site is social, enabling customers to share potential purchases within a shopper's network.

Bodymetrics (www.bodymetrics.com) is a good example of mass customization. Bodymetrics provides a "body scanner" that customers can access either at home or in a store. This technology scans the customer's body, captures more than 150 measurements, and produces a digital replica of the customer's size and shape. This scan is then used to provide made-to-measure jeans and swimsuits for women and men.

Toshiba has developed a "digital changing booth" that lets customers virtually try on clothes through a display. The system uses an off-the-shelf 3D scanner and a camera to analyze the customer's measurements. It then sizes the clothes to fit. A companion app uses the customer's mobile device to let him or her mix and match outfits or place an order.

Sources: Compiled from "Japan's 'Virtual Dressing Rooms,'" *BBC News*, January 23, 2015; J. Ersing, "Clothing Stores Are Setting a Powerful Example that All Businesses Should Follow," *Identities.mic*, January 8,

2015; N. Laskowski, "Fashion Tech Startups Use Data Science to Build Virtual Dressing Rooms," *Tech Target*, January 14, 2015; L. Wang, "Can Technology Solve the Fit Problem in Fashion E-Commerce?" *Business of Fashion*, August 12, 2014; E. Brooke, "8 Startups Trying to Help You Find Clothing that Fits," *Fashionista*, July 22, 2014; R. Shah, "Fixing How Clothes Fit You Can Reshape Online Retail Logistics," *Forbes*, April 11, 2014; "Gina Mancuso, LoveThatFit," *Charlottesville Tomorrow*, March 24, 2014; V. Woollaston, "The End of Online Returns? App Lets You See How Clothes Will Fit Based on Items You Already Own," *Daily Mail*, March 17, 2014;

Questions

1. Look ahead to Porter's five strategies for competitive advantage. Take each of the example companies in this case, and identify which of Porter's strategies that company is using.

2. Do the systems these companies are using constitute strategic information systems? Why or why not?

E-Business and E-Commerce. Conducting business electronically is an essential strategy for companies that are competing in today's business environment. *Electronic commerce* (EC or e-commerce) describes the process of buying, selling, transferring, or exchanging products, services, or information via computer networks, including the Internet. *E-business* is a somewhat broader concept. In addition to the buying and selling of goods and services, e-business also refers to servicing customers, collaborating with business partners, and performing electronic transactions within an organization. Chapter 9 focuses extensively on this topic. In addition, e-commerce applications appear throughout the text.

You now have a general overview of the pressures that affect companies in today's business environment and the responses that they choose to manage these pressures. To plan for the most effective responses, companies formulate strategies. In the new digital economy, these strategies rely heavily on information technology, especially strategic information systems. You examine these topics in the next section.

Before you go on...

1. What are the characteristics of the modern business environment?

2. Discuss some of the pressures that characterize the modern global business environment.

3. Identify some of the organizational responses to these pressures. Are any of these responses specific to a particular pressure? If so, which ones?

Apply the Concept 2.1

LEARNING OBJECTIVE 2.1 Identify effective IT responses to different kinds of business pressures.

STEP 1: Background (Here is what you are learning.)

Businesses face immense pressures today from every angle imaginable. The market is constantly shifting, technology becomes obsolete almost as quickly as it is implemented, society expects businesses to take more responsibility for the communities their work impacts, and legal compliance

is required. Businesses increasingly employ cutting-edge technologies to navigate these difficult waters.

STEP 2: Activity (Here is what you do.)

Pick one business pressure from each of the three broad categories presented in the chapter: Market, Technology, and Societal/Political/Legal. Now search for a real-world business story related to each of the pressures you have chosen.

2.2 Competitive Advantage and Strategic Information Systems

A *competitive strategy* is a statement that identifies a business's approach to compete, its goals, and the plans and policies that will be required to carry out those goals (Porter, 1985).[1] A strategy, in general, can apply to a desired outcome, such as gaining market share. A competitive strategy focuses on achieving a desired outcome when competitors want to prevent you from reaching your goal. Therefore, when you create a competitive strategy, you must plan your own moves, but you must also anticipate and counter your competitors' moves.

Through its competitive strategy, an organization seeks a competitive advantage in an industry. That is, it seeks to outperform its competitors in a critical measure such as cost, quality, and time-to-market. Competitive advantage helps a company function profitably with a market and generate larger-than-average profits.

Competitive advantage is increasingly important in today's business environment, as you will note throughout the text. In general, the *core business* of companies has remained the same. That is, information technologies simply offer tools that can enhance an organization's success through its traditional sources of competitive advantage, such as low cost, excellent customer service, and superior supply chain management. Strategic information systems (SISs) provide a competitive advantage by helping an organization implement its strategic goals and improve its performance and productivity. Any information system that helps an organization either achieve a competitive advantage or reduce a competitive disadvantage qualifies as a strategic information system.

Porter's Competitive Forces Model

The best-known framework for analyzing competitiveness is Michael Porter's competitive forces model (Porter, 1985). Companies use Porter's model to develop strategies to increase their competitive edge. Porter's model also demonstrates how IT can make a company more competitive.

Porter's model identifies five major forces that can endanger or enhance a company's position in a given industry. Figure 2.2 highlights these forces. Although the Web has changed the nature of competition, it has not changed Porter's five fundamental forces. In fact, what makes these forces so valuable as analytical tools is that they have not changed for centuries. Every competitive organization, no matter how large or small, or what business it is in, is driven by these forces. This observation applies even to organizations that you might not consider competitive, such as local governments. Although local governments are not for-profit enterprises, they compete for businesses to locate in their districts, for funding from higher levels of government, for employees, and for many other things.

[1] Porter, M.E. (1985) *Competitive Advantage*, Free Press, New York.

Significantly, Porter (2001)[2] concludes that the *overall* impact of the Web is to increase competition, which generally diminishes a firm's profitability. Let's examine Porter's five forces and the ways that the Web influences them.

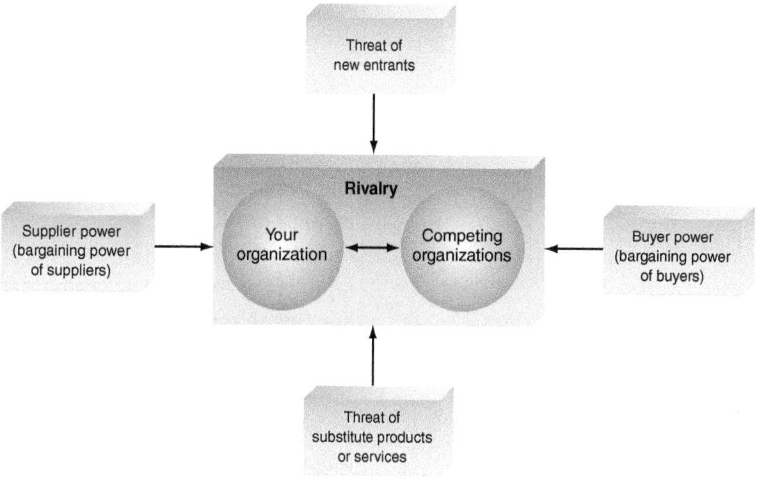

1. *The threat of entry of new competitors.* The threat that new competitors will enter your market is high when entry is easy and low when there are significant barriers to entry. An **entry barrier** is a product or service feature that customers have learned to expect from organizations in a certain industry. A competing organization must offer this feature in order to survive in the marketplace. There are many types of entry barriers. Consider, for example, legal requirements such

FIGURE 2.2 Porter's competitive forces model.

as admission to the bar to practice law or a license to serve liquor, where only a certain number of licenses are available.

Suppose you want to open a gasoline station. In order to compete in that industry, you would have to offer pay-at-the-pump service to your customers. Pay-at-the-pump is an IT-based barrier to entering this market because you must offer it for free. The first gas station that offered this service gained first-mover advantage and established barriers to entry. This advantage did not last, however, because competitors quickly offered the same service and thus overcame the entry barrier.

For most firms, the Web *increases* the threat that new competitors will enter the market because it sharply reduces traditional barriers to entry, such as the need for a sales force or a physical storefront. Today, competitors frequently need only to set up a Web site. This threat of increased competition is particularly acute in industries that perform an *intermediation role*, which is a link between buyers and sellers (e.g., stock brokers and travel agents), as well as in industries where the primary product or service is digital (e.g., the music industry). In addition, the geographical reach of the Web enables distant competitors to compete more directly with an existing firm.

In some cases, the Web increases barriers to entry. This scenario occurs primarily when customers have come to expect a nontrivial capability from their suppliers. For example, the first company to offer Web-based package tracking gained a competitive advantage from that service. Competitors were forced to follow.

2. *The bargaining power of suppliers.* Supplier power is high when buyers have few choices from whom to buy and low when buyers have many choices. Therefore, organizations would rather have more potential suppliers so that they will be in a stronger position to negotiate price, quality, and delivery terms.

The Internet's impact on suppliers is mixed. On the one hand, it enables buyers to find alternative suppliers and to compare prices more easily, thereby reducing the supplier's bargaining power. On the other hand, as companies use the Internet to integrate their supply chains, participating suppliers prosper by locking in customers.

3. *The bargaining power of customers (buyers).* Buyer power is high when buyers have many choices from whom to buy and low when buyers have few choices. For example, in the past, there were few locations where students could purchase textbooks (typically, one or two campus bookstores). In this situation, students had low buyer power. Today, the Web provides students with access to a multitude of potential suppliers as well as detailed information about textbooks. As a result, student buyer power has increased dramatically.

In contrast, *loyalty programs* reduce buyer power. As their name suggests, loyalty programs reward customers based on the amount of business they conduct with a particular

---

[2] Porter, M.E. (2001) "Strategy and the Internet," *Harvard Business Review*, March.

organization (e.g., airlines, hotels, rental car companies). Information technology enables companies to track the activities and accounts of millions of customers, thereby reducing buyer power. That is, customers who receive "perks" from loyalty programs are less likely to do business with competitors. (Loyalty programs are associated with customer relationship management, which you will study in Chapter 12.)

4. *The threat of substitute products or services.* If there are many alternatives to an organization's products or services, then the threat of substitutes is high. If there are few alternatives, then the threat is low. Today, new technologies create substitute products very rapidly. For example, customers today can purchase wireless telephones instead of landline telephones, Internet music services instead of traditional CDs, and ethanol instead of gasoline for their cars.

   Information-based industries experience the greatest threat from substitutes. Any industry in which digitized information can replace material goods (e.g., music, books, software) must view the Internet as a threat because the Internet can convey this information efficiently and at low cost and high quality.

   Even when there are many substitutes for their products, however, companies can create a competitive advantage by increasing switching costs. *Switching costs* are the costs, in money and time, imposed by a decision to buy elsewhere. For example, contracts with smartphone providers typically include a substantial penalty for switching to another provider until the term of the contract expires (quite often, two years). This switching cost is monetary.

   As another example, when you buy products from Amazon, the company develops a profile of your shopping habits and recommends products targeted to your preferences. If you switch to another online vendor, that company will need time to develop a profile of your wants and needs. In this case, the switching cost involves time rather than money.

5. *The rivalry among existing firms in the industry.* The threat from rivalry is high when there is intense competition among many firms in an industry. The threat is low when the competition is among fewer firms and is not as intense.

   In the past, proprietary information systems—systems that belong exclusively to a single organization—have provided strategic advantage to firms in highly competitive industries. Today, however, the visibility of Internet applications on the Web makes proprietary systems more difficult to keep secret. In simple terms, when I see my competitor's new system online, I will rapidly match its features to remain competitive. The result is fewer differences among competitors, which leads to more intense competition in an industry.

   To understand this concept, consider the highly competitive grocery industry, where Walmart, Kroger, Safeway, and other companies compete essentially on price. Some of these companies have IT-enabled loyalty programs in which customers receive discounts and the store gains valuable business intelligence on customers' buying preferences. Stores use this business intelligence in their marketing and promotional campaigns. (You will learn about business intelligence in Chapter 5.)

   Grocery stores are also experimenting with wireless technologies such as *radio-frequency identification* (RFID, discussed in Chapter 10) to speed up the checkout process, track customers through the store, and notify customers of discounts as they pass by certain products. Grocery companies also use IT to tightly integrate their supply chains for maximum efficiency and thus reduce prices for shoppers.

   Established companies can also gain a competitive advantage by allowing customers to use data from the company's products to improve their own performance. For example, Babolat (www.babolat.com), a manufacturer of sports equipment, has developed its Babolat Play Pure Drive system. The system has sensors embedded into the handle of its tennis rackets. A smartphone app utilizes the data from the sensors to monitor and evaluate ball speed, spin, and impact location to give tennis players valuable feedback.

   Competition also is being affected by the extremely low variable cost of digital products. That is, once a digital product has been developed, the cost of producing additional "units" approaches zero. Consider the music industry as an example. When artists record music, their songs are captured in digital format. Physical products, such as CDs or DVDs of the songs for sale in music stores, involve costs. The costs of a physical distribution channel are much higher than those involved in delivering the songs digitally over the Internet.

In fact, in the future companies might give away some products for free. For example, some analysts predict that commissions for online stock trading will approach zero because investors can search the Internet for information to make their own decisions regarding buying and selling stocks. At that point, consumers will no longer need brokers to give them information that they can obtain themselves, virtually for free.

Porter's Value Chain Model

Organizations use Porter's competitive forces model to design general strategies. To identify specific activities where they can use competitive strategies for greatest impact, they use his value chain model (1985). A value chain is a sequence of activities through which the organization's inputs, whatever they are, are transformed into more valuable outputs, whatever they are. The value chain model identifies points where an organization can use information technology to achieve competitive advantage (see Figure 2.3).

According to Porter's value chain model, the activities conducted in any organization can be divided into two categories: primary activities and support activities. Primary activities relate to the production and distribution of the firm's products and services. These activities create value for which customers are willing to pay. The primary activities are buttressed by support activities. Unlike primary activities, support activities do not add value directly to the firm's products or services. Rather, as their name suggests, they contribute to the firm's competitive advantage by supporting the primary activities.

Next, you will see examples of primary and support activities in the value chain of a manufacturing company. Keep in mind that other types of firms, such as transportation, healthcare, education, retail, and others, have different value chains. The key point is that *every* organization has a value chain.

In a manufacturing company, primary activities involve purchasing materials, processing the materials into products, and delivering the products to customers. Manufacturing companies typically perform five primary activities in the following sequence:

1. Inbound logistics (inputs)
2. Operations (manufacturing and testing)
3. Outbound logistics (storage and distribution)

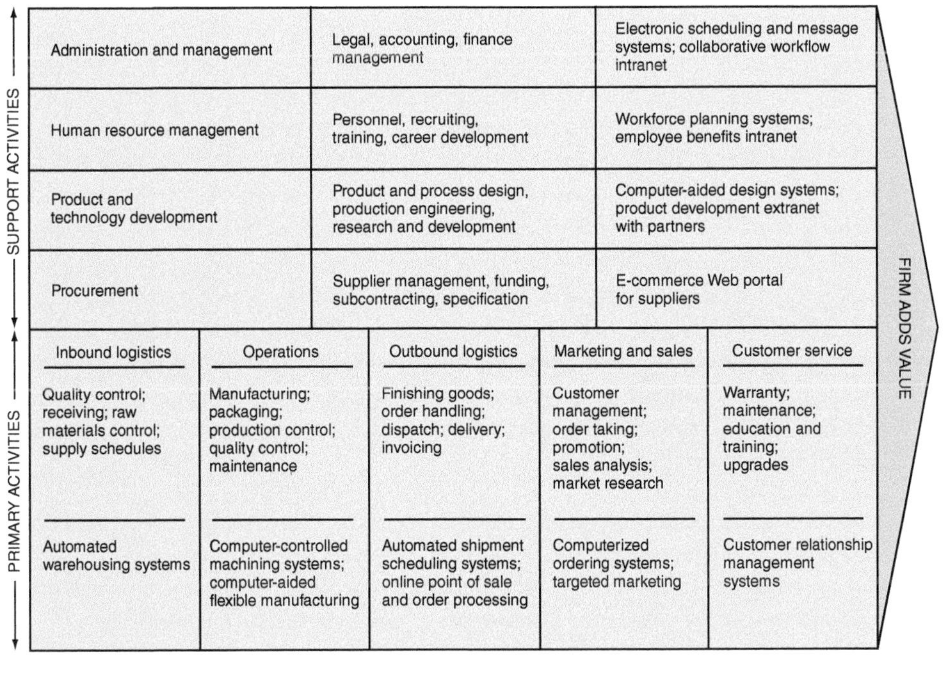

FIGURE 2.3 Porter's value chain model.

SUPPORT ACTIVITIES		
Administration and management	Legal, accounting, finance management	Electronic scheduling and message systems; collaborative workflow intranet
Human resource management	Personnel, recruiting, training, career development	Workforce planning systems; employee benefits intranet
Product and technology development	Product and process design, production engineering, research and development	Computer-aided design systems; product development extranet with partners
Procurement	Supplier management, funding, subcontracting, specification	E-commerce Web portal for suppliers

Inbound logistics	Operations	Outbound logistics	Marketing and sales	Customer service
Quality control; receiving; raw materials control; supply schedules	Manufacturing; packaging; production control; quality control; maintenance	Finishing goods; order handling; dispatch; delivery; invoicing	Customer management; order taking; promotion; sales analysis; market research	Warranty; maintenance; education and training; upgrades
Automated warehousing systems	Computer-controlled machining systems; computer-aided flexible manufacturing	Automated shipment scheduling systems; online point of sale and order processing	Computerized ordering systems; targeted marketing	Customer relationship management systems

PRIMARY ACTIVITIES

FIRM ADDS VALUE

    4. Marketing and sales

    5. Services

As work progresses in this sequence, value is added to the product in each activity. Specifically, the following steps occur:

1. The incoming materials are processed (in receiving, storage, and so on) in activities called *inbound logistics.*

2. The materials are used in operations, where value is added by turning raw materials into products.

3. These products are prepared for delivery (packaging, storing, and shipping) in the out-bound logistics activities.

4. Marketing and sales sell the products to customers, increasing product value by creating demand for the company's products.

5. Finally, the company performs after-sales service for the customer, such as warranty service or upgrade notification, adding further value.

As noted above, these primary activities are buttressed by support activities. Support activities consist of the following:

1. The firm's infrastructure (accounting, finance, management)

2. Human resources management

3. Product and technology development (R&D)

4. Procurement

Each support activity can be applied to any or all of the primary activities. In addition, the support activities can also support one another.

    A firm's value chain is part of a larger stream of activities, which Porter calls a **value system**. A value system, or an *industry value chain*, includes the suppliers that provide the inputs necessary to the firm along with their value chains. After the firm creates products, these products pass through the value chains of distributors (which also have their own value chains), all the way to the customers. All parts of these chains are included in the value system. To achieve and sustain a competitive advantage, and to support that advantage with information technologies, a firm must understand every component of this value system.

Strategies for Competitive Advantage

Organizations continually try to develop strategies to counter the five competitive forces identified by Porter. You will learn about five of those strategies here. Before we go into specifics, however, it is important to note that an organization's choice of strategy involves trade-offs. For example, a firm that concentrates only on cost leadership might not have the resources available for research and development, leaving the firm unable to innovate. As another example, a company that invests in customer happiness (customer orientation strategy) will experience increased costs.

    Companies must select a strategy and then stay with it, because a confused strategy cannot succeed. This selection, in turn, decides how a company will utilize its information systems. A new information system that can improve customer service but will increase costs slightly will be welcomed at a high-end retailer such as Nordstrom's, but not at a discount store such as Walmart. The following list presents the most commonly used strategies. **Figure 2.4** provides an overview of these strategies.

1. *Cost leadership strategy.* Produce products and/or services at the lowest cost in the industry. An example is Walmart's automatic inventory replenishment system, which enables Walmart to reduce inventory storage requirements. As a result, Walmart stores use floor space only to sell products, and not to store them, thereby reducing inventory costs.

2. *Differentiation strategy.* Offer different products, services, or product features than your competitors. Southwest Airlines, for example, has differentiated itself as a low-cost, short-haul, express airline. This has proved to be a winning strategy for competing in the highly competitive airline industry.

3. *Innovation strategy.* Introduce new products and services, add new features to existing products and services, or develop new ways to produce them. A classic example is the introduction of automated teller machines (ATMs) by Citibank. The convenience and cost-cutting features of this innovation gave Citibank a huge advantage over its competitors. Like many innovative products, the ATM changed the nature of competition in the banking industry. Today, an ATM is a competitive *necessity* for any bank. Another excellent example is Apple's rapid introduction of innovative products.

4. *Operational effectiveness strategy.* Improve the manner in which a firm executes its internal business processes so that it performs these activities more effectively than its rivals. Such improvements increase quality, productivity, and employee and customer satisfaction while decreasing time to market.

5. *Customer orientation strategy.* Concentrate on making customers happy. Web-based systems are particularly effective in this area because they can create a personalized, one-to-one relationship with each customer. Amazon (www.amazon.com), Apple (www.apple.com), and Starbucks (www.starbucks.com) are classic examples of companies devoted to customer satisfaction.

Cost Leader
I can sell at a lower cost than you can.

Differentiation
I am better because I am different.

Innovation
I'm doing something new and you can't catch up.

Operational Effectiveness
I can do the same thing more efficiently than you can.

Customer Oriented
I treat my customers better than you do.

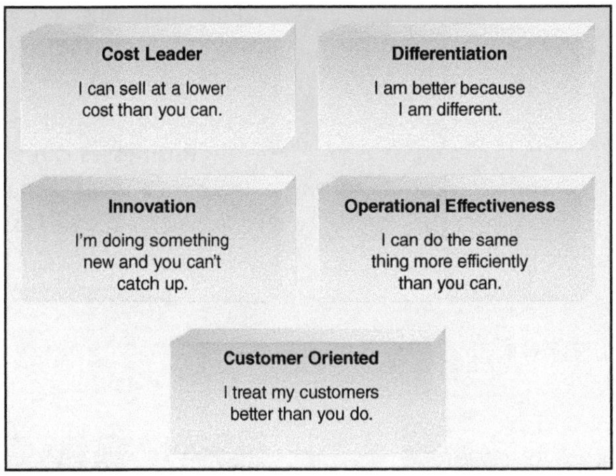

FIGURE 2.4 Strategies for competitive advantage.

Business–Information Technology Alignment

The best way for organizations to maximize the strategic value of IT is to achieve business–information technology alignment. In fact, the "holy grail" of organizations is business–information technology alignment, or strategic alignment (which we will call simply *alignment*). **Business-information technology alignment (business-IT alignment)** is the tight integration of the IT function with the organization's strategy, mission, and goals. That is, the IT function directly supports the business objectives of the organization. There are six characteristics of excellent alignment:

1. Organizations view IT as an engine of innovation that continually transforms the business, often creating new revenue streams.

2. Organizations view their internal and external customers and their customer service function as supremely important.

3. Organizations rotate business and IT professionals across departments and job functions.

4. Organizations provide overarching goals that are completely clear to each IT and business employee.

5. Organizations ensure that IT employees understand how the company makes (or loses) money.

6. Organizations create a vibrant and inclusive company culture.

Unfortunately, many organizations fail to achieve this type of close alignment. In fact, according to a McKinsey & Company survey on IT strategy and spending, only 16 percent of the IT and business executives who participated agreed that their organization had adequate alignment between IT and the business. Given the importance of business–IT alignment, why do so many organizations fail to implement this policy? The major reasons are the following:

- Business managers and IT managers have different objectives.
- The business and IT departments are ignorant of the other group's expertise.
- A lack of communication.

Put simply, business executives often know little about information technology, and IT executives understand the technology but may not understand the real needs of the business. One solution to this problem is to foster a collaborative environment in organizations so that business and IT executives can communicate freely and learn from each other.

Businesses can also utilize enterprise architecture to foster alignment. Originally developed as a tool to organize a company's IT initiatives, the enterprise architecture concept has evolved to encompass both a technical specification (the information and communication technologies and the information systems used in an organization) and a business specification (a collection of core business processes and management activities).

Before you go on...

1. What are strategic information systems?
2. According to Porter, what are the five forces that could endanger a firm's position in its industry or marketplaces?
3. Describe Porter's value chain model. Differentiate between Porter's competitive forces model and his value chain model.
4. What strategies can companies use to gain competitive advantage?
5. What is business–IT alignment?
6. Give examples of business–IT alignment at your university, regarding student systems. (*Hint:* What are the "business" goals of your university with regard to student registration, fee payment, grade posting, etc.?)

Apply the Concept 2.2

LEARNING OBJECTIVE 2.2 Describe the strategies that organizations typically adopt to counter Porter's five competitive forces.

STEP 1: Background

This section has exposed you to Porter's five forces model, which explains how various forces can affect an organization. The threat of entry of new competitors, bargaining power of suppliers, bargaining power of customers, threat of substitute products or services, and rivalry among existing firms in the industry all have an impact on the organization's success. Based on this model, the chapter presents five strategies for competitive advantage: cost leadership, differentiation, innovation, operational effectiveness, and customer orientation.

Walmart is a worldwide company that focuses on a cost-leadership strategy. Review the ways Walmart uses the five forces (or controls them) to maintain their position as a global cost leader. Although it may be somewhat easy to perform this exercise with a global giant like Walmart, it is very difficult to apply these concepts to small businesses.

STEP 2: Activity

Visit your favorite restaurant, and ask to speak to the manager. Asking only a few questions, evaluate whether the manager has a grasp of the five forces model. Do *not* ask anything specifically about Porter. Rather, inquire about rivals, substitutes, customers' bargaining power, suppliers' power, and so on. A good manager should be familiar with these concepts regardless of whether he or she uses the term "*Porter's five forces.*" Finally, ask the manager what strategy he or she uses. Then, try to classify that strategy as a cost leadership, differentiation, innovation, operational effectiveness, and customer orientation strategy.

STEP 3: Deliverable

Identify which of the five forces are at work based on the manager's feedback. Then, describe the strategies that COULD help deal with these particular forces, and explain IF this is what the restaurant is currently attempting to do. If it is not, then explain what they should do differently. Your submission will have two parts: (1) a definition of the forces, and (2) a description of the strategies at play in response to those forces.

What's in IT for me?

For All Majors

All functional areas in any organization must work together in an integrated fashion in order for the firm to respond adequately to business pressures. These responses typically require each functional area to utilize a variety of information systems to support, document, and manage cross-functional business processes. In today's competitive global marketplace, the timeliness and accuracy of these responses are even more critical.

Closely following this discussion, all functional areas must work together for the organization to gain competitive advantage in its marketplace. Again, the functional areas use a variety of strategic information systems to achieve this goal. BPR and BPI process change efforts contribute to the goal as well.

You have seen why companies must be concerned with strategic advantage. But why is this chapter so important for you? There are several reasons. First, the business pressures you have learned about have an impact on your organization, but they also affect you

as an individual. So, it is critical that you understand how information systems can help you, and eventually your organization, respond to these pressures.

In addition, achieving competitive advantage is essential for your organization's survival. In many cases, you, your team, and all your colleagues will be responsible for creating a competitive advantage. Therefore, having general knowledge about strategy and about how information systems affect the organization's strategy and competitive position will help you in your career.

You also need a basic knowledge of your organization's strategy, mission, and goals, as well as its business problems and how it makes (or loses) money. You now know how to analyze your organization's strategy and value chain, as well as the strategies and value chains of your competitors. You also have acquired a general knowledge of how information technology contributes to organizational strategy. This knowledge will help you to do your job better, to be promoted more quickly, and to contribute significantly to the success of your organization.

Summary

1. **Identify effective IT responses to different kinds of business pressures.**

   - *Market pressures:* An example of a market pressure is powerful customers. Customer relationship management is an effective IT response that helps companies achieve customer intimacy.

   - *Technology pressures:* An example of a technology pressure is information overload. Search engines and business intelligence applications enable managers to access, navigate, and utilize vast amounts of information.

   - *Societal/political/legal pressures:* An example of a societal/political/legal pressure is social responsibility, such as the state of the physical environment. Green IT is one response that is intended to improve the environment.

2. **Describe the strategies that organizations typically adopt to counter Porter's five competitive forces.**

Porter's five competitive forces:

1. *The threat of entry of new competitors:* For most firms, the Web increases the threat that new competitors will enter the market by reducing traditional barriers to entry. Frequently, competitors need only to set up a Web site to enter a market. The Web can also increase barriers to entry, as when customers come to expect a nontrivial capability from their suppliers.

2. *The bargaining power of suppliers:* The Web enables buyers to find alternative suppliers and to compare prices more easily, thereby reducing suppliers' bargaining power. From a different perspective, as companies use the Web to integrate their supply chains, participating suppliers can lock in customers, thereby increasing suppliers' bargaining power.

3. *The bargaining power of customers (buyers):* The Web provides customers with incredible amounts of choices for products, as well as information about those choices. As a result, the Web increases buyer power. However, companies can implement loyalty programs in which they use the Web to monitor the activities of millions of customers. Such programs reduce buyer power.

4. *The threat of substitute products or services:* New technologies create substitute products very rapidly, and the Web makes information about these products available almost instantly. As a result, industries (particularly information-based industries) are in great danger from substitutes (e.g., music, books, newspapers, magazines, software). However, the Web also can enable a company to build in switching costs, so that it will cost customers time and/or money to switch from your company to a competitor.

5. *The rivalry among existing firms in the industry:* In the past, proprietary information systems provided strategic advantage for firms in highly competitive industries. The visibility of Internet applications on the Web makes proprietary systems more difficult to keep secret. Therefore, the Web makes strategic advantage more short-lived.

The five strategies are as follows:

1. *Cost leadership strategy*—Produce products and/or services at the lowest cost in the industry.

2. *Differentiation strategy*—Offer different products, services, or product features.

3. *Innovation strategy*—Introduce new products and services, put new features in existing products and services, or develop new ways to produce them.

4. *Operational effectiveness strategy*—Improve the manner in which internal business processes are executed so that a firm performs similar activities better than its rivals.

5. *Customer orientation strategy*—Concentrate on making customers happy.

Chapter Glossary

business environment The combination of social, legal, economic, physical, and political factors in which businesses conduct their operations.

business–information technology alignment The tight integration of the IT function with the strategy, mission, and goals of the organization.

competitive advantage An advantage over competitors in some measure such as cost, quality, or speed; leads to control of a market and to larger-than-average profits.

competitive forces model A business framework devised by Michael Porter that analyzes competitiveness by recognizing five major forces that could endanger a company's position.

digital divide The gap between those who have access to information and communications technology and those who do not.

entry barrier Product or service feature that customers expect from organizations in a certain industry; an organization trying to enter this market must provide this product or service at a minimum to be able to compete.

globalization The integration and interdependence of economic, social, cultural, and ecological facets of life, enabled by rapid advances in information technology.

individual social responsibility See **organizational social responsibility**.

make-to-order The strategy of producing customized products and services.

mass customization A production process in which items are produced in large quantities but are customized to fit the desires of each customer.

organizational social responsibility (also individual social responsibility) Efforts by organizations to solve various social problems.

primary activities Those business activities related to the production and distribution of the firm's products and services, thus creating value.

strategic information systems (SISs) Systems that help an organization gain a competitive advantage by supporting its strategic goals and/or increasing performance and productivity.

support activities Business activities that do not add value directly to a firm's product or service under consideration but support the primary activities that do add value.

value chain A sequence of activities through which the organization's inputs, whatever they are, are transformed into more valuable outputs, whatever they are.

value chain model Model that shows the primary activities that sequentially add value to the profit margin; also shows the support activities.

value system Includes the producers, suppliers, distributors, and buyers, all with their value chains.

Discussion Questions

1. Explain why IT is both a business pressure and an enabler of response activities that counter business pressures.

2. What does a flat world mean to you in your choice of a major? In your choice of a career? Will you have to be a "lifelong learner"? Why or why not?

3. What might the impact of a flat world be on your standard of living?

4. Is IT a strategic weapon or a survival tool? Discuss.

5. Why might it be difficult to justify a strategic information system?

6. Describe the five forces in Porter's competitive forces model, and explain how increased access to high-speed Internet has affected each one.

7. Describe Porter's value chain model. What is the relationship between the competitive forces model and the value chain model?

8. Describe how IT can be used to support different value chains for different companies.

9. Discuss the idea that an information system by itself can rarely provide a sustainable competitive advantage.

Problem-Solving Activities

1. Surf the Internet for information about the Department of Homeland Security. Examine the available information, and comment on the role of information technologies in the department.

2. Experience mass customization by designing your own shoes at www .nike.com, your car at www.jaguar.com, your CD at www.easternrecording .com, your business card at www.iprint.com, and your diamond ring at www.bluenile.com. Summarize your experiences.

3. Access www.go4customer.com. What does this company do and where is it located? Who are its customers? Provide examples of how a U.S. company would use its services.

4. Enter Walmart China (www.wal-martchina.com/english/index.htm). How does Walmart China differ from your local Walmart (consider products, prices, services, etc.)? Describe these differences.

5. Apply Porter's value chain model to Costco (www.costco.com). What is Costco's competitive strategy? Who are Costco's major competitors? Describe Costco's business model. Describe the tasks that Costco must accomplish for each primary value chain activity. How would Costco's information systems contribute to Costco's competitive strategy, given the nature of its business?

6. Apply Porter's value chain model to Dell (www.dell.com). What is Dell's competitive strategy? Who are Dell's major competitors? Describe Dell's business model. Describe the tasks that Dell must accomplish for each primary value chain activity. How would Dell's information systems contribute to Dell's competitive strategy, given the nature of its business?

Closing Case 1

MIS Football Teams Use Virtual Reality

The Problem

College and professional football teams have a unique set of problems. First and foremost, teams would like to reduce the physical wear and tear of drills and practices on their players. In the National Football League (NFL), the most recent Collective Bargaining Agreement (2011) reduced the number of off-season practices, prohibited training camp "two-a-day" practices, and limited the number of contact practices in both the preseason and the regular season.

At the same time, however, players must learn the playbook as quickly and thoroughly as possible. However, when football teams practice, the time on the field for repetitions ("reps") is limited. It is particularly important for the starting players to participate in reps together.

Specifically, consider quarterbacks, arguably the most important position on a football team. Young quarterbacks are often thrown into live action before they are ready because starters are injured. This situation compresses the amount of time available for young quarterbacks to learn enough to make correct decisions, let alone have a chance of winning.

A Potential Solution

Teams are beginning to use an immersive virtual reality experience that makes players feel and think as if they are actually on the practice field. *Virtual reality* (VR) is a set of information technologies that simulate physical presence in the real world, including sight, smell, sound, and touch. Modern VR environments are presented on stereoscopic, head-mounted displays—for example, the Oculus Rift, now owned by Facebook; www.oculus.com—to realistically create an artificial experience such as a video game. VR environments can also create a lifelike, real-world experience such as football. As of July 2015, two companies were providing VR experiences for professional, college, and high school football programs: STriVR Labs (http://strivrlabs.com) and EON Sports (www.eonsportsvr.com).

Here is how these experiences work from the perspective of a quarterback. When he puts on the Oculus Rift headset and the headphones, he is standing in his position on the practice field. As he scans the field, he recognizes the defensive alignment, and he observes how his offense is positioned. He turns around, and he sees that his running back is waiting for the handoff. A voice calls the play, the ball is snapped, and a play unfolds. As the play progresses, the quarterback can scan the defense to determine the type of coverage. One quarterback noted, "It is like watching film, but you are actually there on the field. I feel like I am actually in the scrimmage."

The systems offer a fully immersive, 360-degree view for players and coaches as teams run through plays on a practice field, providing simulated bodies with natural body movements. In addition, players can hear coaches talking as well as the things they would normally hear on the practice field. Staff members spend many hours turning the video into useful virtual reality footage.

The systems gather video from multiple cameras on four-foot tripods placed around the scrimmage on both the offensive and defensive sides. The cameras capture live plays and content from teams' practices and then, via their software, produce three-dimensional video for players through an Oculus Rift headset and headphones. The VR technology essentially has football players walking through real-game experiences.

Although the systems work for every player, quarterback was the logical starting point. The systems initially were utilized as a method to train quarterbacks with mental exercises to reinforce actual practice repetitions. They quickly expanded for use with other positions, because they are invaluable in improving players' reaction times and decision making.

STriVR and EON clients include college teams such as Stanford, Auburn, Clemson, Dartmouth, Vanderbilt, Kansas, Mississippi, and UCLA, as well as the National Football League's Dallas Cowboys and New England Patriots. The first pick in the 2015 NFL Draft, Jameis Winston of the Tampa Bay Buccaneers, trained using the EON system. Further, nearly 100 high school football programs are using VR packages.

STriVR and EON have concentrated on building libraries of basic plays for their clients. After shooting video at various practices, the companies deliver the VR footage to the teams within a few weeks. However, in the near future, the companies hope to reduce the turn-around time, allowing teams to use VR video tailored to specific game plans.

There are other uses for VR technology in football programs, including:

- Teaching incoming freshmen and preparing backup players who do not get as many reps as the starters.
- Providing value in recruiting, because coaches could take laptops, VR headsets, and headphones on the road. Without visiting a campus, recruits could be virtually standing in a locker room with potential teammates, listening to a pregame pep talk. They could then be in the tunnel, racing onto the field with the other players, or on the sidelines during a game.
- Helping injured players—instead of pushing their bodies through a real practice, they could work on their reps and their mental exercises virtually.

The Results

The use of virtual reality technology in sports in just beginning. However, one NFL executive told STriVR to charge $250,000 per year to professional football teams because teams using the technology would be "picking up half a coach."

Finally, STriVR and EON have plans for basketball and baseball in the near future.

Sources: Compiled from S. Wagner-McGough, "Report: Patriots Will Arm Themselves with Virtual Reality Technology," *CBS Sports*, July 23, 2015; S. Springer, "Patriots Poised to Enhance Practice with Virtual Reality Technology," *The Boston Globe*, July 22, 2015; M. Lelinwalla, "All You Need to Know about Virtual Reality Training in College Football and the NFL," *Tech Times*, June 29, 2015; G. Schroeder, "Virtual Reality Becomes a Reality for College Football," *USA Today*, June 9, 2015; B. Fischer, "Use of Virtual-Reality Training Continues to Grow in College Football," *NFL.com*, June 8, 2015; B. Wallace, "Tackling Tech: Why Virtual Reality Will Become Reality for the NFL," *www.patriots.com*, May 28, 2015; B. Feldman, "'I Was Blown Away': Welcome to Football's Quarterback Revolution," *Fox Sports*, March 11, 2015; M. Tait, "KU Becomes Pioneer in Using Virtual Reality to Enhance Football Program," *Tale of the Tait KUsports.com*, March 26, 2013; N. Davis, "NFL, Players Announce New 10-Year Labor Agreement," *USA Today*, July 25, 2011; http://strivrlabs.com, accessed July 22, 2015.

Questions

1. In what other ways could professional and college football programs use virtual reality systems? (*Hint:* Consider the fan experience.)

2. Are STriVR and EON strategic information systems for any football program? Why or why not? Support your answer with specific examples.

3. Will STriVR and EON become competitive necessities for football programs? Why or why not? Support your answer with specific examples.

Closing Case 2

 Bank of America Transforms Its Information Technology

The Problem

Many economists classify the financial crisis of 2007-2008 as the worst financial crisis since the Great Depression of the 1930s. The crisis threatened to bring about the collapse of large financial institutions, which was prevented only by the bailout of banks by national governments. To stabilize the U.S. financial system, the U.S. government invested huge sums in institutions it considered to be critical to the functioning of the entire financial system; that is, "too big to fail."

One of these institutions was the Bank of America (BofA; www.bankofamerica.com), which received $45 billion in bailout funds. (*Note:* Bank of American repaid the entire amount in December 2009). The bank paid a further $17 billion in August 2014 to settle charges of mortgage fraud stemming from poor lending practices leading up to the financial crisis.

After the crisis, BofA executives directed the bank to take measures to eliminate the problems that led to its near-death experience in the financial crisis. Many of these measures involved BofA's information technology.

A Multipart Solution

BofA developed a series of strategic goals for its IT function: (1) standardize its IT infrastructure, (2) streamline applications, (3) develop customer-focused innovations, and (4) streamline the physical infrastructure. BofA's IT organization, called Global Technology and Operations, was directly tasked with achieving the first three goals.

IT Infrastructure. In the past, the IT department typically allocated separate servers in its data centers for each line of business, such as its mortgage business and its trading applications. To improve efficiency and reduce costs, the bank's first strategic goal was to create a standardized, shared IT infrastructure that all business units could readily access. As a result, BofA closed down 20 data centers and implemented a private cloud. (We discuss cloud computing in detail in Plug IT In 4.)

The business goals of moving the IT infrastructure to a private cloud were to enable the bank to respond more quickly to changing business conditions and to cut costs—as much as 50 percent from the bank's current data center costs. The cloud approach also enabled the bank to perform more computing tasks with less hardware. In addition it increased the ability of the bank's network, storage, and server capacity to scale up or scale down as business conditions dictate. Essentially, the cloud gives the bank more flexibility and speed to react to changes in the bank's dynamic business environment.

Corporate data often reside on specific servers in a single location. In contrast, data in a cloud environment may be stored on shared servers in multiple locations. This arrangement requires more complex security controls and compliance reporting. BofA must be able to prove to auditors that it is securely managing sensitive data such as bank account numbers and credit card information in its cloud. In fact, to improve information security and regulatory compliance, the bank is experimenting with tagging or labeling each piece of data so that it can follow the data across its global network, tracking anyone who has had access to it or has made changes to it.

Applications. Under a four-year plan implemented in 2010, BofA retired more than 18,000 applications, many of them left over from its acquisitions of other companies. For example, the bank spent $100 million to consolidate 5 Merrill Lynch financial adviser applications into one. (BofA acquired Merrill Lynch in 2013.) Further, users at corporate clients in 140 countries now access BofA's CashPro Online portal in 11 languages. The portal replaced hundreds of applications, including liquidity management, currency conversion, wire transfers, and many others. The bank also consolidated 22 collateral management systems into one and 8 teller systems into one.

Simplifying its IT infrastructure and reducing the license and support costs of thousands of applications have enabled the bank to invest a larger percentage of its $9 billion annual IT budget on new, innovative applications. In fact, BofA has doubled its spending on new development since 2009.

Innovative Customer Service. The bank's customers stated they wanted their bank to be "where they are." In response, the bank launched new versions of its customer smartphone and iPad app in 2014. The app provides three features:

1. *Account information and transactional capabilities.* For example, customers must be able to view account details and transfer funds on any device from wherever they are. Further, customers can order new debit and credit cards, view their available card credit, schedule appointments, modify scheduled bill payments, order copies of posted checks, and perform many other functions.

2. *Service.* For example, if bank customers are traveling internationally, then they should be able to place a travel notification on their accounts via a mobile device rather than having to call the bank to speak to a customer service representative.

3. *Mobile payments and commerce.* BofA is offering services such as its clearXchange person-to-person payments network jointly with JP-Morgan Chase and Wells Fargo. In addition, the bank offers its BankAmeriDeals merchant-funded rewards program, which allows customers to receive coupons from retailers by clicking on offers sent directly to their online banking accounts.

By July 2015, the app had 15 million users and was growing by more than 200,000 customers per month. In the second quarter of 2015, BofA managed a record 19 million deposits made from mobile devices. This amount is growing at a rate of 50 percent per year.

Physical Infrastructure. To reduce costs, BofA analyzed its network of banking centers; that is, bank branch locations and ATMS. The bank tracked every transaction by customer, location, time, and channel. It then stored the information for 60 months—a total of more than 20 terabytes of data. For security purposes, the bank removed all details that would identify any individual. In addition to tracking customer

activity, the bank examined the capacity of each branch and ATM, the costs of each location, each branch's total revenues, annual sales, and first-year revenue sales to a new customer. Based on the results of the analysis, BofA was able to reduce its banking centers from 6,151 in 2008 to fewer than 5,000 by July 2015. The bank also reduced its annual branch and ATM expenses by nearly 15 percent from $5.5 billion to $4.7 billion.

Interestingly, beginning in 2009 Bank of America IT executives meet annually with 40 technology startups in Silicon Valley to learn about new products. Over the years, the bank has decided to do business with about 17 percent of these startups. BofA's work with startups balances the bank's need for scale and reliability against its need for new ideas.

BofA has high expectations for these vendors. The bank requires open standards and interoperability. It also requires technology contracts in which costs scale down as well as up. Finally, technology vendors must share BofA's risk and regulatory rules, including, in some cases, agreeing to contracts where vendors share in the liability if their technology causes problems that lead to losses or fines for the bank.

The Results

The IT transformation is ongoing, but the bank's financial results seem sound. In July 2015, Bank of American was the country's second-largest bank, with approximately $2.1 trillion in assets. Further, the bank reported net income of $5.3 billion in the second quarter of that year.

Sources: Compiled from H. Clancy, "This Fortune 500 Bank's Patents Are Cited by Apple, Google, and Nike," *Fortune*, June 29, 2015; R. King, "Bank of America's Data Initiative Follows Internet Companies into the Cloud," *The Wall Street Journal*, March 6, 2015; C. Murphy, "How Bank of America Taps Tech Startups," *InformationWeek*, December 1, 2014; R. Preston, "IT Chief of the Year: Bank of America's Cathy Bessant," *InformationWeek*, December 1, 2014; T. Groenfeldt, "Bank of America's Data Mapping Adds $1 Per Share," *Forbes*, August 21, 2014; C. Murphy, "Bank of America's 'Why Stop There?' Cloud Strategy," *InformationWeek*, February 4, 2014; D. Campbell, "Bank of America Finishes Merger of Merrill Lynch into Parent," *Bloomberg Business*, October 1, 2013; B. Yurcan, "The Future of Moble at Bank of America," *InformationWeek*, March 25, 2013; P. Crosman, "Inside BofA's IT Makeover," *American Banker*, September 1, 2011; "BofA Repays All of Government Funds," *MSNBC*, December 10, 2009; www.bankofamerica.com, accessed July 25, 2015.

Questions

1. What is the relationship between the development of mobile banking customer applications and the closing of banking centers?

2. Refer to Porter's strategies for competitive advantage. Which strategy (or strategies) is (are) the Bank of America pursuing? Provide specific examples to support your answer.

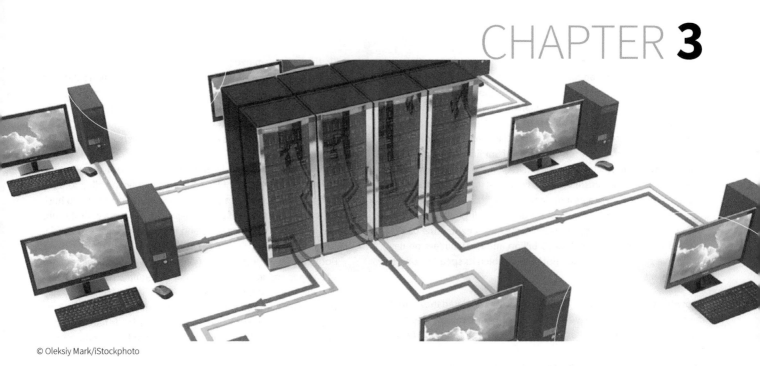

© Oleksiy Mark/iStockphoto

Data and Knowledge Management

LEARNING OBJECTIVES

3.1 Discuss ways that common challenges in managing data can be addressed using data governance.

3.2 Discuss the advantages and disadvantages of relational databases.

3.3 Define *Big Data* and its basic characteristics.

3.4 Explain the elements necessary to successfully implement and maintain data warehouses.

3.5 Describe the benefits and challenges of implementing knowledge management systems in organizations.

Opening Case

 Database Saves the State of Washington Medicaid Dollars

When a patient is admitted to the emergency room (ER) of a hospital, his physician may never have seen him before. Nevertheless, she must diagnose his problem very quickly. If the physician already knew the patient's medical history, then her examination and subsequent diagnosis would be faster, less expensive, and more accurate.

As the Affordable Care Act expands Medicaid to an increasing number of patients, the need for states to control ER costs becomes more critical. Many Medicaid patients visit hospital ERs too many times. In fact, in the state of Washington, patients who went to the ER more than four times in one year comprise 20 percent of all ER visits paid for by Medicaid.

To address this problem, the State of Washington implemented the Emergency Department Information Exchange (EDIE), a database that contains the records of each patient treated in every hospital ER in the state. The database enables physicians to track patients' ER visits to multiple hospitals.

The state experienced some difficulties implementing the database. In the past, some state hospitals had attempted to create regional databases. However, many hospitals did not join these efforts, fearing they would lose both patients and Medicaid dollars.

In response, the state announced that it would no longer reimburse hospitals for more than three non-emergency ER visits by a Medicaid recipient each year. Physicians and hospitals successfully sued the state, claiming the policy was arbitrary and would increase the hospitals' costs.

The state's Medicaid office responded by creating a list of 500 medical problems—for example, acute bronchitis, urinary tract infections, and headaches—that it would no longer reimburse as emergency care. The state argued that those complaints could be treated in doctors' offices or clinics.

Hospitals objected to this list because patients who were not treated in hospitals would reduce hospitals' income. As a result, the state adopted the EDIE database as a compromise. The EDIE database meets federal health privacy laws by allowing only approved medical staff members to access data on patients under their care. When a patient registers at an ER anywhere in the state, the attending physician and nurses immediately receive a fax (some hospitals still use fax machines) or an e-mail from the database. The report lists all of the patient's recent ER admissions, diagnoses, and treatments.

Further, when patients leave the ER, the database helps physicians track their care. One hospital sends paramedics to check on high-risk patients. Other hospitals hire care coordinators to ensure that patients make appointments with a family doctor or specialist. Still other hospitals discovered that many of their ER patients needed help managing pain, so they set up a pain-management clinic.

In addition, the database has helped reduce the prescription of narcotics in the state's ERs by 24 percent in its first year of use, in large part because patients cannot visit multiple health facilities to obtain prescriptions. More than 400 primary care physicians have signed up to receive automatic notifications when one of their patients is admitted to the ER. The state is signing up more family doctors as well as community and mental health clinics.

Physicians can now send many of their patients to clinics or other less expensive care centers rather than ERs. Data released in March 2014 indicate that ER visits by Medicaid patients dropped 10 percent in the 2013 fiscal year, and the rate of ER visits that resulted in a non-acute diagnosis decreased more than 14 percent. The state credits the database for a substantial amount of the state's $33.7 million reduction in 2013 Medicaid costs.

Sources: Compiled from "EDIE and PMP Integration," *American College of Emergency Physicians*, August 11, 2015; "How Big Data Can Reduce ER Visits," *Real Business*, October 23, 2014; J. Creswell, "Doctors Find Barriers to Sharing Digital Medical Records," *The New York Times*, September 30, 2014; T. Bannow, "Oregon Hospitals Begin Sharing ER Data," *The Bend Bulletin*, September 18, 2014; "Report Finds Data Sharing Popular Among Hospitals," *ClinicalKey*, September 12, 2014; R. Daly, "EHR Data Sharing Challenges Hospitals," *Healthcare Financial Management Association*, August 7, 2014; D. Gorenstein, "Data: The Secret Ingredient in Hospital Cooperation," *Marketplace.org*, June 5, 2014; K. Weise, "Hospitals Share Data to Stop ER Abusers," *Bloomberg BusinessWeek*, April 7-13, 2014; "Emergency Department Partnership Is Improving Care and Saving Medicaid Funds," *Washing State Hospital Association*, March 20, 2014; E. Rizzo, "When Hospitals Share Data, Who Benefits?" *Becker's Hospital Review*, March 12, 2014; "When Hospitals Share Patient Records, Emergency Patients Benefit, Study Suggests," *University of Michigan Health System*, January 24, 2014.

Questions

1. Describe additional benefits (beyond those discussed in the case) of the State of Washington's EDIE database.

2. Describe potential disadvantages of the State of Washington's EDIE database.

Introduction

Information technologies and systems support organizations in managing—that is, acquiring, organizing, storing, accessing, analyzing, and interpreting—data. As you noted in Chapter 1, when these data are managed properly, they become *information* and then *knowledge*. As you see in the chapter's opening case, information and knowledge are invaluable organizational resources that can provide any organization with a competitive advantage.

So, just how important are data and data management to organizations? From confidential customer information, to intellectual property, to financial transactions, to social media posts, organizations possess massive amounts of data that are critical to their success. Of course, to benefit from these data, they need to manage them effectively. This type of management, however, comes at a huge cost. According to Symantec's (www.symantec.com) State of Information Survey, digital information costs organizations worldwide over $1 trillion annually, and it makes up roughly *half* of an organization's total value. The survey found that large organizations spend an average of some $40 million annually to maintain and utilize data, and small-to-medium-sized businesses spend almost $350,000.

Despite the monetary value of data, some organizations are building their business models on giving data away for free. IT's About Business 3.1 shows how Jana is bringing Internet access to the developing world using this practice.

IT's About Business 3.1

MKT Giving Data Away for Free

The rapid increase in the number of new smartphones in developing countries has not been accompanied by a corresponding increase in mobile marketing because wireless data are still too expensive. In Africa and Asia, for example, prepaid plans are the norm, not contracts, meaning that most mobile users pay as they go, buying small amounts of minutes and data.

The cost of wireless access in developing countries may seem affordable by American standards, but it's not when compared with average incomes. In India, for example, a gigabyte of 3G data costs just $4, compared with about $20 in the United States. A smartphone in India can cost as little as $40, and the average monthly bill is $7. But in many developing countries, the minimum wage is just 20 cents an hour. In India, only 57 percent of smartphone owners use data, and the average monthly use is just 80 megabytes, compared with 800 for the average American. In the United States, mobile data costs 1 to 2 percent of a person's average wage, compared with 10 percent in Brazil and more than 33 percent in Africa.

One company is trying to help emerging market consumers access the Internet more cheaply. Jana (http://jana.com) is a mobile startup that has business relationships with 237 telecommunications operators in 102 countries, giving the startup access to 3.5 billion mobile phones. In 2014, Jana deployed Marketplace, a service that allows marketers to send ads to mobile users around the world at no cost to the user. The ads can be either short videos or app install ads.

For many millions of people in the developing world, Jana is an entry point to the mobile Web. Jana's mCent (www.mcent.com) app rewards mobile users with data in exchange for trying out apps and allowing Jana to collect personal information, such as their usage history and which friends they persuaded to sign up for the service. The app developers pay for the data rewards and Jana takes a cut. For example, in India, mobile customers can sign up for the chat app LINE (http://line.me/en/) and receive 13 rupees worth of data, and sign up for the music service Saavn (www.saavn.com) and get 28 rupees worth of data. Thus, users acquire free data with which to surf the Web.

mCent's popularity exploded, ranking it India's fifth most popular app in just 12 months. It helped Jana turn a profit by early 2015. Approximately 50 percent of Jana's revenue comes from China's Tencent, Amazon, and Twitter, with the remainder (more than 1500 apps) coming from many other companies.

Jana released its Marketplace platform in an attempt to solve the difficult mobile economics problem in emerging markets. More cell towers would help increase bandwidth, but carriers in the developing world are limited by narrow profit margins, increasing competition, and low capital budgets. In many countries, the average revenue per user is decreasing as impoverished people increasingly access wireless networks.

In addition to increasing its profits, Jana's goal is to provide free Internet service to billions of people. The startup is facing intense competition in this effort.

One solution to the Internet access problem is *zero-rating*—also called *sponsored data*—systems. With zero-rating, Web-based companies establish deals with Internet service providers whereby they pay for the cost of accessing their sites. Facebook, Google, and WhatsApp have used zero-rating for some time with bare-bones services such as Facebook Zero, a text-only version with no images. In a move to make its Android apps more accessible, Google has created a data-sponsorship program.

The zero-rating system has its critics because larger apps with deeper pockets to pay for data have an unfair advantage over smaller apps that do not. Also, some users are not aware of what the Internet is and how it usually works. In Indonesia, for example, 11 percent of Facebook Zero users said they didn't know that they were on the Internet. In fact, Indian critics have protested Facebook's Internet.org app, saying that the fact that it lets smartphone users browse certain sites for free misleads consumers into knowing how open the Web can be.

Jana maintains that the objections to zero-rating systems do not apply to its mCent app. The reason is that after signing up for a sponsored app, consumers can use their free data however they like, including any app, Web site, or video clip.

Critics say that companies going into emerging markets used sponsored data to increase data consumption, while impoverished consumers who are just getting to know the Internet and how it works risk being exploited.

Significantly, mCent users can also be exploited because they may download many apps they're not interested in so that they can receive free data. Jana attempts to avoid this problem by personalizing mCent to users and by tracking the time that users spend on the apps they download.

Sources: Compiled from "Facebook's Internet.org 'Not Scalable' Claims Rival Startup mCent," *Mobile World Live*, September 9, 2015; N. Pahwa, "Google Joins Facebook in Trying to Prevent IAMAI from Taking Strong Anti-Zero Rating Stand," *Medianama*, August 20, 2015; P. Olson, "This App Is Cashing in on Giving the World Free Data," *Forbes*, July 29, 2015; N. Alawadhi, "Google Puts Zero Rating Plan in India on Backburner for Fear of Backlash," *The Times of India*, May 28, 2015; S. Vijayakumar, "Jana Is in Full Support of Net Neutrality," *The Hindu*, May 8, 2015; J. Nanos, "Mobile App Marketplace Jana Pushes Deeper into the Developing World," *The Boston Globe*, May 6, 2015; M. Godwin, "What the 'Zero Rating' Debate Reveals about Net Neutrality," *Reason.com*, April 8, 2015; A. Howard, "Zero Rating Poses a Conundrum for Net Neutrality Advocates around the World," *TechRepublic*, January 23, 2015; A. Drossos, "Forget Fast Lanes. The Real Threat Net-Neutrality Is Zero-Rated Content," *GigaOM*, April 26, 2014; M. Bergen, "Mobile Startup Jana Launches Tool to Reach Next Billion Consumers, on Their Phones," *Advertising Age*, March 19, 2014; "Why Jana Will Help Marketers Reach the Next Billion Customers," *vivaki.com*, July 15, 2013; http://jana.com, www.mcent.com, accessed October 11, 2015.

Questions

1. At first glance, giving away data for free seems to be a questionable business strategy. Describe how Jana's business model makes this practice a success.

2. Why are Facebook and Google so interested in bringing Internet access to the developing world?

3. Discuss the pros and cons of the zero-rating system.

4. Is Jana correct in claiming that its system is not really a zero-rating system? Why or why not?

This chapter will examine the processes whereby data are transformed first into information and then into knowledge. Managing data is critically important in all organizations. Few business professionals are comfortable making or justifying business decisions that are not based on solid information. This is especially true today, when modern information systems make access to that information quick and easy. For example, we have information systems that format data in a way that managers and analysts can easily understand. Consequently, these professionals can access these data themselves and then analyze them according to their needs. The result is useful *information*. Managers can then apply their experience to use this information to address a business problem, thereby producing *knowledge*. Knowledge management, enabled by information technology, captures and stores knowledge in forms that all organizational employees can access and apply, thereby creating the flexible, powerful "learning organization."

Organizations store data in databases. Recall from Chapter 1 that a *database* is a collection of related data files or tables containing data. We discuss databases in Section 3.2.

Clearly, data and knowledge management are vital to modern organizations. But, why should *you* learn about them? The reason is that you will play an important role in the development of database applications. The structure and content of your organization's database depend on how users (you) define your business activities. For example, when database developers in the firm's MIS group build a database, they use a tool called entity-relationship (ER) modeling. This tool creates a model of how users view a business activity. When you understand how to create and interpret an ER model, then you can evaluate whether the developers have captured your business activities correctly.

Keep in mind that decisions about data last longer, and have a broader impact, than decisions about hardware or software. If decisions concerning hardware are wrong, then the equipment can be replaced relatively easily. If software decisions turn out to be incorrect, they can be modified, though not always painlessly or inexpensively. Database decisions, in contrast, are much harder to undo. Database design constrains what the organization can do with its data for a long time. Remember that business users will be stuck with a bad database design, while the programmers who created the database will quickly move on to their next projects.

Further, consider that databases typically underlie the enterprise applications that users access. If there are problems with organizational databases, it is unlikely that any applications will be able to provide the necessary functionality for users. Databases are difficult to set up properly and to maintain. They are also the component of an information system that is most likely to receive the blame for poor performance of the system, and the least likely to be recognized for excellent performance of the system. This is why it is so important to get database designs right the first time—and you will play a key role in these designs.

In addition, you might want to create a small, personal database using a software product such as Microsoft Access. In that case, you will need to be familiar with at least the basics of the product.

After the data are stored in your organization's databases, they must be accessible to users in a form that helps them make decisions. Organizations accomplish this objective by developing *data warehouses*. You should become familiar with data warehouses because they are invaluable decision-making tools. We discuss data warehouses in Section 3.4.

You will also make extensive use of your organization's knowledge base to perform your job. For example, when you are assigned a new project, you will likely research your firm's knowledge base to identify factors that contributed to the success (or failure) of previous, similar projects. We discuss knowledge management in Section 3.5.

You begin this chapter by examining the multiple problems involved in managing data. You then study the database approach that organizations use to help solve these problems. You turn your attention to Big Data, which organizations must manage in today's business environment. Next, you study data warehouses and data marts, and you learn how to utilize them for decision making. You finish the chapter by examining knowledge management.

3.1 | Managing Data

All IT applications require data. These data should be of high quality, meaning that they should be accurate, complete, timely, consistent, accessible, relevant, and concise. Unfortunately, the process of acquiring, keeping, and managing data is becoming increasingly difficult.

The Difficulties of Managing Data

Because data are processed in several stages and often in multiple locations, they are frequently subject to problems and difficulties. Managing data in organizations is difficult for many reasons.

First, the amount of data increases exponentially with time. Much historical data must be kept for a long time, and new data are added rapidly. For example, to support millions of customers, large retailers such as Walmart have to manage petabytes of data. (A petabyte is approximately 1,000 terabytes, or trillions of bytes; see Plug IT In 2.)

In addition, data are also scattered throughout organizations, and they are collected by many individuals using various methods and devices. These data are frequently stored in numerous servers and locations and in different computing systems, databases, formats, and human and computer languages.

Another problem is that data are generated from multiple sources: internal sources (for example, corporate databases and company documents); personal sources (for example, personal thoughts, opinions, and experiences); and external sources (for example, commercial databases, government reports, and corporate Web sites). Data also come from the Web, in the form of clickstream data. **Clickstream data** are those data that visitors and customers produce when they visit a Web site and click on hyperlinks (described in Chapter 4). Clickstream data provide a trail of the users' activities in the Web site, including user behavior and browsing patterns.

Adding to these problems is the fact that new sources of data, such as blogs, podcasts, videocasts, and RFID tags and other wireless sensors, are constantly being developed and the data these technologies generate must be managed. In addition, data degrade over time. For example, customers move to new addresses or change their names, companies go out of business or are bought, new products are developed, employees are hired or fired, and companies expand into new countries.

Data are also subject to *data rot*. Data rot refers primarily to problems with the media on which the data are stored. Over time, temperature, humidity, and exposure to light can cause physical problems with storage media and thus make it difficult to access the data. The second aspect of data rot is that finding the machines needed to access the data can be difficult. For example, it is almost impossible today to find 8-track players. Consequently, a library of 8-track tapes has become relatively worthless, unless you have a functioning 8-track player or you convert the tapes to a modern medium such as CDs.

Data security, quality, and integrity are critical, yet they are easily jeopardized. In addition, legal requirements relating to data differ among countries as well as among industries, and they change frequently.

Another problem arises from the fact that, over time, organizations have developed information systems for specific business processes, such as transaction processing, supply chain management, and customer relationship management. Information systems that specifically support these processes impose unique requirements on data, which results in repetition and conflicts across the organization. For example, the marketing function might maintain information on customers, sales territories, and markets. These data might be duplicated within the billing or customer service functions. This situation can produce inconsistent data within the enterprise. Inconsistent data prevent a company from developing a unified view of core business information—data concerning customers, products, finances, and so on—across the organization and its information systems.

Two other factors complicate data management. First, federal regulations—for example, the Sarbanes–Oxley Act of 2002—have made it a top priority for companies to better account for how they are managing information. Sarbanes–Oxley requires that (1) public companies evaluate and disclose the effectiveness of their internal financial controls and (2) independent auditors for these companies agree to this disclosure. The law also holds CEOs and CFOs personally responsible for such disclosures. If their companies lack satisfactory data management policies and fraud or a security breach occurs, the company officers could be held liable and face prosecution.

Second, companies are drowning in data, much of which is unstructured. As you have seen, the amount of data is increasing exponentially. To be profitable, companies must develop a strategy for managing these data effectively.

An additional problem with data management is Big Data. Big Data is so important that we devote the entire Section 3.3 to this topic.

Data Governance

To address the numerous problems associated with managing data, organizations are turning to data governance. **Data governance** is an approach to managing information across an entire organization. It involves a formal set of business processes and policies that are designed to ensure that data are handled in a certain, well-defined fashion. That is, the organization follows unambiguous rules for creating, collecting, handling, and protecting its information. The objective is to make information available, transparent, and useful for the people who are authorized to access it, from the moment it enters an organization until it is outdated and deleted.

One strategy for implementing data governance is master data management. **Master data management** is a process that spans all organizational business processes and applications. It provides companies with the ability to store, maintain, exchange, and synchronize a consistent, accurate, and timely "single version of the truth" for the company's master data.

Master data are a set of core data, such as customer, product, employee, vendor, geographic location, and so on, that span the enterprise information systems. It is important to distinguish between master data and transaction data. *Transaction data*, which are generated and captured by operational systems, describe the business's activities, or transactions. In contrast, master data are applied to multiple transactions and are used to categorize, aggregate, and evaluate the transaction data.

Let's look at an example of a transaction: You (Mary Jones) purchase one Samsung 42-inch plasma television, part number 1234, from Bill Roberts at Best Buy, for $2,000, on April 20, 2015. In this example, the master data are "product sold," "vendor," "salesperson," "store," "part number," "purchase price," and "date." When specific values are applied to the master data, then a transaction is represented. Therefore, transaction data would be, respectively, "42-inch plasma television," "Samsung," "Best Buy," "Bill Roberts," "1234," "$2,000," and "April 20, 2015."

An example of master data management is Dallas, Texas, which implemented a plan for digitizing the city's public and private records, such as paper documents, images, drawings, and video and audio content. The master database can be utilized by any of the 38 government departments that have appropriate access. The city is also integrating its financial and billing processes with its customer relationship management program. (You will learn about customer relationship management in Chapter 12.)

How will Dallas utilize this system? Imagine that the city experiences a water-main break. Before it implemented the system, repair crews had to search City Hall for records that were filed haphazardly. Once the workers found the hard-copy blueprints, they would take them to the site and, after examining them manually, would decide on a plan of action. In contrast, the new system delivers the blueprints wirelessly to the laptops of crews in the field, who can magnify or highlight areas of concern to generate a rapid response. This process reduces the time it takes to respond to an emergency by several hours.

Along with data governance, organizations use the database approach to efficiently and effectively manage their data. We discuss the database approach in Section 3.2.

Before you go on…

1. What are some of the difficulties involved in managing data?
2. Define *data governance, master data,* and *transactional data*.

Apply the Concept 3.1

LEARNING OBJECTIVE 3.1 Discuss ways that common challenges in managing data can be addressed using data governance.

STEP 1: Background (Here is what you are learning.)

The amount of data we create today is absolutely mind-boggling. EMC is a global company that focuses on helping organizations manage their data. Recently, the company sponsored a study to determine exactly how big the "digital universe" actually is and to envision its projected growth. There are some amazing findings in this study that point to a dramatic growth in data and an increase in virtual data centers. In the future, it will be possible to run your information systems in data centers that do not operate on your premises.

STEP 2: Activity (Here is what you do)

Visit YouTube and search for a video titled "The Digital Universe and You" by EMC. Although the video is somewhat dated (December, 2012), the concepts it presents are still valid. Watch this five-minute video, and consider how the trends it presents relate to the challenges discussed in this section. Now, imagine that your parents own their own business. It is successful, but it is also struggling under pressure to upgrade IT services for its employees and customers. How could you help them to look ahead to the future rather than keeping the status quo?

STEP 3: Deliverable (Here is what you turn in.)

Write an e-mail to your parents to explain how data and data management are likely to evolve over the next 10 years. Describe the common challenges they face, and discuss how data governance can help address these issues. Also, based on the video, highlight the qualities they should look for in new employees. Finally, identify the types of training they should provide for their current employees.

Submit your e-mail to your instructor.

3.2 | The Database Approach

From the mid-1950s, when businesses first adopted computer applications, until the early 1970s, organizations managed their data in a *file management environment*. This environment evolved because organizations typically automated their functions one application at a time. Therefore, the various automated systems developed independently from one another, without any overall planning. Each application required its own data, which were organized in a data file.

A **data file** is a collection of logically related records. In a file management environment, each application has a specific data file related to it. This file contains all of the data records the application requires. Over time, organizations developed numerous applications, each with an associated, application-specific data file.

For example, imagine that most of your information is stored in your university's central database, but a club to which you belong maintains its own files, the athletics department has separate files for student athletes, and your instructors maintain grade data on their personal computers. It is easy for your name to be misspelled in one of these databases or files. Similarly, if you move, then your address might be updated correctly in one database or file but not in others.

Using databases eliminates many problems that arose from previous methods of storing and accessing data, such as file management systems. Databases are arranged so that one set of software programs—the database management system—provides all users with access to all of the data. (You will study database management systems later in this chapter.) Database systems minimize the following problems:

- *Data redundancy:* The same data are stored in multiple locations.
- *Data isolation:* Applications cannot access data associated with other applications.
- *Data inconsistency:* Various copies of the data do not agree.

In addition, database systems maximize the following:

- *Data security*: Because data are "put in one place" in databases, there is a risk of losing a lot of data at one time. Therefore, databases must have extremely high security measures in place to minimize mistakes and deter attacks.
- *Data integrity*: Data meet certain constraints; for example, there are no alphabetic characters in a Social Security number field.
- *Data independence*: Applications and data are independent of one another; that is, applications and data are not linked to each other, so all applications are able to access the same data.

Figure 3.1 illustrates a university database. Note that university applications from the registrar's office, the accounting department, and the athletics department access data through the database management system.

A database can contain vast amounts of data. To make these data more understandable and useful, they are arranged in a hierarchy. We take a closer look at this hierarchy in the next section.

The Data Hierarchy

Data are organized in a hierarchy that begins with bits and proceeds all the way to databases (see Figure 3.2). A bit (*binary digit*) represents the smallest unit of data a computer can process. The term *binary* means that a bit can consist only of a 0 or a 1. A group of eight bits, called a byte, represents a single character. A byte can be a letter, a number, or a symbol. A logical grouping of characters into a word, a small group of words, or an identification number is called a field. For example, a student's name in a university's computer files would appear in the "name" field, and her or his Social Security number would appear in the "Social Security number" field. Fields can also contain data other than text and numbers. They can contain an image, or any other type of multimedia. Examples are a motor vehicle department's licensing database that contains a driver's photograph and a field that contains a voice sample to authorize access to a secure facility.

A logical grouping of related fields, such as the student's name, the courses taken, the date, and the grade, comprises a record. In the Apple iTunes Store, a song is a field in a record, with other fields containing the song's title, its price, and the album on which it appears. A logical grouping of related records is called a data file or a table. For example, a grouping of the

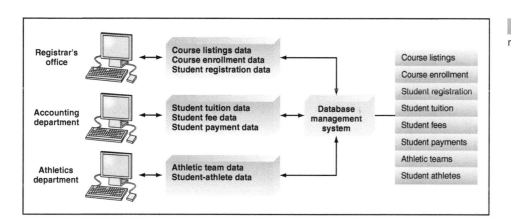

FIGURE 3.1 Database management system.

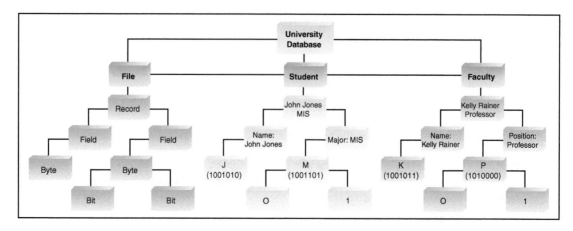

FIGURE 3.2 Hierarchy of data for a computer-based file.

records from a particular course, consisting of course number, professor, and students' grades, would constitute a data file for that course. Continuing up the hierarchy, a logical grouping of related files constitutes a *database*. Using the same example, the student course file could be grouped with files on students' personal histories and financial backgrounds to create a student database. In the next section, you will learn about relational database model.

The Relational Database Model

A **database management system (DBMS)** is a set of programs that provide users with tools to create and manage a database. Managing a database refers to the processes of adding, deleting, accessing, modifying, and analyzing data stored in a database. An organization can access the data by using query and reporting tools that are part of the DBMS or by using application programs specifically written to perform this function. DBMSs also provide the mechanisms for maintaining the integrity of stored data, managing security and user access, and recovering information if the system fails. Because databases and DBMSs are essential to all areas of business, they must be carefully managed.

There are a number of different database architectures, but we focus on the relational database model because it is popular and easy to use. Other database models (for example, the hierarchical and network models) are the responsibility of the MIS function and are not used by organizational employees. Popular examples of relational databases are Microsoft Access and Oracle.

Most business data—especially accounting and financial data—traditionally were organized into simple tables consisting of columns and rows. Tables allow people to compare information quickly by row or column. In addition, users can retrieve items rather easily by locating the point of intersection of a particular row and column.

The **relational database model** is based on the concept of two-dimensional tables. A relational database generally is not one big table—usually called a *flat file*—that contains all of the records and attributes. Such a design would entail far too much data redundancy. Instead, a relational database is usually designed with a number of related tables. Each of these tables contains records (listed in rows) and attributes (listed in columns).

To be valuable, a relational database must be organized so that users can retrieve, analyze, and understand the data they need. A key to designing an effective database is the data model. A **data model** is a diagram that represents entities in the database and their relationships. An **entity** is a person, place, thing, or event—such as a customer, an employee, or a product—about which information is maintained. Entities can typically be identified in the user's work environment. A record generally describes an entity. An **instance** of an entity refers to each row in a relational table, which is a specific, unique representation of the entity. For example, your university's student database contains an entity called student. An instance of the student entity would be a particular student. For instance, you are an instance of the student entity in your university's student database.

Each characteristic or quality of a particular entity is called an attribute. For example, if our entities were a customer, an employee, and a product, entity attributes would include customer name, employee number, and product color.

Consider the relational database example about students diagrammed in Figure 3.3. The table contains data about the entity called students. As you can see, each row of the table corresponds to one student record. (You have your own row in your university's student database.) Attributes of the entity are student name, undergraduate major, grade point average, and graduation date. The rows are the records on Sally Adams, John Jones, Jane Lee, Kevin Durham, Juan Rodriguez, Stella Zubnicki, and Ben Jones. Of course, your university keeps much more data on you than our example shows. In fact, your university's student database probably keeps hundreds of attributes on each student.

Every record in the database must contain at least one field that uniquely identifies that record so that it can be retrieved, updated, and sorted. This identifier field (or attribute) is called the primary key. For example, a student record in a U.S. university would use a unique student number as its primary key. (*Note:* In the past, your Social Security number served as the primary key for your student record. However, for security reasons, this practice has been discontinued.) You see that Sally Adams is uniquely identified by her student ID of 012345.

In some cases, locating a particular record requires the use of secondary keys. A secondary key is another field that has some identifying information, but typically does not identify the record with complete accuracy. For example, the student's major might be a secondary key if a user wanted to identify all of the students majoring in a particular field of study. It should not be the primary key, however, because many students can have the same major. Therefore, it cannot uniquely identify an individual student.

A foreign key is a field (or group of fields) in one table that uniquely identifies a row of another table. A foreign key is used to establish and enforce a link between two tables. We discuss foreign keys in more detail in Plug IT In 3.

Organizations implement databases to efficiently and effectively manage their data. There are a variety of operations that can be performed on databases. We look at three of these operations in detail in Plug IT In 3: query languages, normalization, and joins.

As we noted earlier in this chapter, organizations must manage huge quantities of data. Such data consist of structured and unstructured data and are called Big Data (discussed in Section 3.3). Unstructured data refers to data that does not reside in a traditional relational database. Examples of unstructured data include e-mail messages, word processing documents, videos, images, audio files, PowerPoint presentations, Facebook posts, tweets, snaps, ratings and recommendations, and Web pages. Industry analysts estimate that 80 to 90 percent of the data in an organization is unstructured. To manage Big Data, many organizations are using special types of databases, which we also discuss in Section 3.3.

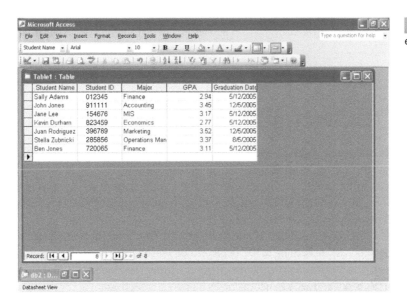

FIGURE 3.3 Student database example.

Because databases typically process data in real time (or near real time), it is not practical to allow users access to the databases. After all, the data will change while the user is looking at them! As a result, data warehouses have been developed to allow users to access data for decision making. You will learn about data warehouses in Section 3.4.

Before you go on...

1. What is a data model?
2. What is a primary key? A secondary key?
3. What is an entity? An attribute? An instance?
4. What are the advantages and disadvantages of relational databases?

Apply the Concept 3.2

LEARNING OBJECTIVE 3.2 Discuss the advantages and disadvantages of relational databases.

STEP 1: Background

This section has introduced you to the advantages and disadvantages of using a relational database. This is one of those concepts that cannot really be appreciated until you work through the process of designing a database. Even though very few people go on to become database administrators, it is still valuable to have some understanding of how a database is built and administered. In this activity, you will be presented with a scenario, and you will then apply the concepts you have just read about. In the process, you will develop a solid foundation to discuss the advantages and disadvantages of relational databases.

STEP 2: Activity

You are employed as the coordinator of multiple ongoing projects within a company. Your responsibilities include keeping track of the company's commercial projects, its employees, and the employees' participation in each project. Usually, a project will have multiple team members, but some projects have not been assigned to any team members. For each project, the company must keep track of the project's title, description, location, estimated budget, and due date.

Each employee can be assigned to one or more projects. Some employees can also be on leave and therefore will not be working on any assignments. Project leaders usually need to know the following information about their team members: name, address, phone number, Social Security number, highest degree attained, and his/her expertise (for example, IS, accounting, marketing, finance).

Your manager has instructed you to present an overview of the advantages and disadvantages of a database that would support the company's efforts to manage the data described in this scenario. At a minimum, you should define the tables and the relationships among the key variables to provide structure to the information that would be included in the database.

STEP 3: Deliverable

Using the relational database design you created in Step 2, prepare a discussion of the advantages and disadvantages of this database. How will it benefit the company? What additional challenges might it create?

Submit your design and your discussion to your instructor.

3.3 | Big Data

We are accumulating data and information at an increasingly rapid pace from many diverse sources. In fact, organizations are capturing data about almost all events—including events that, in the past, firms never used to think of as data at all, such as a person's location, the vibrations and temperature of an engine, and the stress at numerous points on a bridge—and then analyzing those data.

Organizations and individuals must process a vast amount of data that continues to rapidly increase. According to IDC (a technology research firm; www.idc.com), the world generates exabytes of data each year (an exabyte is 1 trillion terabytes). Furthermore, the amount of data produced worldwide is increasing by 50 percent each year.

As recently as the year 2000, only 25 percent of the stored information in the world was digital. The other 75 percent was analog; that is, it was stored on paper, film, vinyl records, and the like. By 2015, the amount of stored information in the world was over 98 percent digital and less than 2 percent nondigital.

As we discussed at the beginning of the chapter, we refer to the superabundance of data available today as Big Data. That is, Big Data is a collection of data so large and complex that it is difficult to manage using traditional database management systems. (We capitalize *Big Data* to distinguish the term from large amounts of traditional data.)

Essentially, Big Data is about predictions. Predictions do not come from "teaching" computers to "think" like humans. Instead, predictions come from applying mathematics to huge quantities of data to infer probabilities. Consider these examples:

- The likelihood that an e-mail message is spam;
- The likelihood that the typed letters "teh" are supposed to be "the";
- The likelihood that the trajectory and velocity of a person jaywalking indicates that he will make it across the street in time, meaning that a self-driving car need only slow down slightly.

Big Data systems perform well because they contain huge amounts of data on which to base their predictions. Moreover, these systems are configured to improve themselves over time by searching for the most valuable signals and patterns as more data are input.

Defining Big Data

It is difficult to define Big Data. Here we present two descriptions of the phenomenon. First, the technology research firm Gartner (www.gartner.com) defines Big Data as diverse, high-volume, high-velocity information assets that require new forms of processing to enable enhanced decision making, insight discovery, and process optimization. Second, the Big Data Institute (TBDI; https://thebigdatainstitute.wordpress.com/) defines Big Data as vast datasets that:

- Exhibit variety;
- Include structured, unstructured, and semi-structured data;
- Are generated at high velocity with an uncertain pattern;
- Do not fit neatly into traditional, structured, relational databases; and
- Can be captured, processed, transformed, and analyzed in a reasonable amount of time only by sophisticated information systems.

Big Data generally consists of the following:

- Traditional enterprise data—examples are customer information from customer relationship management systems, transactional enterprise resource planning data, Web store transactions, operations data, and general ledger data.
- Machine-generated/sensor data—examples are smart meters; manufacturing sensors; sensors integrated into smartphones, automobiles, airplane engines, and industrial machines; equipment logs; and trading systems data.
- Social data—examples are customer feedback comments; microblogging sites such as Twitter; and social media sites such as Facebook, YouTube, and LinkedIn.
- Images captured by billions of devices located throughout the world, from digital cameras and camera phones to medical scanners and security cameras.

Let's take a look at a few specific examples of Big Data:

- In 2015 Google was processing more than 27 petabytes of data every day.
- Facebook members upload more than 10 million new photos every hour. In addition, they click a "like" button or leave a comment nearly 3 billion times every day.

- The 800 million monthly users of Google's YouTube service upload more than an hour of video every second.
- The number of messages on Twitter is growing at 200 percent every year. By mid-2015, the volume exceeded 550 million tweets per day.

Characteristics of Big Data

Big Data has three distinct characteristics: volume, velocity, and variety. These characteristics distinguish Big Data from traditional data:

1. *Volume:* We have noted the huge volume of Big Data. Consider machine-generated data, which are generated in much larger quantities than nontraditional data. For instance, sensors in a single jet engine can generate 10 terabytes of data in 30 minutes. (See our discussion of the Internet of Things in Chapter 10.) With more than 25,000 airline flights per day, the daily volume of data from just this single source is incredible. Smart electrical meters, sensors in heavy industrial equipment, and telemetry from automobiles compound the volume problem.

2. *Velocity:* The rate at which data flow into an organization is rapidly increasing. Velocity is critical because it increases the speed of the feedback loop between a company, its customers, its suppliers, and its business partners. For example, the Internet and mobile technology enable online retailers to compile histories not only on final sales, but on their customers' every click and interaction. Companies that can quickly utilize that information—for example, by recommending additional purchases—gain competitive advantage.

3. *Variety:* Traditional data formats tend to be structured and relatively well described, and they change slowly. Traditional data include financial market data, point-of-sale transactions, and much more. In contrast, Big Data formats change rapidly. They include satellite imagery, broadcast audio streams, digital music files, Web page content, scans of government documents, and comments posted on social networks.

Irrespective of their source, structure, format, and frequency, Big Data are valuable. If certain types of data appear to have no value today, it is because we have not yet been able to analyze them effectively. For example, several years ago when Google began harnessing satellite imagery, capturing street views, and then sharing these geographical data for free, few people understood its value. Today, we recognize that such data are incredibly valuable because analyses of Big Data yield deep insights. We discuss analytics in detail in Chapter 5.

Issues with Big Data

Despite its extreme value, Big Data does have issues. In this section, we take a look at data integrity, data quality, and the nuances of analysis that are worth noting.

Big Data Can Come from Untrusted Sources. As we discussed above, one of the characteristics of Big Data is variety, meaning that Big Data can come from numerous, widely varied sources. These sources may be internal or external to the organization. For instance, a company might want to integrate data from unstructured sources such as e-mails, call center notes, and social media posts with structured data about its customers from its data warehouse. The question is, How trustworthy are those external sources of data? For example, how trustworthy is a tweet? The data may come from an unverified source. Further, the data itself, reported by the source, can be false or misleading.

Big Data Is Dirty. Dirty data refers to inaccurate, incomplete, incorrect, duplicate, or erroneous data. Examples of such problems are misspelling of words and duplicate data such as retweets or company press releases that appear numerous times in social media.

Suppose a company is interested in performing a competitive analysis using social media data. The company wants to see how often a competitor's product appears in social media outlets as well as the sentiments associated with those posts. The company notices that the number of positive posts about the competitor is twice as large the number of positive posts about itself. This finding could simply be a case where the competitor is pushing out its press releases to multiple sources, in essence "blowing its own horn." Alternatively, the competitor could be getting many people to retweet an announcement.

Big Data Changes, Especially in Data Streams. Organizations must be aware that data quality in an analysis can change, or the data itself can change, because the conditions under which the data are captured can change. For instance, imagine a utility company that analyzes weather data and smart-meter data to predict customer power usage. What happens when the utility is analyzing this data in real time and it discovers data missing from some of its smart meters?

Managing Big Data

Big Data makes it possible to do many things that were previously impossible; for example, to spot business trends more rapidly and accurately, prevent disease, track crime, and so on. When properly analyzed, Big Data can reveal valuable patterns and information that were previously hidden because of the amount of work required to discover them. Leading corporations, such as Walmart and Google, have been able to process Big Data for years, but only at great expense. Today's hardware, cloud computing (see Plug IT In 4), and open-source software make processing Big Data affordable for most organizations.

The first step for many organizations toward managing data was to integrate information silos into a database environment and then to develop data warehouses for decision making. (An *information silo* is an information system that does not communicate with other, related information systems in an organization.) After completing this step, many organizations turned their attention to the business of information management—making sense of their proliferating data. In recent years, Oracle, IBM, Microsoft, and SAP have spent billions of dollars purchasing software firms that specialize in data management and business intelligence. (You will learn about business intelligence in Chapter 5.)

In addition to existing data management systems, today many organizations employ NoSQL databases to process Big Data. Think of them as "not only SQL" (structured query language) databases. (We discuss SQL in Plug IT In 3.)

As you have seen in this chapter, traditional relational databases such as Oracle and MySQL store data in tables organized into rows and columns. Recall that each row is associated with a unique record and each column is associated with a field that defines an attribute of that account.

In contrast, NoSQL databases can manipulate structured as well as unstructured data and inconsistent or missing data. For this reason, NoSQL databases are particularly useful when working with Big Data. Many products utilize NoSQL databases, including Cassandra (http://cassandra.apache.org), CouchDB (http://couchdb.apache.org), and MongoDB (www .mongodb.org).

Hadoop (http://hadoop.apache.org) is not a type of database, but rather a collection of programs that allow storage, retrieval, and analysis of very large datasets using massively parallel processing. Massively parallel processing is the coordinated processing of an application by multiple processors that work on different parts of the application, with each processing using its own operating system and memory. As such, Hadoop enables the processing of NoSQL databases, which can be spread across thousands of servers without a reduction in performance. For example, a large database application which could take 20 hours of processing time on a centralized relational database system may only take a few minutes when using Hadoop's parallel processing. IT's About Business 3.2 shows how TrueCar uses Hadoop to manage its rapidly growing amount of data.

MapReduce refers to the software procedure of dividing an analysis into pieces that can be distributed across different servers in different locations. MapReduce first distributes the analysis (map) and then collects and integrates the results back into one report (reduce).

IT's About Business 3.2

MKT TrueCar Uses Hadoop

TrueCar (www.truecar.com) is an automotive pricing and information Web site for buyers and dealers of new and used cars. Via its e-commerce Web site, the company provides buyers with information on how much other customers have paid for cars in addition to upfront pricing and access to a network of more than 10,000 TrueCar dealers. Participating dealerships pay TrueCar when customers purchase a car from them through the site.

MIS Founded in 2005, TrueCar grew very rapidly, but its data management infrastructure did not keep pace. TrueCar decided to implement Hadoop, for two reasons. First, the software tool is an economical way to store data, and it's compatible with several analytics tools.

Second, TrueCar experienced problems in using traditional relational databases to analyze very large amounts of rapidly accumulating data. For example, the car data vary greatly in structure, meaning that some of the data are structured and some are unstructured. Examples of the company's structured data are car brand, car name, car color, and car price. Examples of unstructured data are customer comments and images of cars. This data variability had created problems for TrueCar's existing infrastructure. Essentially, the company is using Hadoop to pursue new data-driven business models specifically developed to exploit all of the information assets available to them.

TrueCar went on to create a 2-petabyte Hadoop data lake storage repository that currently holds information on vehicles, transactions, registrations, customers' buying behaviors, and many additional variables. A *data lake* stores vast amounts of data in their native (original) format until they are needed, rather than forcing the integration of large volumes of data before analysis. Examples of these raw data are documents in .doc, .txt, or .rtf formats; Adobe Photoshop documents in .psd formats; images in .jpg and .gif formats; and video in .mp4 format.

Hadoop allows TrueCar to work with rapidly increasing amounts of data. In fact, TrueCar was managing 24 times as much data by the end of 2014 as it was a year earlier. Those data originated from 12,000 data sources and contain 65 billion data points. Of the 2 petabytes in its Hadoop data lake, TrueCar has 600 terabytes in active use at any one time, involving more than 20 million buyer profiles. Hadoop provides TrueCar customers with an advanced, multidimensional, real-time search capability to help them find their perfect cars.

An early example of TrueCar's use of Hadoop was to manage 700 million car photos every day. The firm notes that if there is no image of a vehicle, then there is no sale.

TrueCar is also using Hadoop to make money from "exhaust data," which is information resulting as a byproduct of normal operations. For example, the company collects exhaust data about actual and potential car buyers who visit its Web site. TrueCar analyzes that data and provides pricing and Web sales tips to its network of car dealers.

TrueCar has experienced problems implementing Hadoop. For example, TrueCar sells a "white label" or generic version of its platform to other companies, such as banks, to rebrand as their own. But the white label version requires security features that Hadoop does not currently support. Third-party clients such as banks and financial institutions must comply with regulations and privacy laws in order for Hadoop data to work. Because of these particular data requirements, TrueCar is closely monitoring the development of new features in Hadoop such as enhanced security features and the ability to track metadata.

Because the Hadoop data lake holds all of the data in a single location, TrueCar can perform a variety of valuable analytics strategies. For instance, one analysis revealed a positive link between the size of a Web cache and sales. A Web cache temporarily stores Web documents, such as images, to speed up the loading of Web pages. The analysis found that the larger the Web caches, the faster the page loads, the more satisfied the customer is, and the greater the likelihood of a purchase.

This is one example of how TrueCar's analytics now include "dark data," which organizations typically deleted, overlooked, or ignored. That is, the sizes of Web caches were largely ignored in the past, but today they are considered valuable.

And how is TrueCar doing? As of July 2015, more than two million vehicles had been bought from TrueCar-certified dealers.

Sources: Compiled from K. Korosec, "TrueCar Helps Sam's Club Get into the Car Business," *Fortune*, September 3, 2015; C. Bruce, "Scott Painter Stepping Down as TrueCar CEO by Year End," *Autoblog*, August 10, 2015; D. Undercoffler, "TrueCar Works on Relationships," *Automotive News*, July 27, 2015; "TrueCar Announces Its Users Have Bought over 2 Million Vehicles from TrueCar Certified Dealers," *PR Newswire*, June 29, 2015; D. Levin, "TrueCar, Facing Lawsuits, Sees Share Price Decline for Most of 2015," *TheStreet*, June 20, 2015; D. Needle, "Hadoop Summit: Wrangling Big Data Requires Novel Tools, Techniques," *eWeek*, June 10, 2015; D. Undercoffler, "Dealers vs. TrueCar: The Saga Continues," *Automotive News*, June 1, 2015; J. Vaughan, "Hadoop Fuels TrueCar's Data-Driven Business Model," *TechTarget*, November 21, 2014; "TrueCar: Over 1 Million Cars Sold through Affinity Auto Buying Programs," *InsuranceNewsNet*, June 13, 2014; www.truecar.com, accessed October 10, 2015.

Questions

1. Describe how Hadoop manages Big Data in its data lake.
2. Discuss why relational databases experienced problems with the variety of data that TrueCar has to manage and analyze.
3. What are the benefits of Big Data to TrueCar?

Putting Big Data to Use

Organizations must manage Big Data and gain value from it. There are several ways to do this.

Making Big Data Available. Making Big Data available for relevant stakeholders can help organizations gain value. For example, consider open data in the public sector. Open data is accessible public data that individuals and organizations can use to create new businesses and solve complex problems. In particular, government agencies gather very large amounts of data, some of which is Big Data. Making that data available can provide economic benefits. The Open Data 500 study at the GovLab at New York University found some 500 examples of U.S.-based companies whose business models depend on analyzing open government data. Another example of making Big Data available occurred in the fight against the Ebola virus, as you see in IT's About Business 3.3.

IT's About Business 3.3

Combining Big Data and Open Data to Fight Ebola

In December 2013, an outbreak of the Ebola virus began in the West African nation of Guinea and then spread to the neighboring countries of Liberia and Sierra Leone. In mid-2014, the World Health Organization (WHO; www.who.it) declared the outbreak a public health emergency of international concern. A dysfunctional healthcare system, a mistrust of government officials after years of armed conflict, local burial customs that include washing the body after death, widespread poverty, severely limited health and infrastructure resources, and the delay in responding to the outbreak for several months all contributed to the failure to control the epidemic. The outbreak became the largest recorded occurrence of Ebola.

The unprecedented scope of the outbreak, coupled with the fact that the Ebola virus incubates between 2 and 21 days before the victim knows they are infected, made it extremely difficult to determine how and where the disease would spread. This situation presented an enormous challenge for the humanitarian agencies providing care to those most in need. For example, out of a population of four million, Liberia had only 200 physicians. As a result, the integration of open data from governments, Big Data, analytics software, and the willingness to collaborate across traditional geopolitical boundaries was essential in the fight against the disease.

IBM's research lab in Africa (www.research.ibm.com/labs/africa/) developed a citizen engagement and analytics system that enables citizens to report their concerns directly to government agencies. In addition, IBM provided staff who volunteered to identify and classify all sources of open Ebola-related data in the Ebola Open Data Repository (www.eboladata.org). The system provides information on the daily experiences of communities to governments and aid agencies in the hopes of helping to stop the spread of the disease.

Launched in collaboration with Sierra Leone's Open Government initiative (www.ogi.gov.sl), Cambridge University's Africa's Voices project, telecommunications company Airtel (www.airtel.com), and Kenya's Echo Mobile (www.echomobile.org), IBM's system incorporates data from a number of sources. For example, wireless carriers gather data from cell phones and make it anonymous before providing it to researchers. Specifically, Airtel set up a toll-free number that citizens used to report Ebola-related matters via short message service (SMS) or voice calls.

Utilizing IBM's cloud-based analytics software, the system highlighted and correlated trends found among all messages. The text message and voice data identify location, so the system can show heatmaps that link public mobile call data with specific locations. (A *heatmap* is a graphical representation of data that represents individual data values as colors.) The analytics process provided an overview of regional population movements that helped predict the spread of Ebola. The cell phone data models and WHO reports were used to focus on the best ways to prevent the spread and provide healthcare.

Integrating other information, such as social media, hospital updates, health clinic and physician reports, media reports, transactional data from retailers and pharmacies, and flight records, authorities used analytics software to determine where and how to respond to the crisis. The system also integrated open data from governments that assisted in relief efforts, such as census data and other data concerning roads, airports, schools, and medical facilities. Finally, it enabled healthcare workers to pinpoint previously unanticipated trends and reduce the spread of the disease, thereby limiting the number of deaths.

The system also allowed authorities to home in on areas with suspected Ebola cases that might need medical supplies and electricity. It also assisted in the stark tasks of collecting bodies and performing burials. In addition, the system provided data for governments to use in requesting international aid, particularly more testing facilities and equipment.

Sources: Compiled from "Ebola Situation Report," *World Health Organization Report*, September 30, 2015; K. Dvorak, "Researchers Turn to Big Data, Social Media to Track Ebola," *FierceHealthIT*, May 13, 2015; M. Shacklett, "Fighting Ebola with a Holistic Vision of Big Data," *TechRepublic*, March 23, 2015; B. Rossi, "How Big Data Is Beating Ebola," *Information Age*, March 5, 2015; E. Malykhina, "IBM Brings Open Data Tech to Ebola Fight," *InformationWeek*, November 10, 2014; "Ebola and Big Data: Call for Help," *The Economist*, October 25, 2014; M. Wall, "Ebola: Can Big Data Analytics Help Contain Its Spread?" *BBC News*, October 15, 2014; D. Richards, "How Big Data Could Help Stop the Ebola Outbreak," *CNBC*, October 1, 2014; "How Big Data Can Help Beat Ebola," *IBM Smarter Planet*, August, 2014; L. Gilpin, "How an Algorithm Detected the Ebola Outbreak a Week Early, and What It Could Do Next," *TechRepublic*, August 26, 2014; www.who.int, accessed October 13, 2015.

Questions

1. Provide examples of open data mentioned in this case.
2. Provide examples of Big Data mentioned in this case.
3. Why was the integration of open data and Big Data essential to help lessen the impact of the Ebola virus?

Enabling Organizations to Conduct Experiments. Big Data allows organizations to improve performance by conducting controlled experiments. For example, Amazon (and many other companies such as Google and LinkedIn) constantly experiments by offering slight different "looks" on its Web site. These experiments are called A/B experiments, because each experiment has only two possible outcomes. Here is an example of an A/B experiment at Etsy .com, an online marketplace for vintage and handmade products.

MKT   When Etsy analysts noticed that one of its Web pages attracted customer attention but failed to keep it, they looked more closely at the page. They found that the page had few "calls to action." (A call to action is an item, such as a button, on a Web page that enables a customer to do something.) On this particular Etsy page, customers could leave, buy, search, or click on two additional product images. The analysts decided to show more product images on the page.

Consequently, one group of visitors to the page saw a strip across the top of the page that displayed additional product images. Another group of page visitors saw only the two original product images. On the page with additional images, customers viewed more products and bought more products. The results of this experiment revealed valuable information to Etsy.

Micro-Segmentation of Customers. Segmentation of a company's customers means dividing them up into groups that share one or more characteristics. Micro-segmentation simply means dividing customers up into very small groups, or even down to the individual level.

MKT   For example, Paytronix Systems (www.paytronix.com) provides loyalty and rewards program software for thousands of different restaurants. Paytronix gathers restaurant guest data from a variety of sources beyond loyalty and gift programs, including social media. Paytronix analyzes this Big Data to help its restaurant clients micro-segment their guests. Restaurant managers are now able to more precisely customize their loyalty and gift programs. In doing so, the managers are noting improved performance in their restaurants in terms of profitability and customer satisfaction.

Creating New Business Models. Companies are able to use Big Data to create new business models. For example, a commercial transportation company operated a large fleet of **POM**   large, long-haul trucks. The company recently placed sensors on all its trucks. These sensors wirelessly communicate large amounts of information to the company, a process called *telematics.* The sensors collect data on vehicle usage (including acceleration, braking, cornering, etc.), driver performance, and vehicle maintenance.

By analyzing this Big Data, the transportation company was able to improve the condition of its trucks through near-real-time analysis that proactively suggested preventive maintenance. In addition, the company was able to improve the driving skills of its operators by analyzing their driving styles.

The transportation company then made its Big Data available to its insurance carrier. Using this data, the insurance carrier performed risk analysis on driver behavior and the condition of the trucks, resulting in a more precise assessment. The insurance carrier offered the transportation company a new pricing model that lowered the transportation company's premiums by 10 percent.

Organizations Can Analyze More Data. In some cases, organizations can even process all the data relating to a particular phenomenon, meaning that they do not have to rely as much on sampling. Random sampling works well, but it is not as effective as analyzing an entire dataset. In addition, random sampling has some basic weaknesses. To begin with, its accuracy depends on ensuring randomness when collecting the sample data. However, achieving such randomness is problematic. Systematic biases in the process of data collection can cause the results to be highly inaccurate. For example, consider political polling using landline phones. This sample tends to exclude people who use only cell phones. This bias can seriously skew the results because cell phone users are typically younger and more liberal than people who rely primarily on landline phones.

Big Data Used in the Functional Areas of the Organization

In this section, we provide examples of how Big Data is valuable to various functional areas in the firm.

Human Resources. Employee benefits, particularly healthcare, represent a major business expense. Consequently, some companies have turned to Big Data to better manage these benefits. Caesars Entertainment (www.caesars.com), for example, analyzes health-insurance claim data for its 65,000 employees and their covered family members. Managers can track thousands of variables that indicate how employees use medical services, such as the number of emergency room visits and whether employees choose a generic or brand name drug.

HRM

Consider the following scenario: Data revealed that too many employees with medical emergencies were being treated at hospital emergency rooms rather than at less-expensive urgent-care facilities. The company launched a campaign to remind employees of the high cost of emergency room visits, and they provided a list of alternative facilities. Subsequently, 10,000 emergencies shifted to less-expensive alternatives, for a total savings of $4.5 million.

Big Data is also having an impact on *hiring*. An example is Catalyst IT Services (www .catalystdevworks.com), a technology outsourcing company that hires teams for programming jobs. Traditional recruiting is typically too slow, and hiring managers often subjectively choose candidates who are not the best fit for the job. Catalyst addresses this problem by requiring candidates to fill out an online assessment. It then uses the assessment to collect thousands of data points about each candidate. In fact, the company collects more data based on *how* candidates answer than on *what* they answer.

For example, the assessment might give a problem requiring calculus to an applicant who is not expected to know the subject. How the candidate responds—laboring over an answer, answering quickly and then returning later, or skipping the problem entirely—provides insight into how that candidate might deal with challenges that he or she will encounter on the job. That is, someone who labors over a difficult question might be effective in an assignment that requires a methodical approach to problem solving, whereas an applicant who takes a more aggressive approach might perform better in a different job setting.

The benefit of this big-data approach is that it recognizes that people bring different skills to the table and that there is no one-size-fits-all person for any job. Analyzing millions of data points can reveal which attributes candidates bring to specific situations.

As one measure of success, employee turnover at Catalyst averages about 15 percent per year, compared with more than 30 percent for its U.S. competitors and more than 20 percent for similar companies overseas.

Product Development. Big Data can help capture customer preferences and put that information to work in designing new products. For example, Ford Motor Company (www.ford.com) was considering a "three blink" turn indicator that had been available on its European cars for years. Unlike the turn signals on its U.S. vehicles, this indicator flashes three times at the driver's touch and then automatically shuts off.

MKT

Ford decided that conducting a full-scale market research test on this blinker would be too costly and time consuming. Instead, it examined auto-enthusiast Web sites and owner forums to discover what drivers were saying about turn indicators. Using text-mining algorithms, researchers culled more than 10,000 mentions and then summarized the most relevant comments.

The results? Ford introduced the three-blink indicator on the new Ford Fiesta in 2010, and by 2013 it was available on most Ford products. Although some Ford owners complained online that they have had trouble getting used to the new turn indicator, many others defended it. Ford managers note that the use of text-mining algorithms was critical in this effort because they provided the company with a complete picture that would not have been available using traditional market research.

Operations. For years, companies have been using information technology to make their operations more efficient. Consider United Parcel Service (UPS). The company has long relied on data to improve its operations. Specifically, it uses sensors in its delivery vehicles that can,

POM

among other things, capture the truck's speed and location, the number of times it is placed in reverse, and whether the driver's seat belt is buckled. These data are uploaded at the end of each day to a UPS data center, where they are analyzed overnight. By combining GPS information and data from sensors installed on more than 46,000 vehicles, UPS reduced fuel consumption by 8.4 million gallons, and it cut 85 million miles off its routes.

MKT

Marketing. Marketing managers have long used data to better understand their customers and to target their marketing efforts more directly. Today, Big Data enables marketers to craft much more personalized messages.

The United Kingdom's InterContinental Hotels Group (IHG; www.ihg.com) has gathered details about the members of its Priority Club rewards program, such as income levels and whether members prefer family-style or business-traveler accommodations. The company then consolidated all this information with information obtained from social media into a single data warehouse. Using its data warehouse and analytics software, the hotelier launched a new marketing campaign. Where previous marketing campaigns generated, on average, between 7 and 15 customized marketing messages, the new campaign generated more than 1,500. IHG rolled out these messages in stages to an initial core of 12 customer groups, each of which is defined by 4,000 attributes. One group, for instance, tends to stay on weekends, redeem reward points for gift cards, and register through IHG marketing partners. Utilizing this information, IHG sent these customers a marketing message that alerted them to local weekend events.

The campaign proved to be highly successful. It generated a 35 percent higher rate of customer conversions, or acceptances, than previous, similar campaigns.

POM

Government Operations. With 55 percent of the population of the Netherlands living under the threat of flooding, water management is critically important to the Dutch government. The government operates a sophisticated water management system, managing a network of dykes or levees, canals, locks, harbors, dams, rivers, storm-surge barriers, sluices, and pumping stations.

In its water management efforts, the government makes use of a vast number of sensors embedded in every physical structure used for water control. The sensors generate at least 2 petabytes of data annually. As the sensors are becoming cheaper, the government is deploying more of them, increasing the amount of data generated.

In just one example of the use of sensor data, sensors in dykes can provide information on the structure of the dyke, how well it is able to handle the stress of the water it controls, and whether it is likely to fail. Further, the sensor data are providing valuable insights for new designs for Dutch dykes. The result is that Dutch authorities have reduced the costs of managing water by 15 percent.

Before you go on…

1. Define Big Data.
2. Describe the characteristics of Big Data.
3. Describe how companies can use Big Data to gain competitive advantage.

Apply the Concept 3.3

LEARNING OBJECTIVE 3.3 Define Big Data and its basic characteristics.

STEP 1: Background

This section describes Big Data as an ongoing phenomenon that is providing businesses with access to vast amounts of

information. The key "ingredients" that make the Big Data phenomenon a reality are volume, velocity, and variety.

STEP 2: Activity

TIBCO (www.tibco.com) is a company that provides a real-time event-processing software platform that brings customers and vendors together in a very interactive and engaging way. It uses vast amounts of data (volume), in real time (velocity), from multiple sources (variety) to bring this solution to its customers. Visit YouTube, and search for two videos —"Deliver Personalized Retail Experiences Using Big Data" and "Harnessing Big Data and Social Media to Engage Customers"—both by user "TIBCOSoftware."

As you view these videos, watch carefully for the three "ingredients" mentioned above.

STEP 3: Deliverable

Choose one of the videos mentioned in Step 2, and write a review. In your review, define Big Data, and discuss its basic characteristics relative to the video. Also in your review, note the functional areas of an organization referred to in each video.

Submit your review to your instructor.

3.4 | Data Warehouses and Data Marts

Today, the most successful companies are those that can respond quickly and flexibly to market changes and opportunities. A key to this response is the effective and efficient use of data and information by analysts and managers. The challenge is providing users with access to corporate data so that they can analyze the data to make better decisions. Let's look at an example. If the manager of a local bookstore wanted to know the profit margin on used books at her store, she could obtain that information from her database, using SQL or QBE. However, if she needed to know the trend in the profit margins on used books over the past 10 years, she would have to construct a very complicated SQL or QBE query.

This example illustrates several reasons why organizations are building data warehouses and/or data marts. First, the bookstore's databases contain the necessary information to answer the manager's query, but this information is not organized in a way that makes it easy for her to find what she needs. Second, the organization's databases are designed to process millions of transactions every day. Therefore, complicated queries might take a long time to answer, and they also might degrade the performance of the databases. Third, transactional databases are designed to be updated. This update process requires extra processing. Data warehouses and data marts are read-only, and the extra processing is eliminated because data already contained in the data warehouse are not updated. Fourth, transactional databases are designed to access a single record at a time. Data warehouses are designed to access large groups of related records.

As a result of these problems, companies are using a variety of tools with data warehouses and data marts to make it easier and faster for users to access, analyze, and query data. You will learn about these tools in Chapter 5 on Business Analytics.

Describing Data Warehouses and Data Marts

In general, data warehouses and data marts support business intelligence (BI) applications. As you will see in Chapter 5, business intelligence encompasses a broad category of applications, technologies, and processes for gathering, storing, accessing, and analyzing data to help business users make better decisions. A **data warehouse** is a repository of historical data that are organized by subject to support decision makers in the organization.

Because data warehouses are so expensive, they are used primarily by large companies. A **data mart** is a low-cost, scaled-down version of a data warehouse that is designed for the end-user needs in a strategic business unit (SBU) or an individual department. Data marts can be implemented more quickly than data warehouses, often in less than 90 days. Further, they support local rather than central control by conferring power on the user group. Typically, groups that need a single or a few BI applications require only a data mart, rather than a data warehouse.

The basic characteristics of data warehouses and data marts include the following:

- *Organized by business dimension or subject.* Data are organized by subject—for example, by customer, vendor, product, price level, and region. This arrangement differs from transactional systems, where data are organized by business process, such as order entry, inventory control, and accounts receivable.

- *Use online analytical processing.* Typically, organizational databases are oriented toward handling transactions. That is, databases use *online transaction processing* (OLTP), where business transactions are processed online as soon as they occur. The objectives are speed and efficiency, which are critical to a successful Internet-based business operation. Data warehouses and data marts, which are designed to support decision makers but not OLTP, use OLTP. Online analytical processing involves the analysis of accumulated data by end users. We consider OLAP in greater detail in Chapter 5.

- *Integrated.* Data are collected from multiple systems and then integrated around subjects. For example, customer data may be extracted from internal (and external) systems and then integrated around a customer identifier, thereby creating a comprehensive view of the customer.

- *Time variant.* Data warehouses and data marts maintain historical data (i.e., data that include time as a variable). Unlike transactional systems, which maintain only recent data (such as for the last day, week, or month), a warehouse or mart may store years of data. Organizations utilize historical data to detect deviations, trends, and long-term relationships.

- *Nonvolatile.* Data warehouses and data marts are nonvolatile—that is, users cannot change or update the data. Therefore, the warehouse or mart reflects history, which, as we just saw, is critical for identifying and analyzing trends. Warehouses and marts are updated, but through IT-controlled load processes rather than by users.

- *Multidimensional.* Typically the data warehouse or mart uses a multidimensional data structure. Recall that relational databases store data in two-dimensional tables. In contrast, data warehouses and marts store data in more than two dimensions. For this reason, the data are said to be stored in a multidimensional structure. A common representation for this multidimensional structure is the *data cube*.

The data in data warehouses and marts are organized by *business dimensions*, which are subjects such as product, geographic area, and time period that represent the edges of the data cube. If you look ahead to Figure 3.6 for an example of a data cube, you see that the product dimension is comprised of nuts, screws, bolts, and washers; the geographic area dimension is comprised of East, West, and Central; and the time period dimension is comprised of 2013, 2014, and 2015. Users can view and analyze data from the perspective of these business dimensions. This analysis is intuitive because the dimensions are presented in business terms that users can easily understand.

A Generic Data Warehouse Environment

The environment for data warehouses and marts includes the following:

- Source systems that provide data to the warehouse or mart
- Data-integration technology and processes that prepare the data for use
- Different architectures for storing data in an organization's data warehouse or data marts
- Different tools and applications for the variety of users. (You will learn about these tools and applications in Chapter 5.)
- Metadata, data-quality, and governance processes that ensure that the warehouse or mart meets its purposes

Figure 3.4 depicts a generic data warehouse/data mart environment. Let's drill down into the component parts.

Source Systems. There is typically some "organizational pain" (i.e., business need) that motivates a firm to develop its BI capabilities. Working backward, this pain leads to information

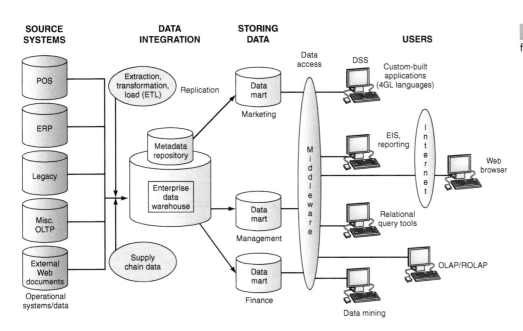

FIGURE 3.4 Data warehouse framework.

requirements, BI applications, and source system data requirements. The data requirements can range from a single source system, as in the case of a data mart, to hundreds of source systems, as in the case of an enterprisewide data warehouse.

Modern organizations can select from a variety of source systems, including: operational/transactional systems, enterprise resource planning (ERP) systems, Web site data, third-party data (e.g., customer demographic data), and more. The trend is to include more types of data (e.g., sensing data from RFID tags). These source systems often use different software packages (e.g., IBM, Oracle) and store data in different formats (e.g., relational, hierarchical).

A common source for the data in data warehouses is the company's operational databases, which can be relational databases. To differentiate between relational databases and multi-dimensional data warehouses and marts, imagine your company manufactures four products—nuts, screws, bolts, and washers—and has sold them in three territories—East, West, and Central—for the previous three years—2013, 2014, and 2015. In a relational database, these sales data would resemble Figure 3.5(a) through (c). In a multidimensional database, in contrast, these data would be represented by a three-dimensional matrix (or data cube), as depicted in Figure 3.6. This matrix represents sales *dimensioned by* products and regions and year. Notice that Figure 3.5(a) presents only sales for 2013. Sales for 2014 and 2015 are presented in Figure 3.5(b) and (c), respectively. Figure 3.7(a) through (c) illustrates the equivalence between these relational and multidimensional databases.

FIGURE 3.5 Relational databases.

(a) 2013

Product	Region	Sales
Nuts	East	50
Nuts	West	60
Nuts	Central	100
Screws	East	40
Screws	West	70
Screws	Central	80
Bolts	East	90
Bolts	West	120
Bolts	Central	140
Washers	East	20
Washers	West	10
Washers	Central	30

(b) 2014

Product	Region	Sales
Nuts	East	60
Nuts	West	70
Nuts	Central	110
Screws	East	50
Screws	West	80
Screws	Central	90
Bolts	East	100
Bolts	West	130
Bolts	Central	150
Washers	East	30
Washers	West	20
Washers	Central	40

(c) 2015

Product	Region	Sales
Nuts	East	70
Nuts	West	80
Nuts	Central	120
Screws	East	60
Screws	West	90
Screws	Central	100
Bolts	East	110
Bolts	West	140
Bolts	Central	160
Washers	East	40
Washers	West	30
Washers	Central	50

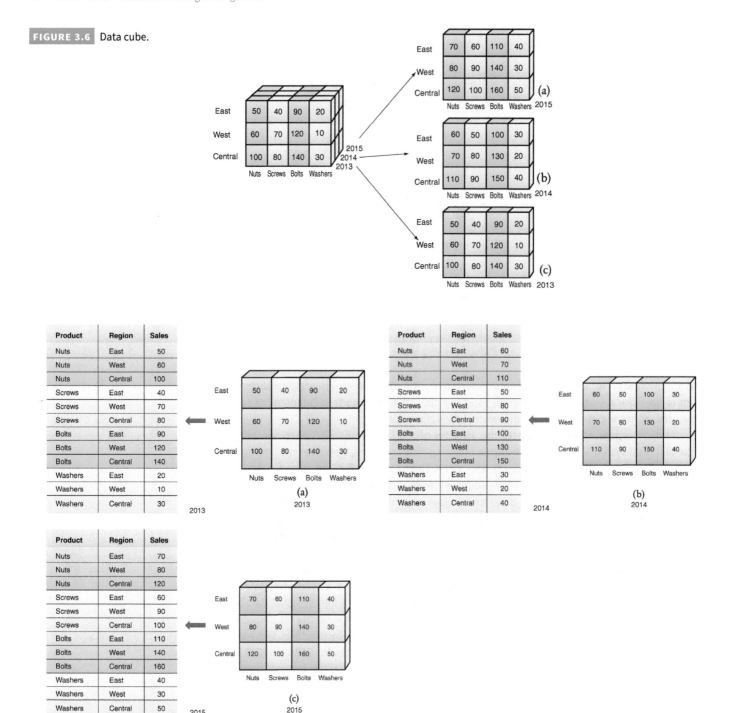

FIGURE 3.6 Data cube.

FIGURE 3.7 Equivalence between relational and multidimensional databases.

Unfortunately, many source systems that have been in use for years contain "bad data" (e.g., missing or incorrect data) and are poorly documented. As a result, data-profiling software should be used at the beginning of a warehousing project to better understand the data. For example, this software can provide statistics on missing data, identify possible primary and foreign keys, and reveal how derived values (e.g., column 3 = column 1 + column 2) are calculated. Subject area database specialists (e.g., marketing, human resources) can also assist in understanding and accessing the data in source systems.

Organizations need to address other source systems issues as well. Often there are multiple systems that contain some of the same data and the best system must be selected as the source system. Organizations must also decide how granular (i.e., detailed) the data should be. For example, does the organization need daily sales figures or data at the individual trans-action level? The conventional wisdom is that it is best to store data at a highly granular level because someone will likely request the data at some point.

Data Integration. In addition to storing data in their source systems, organizations need to *extract* the data, *transform* them, and then *load* them into a data mart or warehouse. This process is often called ETL, although the term *data integration* is increasingly being used to reflect the growing number of ways that source system data can be handled. For example, in some cases, data are extracted, loaded into a mart or warehouse, and then transformed (i.e., ELT rather than ETL).

Data extraction can be performed either by handwritten code (e.g., SQL queries) or by commercial data-integration software. Most companies employ commercial software. This software makes it relatively easy to specify the tables and attributes in the source systems that are to be used, map and schedule the movement of the data to the target (e.g., a data mart or warehouse), make the required transformations, and ultimately load the data.

After the data are extracted they are transformed to make them more useful. For exam-ple, data from different systems may be integrated around a common key, such as a customer identification number. Organizations adopt this approach to create a 360-degree view of all of their interactions with their customers. As an example of this process, consider a bank. Cus-tomers can engage in a variety of interactions: visiting a branch, banking online, using an ATM, obtaining a car loan, and more. The systems for these touch points—defined as the numerous ways that organizations interact with customers, such as e-mail, the Web, direct contact, and the telephone—are typically independent of one another. To obtain a holistic picture of how customers are using the bank, the bank must integrate the data from the various source sys-tems into a data mart or warehouse.

Other kinds of transformations also take place. For example, format changes to the data may be required, such as using *male* and *female* to denote gender, as opposed to 0 and 1 or M and F. Aggregations may be performed, say on sales figures, so that queries can use the summa-ries rather than recalculating them each time. Data-cleansing software may be used to "clean up" the data; for example, eliminating duplicate records for the same customer.

Finally, data are loaded into the warehouse or mart during a specific period known as the "load window." This window is becoming smaller as companies seek to store ever-fresher data in their warehouses. For this reason, many companies have moved to real-time data warehous-ing where data are moved (using data-integration processes) from source systems to the data warehouse or mart almost instantly. For example, within 15 minutes of a purchase at Walmart, the details of the sale have been loaded into a warehouse and are available for analysis.

Storing the Data. A variety of architectures can be used to store decision-support data. The most common architecture is *one central enterprise data warehouse*, without data marts. Most organizations use this approach, because the data stored in the warehouse are accessed by all users and represent the *single version of the truth*.

Another architecture is *independent data marts*. This architecture stores data for a single application or a few applications, such as marketing and finance. Limited thought is given to how the data might be used for other applications or by other functional areas in the organiza-tion. This is a very application-centric approach to storing data.

The independent data mart architecture is not particularly effective. Although it may meet a specific organizational need, it does not reflect an enterprise-wide approach to data man-agement. Instead, the various organizational units create independent data marts. Not only are these marts expensive to build and maintain, but they often contain inconsistent data. For example, they may have inconsistent data definitions such as: What is a customer? Is a particu-lar individual a potential or current customer? They might also use different source systems (which may have different data for the same item, such as a customer address). Although inde-pendent data marts are an organizational reality, larger companies have increasingly moved to data warehouses.

Still another data warehouse architecture is the *hub and spoke*. This architecture contains a central data warehouse that stores the data plus multiple dependent data marts that source their data from the central repository. Because the marts obtain their data from the central repository, the data in these marts still comprise the *single version of the truth* for decision-support purposes.

The dependent data marts store the data in a format that is appropriate for how the data will be used and for providing faster response times to queries and applications. As you have learned, users can view and analyze data from the perspective of business dimensions and measures. This analysis is intuitive because the dimensions are in business terms, easily understood by users.

Metadata. It is important to maintain data about the data, known as *metadata*, in the data warehouse. Both the IT personnel who operate and manage the data warehouse and the users who access the data need metadata. IT personnel need information about data sources; database, table, and column names; refresh schedules; and data-usage measures. Users' needs include data definitions, report/query tools, report distribution information, and contact information for the help desk.

Data Quality. The quality of the data in the warehouse must meet users' needs. If it does not, users will not trust the data and ultimately will not use it. Most organizations find that the quality of the data in source systems is poor and must be improved before the data can be used in the data warehouse. Some of the data can be improved with data-cleansing software, but the better, long-term solution is to improve the quality at the source system level. This approach requires the business owners of the data to assume responsibility for making any necessary changes to implement this solution.

To illustrate this point, consider the case of a large hotel chain that wanted to conduct targeted marketing promotions using zip code data it collected from its guests when they checked in. When the company analyzed the zip code data, they discovered that many of the zip codes were 99999. How did this error occur? The answer is that the clerks were not asking customers for their zip codes, but they needed to enter something to complete the registration process. A short-term solution to this problem was to conduct the marketing campaign using city and state data instead of zip codes. The long-term solution was to make certain the clerks entered the actual zip codes. The latter solution required the hotel managers to take the responsibility for making certain their clerks enter the correct data.

Governance. To ensure that BI is meeting their needs, organizations must implement *governance* to plan and control their BI activities. Governance requires that people, committees, and processes be in place. Companies that are effective in BI governance often create a senior-level committee comprised of vice presidents and directors who (1) ensure that the business strategies and BI strategies are in alignment, (2) prioritize projects, and (3) allocate resources. These companies also establish a middle management–level committee that oversees the various projects in the BI portfolio to ensure that these projects are being completed in accordance with the company's objectives. Finally, lower level operational committees perform tasks such as creating data definitions and identifying and solving data problems. All of these committees rely on the collaboration and contributions of business users and IT personnel.

Users. Once the data are loaded in a data mart or warehouse, they can be accessed. At this point the organization begins to obtain business value from BI; all of the prior stages constitute creating BI infrastructure.

There are many potential BI users, including IT developers; frontline workers; analysts; information workers; managers and executives; and suppliers, customers, and regulators. Some of these users are *information producers* whose primary role is to create information for other users. IT developers and analysts typically fall into this category. Other users—including managers and executives—are *information consumers*, because they utilize information created by others.

Companies have reported hundreds of successful data-warehousing applications. You can read client success stories and case studies at the Web sites of vendors such as NCR Corp. (www.ncr.com) and Oracle (www.oracle.com). For a more detailed discussion, visit the

Data Warehouse Institute (http://tdwi.org). The benefits of data warehousing include the following:

- End users can access needed data quickly and easily via Web browsers because these data are located in one place.
- End users can conduct extensive analysis with data in ways that were not previously possible.
- End users can obtain a consolidated view of organizational data.

These benefits can improve business knowledge, provide competitive advantage, enhance customer service and satisfaction, facilitate decision making, and streamline business processes.

Despite their many benefits, data warehouses have some limitations. First, they can be very expensive to build and to maintain. Second, incorporating data from obsolete mainframe systems can be difficult and expensive. Finally, people in one department might be reluctant to share data with other departments.

Before you go on…

1. Differentiate between data warehouses and data marts.
2. Describe the characteristics of a data warehouse.
3. What are three possible architectures for data warehouses and data marts in an organization?

Apply the Concept 3.4

LEARNING OBJECTIVE 3.4 Explain the elements necessary to successfully implement and maintain data warehouses.

STEP 1: Background

A set of general ingredients is required for organizations to effectively utilize the power of data marts and data warehouses. Figure 3.4 presents this information. Healthcare as an industry has not been centralized for many business, legal and ethical reasons. However, the overall health implications of a centralized data warehouse are unimaginable.

STEP 2: Activity

Visit http://www.wiley.com/go/rainer/MIS4e/applytheconcept, and read the article in *WIRED* magazine from March 6, 2014, titled "Gadgets Like Fitbit Are Remaking How Doctors Treat You." As you read this article, you will see that several key ingredients exist, though no one has built a medical data warehouse as described

in the article. (The term "warehouse" is not used, but the concept is applicable.) Also, although the article seems to focus on real-time data usage, imagine the possibilities of compiling years of this type of data in a data warehouse.

STEP 3: Deliverable

To demonstrate that you recognize the environmental factors necessary to implement and maintain a data warehouse, imagine that the date is exactly five years in the future. Write a newspaper article titled "Data from Gadgets Like Fitbit Remade How Doctors Treated Us." In your article imagine that all of the ingredients necessary in the environment have come together. Discuss what the environment was like five years ago (today) and how things have evolved to create the right mix of environmental factors.

Be aware that there is no right/wrong answer to this exercise. The objective is for you to recognize the necessary environment for a successful data warehouse implementation. The healthcare-related example simply provides a platform to accomplish this task.

3.5 | Knowledge Management

As we have noted throughout this text, data and information are critically important organizational assets. Knowledge is a vital asset as well. Successful managers have always valued and utilized intellectual assets. These efforts were not systematic, however, and they did not ensure that knowledge was shared and dispersed in a way that benefited the overall organization.

Moreover, industry analysts estimate that most of a company's knowledge assets are not housed in relational databases. Instead, they are dispersed in e-mail, word-processing documents, spreadsheets, presentations on individual computers, and in people's heads. This arrangement makes it extremely difficult for companies to access and integrate this knowledge. The result frequently is less-effective decision making.

Concepts and Definitions

Knowledge management (KM) is a process that helps organizations manipulate important knowledge that comprises part of the organization's memory, usually in an unstructured format. For an organization to be successful, knowledge, as a form of capital, must exist in a format that can be exchanged among persons. In addition, it must be able to grow.

Knowledge. In the information technology context, knowledge is distinct from data and information. As you learned in Chapter 1, data are a collection of facts, measurements, and statistics; information is organized or processed data that are timely and accurate. Knowledge is information that is *contextual*, *relevant*, and *useful*. Simply put, knowledge is information in action. **Intellectual capital** (or **intellectual assets**) is another term for knowledge.

To illustrate, a bulletin listing all of the courses offered by your university during one semester would be considered *data*. When you register, you process the data from the bulletin to create your schedule for the semester. Your schedule would be considered *information*. Awareness of your work schedule, your major, your desired social schedule, and characteristics of different faculty members could be construed as *knowledge*, because it can affect the way you build your schedule. You see that this awareness is contextual and relevant (to developing an optimal schedule of classes) as well as useful (it can lead to changes in your schedule). The implication is that knowledge has strong experiential and reflective elements that distinguish it from information in a given context. Unlike information, knowledge can be utilized to solve a problem.

Numerous theories and models classify different types of knowledge. In the next section, we will focus on the distinction between explicit knowledge and tacit knowledge.

Explicit and Tacit Knowledge. **Explicit knowledge** deals with more objective, rational, and technical knowledge. In an organization, explicit knowledge consists of the policies, procedural guides, reports, products, strategies, goals, core competencies, and IT infrastructure of the enterprise. In other words, explicit knowledge is the knowledge that has been codified (documented) in a form that can be distributed to others or transformed into a process or a strategy. A description of how to process a job application that is documented in a firm's human resources policy manual is an example of explicit knowledge.

In contrast, **tacit knowledge** is the cumulative store of subjective or experiential learning. In an organization, tacit knowledge consists of an organization's experiences, insights, expertise, know-how, trade secrets, skill sets, understanding, and learning. It also includes the organizational culture, which reflects the past and present experiences of the organization's people and processes, as well as the organization's prevailing values. Tacit knowledge is generally imprecise and costly to transfer. It is also highly personal. Finally, because it is unstructured, it is difficult to formalize or codify, in contrast to explicit knowledge. A salesperson who has worked with particular customers over time and has come to know their needs quite well would possess extensive tacit knowledge. This knowledge is typically not recorded. In fact, it might be difficult for the salesperson to put into writing, even if he or she were willing to share it.

Knowledge Management Systems

The goal of knowledge management is to help an organization make the most productive use of the knowledge it has accumulated. Historically, management information systems have focused on capturing, storing, managing, and reporting explicit knowledge. Organizations now realize they need to integrate explicit and tacit knowledge into formal information systems. **Knowledge management systems (KMSs)** refer to the use of modern information technologies—the Internet, intranets, extranets, databases—to systematize, enhance, and expedite intrafirm and interfirm knowledge management. KMSs are intended to help an organization cope with turnover, rapid change, and downsizing by making the expertise of the organization's human capital widely accessible. IT's About Business 3.4 illustrates how Performance Bicycle implemented the Learning Center, a knowledge management system.

IT's About Business 3.4

MKT Performance Bicycle Leverages Its
MIS Employees' Knowledge

Performance Bicycle (PB; www.performancebike.com) is a leading retailer of cycling products. The company has 2,200 employees and more than 100 stores in 20 states. It also has a print catalog and sells more than 10,000 products on its Web site.

The company wanted to use the Web to increase its customer base as part of its long-term business plan. PB knew that its e-commerce site could extend its reach beyond its brick-and-mortar stores. To do this, it would need more than just great products.

Performance Bicycle decided to leverage its employees' passion for cycling. Most of them keep bikes in their offices or cubicles. By using the staff's knowledge and enthusiasm, PB could motivate new customers and cement its reputation as a cycling expert. Significantly, the company recognized that although its employees' knowledge is extremely valuable, it was also largely untapped. The challenge confronting Performance Bicycle was to capture this knowledge and share it with its customers in an engaging way. PB addressed this challenge by launching its Learning Center.

To make its employees' knowledge available to customers on its Web site, Performance Bicycle added a knowledge management system, called the Learning Center, where staff share their expertise, tips, and tricks via videos, articles, and how-to guides. Key to the Learning Center's success is its seamless integration with e-commerce, allowing customers to easily find products and the relevant multimedia content about them. For example, customers interested in performing maintenance on their bike can watch a how-to video and then click directly to the replacement parts they'll need to order.

Performance Bicycle conducted knowledge-transfer sessions to obtain the knowledge for the Learning Center. PB has an editorial team that reviews content produced by employees, including articles and video guides. When publishing the content to the Learning Center, the editorial team makes links to relevant pages on the e-commerce site. When new products are added for sale, the editorial team links back to relevant Learning Center content.

For Performance Bicycle employees and customers alike, cycling is a lifestyle. Its e-commerce site and Learning Center have helped forge its reputation as a leading cycling authority. The site succeeds in inspiring both experienced and new cyclists, and helps them navigate the otherwise bumpy road of a wide range of products.

And the bottom line? Within just four months of the Learning Center going live, traffic on PB's site tripled. The Learning Center is now referring more than 40 percent of all of the company's direct online sales. Meanwhile, PB has begun to implement the Learning Center as a mobile application to further improve the customer experience.

Sources: Compiled from A. Dow, "Top Takeaways for Retail from VMworld," *VMware Blogs*, September 15, 2015; "Consumer and Retail Companies Must Focus on Distribution and Localization in Emerging Markets," *M-Brain*, July 5, 2015; E. Tucker, "Positive Stories about Working in Retail," *APQC.org*, April 29, 2015; T. Hussein and S. Khan, "Knowledge Management: An Instrument for Implementation in Retail Marketing," *MATRIX Academic International Online Journal of Engineering and Technology*, April, 2015; "Performance Bike: Architecting a Customer Learning Center," *Sirius Digital Experience*, 2015; A. Pickrell, "Putting the 'Perform' in Performance Bicycle," *IBM Amplify*, 2015; J. Gregoire, "5 Challenges, Opportunities, and Imperatives for Retailers in 2015," *CPC Strategy*, October 8, 2014; "Performance Bicycle," *IBM Smarter Commerce*, April 22, 2014; "Performance Bicycle Launches Learning Center," *MarketWatch*, September 25, 2013; www.performancebike.com, accessed September 26, 2015.

Questions

1. Describe several ways in which Performance Bicycle incorporates employee knowledge in its customer experience.

2. Is Performance Bicycle capturing and using its employee's tacit knowledge or explicit knowledge? Explain your answer.

Organizations can realize many benefits with KMSs. Most importantly, they make **best practices**—the most effective and efficient ways of doing things—readily available to a wide range of employees. Enhanced access to best-practice knowledge improves overall organizational performance. For example, account managers can now make available their tacit knowledge about how best to manage large accounts. The organization can then utilize this knowledge when it trains new account managers. Other benefits include improved customer service, more efficient product development, and improved employee morale and retention.

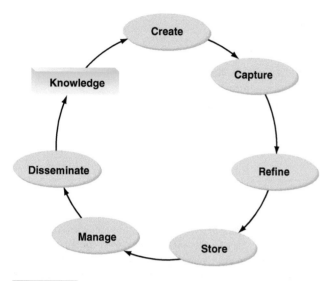

FIGURE 3.8 **FIGURE 3.8** The knowledge management system cycle.

At the same time, however, implementing effective KMSs presents several challenges. First, employees must be willing to share their personal tacit knowledge. To encourage this behavior, organizations must create a knowledge management culture that rewards employees who add their expertise to the knowledge base. Second, the organization must continually maintain and upgrade its knowledge base. Specifically, it must incorporate new knowledge and delete old, outdated knowledge. Finally, companies must be willing to invest in the resources needed to carry out these operations.

The KMS Cycle

A functioning KMS follows a cycle that consists of six steps (see Figure 3.8). The reason the system is cyclical is that knowledge is dynamically refined over time. The knowledge in an effective KMS is never finalized because the environment changes over time and knowledge must be updated to reflect these changes. The cycle works as follows:

1. *Create knowledge.* Knowledge is created as people determine new ways of doing things or develop know-how. Sometimes external knowledge is brought in.
2. *Capture knowledge.* New knowledge must be identified as valuable and be represented in a reasonable way.
3. *Refine knowledge.* New knowledge must be placed in context so that it is actionable. This is where tacit qualities (human insights) must be captured along with explicit facts.
4. *Store knowledge.* Useful knowledge must then be stored in a reasonable format in a knowledge repository so that other people in the organization can access it.
5. *Manage knowledge.* Like a library, the knowledge must be kept current. It must be reviewed regularly to verify that it is relevant and accurate.
6. *Disseminate knowledge.* Knowledge must be made available in a useful format to anyone in the organization who needs it, anywhere and anytime.

Before you go on...

1. What is knowledge management?
2. What is the difference between tacit knowledge and explicit knowledge?
3. Describe the knowledge management system cycle.

Apply the Concept 3.5

LEARNING OBJECTIVE 3.5 Describe the benefits and challenges of implementing knowledge management systems in organizations.

STEP 1: Background

As you have learned in this text, data are captured, stored, analyzed, and shared to create knowledge within organizations. This knowledge is exposed in meetings when colleagues are interpreting the information they received from the latest report,

in employee presentations, in e-mail among coworkers, and in numerous other scenarios. The problem many organizations face is that there are massive amounts of knowledge that are created and shared, but this information is not stored in a centralized, searchable format.

STEP 2: Activity

Visit http://www.wiley.com/go/rainer/MIS4e/applytheconcept, and click on the links provided for Apply the Concept 3.5. They will take you to two YouTube videos: "Discover What You Know" by user "Ken Porter" and "Lee Bryant—Knowledge Management" by user "usnowfilm." Both videos illustrate the importance of capturing knowledge within an organization so it can be shared with the right person at the right time to support effective decision making.

STEP 3: Deliverable

Write a short paragraph or two to discuss the benefits and challenges faced by companies when they attempt to implement a knowledge management system. How many of these elements are technical, and how many are social? Also, discuss the ways that companies can use Web 2.0 technologies to help capture and share knowledge.

Submit this essay to your instructor.

What's in IT for me?

ACCT For the Accounting Major

The accounting function is intimately concerned with keeping track of the transactions and internal controls of an organization. Modern databases enable accountants to perform these functions more effectively. Databases help accountants manage the flood of data in today's organizations so that they can keep their firms in compliance with the standards imposed by Sarbanes–Oxley.

Accountants also play a role in cost justifying the creation of a knowledge base and then auditing its cost-effectiveness. In addition, if you work for a large CPA company that provides management services or sells knowledge, you will most likely use some of your company's best practices that are stored in a knowledge base.

FIN For the Finance Major

Financial managers make extensive use of computerized databases that are external to the organization, such as CompuStat or Dow Jones, to obtain financial data on organizations in their industry. They can use these data to determine if their organization meets industry benchmarks in return on investment, cash management, and other financial ratios.

Financial managers, who produce the organization's financial status reports, are also closely involved with Sarbanes–Oxley. Databases help these managers comply with the law's standards.

MKT For the Marketing Major

Databases help marketing managers access data from the organization's marketing transactions, such as customer purchases, to plan targeted marketing campaigns and to evaluate the success of previous campaigns. Knowledge about customers can make the difference between success and failure. In many databases and knowledge bases, the vast majority of information and knowledge concerns customers, products, sales, and marketing. Marketing managers regularly use an organization's knowledge base, and they often participate in its creation.

POM For the Production/Operations Management Major

Production/operations personnel access organizational data to determine optimum inventory levels for parts in a production process. Past production data enable production/operations management (POM) personnel to determine the optimum configuration for assembly lines. Firms also collect quality data that inform them not only about the quality of finished products but also about quality issues with incoming raw materials, production irregularities, shipping and logistics, and after-sale use and maintenance of the product.

Knowledge management is extremely important for running complex operations. The accumulated knowledge regarding scheduling, logistics, maintenance, and other functions is very valuable. Innovative ideas are necessary for improving operations and can be supported by knowledge management.

HRM For the Human Resources Management Major

Organizations keep extensive data on employees, including gender, age, race, current and past job descriptions, and performance evaluations. HR personnel access these data to provide reports to government agencies regarding compliance with federal equal opportunity guidelines. HR managers also use these data to evaluate hiring practices, evaluate salary structures, and manage any discrimination grievances or lawsuits brought against the firm.

Databases help HR managers provide assistance to all employees as companies turn over more and more decisions about healthcare and retirement planning to the employees themselves. The employees can use the databases for help in selecting the optimal mix among these critical choices.

HR managers also need to use a knowledge base frequently to find out how past cases were handled. Consistency in how employees are treated not only is important, but it also protects the company against legal actions. In addition, training for building, maintaining, and using the knowledge system sometimes is the responsibility of the HR department. Finally, the HR department might be responsible for compensating employees who contribute their knowledge to the knowledge base.

MIS For the MIS Major

The MIS function manages the organization's data as well as the databases. MIS database administrators standardize data names by using the data dictionary. This process ensures that all users understand which data are in the database. Database personnel also help users access needed data and generate reports with query tools.

Summary

1. Discuss ways that common challenges in managing data can be addressed using data governance.

The following are three common challenges in managing data:

- Data are scattered throughout organizations and are collected by many individuals using various methods and devices. These data are frequently stored in numerous servers and locations and in different computing systems, databases, formats, and human and computer languages.

- Data come from multiple sources.

- Information systems that support particular business processes impose unique requirements on data, which results in repetition and conflicts across an organization.

One strategy for implementing data governance is master data management. Master data management provides companies with the ability to store, maintain, exchange, and synchronize a consistent, accurate, and timely "single version of the truth" for the company's core master data. Master data management manages data gathered from across an organization, manages data from multiple sources, and manages data across business processes in an organization.

2. Discuss the advantages and disadvantages of relational databases.

Relational databases allow people to compare information quickly by row or column. In addition, items are easy to retrieve by finding the point of intersection of a particular row and column. On the other hand, large-scale relational databases can be composed of many interrelated tables, making the overall design complex with slow search and access times.

3. Define Big Data and its basic characteristics.

Big Data is composed of high volume, high velocity, and high variety information assets that require new forms of processing to enable enhanced decision making, insight discovery, and process optimization. Big Data has three distinct characteristics, which are volume, velocity, and variety. These characteristics distinguish Big Data from traditional data:

- *Volume:* Big Data consists of vast quantities of data.

- *Velocity:* Big Data flows into an organization at incredible speeds.

- *Variety:* Big Data includes a huge variety of different data in differing data formats.

4. Explain the elements necessary to successfully implement and maintain data warehouses.

To successfully implement and maintain a data warehouse, an organization must:

- Link source systems that provide data to the warehouse or mart.

- Prepare the necessary data for the data warehouse using data integration technology and processes.

- Decide on an appropriate architecture for storing data in the data warehouse or data mart.

- Select the tools and applications for the variety of organizational users.

- Ensure that metadata, data quality, and governance processes are in place to ensure that the data warehouse or mart meets its purposes.

5. Describe the benefits and challenges of implementing knowledge management systems in organizations.

Organizations can realize many benefits with KMSs, including:

- Best practices are readily available to a wide range of employees.

- Improved customer service;

- More efficient product development; and

- Improved employee morale and retention.

Challenges to implementing KMSs include:

- Employees must be willing to share their personal tacit knowledge.

- Organizations must create a knowledge management culture that rewards employees who add their expertise to the knowledge base.

- The knowledge base must be continually maintained and updated.

- Companies must be willing to invest in the resources needed to carry out these operations.

Chapter Glossary

Dattribute Each characteristic or quality of a particular entity.

best practices The most effective and efficient ways to do things.

Big Data A collection of data so large and complex that it is difficult to manage using traditional database management systems.

bit A binary digit—that is, a 0 or a 1.

byte A group of eight bits that represents a single character.

clickstream data Data collected about user behavior and browsing patterns by monitoring users' activities when they visit a Web site.

data file (also table) A collection of logically related records.

data governance An approach to managing information across an entire organization.

data mart A low-cost, scaled-down version of a data warehouse that is designed for the end-user needs in a strategic business unit (SBU) or a department.

data model A diagram that represents entities in the database and their relationships.

data warehouse A repository of historical data that are organized by subject to support decision makers in the organization.

database management system (DBMS) The software program (or group of programs) that provides access to a database.

entity Any person, place, thing, or event of interest to a user.

explicit knowledge The more objective, rational, and technical types of knowledge.

field A characteristic of interest that describes an entity.

foreign key A field (or group of fields) in one table that uniquely identifies a row (or record) of another table.

instance Each row in a relational table, which is a specific, unique representation of the entity.

intellectual capital (or intellectual assets) Other terms for knowledge.

knowledge management (KM) A process that helps organizations identify, select, organize, disseminate, transfer, and apply information and expertise that are part of the organization's memory and that typically reside within the organization in an unstructured manner.

knowledge management systems (KMSs) Information technologies used to systematize, enhance, and expedite intra- and interfirm knowledge management.

master data A set of core data, such as customer, product, employee, vendor, geographic location, and so on, that spans an enterprise's information systems.

master data management A process that provides companies with the ability to store, maintain, exchange, and synchronize a consistent, accurate, and timely "single version of the truth" for the company's core master data.

multidimensional structure Storage of data in more than two dimensions; a common representation is the data cube.

primary key An field (or attribute) of a record that uniquely identifies that record so that it can be retrieved, updated, and sorted.

record A grouping of logically related fields.

relational database model Data model based on the simple concept of tables in order to capitalize on characteristics of rows and columns of data.

secondary key A field that has some identifying information, but typically does not uniquely identify a record with complete accuracy.

table A grouping of logically related records.

tacit knowledge The cumulative store of subjective or experiential learning, which is highly personal and hard to formalize.

unstructured data Data that does not reside in a traditional relational database.

Discussion Questions

1. Is Big Data really a problem on its own, or are the use, control, and security of the data the true problems? Provide specific examples to support your answer.

2. What are the implications of having incorrect data points in your Big Data? What are the implications of incorrect or duplicated customer data? How valuable are decisions that are based on faulty information derived from incorrect data?

3. Explain the difficulties involved in managing data.

4. What are the problems associated with poor-quality data?

5. What is master data management? What does it have to do with high-quality data?

6. Explain why master data management is so important in companies that have multiple data sources.

7. Describe the advantages and disadvantages of relational databases.

8. Explain why it is important to capture and manage knowledge.

9. Compare and contrast tacit knowledge and explicit knowledge.

Problem-Solving Activities

1. Access various employment Web sites (e.g., www.monster.com and www.dice.com) and find several job descriptions for a database administrator. Are the job descriptions similar? What are the salaries offered in these positions?

2. Access the Web sites of several real estate companies. Find the sites that take you through a step-by-step process for buying a home, that provide virtual reality tours of homes in your price range (say, $200,000 to $250,000) and location, that provide mortgage and interest rate calculators, and that offer financing for your home. Do the sites require that you register to access their services? Can you request that an e-mail be sent to you when properties in which you might be interested become

available? How does the process outlined influence your likelihood of selecting this company for your real estate purchase?

3. It is possible to find many Web sites that provide demographic information. Access several of these sites and see what they offer. Do the sites differ in the types of demographic information they offer? If so, how? Do the sites require a fee for the information they offer? Would demographic information be useful to you if you wanted to start a new business? If so, how and why?

4. Search the Web for uses of Big Data in homeland security. Specifically, read about the spying by the U.S. National Security Agency (NSA). What role did technology and Big Data play in this questionable practice?

5. Visit the website for HowStuffWorks (www.howstuffworks.com), and search for "Big Data: Friend or Foe?" What points does this article present concerning the delicate balance between shared data and customer privacy?

6. Access the Web sites of IBM (www.ibm.com), Sybase (www.sybase.com), and Oracle (www.oracle.com), and trace the capabilities of their latest data management products, including Web connections.

7. Enter the Web site of the Gartner Group (www.gartner.com). Examine the company's research studies pertaining to data management. Prepare a report on the state of the art.

8. Calculate your personal digital footprint at http://www.emc.com/digital_universe/downloads/web/personal-ticker.htm.

9. Diagram a knowledge management system cycle for a fictional company that sells customized T-shirts to students.

Closing Case 1

POM Tracking Pot from Seed to Customer

The Problem

When Colorado's Amendment 64 legalized recreational marijuana in 2012, most of its support came from voters in Denver and its surrounding metropolitan area, and not from the state's more rural areas. As a result, Colorado remains divided over the drug, which is still illegal under federal law (as of October 2015).

In fact, of 321 municipalities in Colorado, 228 "opted out" of allowing marijuana. Local officials and law enforcement throughout the state, unconvinced of the benefits of legalizing marijuana, have tried to push back against legalization, citing the federal government's ban on the drug. Meanwhile, investors, business owners, tourists, and many Colorado residents argue that legal recreational marijuana has benefited the state.

At least partially in response to this ongoing debate, Colorado has placed strict regulations on all aspects of the marijuana production process. These regulations mandate that producers and distributors track each plant throughout its lifecycle. The problem was how to implement these regulations in an efficient, accountable, cost-effective manner.

The IT Solution

Colorado's marijuana growers and distributors are having to adjust to regulations concerning their newly legitimate businesses. Under the state's rules, growers must put a microchip on each plant so it can be recorded and monitored in Colorado's Marijuana Inventory Tracking Solution (MITS).

A yellow radio-frequency identification (RFID) tag placed on each plant enables officials consulting a statewide database to track crops from "bud to blunt." The tags contain 24-digit identification codes, and they are staked into the soil or wrapped around individual plants while they grow. The tags travel with the plants through the grow house, to harvest, and as the pot flowers are dried and cured for flavor. (A *grow house* is a property that is primarily used for the production of marijuana.) For shipment to stores, each strain of marijuana is grouped into a batch that receives its own RFID tag, which remains on the packages until the batch is sold. During scheduled and unscheduled visits to dispensaries or grow houses, state officials use RFID scanners and electronic inventories to ensure that none of the plants goes missing.

Franwell (www.franwell.com), a Florida-based technology company, developed the RFID tag system. Each plant tag costs 45 cents, and the batch package tag costs 25 cents. Growers contend that the tags are expensive. For many growers, however, their biggest frustration is having to enter the data twice: once into their own accounting databases and again into the MITS system, which is not compatible with most other accounting programs. The penalties for mistakes in

entering the data include loss of license and criminal charges. Given that the potential for mistakes is high, growers feel that these penalties are excessively harsh. For example, when a plant dies, growers must follow a lengthy ticketing procedure to document and delete that plant from the system or face severe penalties for a "missing" plant.

Franwell is working to develop a system that integrates with grower databases. The company notes that the water- and chemical-resistant tags are relatively cheap given that orders are usually small.

A spokeswoman for Colorado's marijuana enforcement division maintains that red tape and fees are "part of being regulated." Complaints notwithstanding, one grower stated that RFID tagging and capturing the data in the MITS database is necessary to legitimize the industry.

The plant tags do provide some benefits to growers. Specifically, they offer knowledgeable growers a closer look at which strains are selling well or where a troublesome batch shipped. For example, when a batch of pot-infused gummy bears shipped from Native Roots (http://nativeroots303.com, the largest marijuana dispensary in Colorado) became moldy, the store manager used the data recorded on the MITS database to locate and recall only the rotten gummies. Other growers are installing their own RFID scanners to electronically track each plant's location in their warehouses.

The Results

As of July 2015, the state of Colorado had issued nearly 2,500 licenses for marijuana cultivation, production, and testing facilities and retail stores in both the medical and recreational markets. Marijuana brought in nearly $80 million for the state in taxes and fees during the 2015 fiscal year. The revenue comes from a 2.9 percent retail and medical marijuana sales tax, a 10 percent retail marijuana special sales tax, and a 15 percent marijuana excise tax, plus application and license fees for retail and medical marijuana.

Those figures did not keep track of the economic contributions of thousands of tourists who come to Colorado partly for its marijuana. In fact, according to Colorado's Marijuana Enforcement Division, up to 90 percent of recreational marijuana sales in some areas, particularly mountain resort towns, are made to tourists.

In November 2014, Oregon legalized nonmedical cultivation and uses of marijuana beginning in July 2015. (The state had previously allowed small amounts of marijuana to be used for medical purposes.) The state is planning to use an RFID system similar to Colorado's to monitor marijuana production and distribution.

Sources: Compiled from R. Grenoble, "Revenue from Colorado Marijuana Tax Expected to Double in 2015," *The Huffington Post*, September 21, 2015; K. Wyatt, "Colorado Pot Growers Save Big Bucks on Tax Holiday Caused by Quirk in State Law," *US News and World Report*, September 16, 2015; J. Frank, "Ahead of 2015 Vote, Campaign Pushes Marijuana Tax Question in Colorado," *The Denver Post*, September 13, 2015; C. Cooper, "Colorado Profits, But Still Divided on Legal Weed," *The Center for Public Integrity*, August 16, 2015; R. Baca, "Colorado Pot Sales Spike in June, Top $50 Million for First Time," *The Cannabist*, August 13, 2015; H. Borrud, "Oregon Pot Tracking System Will Use RFID Technology," *East Oregonian*, June 14, 2015; S. Lohmeyer, "States Turn to Tech for Tracking Marijuana," *GCN.com*, May 26, 2015; K. Mulvaney, "Advocate Says Colorado Received $60 Million in Taxes and Fees from Marijuana in 2014," *Providence Journal*, January 11, 2015; K. Weise, "Tracking Colorado's Legal Pot, Plant by Plant,"

Bloomberg BusinessWeek, March 17-23, 2014; R. Hiscott, "RFID Tags Track Marijuana from Seed to Sale in Colorado," *Mashable*, February 11, 2014.

Questions

1. Describe how database technology plays an important role enabling Colorado to closely monitor the marijuana production and distribution process.

2. Describe potential disadvantages in using RFID tags to monitor marijuana production and distribution.

Closing Case 2

POM Big Data and the Treatment of Cancer

The Problem

The global statistics on cancer are sobering. Every year, 8 million people die from cancer, and 14 million people discover they have the disease. Approximately $100 billion is spent on cancer drugs globally. Unfortunately, the majority of cancer treatments are not successful.

Despite years of effort by the medical establishment to persuade doctors and hospitals to embrace electronic medical records (EMRs), oncology data have remained difficult to access and use. (*Oncology* is the branch of medicine that deals with the study and treatment of cancer.)

Data on a single cancer patient can come from multiple sources, including internists, oncologists, radiologists, surgeons, and laboratory and pathology reports. Even when the data are digitized, they are often in an unstructured format. Rather than being organized in databases, the data are often in multiple, inconsistent formats across different lab reports and records. Making matters worse, much data remain hidden in reports that have been written by hand and scanned, in audio recordings, and in low-resolution PDF files printed from fax machines. Finally, incompatible systems and strict privacy regulations—for example, the Health Insurance Portability and Accountability Act, or HIPAA—that govern personal health information make it even more difficult for data to be shared across thousands of oncology practices.

Only a small fraction of cancer patient treatment data are being collected systematically. Those data are typically collected from randomized clinical trials, which cover only 4 percent of adult cancer patients.

A Proposed IT Solution

Flatiron Health (Flatiron; www.flatiron.com) wants to help doctors develop better treatment options for cancer. Founded in 2012, Flatiron essentially fights cancer with organized data. With its OncologyCloud, the company is helping oncologists enhance patient care. The company collects, organizes, and standardizes much of the information for the 96 percent of patients not included in clinical trials and then offers those data back to physicians in a format that can be analyzed.

The two Flatiron founders began their startup by visiting 60 cancer centers, speaking directly with experts, and visiting patients with physicians. Working with oncology experts, they decided that the most pressing need in cancer treatment was to organize the massive volumes of clinical data that are scattered in the filing systems of oncology treatment centers throughout the country. They proposed to collect the data—both digital and otherwise—and then organize them,

aggregate them, and provide them to physicians, who can use the data to make better decisions about how to treat their patients.

In theory, electronic medical records (EMRs) were supposed to make such data aggregation and integration easier. Unfortunately, those benefits have not totally materialized. In fact, more than 25 percent of U.S. medical records remain in hard-copy format.

The Flatiron founders spent more than two years building what they call a *data model*, which is their strategy to organize clinical information into categories. Working with a team of physicians, they decided to focus initially on one type of cancer: colon cancer. Using published clinical trials, they extracted more than 350 data categories, including demographics, geographic location, cancer stages, biological markers of disease, and responses to therapies. Then they repeated the process for other forms of cancer.

To automate the process of extracting data from medical records, which can be labor intensive, Flatiron used matching algorithms targeted at pinpointing values in lab reports. They also utilized natural-language processing to enable computers to read documents and extract data from them. Such systems must be trained. To accomplish this task, Flatiron hired a team of 60 nurses to enter data on 500 patients by hand, creating a "training set" that was used to detect errors in data that had been collected automatically. Data collection errors were then fed back into the system as inputs to help improve the automated collection process.

The Results

Using Flatiron's OncologyCloud, oncologists are able to see the most effective therapies for the most patients in similar circumstances. Further, these physicians are able to evaluate their own treatment outcomes against those of other specialists across the nation and then quickly correct any deficiencies. The OncologyCloud also highlights cost-effective therapies and wasteful healthcare spending. Finally, the system helps to match patients with suitable clinical trials, hopefully speeding up the development and approval of new medicines.

In 2014, Flatiron acquired Altos Solutions, which developed the first oncology-specific electronic medical record. This acquisition gave Flatiron a larger installed base and closer contact with physicians. By October 2015 Flatiron systems were being used in 210 cancer centers that collectively see about 300,000 new patients every year. Further, in 2014 Google invested more than $100 million in Flatiron via Google Ventures, the company's venture capital unit.

In 2015, Flatiron and Guardant Health (www.guardanthealth.com) began to collaborate to enable more effective cancer treatment. Flatiron will provide the structure and all of the clinical trial information for the OncologyCloud. Guardant's commercially available cancer screening product, Guardant360, will be used to collect data from patients' blood samples in a much more efficient manner than was previously possible.

And the bottom line? In 2014, nearly 1.7 million Americans were newly diagnosed with cancer. If oncologists using the OncologyCloud could improve the patient survival rate by 5 percent, they would save tens of thousands of lives every year.

Sources: Compiled from L. Ramsey, "Cancer Treatment Is on the Brink of a Data Revolution," *Business Insider*, September 22, 2015; N. Versel, "GuardantHealth, Flatiron Health to Link Genomics, Analytics for Personalized Cancer Care," *MedCityNews*, August 19, 2015; C. Magee, "GuardantHealth and Flatiron Health Team Up to Cure Cancer with Big Data," *TechCrunch*, August 19, 2015; "Fighting Cancer with Big Data," *The Rambus Blog*, August 10, 2015; T. Stephens, "California Initiative to Advance Precision Medicine Funds UC Santa Cruz Pediatric Cancer Project," *University of California at Santa Cruz News Center*, August 3, 2015; B. Marr, "How Big Data Is Transforming the Fight Against Cancer," *Forbes*, June 28, 2015; "Varian Medical Systems and Flatiron Health to Develop Next Generation of Cloud-Based Oncology Software," *Flatiron Health Press Release*, May 26, 2015; "Foundation Medicine and Flatiron Health Collaborate to Develop First In-Class Data Platform to Accelerate Precision Medicine for Cancer," *Foundation Medicine*, December 2, 2014; M. Helft, "Can Big Data Cure Cancer?" *Fortune*, August 11, 2014; S. Baum, "Flatiron Health Finds Ideal Match with Duke Cancer Care Research Director," *MedCityNews*, July 2, 2014; K. Noyes, "Flatiron Health's Bold Proposition to Fight Cancer with Big Data," *Fortune*, June 12, 2014; N. Taylor, "Buzz: Google Ventures Leading $100M Round in Oncology Big Data Platform," *FierceBioTechIT*, May 5, 2014; www.flatiron.com, www.guardanthealth.com, accessed August 26, 2015.

Questions

1. Describe the Big Data issues in this case.

2. How does Flatiron use Big Data in its attempt to improve cancer treatment?

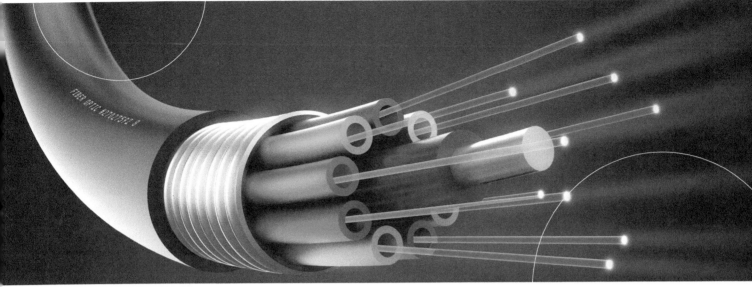

CHAPTER 4

Henrik5000/iStockphoto

Telecommunications and Networking

LEARNING OBJECTIVES

4.1 Compare and contrast the major types of networks.

4.2 Describe the wireline communications media and transmission technologies.

4.3 Describe the most common methods for accessing the Internet.

4.4 Explain the impact that discovery network applications have had on business and everyday life.

4.5 Explain the impact that communication network applications have had on business and everyday life.

4.6 Explain the impact that collaboration network applications have had on business and everyday life.

4.7 Explain the impact that educational network applications have had on business and everyday life.

Opening Case

 What to Do About Landline Telephones?

MKT The Problem

Large telecommunications companies such as AT&T (www.att.com) and Verizon Communications (www.verizon.com) want to get rid of their twisted-pair copper wire networks (discussed later in this chapter), called plain old telephone system, or POTS, and to replace them with Internet Protocol (IP) systems that will use the same wired and wireless broadband networks that provide Internet access, cable television, and telephone service to your home. There are several reasons why these large carriers find this transition desirable.

First, the U.S. government has a universal service guarantee, established by the Communications Act of 1934, that mandates that every resident have a baseline level of telecommunications services. The Federal Communications Commission (FCC) recognizes that telephone services provide a vital link to emergency services, government services, and surrounding communities. Because of the universal service guarantee, carriers frequently must operate expensive copper twisted-pair phone lines in rural areas to support small populations when it would be less expensive to provide cellular coverage. The carriers are compensated for these costs through a tax on customers' phone bills called the Universal Service Fund.

Second, many Americans either have gotten rid of their landline telephones or are preparing to do so. In fact, only 8 percent of U.S. households rely exclusively on a landline telephone. As the carriers' revenues decrease due to the falling number of POTS subscribers, the costs of maintaining the old POTS network are increasing. Put simply, landlines are becoming much less profitable.

Third, carriers want to increase their stock prices. The stock market favors companies with high revenue growth and punishes those that exhibit either no growth or declining revenues. Because POTS networks inhibit revenue growth and profitability, they tend to hold down the stock prices of companies like AT&T and Verizon.

In Mantoloking, New Jersey, Verizon wants to replace its POTS network, which Hurricane Sandy destroyed in 2012, with the company's wireless Voice Link. This operation would make Mantoloking the first U.S. community to be completely without POTS. However, not all residents favor this scenario for reasons we discuss later in this case. In addition, New Jersey's state legislature has concerns about, for example, inoperable building alarm systems because wireless systems cannot manage these systems. Verizon tried to implement the same process on Fire Island, New York, when its POTS was destroyed. Public opposition, however, forced the company to install fiber-optic cable.

For people living in rural areas, where cell towers are few and wireless capabilities are limited, eliminating POTS could create serious problems. In contrast, residents in metropolitan areas do not really have to worry about the end of POTS because high-speed wireline and wireless services are readily available replacements.

Despite industry pressures to eliminate POTS, there are several arguments in favor of keeping these networks. First, consider safety. When you call 911 from a landline telephone, the emergency operator knows your exact address. In contrast, wireless phones do not provide this specific location data, even if they contain GPS systems. Consequently, operators can respond more effectively to emergency calls from POTS networks than to calls from IP networks.

Second, POTS does not require power for landline phones to work. This advantage is critical in the event of a natural disaster, when cell towers are quickly jammed or become inoperable.

These issues concern the FCC. Because universal access for U.S. citizens is a key principle, the agency is unwilling to let telecommunications companies drop geographically undesirable customers. Instead, telecommunication companies must obtain FCC approval to completely eliminate services. The agency will not grant this approval unless there is a viable competitor to provide communications to people who have none. Many rural areas do not have viable competitors. That is the crux of the problem: The carriers want to eliminate their existing POTS networks, but the universal service guarantee makes that process extremely difficult.

Proposed Solutions

Although the FCC frequently denies permission to companies to eliminate POTS, it does allow carriers to experiment with the removal of landline telephones. To protect the universal service guarantee, however, carriers must meet certain FCC standards during these trials:

- Public safety communications must be available regardless of which technology is used;
- All Americans must have access to affordable communications services;
- Competition in the marketplace must provide choice for consumers and businesses;
- Consumer protection must be paramount.

On February 28, 2014, AT&T announced a trial program to eliminate landline telephones in Carbon Hill, Alabama, (population 2,071) and offer broadband and Voice-over-Internet-Protocol (VoIP) services in their place. The company and the FCC want to use this trial to learn several things: (a) how households will reach 911, (b) how small businesses will connect to customers, (c) how people with medical monitoring devices or home alarms will be certain that they are connected to a reliable network, and (d) the costs of converting from POTS to IP networks.

An additional challenge for AT&T in the Carbon Hill trial is that 4 percent of the residential customers are located too far away from AT&T facilities to receive broadband service. The carrier is investigating strategies to provide telephone service for these residents.

In addition to these trials, by September 2015, approximately 30 states had passed or were considering laws that restrict state government oversight of POTS networks. These laws eliminate the "carrier of last resort" rules. (A *carrier of last resort* is a telecommunications provider that is required by law to provide service to any customer in a service area who requests it, even if serving that customer is not economically viable at existing rates.) This move would abolish the universal service guarantee that gives every U.S. resident access to affordable telephone service. These states argue that telecommunications resources should be directed to developing modern telephone technologies rather than to supporting POTS networks.

The Results

As of September 2015, the outcome of the carriers' experiments and the state legislation remained largely unknown. However, it appears that the move away from POTS networks toward IP networks will continue.

Sources: J. Balmert, "Kasich Proposal Could Eliminate Landlines," *Cincinnati.com*, June 22, 2015; J. Wernau and E. Hirst, "Phone Companies Would Like to Cut Your Landline Cord for You," *Chicago Tribune*, December 18, 2014; "Carbon Hill, Alabama – 'The City with a Future' (Without Landlines)," *nojitter.com*, November 28, 2014; "Local Woman Fights Statewide Plan to Eliminated Landline Phones," *myFOXDetroit*, October 17, 2014; K. Vlahos, "FCC Tests Ways to Kill the Telephone Wire," *Digital Trends*, June 15, 2014; D. Weil, "AT&T Begins Process to Eliminate Some Landlines," *Newsmax*, April 8, 2014; J. Waters, "Prepare to Hang Up the Phone, Forever," *Wall Street Journal*, March 29, 2014; B. Dyas, "11 Reasons to Bring Back Landlines in 2014 (Seriously)," *The Huffington Post*, January 23, 2014; "Opponents Say Bill to Eliminate Landline Service Threatens Public Safety," *ABC News*, December 9, 2013; M. Anders, "Controversial Landline Phone Legislation Passes Michigan Senate Committee," *mLive.com*, December 3, 2013; B. Fung, "We Spend Billions a Year Maintaining Phone Lines (Almost) Nobody Depends On. Should We Get Rid of Them?" *The Washington Post*, October 8, 2013; M. Cherney, "When Will the Old Phone Networks Die? Not Soon," *InformationWeek*, April 8, 2013; www.fcc.gov, accessed September 14, 2015.

1. Should the large carriers be able to eliminate their POTS networks?

   a. Debate this argument from the viewpoint of the large telecommunications carriers.

   b. Debate this argument from the viewpoint of rural customers.

2. Why are wireless networks unable to take over all of the functions of POTS networks at this time (September 2015)?

Introduction

In addition to networks being essential in your personal lives, there are three fundamental points about network computing you need to know. First, in modern organizations computers do not work in isolation. Rather, they constantly exchange data with one another. Second, this exchange of data—facilitated by telecommunications technologies—provides companies with a number of very significant advantages. Third, this exchange can take place over any distance and over networks of any size.

Without networks, the computer on your desk would be merely another productivity-enhancement tool, just as the typewriter once was. The power of networks, however, turns your computer into an amazingly effective tool for accessing information from thousands of sources, thereby making both you and your organization more productive. Regardless of the type of organization (profit/not-for-profit, large/small, global/local) or industry (manufacturing, financial services, healthcare), networks in general, and the Internet in particular, have transformed—and will continue to transform—the way we do business.

Networks support new and innovative ways of doing business, from marketing to supply chain management to customer service to human resources management. In particular, the Internet and private intranets—a network located within a single organization that uses Internet software and TCP/IP protocols—have an enormous impact on our lives, both professionally and personally.

For all organizations regardless of their size, having a telecommunications and networking system is no longer just a source of competitive advantage. Rather, it is necessary for survival.

Computer networks are essential to modern organizations for many reasons. First, networked computer systems enable organizations to become more flexible so that they can adapt to rapidly changing business conditions. Second, networks allow companies to share hardware, computer applications, and data across the organization and among different organizations. Third, networks make it possible for geographically dispersed employees and workgroups to share documents, ideas, and creative insights. This sharing encourages teamwork, innovation, and more efficient and effective interactions. In addition, networks are a critical link between businesses, their business partners, and their customers.

Clearly, networks are essential tools for modern businesses. But, why do *you* need to be familiar with networks? The simple fact is that if you operate your own business or work in a business, you cannot function without networks. You will need to communicate rapidly with your customers, business partners, suppliers, employees, and colleagues. Until about 1990, you would have used the postal service or the telephone system with voice or fax capabilities for business communication. Today, however, the pace of business is much faster—almost real time. To keep up with this incredibly fast pace, you will need to use computers, e-mail, the Internet, cell phones, and mobile devices. Furthermore, all of these technologies will be connected via networks to enable you to communicate, collaborate, and compete on a global scale.

Networking and the Internet are the foundations for commerce in the twenty-first century. Recall that one important objective of this book is to help you become an informed user of information systems. Knowledge of networking is an essential component of modern business literacy. In fact, as you see in IT's About Business 4.1, a robust telecommunications infrastructure is essential for entire nations as well.

IT's About Business 4.1

MIS The Least Connected Country on Earth

Eritrea, a nation of six million people, is located on Africa's east coast, bordered by Sudan, Djibouti, and Ethiopia. The country has been ruled by a dictatorship since it achieved independence in 1993. Since 2009, Reporters Without Borders (www.rsf.org) has ranked Eritrea at the bottom of its press freedom index.

Eritrea is also the least-connected country on earth, according to data compiled by the United Nations International Telecommunication Union (ITU; www.itu.int). Eritreans are allowed to make international calls and to use the Internet. However, according to ITU data, only 1 percent of Eritreans have a landline, and only 5.6 percent have a cell phone. Both of these percentages are the lowest in the world.

The country's only telecommunications provider, Eritrea Telecommunication Services (EriTel; www.eritel.com.er), is controlled by the government. Customers must ask permission from local authorities to own a cell phone, and pay 200 nakfa ($13.29) to apply. Citizens who are fulfilling compulsory military service aren't given permission to have a cell phone. To activate their phone, customers pay EriTel the equivalent of $33.60. When they add minutes to their phone, that costs at least $3.65 every time. Because the average Eritrean earns roughly $500 a year, this expense is prohibitive to most.

Robert Van Buskirk, a Fulbright scholar from the United States, set up the country's first unofficial e-mail service in the mid-1990s. He used international phone calls to send e-mails between a computer at the University of Asmara—Eritrea's capital city—and a computer in California. For a couple of years, he singlehandedly operated the entire country's e-mail service.

As of September 2015, less than 1 percent of Eritreans are connected, according to the ITU. Access is available in just a few places. However, Internet connections are almost always dial-up, and they are extremely slow. Eritrea was also the last African country to establish a satellite connection to the Internet. Further, the country is one of only two African coastal nations with no fiber-optic connections. Only about 150 landline broadband connections exist, and only a handful of residences have Internet access, mostly dial-up connections costing about $200 a month.

Eritreans can get public Internet access in about 100 Internet cafés throughout the country. There is often a wait to use one of about 10 computers in each café. Users pay roughly $1.34 to be online for an hour, the equivalent of seven loaves of bread. Some cafés download American movies and TV shows and show them in the evenings for a fee.

Significantly, despite the government's severe repression of press freedom, there seems to be little censorship of the Internet. One likely reason is that high costs and long download times have marginalized the use of the Internet as a protest vehicle. Another possible reason is that the country is experiencing severe economic difficulties, and the government may recognize that strengthening the country's telecommunications would help improve the economy. In addition, the government wants to improve tourism. This goal would require a greatly improved telecommunications infrastructure as well.

Sources: Compiled from "Eritrea—Telecoms, Mobile, and Broadband—Market Insights and Statistics," *budde.com.au*, June 4, 2015; Y. Abselom, "Eritrea Blossoming Beautifully at 24," *Geeska Afrika Online*, May 10, 2015; "Sadly, Eritrea Remains at Tail of All World Indexes," *harnnet.org*, January 12, 2015; "Eritrea Telecommunication Report 2015," *Business Monitor International*, December 24, 2014; "Eritrea: Stronger Private Sector, Qualified Workforce, International Integration Needed, Says AFDB," *Caperi.com*, October 8, 2014; C. Winter and B. Haile, "The World…Eritrea," *Bloomberg BusinessWeek*, June 30 – July 6, 2014; C. Winter, "Eritrea's Communications Disconnect," *Bloomberg Business Week*, June 26, 2014.R. Atkinson and L. Stewart, "The Economic Benefits of Information and Communications Technology," *Information Technology & Innovation Foundation*, May 14, 2013.

Questions

1. Describe the impacts of a lack of telecommunications infrastructure on Eritrea.

2. Besides improving the economy, what other areas of Eritrean life would be impacted by a greatly improved telecommunications infrastructure?

3. Can the government of Eritrea allow an improved telecommunications infrastructure while maintaining strict control over communications and information? Why or why not? Support your answer.

You begin this chapter by learning what a computer network is and by identifying the various types of networks. You then study network fundamentals, and you next turn your attention to the basics of the Internet and the World Wide Web. You conclude by examining the many network applications available to individuals and organizations—that is, what networks help you do.

4.1 | What Is a Computer Network?

A computer network is a system that connects computers and other devices (e.g., printers) via communications media so that data and information can be transmitted among them. Voice and data communication networks are continually becoming faster—that is, their bandwidth is increasing—and cheaper. Bandwidth refers to the transmission capacity of a network; it is stated in bits per second. Bandwidth ranges from narrowband (relatively low transmission capacity) to broadband (relatively high network capacity).

The telecommunications industry itself has difficulty defining the term broadband. In February 2015, the Federal Communications Commission (FCC) proposed new rules defining broadband as the transmission capacity of a communications medium (discussed later in this chapter) faster than 25 megabits per second (Mbps) for download (transmission speed for material coming to you from an Internet server, such as a movie streamed from Netflix) and 4 Mbps for upload (transmission speed for material that you upload to an Internet server such as a Facebook post). The definition of broadband remains fluid, however, and it will undoubtedly continue to change to reflect greater transmission capacities in the future.

You are likely familiar with certain types of broadband connections, such as *digital subscriber line (DSL)* and cable to your homes and dorms. DSL and cable fall within the range of transmission capacity mentioned here and are thus defined as broadband connections.

The various types of computer networks range from small to worldwide. They include (from smallest to largest) personal area networks (PANs), local area networks (LANs), metropolitan area networks (MANs), wide area networks (WANs), and the ultimate WAN, the Internet. PANs are short-range networks—typically a few meters—that are used for communication among devices close to one person. They can be wired or wireless. (You will learn about wireless PANs in Chapter 10.) MANs are relatively large computer networks that cover a metropolitan area. MANs fall between LANs and WANs in size. WANs typically cover large geographical areas; in some cases they can span the entire planet.

Local Area Networks

Regardless of their size, networks represent a compromise among three objectives: speed, distance, and cost. Organizations typically must select two of the three. To cover long distances, organizations can have fast communication if they are willing to pay for it, or cheap communication if they are willing to accept slower speeds. A third possible combination of the three trade-offs is fast, cheap communication with distance limitations. This is the idea behind local area networks.

A local area network (LAN) connects two or more devices in a limited geographical region, usually within the same building, so that every device on the network can communicate with every other device. Most LANs today use Ethernet (discussed later in this chapter). Figure 4.1 illustrates an Ethernet LAN that consists of four computers, a server, and a printer,

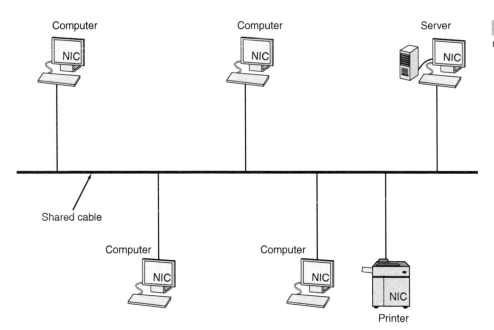

FIGURE 4.1 Ethernet local area network.

all of which connect via a shared cable. Every device in the LAN has a *network interface card* (NIC) that allows the device to physically connect to the LAN's communications medium. This medium is typically unshielded twisted-pair wire (UTP).

Although it is not required, many LANs have a file server or network server. The server typically contains various software and data for the network. It also houses the LAN's network operating system, which manages the server and routes and manages communications on the network.

Wide Area Networks

When businesses have to transmit and receive data beyond the confines of the LAN, they use wide area networks. The term *wide area network* did not even exist until local area networks appeared. Before that time, what we call a wide area network today was simply called a "network."

A **wide area network (WAN)** is a network that covers a large geographical area. WANs typically connect multiple LANs. They are generally provided by common carriers such as telephone companies and the international networks of global communications services providers. Examples of these providers include AT&T (www.att.com) in the United States, Deutsche Telekom in Germany (www.telekom.com), and NTT Communications (www.ntt.com) in Japan.

WANs have large capacity, and they typically combine multiple channels (e.g., fiber-optic cables, microwave, and satellite). The Internet is an example of a WAN.

WANs also contain **routers**—a communications processor that routes messages from a LAN to the Internet, across several connected LANs, or across a WAN such as the Internet.

Enterprise Networks

Organizations today have multiple LANs and may have multiple WANs. All of these networks are interconnected to form an enterprise network. **Figure 4.2** displays a model of enterprise computing. Note that the enterprise network in the figure has a backbone network. Corporate **backbone networks** are high-speed central networks to which multiple smaller networks (such as LANs and smaller WANs) connect. The LANs are called *embedded LANs* because they connect to the backbone WAN.

Unfortunately, traditional networks can be rigid and lack the flexibility to keep pace with increasing business networking requirements. The reason for this problem is that the functions of traditional networks are distributed across physical routers and devices (i.e., hardware). This process means that to implement changes, each network device must be configured individually. In some cases, devices must be configured manually. *Software-defined networks* (SDN) are an emerging technology that is becoming increasingly important to help organizations manage their data flows across their enterprise networks.

With SDN, decisions controlling how network traffic flows across network devices are managed centrally by software. The software dynamically adjusts data flows to meet business and application needs.

Think of traditional networks as the road system of a city in 1920. Data packets are the cars that travel through the city. A traffic officer (physical network devices) controls each intersection and directs traffic by recognizing the turn signals, and size and shape of the vehicles passing through the intersection. The officers can direct only the traffic at their intersection. They do not know the overall traffic volume in the city nor do they know traffic movement across the city. Therefore, it is difficult to control the city's traffic patterns as a whole and to manage peak-hour traffic. When problems occur, the city must communicate with each individual officer via radio.

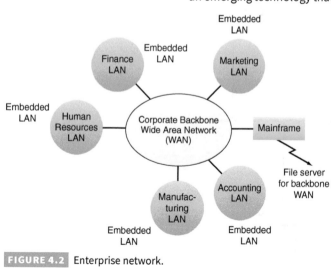

FIGURE 4.2 Enterprise network.

Now think of SDN as the road system of a modern city. Each traffic officer is replaced by a traffic light and a set of electronic vehicle counters, which are connected to central monitoring and control software. As such, the city's traffic can be instantly and centrally controlled. The control software can direct traffic differently at various times of the day (say, rush hours). The software monitors traffic flow and automatically changes the traffic lights to help traffic flow through the city with minimal disruption.

Before you go on...

1. What are the primary business reasons for using networks?
2. What are the differences between LANs and WANs?
3. Describe an enterprise network.

Apply the Concept 4.1

LEARNING OBJECTIVE 4.1 Compare and contrast the major types of networks.

STEP 1: Background (Here is what you are learning.)

Section 4.1 has introduced you to the different types of networks that connect businesses around the world. These networking capabilities enable modern organizations to operate over many geographic locations. Frequently, a company's headquarters are located in one city with various branches in other countries. In addition, employees often work from home rather than commute to a physical office. The computer network is the technology that allows all of this to happen. For a network to function, a few components are required. In this activity, you will place these components in the appropriate places to create a computer network.

STEP 2: Activity (Here is what you do.)

Consider the following company, called JLB TechWizards, and these potential network components.

1. *Headquarters:* JLB TechWizards manufactures, sells, and services computer equipment. The company's headquarters, ocated in Chicago, house several key functions including marketing, accounting, HR, and manufacturing. Each office has a number of PCs that connect to the main server. All offices share data and printers.

2. *Salesforce:* The company has 15 technicians who service equipment sold within the United States. Each technician has a laptop that must connect to the database at headquarters about three hours each day to check inventory, enter repairs, and place orders. Technicians are constantly on the road, and they need to be able to check inventory whether they are in a hotel or at a customer site. In addition, each evening the technicians must log on to check for updates and to post their daily activities.

3. *Employees from home:* JLB TechWizards has a number of employees who work from home part time on flextime. These employees must have a fast, secure connection because some of them are dealing with financial data stored in the main computer and its databases at headquarters. They all live within 20 miles of their workplace.

STEP 3: Deliverable (Here is what you turn in.)

Use the description of JLB TechWizards presented above to compare and contrast the types of networks discussed in this section. Explain how these networks will or will not meet the needs of each situation. A table may be useful to present this information, but it is not required. Create a Word document with your description and explanations and submit it to your instructor.

4.2 | Network Fundamentals

In this section, you will learn the basics of how networks actually operate. You begin by studying wireline communications media, which enable computers in a network to transmit and receive data. You conclude this section by looking at network protocols and types of network processing.

Today, computer networks communicate via digital signals, which are discrete pulses that are either on or off, representing a series of *bits* (0s and 1s). This quality allows digital signals to convey information in a binary form that can be interpreted by computers.

The U.S. public telephone system (called the plain old telephone system or POTS) was originally designed as an analog network to carry voice signals or sounds in an analog wave format (see the chapter opening case). In order for this type of circuit to carry digital information, that information must be converted into an analog wave pattern by a *dial-up modem*. Dial-up modems are almost extinct in most parts of the developed world.

Cable modems are modems that operate over coaxial cable—for example, cable TV. They offer broadband access to the Internet or corporate intranets. Cable modem speeds vary widely. Most providers offer bandwidth between 1 and 6 million bits per second (Mbps) for downloads (from the Internet to a computer) and between 128 and 768 thousand bits per second (Kbps) for uploads. Cable modem services share bandwidth among subscribers in a locality. That is, the same cable line connects to many households. Therefore, when large numbers of neighbors access the Internet at the same time, cable speeds can decrease significantly.

DSL modems operate on the same lines as voice telephones and dial-up modems. DSL modems always maintain a connection, so an Internet connection is immediately available.

Communications Media and Channels

Communicating data from one location to another requires some form of pathway or medium. A **communications channel** is such a pathway. It is comprised of two types of media: cable (twisted-pair wire, coaxial cable, or fiber-optic cable) and broadcast (microwave, satellite, radio, or infrared).

Wireline media or **cable media** use physical wires or cables to transmit data and information. Twisted-pair wire and coaxial cables are made of copper, and fiber-optic cable is made of glass. The alternative is communication over **broadcast media** or **wireless media**. The key to mobile communications in today's rapidly moving society is data transmissions over electromagnetic media—the "airwaves." In this section, you will study the three wireline channels. **Table 4.1** summarizes the advantages and disadvantages of each of these channels. You will become familiar with wireless media in Chapter 10.

Twisted-Pair Wire. The most prevalent form of communications wiring—twisted-pair wire—is used for almost all business telephone wiring. As the name suggests, it consists of strands of copper wire twisted in pairs (see **Figure 4.3**). Twisted-pair wire is relatively inexpensive to purchase, widely available, and easy to work with. However, it also has some significant disadvantages. Specifically, it is relatively slow for transmitting data, it is subject to interference from other electrical sources, and it can be easily tapped by unintended receivers to gain unauthorized access to data.

TABLE 4.1 Advantages and Disadvantages of Wireline Communications Channels

Channel	Advantages	Disadvantages
Twisted-pair wire	Inexpensive	Slow (low bandwidth)
	Widely available	Subject to interference
	Easy to work with	Easily tapped (low security)
Coaxial cable	Higher bandwidth than twisted-pair	Relatively expensive and inflexible
		Easily tapped (low to medium security)
	Less susceptible to electromagnetic interference	Somewhat difficult to work with
Fiber-optic cable	Very high bandwidth	Difficult to work with (difficult to splice)
	Relatively inexpensive	
	Difficult to tap (good security)	

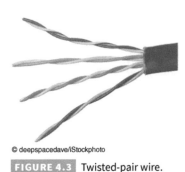

© deepspacedave/iStockphoto

FIGURE 4.3 Twisted-pair wire.

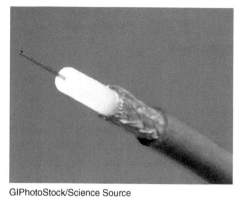

Cross-section view

How coaxial cable looks to us

FIGURE 4.4 Two views of coaxial cable.

Coaxial Cable. Coaxial cable (Figure 4.4) consists of insulated copper wire. Compared with twisted-pair wire, it is much less susceptible to electrical interference, and it can carry much more data. For these reasons, it is commonly used to carry high-speed data traffic as well as television signals (thus the term *cable TV*). However, coaxial cable is more expensive and more difficult to work with than twisted-pair wire. It is also somewhat inflexible.

Fiber Optics. Fiber-optic cable (Figure 4.5) consists of thousands of very thin filaments of glass fibers that transmit information via light pulses generated by lasers. The fiber-optic cable is surrounded by cladding, a coating that prevents the light from leaking out of the fiber.

Fiber-optic cables are significantly smaller and lighter than traditional cable media. They also can transmit far more data, and they provide greater security from interference and tapping. As of early-2015, optical fiber had reached data transmission rates of more than 50 trillion bits (terabits) per second in laboratory experiments. Fiber-optic cable is typically used as the backbone for a network, whereas twisted-pair wire and coaxial cable connect the backbone to individual devices on the network.

Network Protocols

Computing devices that are connected to the network must access and share the network to transmit and receive data. These devices are often referred to as *nodes* of the network. They work together by adhering to a common set of rules and procedures—known as a protocol—that enable them to communicate with one another. The two major protocols are the Ethernet and Transmission Control Protocol/Internet Protocol.

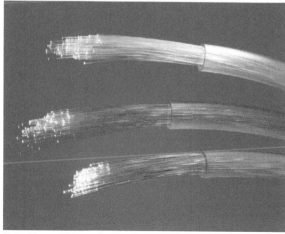

FIGURE 4.5 Two views of fiber-optic cable.

Cross-section view

How fiber-optic cable looks to us

Ethernet. A common LAN protocol is Ethernet. Many organizations use 100-gigabit Ethernet, where the network provides data transmission speeds of 100 gigabits (100 billion bits) per second. The 400-gigabit Ethernet is projected to be in service in 2017.

Transmission Control Protocol/Internet Protocol. The **Transmission Control Protocol/Internet Protocol (TCP/IP)** is the protocol of the Internet. TCP/IP uses a suite of protocols, the main ones being the Transmission Control Protocol (TCP) and the Internet Protocol (IP). The TCP performs three basic functions: (1) It manages the movement of data packets (see below) between computers by establishing a connection between the computers, (2) it sequences the transfer of packets, and (3) it acknowledges the packets that have been transmitted. The **Internet Protocol (IP)** is responsible for disassembling, delivering, and reassembling the data during transmission.

Before data are transmitted over the Internet, they are divided into small, fixed bundles called *packets*. The transmission technology that breaks up blocks of text into packets is called *packet switching*. Each packet carries the information that will help it reach its destination—the sender's IP address, the intended receiver's IP address, the number of packets in the message, and the sequence number of the particular packet within the message. Each packet travels independently across the network and can be routed through different paths in the network. When the packets reach their destination, they are reassembled into the original message.

It is important to note that packet-switching networks are reliable and fault tolerant. For example, if a path in the network is very busy or is broken, packets can be dynamically ("on the fly") rerouted around that path. Also, if one or more packets do not get to the receiving computer, then only those packets need to be resent.

Why do organizations use packet switching? The main reason is to achieve reliable end-to-end message transmission over sometimes unreliable networks that may have short-acting or long-acting problems.

The packets use the TCP/IP protocol to carry their data. TCP/IP functions in four layers (see Figure 4.6). The *application layer* enables client application programs to access the other layers, and it defines the protocols that applications use to exchange data. One of these application protocols is the **Hypertext Transfer Protocol (HTTP)**, which defines how messages are formulated and how they are interpreted by their receivers. (We discuss hypertext in Section 4.3.) The *transport layer* provides the application layer with communication and packet services. This layer includes TCP and other protocols. The *Internet layer* is responsible for addressing, routing, and packaging data packets. The IP is one of the protocols in this layer. Finally, the *network interface layer* places packets on, and receives them from, the network medium, which can be any networking technology.

Two computers using TCP/IP can communicate even if they use different hardware and software. Data sent from one computer to another proceed downward through all four layers,

FIGURE 4.6 The four layers of the TCP/IP reference model.

Email: Sending a Message via SMPT (Simple Mail Transfer Protocol)	Application	Email: Message received
Break Message into packets and determine order	Transport	Packets reordered and replaced (if lost)
Assign sending and receiving IP addresses and apply to each packet	Internet	Packets routed through internal network to desired IP address
Determine path across network/ Internet to intended destination	Network Interface	Receipt of packets

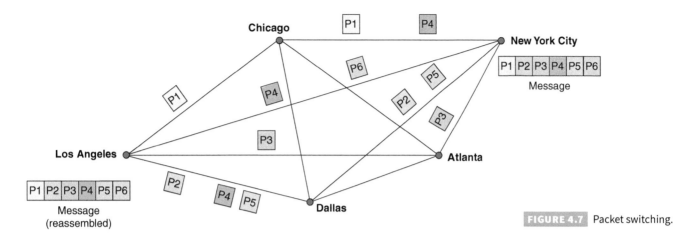

FIGURE 4.7 Packet switching.

beginning with the sending computer's application layer and going through its network interface layer. After the data reach the receiving computer, they travel up the layers.

TCP/IP enables users to send data across sometimes unreliable networks with the assurance that the data will arrive in uncorrupted form. TCP/IP is very popular with business organizations because of its reliability and the ease with which it can support intranets and related functions.

Let's look at an example of packet switching across the Internet. Figure 4.7 illustrates a message being sent from New York City to Los Angeles over a packet-switching network. Note that the different colored packets travel by different routes to reach their destination in Los Angeles, where they are reassembled into the complete message.

Types of Network Processing

Organizations typically use multiple computer systems across the firm. Distributed processing divides processing work among two or more computers. This process enables computers in different locations to communicate with one another via telecommunications links. A common type of distributed processing is client/server processing. A special type of client/server processing is peer-to-peer processing.

Client/Server Computing. Client/server computing links two or more computers in an arrangement in which some machines, called *servers*, provide computing services for user PCs, called *clients*. Usually, an organization performs the bulk of its processing or application/data storage on suitably powerful servers that can be accessed by less powerful client machines. The client requests applications, data, or processing from the server, which acts on these requests by "serving" the desired commodity.

Client/server computing leads to the ideas of "fat" clients and "thin" clients. As discussed in Plug IT In 2, *fat clients* have large storage and processing power and therefore can run local programs (such as Microsoft Office) if the network goes down. In contrast, *thin clients* may have no local storage and only limited processing power. Thus, they must depend on the network to run applications. For this reason, they are of little value when the network is not functioning.

Peer-to-Peer Processing. Peer-to-peer (P2P) processing is a type of client/server distributed processing where each computer acts as *both* a client and a server. Each computer can access (as assigned for security or integrity purposes) all files on all other computers.

There are three basic types of peer-to-peer processing. The first type accesses unused CPU power among networked computers. An application of this type is SETI@home (http://setiathome.ssl.berkeley.edu). These applications are from open-source projects, and they can be downloaded at no cost.

The second form of peer-to-peer is real-time, person-to-person collaboration, such as Microsoft SharePoint Workspace (http://office.microsoft.com/en-us/sharepoint-workspace).

This product provides P2P collaborative applications that use buddy lists to establish a connection and allow real-time collaboration within the application.

The third peer-to-peer category is advanced search and file sharing. This category is characterized by natural language searches of millions of peer systems. It enables users to discover other users, not just data and Web pages. One example of this category is BitTorrent.

BitTorrent (www.bittorrent.com) is an open-source, free, peer-to-peer file-sharing application that simplifies the problem of sharing large files by dividing them into tiny pieces, or "torrents." BitTorrent addresses two of the biggest problems of file sharing: (1) downloading bogs down when many people access a file at once, and (2) some people leech, meaning they download content but refuse to share it. BitTorrent eliminates the bottleneck by enabling all users to share little pieces of a file at the same time—a process called *swarming*. The program prevents leeching because users must upload a file while they download it. Thus, the more popular the content, the more efficiently it travels over a network.

Before you go on...

1. Compare and contrast the three wireline communications channels.
2. Describe the various technologies that enable users to send high-volume data over any network.
3. Describe the Ethernet and TCP/IP protocols.
4. Differentiate between client/server computing and peer-to-peer processing.

Apply the Concept 4.2

LEARNING OBJECTIVE 4.2 Describe the wireline communications media and transmission technologies.

STEP 1: Background

Section 4.2 covers network channels, protocols, and other network fundamentals. These computer networks enable businesses to receive and share information with customers, suppliers, and employees. Made up of several possible cable types and protocols, they are quite literally the backbone of modern businesses.

STEP 2: Activity

Imagine that you work in the billing department of a midsized hospital. Recently, your supervisor stated that hospital growth had created a need for office space to be repurposed, and your work would now be done from home. You would be reimbursed for any expenses involved in preparing your home office, and

your home Internet (required connection speed of 1.5 MB/sec minimum) would also be reimbursed quarterly. The only requirement is that you finalize the same number of bills each day from home as you did in the office. You can schedule your own time, as long as your work gets done.

Visit http://www.wiley.com/go/rainer/MIS4e/applytheconcept to watch a few videos about telecommuting.

STEP 3: Deliverable

Describe the wireline communication media and the transmission technologies (protocols) that you will need to be able to telecommute. Your description should (at a minimum) include the home Internet connection, use of the Web, and connections within the office. It should also describe the protocols that operate to support these connections. Submit your description to your instructor.

4.3 | The Internet and the World Wide Web

The **Internet ("the Net")** is a global WAN that connects approximately one million organizational computer networks in more than 200 countries on all continents, including Antarctica. It has become so widespread that it features in the daily routine of some three billion people. Participating computer systems include smartphones, PCs, LANs, databases, and mainframes.

The computers and organizational nodes on the Internet can be of different types and makes. They are connected to one another by data communications lines of different speeds. The primary network connections and telecommunications lines that link the nodes are referred to as the Internet backbone. For the Internet, the backbone is a fiber-optic network that is operated primarily by large telecommunications companies.

As a network of networks, the Internet enables people to access data in other organizations and to communicate, collaborate, and exchange information seamlessly around the world, quickly and inexpensively. Thus, the Internet has become a necessity for modern businesses.

The Internet grew out of an experimental project of the Advanced Research Project Agency (ARPA) of the U.S. Department of Defense. The project began in 1969 as the *ARPAnet*. Its purpose was to test the feasibility of a WAN over which researchers, educators, military personnel, and government agencies could share data, exchange messages, and transfer files.

Today, Internet technologies are being used both within and among organizations. An intranet is a network that uses Internet protocols so that users can take advantage of familiar applications and work habits. Intranets support discovery (easy and inexpensive browsing and search), communication, and collaboration inside an organization.

In contrast, an extranet connects parts of the intranets of different organizations. In addition, it enables business partners to communicate securely over the Internet using virtual private networks (VPNs) (explained in Chapter 7). Extranets offer limited accessibility to the intranets of participating companies, as well as necessary interorganizational communications. They are widely used in the areas of business-to-business (B2B) electronic commerce (see Chapter 9) and supply chain management (SCM) (see Chapter 13).

No central agency manages the Internet. Instead, the costs of its operation are shared among hundreds of thousands of nodes. Thus, the cost for any one organization is small. Organizations must pay a small fee if they wish to register their names, and they need to install their own hardware and software to operate their internal networks. The organizations are obliged to move any data or information that enter their organizational network, regardless of the source, to their destination, at no charge to the senders. The senders, of course, pay the telephone bills for using either the backbone or regular telephone lines.

Accessing the Internet

You can access the Internet in several ways. From your place of work or your university, you can utilize your organization's LAN. A campus or company backbone connects all of the various LANs and servers in the organization to the Internet. You can also log onto the Internet from your home or on the road, using either wireline or wireless connections.

Connecting via an Online Service. You can also access the Internet by opening an account with an Internet service provider. An Internet service provider (ISP) is a company that provides Internet connections for a fee. Large ISPs include Comcast (www.comcast.com), AT&T (www.att.com), Time Warner Cable (www.timewarnercable.com) and Verizon (www .verizon.com).

ISPs connect to one another through network access points (NAPs). NAPs are exchange points for Internet traffic. They determine how traffic is routed. NAPs are key components of the Internet backbone. Figure 4.8 displays a schematic of the Internet. The white links at the top of the figure represent the Internet backbone; the brown dots where the white links meet are the NAPs.

Connecting via Other Means. There have been several attempts to make access to the Internet cheaper, faster, and easier. For example, terminals known as Internet kiosks have been located in such public places as libraries and airports (and even in convenience stores in some countries) for use by people who do not have their own computers. Accessing the Internet from smartphones and tablets is common, and fiber-to-the-home (FTTH) is growing rapidly. FTTH involves connecting fiber-optic cable directly to individual homes. Table 4.2 summarizes the various means of connecting to the Internet. Satellite connections and Google Fiber are worth noting in more detail.

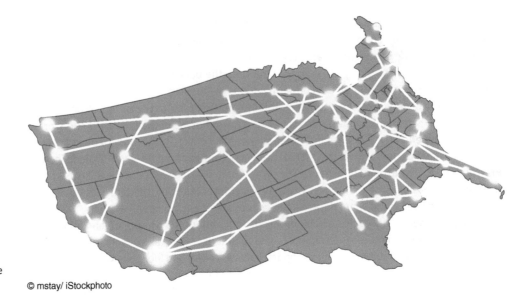

FIGURE 4.8 Internet (backbone in white).

TABLE 4.2 Internet Connection Methods

Service	Description
Dial-up	Still used in the United States where broadband is not available
DSL	Broadband access via telephone companies
Cable modem	Access over your cable TV coaxial cable. Can have degraded performance if many of your neighbors are accessing the Internet at once
Satellite	Access where cable and DSL are not available
Wireless	Very convenient, and WiMAX will increase the use of broadband wireless
Fiber-to-the-home (FTTH)	Expensive and usually placed only in new housing developments

Connecting via satellite. In January 2015, OneWeb (http://oneweb.world) announced that it would build a micro-satellite network to bring Internet access to all corners of the globe. OneWeb aims to target rural markets, emerging markets, and in-flight Internet services on airlines. The company plans to create a network of 648 small satellites, each weighing some 285 pounds and orbiting 750 miles above the Earth. OneWeb plans to launch its Internet over satellite service in 2018.

On the other hand, Elon Musk (the founder of Tesla Motorcars and SpaceX) announced his plans to launch 4000 satellites into low earth orbit by 2021. Musk said his Internet-over-satellite service was intended to be the primary means of long-distance Internet traffic for people in sparsely populated areas.

Google Fiber. Cable distribution giants such as Verizon (www.verizon.com), Time Warner Cable (www.timewarnercable.com), and Comcast (www.comcast.com) enjoy healthy profit margins on their Internet services. None of these companies, however, appears to have plans to extend fiber-to-the-home services to additional geographical areas. Rather, their business goal is to sign up more people in their existing service areas. They have adopted this strategy because focusing on existing service areas adds the most revenue without increasing the companies' capital costs. Essentially, there are no compelling business incentives for the established cable companies to expand their service offerings. This policy is unfortunate because most Americans have no choice but to do business with their local cable company. To compound this problem, few outside companies have the money to compete with the existing, cash-heavy telecommunications companies who control existing cable networks.

Today, Google is installing and operating ultrafast fiber-optic cable service, known as Google Fiber (http://fiber.google.com), in U.S. cities. Google Fiber was first deployed to homes in Kansas City (Kansas and Missouri). By May 2016, Google Fiber was operating in nine U.S. cities. Significantly, about seven months after Google announced its intentions to bring Fiber to Austin, AT&T announced it was introducing 1-Gbps service in the same city.

Addresses on the Internet. Each computer on the Internet has an assigned address, called the Internet Protocol (IP) address, that distinguishes it from all other computers. The IP address consists of sets of numbers, in four parts, separated by dots. For example, the IP address of one computer might be 135.62.128.91. You can access a Web site by typing this number in the address bar of your browser.

Currently, there are two IP addressing schemes. The first scheme, IPv4, is the most widely used. IP addresses using IPv4 consist of 32 bits, meaning that there are 2^{32} possibilities for IP addresses, or 4,294,967,295 distinct addresses. Note that the IP address in the preceding paragraph (135.62.128.91) is an IPv4 address. At the time that IPv4 was developed, there were not as many computers that need addresses as there are today. Therefore, a new IP addressing scheme has been developed, IPv6.

IP addresses using IPv6 consist of 128 bits, meaning that there are 2^{128} possibilities for distinct IP addresses, which is an unimaginably large number. IPv6, which is replacing IPv4, will accommodate the rapidly increasing number of devices that need IP addresses, such as smartphones.

IP addresses must be unique so that computers on the Internet know where to find one another. The Internet Corporation for Assigned Names (ICANN) (www.icann.org) coordinates these unique addresses throughout the world. Without that coordination, we would not have one global Internet.

ICANN planned to transition its functions to a "global multistakeholder community" in 2015. In September 2015, the American Registry for Internet Numbers (ARIN; www.arin.net), the organization responsible for issuing IP addresses in North America, announced that it had run out of freely available IPv4 addresses. This situation will not affect normal Internet users, but it will put more pressure on Internet service providers, software companies, and large organizations to accelerate their migration to IPv6.

Because the numeric IP addresses are difficult to remember, most computers have names as well. ICANN accredits certain companies called *registrars* to register these names, which are derived from a system called the domain name system (DNS). Domain names consist of multiple parts, separated by dots, that are read from right to left. For example, consider the domain name *business.auburn.edu*. The rightmost part (or zone) of an Internet name is its top-level domain (TLD). The letters *edu* in business.auburn.edu indicate that this is an educational site. The following are popular U.S. TLDs:

com	commercial sites
edu	educational sites
mil	military government sites
gov	civilian government sites
org	organizations

To conclude our domain name example, *auburn* is the name of the organization (Auburn University), and *business* is the name of the particular machine (server) within the organization to which the message is being sent.

A top-level domain (TLD) is the domain at the highest level in the hierarchical Domain Name System of the Internet. The top-level domain names are located in the root zone (rightmost zone) of the name. Management of most TLDs is delegated to responsible organizations by ICANN. ICANN operates the Internet Assigned Numbers Authority (IANA), which is in charge of maintaining the DNS root zone. Today, IANA distinguishes the following groups of TLDs:

- Country-code top-level domains (ccTLD): Two letter domains established for countries or territories. For example, *de* stands for Germany, *it* for Italy, and *ru* for Russia.

- Internationalized country code top-level domains (IDN ccTLD): These are ccTLDs in non-Latin character sets (e.g., Arabic or Chinese).
- Generic top-level domains (gTLD): Top-level domains with three or more characters. gTLDs initially consisted of .gov, .edu, .com, .mil, .org, and .net. In late 2000, ICANN introduced .aero, .biz, .coop, .info, .museum, .name, and .pro.

The Future of the Internet

Researchers assert that if Internet bandwidth is not improved rapidly, then within a few years the Internet will be able to function only at a much reduced speed. The Internet sometimes is too slow for data-intensive applications such as full-motion video files (movies) and large medical files (X-rays). In addition, the Internet is unreliable and is not secure. As a result, Internet2 has been developed by many U.S. universities collaborating with industry and government. Internet2 develops and deploys advanced network applications such as remote medical diagnosis, digital libraries, distance education, online simulation, and virtual laboratories. It is designed to be fast, always on, everywhere, natural, intelligent, easy, and trusted. Note that Internet2 is not a separate physical network from the Internet. At the end of 2014, Internet2 had over 500 members, including 252 institutions of higher education and 82 members from industry. For more details, see www.internet2.edu.

The World Wide Web

Many people equate the Internet with the World Wide Web. However, they are not the same thing. The Internet functions as a transport mechanism, whereas the World Wide Web is an application that uses those transport functions. Other applications, such as e-mail, also run on the Internet.

The World Wide Web (The Web, WWW, or W3) is a system of universally accepted standards for storing, retrieving, formatting, and displaying information via a client/server architecture. The Web handles all types of digital information, including text, hypermedia, graphics, and sound. It uses graphical user interfaces (GUIs) (explained in Plug IT In 2), so it is very easy to navigate.

Hypertext is the underlying concept defining the structure of the World Wide Web. Hypertext is the text displayed on a computer display or other electronic device with references, called hyperlinks, to other text that the reader can immediately access, or where text can be revealed progressively at additional levels of details. A hyperlink is a connection from a hypertext file or document to another location or file, typically activated by clicking on a highlighted word or image on the screen, or by touching the screen.

Organizations that wish to offer information through the Web must establish a *home page*, which is a text and graphical screen display that usually welcomes the user and provides basic information on the organization that has established the page. In most cases, the home page will lead users to other pages. All the pages of a particular company or individual are collectively known as a Web site. Most Web pages provide a way to contact the organization or the individual. The person in charge of an organization's Web site is its *Webmaster*. (*Note: Webmaster* is a gender-neutral title.)

To access a Web site, the user must specify a uniform resource locator (URL), which points to the address of a specific resource on the Web. For instance, the URL for Microsoft is http://www.microsoft.com. Recall that HTTP stands for hypertext transport protocol. The remaining letters in this URL—www.microsoft.com—indicate the domain name that identifies the Web server that stores the Web site.

Users access the Web primarily through software applications called browsers. Browsers provide a graphical front end that enables users to point-and-click their way across the Web, a process called *surfing*. Web browsers became a means of universal access because they deliver the same interface on any operating system on which they run.

Before you go on...

1. Describe the various ways that you can connect to the Internet.

2. Identify each part of an Internet address.

3. Describe the difference between the Internet and the World Wide Web.

4. What are the functions of browsers?

Apply the Concept 4.3

LEARNING OBJECTIVE 4.3 Describe the most common methods for accessing the Internet.

STEP 1: Background

Section 4.3 has explained the difference between the Internet and the World Wide Web. Although many people use these terms interchangeably, they are very different. Most computers today are continuously connected to the Internet, though they are not always accessing the Web. Offices and other places of employment typically set up an Internet connection via a local area network (LAN). However, at home you have several options to consider.

STEP 2: Activity

Visit http://www.wiley.com/go/rainer/MIS4e/applytheconcept, and watch the YouTube videos listed there. These videos go into

a little more detail about the types of connections mentioned in Table 4.2. You will learn about advantages, disadvantages, and things to consider for the different methods of connecting to the Internet.

STEP 3: Deliverable

Imagine that your parents are "technologically challenged" (some of you may not have to imagine). They have just bought a house at the beach, and they are getting ready to set up an Internet connection. At home, there is only one provider, so DSL vs. cable vs. cellular vs. satellite is not an issue. However, there are several options at the beach, and your parents do not know where to begin.

Compose an email to your parents that describes the most common methods for accessing the Internet to help them develop criteria for making their choice.

4.4 | Network Applications: Discovery

Now that you have a working knowledge of what networks are and how you can access them, the key question is: How do businesses use networks to improve their operations? In the next four sections of this chapter, we explore four network applications: discovery, communication, collaboration, and education. These applications, however, are merely a sampling of the many network applications currently available to users. Even if these applications formed an exhaustive list today, they would not do so tomorrow when something new will be developed. Furthermore, placing network applications in categories is difficult because there will always be borderline cases. For example, telecommuting really combines communication and collaboration.

The Internet enables users to access or *discover information* located in databases all over the world. By browsing and searching data sources on the Web, users can apply the Internet's discovery capability to areas ranging from education to government services to entertainment to commerce. Although having access to all this information is a great benefit, it is critically important to realize that there is no quality assurance for information on the Web. The Web is truly democratic in that *anyone* can post information to it. Therefore, the fundamental rule about information on the Web is "User beware!"

In addition, the Web's major strength—the vast stores of information it contains—also presents a major challenge. The amount of information on the Web can be overwhelming, and it doubles approximately each year. As a result, navigating through the Web and gaining access to necessary information are becoming more and more difficult. To accomplish these tasks, people increasingly are using search engines, directories, and portals.

Search Engines and Metasearch Engines

A **search engine** is a computer program that searches for specific information by keywords and then reports the results. A search engine maintains an index of billions of Web pages. It uses that index to find pages that match a set of user-specified keywords. Such indexes are created and updated by *webcrawlers*, which are computer programs that browse the Web and create a copy of all visited pages. Search engines then index these pages to provide fast searches.

In mid-2016, four search engines accounted for almost all searches in the United States. They are, in order, Google (www.google.com), Bing (www.bing.com), Yahoo! (www.yahoo.com), and Ask (www.ask.com). The leading search engine in China is Baidu (www.baidu.com), which claimed approximately three-fourths of the Chinese market in mid-2016.

There are an incredible number of other search engines that are quite useful, many of which perform very specific searches. Examples include: Boardreader (www.boardreader.com), BuzzSumo (www.buzzsumo.com), CrunchBase (www.crunchbase.com), DuckDuckGo (https://duckduckgo.com), and Topsy (www.topsy.com).

For an even more thorough search, you can use a metasearch engine. **Metasearch engines** search several engines at once and then integrate the findings to answer users' queries. Examples are Surf-wax (www.surfwax.com), Metacrawler (www.metacrawler.com), Mamma (www.mamma.com), KartOO (www.kartoo.com), and Dogpile (www.dogpile.com).

Publication of Material in Foreign Languages

Not only is there a huge amount of information on the Internet, but it is also written in many different languages. How, then, do you access this information? The answer is that you use an *automatic translation* of Web pages. Such translation is available to and from all major languages, and its quality is improving with time. Some major translation products are Microsoft's Bing translator (http://www.microsofttranslator.com) and Google (www.google.com/language_tools) (see **Figure 4.9**), as well as products and services available at Trados (www.trados.com).

Companies invest resources to make their Web sites accessible in multiple languages as a result of the global nature of the business environment. That is, multilingual Web sites are now a competitive necessity. When companies are disseminating information around the world, getting that information correct is essential. It is not enough for companies to translate Web content. They must also localize that content and be sensitive to the needs of the people in local markets.

To reach 80 percent of the world's Internet users, a Web site needs to support a minimum of 10 languages: English, Chinese, Spanish, Japanese, German, Korean, French, Italian, Russian, and Portuguese. At 20 cents and more per word, translation services are expensive. Companies supporting 10 languages can spend $200,000 annually to localize information and

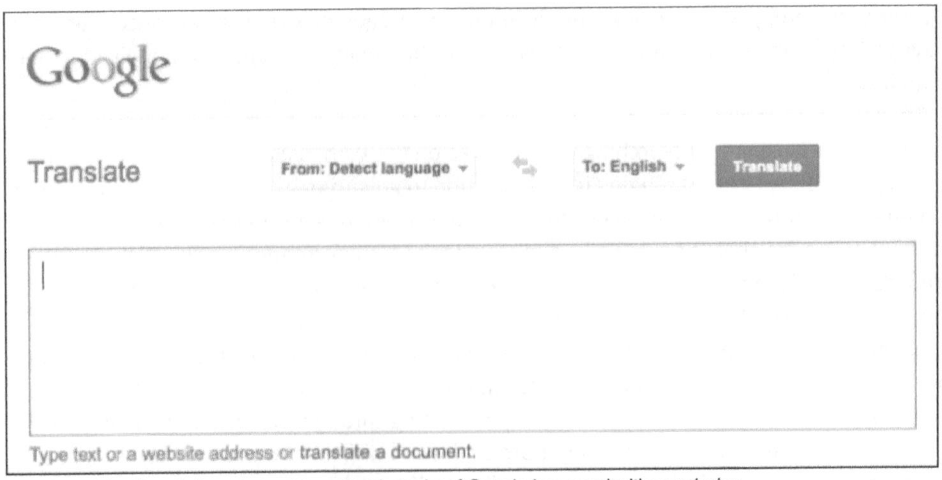

FIGURE 4.9 Google Translate. (Google and the Google logo are registered trademarks of Google Inc., used with permission).

Google and the Google logo are registered trademarks of Google Inc., used with permission another $50,000 to maintain the Web sites. Translation budgets for major multinational companies can run in millions of dollars. Many large companies use Systran S.A. (www.systransoft .com) for high-quality machine translation services.

Portals

Most organizations and their managers encounter information overload. Information is scattered across numerous documents, e-mail messages, and databases at different locations and systems. Finding relevant and accurate information is often time-consuming and may require users to access multiple systems.

One solution to this problem is to use portals. A portal is a Web-based, personalized gateway to information and knowledge that provides relevant information from different IT systems and the Internet using advanced search and indexing techniques. After reading the next section, you will be able to distinguish among four types of portals: commercial, affinity, corporate, and industrywide. The four types of portals are differentiated by the audiences they serve.

A commercial (public) portal is the most popular type of portal on the Internet. It is intended for broad and diverse audiences, and it offers routine content, some of it in real time (e.g., a stock ticker). Examples are Lycos (www.lycos.com) and Microsoft Network (www.msn .com).

In contrast, an affinity portal offers a single point of entry to an entire community of affiliated interests, such as a hobby group or a political party. Your university most likely has an affinity portal for its alumni. Figure 4.10 displays the affinity portal for the University of West Georgia. Other examples of affinity portals are www.techweb.com and www.zdnet.com.

As the name suggests, a corporate portal offers a personalized, single point of access through a Web browser to critical business information located inside and outside an organization. These portals are also known as *enterprise portals*, *information portals*, and *enterprise information portals*. In addition to making it easier to find needed information, corporate portals offer customers and employees self-service opportunities.

Whereas corporate portals are associated with a single company, an industrywide portal serves entire industries. An example is TruckNet (www.truck.net), a portal for the trucking industry and the trucking community, including professional drivers, owner/operators, and trucking companies.

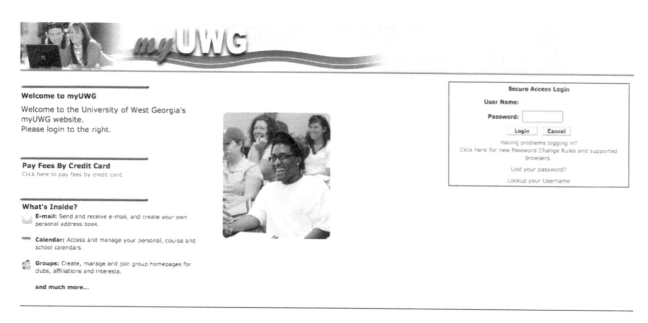

Courtesy of the University of West Georgia.

FIGURE 4.10 University of West Georgia affinity portal. (Courtesy of the University of West Georgia).

Before you go on...

1. Differentiate between search engines and metasearch engines.

2. What are some reasons why publication of material in a number of languages is so important?

3. Describe the various reasons that portals are useful to us.

Apply the Concept 4.4

LEARNING OBJECTIVE 4.4 Explain the impact that discovery network applications have had on business and everyday life.

STEP 1: Background

Section 4.4 has introduced you to the discovery aspect of networks, specifically, the web. Search engines (of all kinds) open up doors of knowledge for anyone with a question. Translation tools allow you to even discover your answer from other languages. These, however, are very broad tools. Portals help to narrow the by focusing your search within a narrow realm of information. They also push very specific information to you rather than waiting on you to request everything.

STEP 2: Activity

Before there were online search tools, there was the library card catalog. It was a method of organizing information in a library so that you could easily retrieve the information needed. Today, research is handled very differently. Visit http://www.wiley.com/go/rainer/MIS4e/applytheconcept to watch a video about the use of the "old school" library card catalog.

STEP 3: Deliverable

Search the web for the book referenced in the YouTube video linked above. Use multiple search engines (such as google.com, yahoo.com, or bing.com), some meta search engines (such as dogpile.com, blingo.com, or excite.com), and your school's library system. Make note of the amount of and type of information you are able to find in just a few minutes about the book referenced in the YouTube video above. Write a paragraph that compares your experience to the card catalog system.

Now think even bigger. If discovery applications have made this much impact on something as simple as finding a book (or information on the book), how much bigger is the impact on business and everyday life? Prepare a second paragraph that discusses the latter question.

Submit both paragraphs to your instructor.

4.5 Network Applications: Communication

The second major category of network applications is communication. There are many types of communication technologies, including e-mail, call centers, chat rooms, and voice. Further, we discuss an interesting application of communication: telecommuting. Note: You will read about other types of communication, blogging and microblogging, in Chapter 8.

Electronic Mail

Electronic mail (e-mail) is the largest-volume application running over the Internet. Studies have found that almost all companies conduct business transactions via e-mail, and the vast majority confirm that e-mail is tied to their means of generating revenue. On the other hand, the amount of e-mail that managers receive has become overwhelming. In fact, too much e-mail can lead to a loss of productivity.

Web-Based Call Centers

Effective personalized customer contact is becoming an important aspect of Web-based customer support. Such service is provided through *Web-based call centers*, also known as *customer care centers*. For example, if you need to contact a software vendor for technical support, you will usually be communicating with the vendor's Web-based call center, using e-mail, a telephone conversation, or a simultaneous voice/Web session. Web-based call centers are sometimes located in foreign countries such as India. Such *offshoring* is an important issue for the U.S. companies. (We discuss offshoring in Chapter 14.)

Significantly, some of the U.S. companies are moving their call center operations back to the United States, for several reasons. First, they believe they have less control of their operations when the centers are located overseas. They must depend on the vendor company to uphold their standards, such as quality of service. A second difficulty is language differences, which can create serious communication problems. Third, companies that manage sensitive information risk breaching customer confidentiality and security. Finally, the call center representatives typically work with many companies. As a result, they may not deliver the same level of customer services that each company requires.

Electronic Chat Rooms

Electronic chat refers to an arrangement whereby participants exchange conversational messages in real time in a chat room. Chat programs allow you to send messages to people who are connected to the same channel of communication at the same time. Anyone can join in the conversation. Messages are displayed on your screen as they arrive.

There are two major types of chat programs. The first type is Web based, which allows you to send messages to Internet users by using a Web browser and visiting a Web chat site (e.g., http://messenger.yahoo.com). The second type is e-mail based (text only); it is called *Internet Relay Chat* (IRC). A business can use IRC to interact with customers, provide online experts for answers to questions, and so on.

Voice Communication

The plain old telephone service (POTS) has been largely replaced by Internet telephony. With Internet telephony, also known as Voice-over-Internet Protocol or VoIP, phone calls are treated as just another kind of data. That is, your analog voice signals are digitized, sectioned into packets, and then sent over the Internet.

Consider Skype (www.skype.com), which provides several VoIP services for free: voice and video calls to users who also have Skype, instant messaging, short message service, voice mail, one-to-one and group chats, and conference calls with up to nine people. As of September 2015, the most current version of Skype offered full-screen, high-definition video calling, Skype Access (to access WiFi hotspots), call transfer to a Skype contact on either a mobile or a landline phone, improved quality of calls, and ease of use. It also provided additional functions for which users pay. For example, SkypeOut allows you to make calls to landline phones and mobile phones. SkypeIn provides a number that your friends can call from any phone, and you pick up the call in Skype.

Vonage (www.vonage.com) also provides VoIP services, but for a fee ($9.99 per month for the first six months and then $28 per month). With Vonage you make and receive calls with your existing home phone through your broadband Internet connection. Your phone actually connects to Vonage instead of an actual phone company. The person whom you are calling does not need to have Vonage or even an Internet connection.

Unified Communications

In the past, organizational networks for wired and wireless data, voice communications, and videoconferencing operated independently, and the IT department managed each network separately. This arrangement increased costs and reduced productivity.

Unified communications (UC) simplifies and integrates all forms of communications—voice, voice mail, fax, chat, e-mail, instant messaging, short message service, presence (location) services, and videoconferencing—on a common hardware and software platform. *Presence services* enable users to know where their intended recipients are and if they are available, in real time.

UC unifies all forms of human and computer communications into a common user experience. For example, UC allows an individual to receive a voice mail message and then read it in his or her e-mail inbox. In another example, UC enables users to seamlessly collaborate with another person on a project, regardless of where the users are located. One user could quickly locate the other user by accessing an interactive directory, determining whether that user is available, engaging in a text messaging session, and then escalating the session to a voice call or even a video call, all in real time.

Telecommuting

Knowledge workers are being called the distributed workforce, or "digital nomads." This group of highly prized workers is now able to work anywhere and anytime, a process called **telecommuting**. Distributed workers are those who have no permanent office at their companies, preferring to work at home offices, in airport lounges, or client conference rooms, or on a high school stadium bleacher. The growth of the distributed workforce is driven by globalization, extremely long commutes to work, rising gasoline prices, ubiquitous broadband communications links (wireline and wireless), and powerful laptop computers and computing devices.

Telecommuting offers a number of potential advantages for employees, employers, and society. For employees, the benefits include reduced stress and improved family life. In addition, telecommuting offers employment opportunities for housebound people such as single parents and persons with disabilities. Benefits for employers include increased productivity, the ability to retain skilled employees, and the ability to attract employees who do not live within commuting distance.

However, telecommuting also has some potential disadvantages. For employees, the

HRM

major disadvantages are increased feelings of isolation, possible loss of fringe benefits, lower pay (in some cases), no workplace visibility, the potential for slower promotions, and lack of socialization. In a 2013 study, researchers at Stanford University found that telecommuting employees are 50 percent less likely to receive a promotion than onsite workers. The researchers concluded that a lack of "face time" with bosses caused careers to stall.

In addition, telecommuting employees often have difficulties "training" their families to understand that they are at work even though they are physically at home. Families have to understand that they should not disturb the telecommuter for anything that they would not have disturbed him or her about in a "real" office. The major disadvantages to employers are difficulties in supervising work and potential data security problems.

Yahoo! CEO Marissa Mayer banned telecommuting in her company in February 2013. Best Buy and HP followed suit that same year. Despite being banned at these three large companies, telecommuting continues to grow.

Before you go on…

1. Discuss the advantages and disadvantages of electronic mail.
2. Why are many companies bringing their call centers back to the United States?
3. Describe Voice-over-Internet Protocol.
4. What are the advantages and disadvantages of telecommuting to you as an individual?

Apply the Concept 4.5

LEARNING OBJECTIVE 4.5 Explain the impact that communication network applications have had on business and everyday life.

STEP 1: Background

Section 4.5 has introduced you to the communication aspect of networks that have radically changed the way humans interact with each other. Most of these methods of communication are even available on our mobile devices now via a cellular connection. Such drastic changes have brought about many struggles and possibilities for businesses.

STEP 2: Activity

The methods that we use to communicate today vary greatly from just 50 years ago. Visit http://www.wiley.com/go/rainer/MIS4e/applytheconcept to watch YouTube video about how communication has changed. While it only goes up to 1965, you will still recognize the situations and the uses of improved communications.

STEP 3: Deliverable

Consider the various uses of communications in the video (work, personal, military, emergency, etc.). How do our modern technologies such as Internet, video, mobile, and text impact what is possible on these types of communication? Create a list of the ways that the technologies discussed in this section have changed the way we communicate on a personal level, at work, in emergencies, and in military situations and give a brief explanation of each. Discuss at least three changes for each area of communication. Submit your answers to your professor.

4.6 | Network Applications: Collaboration

The third major category of network applications is collaboration. Collaboration refers to efforts by two or more entities—that is, individuals, teams, groups, or organizations—who work together to accomplish certain tasks. The term workgroup refers specifically to two or more individuals who act together to perform some task.

Workflow is the movement of information as it progresses through the sequence of steps that make up an organization's work procedures. Workflow management makes it possible to pass documents, information, and tasks from one participant to another in a way that is governed by the organization's rules or procedures. Workflow systems are tools for automating business processes.

If group members are working in different locations, they constitute a virtual group (team). Virtual groups conduct *virtual meetings*—that is, they "meet" electronically. Virtual collaboration (or *e-collaboration*) refers to the use of digital technologies that enable organizations or individuals who are geographically dispersed to collaboratively plan, design, develop, manage, and research products, services, and innovative applications. Organizational employees frequently collaborate virtually with one another. In addition, organizations collaborate virtually with customers, suppliers, and other business partners to become more productive and competitive.

Collaboration can be *synchronous*, meaning that all team members meet at the same time. Teams may also collaborate *asynchronously* when team members cannot meet at the same time. Virtual teams, whose members are located throughout the world, typically must collaborate asynchronously.

A variety of software products are available to support all types of collaboration. Among the most prominent are Google Drive (http://drive.google.com), Microsoft SharePoint Workspace (www.microsoft.com/ Sharepoint/default.mspx), Jive (www.jivesoftware.com), and IBM Lotus Quickr (www.ibm.com/lotus/quickr). In general, these products provide online collaboration capabilities, workgroup e-mail, distributed databases, bulletin whiteboards, electronic text editing, document management, workflow capabilities, instant virtual meetings, application sharing, instant messaging, consensus building, voting, ranking, and various application development tools.

These products also provide varying degrees of content control. Google Drive, Microsoft SharePoint Workspace, and Jive provide for shared content with *version management*, whereas Microsoft SharePoint Workspace and IBM Lotus Quickr offer *version control*. Products that provide version management track changes to documents and provide features to accommodate multiple people working on the same document at the same time. In contrast, version-control systems provide each team member with an account that includes a set of permissions. Document directories are often set up so that users must check out documents before they can edit them. When one team member checks out a document, no other member can access it. Once the document has been checked in, it becomes available to other members.

Collaboration is so important that companies are using information technology to enable the process as much as possible. IT's About Business 4.2 shows how Raytheon uses CAVEs to maximize collaboration.

IT's About Business 4.2

MIS   The Collaboration Environment at Raytheon

The Raytheon Company (www.raytheon.com) is a U.S. defense contractor that manufactures weapons and military and commercial electronics. Raytheon's design and development process was high-tech in that it involved computer-aided design (CAD). But it was still low-tech when it came to collaboration. Raytheon engineers would sit together and look at each other's laptops in an extremely time-consuming process. Now, Raytheon engineers designing missiles work with the company's manufacturing and IT departments, as well as partners and suppliers, using stereoscopic 3-D (S3D) and augmented reality technologies.

Raytheon engineers produce CAD product drawings, which become 3D models. In a manner that could be from Star Trek, the models are displayed on S3D screens called Cave Automatic Virtual Environments, or CAVE. A CAVE is a series of 72 ultrahigh-definition 3-D television sets, stacked eight feet high and arranged in a panorama that stretches over 320 degrees.

There are also portable versions of CAVEs that can be used off site. Regardless of the physical form, engineers wear 3-D eyewear and "step into" the CAVE and enter a virtual reality world. They and others around the world can share in seeing products such as missiles in a three-dimensional environment, such as a simulated battle.

The CAVE allows technical blueprints to come to life, so engineers can not only see an object, but touch and manipulate it as well. CAVE users can make quick changes to technical specifications. Potential Raytheon customers, such as military personnel, can walk into a CAVE and adjust equipment according to their needs. CAVE translates the abstract into the real, using what Raytheon calls "the common language of visualization."

The CAVE technology has changed the way that Raytheon works with clients. Instead of giving a presentation to clients, Raytheon engineers sit with them in a CAVE videoconference and they explore the 3-D models together. The technology allows Raytheon designers to show clients their raw materials on the CAVE screens as easily as if they were being spread out on a boardroom table.

One benefit of CAVEs is that it is far more cost-effective to create virtual missile prototypes than it is to build physical prototypes. Another benefit is that CAVEs speed up the design process and get products to market faster. If engineers suspect that something is wrong with the wiring inside a missile prototype, for example, they can examine the 3-D model inside a CAVE and make adjustments quickly, such as moving wires farther away from a part that gets very hot. That would be expensive and time-consuming to do with a physical missile prototype.

CAVEs have improved the level of teamwork both inside Raytheon and with business partners and suppliers. Interestingly, CAVEs have energized customer presentations. Raytheon can put customers right in the field, using CAVEs to simulate a combat environment complete with a desert, mountains, or ocean, for the ultimate in product demonstration. This helps customers focus on what they're looking for. It can also help Raytheon with a classic "upsell" move – showing customers how one product can serve needs they didn't even know they had. As an example, the company used S3D to simulate a battleship at sea to demonstrate a ship-based missile for a client. The customer was so impressed with that missile's capabilities that it ordered a land-based missile with similar functions. The land-based missile was not on the customer's shopping list going in to the presentation.

Raytheon also takes its CAVEs on the road, encouraging middle school students to get involved in STEM (science, technology, engineering, mathematics). The S3D technology isn't just good for product prototypes, either. Raytheon used it to design and test a missile factory in Huntsville, Alabama. The factory itself produces missiles with state-of-the-art robotics and computer-controlled tools.

CAVEs do present challenges. Converting Raytheon's conventional 2-D images to 3-D images involves time and effort. It's also not possible to entirely escape the physical world, as the company must invest in the space and TV screens needed to construct the large CAVEs.

The benefits of S3D are many. The technology has allowed Raytheon to avoid potential design and mock-up errors, saving considerable amounts of time and money. It's shaved countless hours off the time to engineer and manufacture products. It's cut down on the amount of travel for Raytheon engineers to visit suppliers. It's enabled Raytheon to review and complete designs faster. And it's helped identify potential mechanical defects that might have gone undetected until the product was on the production line.

What's next for Raytheon's S3D? It's working on the next generation of the technology, which will not require CAVE users to don eyewear. The firm is evaluating the virtual-reality headsets from Oculus Rift (www.oculus.com).

Sources: Compiled from J. Meister, "Raytheon Animators Create Simulated Defense Situations," *PDDNet*, September 2, 2015; D. Adams, "Now Showing at Raytheon: Missiles in 3-D," *The Boston Globe*, November 10, 2014; A. Shaheed, "Missile Makers Use Virtual 'CAVE' to Test Weapons," *Fox News*, June 26, 2014; A. Barrie, "Next-Gen Missile Killers Created in a Virtual 'Batcave'," *Fox News*, April 11, 2014; S. O'Neill, "Raytheon 3-D CAVEs Speed Missile Design, Testing," *InformationWeek*, April 1, 2014; "Futuristic Raytheon Alabama Factory Makes Missile with Robots," *madeinalabama.com*, June 18, 2013; www.raytheon.com, accessed September 18, 2015.

Questions

1. Describe the use of information technologies in Raytheon's CAVEs.

2. What are potential disadvantages of using CAVEs in the product design process?

Crowdsourcing

One type of collaboration is crowdsourcing, in which an organization outsources a task to an undefined, generally large group of people in the form of an open call. Crowdsourcing provides many potential benefits to organizations. First, crowds can explore problems—and often resolve them—at relatively low cost, and often very quickly. Second, the organization can tap a wider range of talent than might be present among its employees. Third, by listening to the crowd, organizations gain firsthand insight into their customers' desires. Finally, crowdsourcing taps into the global world of ideas, helping companies work through a rapid design process. Let's look at some examples of crowdsourcing.

- Crowdsourcing help desks: IT help desks are a necessary service on college campuses because students depend on their computers and Internet access to complete their schoolwork and attend class online. At Indiana University at Bloomington, new IT help desks use crowdsourcing to alleviate the cost and pressure of having to answer so many calls. Students and professors post their IT problems on an online forum, where other students and amateur IT experts answer them.   `MIS`

- Recruitment: Champlain College in Vermont developed a Champlain For Reel program, inviting students to share via YouTube videos recounting their experiences at the school and the ways they benefited from their time there. The YouTube channel serves to recruit prospective students and even updates alumni on campus and community events.   `MKT`

- Scitable (www.nature.com/scitable) combines social networking and academic collaboration. Through crowdsourcing, students, professors, and scientists discuss problems, find solutions, and swap resources and journals. Scitable is a free site that lets each individual user turn to crowdsourcing for answers even while helping others.

- Procter & Gamble (P&G) uses InnoCentive (www.innocentive.com), where company researchers post their problems. P&G offers cash rewards to problem solvers.

- SAP's Idea Place (https://ideas.sap.com) generates ideas for not-yet-developed software improvements and innovation. Any person can view the content in the Idea Place. The Idea Place is organized into numerous sessions, or categories, under which the ideas are organized. Once you have posted your idea, other users can vote on it and add comments. Status updates on your idea allow you to follow it as it progresses through the Idea Place. Every idea is reviewed by a team of experts made up of engineers, product managers, and community managers who evaluate the potential for implementation. The ideas with the most votes will receive a higher level of attention from SAP.

Although crowdsourcing has numerous success stories, there are many questions and concerns about this system, including the following:

- Should the crowd be limited to experts? If so, then how would a company go about implementing this policy?

- How accurate is the content created by the nonexperts in the crowd? How is accuracy maintained?

- How is crowd-created content being updated? How can companies be certain the content is relevant?

- The crowd may submit too many ideas, with most of them being worthless. In this scenario, evaluating all of these ideas can be prohibitively expensive. For example, during the BP oil spill in 2010, crowds submitted more than 20,000 suggestions on how to stem the flow of oil. The problem was very technical, so there were many poor suggestions. Nevertheless, despite the fact that BP was under severe time constraints, the company had to evaluate all of the ideas.

- Content contributors may violate copyrights, either intentionally or unintentionally.

- The quality of content (and therefore subsequent decisions) depends on the composition of the crowd. The best decisions may come if the crowd is made up of people with diverse opinions and ideas. In many cases, however, companies do not know the makeup of the crowd in advance.

Electronic Teleconferencing and Video Conferencing

Teleconferencing is the use of electronic communication technology that enables two or more people at different locations to hold a conference. There are several types of teleconferencing. The oldest and simplest is a telephone conference call, where several people talk to one another from multiple locations. The biggest disadvantage of conference calls is that they do not allow the participants to communicate face to face nor can they see graphs, charts, and pictures at other locations.

To overcome these shortcomings, organizations are increasingly turning to video teleconferencing or videoconferencing. In a **videoconference**, participants in one location can view participants, documents, and presentations at other locations. The latest version of videoconferencing, called *telepresence*, enables participants to seamlessly share data, voice, pictures, graphics, and animation by electronic means. Conferees can also transmit data along with voice and video, which allows them to work together on documents and to exchange computer files.

Telepresence systems range from on-premise, high-end systems to cloud-based systems. (We discuss on-premise computing and cloud computing in Plug IT In 4). On-premise, high-end systems are expensive and require dedicated rooms with large high-definition screens to show people sitting around conference tables (see **Figure 4.11**). These systems have advanced audio capabilities that let everyone talk at once without canceling out any voices. These systems also require technical staff to operate and maintain. Examples of high-end systems include Cisco's TelePresence system (www.cisco.com) and Polycom's RealPresence Immersive system (www.polycom.com).

Interestingly, in 2006, Cisco's telepresence system cost approximately $300,000 per installation, but in September 2015 the company offered its system for approximately $20,000. This steep decline in pricing is a good example of Moore's Law in action. (See Plug IT In 2.)

However, having dedicated rooms where telepresence meetings take place is not particularly useful when so many employees work remotely. As a result, companies such as Fuze (www.fuze.com) and BlueJeans Nework (www.bluejeans.com) offer telepresence systems that utilize cloud computing. The cloud delivery model means that Fuze and BlueJeans provide systems that are cheaper, more flexible, and require fewer in-house technical staff to operate and maintain. In addition, Fuze and BlueJeans can deliver their telepresence systems to any device, including smartphones, tablets, and laptop and desktop computers.

Monthly telepresence subscription fees for Fuze and BlueJeans cost $10 to $15 per user per month. In response, Cisco is now offering cloud-based telepresence systems at monthly rates of $25 per user and high-end, conference room telepresence systems at monthly rates of $5,100 per user.

FIGURE 4.11 Telepresence system.

HO Marketwire Photos/NewsCom

Before you go on…

1. Describe virtual collaboration and why it is important to you.

2. Define crowdsourcing and provide two examples of crowdsourcing not mentioned in this section.

3. Identify the business conditions that have made videoconferencing more important.

Apply the Concept 4.6

LEARNING OBJECTIVE 4.6 Explain the impact that collaboration network applications have had on business and everyday life.

STEP 1: Background

As you have seen, collaboration tools impact people inside and outside of the organization. Some collaboration tools allow geographically separated employees to work together while some allow those across the hall to work more effectively. Other tools just allow larger groups to brainstorm and be creative. The big idea here is that there is synergy created when people are able to work together via digital tools that overcome time and space.

STEP: Activity

Brightidea is a company that provides a suite of products that touches on many of the topics in the chapter. Visit http://www

.wiley.com/go/rainer/MIS4e/applytheconcept and watch the YouTube video that introduces the company. Then click the second link to visit the Brightidea website. There are several case studies, videos, and product explanations that will help you understand what this product offers.

STEP 3: Deliverable

As you peruse Brightidea's website, look for evidence that the software supports the topics discussed in this section: workflow, virtual collaboration, crowdsourcing, and teleconferencing. Prepare a set of presentation slides (use any tool at your disposal or at your instructors request) that discusses the impact that collaboration network applications (such as Brightidea's products) have had on businesses. ßPresent your slides to your class and professor.

4.7 | Network Applications: Educational

The fourth major category of network applications consists of education applications. In this section, we discuss e-learning, distance learning, and virtual universities.

E-Learning and Distance Learning

E-learning and distance learning are not the same thing, but they do overlap. E-learning refers to learning supported by the Web. It can take place inside classrooms as a support to conventional teaching, such as when students work on the Web during class. It also can take place in virtual classrooms, in which all coursework is completed online and classes do not meet face-to-face. In these cases, e-learning is a part of distance learning. Distance learning (DL) refers to any learning situation in which teachers and students do not meet face-to-face.

Today, the Web provides a multimedia interactive environment for self-study. Web-enabled systems make knowledge accessible to those who need it, when they need it, anytime, anywhere. For this reason, e-learning and DL can be useful for both formal education and corporate training.

There are many benefits of e-learning. For example, online materials can deliver very current content that is of high quality (created by content experts) and consistent (presented the same way every time). It also gives students the flexibility to learn at any place, at any time, and at their own pace. In corporate training centers that use e-learning, learning time generally is shorter, which means that more people can be trained within a given time frame. This system reduces training costs and eliminates the expense of renting facility space.

Despite these benefits, e-learning has some drawbacks. For one, students must be computer literate. Also, they may miss the face-to-face interaction with instructors and fellow students. In addition, accurately assessing students' work can be problematic because instructors really do not know who completed the assignments.

E-learning does not usually replace the classroom setting. Rather, it enhances it by taking advantage of new content and delivery technologies. Advanced e-learning support environments, such as Blackboard (www.blackboard.com), add value to traditional learning in higher education.

A new form of distance learning has recently appeared, called *massive open online courses* or *MOOCs*. MOOCs are a tool for democratizing higher education. Several factors have contributed to the growth of MOOCs, including improved technology and the rapidly increasing costs of traditional universities. MOOCs are highly automated, complete with computer-graded assignments and exams.

MOOCs have not yet proved that they can effectively teach the thousands of students who enroll in them. In addition, they do not provide revenues for universities. Further, MOOCs can register a mixture of high school students, retirees, faculty, enrolled students, and working professionals. Designing a course that adequately meets the needs of such a diverse student population is difficult. Finally, although initial registrations for a MOOC might exceed 100,000 students, completion rates in any one MOOC tend to be less than 10 percent.

Hundreds of thousands of students around the world who lack access to universities are using MOOCs to acquire sophisticated skills and high-paying jobs without having to pay tuition or obtain a college degree. IT's About Business 4.3 takes a closer look at MOOCs in India.

IT's About Business 4.3

Massive Open Online Courses in India

MOOCs in India With 3.2 million students enrolled in India's universities, there are simply not enough professors to teach everyone in person. Some rural universities cannot even offer essential courses. In many universities, first-year courses are taught by people with just a bachelor's degree. Further, a degree from most of India's 35,000 colleges does not mean a great deal to international employers. India's best hope to address this problem is a greater role for online education.

Today, many fields, particular ones in technical areas, are embracing online education for career advancement. Indian enrollments account for about 8 percent of worldwide activity in Coursera (www.coursera.org) and 12 percent in edX (www.edx.org), the two leading providers of massive open online courses, or MOOCs. Only the U.S.'s share is higher. Coursera's most popular offering in India is a University of Maryland course on how to build mobile applications for Android devices. After that course come Python programming classes from the University of Michigan and Rice University, followed by a Stanford University class on machine learning.

In the United States and Europe, MOOCs have proved to be less revolutionary than first predicted when they became popular in 2012. Rather than displacing traditional undergraduate programs, MOOCs in developed economies find their largest audiences among people eager to learn more about specific subjects.

Among college students and recent graduates in India, online courses from the United States and Europe are immensely popular. They see taking the right technical courses as a means of advancing in their careers. They are also frequently willing to pay $20 to $250 for a certificate that attests to their successful performance on a final exam.

Consider one Indian student who took his country's most difficult college placement exam, the Indian Institutes of Technology (IIT) Joint Entrance Exam. Fewer than 3 percent of the more than 300,000 students who attempted the test qualified for a place at one of the elite Indian Institutes of Technology. This student's score, which placed him in the top 1 percent of exam-takers, gained him entrance to IIT Delhi (www.iitd.ac.in). But he didn't place high enough to qualify for the school's most competitive degree program, computer science. As a result, he was told to major in civil engineering.

He took civil engineering courses, but he didn't want to be a civil engineer, so he took a variety of management courses as well. As a result, he landed his first job after graduation at Wipro (www.wipro.com), one of India's leading information-technology companies. He then enrolled in three online data science classes via Coursera, all taught by Johns Hopkins professors. By earning certificates from the courses, he gained the attention of Dunnhumby (www.dunnhumby.com), one of England's largest customer-analytics companies. He now works for them as a Delhi-based senior analyst.

Companies such as Google, Wipro, Infosys, Infineon, and Microsoft have hired Indian engineers with online-education credentials. Thousands of Indian engineers now list schools such as Stanford, MIT, and Carnegie Mellon on LinkedIn as part of their educational background, based solely on their having completed online courses offered by professors at those U.S. universities.

Eager to establish that India can create its own advanced online classes rather than simply import content from the United States, in 2014 the Ministry of Human Resources Development introduced plans for its own MOOC platform, called Swayam. As of June 2015, only three Swayam courses had been announced. By way of comparison, Coursera and edX each offers more than 500 online classes.

Significantly, Indian professors have noted several limitations in MOOCs. They maintain that making the technology work is the easy part. The greater challenge is to rearrange university priorities so that India's best instructors have enough discretionary time to build MOOCs. Another problem is schools' reluctance to provide academic credit for online learning.

In addition, Indian professors have found that it is difficult to test the depth of students' understanding of the material. The MOOC format requires professors to develop assignments and exams that can be machine-graded, which biases the material toward more superficial questions than a traditional classroom exam would contain. The professors have concluded that students are more likely to gain an "awareness" of a field than to acquire in-depth knowledge.

The All India Council for Technical Education is working to establish new guidelines that would allow students to earn 15 percent of their credits online. One proposal would permit outlying colleges to use a blended model, in which online instruction supplements class lectures and discussions. That approach has been incorporated into the 2015-2016 academic year, with 50 of India's autonomous institutes working with IIT Bombay to offer blended MOOCs in three subjects: Introduction to Computer Programming, Thermodynamics, and Quantum Mechanics and Quantum Computation.

Sources: Compiled from P. Newton, "How MOOCs Are Impacting India's Business Education," *IntelligenceHQ*, August 12, 2015; G. Anders, "India Loves MOOCs," *MIT Technology Review*, July 27, 2015; "SWAYAM—MOOC Initiative by India," *EduWire*, June 7, 2015; "Can MOOCs Improve India's Higher Education?" *discover.isif.asia*, May 26, 2015; F. Nisha and V. Senthil, "MOOCs: Changing Trend Towards Open Distance Learning with Special Reference to India," *Journal of Library & Information Technology*, March, 2015; A. Vishnoi, "MOOCs Platform: PM Narendra Modi's Gift to Nation on I-Day," *India Today*, August 12, 2014; P. Bharti, "Indian HRD Ministry Launches a MOOC Platform—SWAYAM," *EdTechReview*, October 16, 2014; D. Shah, "India Announces Official MOOC Platform 'Swayam'," *Class Central*, October 2, 2014; C. Fox, "Higher, Open Education for India," *OpenSource.com*, August 29, 2013; M. Nair, "MOOCs Click with Indians," *The Times of India*, August 18, 2013.

Questions

1. Discuss possible quality control issues with MOOCs in India. For each issue, explain how you would solve the problem.
2. Discuss the possible impacts of MOOCs on traditional higher education in India.
3. Would you be willing to enroll in a MOOC as a full-time student at your university? Why or why not?
4. Would you be willing to enroll in a MOOC after you graduate? Why or why not?

Virtual Universities

Virtual universities are online universities in which students take classes via the Internet either at home or in an off-site location. A large number of existing universities offer online education of some form. Some universities, such as the University of Phoenix (www.phoenix.edu), California Virtual Campus (www.cvc.edu), and the University of Maryland (www.umuc.edu), offer thousands of courses and dozens of degrees to students worldwide, all of them online. Other universities offer limited online courses and degrees, but they employ innovative teaching methods and multimedia support in the traditional classroom.

Before you go on...

1. Describe the differences between e-learning and distance learning.
2. What are virtual universities? Would you be willing to attend a virtual university? Why or why not?

Apply the Concept 4.7

LEARNING OBJECTIVE 4.7 Explain the impact that educational network applications have had on business and everyday life.

STEP 1: Background

Imagine that you are an expert in math. Someone hands you a piece of chalk and a chalkboard and gives you a task of creating an educational experience to share your knowledge with other people. You would probably create a traditional classroom. Now imagine that you are not handed chalk, but the Internet, video

capabilities, file sharing, collaboration, tools, and more! Imagine the possibilities!

STEP 2: Activity

Visit http://www.wiley.com/go/rainer/MIS4e/applytheconcept and visit the Web site about Brightspace. Be sure to look at the video about how technology has changed education. Brightspace (you may have heard it called by its former name, Desire2Learn) is a learning management system that several schools use as a platform to offer educational activities using the digital tools available today.

This platform can be used to offer e-learning experiences, distance learning opportunities, or fully virtual classrooms.

There are many discussions about how these educational network applications impact individual's everyday life. Single parents are able to go to school using educational network applications. Working professionals are able to pursue graduate degrees online. But what about the impact on businesses?

STEP 3: Deliverable

Many organizations use these tools to facilitate mandatory training or for onboarding new employees. Visit http://www.wiley.com/go/rainer/MIS4e/applytheconcept and view the second link about Brightspace's enterprise offerings. Research their site to create and discuss a list of five ways that educational network applications impact businesses.

What's in IT for me?

ACCT For the Accounting Major

Accounting personnel use corporate intranets and portals to consolidate transaction data from legacy systems to provide an overall view of internal projects. This view contains the current costs charged to each project, the number of hours spent on each project by individual employees, and an analysis of how actual costs compare with projected costs. Finally, accounting personnel use Internet access to government and professional Web sites to stay informed on legal and other changes affecting their profession.

FIN For the Finance Major

Corporate intranets and portals can provide a model to evaluate the risks of a project or an investment. Financial analysts use two types of data in the model: historical transaction data from corporate databases via the intranet and industry data obtained via the Internet. In addition, financial services firms can use the Web for marketing and to provide services.

MKT For the Marketing Major

Marketing managers use corporate intranets and portals to coordinate the activities of the sales force. Sales personnel access corporate portals via the intranet to discover updates on pricing, promotion, rebates, customer information, and information about competitors. Sales staff can also download and customize presentations for their customers. The Internet, particularly the Web, opens a completely new marketing channel for many industries. Just how advertising, purchasing, and information dispensation should occur appears to vary from industry to industry, product to product, and service to service.

POM For the Production/Operations Management Major

Companies are using intranets and portals to speed product development by providing the development team with three-dimensional models and animation. All team members can access the models for faster exploration of ideas and enhanced feedback. Corporate portals, accessed via intranets, enable managers to carefully supervise their inventories as well as real-time production on assembly lines. Extranets are also proving valuable as communication formats for joint research and design efforts among companies. The Internet is also a great source of cutting-edge information for POM managers.

HRM For the Human Resources Management Major

Human resources personnel use portals and intranets to publish corporate policy manuals, job postings, company telephone directories, and training classes. Many companies deliver online training obtained from the Internet to employees through their intranets. Human resources departments use intranets to offer employees healthcare, savings, and benefit plans, as well as the opportunity to take competency tests online. The Internet supports worldwide recruiting efforts; it can also be the communications platform for supporting geographically dispersed work teams.

MIS For the MIS Major

As important as the networking technology infrastructure is, it is invisible to users (unless something goes wrong). The MIS function is responsible for keeping all organizational networks up and running all the time. MIS personnel, therefore, provide all users with an "eye to the world" and the ability to compute, communicate, and collaborate anytime, anywhere. For example, organizations have access to experts at remote locations without having to duplicate that expertise in multiple areas of the firm. Virtual teaming allows experts physically located in different cities to work on projects as though they were in the same office.

Summary

1. Compare and contrast the two major types of networks.

The two major types of networks are local area networks (LANs) and wide area networks (WANs). LANs encompass a limited geographical area and are usually composed of one communications medium. In contrast, WANs encompass a broad geographical area and are usually composed of multiple communications media.

2. Describe the wireline communications media and channels.

Twisted-pair wire, the most prevalent form of communications wiring, consists of strands of copper wire twisted in pairs. It is relatively inexpensive to purchase, widely available, and easy to work with. However, it is relatively slow for transmitting data, it is subject to interference from other electrical sources, and it can be easily tapped by unintended receivers.

Coaxial cable consists of insulated copper wire. It is much less susceptible to electrical interference than is twisted-pair wire and it can carry much more data. However, coaxial cable is more expensive and more difficult to work with than twisted-pair wire. It is also somewhat inflexible.

Fiber-optic cables consist of thousands of very thin filaments of glass fibers that transmit information via light pulses generated by lasers. Fiber-optic cables are significantly smaller and lighter than traditional cable media. They can also transmit far more data, and they provide greater security from interference and tapping. Fiber-optic cable is often used as the backbone for a network, whereas twisted-pair wire and coaxial cable connect the backbone to individual devices on the network.

3. Describe the most common methods for accessing the Internet.

Common methods for connecting to the Internet include dial-up, DSL, cable modem, satellite, wireless, and fiber to the home.

4. Explain the impact that discovery network applications have had on business and everyday life.

Discovery involves browsing and information retrieval, and provides users the ability to view information in databases, download it, and/or process it. Discovery tools include search engines, directories, and portals. Discovery tools enable business users to efficiently find needed information.

5. Explain the impact that communication network applications have had on business and everyday life.

Networks provide fast, inexpensive *communications*, via e-mail, call centers, chat rooms, voice communications, and blogs. Communications tools provide business users with a seamless interface among team members, colleagues, business partners, and customers.

Telecommuting is the process whereby knowledge workers are able to work anywhere and anytime. Telecommuting provides flexibility for employees, with many benefits and some drawbacks.

6. Explain the impact that collaboration network applications have had on business and everyday life.

Collaboration refers to mutual efforts by two or more entities (individuals, groups, or companies) who work together to accomplish tasks. Collaboration is enabled by workflow systems. Collaboration tools enable business users to collaborate with colleagues, business partners, and customers.

7. Explain the impact that educational network applications have had on business and everyday life.

E-learning refers to learning supported by the Web. Distance learning refers to any learning situation in which teachers and students do not meet face-to-face. E-learning provides tools for business users to enable their lifelong learning.

Virtual universities are online universities in which students take classes via the Internet at home or an off-site location. Virtual universities make it possible for students to obtain degrees while working full time, thus increasing their value to their firms.

Chapter Glossary

affinity portal A Web site that offers a single point of entry to an entire community of affiliated interests.

analog signals Continuous waves that transmit information by altering the amplitude and frequency of the waves.

backbone networks High-speed central networks to which multiple smaller networks (e.g., LANs and smaller WANs) connect.

bandwidth The transmission capacity of a network, stated in bits per second.

broadband The transmission capacity of a communications medium faster than 4 Mbps.

broadcast media (also called **wireless media**) Communications channels that use electromagnetic media (the "airwaves") to transmit data.

browsers Software applications through which users primarily access the Web.

cable media (also called **wireline media**) Communications channels that use physical wires or cables to transmit data and information.

chat room A virtual meeting place where groups of regulars come to "gab" electronically.

client/server computing Form of distributed processing in which some machines (servers) perform computing functions for end-user PCs (clients).

clients Computers, such as users' personal computers, that use any of the services provided by servers.

coaxial cable Insulated copper wire; used to carry high-speed data traffic and television signals.

collaboration Mutual efforts by two or more individuals who perform activities in order to accomplish certain tasks.

commercial (public) portal A Web site that offers fairly routine content for diverse audiences; offers customization only at the user interface.

communications channel Pathway for communicating data from one location to another.

computer network A system that connects computers and other devices via communications media so that data and information can be transmitted among them.

corporate portal A Web site that provides a single point of access to critical business information located inside and outside of an organization.

crowdsourcing A process in which an organization outsources a task to an undefined, generally large group of people in the form of an open call.

digital signals A discrete pulse, either on or off, that conveys information in a binary form.

distance learning (DL) Learning situations in which teachers and students do not meet face-to-face.

distributed processing Network architecture that divides processing work between two or more computers, linked together in a network.

domain name system (DNS) The system administered by the Internet Corporation for Assigned Names (ICANN) that assigns names to each site on the Internet.

domain names The name assigned to an Internet site, consisting of multiple parts, separated by dots, which are translated from right to left.

e-learning Learning supported by the Web; can be done inside traditional classrooms or in virtual classrooms.

enterprise network An organization's network composed of interconnected multiple LANs and WANs.

Ethernet A common local area network protocol.

extranet A network that connects parts of the intranets of different organizations.

fiber-optic cable A communications medium consisting of thousands of very thin filaments of glass fibers, surrounded by cladding, that transmit information via light pulses generated by lasers.

file server (also called network server) A computer that contains various software and data files for a local area network and contains the network operating system.

hyperlink A connection from a hypertext file or document to another location or file, typically activated by clicking on a highlighted word or image on the screen, or by touching the screen.

hypertext Text displayed on a computer display with references, called hyperlinks, to other text that the reader can immediately access.

Hypertext Transport Protocol (HTTP) The communications standard used to transfer pages across the WWW portion of the Internet; defines how messages are formulated and transmitted.

industrywide portal A Web-based gateway to information and knowledge for an entire industry.

Internet (the Net) A massive global WAN that connects approximately 1 million organizational computer networks in more than 200 countries on all continents, including Antarctica, and features in the daily routine of almost 2 billion people. Participating computer systems include smartphones, PCs, LANs, databases, and mainframes.

Internet backbone The primary network connections and telecommunications lines that link the computers and organizational nodes of the Internet.

Internet Protocol (IP) A set of rules responsible for disassembling, delivering, and reassembling packets over the Internet.

Internet Protocol (IP) address An assigned address that uniquely identifies a computer on the Internet.

Internet service provider (ISP) A company that provides Internet connections for a fee.

Internet telephony (Voice-over-Internet Protocol or VoIP) The use of the Internet as the transmission medium for telephone calls.

Internet2 A new, faster telecommunications network that deploys advanced network applications such as remote medical diagnosis, digital libraries, distance education, online simulation, and virtual laboratories.

intranet A private network that uses Internet software and TCP/IP protocols.

local area network (LAN) A network that connects communications devices in a limited geographic region, such as a building, so that every user device on the network can communicate with every other device.

metasearch engine A computer program that searches several engines at once and integrates the findings of the various search engines to answer queries posted by users.

modem Device that converts signals from analog to digital and vice versa.

network access points (NAPs) Computers that act as exchange points for Internet traffic and determine how traffic is routed.

network server See file server.

packet switching The transmission technology that divides blocks of text into packets.

peer-to-peer (P2P) processing A type of client/server distributed processing that allows two or more computers to pool their resources, making each computer both a client and a server.

portal A Web-based personalized gateway to information and knowledge that provides information from disparate information systems and the Internet, using advanced search and indexing techniques.

protocol The set of rules and procedures governing transmission across a network.

router A communications processor that routes messages from a LAN to the Internet, across several connected LANs, or across a wide area network such as the Internet.

search engine A computer program that searches for specific information by keywords and reports the results.

servers Computers that provide access to various network services, such as printing, data, and communications.

telecommuting A work arrangement whereby employees work at home, at the customer's premises, in special workplaces, or while traveling, usually using a computer linked to their place of employment.

teleconferencing The use of electronic communication that allows two or more people at different locations to have a simultaneous conference.

Transmission Control Protocol/Internet Protocol (TCP/IP) A file transfer protocol that can send large files of information across sometimes unreliable networks with assurance that the data will arrive uncorrupted.

twisted-pair wire A communications medium consisting of strands of copper wire twisted together in pairs.

unified communications Common hardware and software platform that simplifies and integrates all forms of communications—voice, e-mail, instant messaging, location, and videoconferencing—across an organization.

uniform resource locator (URL) The set of letters that identifies the address of a specific resource on the Web.

videoconference A virtual meeting in which participants in one location can see and hear participants at other locations and can share data and graphics by electronic means.

virtual collaboration The use of digital technologies that enable organizations or individuals to collaboratively plan, design, develop, manage, and research products, services, and innovative information systems and electronic commerce applications.

virtual group (team) A workgroup whose members are in different locations and who meet electronically.

virtual universities Online universities in which students take classes via the Internet at home or at an off-site location.

Voice-over-Internet Protocol (VoIP) See **Internet telephony**.

Web site Collectively, all of the Web pages of a particular company or individual.

wide area network (WAN) A network, generally provided by common carriers, that covers a wide geographical area.

wireless media See **broadcast media**.

wireline media See **cable media**.

workgroup Two or more individuals who act together to perform some task, on either a permanent or on a temporary basis.

workflow The movement of information as it flows through the sequence of steps that make up an organization's work procedures.

World Wide Web (the Web, WWW, or W3) A system of universally accepted standards for storing, retrieving, formatting, and displaying information via a client/server architecture; it uses the transport functions of the Internet.

Discussion Questions

1. What are the implications of having fiber-optic cable to everyone's home?

2. What are the implications of BitTorrent for the music industry? For the motion picture industry?

3. Discuss the pros and cons of P2P networks.

4. Should the Internet be regulated? If so, by whom?

5. Discuss the pros and cons of delivering this book over the Internet.

6. Explain how the Internet works. Assume you are talking with someone who has no knowledge of information technology (in other words, keep it very simple).

7. How are the network applications of communication and collaboration related? Do communication tools also support collaboration? Give examples.

8. Search online for the article from *The Atlantic*: "Is Google Making Us Stupid?" *Is* Google making us stupid? Support your answer.

9. *Network neutrality* is an operating model under which Internet service providers (ISPs) must allow customers equal access to content and applications, regardless of the source or nature of the content. That is, Internet backbone carriers must treat all Web traffic equally, not charging different rates by user, content, site, platform, or application.

   Telecommunications and cable companies want to replace network neutrality with an arrangement in which they can charge differentiated prices based on the amount of bandwidth consumed by the content

that is being delivered over the Internet. ISPs further contend that net neutrality hinders U.S. international competitiveness by decreasing innovation and discouraging capital investments in new network technologies. Without such investments and innovations, ISPs will be unable to handle the exploding demand for Internet and wireless data transmission.

From the opposite perspective, proponents of network neutrality argue that the risk of censorship increases when network providers can selectively block or slow access to certain content, such as access to competing low-cost services such as Skype and Vonage. They also assert that a neutral Internet encourages innovation. Finally, they contend that the neutral Internet has helped to create many new businesses.

   a. How do you feel about the net neutrality issue?

   b. Do you believe heavier bandwidth users should pay for more bandwidth?

   c. Do you believe wireless carriers should operate under different rules than wireline carriers?

   d. Evaluate your own bandwidth usage. (For example: Do you upload and download large files, such as movies?) If network neutrality were to be eliminated, what would the impact be for you?

10. Should businesses monitor network usage? Do see a problem with employees using company-purchased bandwidth for personal use? Please explain your answer.

Problem-Solving Activities

1. Calculate how much bandwidth you consume when using the Internet every day. How many e-mails do you send daily and what is the size of each? (Your e-mail program may have e-mail file size information.) How many music and video clips do you download (or upload) daily and what is the size of each? If you view YouTube often, surf the Web to find out the size of a typical YouTube file. Add up the number of e-mail, audio, and video files you transmit or receive on a typical day. When you have calculated your daily Internet usage, determine if you are a "normal" Internet user or a "power" Internet user. What impact does network neutrality have on you as a "normal" user? As a "power" user?

2. Access several P2P applications, such as SETI@home. Describe the purpose of each application, and indicate which ones you would like to join.

3. Access http://ipv6.com and www.ipv6news.info and learn about more advantages of IPv6.

4. Access www.icann.org and learn more about this important organization.

5. Set up your own Web site using your name for the domain name (e.g., KellyRainer).

    a. Explain the process for registering a domain.

    b. Which top-level domain will you use and why?

6. Access www.icann.org and obtain the name of an agency or company that can register a domain for the TLD that you selected. What is the name of that agency or company?

7. Access the Web site for that agency or company (in question 6) to learn the process that you must use. How much will it initially cost to register your domain name? How much will it cost to maintain that name in the future?

8. You plan to take a two-week vacation in Australia this year. Using the Internet, find information that will help you plan the trip. Such information includes, *but is not limited to*, the following:

    a. Geographical location and weather conditions at the time of your trip

    b. Major tourist attractions and recreational facilities

    c. Travel arrangements (airlines, approximate fares)

    d. Car rental; local tours

    e. Alternatives for accommodation (within a moderate budget) and food

    f. Estimated cost of the vacation (travel, lodging, food, recreation, shopping, etc.)

    g. Country regulations regarding the entrance of your dog

    h. Shopping

    i. Passport information (either to obtain one or to renew one)

    j. Information on the country's language and culture

    k. What else do you think you should research before going to Australia?

9. From your own experience or from the vendor's information, list the major capabilities of Lotus Notes/Domino. Do the same for Microsoft Exchange. Compare and contrast the products. Explain how the products can be used to support knowledge workers and managers.

10. Visit Web sites of companies that manufacture telepresence products for the Internet. Prepare a report. Differentiate between telepresence products and videoconferencing products.

11. Access Google (or YouTube) videos and search for "Cisco Magic." This video shows Cisco's next-generation telepresence system. Compare and contrast it with current telepresence systems.

12. Access the Web site of your university. Does the Web site provide high-quality information (right amount, clear, accurate, etc.)? Do you think a high-school student who is thinking of attending your university would feel the same way?

13. Compare and contrast Google Sites (www.google.com/sites) and Microsoft Office Live (www.liveoffice.com). Which site would you use to create your own Web site? Explain your choice.

14. Access the Web site of the Recording Industry Association of America (www.riaa.com). Discuss what you find there regarding copyright infringement (i.e., downloading music files). How do you feel about the RIAA's efforts to stop music downloads? Debate this issue from your point of view and from the RIAA's point of view.

15. Research the companies involved in Internet telephony (Voice-over IP). Compare their offerings as to price, necessary technologies, ease of installation, and so on. Which company is the most attractive to you? Which company might be the most attractive for a large company?

16. Access various search engines other than Google. Search for the same terms on several of the alternative search engines and on Google. Compare the results on breadth (number of results found) and precision (results are what you were looking for).

17. Second Life (www.secondlife.com) is a three-dimensional, online world built and owned by its residents. Residents of Second Life are avatars who have been created by real people. Access Second Life, learn about it, and create your own avatar to explore this world. Learn about the thousands of people who are making "real-world" money from operations in Second Life.

18. Access Microsoft's Bing translator (http://www.microsofttranslator.com) or Google (www.google.com/language_tools) translation pages. Type in a paragraph in English and select, for example, English-to-French. When you see the translated paragraph in French, copy it into the text box, and select French-to-English. Is the paragraph that you first entered the same as the one you are looking at now? Why or why not? Support your answer.

Closing Case 1

POM   Using Technology for Sustainable Seafood

MKT   **The Problem**

MIS   To avoid a tariff of approximately 65 percent imposed on low-priced imports of fish, some foreign seafood businesses deliberately mislabel cheaper fish species as more expensive species to mislead inspectors. In one case, a business saved more than $60 million in tariffs by labeling Asian catfish as grouper. In 2013 Oceana (www.oceana.org), a nonprofit U.S. organization, performed DNA tests on 1,200 fish samples and found that one-third had been mislabeled.

Researchers tend to identify seafood fraud with foreign fisheries. A large majority of the seafood consumed in the United States is imported from countries with loose aquaculture laws, with Thailand and Vietnam being the worst offenders.

The Pew Charitable Trusts (www.pewtrusts.org) estimates that one of every five fish taken from the ocean is caught illegally. This practice depletes stocks of certain species (e.g., tuna) to levels that threaten their survival. Whether it is to avoid fines for fishing without permits or for exceeding their quotas or to boost profits, fishermen often try to pass off one type of fish as another.

Potential Solutions

For decades, DNA sequencing has been the only tool that can positively identify the correct species of fish. However, the process takes at least 12 hours, which is too much time for most wholesale buying decisions. Today, however, Grouperchek, a portable technology, can accurately identify one species of fish—grouper—in 45 minutes, for only $30. Grouperchek developers are working to expand the technology's capabilities to other species of fish.

Shellcatch (www.shellcatch.com) is providing another solution. The San Francisco-based startup is taking advantage of the increasing demand for sustainable seafood. The company hopes that its technology will combat the overfishing and fraud that threaten the international seafood trade. Shellcatch claims that its technology lets consumers know the people behind the fish they are eating.

Shellcatch is trying to fill a gap in the marketplace. Many countries already require large commercial fishing boats to be equipped with either vessel-monitoring systems or human observers to certify that the boats are not straying into protected areas. However, these systems are too expensive. In addition, they are often logistically impossible to implement across millions of small fishing boats.

In the past, Chilean fishermen have fished for flounder and abalone using nets, hooks, and their accumulated knowledge of their craft. Today, they also utilize satellite networks and cloud computing to earn the best possible price for their catch. Approximately 250 Chilean fishermen have signed on to use Shellcatch technology. The Chilean office of the Nature Conservancy provided $106,000 in grant support and training for to help fishermen deploy Shellcatch's equipment on their boats.

Fishing boats using Shellcatch have a small GPS-enabled camera that records which types of fish they catch and where. On the dock, the fishermen weigh their catches on a video-equipped scale and tag them with unique Shellcatch bar codes and Quick Response (QR) codes. The data are then uploaded into the cloud, where a diner at a restaurant can retrieve them by waving a smartphone over the menu. Diners can also access photos of the fisherman making the catch, which is a detail calculated to appeal to consumers who want to know the identity and origin of their food. One restaurant owner notes that many of her customers like to find out information about the fish on their tables, even down to the particular cove where the fish was caught.

Shellcatch's hardware is suitable for small boats. The device is compact and waterproof, and it has a long battery life, so it can be used on boats with no power source. The software is constantly upgraded, to further automate the monitoring process. Shellcatch uses video analytics, which, for instance can detect whether sea turtles are being accidentally caught in fishing nets. The Mexican government, which is facing the threat of U.S. trade sanctions over the rising death toll of endangered loggerhead sea turtles in the Northern Pacific, is paying Shellcatch to monitor 16 fishing boats. The U.S. claims that Mexican fishermen are catching the turtles in their nets; Mexico denies the charges. Shellcatch has announced that it will soon begin monitoring an additional 200 boats in Mexican waters.

The Results

Chilean fishermen who use Shellcatch claim they earn a 25 percent premium, on average, for their catch from upscale restaurants and supermarkets that want to know in which waters their fish are caught. The fishermen also believe that Shellcatch can help reverse years of overfishing. The reason is they can catch fewer fish and still earn the same amount of money.

Shellcatch's business plan is to eventually make a profit by selling its services to fishermen who want to sell traceable fish. In 2015, some of the Chilean fishermen the company had recruited did indeed begin paying for the service. In addition, Shellcatch has established relationships with more than 50 restaurants, supermarkets, and stores in Chile that purchase seafood verified by the system.

The company's business plan also includes marketing the data it collects to governments, environmental organizations, restaurant owners, retailers, and distributors. The firm could also benefit from President Obama's recent push to clean up the seafood trade by promoting the creation of a system that tracks fish from the boat to the plate. In addition, Shellcatch is expanding its operations to Peru, and it plans to expand to other countries.

Sources: Compiled from D. Bank, "Bountiful Catch for Sustainable Seafood Investors: Finalists in Fish 2.0 Competition," *The Huffington Post*, September 16, 2015; "37 Innovative Seafood Companies to Pitch at Fish 2.0 Finals," *Fish 2.0*, September 14, 2015; The Green Man, "Consumers Can See Who Caught Their Fish," *The Vancouver Sun blogs*, June 2, 2015; C. Elton, "Tracing the Fish on Your Plate Back to the Sea," *Bloomberg BusinessWeek*, May 25-31, 2015; M. Fontanazza, "Untangling the Net of Seafood Fraud," *Food Safety Tech*, April 14, 2015; N. Lou, "Bait and Switch: The Fraud Crisis in the Seafood Industry," *The Atlantic*, March 19, 2015; D. Abel, "U.S. Aims to Curb Seafood Fraud," *The Boston Globe*, March 16, 2015; C. Rentz, "Seafood Fraud Cases Plummet as NOAA Cuts Investigators," *Portland Press Herald*, December 12, 2014; R. Jordan, "Trash to Treasure: Stanford Researcher Tells a Seafood Story," *Stanford News Service*, March 18, 2014; "SmartFish: Catching Gold in the Fish Market," *National Geographic*, November 1, 2013; www.shellcatch.com, www.fish20.org, accessed September 18, 2015.

Questions

1. Describe how the Shellcatch technology benefits fishermen, consumers, and the environment.

2. What are the potential disadvantages of the Shellcatch technology for fishermen?

Closing Case 2

 MKT Local Language Web Sites in India

The Problem

The World Bank (www.worldbank.org) estimates that 80 percent of online content is available in only 1 of 10 languages: English, Chinese, Spanish, Japanese, Arabic, Portuguese, German, French, Russian, and Korean. Roughly three billion people speak one of these as their first language. However, more than half of all online content is written in English, which is understood by only 21 percent of the world's population.

Consider India, whose citizens speak roughly 425 languages and dialects. Industry analysts estimate that less than 0.1 percent of all Web content is composed in Hindi, the first language of approximately 260 million people.

Companies such as Amazon (www.amazon.com) and SoftBank (www.softbank.com) are investing in India to take advantage of rapid increases in Web usage. Since 2013, an additional 100 million Indians have begun accessing the Web, for a total of more than 350 million as of September 2015. In fact, India now is second only to China in total number of Internet users. Further, the Internet & Mobile Association of India (www.iamai.in) predicts that more than 500 million Indians will access the Internet by 2017.

Unfortunately, a large proportion of India's population cannot make use of any existing online offerings. Almost all the Web sites in India are available only in English, a language that is familiar to many middle-class city dwellers but not to a large segment of the country's population. Roughly one-third of the Indians online do not speak English, and they are poorly served because of the lack of localized content.

Consider the case of a resident of the city of Chennai who is a native speaker of Tamil, a language common in India's southern states. His knowledge of English is very limited. He can check his e-mail online and can sometimes use the Internet to look up addresses and phone numbers, but that is about all he can do. Even Indian Web sites that focus on his major interests—yoga, movies, and sports—are of little use to him, because they are written primarily in English. As a result, he depends on books and Tamil newspapers.

Adding to these problems, among India's smartphone users, fewer than 40 percent have devices that can display Hindi, the most common local language. Support for India's nine other major languages is even more limited.

Potential Solutions

U.S. companies seeking to expand in India must be able to manage the language problem, and Google (www.google.com) has taken the lead. Google has been able to expand its language options without having to hire many new workers because the company already has employees from throughout India whom it has enlisted for these projects.

In November 2014, Google announced partnerships with 18 Indian companies, including Process Nine Technologies (www.process9.com) and Reverie Language Technologies (http://go.reverieinc.com), to develop online content in languages other than English. Google is also targeting ads to non-English speakers. In December 2014, the firm introduced AdSense in Hindi, enabling owners of Hindi-language Web sites to purchase Hindi keywords.

Google also made India the first market for its Android One smartphones, priced at about $100. Google worked with Indian phone manufacturers such as Micromax (www.micromaxinfo.com) and Karbonn (www.karbonnmobiles.com) to develop the phones. The Android One supports English and Hindi. In addition, it will add five more local languages when Google releases the next version of its mobile operating system. The Android One also supports Hindi voice-search capabilities.

Other companies are pursuing local-language options as well. In 2014, Microsoft (www.microsoft.com) began offering users the ability to input Hindi text on their mobile phones. Also in 2014, Facebook

announced a contest to encourage developers to create local-language mobile apps. Mozillla, which controls the open-source browser Firefox, is using India as a testing ground for software that customers who buy Firefox-branded smartphones can use to create local-language Web sites and apps.

Among Indian companies, e-commerce Web site Snapdeal (www.snapdeal.com) is a leader, introducing Hindi and Tamil versions in 2014. The country's other two large e-commerce companies, Amazon India and Indian rival Flipkart, are available only in English.

India's government is principally working on more basic issues, such as helping more Indians gain access to the Internet. Prime Minister Modi's government is promoting an $18 billion Digital India campaign (www.digitalindia.gov.in) to expand broadband Internet access and services. However, the government's program to connect 250,000 villages to the Web by 2016 is far behind schedule.

Industry analysts note one outstanding opportunity for Modi's government to pursue, Indian Railways. About 23 million people per day ride Indian Railways (www.indianrail.gov.in), including millions of speakers of Tamil, Bengali, Gujarati, and other local languages. However, the Indian Railways Web site is available only in English and Hindi.

The Results

In March 2015, ongoing monitoring by W3Techs (http://w3techs.com) revealed that more than half of the most visited Web sites in India still had English-language homepages. Therefore, it appears that progress in producing local-language content will remain slow.

Sources: Compiled from "Usage of Content Languages for Web Sites," *http://w3techs.com*, retrieved September 19, 2015; "India Internet Userbase Crosses 350-mn Milestone in June," *Deccan Herald*, September 2, 2015; "India's Internet User Base at 350 Million, to Reach 503 Million by 2017," *Press Trust of India*, July 20, 2015; N. Najar, "India's Leader Maps Out a More Robust Digital Future," *The New York Times*, July 5, 2015; "PM Modi Launches Digital India Campaign: Asks Why Can't Google Be Made in India," *The Economic Times*, July 1, 2015; M. Orcutt, "The Online Language Barrier," *MIT Technology Review*, March 6, 2015; B. Einhorn, M. Sharma, and G. Nagarajan, "Imagine How Hard It Would Be to Use the Internet If You Could Read Only One-Third of It," *Bloomberg BusinessWeek*, January 19-25, 2015; M. Chanchani, "Top E-Tailers Launching Sites in Regional Languages to Woo Customers," *The Economic Times*, July 3, 2014; P. Mishra, "Snapdeal Launches Local Language Site as Indian E-Commerce Goes Native," *TechCrunch*, January 30, 2014.

Questions

1. Suppose that approximately 500 million Indians have access to Web sites in their native languages by 2017. What are the implications for you as students?

2. Why is it so important for U.S. companies to be able to provide content in local languages around the world?

Business Analytics

LEARNING OBJECTIVES

5.1 Use a decision support framework to demonstrate how technology supports managerial decision making at each phase of the decision-making process.

5.2 Describe each phase of the business analytics process.

5.3 Describe each of the various analytics tools and examples of their uses.

5.4 Provide a definition and a use case example for descriptive analytics, predictive analytics, and prescriptive analytics.

Opening Case

Rent the Runway

POM On average, an American woman buys 64 new pieces of clothing per year—half of which she will wear only one time. Facebook and Instagram are actually making matters worse. Today, women often feel that they cannot wear an outfit repeatedly because their friends have seen that outfit on social media. Moreover, fashion industry analysts note that new fashion trends in women's apparel emerge on average every 10 weeks. Therefore, if a woman wants to feel that she is in step with fashion, she would need to change at least part of her wardrobe that frequently.

A major trend in today's economy is a transition from ownership to subscribing and sharing. At least one company has implemented this business model in the fashion industry. Located at the intersection of the sharing economy, Facebook, and Instagram, Rent the Runway (RTR; www.renttherunway.com) buys designer dresses wholesale and rents them over the Web for a night or two, charging only a fraction of the price of the dress. For instance, an RTR customer can wear a Calvin Klein gown that costs thousands of dollars for only $70. In 2015, RTR launched a subscription service called Unlimited that allows customers to borrow up to three accessories (sunglasses, bags, jackets) for as long as they want for $99 per month.

When RTR merchandisers decide whether to buy a new dress, they follow a list of 40 data points such as fabric, zippers, stitching, and shape to determine whether the dress will hold up to the rigors of multiple rentals. The longer the lifespan, the higher the return on capital. In mid-2015, RTR averaged 30 turns (rentals) per dress.

Delivering a delicate designer dress is a difficult, complicated, and expensive operation. The dresses must arrive on time and in perfect condition. One mistake—a late arrival, an unsightly stain, a poor fit—creates a customer relations nightmare. To accomplish the firm's goals, every day RTR algorithms analyze more than 65,000 dresses and 25,000 earrings, bracelets, and necklaces as they move around the country among the firm's five million members. The algorithms enable RTR to ship out 60 percent of the dresses the same day they arrive. In the RTR warehouse, employees sort returns, remove all kinds of stains, sterilize jewelry, and mend tears in clothing. The RTR process works like this:

- Customers return thousands of dresses in barcoded envelopes.
- Employees scan the dresses into the RTR analytics and logistics systems.
- Workers inspect the dresses and sort them into bins marked for regular cleaning, stain removal, or repairs.
- Employees who are part chemists and part artists remove stains from clothing, extending the life of the dresses. A database suggests the optimal chemicals to use for each type of stain and each type of material.
- Automated cleaning machines sterilize and smooth gowns in one minute. (RTR operates the largest dry-cleaning operation in the United States.)
- Seamstresses repair tears, reattach beads, and replace sequins to get gowns ready for wear.
- Orders are assembled and checked for accuracy. The system forecasts dress demand to choose the most cost-effective shipping method for customer returns (ground or overnight air).
- Dresses are double-bagged and mailed to the next customer. To ensure a good fit, customers receive the same dress in two sizes at no extra cost.

With every dress it rents, RTR's analytics algorithms learn more about effective strategies to track the location of each item, forecast demand, select shipping methods, set prices, and control inventory. RTR's algorithms also examine customer reviews to learn which dresses women are renting for certain occasions. They then forecast demand to determine whether the prepaid shipping label that goes with a dress should require the customer to return the dress overnight or whether a three-day return, which costs less, is sufficient.

RTR operates five physical retail locations in the United States—New York City (Flatiron and Soho), Chicago, Las Vegas, and Washington, DC. The company plans to add another 10 locations over the next few years. Prices in the retail stores are identical to online prices. RTR is opening these stores to help alleviate the fears that women have when trying new brands. In addition, in-store customers are likely to explore more styles than they might discover online.

In 2014 the total value of RTR dress and accessory rentals exceeded $800 million, and the company earned $50 million in revenue. Revenue is expected to increase to $80 million in 2015. The number of customers, amount of repeat business, and rental volume doubled in 2014 and are projected to double again in 2015. By mid-2015, RTR had raised $116 million in venture capital funding.

RTR predicts that in 5 to 10 years women's closets will look very different. There will be one portion filled with clothes that she owns and another portion that will be in constant rotation, filled with rented items. Also, RTR predicts that women might go on vacation without taking a suitcase. Instead, they will arrive at their hotel rooms with only one small bag, and they will find their closets already filled with rented clothing from RTR.

Further, the founders envision RTR as a marketplace for retailers and brands to rent unsold inventory instead of shipping it to discount retailers. Their overall strategy is to build the Amazon of retail.

Sources: Compiled from P. Vasan, "Rent the Runway's Designer Closet Tops $800 Million," *CNBC*, July 25, 2015; D. Silver, "A High-End Version of Rent the Runway Is Headed to the Hamptons This Summer," *Observer*, June 4, 2015; E. Nagy, "Rent the Runway's Formula for Finding and Fostering Women Leaders," *Fast Company*, May 13, 2015; L. King, "Be Authentic: Rent the Runway's CEO on How to Win," *Forbes*, March 28, 2015; J. D'Onfro, "Why the CEO of a $400 Million E-Commerce Company Wants UPS and FedEx 'Out of Business,'" *Business Insider*, March 18, 2015; J. D'Onfro, "This Startup Founder Wants You to Be Able to Go on a Vacation Without Packing a Suitcase," *Business Insider*, March 14, 2015; R. King, "Q&A: How Rent the Runway Dazzles Shoppers with Data," *ZDNet*, February 20, 2015; A. Agarwal, "The Key to Successful Commerce Businesses Is Supply Chain," *TechCrunch*, December 24, 2014; S. Bertoni, "The Billion-Dollar Dress," *Forbes*, September 8, 2014; A. Samuel, "Established Companies, Get Ready for the Collaborative Economy," *Harvard Business Review*, March 4, 2014; www.renttherunway.com, accessed August 24, 2015.

Questions

1. Describe the descriptive analytics applications of Rent the Runway's business model.

2. Describe the predictive analytics applications of Rent the Runway's business model.

3. Describe a possible prescriptive analytics application for Rent the Runway.

4. What companies and industries are in danger of being disrupted by Rent the Runway? (Hint: Will Rent the Runway change the way that women buy clothes?)

Introduction

The chapter opening case illustrates the importance and far-reaching nature of business analytics applications. **Business analytics (BA)** is the process of developing actionable decisions or recommendations for actions based on insights generated from historical data. Business analytics examines data with a variety of tools and techniques, formulates descriptive, predictive, and prescriptive models, and communicates these results to organizational decision makers. Business analytics can answer questions such as: What happened, how many, how often, where the problem is, what actions are needed, why is this happening, what will happen if these trends continue, what will happen next, what is the best (or worst) that can happen, and what actions should the organization take to achieve various successful business outcomes?

There is a great deal of confusion between the terms *business analytics* and *business intelligence*. Business intelligence (BI) has been defined as a broad category of applications, technologies, and processes for gathering, storing, accessing, and analyzing data to help business users make better decisions. Many experts argue that the terms should be used interchangeably. We agree. However, for simplicity we use the term business analytics (BA) throughout this chapter.

This chapter describes information systems (ISs) that support *decision making*. Essentially all organizational information systems support decision making (refer to Figure 1.4 and Chapter 11). Fundamental organizational ISs such as transaction processing systems, functional area information systems, and enterprise resource planning systems provide a variety of reports that help decision makers. This chapter focuses on business analytics systems, which provide critically important support to the vast majority of organizational decision makers.

The chapter begins by reviewing the manager's job and the nature of modern managerial decisions. This discussion will help you to understand why managers need computerized support. The chapter then introduces the business analytics process and addresses each step in that process in turn.

It is impossible to overstate the importance of business analytics within modern organizations. Recall from Chapter 1 that the essential goal of information systems is to provide the right information to the right person, in the right amount, at the right time, in the right format. In essence, BA achieves this goal. Business analytics systems provide actionable business results that decision makers can act on in a timely fashion.

It is also impossible to overstate the importance of your input into the BA process within an organization, for several reasons. First, you (the user community) will decide what data should be stored in your organization's data warehouse. You will then work closely with the MIS department to obtain these data.

Further, you will use your organization's BA applications, probably from your first day on the job. With some BA tools such as data mining and decision support systems, you will decide how you want to analyze the data (user-driven analysis). With BA presentation applications such as dashboards, you will decide which data you need and in which format. Again, you will work closely with your MIS department to ensure that these applications meet your needs.

In addition, a significant change is taking place within the BA environment. In the past, organizations used BA only to support management. Today, however, BA applications are increasingly available to front-line personnel (e.g., call center operators), suppliers, customers, and even regulators. These groups rely on BA to provide them with the most current information.

Much of this chapter is concerned with large-scale BA applications. You should keep in mind, however, that smaller organizations, and even individual users, can implement small-scale BA applications as well.

After you finish this chapter, you will have a basic understanding of decision making, the BA process, and the incredibly broad range of BA applications employed in modern organizations. This knowledge will enable you to immediately and confidently provide input into your organization's BA processes and applications. Further, this chapter will help you use your organization's BA applications to effectively analyze data and thus make better decisions. We hope that this chapter will help you to *"ask the next question."* Enjoy!

5.1 Managers and Decision Making

Management is a process by which an organization achieves its goals through the use of resources (people, money, materials, and information). These resources are considered to be *inputs*. Achieving the organization's goals is the *output* of the process. Managers oversee this process in an attempt to optimize it. A manager's success often is measured by the ratio between the inputs and outputs for which he or she is responsible. This ratio is an indication of the organization's productivity.

The Manager's Job and Decision Making

To appreciate how information systems support managers, you first must understand the manager's job. Managers do many things, depending on their position in the organization, the type and size of the organization, the organization's policies and culture, and the personalities of the managers themselves. Despite these variations, however, all managers perform three basic roles (Mintzberg, 1973):[1]

1. *Interpersonal roles:* Figurehead, leader, liaison
2. *Informational roles:* Monitor, disseminator, spokesperson, analyzer
3. *Decisional roles:* Entrepreneur, disturbance handler, resource allocator, negotiator

Early information systems primarily supported the informational roles. In recent years, however, information systems have been developed that support all three roles. In this chapter, you will focus on the support that IT can provide for decisional roles.

A decision refers to a choice among two or more alternatives that individuals and groups make. Decisions are diverse and are made continuously. Decision making is a systematic process. Economist Herbert Simon (1977)[2] described decision making as composed of three major phases: intelligence, design, and choice. Once the choice is made, the decision is implemented. Figure 5.1 illustrates this process, highlighting the tasks that are in each phase. Note that there

FIGURE 5.1 The process and phases in decision making.

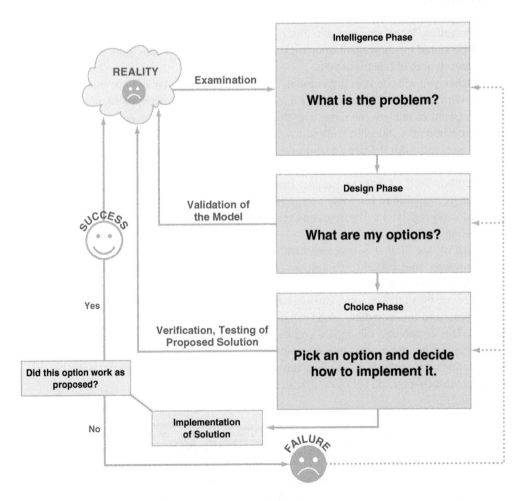

[1] Mintzberg, H. (1973) *The Nature of Managerial Work*, Harper & Row, New York.
[2] Simon, H.A. (1977) *The New Science of Management Decision*, Prentice-Hall, Englewood Cliffs, NJ.

is a continuous flow of information from intelligence, to design, to choice (bold lines). At any phase, however, there may be a return to a previous phase (broken lines).

This model of decision making is quite general. Undoubtedly, you have made decisions where you did not construct a model of the situation, validate your model with test data, or conduct a sensitivity analysis. The model we present here is intended to encompass *all* of the conditions that might occur when making a decision. For some decisions, some steps or phrases may be minimal, implicit (understood), or completely absent.

The decision-making process starts with the *intelligence phase*, in which managers examine a situation and then identify and define the problem or opportunity. In the *design phase*, decision makers construct a model for addressing the situation. They perform this task by making assumptions that simplify reality and by expressing the relationships among all of the relevant variables. Managers then validate the model by using test data. Finally, decision makers set criteria for evaluating all of the potential solutions that are proposed. The *choice phase* involves selecting a solution or course of action that seems best suited to resolve the problem. This solution (the decision) is then implemented. Implementation is successful if the proposed solution solves the problem or seizes the opportunity. If the solution fails, then the process returns to the previous phases. Computer-based decision support assists managers in the decision-making process.

Why Managers Need IT Support

Making good decisions is very difficult without solid information. Information is vital for each phase and activity in the decision-making process. Even when information is available, however, decision making is difficult due to the following trends:

- The *number of alternatives* is constantly *increasing*, due to innovations in technology, improved communications, the development of global markets, and the use of the Internet and e-business. A key to good decision making is to explore and compare many relevant alternatives. The greater the number of alternatives, the more a decision maker needs computer-assisted searches and comparisons.

- Most decisions must be made *under time pressure*. It often is not possible to manually process information fast enough to be effective.

- Due to increased uncertainty in the decision environment, decisions are becoming more complex. It is usually necessary to *conduct a sophisticated analysis* in order to make a good decision.

- It often is necessary to rapidly access remote information, consult with experts, or conduct a group decision-making session, all without incurring major expenses. Decision makers, as well as the information they need to access, can be situated in different locations. Bringing everything together quickly and inexpensively represents a serious challenge.

These trends create major difficulties for decision makers. Fortunately, as you will see throughout this chapter, computerized decision support can be of enormous help.

Next you will learn about two aspects of decision making that place our discussion of BA in context—problem structure and the nature of the decisions.

A Framework for Computerized Decision Analysis

To better understand business analytics, note that various types of decisions can be placed along two major dimensions: problem structure and the nature of the decision (Gorry and Scott Morton, 1971).[3] Figure 5.2 provides an overview of decision making along these two dimensions.

Problem Structure. The first dimension is *problem structure*, where decision-making processes fall along a continuum ranging from highly structured to highly unstructured (see the

[3] Gorry, G.A. and Scott Morton, M. (1971) "A Framework for Management Information Systems," *Sloan Management Review*, Fall, 21–36.

FIGURE 5.2 Decision support framework.

THE NATURE OF DECISIONS

PROBLEM STRUCTURE	Operational Control	Management Control	Strategic Planning
Structured	Accounts receivable Accounts payable Order entry 1	Budget analysis Short-term forecasting Personnel reports Make-or-buy analysis 2	Financial management Investment portfolio Warehouse location 3
Semistructured	Production scheduling, Inventory control 4	Credit evaluation Budget preparation Plant layout Project scheduling Reward system Design 5	Building a new plant Mergers and acquisitions New product planning Compensation planning HR policies 6
Unstructured	Building software Approving loans Operating a help desk 7	Negotiating Recruiting an executive Lobbying 8	R & D planning New technology development Social responsibility planning 9

left column in Figure 5.2). *Structured decisions* deal with routine and repetitive problems for which standard solutions exist, such as inventory control. In a structured decision, the first three phases of the decision process—intelligence, design, and choice—are laid out in a particular sequence, and the procedures for obtaining the best (or at least a good enough) solution are known. These types of decisions are candidates for decision automation.

At the other extreme of complexity are *unstructured decisions*. These decisions are intended to deal with "fuzzy," complex problems for which there are no cut-and-dried solutions. An unstructured decision is one in which there is no standardized procedure for carrying out any of the three phases. In making such a decision, human intuition and judgment often play an important role. Typical unstructured decisions include planning new service offerings, hiring an executive, and choosing a set of research and development (R&D) projects for the coming year. Although BA cannot make unstructured decisions, it can provide information that assists decision makers.

Located between structured and unstructured decisions are *semistructured* decisions, in which only some of the decision-process phases are structured. Semistructured decisions require a combination of standard solution procedures and individual judgment. Examples of semistructured decisions are evaluating employees, setting marketing budgets for consumer products, performing capital acquisition analysis, and trading bonds.

The Nature of Decisions. The second dimension of decision support deals with the *nature of decisions*. All managerial decisions fall into one of three broad categories:

1. *Operational control:* Executing specific tasks efficiently and effectively
2. *Management control:* Acquiring and using resources efficiently in accomplishing organizational goals
3. *Strategic planning:* The long-range goals and policies for growth and resource allocation

These categories are displayed along the top row of Figure 5.2.

The Decision Matrix. The three primary classes of problem structure and the three broad categories of the nature of decisions can be combined in a decision-support matrix that consists of nine cells, as diagrammed in Figure 5.2. Lower-level managers usually perform the tasks in cells 1, 2, and 4. The tasks in cells 3, 5, and 7 are usually the responsibility of middle managers and professional staff. Finally, the tasks in cells 6, 8, and 9 are generally carried out by senior executives.

Today, it is difficult to state that certain organizational information systems support certain cells in the decision matrix. The fact is that the increasing sophistication of information systems means that essentially any information system can be useful to any decision maker, regardless of his or her level in the organization or function in the organization. As you study this chapter, you will see that business analytics is applicable across all cells of the decision matrix.

Before you go on…

1. Describe the decision-making process proposed by Simon.

2. You are registering for classes next semester. Apply the decision-making process to your decision about how many and which courses to take. Is your decision structured, semistructured, or unstructured? Support your answer.

3. Consider your decision-making process when registering for classes next semester. Explain how information technology supports (or does not support) each phase of this process.

Apply the Concept 5.1

LEARNING OBJECTIVE 5.1 Use a decision support framework to demonstrate how technology supports managerial decision making at each phase of the decision-making process.

STEP 1: Background (Here is what you are learning.)

If you look back through this section, you will see that Henry Mintzberg's 1973 book, *The Nature of Managerial Work*, was referenced when the three basic roles of a manager were presented. This text focuses on the decisional role because that is the one that is most supported by information systems. However, Mintzberg's work goes well beyond the decisional role.

STEP 2: Activity (Here is what you do.)

Visit http://www.wiley.com/go/rainer/MIS4e/applytheconcept, and click on the link provided for Apply the Concept 5.1. The link will take you to a YouTube video titled "Data-Driven Decision Making" by user "minnetonka schools." This video mentions a strategic plan, operational control, and decisional control. As you view the video, make certain to watch for these key points, and pay special attention to how they are supported by data.

STEP 3: Deliverable (Here is what you turn in.)

Write a short paper (a couple of paragraphs is plenty) for your professor that will identify the phases in the decision-making process for Minnetonka Schools. Be sure to demonstrate how technology supports their decision making in each phase.

5.2 | The Business Analytics Process

As previously defined, **business analytics** is the process of developing actionable decisions or recommendations for actions based upon insights generated from historical data. Business analytics encompasses not only applications, but also technologies and processes. It includes both "getting data in" (to a data mart or warehouse) and "getting data out" (through BA applications).

Figure 5.3 illustrates the BA process in an organization. As you see in the figure, the BA process requires multiple steps, technologies, tools, and models. Let's look at each step of Figure 5.3 in turn, from left to right.

The entire BA process begins with a business problem, known as *pain points* to practicing managers. When organizations face business problems, they often turn to business analytics.

Before we begin our discussion of the BA process, let's emphasize the importance of the technologies that enable the entire process (see Figure 5.3). These technologies, all of which are improving exponentially, include microprocessors, storage, and networks.

Microprocessors (or chips) are becoming increasingly powerful (see Plug IT In 2). For example, specialized graphics processing units (GPUs) are essential to neural networks, an analytics

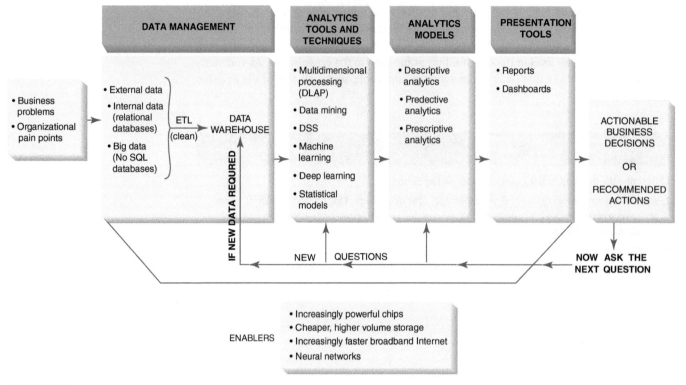

FIGURE 5.3 The Business Analytics Process

tool that we discuss in Plug IT In 5. Digital storage capacity and access speed are both increasing exponentially. These advances are driving the cost of storage down exponentially as well. Transmission speed (bandwidth; see Chapter 4) in computer networks, particularly the Internet, is also increasing exponentially. As a result, decision makers are able to collaborate on difficult, time-sensitive decisions regardless of their locations.

To actually begin the BA process, an organization must have data (and lots of it!). As you saw from our discussion of enabling technologies, organizations are now able to analyze rapidly increasing amounts of data. As you learned in Chapter 3, these data originate from internal sources (e.g., structured data in relational databases) and external sources (e.g., unstructured data from social media). Organizations are now able to combine and analyze structured and unstructured data from many sources in the form of Big Data. At this point, organizations integrate and "clean" these data into data marts and data warehouses (see Chapter 3) through a process called extract, transform, and load (ETL). The data in the data warehouse are now available to be analyzed by a variety of analytics tools and techniques.

There are numerous analytics tools and techniques available to decision makers. These tools include Excel, decision-support systems, online analytical processing (OLAP), data mining, machine learning, deep learning, and neural networks. We discuss the first four in Section 5.3, and the last three in Plug IT In 5. Note that there are many statistical modeling tools available in analytics software packages. These tools are beyond the scope of this chapter.

Organizations can apply analytics tools and techniques to data in the form of three possible analytics models: descriptive analytics, predictive analytics, and prescriptive analytics. We discuss these three models in Section 5.4.

All three models will produce results, which must be communicated to decision makers in the organization. In general, data scientists will use various analytics tools and techniques to examine analytics models. Many organizations have employees who "translate" the results of the analytics models into business terms for the decision makers. These translators often use presentation tools in the form of dashboards to get the message across visually (see Section 5.4).

What is interesting about the analytics process is that once the results are obtained and presented, decision makers must be ready to "ask the next question." Everyone involved in the BA process must use their creativity and intuition at this point. In addition, the results of the BA process almost always will lead to new, unanswered questions. To address these questions, the BA process starts over at the data management stage.

The Scope of Business Analytics

The use of BA in organizations varies considerably. In smaller organizations, BA may be limited to Excel spreadsheets. In larger ones, BA often is enterprisewide, and it includes applications such as data mining/predictive analytics, dashboards, and data visualization. It is important to recognize that the importance of BA to organizations continues to grow. In fact, it is not an exaggeration to assert that for many firms, BA is now a requirement for competing in the marketplace.

Not all organizations use BA in the same way. For example, some organizations employ only one or a few applications, whereas others utilize enterprisewide BA. In general, there are three specific analytics targets that represent different levels of change. These targets differ in terms of their focus; scope; level of sponsorship, commitment, and required resources; technical architecture; impact on personnel and business processes; and benefits.

The Development of One or a Few Related Analytics Applications. This target is often a point solution for a departmental need, such as campaign management in marketing. Sponsorship, approval, funding, impacts, and benefits typically occur at the departmental level. For this target, organizations usually create a data mart to store the necessary data. Organizations must be careful that the data mart—an "independent" application—does not become a "data silo" that stores data that are inconsistent with, and cannot be integrated with, data used elsewhere in the organization.

The Development of Infrastructure to Support Enterprisewide Analytics. This target supports both current and future analytics needs. A crucial component of analytics at this level is an enterprise data warehouse. Because it is an enterprisewide initiative, senior management often provides sponsorship, approval, and funding. In addition, the impacts and benefits are felt throughout the organization.

An example of this target is the 3M Corporation. Traditionally, 3M's various divisions had operated independently, using separate decision-support platforms. Not only was this arrangement costly, but it prevented 3M from integrating the data and presenting a "single face" to its customers. For example, sales representatives did not know whether or how business customers were interacting with other 3M divisions. The solution was to develop an enterprise data warehouse that enabled 3M to operate as an integrated company. As an added benefit, the costs of implementing this system were offset by savings resulting from the consolidation of the various platforms.

`MKT`

Support for Organizational Transformation. With this target, a company uses business analytics to fundamentally transform the ways it competes in the marketplace. Business analytics supports a new business model, and it enables the business strategy. Because of the scope and importance of these changes, critical elements such as sponsorship, approval, and funding originate at the highest organizational levels. The impact on personnel and processes can be significant, and the benefits accrue across the organization.

Harrah's Entertainment (a brand of Caesars Entertainment; www.caesars.com) provides a good example of this analytics target. Harrah's developed a customer loyalty program known as Total Rewards. To implement the program, Harrah's created a data warehouse that integrated data from casino, hotel, and special event systems (e.g., wine-tasting weekends) across all the various customer touchpoints (e.g., slot machines, table games, and Internet). Harrah's utilized these data to reward loyal customers and to reach out to them in personal and appealing ways, such as through promotional offers. These efforts helped the company to become a leader in the gaming industry.

`MKT`

IT's About Business 5.1 describes business analytics applications at Darden Restaurants, Twiddy & Company, and Point Defiance Zoo & Aquarium. As you read about the three companies, think about the following:

1. What is the scope of business analytics in each company?
2. After you have studied Section 5.4, what is (are) the business analytics model(s) that each company is using?

IT's About Business 5.1

POM Darden Restaurants

MKT Darden Restaurants (www.darden.com) encompasses seven brands—Olive Garden, Longhorn Steakhouse, Bahama Breeze, Seasons 52, The Capital Grill, Eddie V's, and Yard House. The company owns and operates more than 1,500 restaurants, employs more than 150,000 people, and serves more than 320 million meals every year.

The company needed a more effective strategy to gather data about what was happening in individual restaurants than simply calling restaurant managers on the telephone at the end of every day. As a result, Darden implemented a Check-Level Analytics system to improve decision making. The system collects information about patrons from the time they arrive until they settle the bill.

The restaurant chain analyzes these types of data, among others:

- How long it takes for a guest to be seated or given a wait time.
- The length of the cook time. Darden calculates cook times for each menu item so that each restaurant can pace both the meal and the food preparation.
- The name of the server who served the guest.
- What time the customer paid the check.
- How much time the guest spent in the restaurant.

Darden links all of these data to the guest satisfaction survey, should the guest complete it. In this way, Darden can get a better picture of what its customers experience in all of its restaurants.

Darden's goal is to better understand its guests. For example:

- When is the best time to offer early-bird specials or happy hour to fill more tables?
- How effective are any specials?
- What is the optimal physical configuration of the restaurant to reduce wait times?
- Are too many two-place tables sitting empty while parties of four wait for tables?
- How much is wait time reduced, and how many more tables can be turned, by adding servers or kitchen staff during busy times?
- What special requests do guests have—for example, a seat by the window or a private corner—that the restaurant cannot accommodate?
- Who are your guests? Is this their first visit? Are they celebrating a special occasion? How did they hear about you?

Darden's use of analytics has produced results. The restaurant company has saved at least $20 million.

MKT Twiddy & Company

Travelers to the Outer Banks of North Carolina can search more than 1,000 homes to rent on the islands through Twiddy & Company (www.twiddy.com). Twiddy has two business goals: to ensure that travelers enjoy their stay and that homeowners maximize their profit.

Over the years, Twiddy had used spreadsheets to accumulate operational data. The company invested $40,000 in BA tools from SAS (www.sas.com) to integrate these data into an analyzable format. Before implementing SAS analytics, about the only thing that Twiddy could tell its homeowners was what dates their homes were available to rent. Now, Twiddy can analyze data on market and seasonal trends, and property locations and sizes, to suggest optimal prices to homeowners for any particular week.

Twiddy bookings increased and the size of its property inventory rose by more than 10 percent after the company began using SAS. While revenues increased, costs decreased by 15 percent, thanks to a reduction in invoice processing errors and the automation of service schedules. The total savings? About $50,000 since using the SAS analytics.

POM Point Defiance Zoo & Aquarium

MKT For Point Defiance Zoo & Aquarium (www.pdza.org), located in Tacoma, Washington, the biggest business problem is the weather. Specifically, unpredictable weather makes estimating zoo attendance extremely difficult. Historically, Point Defiance used standard weather forecasts to predict attendance, with mixed results.

Attendance is critical to the success of zoos. Therefore, Point Defiance partnered with IBM (www.ibm.com) and analytics firm BrightStar Partners (www.brightstarpartners.com). The zoo compared its attendance records for the past several years with historical weather data collected by the National Weather Service (www.weather.gov). Now, for any given weekend, the zoo can estimate attendance with an impressive amount of accuracy. The zoo uses these predictions to flexibly schedule its staffing. How effective is this system? For Memorial Day 2014, the projected attendance was within 113 people of the actual attendance—that is pretty accurate.

The analytics software doesn't just use weather data—it collects information on zoo guests to help target its marketing campaigns. For example, the system analyzed the zip codes of the most regular patrons and targeted membership discounts to them, which boosted membership by 13 percent in the first three months of 2014. Point Defiance sold $60,000 worth of memberships by spending just $4,000.

Point Defiance also analyzed data about online ticket sales and found that many people bought tickets in the evenings and mornings when they weren't at work. As a result, the zoo implemented time-limited deals, which helped boost its online ticket sales by 771 percent since 2013. Even in-person ticket sales got a boost, setting records during the same time period.

Sources: Compiled from M. Harper, "The Future of Customer Data for Restaurants," *Applied Predictive Technologies*, August 5, 2015; R. Delgado, "How Restaurants Are Using Big Data," *SmartData Collective*, May 6, 2015; C. Brubaker, "Not Taking Advantage of Restaurant Analytics Is Costing You Money," *Swipely*, April 20, 2015; "New Benchmarking Reports Help Twiddy Boost Email Open Rates by 500%," *Google Analytics Blog*, September 10, 2014; R. Lahiri and M. DeRosa, "How Data Analytics Can Improve Real Property Management," *FCW: The Business of Federal Technology*, September 2, 2014; J. Martindale, "Animals Inspire Analytics Innovation," *All Analytics*, August 21, 2014; E. Alton, "What Big Data Means for Animal Attractions," *Entertainment Designer*, July 18, 2014;

J. O'Brien, "5 Ways Big Data Is Changing Real Estate," *Mashable*, July 9, 2014; K. Kelleher, "Big Data, Small Budget," *Inc.*, July/August, 2014; M. Heller, "How Data Analytics Is Transforming the Real-Estate Industry," *CIO*, May 28, 2014; D. Carr, "Darden Seeks Integrated View of Customers across Brands," *InformationWeek*, April 1, 2014; "Restaurant Analytics: Uncovering Answers to Grow Your Business," Teradata, 2013; www.darden.com, www.twiddy.com, www.pdza.org, accessed August 28, 2015.

Questions

1. What is the scope of business analytics for each company?
2. Describe how Darden Restaurants might employ predictive and prescriptive analytics.
3. Describe how Twiddy & Company might employ predictive and prescriptive analytics.
4. Describe how Point Defiance might employ prescriptive analytics.

Before you go on...

1. Describe the business analytics process.
2. Describe the three business analytics targets.

Apply the Concept 5.2

LEARNING OBJECTIVE 5.2 Describe each phase of the business analytics process.

STEP 1: Background

In this section you have learned that BA is a concept that encompasses everything from the collection, analysis, and dissemination of data to the technology tools that enable this process to take place. In particular, organizations use BA to support:

- Specific departmental needs, and
- Organizational change.

STEP 2: Activity

There are several companies that provide data management and BA tools to help make decisions. Two of these companies are Avitas and Intricity. Visit http://www.wiley.com/go/rainer/MIS4e/applytheconcept to watch a short YouTube video about BA by each of these companies. While you watch, look for examples of how their tools support departments, enterprises, and/or organizational change.

STEP 3: Deliverable

Write a short description of how Avitas and Intricity help users work through the BA process (see Figure 5.3). Try to show how the process is supported, but also be aware that there might be gaps. Make note of any areas for improvement as well, if you find any.

5.3 | Business Analytics Tools

A variety of BA tools for analyzing data are available. They include Excel, multidimensional analysis (also called OLAP), data mining, and decision-support systems. There are also numerous statistical tools that business analytics models employ. These tools include linear and multiple regression, time series models, classification, clustering, and many others. A discussion of these diverse models, however, is beyond the scope of our discussion.

Excel

The most popular BA tool by far is Excel. For years, BA vendors "fought" against the use of Excel. Eventually, however, they decided to "join it" by designing their software so that it interfaces with Excel. How does this process work? Essentially, users download plug-ins that add functionality (e.g., the ability to list the top 10 percent of customers, based on purchases) to Excel. This process can be thought of as creating "Excel on steroids." Excel then connects to the vendor's application server—which provides additional data analysis capabilities—which in turn connects to a backend database, such as a data mart or warehouse. This arrangement gives Excel users the functionality and access to data typical of sophisticated BA products, while allowing them to work with a familiar tool—Excel. Due to advances in the functionality of Excel, the following BA tools can often be accomplished by using this software package.

Multidimensional Analysis or Online Analytical Processing

Some BA applications include online analytical processing, also referred to as multidimensional analysis capabilities. OLAP involves "slicing and dicing" data stored in a dimensional format, drilling down in the data to greater detail, and aggregating the data.

Consider our example from Chapter 3. Recall Figure 3.6 illustrating the data cube. The product is on the *x*-axis, geography is on the *y*-axis, and time is on the *z*-axis. Now, suppose you want to know how many nuts the company sold in the West region in 2013. You would slice and dice the cube, using *nuts* as the specific measure for product, *West* as the measure for geography, and *2013* as the measure for time. The value or values that remain in the cell(s) after our slicing and dicing is (are) the answer to our question. As an example of drilling down, you also might want to know how many nuts were sold in January 2013. Alternatively, you might want to know how many nuts were sold during 2013–2015, which is an example of aggregation, also called "rollup."

Data Mining

Data mining refers to the process of searching for valuable business information in a large database, data warehouse, or data mart. Data mining can perform two basic operations: (1) predicting trends and behaviors and (2) identifying previously unknown patterns. Business analytics applications typically provide users with a view of what has happened; data mining helps to explain *why* it is happening, and it predicts what will happen in the future.

Regarding the first operation, data mining automates the process of finding predictive information in large databases. Questions that traditionally required extensive hands-on analysis now can be answered directly and quickly from the data. For example, *targeted marketing* relies on predictive information. Data mining can use data from past promotional mailings to identify those prospects who are most likely to respond favorably to future mailings. Another business problem that uses predictive information is the forecasting of bankruptcy and other forms of default.

MKT

Data mining can also identify previously hidden patterns in a single step. For example, it can analyze retail sales data to discover seemingly unrelated products that people often purchase together. The classic example is beer and diapers. Data mining found that young men tend to buy beer and diapers at the same time when shopping at convenience stores.

One significant predictive analytics operation is detecting fraudulent credit card transactions. Over time a pattern emerges of the typical ways you use your credit card and your typical shopping behaviors—the places in which you use your card, the amounts you spend, and so on. If your card is stolen and used fraudulently, then the usage often varies noticeably from your established pattern. Data-mining tools can discern this difference and bring the issue to your attention.

FIN

Numerous data-mining applications are used in business and in other fields. According to a Gartner report (www.gartner.com), most Fortune 1000 companies worldwide currently use data mining, as the following representative examples illustrate. Note that in most cases the purpose of data mining is to identify a business opportunity in order to create a sustainable competitive advantage.

POM

- *Retailing and sales:* Predicting sales, preventing theft and fraud, and determining correct inventory levels and distribution schedules among outlets. For example, retailers such as AAFES (stores on military bases) use Fraud Watch from SAP (www.sap.com) to combat fraud by employees in their 1,400 stores.

- *Banking:* Forecasting levels of bad loans and fraudulent credit card use, predicting credit card spending by new customers, and determining which kinds of customers will best respond to (and qualify for) new loan offers.

FIN

- *Manufacturing and production:* Predicting machinery failures and finding key factors that help optimize manufacturing capacity.

POM

- *Insurance:* Forecasting claim amounts and medical coverage costs, classifying the most important elements that affect medical coverage, and predicting which customers will buy new insurance policies. (See IT's About Business 5.2.)

POM

- *Policework:* Tracking crime patterns, locations, and criminal behavior; identifying attributes to assist in solving criminal cases. Consider PredPol (www.predpol.com), the predictive policing company. After deploying PredPol, the Los Angeles Police Department's Foothill Division noted a 20 percent decrease in crimes year over year from January 2013 to January 2014.

POM

- *Healthcare:* Correlating demographics of patients with critical illnesses and developing better insights on how to identify and treat symptoms and their causes. In March 2013, Microsoft and Stanford University announced that they had mined the search data of millions of users to successfully identify unreported side effects of certain medications.

- *Marketing:* Classifying customer demographics that can be used to predict which customers will respond to a mailing or buy a particular product.

MKT

- *Politics:* In his FiveThirtyEight blog, Nate Silver famously analyzed polling and economic data to predict the results of the 2008 presidential election, calling 49 out of 50 states correctly. He then correctly predicted all 50 states in the 2012 presidential election.

- *Weather:* The National Weather Service is predicting weather with increasing accuracy and precision.

MKT

- *Higher education:* Desire2Learn (www.desire2learn.com) provides an application called Degree Compass that recommends courses based on students' majors, transcripts, and past course success rates. In March 2013, Degree Compass reported a 92 percent accuracy rate across four universities in predicting the grade that a student would receive in a course.

- *Social good:* As you read about in IT's About Business 5.4, Simpa Networks sells solar-as-a-service to poor households and small businesses. Simpa partnered with DataKind (www.datakind.org) whose data scientists analyzed Simpa's historical customer data to help Simpa assess potential customers.

Decision Support Systems

Decision support systems (DSSs) combine models and data to analyze semistructured problems and some unstructured problems that involve extensive user involvement. **Models** are simplified representations, or abstractions, of reality. Decision support systems enable business managers and analysts to access data interactively, to manipulate these data, and to conduct appropriate analyses.

Decision support systems can enhance learning and contribute to all levels of decision making. DSSs also employ mathematical models. Finally, they have the related capabilities of sensitivity analysis, what–if analysis, and goal-seeking analysis, which you will learn about next. You should keep in mind that these three types of analysis are useful for any type of decision-support application. Excel, for example, supports all three.

To learn about DSS and the three types of analysis, let's look at an example. Blue Nile (www.bluenile.com) is an online retailer of certified diamonds. The firm's website has a built-in decision support system to help customers find the diamond that best meets their needs. Blue Nile's DSS provides an excellent example of sensitivity analysis, what-if analysis, and goal-seeking analysis.

Access the Blue Nile website and click on "Diamonds" in the upper left corner. On the drop-down box, you will see "Search for diamonds." There are many types of diamonds, but for this example click on "Round." You will see:

- The number of round diamonds available for sale, again in the upper left corner. When we accessed the Blue Nile DSS, the firm offered 112,333 round diamonds for sale.
- Five slide bars labeled: Price, Carat, Cut, Color, and Clarity. Each slide bar represents a variable in Blue Nile's DSS.
- A list of each diamond accompanied by a value for each of the five variables. This list constitutes the data (all round diamonds available for sale) for your analyses.

Keep in mind that when you experiment with the Blue Nile DSS, the number of round diamonds available will vary from what we obtained when we accessed the DSS and performed the analyses. The reason is that the Blue Nile website is updated in near real-time as the company sells its diamonds.

Sensitivity Analysis. Sensitivity analysis examines how sensitive an output is to any change in an input while keeping other inputs constant. Sensitivity analysis is valuable because it enables the system to adapt to changing conditions and to the varying requirements of different decision-making situations.

Let's perform *two sensitivity analyses* on the data:

- First, adjust the slide bars for the Carat variable, so that you will see only those round diamonds between 1.00 and 1.50 carats. Keep all the other slide bars in their fully open position. In that way, you keep the other variables constant. Note that the number of round diamonds available decreases dramatically. When we followed this procedure, the number of round diamonds available for sale dropped to 14,009.
- Second, adjust the slide bars for the Color variable, so that you will only see those round diamonds of D, E, and F color. Be sure to open the slide bars for Carat and keep the other slide bars in their fully open position. When we followed this procedure, the number of round diamonds available for sale dropped to 58,993.

Comparing the results of these two sensitivity analyses, we can say that the number of round diamonds for sale is more sensitive to changes in Carat than to changes in Color, with the other variables constant.

What–If Analysis. A model builder must make predictions and assumptions regarding the input data, many of which are based on the assessment of uncertain futures. The results depend on the accuracy of these assumptions, which can be highly subjective. *What–if analysis* attempts to predict the impact of changes in the assumptions (input data) on the proposed solution.

Let's perform a *what-if analysis* on the data. A young man's fiancée has decided that she would like her engagement ring to be between one and two carats, at least a Very Good cut, an F color or better, and a clarity of at least VVS2 (VVS2 means "two very, very small imperfections"). Adjust the slide bars for all four of the variables at once. When we followed this procedure, the number of round diamonds available for sale dropped to 3,830.

Goal-Seeking Analysis. *Goal-seeking analysis* represents a "backward" solution approach. Goal seeking attempts to calculate the value of the inputs necessary to achieve a desired level of output.

Let's perform a *goal-seeking analysis* on the data. When the young man in our example looked at the list of 3,830 diamonds (using the scroll bar on the right side of the list), he noticed that the prices ranged from $6,356 to $10,117. He told his fiancée that he had only $5,000 to invest in a diamond. Consequently, they opened up the slide bars for the Carat, Cut, Color, and Clarity variables and adjusted the slide bar for the Price variable to be between $4,500 and $5,000. When we followed this procedure, the number of round diamonds available for sale dropped to 3,874.

The couple now had the problem of examining the list of diamonds to decide which combination of the four variables would be suitable. They did this be performing several what-if analyses:

- She decided that she really wanted a diamond between one and two carats. After adjusting the Carat slide bar, the number of round diamonds available dropped to 2,035.
- She then decided that she wanted a D, E, or F color. After adjusting the Color slide bar, the number of round diamonds available dropped to 424.
- Next, she chose a Cut that was at least Very Good. After adjusting the Cut slide bar, the number of round diamonds available dropped to 266.
- The couple noticed that all 266 diamonds had a Clarity variable of either SI1 (one small imperfection) or SI2 (two small imperfections). Either they could decide that this level of clarity is acceptable, or go back and perform additional what-if analyses on other variables.

Before you go on…

1. Describe multidimensional analysis.
2. What are the two basic operations of data mining?
3. What is the purpose of decision support systems?

Apply the Concept 5.3

LEARNING OBJECTIVE 5.3 Describe each of the various analytics tools and examples of their uses.

STEP 1: Background

This section has explained that data are more abundant today than ever before. One thing we are learning is that there is much we *can* know that we *do not* know. In fact, there are many questions we are not even aware we should be asking! For such questions, we use multidimensional analysis and data-mining tools to extract valuable insights from the data. When we know the questions, we frequently employ decision support systems to run sensitivity, what-if, or goal-seeking analysis.

STEP 2: Activity

Consider your university. Various departments focus on teaching, student academic support, financial aid, admissions,

recruitment, administration, and much more. Each of these departments has its special purpose, but overall the enterprise exists to support student learning.

Visit your university's website, and look for these various functions. What can you learn about their purpose? Based on this knowledge, what can you imply about the types of BA applications they might use?

STEP 3: Deliverable

Within the context of Higher Education, describe the various tools and provide an example of how each could be used to support your campus. Submit your response to your instructor.

5.4 Business Analytics Models: Descriptive Analytics, Predictive Analytics, and Prescriptive Analytics

Organizations must analyze huge amounts of raw data in order to make sense out of them. This overall process is known as data reduction. *Data reduction* is the conversion of raw data into a smaller amount of more useful information. Descriptive, predictive, and prescriptive analytics are essentially steps in data reduction.

Descriptive Analytics

Descriptive analytics are the first step in data reduction. Industry analysts estimate that the majority of business analytics are descriptive. **Descriptive analytics** summarize what has happened in the past and allow decision makers to learn from past behaviors. Common examples of descriptive analytics are reports that provide historical insights regarding an organization's production, financials, operations, sales, finance, inventory, and customers.

MKT

For example, Fandango (www.fandango.com), the leading online ticket seller for movie theaters, wants to analyze the movie preferences of its customers during the past year. The firm sells millions of tickets to approximately 20,000 movie theaters across the United States. Fandango captures data about customers, movie theaters, ticket sales, and show times. Using a sample of movie titles, Fandango analysts can investigate the correlations among total sales for different movies. Using a sample of moviegoers, they can calculate the average ticket sales for a week, the most popular movie, the distribution of customers among the movie genres, the busiest hours of the day in the movie theater, and many other analyses. These descriptive analyses help Fandango set ticket prices, offer discounts for certain movies or show times, and assign show times of the same movie in different theaters.

For other examples of descriptive analytics, see this chapter's opening case, closing case 1, closing case 2, and all IT's About Business. IT's About Business 5.2 shows how Esurance successfully employs descriptive analytics to provide personalized quotes to prospective customers.

IT's About Business 5.2

Esurance Uses Analytics to Provide Personalized Quotes

MKT Esurance (www.esurance.com) sells automobile insurance directly to consumers online and over the telephone. The firm offers services to almost 90 percent of the U.S. population in 40 states. The insurer also functions as a shopping and comparison site for customers in the 10 remaining states. Esurance is a wholly owned subsidiary of Allstate (www.allstate.com).

For most customers, choosing the right insurance is complicated. Esurance wanted to make it easier for its Web customers to make choices quickly and knowledgeably. Specifically, Esurance wanted to make the online purchasing process equivalent to a face-to-face meeting with an insurance agent. As a result, the company developed an analytics software package called the Coverage Rules Engine (CRE).

The CRE integrates and analyzes data from two sources. First, Esurance staff members formulate business rules by analyzing queries against the historical information in the firm's database and by talking with Esurance's agents, who assist customers online, over the phone, and in person. The insurer spent about 18 months adding business rules to the CRE. Second, the CRE relies on the answers from a questionnaire filled out by customers. These answers produce about 55 variables that the CRE can utilize to modify the initial package presentation. By analyzing the two types of data, the CRE can provide almost unlimited customization—up to 8 billion possible packages of coverage.

Consider this example of how Esurance uses its CRE. A common business practice is "upselling"—promoting additional products or services to customers after they've made their initial purchase. Esurance noted that in the insurance business, agents

dealing with customers in person would often suggest they add towing and roadside emergency insurance, which was a popular add-on. But Esurance customers on the Web would rarely add towing to their packages. Consequently, Esurance conducted an experiment. The company added a button on its site that asked customers before completing their transaction if they wanted to add towing to their policies. If not, they just completed their purchase. With this new feature, many customers did select the towing option, just like with in-person sales.

Thanks to CRE, shopping for insurance online is becoming more and more like the experience with an agent face-to-face. Descriptive analytics help Esurance to instantly customize and present the packages and options that are most likely to succeed with the customer. The company continuously monitors how well the CRE is doing by comparing the numbers of customers who buy a policy with those who leave the site without making a purchase.

Esurance also wants to make sure customers don't buy too little or too much insurance. It's convinced that the CRE comes up with the right combination for each customer. Not only does Esurance feel that its quotes and packages are optimal, but that they are provided in half the time (15 minutes) that another online car insurer (GEICO) advertises.

Although the CRE platform cost $1 million to develop and implement, the company has saved between $500,000 and $1 million annually in further IT costs, including any subscriptions to analytics software-as-a-service (SaaS).

Sources: Compiled from C. Babcock, "Esurance Puts Analytics Closer to the Customer," *InformationWeek*, April 28, 2015; D. Jergler, "Google Compare May Go Beyond Auto Insurance," *Insurance Journal*,

March 11, 2015; G. Bartholomew, "Demystifying the Rate Madness in Insurance Advertising," *EagleEye Analytics*, October 17, 2014; S. Overby, "Progressive Insurance Uses Data Analytics to Fine-Tune Ad Strategy," *CIO*, September 28, 2014; R. Clarke and A. Libarikian, "Unleashing the Value of Advance Analytics in Insurance," *McKinsey*, August, 2014; D. Wing, "Evolution of Homeowners Data and Analytics," *Verisk Analytics*, Quarter 2, 2014; C. Boulton, "Auto Insurers Bank on Big Data to Drive New Business," *The Wall Street Journal*, February 20, 2013; www.esurance.com, accessed August 28, 2015.

Questions

1. Describe how Esurance's CRE analytics package contributes to the customer's experience.

2. Provide an example of a predictive analytics application that Esurance could implement.

3. Provide an example of a prescriptive analytics application that Esurance could implement.

The emergence of technology for capturing, storing, and using real-time data (e.g., the Internet of Things, see Chapter 10) has enabled real-time BA users to employ analytics models to analyze data in real time. In addition, it helps organizations to make decisions and to interact with customers in new ways. Real-time BA is closely related to descriptive analytics because the focus of decisions is real time, rather than at some point in the future. IT's About Business 5.3 illustrates how TaKaDu uses sensor data as inputs into real-time analytics software to monitor the pipes of water utilities.

IT's About Business 5.3

TaKaDu's Dashboard Helps to Conserve Water

POM Israel is a desert nation that has been dealing with a drought caused by record-low rainfall since 2008. Therefore, freshwater sources in Israel and the surrounding region are precious. Israelis use water from three sources: recycled wastewater (about 85 percent); a reservoir, filled by pipelines from the Sea of Galilee 90 miles to the north (some 10 percent); and desalination (approximately 5 percent).

Regardless of the source of water, the pipes carrying this precious resource are all-important. About one third of water distributed by utilities around the world is lost to leaks. Consequently, the ability to detect leaks instantly is the most valuable conservation technology.

In 2008, startup TaKaDu (www.takadu.com) designed cloud-based analytics software that utilizes raw data from smart sensors placed in the pipes of the water network. (See our discussion of the Internet of Things in Chapter 10.) These sensors monitor the flow rates, pressure, and quality of the water, and they identify problems in the meters, valves, pipes, and other system equipment. The software's algorithms then analyze these data to determine when and where water is leaking. As an added benefit, the sensors can detect weaknesses in the pipes that could lead to future leaks. Consequently they enable utilities to prevent leaks before they occur.

TaKaDu provides its results in the form of dashboards on employee smart phones. By scanning the dashboards, company employees monitor whether the meters are accurate, the water quality and pressure are optimal, the water flow is normal, and the pumps are operating properly. How do employees know if the water flow is normal and therefore when use is abnormal? The TaKaDu software determines a baseline of regular use throughout the day. For example, it establishes that water use is highest when people are typically at home—in the mornings before they go to work and in the evenings when they return.

The software also considers local factors. At a Dutch utility, for instance, the system noted regular peaks of flow one Friday afternoon. It turned out that increased water use happened during breaks in play during a World Cup game between the Netherlands and Spain, when fans used their bathrooms.

In addition to leaks and use patterns, TaKaDu software can also help pinpoint problems that could be due to theft. A utility in Melbourne, Australia, Unitywater (www.unitywater.com), detected spikes of water coming from a fire hydrant. Officials discovered that a strawberry farmer was siphoning water from the hydrant. Network-wide, Unitywater saved more than one billion liters of water in the first 12 months of implementing the TaKaDu system, with a value of more than $2 million. The utility saves not only money, but time, because it now takes 60 percent less time to repair problems.

TaKaDu software is most effective when it works with other systems. For example, it complements the sound equipment developed by the technology company Aquarius Spectrum (www.aquarius-spectrum.com). TaKaDu software identifies the location of a leak within a neighborhood, and then Aquarius's technology detects the exact pipe that the leak is coming from. Another company, Curapipe (www.curapipe.com), has technology that plugs leaks automatically without the need for digging.

TaKaDu has helped Israel to enjoy higher agricultural yields during the current drought than the country had previously achieved in nondrought years. Recall that global utilities tend to lose 30 percent of the water they distribute. That figure is just 10 percent for Jerusalem's utility, Hagihon, since implementing TaKaDu. In mid-2015, Israel even enjoyed a water surplus, some of which (about 150 million cubic meters per year) it pumps to Jordan and the Palestinian Authority.

By mid-2015, TaKaDu software had been adopted by 14 other utilities in cities ranging from Campo Grande, Brazil, to Bilbao, Spain. In 2015, Australia's largest utility, Sydney Water (www.sydneywater.com.au), adopted the system as well. Also in 2015, TaKaDu introduced its service for U.S. utilities that monitor water quality, an activity that is closely regulated by the U.S. Environmental Protection Agency.

Unfortunately, despite this progress, in mid-2015 only 1 out of 5 utilities worldwide were using smart sensors in their water networks, and in the United States, it's an even lower proportion. But TaKaDu expects the use of its technology will increase, especially among American utilities, as the cost of hardware declines, networks age, and droughts become more common.

Sources: Compiled from "3M Partners with TaKaDu to Offer Water Utilities a More Complete Solution," *TaKaDu Press Release*, August 26, 2015; D. Asper, "TaKaDu's Water-Saving Technology Saves Australia Millions of Dollars," *NoCamels*, April 6, 2015; J. Foreshew, "TaKaDu Helps Keep Water Flowing for Unitywater," *The Australian Business Review*, March 31, 2015; A. Little, "Anybody Call a Plumber?" *Bloomberg BusinessWeek*, January 12-18, 2015; J. Neeman, J. Buxton, and K. Cornish, "Water Utilities Turn to New Technologies to Increase Intelligence in Systems," *Breaking Energy*, December 4, 2014; H. Moreno, "Transforming Utilities Using Data Analytics," *Forbes*, September 30, 2014; S. Udasin, "Hagihon, TaKaDu Sign Contract for Jerusalem Water Management," *The Jerusalem Post*, September 10, 2014; J. Ollagnier, "Water Utilities: Can They Use Analytics for Smart Monitoring?" *Accenture*, March 28, 2014; www.takadu.com, accessed August 27, 2015.

Questions

1. How does the TaKaDu system utilize the Internet of Things? (Hint: See Chapter 10.)

2. Provide an example of how TaKaDu uses its system for predictive analytics.

3. Provide an example of how TaKaDu could use its system for prescriptive analytics.

4. Refer to Chapter 2. Is the TaKaDu system a strategic information system for Jerusalem? Why or why not?

Predictive Analytics

Predictive analytics are the next step in data reduction. **Predictive analytics** utilize a variety of analytics techniques and tools to examine recent and historical data in order to detect patterns and predict future outcomes and trends. Predictive analytics provide estimates about the likelihood of a future outcome.

The purpose of predictive analytics is *not* to tell decision makers what will happen in the future. Predictive analytics can only forecast what *might* happen in the future, because predictive analytics are based on probabilities.

MKT Continuing our example of Fandango. How does the ticket seller know when to send e-mails to its members with discount offers for a specific movie on a specific day? Consider John Jones. Predictive analytics tools analyze terabytes of data to determine that while John likes science fiction movies, he has not seen the latest science fiction movie, which has been in theaters since the previous Friday.

Predictive analytics are used throughout organizations in every industry. Let's look at some examples.

MKT • Predictive analytics drive the coupons you receive at the grocery cash register. In the United Kingdom, grocery giant Tesco (www.tesco.com) predicts which discounts will be redeemed in order to target more than 100 million personalized coupons annually at cash registers in 13 countries. This process increased coupon redemption rates by a factor of 3.6 over previous methods.

MKT • Websites predict which ads you will click in order to instantly choose which ad to show you, a process that drives millions of dollars in new revenue.

• President Obama was re-elected in 2012 with the help of voter prediction. His campaign predicted which voters would be positively persuaded by campaign contact, and which voters would be negatively impacted.

• Leading online dating companies Match (www.match.com), OKCupid (www.okcupid.com), and eHarmony (www.eharmony.com) predict which prospect on your screen will be the most compatible with you.

• Student essay grade prediction has been developed for automatic grading. The system grades as accurately as human graders.

MKT • Wireless carriers predict how likely it is you will cancel and defect to a competitor (churn), possibly before you have decided to do so. The predictions are based on factors such as dropped calls, your phone usage, your billing information, and whether your contacts have already defected.

POM • Allstate Insurance tripled the accuracy of predicting bodily injury liability from car crashes based on the characteristics of the insured vehicle. This process results in approximately $40 million annual savings.

• Stanford University data scientists used predictive analytics to diagnose breast cancer better than human physicians by discovering an innovative method that takes into account a greater number of contributing factors in a tissue sample.

- Officials in Oregon and Pennsylvania are using predictive analytics to assess the risk that a convict will offend again.

- Financial services firms use predictive analytics to produce credit scores. They use these scores to determine the probability of customers making future credit payments on time. **FIN**

- Other examples of predictive analytics include understanding how sales might close at the end of the year, predicting what items customers will purchase together, and forecasting inventory levels based on a large number of variables.

- Sentiment analysis is another type of predictive analysis. The input to this type of model is plain text (e.g., ratings, recommendations, tweets, Facebook posts) and the output of the model is a sentiment score. This score can be positive or negative. This score could also be a number between -1 and $+1$, indicating the degree of positivity or negativity.

For other examples of descriptive analytics, see this chapter's opening case, closing case 1, closing case 2, and all IT's About Business. IT's About Business 5.4 illustrates how a startup company in India uses analytics to predict which of its customers will be a good credit risk.

IT's About Business 5.4

POM Simpa Networks Provide Solar Energy to India's Poor

MKT Worldwide, approximately 1.6 billion people do not have access to electricity, and another 1 billion have only unreliable access. Many of these people depend on kerosene lanterns and battery-powered flashlights for light. Moreover, these same people often earn less than $10 per day, and they spend up to 30 percent of their incomes on inefficient and expensive means of accessing electricity.

The lack of electricity is particularly acute in India, with 75 million families not having access. Consequently, these people rely on "dirty" fuels such as kerosene, which they use in lamps. There is hope, however. There are effective alternatives to electricity, such as solar power, which can meet the needs of homes and small businesses.

To address these energy needs, Simpa Networks (www.simpanetworks.com), a startup technology company founded in 2010, sells solar power not as a system but as a service, to rural households and businesses. Its mission is to bring sustainable energy to those who currently do not have enough money to pay for their energy needs.

Simpa's customers use the "Progressive Purchase" pricing model. Under this model, the consumer makes a series of payments, each of which unlocks the solar home system for a specified amount of energy consumption. When the prepaid consumption is exhausted, the solar home system is temporarily disabled until the customer makes another payment. When the consumer has fully paid the total purchase price of the product, then Simpa restores full functionality. The system is permanently unlocked, and it produces energy for free.

Simpa's problem is that, because it has limited resources, it must be selective in deciding which families and businesses to support. As a result, the company turned to DataKind for help. DataKind (www.datakind.org) is a nonprofit organization that connects data scientists with organizations working to address humanitarian issues.

DataKind's scientists used Simpa's historical data on customer energy usage and payment behavior as inputs into a credit-scoring model that helps Simpa better assess new customers. The objective is to offer the most appropriate services and support.

That is, the model enables Simpa to become "smarter" in selecting customers. The model also enables Simpa to take risks when lending to rural farmers who cannot turn to banks for loans.

Simpa's solar-as-a-service has resulted in huge time savings for those doing farming and household tasks such as cooking and cleaning. The system also has health benefits, including better quality of light and better air quality thanks to reduced kerosene fumes and wood smoke. Prior to Simpa's system, approximately 80 percent of energy-poor individuals suffered eye irritation from fumes. After customers deployed the system, that number fell to 28 percent. Further, fire accidents dropped to zero. The system also helps increase sales in shops that can stay open longer thanks to cheaper energy.

By mid-2015, Simpa's clean, reliable energy could be found in more than 63,000 rural households and small businesses in India. The credit-scoring model helped Simpa provide its system to the optimal mix of customers. In that way, the company was able to receive an excellent return on its investment and, in turn, help additional families and businesses.

Sources: Compiled from M. Barlow, "Data and Social Good," *O'Reilly*, August 15, 2015; "Simpa Networks: Making Solar Power Affordable in Rural India," *OPIC*, 2014; J. Novet, "DataKind's Do-Good Data-Science Projects Arrive in 5 More Cities," *Venture Beat*, August 21, 2014; B. Prows, "Rural Solar Energy Lights India's Future," *MobileBeyond*, July 12, 2014; A. Satter, "Watch How Solar Power Is Transforming Rural India," *Think Progress*, July 10, 2014; "We Envision a World without Energy Poverty by 2030: Bijli Program Update," *The Climate Group*, July 3, 2014; "Affordable Pay-As-You-Go Solar Power for India's Energy-Poor Homes," *ADB Knowledge Showcases*, August 2013; www.datakind.org, www.simpanetworks.com accessed August 28, 2015.

Questions

1. Describe how Simpa Networks uses descriptive analytics to further its mission.

2. How does predictive analytics help Simpa Networks provide solar energy to India's underserved population?

2. Describe how Simpa Networks could use prescriptive analytics to further its mission.

Prescriptive Analytics

Prescriptive analytics go beyond descriptive and predictive models by recommending one or more courses of action and showing the likely outcome of each decision. Predictive analytics does not predict one possible future, but rather multiple future outcomes based on the decision maker's actions. Prescriptive analytics attempt to quantify the effect of future decisions in order to advise on possible outcomes before the decisions are actually made.

Some companies are successfully using prescriptive analytics to optimize production, scheduling, and inventory along the supply chain to make sure that they deliver the right products at the right time in order to optimize the customer experience.

Prescriptive analytics requires a predictive model with two additional components: actionable data and a feedback system that tracks the outcome produced by the action taken. Because a prescriptive model is able to predict the possible consequences based on different choices of action, it can also recommend the best course of action for any pre-specified outcome.

POM Continuing with the Fandango example: The company uses prescriptive analytics to be able to change ticket price offerings every hour. Fandango has learned when the most desirable movie times are by analyzing millions of show times instantaneously. This data is then used to set an optimal price at any given time, based on the supply of show times and the demand for movie tickets. This process maximizes profits. The data from each show provides the feedback as to the contribution of each ticket price to profits.

For examples of prescriptive analytics, see this chapter's two closing cases. Pay particular attention to how the organizations in these two cases progress from descriptive analytics, to predictive analytics, and then on to prescriptive analytics.

Presentation Tools

After applying BA models, the results are presented to users in visual formats such as text, graphics, and tables. This process, known as *data visualization*, makes IT applications more attractive and understandable to users. A variety of visualization methods and software packages that support decision making are available. Dashboards are the most common BA presentation tool. We also take a look at another valuable data visualization tool: geographic information systems.

Dashboards. Dashboards evolved from executive information systems, which were information systems designed specifically for the information needs of top executives. Today, however, many employees, business partners, and customers use digital dashboards.

A **dashboard** provides easy access to timely information and direct access to management reports. It is user friendly, it is supported by graphics, and, most importantly, it enables managers to examine exception reports and drill down into detailed data. Table 5.1 summarizes the various capabilities common to many dashboards. Moreover, some of the capabilities discussed in this section have been incorporated into many BA products, as illustrated in Figure 5.4.

One outstanding example of a dashboard is Bloomberg LP (www.bloomberg.com), a privately held company, that provides a subscription service that sells financial data, software to analyze these data, trading tools, and news (electronic, print, TV, and radio). All of this information is accessible through a color-coded Bloomberg keyboard that displays the desired information on a computer screen, either the user's screen or one that Bloomberg provides. Users can also set up their own computers to access the service without a Bloomberg keyboard. The subscription service plus the keyboard is called the Bloomberg Terminal. It literally represents a do-it-yourself dashboard, because users can customize their information feeds as well as the look and feel of those feeds (see Figure 5.5).

In another example, a human resources dashboard/scorecard developed by iDashboards, one of the leading BA software vendors. At a glance, users can see employee productivity, hours, team, department, and division performance in graphical, tabular, summary, and detailed

TABLE 5.1   The Capabilities of Dashboards

Capability	Description
Drill down	The ability to go to details, at several levels; it can be done by a series of menus or by clicking on a drillable portion of the screen.
Critical success factors (CSFs)	The factors most critical for the success of business. These can be organizational, industry, departmental, or for individual workers.
Key performance indicators	The specific measures of CSFs.
Status access	The latest data available on KPI or some other metric, often in real time.
Trend analysis	Short-, medium-, and long-term trend of KPIs or metrics, which are projected using forecasting methods.
Exception reporting	Reports highlight deviations larger than certain thresholds. Reports may include only deviations.

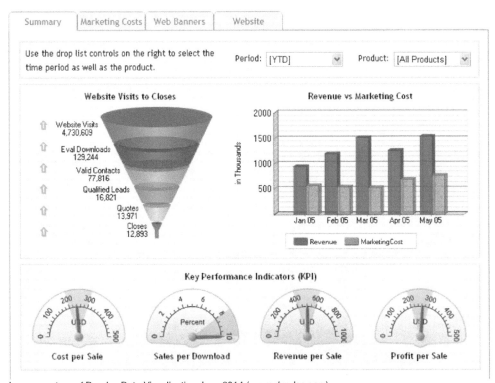

FIGURE 5.4 Sample performance dashboard.

Image courtesy of Dundas Data Visualization, Inc., 2014 (*www.dundas.com*).

form. The selector box to the left enables the user to easily change between specific analyses to compare their performance.

A unique and interesting application of dashboards to support the informational needs of executives is the Management Cockpit. Essentially, a Management Cockpit is a strategic management room containing an elaborate set of dashboards that enable top-level decision makers to pilot their businesses better. The goal is to create an environment that encourages more efficient management meetings and boosts team performance via effective communication. To help achieve this goal, the dashboard graphically displays KPIs and information relating to critical success factors on the walls of a meeting room called the *Management Cockpit Room* (see Figure 5.6). The cockpit-like arrangement of instrument panels and displays helps managers visualize how all of the different factors in the business interrelate.

FIGURE 5.5 Bloomberg Terminal.

Carlos Osario/Zuma Press.

FIGURE 5.6 Management Cockpit.

The Management Cockpit is a registered trademark of SAP, created by Professor Patrick M. Georges.

Within the room, the four walls are designated by color: Black, Red, Blue, and White. The Black Wall displays the principal success factors and financial indicators. The Red Wall measures market performance. The Blue Wall projects the performance of internal processes and employees. Finally, the White Wall indicates the status of strategic projects. The Flight Deck, a six-screen, high-end PC, enables executives to drill down to detailed information. External information needed for competitive analyses can easily be imported into the room.

Board members and other executives hold meetings in the Management Cockpit Room. Managers also meet there with the comptroller to discuss current business issues. The Management Cockpit can implement various what–if scenarios for this purpose. It also provides a common basis for information and communication. Finally, it supports efforts to translate a corporate strategy into concrete activities by identifying performance indicators.

Geographic Information Systems. A geographic information system (GIS) is a computer-based system for capturing, integrating, manipulating, and displaying data using digitized maps. Its most distinguishing characteristic is that every record or digital object has an identified geographical location. This process, called *geocoding*, enables users to generate information for planning, problem solving, and decision making. In addition, the graphical format makes it easy for managers to visualize the data. There are countless applications of GISs to improve decision making in both the public and private sectors.

Children's National Health System offers injury prevention advice to the community. Clinicians have found that using geospatial data helps them accomplish this mission. The healthcare center integrated its existing electronic health records system with GIS software from ESRI (www.esri.com) to display health data with geospatial coordinates. One of the integrated system's first projects focused on pediatric burn cases.

GIS mapping enabled the clinic to identify the hotspots where injuries were occurring on a map. That map allowed staff members to develop prevention programs tailored to the demographics of areas with high rates of injuries. For example, if the system identifies a cluster of children with burns in an Hispanic neighborhood, the staff will work with community groups to provide parents with Spanish-language information about safety.

The new system has produced results. The clinic is seeing fewer burn patients overall and fewer patients requiring high-level burn care. Children's National Health System is now using its system to map concentrations of other medical conditions, such as obesity and asthma.

Before you go on...

1. Differentiate among descriptive analytics, predictive analytics, and prescriptive analytics.

2. What is a dashboard? Why are dashboards so valuable to employees?

Apply the Concept 5.4

LEARNING OBJECTIVE 5.4 Provide a definition and a use case example for descriptive analytics, predictive analytics, and prescriptive analytics.

STEP 1: Background

Section 5.4 discusses descriptive, predictive, and prescriptive analytics. Descriptive analytics describe what has happened, predictive analytics predicts what might happen, and prescriptive analytics prescribes probabilities to future outcomes based on future activities.

STEP 2: Activity

Visit http://www.wiley.com/go/rainer/MIS4e/applytheconcept, and click on the link provided for Apply the Concept 5.4. This link will take you to a video that describes prescriptive analytics to help a rock climber determine the best path to the top based on certain decisions. While this is a simple example, it illustrates the need to think past the next choice and to see how this choice will impact the overall probability of reaching the desired outcome.

STEP 3: Deliverable

Based on the video and any of your own Web research, describe and give examples of how a rock climber might use descriptive analytics, predictive analytics, and prescriptive analytics to determine the best path to the goal.

What's in IT for me?

ACCT   For the Accounting Major

BA is used extensively in auditing to uncover irregularities. It also is used to uncover and prevent fraud. CPAs use BA for many of their duties, ranging from risk analysis to cost control.

FIN   For the Finance Major

People have been using computers for decades to solve financial problems. Innovative BA applications have been created for activities such as making stock market decisions, refinancing bonds, assessing debt risks, analyzing financial conditions, predicting business failures, forecasting financial trends, and investing in global markets.

MKT   For the Marketing Major

Marketing personnel utilize BA in many applications, from planning and executing marketing campaigns, to allocating advertising budgets, to evaluating alternative routings of salespeople. New marketing approaches such as targeted marketing and database marketing depend heavily on IT in general, and on data warehouses and business intelligence applications in particular.

POM   For the Production/Operations Management Major

BA supports complex operations and production decisions from inventory control, to production planning, to supply chain integration.

HRM   For the Human Resources Management Major

Human resources personnel use BA for many of their activities. For example, BA applications can find resumes of applicants posted on the Web and sort them to match needed skills and to support management succession planning.

MIS   For the MIS Major

MIS provides the data infrastructure used in BA. MIS personnel are also involved in building, deploying, and supporting BA applications.

Summary

1. **Use a decision support framework to demonstrate how technology supports managerial decision making at each phase of the decision-making process.**

When making a decision, either organizational or personal, the decision maker goes through a three-step process: intelligence, design, and choice. When the choice is made, the decision is implemented. In general, it is difficult to state which information systems support specific decision makers in an organization. Modern information systems, particularly business analytics systems, are available to support everyone in an organization.

2. **Describe each phase of the business analytics process.**

Business analytics is the process of developing actionable decisions or recommendations for actions based on insights generated from historical data. The phases in the business analytics process are shown in FIGURE 5.3 and include data management, analytics tools and techniques, analytics models, and presentation tools.

3. **Describe each of the various analytics tools and examples of their uses.**

These techniques and tools include Excel, decision support systems, online analytical processing (OLAP), data mining, machine learning, deep learning, and neural networks. We discuss the first four in Section 5.3, and the last three in Plug IT In 5. Note that there are many statistical modeling tools available in analytics software packages. These tools are beyond the scope of this chapter

4. **Provide a definition and a use case example for descriptive analytics, predictive analytics, and prescriptive analytics.**

Descriptive analytics summarize what has happened in the past and allow decision makers to learn from past behaviors. Predictive analytics utilize a variety of analytics techniques and tools to examine recent and historical data in order to detect patterns and predict future outcomes and trends. Prescriptive analytics go beyond descriptive and predictive models by recommending one or more courses of action and showing the likely outcome of each decision. We leave the examples of each analytics model to you.

Chapter Glossary

business analytics (BA) The process of developing actionable decisions or recommendations for actions based on insights generated from historical data.

business intelligence (BI) A broad category of applications, technologies, and processes for gathering, storing, accessing, and analyzing data to help business users make better decisions.

dashboard A business analytics presentation tool that provides rapid access to timely information and direct access to management reports.

data mining The process of searching for valuable business information in a large database, data warehouse, or data mart.

decision A choice that individuals and groups make among two or more alternatives.

decision support systems (DSSs) Business intelligence systems that combine models and data in an attempt to solve semistructured and some unstructured problems with extensive user involvement.

descriptive analytics A type of business analytics that summarize what has happened in the past and allow decision makers to learn from past behaviors.

geographic information system (GIS) A computer-based system for capturing, integrating, manipulating, and displaying data using digitized maps.

management A process by which organizational goals are achieved through the use of resources.

model (in decision making) A simplified representation, or abstraction, of reality.

multidimensional data analysis See online analytical processing (OLAP).

online analytical processing (OLAP) (or multidimensional data analysis) A set of capabilities for "slicing and dicing" data using dimensions and measures associated with the data.

predictive analytics A type of business analytics that utilize a variety of analytics tools to examine recent and historical data in order to detect patterns and predict future outcomes and trends.

prescriptive analytics A type of business analytics that recommend one or more courses of action and showing the likely outcome of each decision.

productivity The ratio between the inputs to a process and the outputs from that process.

Discussion Questions

1. Your company is considering opening a new factory in China. List several typical activities involved in each phase of the decision (intelligence, design, and choice).

2. Recall that a market basket analysis (a type of data mining) of convenience store purchases revealed that customers tended to buy beer and diapers at the same time when they shopped. Now that the analysis uncovered this relationship exists, provide a rationale for it. Note: You will have to decide what the next question is.

3. American Can Company announced that it was interested in acquiring a company in the health maintenance organization (HMO) field. Two decisions were involved in this act: (1) the decision to acquire an HMO, and (2) the decision of which HMO to acquire. How can the use of BA assist the company in this endeavor?

4. Discuss the strategic benefits of business analytics.

5. In early 2012, *The New York Times* reported the story of a Target data scientist who was able to determine if a customer was pregnant based on her pattern of previous purchases.

   a. Describe the business analytics models that the data scientist used.

   b. Refer to Chapter 6 and discuss the ethics of Target's analytics process.

   c. Research the story and note the unintended consequences of Target's analytics process.

6. Consider the admissions process at your university. Your university's admissions process involves the analysis of many variables to decide whom to admit to each year's freshman class. Contact your admissions office and gather information on the variables used in the admissions process. As you recall from applying at your university, typical variables would include high school attended, high school grade point average, standardized test scores such as ACT or SAT, and many others. (Do not be surprised if there are variables that your admissions office cannot provide.)

   a. Provide an example of how your admissions office uses descriptive analytics in the admissions process. Use the variables you have found in your example.

   b. Provide an example of how your admissions office uses predictive analytics in the admissions process. Use the variables you have found in your example.

   c. Provide an example of how your admissions office uses prescriptive analytics in the admissions process. Use the variables you have found in your example.

Closing Case 1

Analytics in the National Basketball Association

POM The Problem

Historically the primary method of judging how well a player or team was performing was the "eye test." This term refers to the intuitive feeling that people with long experience in a sport acquired from watching games and practices. Today, professional sports teams are utilizing analytics to provide data-driven judgments.

The analytics revolution in professional sports began in baseball, as highlighted in the book and the movie *Moneyball*. Baseball is a relatively simple sport to analyze statistically because it centers on a sequence of one-on-one confrontations between a batter and a pitcher. Further, each play has an obvious start point and end point. Statisticians call each of those plays a "state."

In contrast the discrete, state-to-state action in baseball, basketball is a constant flow. Players switch instantly from offense to defense.

Moreover, regardless of a player's position, he or she can be anywhere on the court at any time. The game has no states, so analysts could not statistically determine the odds of a given outcome (e.g., a player making a shot).

Consequently, modern analytics focuses on the locations and movement of the players and the ball. Essentially, analytics in the National Basketball Association (NBA; www.nba.com) is a mapping and data visualization problem. The challenge is to visually depict data about movement through space and time; that is, to make numbers visible.

The Solution

The First System. Kirk Goldsberry, a longtime basketball fan with a Ph.D. in geography, undertook the task of developing analytics software for professional basketball. First, he divided the 1,284 square feet of the court where players actually shoot—the area that stretches from just outside the three-point line (roughly 25 feet) to the basket—into cells. Then he searched for data.

Obtaining the relevant data for accurate analysis was difficult. Tracking 10 players in constant motion is not a simple process. On ESPN.com, Goldsberry found statistics for every shot taken in the NBA, including who took the shot, from where, and whether it went in the basket. He then developed a database with the spatial coordinates for all 700,000 shots taken in every NBA game from 2006 to 2011.

Goldsberry next analyzed his data to generate maps that showed where a given player shot, how often, and whether or not the shot was good. Goldsberry called his system CourtVision. This system revealed differences in players that had not been previously quantified. For example, Ray Allen, one of the NBA's best shooters, had several areas where he made a high percentage of his shots from three-point range. However, he rarely attempted any mid-range shots.

For the first time, fans could see the types of shots their favorite players took as well as the relative value of those shots. However, CourtVision did not take into account variables such as who the defender was or what else was happening on the court. Nevertheless, Goldsberry's system provided team management with an initial tool to evaluate players.

Today's System. The next opportunity to collect data came when a company called Stats (www.stats.com) developed a six-camera setup for basketball. The camera system, which is now employed in all 29 NBA arenas, tracks each player on the court throughout every game. It therefore provides a complete view of the entire game, including tracking individual players and ball possession.

Stats offered its data to Goldsberry. The data were more specific than the data Goldsberry had obtained from ESPN.com. Once Goldsberry had the data, he could analyze them to answer any number of questions.

- Players who "draw the defense" can be quantified as ones who pass the ball effectively when two or more players are guarding them.
- "Getting good spacing" visualizes which players control which parts of the court.
- "On-ball defense" assesses how effectively a player defending the ball decreases his opponent's chance of scoring.

In addition, analyzing the camera data enabled Goldsberry to understand one of the most difficult aspects of basketball: defense. Historically, teams had relied on counting statistics—for example, how many steals, how many blocks—to capture a player's defensive value. The new system provided a much more sophisticated picture of the game.

Goldsberry began by observing that the area right around the basket is the most important real estate on the court to defend because this area is where offensive players shoot the highest percentage. Therefore, he analyzed how effectively defenders within five feet of the basket were able to prevent opponents from scoring. He found that the average NBA defender allowed a shooting percentage of 49.7 in that area.

Utilizing his new data, Goldsberry identified two classes of defense. In the first type, defenders blocked or altered their opponents' shots – that is, they reduced "shooting efficiency." In the 2014 NBA season, for example, Indiana Pacers center Roy Hibbert and Milwaukee Bucks center Larry Sanders led the NBA, holding opponents to 38 percent.

The second approach to defense was more subtle. Goldsberry found that some players reduced the frequency of their opponents' shots, not just their efficiency. By comparing the average rate of shots to the rate when specific defenders were guarding the area, he could calculate when the number of shots decreased. Again in the 2014 NBA season, the best player at this type of defense was Houston Rockets center Dwight Howard, who caused opposing teams to shoot 9 percent less frequently around the basket. As opponents shot less often around the basket, they took more mid-range shots, which are the least productive shots in the NBA.

The Results

Goldsberry essentially divided basketball games into slices of time and then employed the same kinds of analyses that analysts had been applying to the states in baseball. He could then quantify the value—in terms of points—of every move on the court, from an entry pass into the post (the area close to the basket) to a drive to the basket. These analyses created a new method to evaluate everything a player and team does.

Let's consider one example, the Houston Rockets. Utilizing the results of its analytics software, the team rarely shoots long-range two-point jump shots, because the Rockets believe this type of shot is among the worst strategies in basketball. The shots are too far away from the basket to be a high-probability scoring opportunity, yet not far enough (behind the three-point line) to be awarded an extra point for the risk in taking an even longer shot.

Analytics are impacting not only the Rockets, but the entire NBA as well. For instance, in January 2015 NBA data analysis revealed that players attempted more three-point shot attempts than free throws. In fact, three three-point shot defines the shift to analytics in the NBA. It is not a coincidence that the Golden State Warriors, the 2015 NBA champions, were the league's best three-point shooting team during the regular season.

Sources: Compiled from "NBA Teams That Have Analytics Department," *NBAStuffer.com*, August 17, 2015; T. Ross, "Welcome to Smarter Basketball," *The Atlantic*, June 25, 2015; K. Mehta, "Data and the NBA: A Slam Dunk Approach to Basketball," *umbel.com*, June 22, 2015; C. Benjamin, "The 4 Fallacies of NBA Analytics," *Men's Journal,* June 3, 2015; S. Hammer, "Analytics Key to Modern NBA Success," *The Miscellany News*, May 6, 2015; M. Lawrence, "Big Data's Air-Ball: Five Questions about Players that NBA Analytics Can't Answer," *Forbes*, February 27, 2015; B. Alamar, "The Inside Man: NBA Analytics," *ESPN.com*, February 25, 2015; M. McClusky, "This Guy's Quest to Track Every Shot in the NBA Changed Basketball Forever," *Wired*, November, 2014; T. Moynihan, "The NBA's New High-Tech Control Center Is a Hoops Fan's Dream," *Wired*, October 28, 2014; R. Simmons, "Golden State Warriors at the Forefront of NBA Data Analysis," *SFGate*, September 14, 2014; B. Holmes, "New Age of NBA Analytics: Advantage or Overload?" *The Boston Globe*, March 30, 2014; D. Oliver, "How Numbers Have Changed the NBA," *ESPN.com*, November, 15, 2013; www.nba.com, accessed August 25, 2015.

Questions

1. Provide an example of the use of descriptive analytics for an NBA team using Goldberry's system.

2. Provide an example of the use of predictive analytics for an NBA team using Goldberry's system.

3. Provide an example of the use of prescriptive analytics for an NBA team using Goldberry's system.

4. What are the advantages and disadvantages of Goldsberry's system to NBA players? Provide specific examples to support your answer.

Closing Case 2

United Parcel Service Uses Three Types of Analytics

POM   **The Problem**

United Parcel Service (UPS; www.ups.com) is a global organization, with 424,000 employees and nearly 100,000 vehicles. UPS drivers typically make between 120 and 175 "drops" per day. Between any two drops, drivers can take a number of possible paths. With 55,000 routes in the Unites States alone, the total number of possible routes is inconceivably vast. Clearly, it is in the best interest of UPS and its drivers to find the most efficient routes. Therefore, any tiny amount of efficiency that can be gained in daily operations yields significant improvements to the company's bottom line. Essentially, "little" things matter a great deal to UPS.

In addition, UPS must manage a low-margin business as well as a unionized workforce that is compensated at the high end of the industry scale. Significantly, rival FedEx (www.fedex.com) uses independent contractors for its ground network. Consequently, FedEx does not have the burden of expensive employee benefits packages.

Another problem for UPS is that the increase in electronic commerce has shifted an increasing number of UPS's delivery stops from retailers to residences. In fact, UPS expects that residential deliveries will make up half of the company's total deliveries by 2018. Historically, drivers would drop off multiple packages at a retailer. Today, they must make scattered stops to drop off packages at individual houses in a neighborhood. This process involves more routes and is more time consuming.

The Solution

For decades UPS has been using three types of analytics to produce efficiencies:

- Descriptive analytics asks, "Where are we today?"
- Predictive analytics asks, "With our current trajectory, where *will* we be tomorrow?"
- Prescriptive analytics asks, "Where *should* we be tomorrow?"

As UPS has moved from descriptive to predictive to prescriptive analytics, its data needs have increased, the skill set of its people has increased, and the business impact of analytics has increased. We consider these developments below.

Descriptive Analytics. UPS implemented descriptive analytics in the 1990s when the company provided its drivers with hand-held computers, called Delivery Information Acquisition Devices (DIADs). The DIADs enabled UPS to capture detailed data that measured the company's current status. For example, the company measured driving variables in hundredths of a second. Their reasoning was that if they could reduce one mile per driver per day in the United

States alone, that process would add up to $50 million to the bottom line annually.

One drawback to the DIAD system was that the data were scattered across various locations. Specifically, some of the data were with employees, some were located in corporate repositories, some were contained in Excel spreadsheets, and some were distributed throughout the company. However, UPS did not have a predictive model that could help the company "tomorrow."

Predictive Analytics. To address this problem, in 2003 UPS deployed predictive analytics with its Package Flow Technologies system. With this system, drivers started the day with a DIAD that detailed the packages they were to deliver and the order in which they were to deliver those packages. The DIAD became the drivers' assistant. The system enabled UPS to reduce total delivery driving by 85 million miles per year. That process saved the firm 8.5 million gallons of fuel, and it saved the planet from 85,000 metric tons of carbon dioxide going into the atmosphere.

However, drivers had to provide different services from the same vehicle—for example, deferred service and premium service. They had some packages that had to be delivered by 10:30 AM, some that had to be delivered by noon, and some that had to be delivered by 2:00 PM. Drivers therefore had to decide how they were going to service those customers. With so many variables to consider, it was practically impossible for drivers to optimize their routes.

Prescriptive Analytics. UPS realized that it needed to take analytics to the next level. So, in mid-2012, the company began deploying its On-Road Integrated Optimization and Navigation (ORION) system. ORION reorganizes the drivers' routes based on today's customers, today's needs, and today's packages, and it designs deliveries in a very specific, optimized order. ORION takes into account UPS business rules, maps, what time drivers need to be at specific locations, and customer preferences.

When UPS drivers are on the road, they usually travel at speeds of 20–25 miles per hour. Therefore, every mile reduced equates to a savings of 2–3 minutes. Because ORION shortens routes by 7–8 miles per day, this savings enables UPS to deliver more packages.

ORION enhances UPS customer service with more efficient routing, and it allows UPS to offer innovative services and customized solutions. An example of this type of service is UPS My Choice, which gives customers a one-day alert for the time a package is arriving, and allows them to control the timing and location of the delivery. By mid-2015, UPS My Choice had almost 13 million members.

At the beginning of a shift, a UPS driver checks his DIAD, which displays two possible delivery routes. One route uses ORION, and the other uses UPS's traditional combination of work rules, procedures, and analytic tools. Drivers can choose either route, but if they decide not to use ORION, then they will be asked to explain their decisions.

Driver reaction to ORION has been mixed. The experience can frustrate some drivers who might not want to surrender their autonomy or who might not follow ORION's logic in designing their routes.

The Results

In 2013, ORION saved 1.5 million gallons of fuel (on top of the 8.5 million gallons the firm was already saving). UPS gained those savings despite the fact that only 20 percent of its 50,000 drivers had adopted the system. UPS plans to complete the deployment of ORION by the end of 2016. When ORION is fully implemented, the system is expected to reduce the distance driven by its drivers by 100 million miles annually. Further, ORION will produce annual savings of $300 million as well as an additional 10 million gallons of fuel. In addition, ORION will produce further environmental benefits and cost reductions when UPS vehicles outside the United States are equipped with the technology.

UPS continues to look into the future. Interestingly, ORION provides a natural link to driverless vehicles.

However, ORION does not yet perform certain functions. For example, when drivers leave in the morning, the route they have in their DIAD does not change, meaning the system does not update routes if something goes wrong. In addition, ORION also does not take traffic or weather into account. UPS plans to integrate these features into subsequent upgrades of ORION.

Sources: Compiled from C. Powers, "How UPS Augments Its Drivers' Intuition with Predictive Analytics," *ASUG News*, June 9, 2015; E. Siegel, "Predictive Analytics Driving Results, ROI at UPS," *Data Informed*, June 1, 2015; E. Siegel, "Wise Practitioner—Predictive Analytics Interview Series: Jack Levis of UPS," *Predictive Analytics World*, April 28, 2015; J. Berman, "UPS Is Focused on the Future for Its ORION Technology," *Logistics Management*, March 3, 2015; "UPS Moves Up Full ORION Rollout in U.S. Market to the End of 2016," *DC Velocity*, March 2, 2015; J. Gidman, "Algorithm Will Tell All UPS Trucks Where to Go," *Newser*, February 17, 2015; S. Rosenbush and L. Stevens, "At UPS, the Algorithm Is the Driver," *The Wall Street Journal*, February 16, 2015; J. Dix, "How UPS Uses Analytics to Drive Down Costs," *Network World*, December 1, 2014; K. Noyes, "The Shortest Distance Between Two Points? At UPS, It's Complicated," *Fortune*, July 25, 2014; www.ups.com, accessed August 26, 2015.

Questions

1. Explain how DIADs were a descriptive analytics solution for UPS.

2. Explain how the Package Flow Technologies system was a predictive analytics solution for UPS.

3. Explain how the ORION system was a prescriptive analytics solution for UPS.

4. Describe another potential application for the UPS ORION system. That is, what is the next question that UPS managers might ask of the ORION system?

CHAPTER 6

Ethics and Privacy

CHAPTER OUTLINE

6.1 Ethical Issues

6.2 Privacy

LEARNING OBJECTIVES

6.1 Describe ethics, its three fundamental tenets, and the four categories of ethical issues related to information technology.

6.2 Discuss at least one potential threat to the privacy of the data stored in each of three places that store personal data.

Opening Case

 Marriott Blocks Guests' Wi-Fi Access

In many ways, technology is disrupting profitable services that hotels previously provided to their guests, causing hotels to lose these sources of revenue. Consider these examples:

- *Phone calls:* Disrupted by smartphones (see Chapter 10) and Voice-Over Internet Protocol (see Chapter 4);

- *Internet access:* Disrupted by personal Wi-Fi hotspots on smartphones and Mi-Fi (see Chapter 10);

- *Premium television:* Netflix (www.netflix.com), Hulu (www.hulu.com), Amazon Prime (www.amazon.com/prime), and customers streaming their own TiVo (www.tivo.com) recordings have replaced in-room, on-demand movies and some premium sporting events.

- *Room service:* Disrupted by Seamless (www.seamless.com) and Eat24 (http://eat24.com), who deliver food to your door;

- *Laundry and dry cleaning pick-up:* Disrupted by Washio (www.getwashio.com), Postmates (http://postmates.com), and the mobile Web sites of local cleaners themselves who offer pick-up and delivery.

- *Honor bar:* Disrupted by apps such as Instacart (www.instacart.com) that deliver drinks and snacks to your door, possibly for a lower cost than the compact refrigerator in hotel rooms.

To avoid losing revenue, hotels have been forced to devise strategies to compete with these services. Consider hotel chain Marriott (www.marriott.com). Wireless connection rates for Marriott start at

$14.95 per day. For $19.95, guests receive "enhanced high-speed Internet," which includes video chatting, downloading large files, and streaming video. Rather than pay these expensive charges, many guests use their data allotment from their cell phone providers. Marriott was also charging conference organizers and exhibitors between $250 and $1,000 per access point to use the hotel's Wi-Fi connection.

Marriott attempted to maintain its Internet revenues by blocking Wi-Fi access in its hotels' conference areas. Unfortunately for Marriott, this policy generated more problems than income. In 2013, a conference attendee at the Gaylord Opryland Hotel in Nashville, Tennessee—which is managed by Marriott—discovered that the hotel was jamming Wi-Fi devices in its ballrooms, although it was providing access in the guest rooms. The guest complained to the Federal Communications Commission (FCC; www.fcc.gov).

In response, the FCC launched an investigation. In 2014, the agency concluded that Marriott had blocked personal hotspots and was therefore in violation of the Communications Act. The FCC fined the hotel chain $600,000 for these violations. In addition, Marriott had to submit compliance reports to the agency for three years.

Marriott defended its policies by claiming that its objective was to protect its guests from rogue wireless hotspots that could cause degraded service, cyberattacks, and identity theft. The company further contended that the Opryland Hotel's actions were lawful.

In August 2014, Marriott petitioned the FCC to change the Communications Act so the company could continue to block Wi-Fi services in its hotels' conference spaces. The hotel chain asserted this practice was necessary to prevent attendees from launching cyberattacks on the company's network. Many customers were outraged by the petition, claiming that Marriott's request was an attempt to ban Wi-Fi access in hotel rooms and lobbies as well as in conference rooms.

In December 2014, Microsoft, Google, the Consumer Electronics Association (www.ce.org), and others filed comments with the FCC opposing Marriott's Wi-Fi blocking plan. These companies noted that Marriott and other hotels make large amounts of money by charging businesses and individuals expensive rates to connect to the Internet in conference halls and meeting rooms. They contended that these policies were against the public interest, illegal, and malicious. They

further charged that the security claims being made by Marriott were misleading. In response to negative publicity, in January 2015, Marriott issued a statement announcing that it would not block Wi-Fi at any hotel for any reason.

Meanwhile, in a strongly worded statement released the same month, the FCC asserted it would aggressively investigate and act upon unlawful intentional interference with Wi-Fi access in any establishment. Several months later, the commission fined Smart City Holdings (www.smartcity.com) $750,000 for blocking Wi-Fi access at a number of convention centers served by the company in order to force customers to utilize the company's own, expensive Wi-Fi options.

Sources: Compiled from A. Lee, "Marriott Ends Its Bid to Kill Your Wi-Fi Hotspot," *ReadWrite*, February 2, 2015; D. Murphy, "Marriott Abandons FCC Petition for Hotel Wi-Fi Blocking," *PC Magazine*, February 1, 2015; M. Moon, "Marriott Is No Longer Fighting for Permission to Block Wi-Fi Hotspots," *Engadget*, January 31, 2015; B. Brown, "FCC Calls Blocking of Personal Wi-Fi Hotspots 'Disturbing Trend'," *Network World*, January 27, 2015; "FCC to Marriott: Never Try to Block Wi-Fi Again," *CNN Money*, January 27, 2015; "Marriott: You Win, We Won't Block Wi-Fi," *CNN Money*, January 15, 2015; "Marriott Hotels Do U-Turn over Wi-Fi Hotspot Blocks," *BBC News*, January 15, 2015; "Marriott Is Bad, and Should Feel Bad," *The Economist*, January 6, 2015; "Should Hotels Be Allowed to Block Competing Wi-Fi?" *Consumer Traveler*, October 6, 2014; "How This Hotel Made Sure Your Wi-Fi Hotspot Sucked," *ReadWrite*, October 4, 2014; K. Knibbs, "The FCC Fined Marriott $600,000 for Blocking Guests' Wi-Fi," *Gizmodo*, October 3, 2014; www.marriott.com, www.fcc.gov, accessed August 31, 2015.

Questions

1. Discuss the ethicality and legality of Marriott's decision to block Wi-Fi access in conference centers in its hotels.

2. After the FCC found that Marriott had broken the law, did the hotel chain manage the situation correctly? Why or why not? If not, then how should Marriott have handled the situation? That is, what could the hotel chain have done better?

3. Describe the privacy implications of Marriott's trying to force guests to use its Wi-Fi access point.

Introduction

The chapter opening case about Marriott blocking Wi-Fi access addresses the two major issues you will study in this chapter: ethics and privacy. The two issues are closely related to each other and also to IT, and both raise significant questions involving access to information in the digital age. For example: Are the actions of Marriott ethical? Did Marriott violate the privacy of its guests? The answers to these questions are not straightforward. In fact, IT has made finding answers to these questions even more difficult.

You will encounter numerous ethical and privacy issues in your career, many of which will involve IT in some manner. This chapter provides insights into how to respond to these issues. Furthermore, it will help you to make immediate contributions to your company's code of ethics and its privacy policies. You will also be able to provide meaningful input concerning the potential ethical and privacy impacts of your organization's information systems on people within and outside the organization.

For example, suppose your organization decides to adopt social computing technologies (which you will study in Chapter 8) to include business partners and customers in new product development. You will be able to analyze the potential privacy and ethical implications of implementing these technologies.

All organizations, large and small, must be concerned with ethics. In particular, small business (or startup) owners face a very difficult situation when their employees have access to sensitive customer information. There is a delicate balance between access to information and the appropriate use of that information. This balance is best maintained by hiring honest and trustworthy employees who abide by the organization's code of ethics. Ultimately this issue leads to another question: Does the small business, or a startup, even have a code of ethics to fall back on in this type of situation?

6.1 | Ethical Issues

Ethics refers to the principles of right and wrong that individuals use to make choices that guide their behavior. Deciding what is right or wrong is not always easy or clear-cut. Fortunately, there are many frameworks that can help us make ethical decisions.

Ethical Frameworks

There are many sources for ethical standards. Here we consider four widely used standards: the utilitarian approach, the rights approach, the fairness approach, and the common good approach. There are many other sources, but these four are representative.

The *utilitarian approach* states that an ethical action is the one that provides the most good or does the least harm. The ethical corporate action would be the one that produces the greatest good and does the least harm for all affected parties—customers, employees, shareholders, the community, and the physical environment.

The *rights approach* maintains that an ethical action is the one that best protects and respects the moral rights of the affected parties. Moral rights can include the rights to make one's own choices about what kind of life to lead, to be told the truth, not to be injured, and to enjoy a degree of privacy. Which of these rights people are actually entitled to—and under what circumstances—is widely debated. Nevertheless, most people acknowledge that individuals are entitled to some moral rights. An ethical organizational action would be one that protects and respects the moral rights of customers, employees, shareholders, business partners, and even competitors.

The *fairness approach* posits that ethical actions treat all human beings equally, or, if unequally, then fairly, based on some defensible standard. For example, most people might believe it is fair to pay people higher salaries if they work harder or if they contribute a greater amount to the firm. However, there is less certainty regarding CEO salaries that are hundreds or thousands of times larger than those of other employees. Many people question whether this huge disparity is based on a defensible standard or whether it is the result of an imbalance of power and hence is unfair.

Finally, the *common good approach* highlights the interlocking relationships that underlie all societies. This approach argues that respect and compassion for all others is the basis for ethical actions. It emphasizes the common conditions that are important to the welfare of everyone. These conditions can include a system of laws, effective police and fire departments, healthcare, a public educational system, and even public recreation areas.

If we combine these four standards, we can develop a general framework for ethics (or ethical decision making). This framework consists of five steps:

1. Recognize an ethical issue:

    Could this decision or situation damage someone or some group?

    Does this decision involve a choice between a good and a bad alternative?

    Does this issue involve more than simply legal considerations? If so, then in what way?

2. Get the facts:

    What are the relevant facts of the situation?

    Do I have sufficient information to make a decision?

    Which individuals and/or groups have an important stake in the outcome?

    Have I consulted all relevant persons and groups?

3. Evaluate alternative actions:

    Which option will produce the most good and do the least harm? (the utilitarian approach)

    Which option best respects the rights of all stakeholders? (the rights approach)

    Which option treats people equally or proportionately? (the fairness approach)

    Which option best serves the community as a whole, and not just some members? (the common good approach)

4. Make a decision and test it:

    Considering all the approaches, which option best addresses the situation?

5. Act and reflect on the outcome of your decision:

    How can I implement my decision with the greatest care and attention to the concerns of all stakeholders?

    How did my decision turn out, and what did I learn from this specific situation?

Now that we have created a general ethical framework, we will focus specifically on ethics in the corporate environment.

Ethics in the Corporate Environment

Many companies and professional organizations develop their own codes of ethics. A **code of ethics** is a collection of principles intended to guide decision making by members of the organization. For example, the Association for Computing Machinery (www.acm.org), an organization of computing professionals, has a thoughtful code of ethics for its members (see www.acm.org/constitution/code.html).

Keep in mind that different codes of ethics are not always consistent with one another. Therefore, an individual might be expected to conform to multiple codes. For example, a person who is a member of two large professional computing-related organizations may be simultaneously required by one organization to comply with all applicable laws and by the other organization to refuse to obey unjust laws.

Fundamental tenets of ethics include:

Responsibility means that you accept the consequences of your decisions and actions.

Accountability refers to determining who is responsible for actions that were taken.

Liability is a legal concept that gives individuals the right to recover the damages done to them by other individuals, organizations, or systems.

Before you go any further, it is critical that you realize that what is *unethical* is not necessarily *illegal*. For example, a bank's decision to foreclose on a home can be technically legal, but it can raise many ethical questions. In many instances, then, an individual or organization faced with an ethical decision is not considering whether to break the law. As the foreclosure example illustrates, however, ethical decisions can have serious consequences for individuals, organizations, and society at large.

We have witnessed a large number of extremely poor ethical decisions, not to mention outright criminal behavior, at many organizations. During 2001 and 2002, three highly publicized fiascos occurred at Enron, WorldCom, and Tyco. At each company, executives were convicted of various types of fraud for using illegal accounting practices. These actions led to the passage of the Sarbanes–Oxley Act in 2002. Sarbanes–Oxley requires publicly held companies to implement financial controls and company executives to personally certify financial reports.

FIN

Then, the subprime mortgage crisis exposed unethical lending practices throughout the mortgage industry. The crisis also highlighted pervasive weaknesses in the regulation of the U.S. financial industry as well as the global financial system. It ultimately contributed to a deep recession in the global economy. Along these same lines, financier Bernie Madoff was convicted in 2009 of operating a Ponzi scheme and sentenced to 150 years in federal prison. In addition, several of Madoff's employees were convicted in 2014.

Advancements in information technologies have generated a new set of ethical problems. Computing processing power doubles roughly every 18 months, meaning that organizations are more dependent than ever on their information systems. Organizations can store increasing amounts of data at decreasing costs. As a result, they can maintain more data on individuals for longer periods of time. Going further, computer networks, particularly the Internet, enable organizations to collect, integrate, and distribute enormous amounts of information on individuals, groups, and institutions. These developments have created numerous ethical problems concerning the appropriate collection and use of customer information, personal privacy, and the protection of intellectual property. IT's About Business 6.1 illustrates how misuse of information technology at Volkswagen led to a global scandal.

IT's About Business 6.1

Volkswagen and the "Diesel Dupe"

Beginning in 2009, German car manufacturer Volkswagen (VW; http://en.volkswagen.com) launched a global marketing campaign promoting the low emissions of its diesel cars. During this period, global sales of VW diesel cars increased noticeably, and the vehicles won several environmental awards. The low emissions became a critical selling point as consumers and governments became increasingly concerned with pollution and global warming.

On September 18, 2015, the U.S. Environmental Protection Agency (EPA; www.epa.gov) issued a notice of violation of the 1970 Clean Air Act to VW. The agency charged that VW had installed software in millions of its diesel cars that could detect when the cars were undergoing emissions testing and then could alter the performance in order to meet federal standards.

Essentially, Volkswagen had intentionally programmed these diesel engines to activate certain emissions controls only during laboratory emissions testing. During this testing, cars are typically placed on a stationary device called a dynamometer. The programming caused the vehicles' output of pollutants known as nitrogen oxides to meet U.S. emissions standards during laboratory testing. However, during actual driving the software shut down the emissions controls. As a result the cars provided better performance and fuel economy. However, they also produced up to 40 times more nitrogen oxides. Approximately 11 million cars worldwide, manufactured between model years 2009 and 2015 included this programming, known as a "defeat device."

As of this writing the case against Volkswagen appears to be solid. Volkswagen fully acknowledged that they had manipulated the vehicle emission tests after being shown the evidence of the defeat device. Both VW CEO Martin Winterkorn and VW America CEO Michael Horn admitted the charges were valid.

The consequences of the scandal, which became known as the "Diesel Dupe," have been severe. The issue wasn't limited to the United States. Authorities in Britain, Canada, Italy, France, Germany, and South Korea are among those investigating the automaker. These countries are questioning whether any of the emissions testing of VW vehicles was legitimate.

The EPA announced that should the allegations be proved, VW could face fines of up to $37,500 per vehicle, for a total of approximately $18 billion. On September 20, 2015, the company officially stopped selling affected diesel vehicles.

Shortly thereafter, VW announced plans to repair up to 11 million vehicles affected by the scandal. It was unclear whether the repairs would include both software and hardware modifications. The recall began in January 2016, with all of the affected cars projected to be fixed by the end of that year. The carmaker earmarked $18 billion to settle the worldwide costs of the recall, fines, and other repercussions. Of this total, $10 billion were for the company's settlement with car owners in the United States. In addition, Volkswagen established an online service where customers can learn if their car is impacted based on the car's vehicle identification number (VIN).

The timing of the emissions scandal was significant, because the sales of diesel vehicles had already been declining. In Europe, the impact of the scandal could be devastating, perhaps prompting consumers to switch to gasoline-powered cars.

On October 7, 2015, hundreds of class-action lawsuits had been reportedly filed in the United States on behalf of Volkswagen owners, claiming fraud and breach of contract. The lawsuits claimed that diesel vehicles will be worth less money because they will need to be fixed to conform to pollution regulations, due to expected reductions in horsepower and fuel efficiency. By the end of that month, the resale value of the affected cars in the United States had declined between 5 and 16 percent, based on used car auction prices listed in the Kelley Blue Book (www.kbb.com).

Perhaps the most significant element of the VW scandal is that the workaround to improve emissions during testing was programmed into the software that controlled the cars' emissions. Cheating that occurs within the software can be subtle and difficult to detect. The significance of the software cheating could have ramifications in other situations, as similar software is being used in everything from voting machines to electric power distribution. As we give more control of our lives to software, we need better verification and transparency of these technologies.

On September 23, 2015, VW CEO Martin Winterkorn resigned, although he denied any personal wrongdoing. It remained unclear which company executives knew what and when they knew it, although the German newspaper *Der Spiegel* reported that at least 30 people in management positions at VW were aware of the deceit for years. VW denied this allegation.

In November 2015, the EPA announced that it was investigating Audi and Porsche for allegedly using defeat devices on their diesel automobiles. The costs of the Diesel Dupe were to blame for VW's first quarterly loss in 15 years as the company suffered a large writedown. In fact, Volkswagen's stock price declined by as much as 40 percent since the scandal was discovered.

Sources: Compiled from D. Francis, "Analysis: Volkswagen's Emissions Cheat Headache Just Got Worse," *Chicago Tribune*, May 17, 2016; "VW Emissions Scandal: U.S. Regulators Find More Cars with Cheat Tests," *BBC News*, November 3, 2015; T. Pollard, "Volkswagen's Emissions 'Cheat' Software Scandal: The Latest," *Car Magazine*, October 23, 2015; D. Ivory and K. Bradsher, "Regulators Investigating 2nd VW Emissions Program," *The New York Times*, October 9, 2015; N. Bomey, "House Slams 'Arrogance' of VW; CEO Says No Buyback Planned," *USA Today*, October 9, 2015; M. Spector and A. Harder, "VW's U.S. Chief Apologizes, Says Engineers at Fault," *The Wall Street Journal*, October 9, 2015; I. Chapple and M. Thompson, "Volkswagen HQ Raided by German Police," *CNN Money*, October 8, 2015; K. Johnson and J. Willhite, "Volkswagen CFO Is in the Hot Seat," *The*

Wall Street Journal, September 28, 2015; B. Schneier, "Volkswagen Scandal Could Just Be the Beginning," *CNN*, September 28, 2015; "That'll Set You Back at Least $7.3 Billion," *Bloomberg BusinessWeek*, September 28, 2015; "Volkswagen Scandal . . . . in Two Minutes," *CNN Money*, September 28, 2015; T. Claburn, "Volkswagen's New CEO Brings Software Know-How," *InformationWeek*, September 26, 2015; R. Hotten, "Volkswagen: The Scandal Explained," *BBC News*, December 10, 2015; A. Davies, "The Real Winner in the VW Diesel Scandal? Hybrid Cars," *Wired*, September 24, 2015; B. Berman, "What the VW Scandal Means for Clean Diesel," *MIT Technology Review*, September 23, 2015; A. Davies, "VW Owners Aren't Going to Like the Fixes for Their Diesels," *Wired*, September 22, 2015; T. Claburn, "Volkswagen: 11 Million Cars Used Deceptive Emissions Software," *InformationWeek*, September 22, 2015; J. Ewing and C. Davenport, "Volkswagen Stops Selling Cars Facing U.S. Inquiry," *The New York Times*, September 21, 2015; W. Boston, A. Harder, M. Spector, and C. Rogers, "Volkswagen Halts U.S. Sales of Certain Diesel Cars," *The Wall Street Journal*, September 20, 2015; http://en.volkswagen.com, accessed October 31, 2015.

Questions

1. Describe the role that information technology played in Volkswagen's Diesel Dupe.

2. The fundamental tenets of ethics include responsibility, accountability, and liability. Discuss each of these tenets as it applies to the Volkswagen scandal.

Ethics and Information Technology

All employees have a responsibility to encourage ethical uses of information and information technology. Many of the business decisions you will face at work will have an ethical dimension. Consider the following decisions that you might have to make:

- Should organizations monitor employees' Web surfing and e-mail?
- Should organizations sell customer information to other companies?
- Should organizations audit employees' computers for unauthorized software or illegally downloaded music or video files?

The diversity and ever-expanding use of IT applications have created a variety of ethical issues. These issues fall into four general categories: privacy, accuracy, property, and accessibility.

1. *Privacy issues* involve collecting, storing, and disseminating information about individuals.

2. *Accuracy issues* involve the authenticity, fidelity, and correctness of information that is collected and processed.

3. *Property issues* involve the ownership and value of information.

4. *Accessibility issues* revolve around who should have access to information and whether they should pay a fee for this access.

IT's About Business 6.2 illustrates the ethical (and privacy) issues surrounding the European Court of Justice's decision that implemented the "right to be forgotten" in the European Union.

IT's About Business 6.2

Do You Have the Right to Be Forgotten?

In 1998, a lawyer in Spain undergoing financial trouble had to put a piece of property he owned up for auction. This was reported in a Spanish newspaper, *La Vanguardia*. Soon after, the lawyer cleared his debts, but the newspaper article was still accessible online when someone searched his name on Google.

The lawyer in 2010 demanded that the newspaper take down the online articles and that Google remove the links to them. The Spanish Data Protection Agency (www.agpd.es) turned down his request for the newspaper to remove the articles, but it allowed his request that Google not link to them. In 2014, the Spanish agency's decisions were upheld by the European Court of Justice, the superior court for countries of the European Union. The Court of Justice decision went even further, protecting the rights of all individuals in member countries to have Google take down links to any information about them that was deemed "inadequate, irrelevant or no longer relevant, or excessive in relation to the purposes for which they were processed and in the light of the time that has elapsed."

In effect, then, the European Union's highest court had ruled that citizens have a "right to be forgotten" on the Web and can therefore force Google and other search engines to remove outdated or "irrelevant" links about their personal histories from search results. The "right to be forgotten" is the right for individuals to request that information about them be taken offline after it's no longer relevant. Specifically, individuals can ask Google to remove links to news articles, court judgments, and other documents in search results for their name. The court's decision empowers individuals to ask Google or other search operators to take down links to Web pages that are published by third parties, such as newspapers, that contain information relating to them. The decision does not require that the article or the Web site be removed or altered by the original publisher. Rather, the link to this content must be removed.

Subsequent to the courts' decision, requests to remove embarrassing and negative links exploded. By September 2015, roughly 250,000 requests had been submitted. In one instance, a former politician seeking reelection requested the removal of links to articles about his poor behavior while in office. In another scenario, a physician sought to erase negative online reviews.

Not surprisingly, the "right to be forgotten" has created a great deal of controversy. Privacy advocates defend the decision as a reclamation of privacy rights. Opponents contend that, were this policy to be implemented, people's search results would come to resemble official biographies that record only the facts that individuals want other people to know. That situation could be dangerous. Opponents further argue that the court decision fails to identify which criteria the search engines should use to decide which requests to honor. The ruling also does not require that embarrassing material—revealing photographs, court documents, gossip—be erased from the Internet, just from search results.

While the European Court of Justice decision was clear on granting the "right to be forgotten" to all citizens, it was unclear how exactly that would happen. The ruling called for a balance between the privacy rights of individuals and the rights of the public to information. But the decision by Europe's highest court is binding on the courts in member states, which must interpret it as best they can. Consequently, privacy and the "right to be forgotten" could vary from one country to another, potentially generating a great deal of confusion and uncertainty.

As of September 2015, it was not clear how search engines such as Google needed to comply with the EU ruling. Google has a page that allows users to request that certain links be deleted, based on copyright and similar claims. In March 2016, Google announced that it would apply the right to be forgotten to all European Union searches.

Google has implemented a two-part system for complying with the court's decision. The first part created a software infrastructure to remove links. This software enables Google to apply its existing system to delete copyrighted and trademarked works.

In the second part, Google created an administrative system to collect and act on requests to remove links. Internet users in all of the EU countries covered by the decision can fill out a form in one of 25 languages through the local Google site in that country. (The form is not available through the main Google.com homepage based in the United States.) Individuals fill in their name and the links they want removed, and must also explain why they feel the information is objectionable, such as that it is no longer relevant or is out of date. If Google agrees with the petitioner, it notifies the Webmaster of the sites in question and allows those sites to state their case to keep the link.

Each request for link deletion is reviewed by a team of lawyers, paralegals, and others assembled by Google. The reviewers are mainly looking at whether the petitioner is a public or private figure, if the information is from a reputable news organization or government agency, if the petitioner themselves originally published the information, and whether the link relates to political speech or criminal charges.

Meanwhile, another dispute has arisen concerning the scope of the court's ruling. Specifically, France's data regulators determined that it is not sufficient for Google to remove a result from its European search pages (Google.fr, Google.de, etc.). Instead, the company must remove links worldwide by deleting them from its "Google.com" version as well. In response, Google informed the French regulators in September 2015 that it would not implement "right to be forgotten" requests on a worldwide basis. The company argued that although the right to be forgotten is the law in Europe, it is not the law globally. Further, content that is declared illegal under the laws of one country can still be legal in other countries.

Sources: Compiled from C. Lecher, "Google Will Apply the 'Right to Be Forgotten' to All EU Searches Next Week," *The Verge*, March 4, 2016; M. Stern, "UK Orders Google to Censor Links to Articles about 'Right to Be Forgotten,' Removals" *Slate*, August 21, 2015; F. Manjoo, "'Right to Be Forgotten' Online Could Spread," *The New York Times*, August 5, 2015; A. Hern, "Google Says Non to French Demand to Expand Right to Be Forgotten Worldwide," *The Guardian*, July 30, 2015; J. Roberts, "The Right to Be Forgotten from Google? Forget It, Says U.S. Crowd," *Fortune*, March 12, 2015; H. Maycotte, "America's 'Right to Be Forgotten' Fight Heats Up," *Forbes*, September 30, 2014; J. Toobin, "The Solace of Oblivion," *The New Yorker*, September 29, 2014; "Internet Privacy: Do Users Have a 'Right to be Forgotten'?" *The Week*, May 30, 2014; T. Claburn, "Google Ordered to 'Forget,'"

InformationWeek, May 13, 2014; "Google's Legal Blow: What the 'Right to Be Forgotten' Means," *The Wall Street Journal*, May 13, 2014; D. Lee, "What Is the 'Right to Be Forgotten'?" *BBC News*, May 13, 2014; www.google.com, accessed September 7, 2015.

Questions

1. Describe the advantages to individuals of the "right to be forgotten" policy. Provide examples to support your answer.

2. What are the potential long-term disadvantages of the "right to be forgotten" policy? Provide examples to support your answer.

3. Describe the ethicality and legality of the "right to be forgotten" policy.

4. What are the privacy implications of the "right to be forgotten" policy?

Table 6.1 lists representative questions and issues for each of these categories. In addition, Online Ethics Cases presents 14 scenarios that raise ethical issues. These scenarios will provide a context for you to consider situations that involve ethical or unethical behavior.

Many of the issues and scenarios discussed in this chapter involve privacy as well as ethics. In the next section, you will learn about privacy issues in more detail.

TABLE 6.1 A Framework for Ethical Issues

Privacy Issues

What information about oneself should an individual be required to reveal to others?

What kinds of surveillance can an employer use on its employees?

What types of personal information can people keep to themselves and not be forced to reveal to others?

What information about individuals should be kept in databases, and how secure is the information there?

Accuracy issues

Who is responsible for the authenticity, fidelity, and accuracy of the information collected?

How can we ensure that the information will be processed properly and presented accurately to users?

How can we ensure that errors in databases, data transmissions, and data processing are accidental and not intentional?

Who is to be held accountable for errors in information, and how should the injured parties be compensated?

Property Issues

Who owns the information?

What are the just and fair prices for its exchange?

How should we handle software piracy (illegally copying copyrighted software)?

Under what circumstances can one use proprietary databases?

Can corporate computers be used for private purposes?

How should experts who contribute their knowledge to create expert systems be compensated?

How should access to information channels be allocated?

Accessibility issues

Who is allowed to access information?

How much should companies charge for permitting access to information?

How can access to computers be provided for employees with disabilities?

Who will be provided with the equipment needed for accessing information?

What information does a person or an organization have a right to obtain, under what conditions, and with what safeguards?

Before you go on…

1. What does a code of ethics contain?

2. Describe the fundamental tenets of ethics.

Apply the Concept 6.1

LEARNING OBJECTIVE 6.1 Describe ethics, its three fundamental tenets, and the four categories of ethical issues related to information technology.

STEP 1: Background (Here is what you are learning.)

As you begin your career, you need to be aware of the current trends affecting the four areas of concern presented in Section 6.1. Privacy (what people know about you), property (who owns the data about you), accuracy (are the data about you accurate), and accessibility (who can access your data) are major topics in the today's high-tech world. They are especially important in the migration to electronic health records, mobile wallets, social media, and government-run databases, to name a few.

STEP 2: Activity (Here is what you are doing.)

Visit http://www.wiley.com/go/rainer/MIS4e/applytheconcept, and read the article posted on the *Huffington Post* Web site from

November 2013. The article describes an unusual (or not-so-unusual) action on the part of Goldman Sachs. It seems they have decided that their junior bankers should have weekends off!

Understand that it isn't illegal to require your employees to work weekends, nor is it illegal to give them time off. It also isn't illegal to work people 75 hours a week. Many of the talking points in this article focus expressly on ethics. An employer is trying to do the "right" thing, and they have used a new standard to define "right."

STEP 3: Deliverable (Here is what you turn in.)

Summarize the article for your professor. In your summary, make certain to define ethics and to describe how the three fundamental tenets of ethics (responsibility, liability, and accountability) played a role in Goldman Sach's decision. Finally, (not from the article) discuss how these same bankers deal with the four areas of ethical concern with regards to your financial information.

6.2 | Privacy

In general, privacy is the right to be left alone and to be free of unreasonable personal intrusions. Information privacy is the right to determine when, and to what extent, information about you can be gathered and/or communicated to others. Privacy rights apply to individuals, groups, and institutions. The right to privacy is recognized today in all the U.S. states and by the federal government, either by statute or in common law.

Privacy can be interpreted quite broadly. However, court decisions in many countries have followed two rules fairly closely:

1. The right of privacy is not absolute. Privacy must be balanced against the needs of society.

2. The public's right to know supersedes the individual's right of privacy.

These two rules illustrate why determining and enforcing privacy regulations can be difficult.

As we discussed earlier, rapid advances in information technologies have made it much easier to collect, store, and integrate vast amounts of data on individuals in large databases. On an average day, data about you are generated in many ways: surveillance cameras located on toll roads, on other roadways, in busy intersections, in public places, and at work; credit card transactions; telephone calls (landline and cellular); banking transactions; queries to search engines; and government records (including police records). These data can be integrated to produce a digital dossier, which is an electronic profile of you and your habits. The process of forming a digital dossier is called profiling.

Data aggregators, such as LexisNexis (www.lexisnexis.com), ChoicePoint (www.choicepoint .com), and Acxiom (www.acxiom.com), are prominent examples of profilers. These companies collect public data such as real estate records and published telephone numbers, in addition to nonpublic information such as Social Security numbers; financial data; and police, criminal, and motor vehicle records. They then integrate these data to form digital dossiers on most adults in the United States. They ultimately sell these dossiers to law enforcement agencies and companies that conduct background checks on potential employees. They also sell them to companies that want to know their customers better, a process called *customer intimacy*.

Data on individuals can also be used in more controversial manners. For example, a controversial map in California identifies the addresses of donors who supported Proposition 8, the referendum approved by California voters in the 2008 election that outlawed same-sex marriage in that state (see www.eightmaps.com). Gay activists created the map by combining Google's satellite mapping technology with publicly available campaign records that listed Proposition 8 donors who contributed $100 or more. These donors were outraged, claiming that the map invaded their privacy.

Electronic Surveillance

According to the American Civil Liberties Union (ACLU), tracking people's activities with the aid of information technology has become a major privacy-related problem. The ACLU notes that this monitoring, or **electronic surveillance**, is rapidly increasing, particularly with the emergence of new technologies. Electronic surveillance is conducted by employers, the government, and other institutions.

Americans today live with a degree of surveillance that would have been unimaginable just a few years ago. For example, surveillance cameras track you at airports, subways, banks, and other public venues. In addition, inexpensive digital sensors are now everywhere. They are incorporated into laptop webcams, video-game motion sensors, smartphone cameras, utility meters, passports, and employee ID cards. Step out your front door and you could be captured in a high-resolution photograph taken from the air or from the street by Google or Microsoft, as they update their mapping services. Drive down a city street, cross a toll bridge, or park at a shopping mall, and your license plate will be recorded and time-stamped.

Emerging technologies such as low-cost digital cameras, motion sensors, and biometric readers are helping to increase the monitoring of human activity. In addition, the costs of storing and using digital data are rapidly decreasing. The result is an explosion of sensor data collection and storage.

In fact, your smartphone has become a sensor. The average price of a smartphone has increased 17 percent since 2000. However, the phone's processing capability has increased by *13,000 percent* during that time, according to technology market research firm ABI Research (www.abiresearch.com). As you will study in Chapter 10, smartphones can now record video, take pictures, send and receive e-mail, search for information, access the Internet, and locate you on a map, among many other things. Your phone also stores large amounts of information about you that can be collected and analyzed. A special problem arises with smartphones that are equipped with global positioning system (GPS) sensors. These sensors routinely *geotag* photos and videos, embedding images with the longitude and latitude of the location shown in the image. Thus, you could be inadvertently supplying criminals with useful intelligence by posting personal images on social networks or photo-sharing Web sites. These actions would show the criminals exactly where you live.

Another example of how new devices can contribute to electronic surveillance is facial recognition technology. Just a few years ago, this software worked only in very controlled settings such as passport checkpoints. However, this technology can now match faces even in regular snapshots and online images. For example, Intel and Microsoft have introduced in-store digital billboards that can recognize your face. These billboards can keep track of the products you are interested in based on your purchases or browsing behavior. One marketing analyst has predicted that your experience in every store will soon be customized.

Google and Facebook are using facial-recognition software—Google Picasa and Facebook Photo Albums—in their popular online photo-editing and sharing services. Both companies encourage users to assign names to people in photos, a practice referred to as *photo tagging.* Facial-recognition software then indexes facial features. Once an individual in a photo is tagged, the software searches for similar facial features in untagged photos. This process allows the user to quickly group photos in which the tagged person appears. Significantly, the individual is not aware of this process.

Why is tagging important? The reason is that once you are tagged in a photo, that photo can be used to search for matches across the entire Internet or in private databases, including databases fed by surveillance cameras. How could this type of surveillance affect you? As one example, a car dealer can take a picture of you when you step onto the car lot. He or she could then quickly profile you (find out information about where you live, your employment, etc.) on the Web to achieve a competitive edge in making a sale. Even worse, a stranger in a restaurant could photograph you with a smartphone and then go online to profile you for reasons of his or her own. One privacy attorney has asserted that losing your right to anonymity would have a chilling effect on where you go, whom you meet, and how you live your life. IT's About Business 6.3 illustrates another type of surveillance technology employed by law enforcement agencies.

IT's About Business 6.3

MIS The StingRay

The Federal Communications Commission (FCC; www.fcc.gov) has authorized the Harris Corporation (www.harris.com), a defense contractor, to sell a surveillance device that tracks cellphones. The StingRay, the size of a suitcase, acts like a cell tower, emitting signals that can dupe phones up to one mile away into sending identifying information. The device can also capture texts, calls, e-mails, and other data. Harris routinely refuses to discuss the StingRay.

The StingRays are popular among local law enforcement agencies, which have spent millions on them, using part of the more than $35 billion in grants from the Department of Homeland Security (DHS; www.dhs.gov) earmarked for cities, counties, and states to fight terrorism and prepare for emergencies and disasters. The StingRay funding also comes from federal drug enforcement grants and money raised by nonprofit organizations for local police departments.

The American Civil Liberties Union (ACLU; www.aclu.org) claims that cellphone surveillance equipment is owned by at least 44 police forces in 18 states, while other local law enforcement agencies borrow the equipment from federal agencies such as the Federal Bureau of Investigation (FBI; www.fbi.gov) and the Drug Enforcement Administration (DEA; www.dea.gov).

The StingRay technology is a closely guarded secret. The FBI says it must be kept confidential or else criminals and terrorists could try to circumvent it. As a result, law enforcement agencies must sign a nondisclosure agreement before buying a StingRay. There is controversy that the nondisclosure agreements make government practices less transparent. Legal experts claim that these agreements raise important issues of privacy and even constitutional issues.

Because the StingRay can monitor all cellphones within range, civil liberties advocates say that it violates the privacy of innocent people, not just potential criminals who are being targeted. Further, until 2015 police officers could use the devices without informing anyone or having to obtain approval from judges, as they would have to do to obtain phone records.

The secrecy over StingRay has led to unintended consequences. For example, reporters have uncovered cases where the police used a StingRay as part of their routine police work, including locating petty criminals, and then did not reveal the cellphone surveillance tactic to the suspects, their lawyers, or even the judges hearing the cases.

The use of StingRays has stirred up a hornet's nest regarding procedural issues in the justice system. Suspects usually have the right to know what evidence was collected against them and to challenge the legality of the method used to gather that evidence. While police have used StingRays against those suspected of everything from petty crimes to murder, records show that that evidence has been routinely hidden or obscured from the suspects in court. In fact, many such suspects were never even prosecuted. About one-third of cases involving evidence from StingRays are thrown out, even those involving stolen cellphones. Only half of those who were prosecuted are convicted. Even though state law requires that defense attorneys be informed about electronic surveillance, many say they weren't told that a StingRay was involved.

As one example, consider a case in which the police had used a StingRay to locate a man accused of armed robbery. The man's lawyer asked police to demonstrate the technology, which they refused, despite a judge's order that police and prosecutors produce the machine. As a result, the man was allowed to plea bargain for the lesser crime of petty theft.

In September 2015, the U.S. Department of Justice (DOJ; www.doj.gov) mandated that federal agencies had to obtain search warrants to use StingRays. To enhance privacy protections, the policy requires that data gathered via a StingRay be deleted as soon as the cell phone is located. Further, all data must be deleted at least once per day. The policy also forbids federal agencies from using StingRays during criminal investigations to gather data from communication, such as such as e-mails, texts, contact lists, and images. Significantly, the ACLU notes that the policy only applies to federal agencies and not the many state and local police departments that have bought StingRays with federal funds. In that sense, the ACLU argues, the policy does not go far enough.

In response to the objections of the ACLU and the DOJ, federal officials stated that StingRays allow them to monitor dangerous criminals. For example, FBI Director James Comey asserted that the agency uses StingRay to find killers, kidnappers, drug dealers, missing children, and pedophiles.

Sources: Compiled from N. Woolf, "2,000 Cases May Be Overturned Because Police Used Secret StingRay Surveillance," *The Guardian*, September 4, 2015; W. Ashford, "U.S. Cracks Down on Mobile Phone Tracking by Federal Agencies," *Computer Weekly*, September 4, 2015; K. Zetter, "The Feds Need a Warrant to Spy with StingRays from Now On," *Wired*, September 3, 2015; B. Heath, "Police Secretly Track Cellphones to Locate Even Petty Criminals," *USA Today*, August 24, 2015; C. Farivar, "In Rare Move, Silicon Valley County Gov't Kills Stingray Acquisition," *Ars Technica*, May 7, 2015; J. Fenton, "Baltimore Police Say Stingray Phone Tracking Use Exceeds 25,000 Instances," *The Baltimore Sun*, April 20, 2015; M. Richtel, "A Police Gadget Tracks Phones? Shhh! It's Secret," *The New York Times*, March 15, 2015;

K. Klonick, "Stingrays: Not Just for Feds!" *Slate*, November 10, 2014; P. Robison, "Another Privacy Concern: Police Spying on Cell Phones," *Bloomberg BusinessWeek*, October 16, 2014; K. Zetter, "Florida Cops' Secret Weapon: Warrantless Cellphone Tracking," *Wired*, March 3, 2014; R. Gallagher, "Meet the Machines that Steal Your Phone's Data," *Ars Technica*, September 25, 2013.

Questions

1. As technology advances, what are the implications for electronic surveillance?

2. Discuss the legality and ethicality of the police using StingRays for ordinary crime.

3. Discuss the legality and ethicality of federal law enforcement agencies using StingRays to find terrorists.

4. Are your answers to Questions 2 and 3 different? Explain your reasoning.

The scenarios we just considered deal primarily with your personal life. However, electronic surveillance has become a reality in the workplace as well. In general, employees have very limited legal protection against surveillance by employers. The law supports the right of employers to read their employees' e-mail and other electronic documents and to monitor their employees' Internet use. Today, more than three-fourths of organizations routinely monitor their employees' Internet usage. In addition, two-thirds use software to block connections to inappropriate Web sites, a practice called *URL filtering*. Furthermore, organizations are installing monitoring and filtering software to enhance security by blocking malicious software and to increase productivity by discouraging employees from wasting time.

In one organization, the chief information officer (CIO) monitored roughly 13, 000 employees for three months to determine the type of traffic they engaged in on the network. He then forwarded the data to the chief executive officer (CEO) and the heads of the human resources and legal departments. These executives were shocked at the questionable Web sites the employees were visiting, as well as the amount of time they were spending on those sites. The executives quickly decided to implement a URL filtering product.

In general, surveillance is a concern for private individuals regardless of whether it is conducted by corporations, government bodies, or criminals. As a nation, the United States is still struggling to define the appropriate balance between personal privacy and electronic surveillance, especially in situations that involve threats to national security.

Personal Information in Databases

Modern institutions store information about individuals in many databases. Perhaps the most visible locations of such records are credit-reporting agencies. Other institutions that store personal information include banks and financial institutions; cable TV, telephone, and utilities companies; employers; mortgage companies; hospitals; schools and universities; retail establishments; government agencies (Internal Revenue Service, your state, your municipality); and many others.

There are several concerns about the information you provide to these record keepers. Some of the major concerns are as follows:

- Do you know where the records are?
- Are the records accurate?
- Can you change inaccurate data?
- How long will it take to make a change?
- Under what circumstances will the personal data be released?
- How are the data used?
- To whom are the data given or sold?
- How secure are the data against access by unauthorized people?

Information on Internet Bulletin Boards, Newsgroups, and Social Networking Sites

Every day we see more and more *electronic bulletin boards*, *newsgroups*, *electronic discussions* such as chat rooms, and *social networking sites* (discussed in Chapter 8). These sites appear on the Internet, within corporate intranets, and on blogs. A *blog*, short for "Weblog," is an informal, personal journal that is frequently updated and is intended for general public reading. How does society keep owners of bulletin boards from disseminating information that may be offensive to readers or simply untrue? This is a difficult problem because it involves the conflict between freedom of speech on the one hand and privacy on the other. This conflict is a fundamental and continuing ethical issue in the United States and throughout the world.

There is no better illustration of the conflict between free speech and privacy than the Internet. Many Web sites contain anonymous, derogatory information on individuals, who typically have little recourse in the matter. The vast majority of the U.S. firms use the Internet in examining job applications, including searching on Google and on social networking sites. Consequently, derogatory information contained on the Internet can harm a person's chances of being hired.

New information technologies can also present serious privacy concerns. IT's About Business 6.4 shows how life and automobile insurance companies use technology to track individual policy holders.

IT's About Business 6.4

 MIS   **Tracking Data Impacts Life and**
 MKT   **Automobile Insurance**

Life Insurance Only 44 percent of households in the United States own individual life insurance policies, a 50-year low. As a result, John Hancock (www.johnhancock.com) is offering a new type of life insurance program, which the insurer hopes will increase sales.

Life insurance policies are typically underwritten using a snapshot of a person's medical status at the time they apply for the policy. In this way, life insurance is a "one and done" process, unlike health insurance, which requires ongoing medical information to adjust premiums annually.

In its new program, John Hancock will price policies continuously for participating consumers. These customers must agree to continually share their medical data with Hancock. The insurer operates the program in conjunction with Vitality (www.thevitalitygroup .com), a global wellness company.

Similar programs implemented by Vitality in other countries, including Australia, South Africa, and Singapore, have shown impressive results: policyholders are motivated to improve their fitness to bring down their life insurance premiums. Vitality found in a 2014 study that participants who had not been exercising but who underwent a fitness regime for three years reduced their health risk factors by 13 percent. Those who were active before the study but increased their fitness activities cut their health risk factors by 22 percent over the three years.

Holders of the John Hancock life insurance policy through Vitality earn points for various fitness activities that are expected to increase their longevity. The more points they earn, the bigger the discount they receive on their premiums. Participants receive a free Fitbit monitor and they may choose to upload their data to the insurance company. Policyholders receive 1,000 points for being a nonsmoker; 1,000 points for each reading in the "normal" range of

cholesterol, glucose, and blood sugar; 3,120 points over a year for doing a standard workout three times a week or an advanced workout twice a week; and 400 points for getting a flu shot. Ten percent of earned points can be carried over to the next year.

All participants start the program by paying a premium at the "gold" level, which requires 7,000 points per year. The gold-level premium is discounted by about 9 percent over the regular premium. If over the course of the program a participant can't maintain gold status, their premium could increase by up to 1.6 percent each year. If a participant reaches platinum status, which requires 10,000 points a year, the premium goes down by about 0.3 percent per year.

The program does raise questions about the security of consumers' health information and whether it could be used in ways that work against a consumer's best interests. For example:

- Would an insurance company penalize a policyholder whose Fitbit data shows they have symptoms of stress?
- What if insurance underwriters make mistakes or incorrect assumptions in analyzing Fitbit data?
- What happens when insurance companies violate protections guaranteed by the Health Insurance Portability and Accountability Act (HIPAA)? Will they be fined and if so, how much?

Hancock's program also raises privacy concerns. Hancock responds by stating that consumers do not have to send the company any data that they are not comfortable with, although they will not accumulate points for data that they do not share.

And one final interesting question: For most life insurance policyholders, the older they are, the higher their risk. Therefore, why would anyone want to continuously price their policies when they could enjoy level premiums over the years (depending on the policy they purchased)?

Automobile Insurance If you have a clean driving record, you may be paying too much for car insurance. That's because auto insurance companies base rates on statistical averages for characteristics such as age, sex, marital status, location, and the type and age of car. Some drivers get a discount based on how long they have gone accident-free.

Technology now enables drivers to get a break on their auto insurance premiums based on how they actually drive, rather than on statistics. The strategy, called usage-based insurance, lets auto insurers track your driving in exchange for an annual discount on your insurance premium, depending on your driving habits. Participation is voluntary.

The technology works like this. Drivers plug a device into the diagnostic ports in their cars. The tool collects data from the car's computer, such as the time of day, mileage, speed, and acceleration and braking rates. The tool then sends this data to the auto insurance via a cellular network.

State Farm (www.statefarm.com; Drive Safe), Progressive (www.progressive.com; Snapshot), and Allstate (www.allstate .com; Drive Wise) all offer usage-based automobile insurance. Let's take a closer look at Progressive's Snapshot product.

As with the other companies, Progressive drivers plug the device into their cars' data ports. Drivers can earn a discount if their data shows a good driving record after 30 days. The tracking lasts six months, after which drivers return the tool back to the company. They can be eligible to receive a discount of up to 30 percent from then on. Progressive does not raise rates based on any data it collects. Participation in the program is free.

Progressive's usage-based insurance program has been tried by more than 1.4 million people, and about one-third continued with it. Of those who continued, about two-thirds received a discount, usually from 10 to 15 percent. The program currently provides approximately 10 percent of the company's revenue.

As of May 2016, none of the three auto insurers was collecting GPS data, so drivers' locations remained private. Further, the three companies were not raising rates on drivers whose data turned out to be poor.

Privacy is a major concern with these programs. There is a fear that data may end up in the hands of people outside the insurance company or that the data may be used for reasons other than originally intended. For example, auto insurers may have little interest in a driver's location at a certain time on a certain day, but if insurers start to collect and store that data, lawyers may one day subpoena the information. Another privacy concern is that the auto insurers will contribute driver histories into a central industry database. In that case, drivers would have a "driver score" similar to the credit score that FICO (www.myfico.com) maintains. Therefore, when drivers look to purchase automobile insurance, their driver scores will impact the premium cost.

Sources: Compiled from "Automotive Usage-Based Insurance (UBI) Market Report 2015-2025 Insurance Telematics and the Connected Car – Reportlinker Review," *PR Newswire*, October 7, 2015; C. Tuohy, "Health Data Leads to Floating Premiums in Some Life Policies," *InsuranceNewsNet*, July 10, 2015; A. Dart, "The Case for Connected Wearables in Life Insurance," *CSC*, July 3, 2015; "Usage-Based Insurance and Telematics," *National Association of Insurance Commissioners*, April 24, 2015; M. Mapp, "John Hancock's Bargain: Give Us More Data, You Pay Less in Rates," *CNBC*, April 19, 2015; K. Calamur, "John Hancock Hopes You'll Trade Activity Data for Insurance Discounts," *NPR.org*, April 8, 2015; T. Bernard, "Giving Out Private Data for Discount in Insurance," *The New York Times*, April 8, 2015; R. Lieber, "Lower Your Car Insurance Bill, at the Price of Some Privacy," *The New York Times*, August 15, 2014; A. Tanner, "Data Monitoring Saves Some People on Car Insurance, But Some Will Pay More," *Forbes*, August 14, 2013; C. Woodyard and J. O'Donnell, "Your Car May Be Invading Your Privacy," *USA Today*, March 25, 2013; J. Anderson, "Data-Tracking Technology Can Help Lower Your Car Insurance," *Kiplinger*, October 2011; www.johnhancock.com, www.thevitalitygroup.com, accessed September 1, 2015.

Questions

1. Describe the advantages of continuous life insurance underwriting and usage-based automobile insurance to the consumer.

2. Describe the advantages of continuous life insurance underwriting and usage-based automobile insurance to the company.

3. Would you be willing to participate in continuous life insurance? Why or why not?

4. Would you be willing to participate in usage-based automobile insurance? Why or why not?

5. Are your answers to Questions #3 and #4 different? If so, why?

Privacy Codes and Policies

Privacy policies or **privacy codes** are an organization's guidelines for protecting the privacy of its customers, clients, and employees. In many corporations, senior management has begun to understand that when they collect vast amounts of personal information, they must protect it. In addition, many organizations give their customers some voice in how their information is used by providing them with opt-out choices. The **opt-out model** of informed consent permits the company to collect personal information until the customer specifically requests that the data not be collected. Privacy advocates prefer the **opt-in model** of informed consent, which prohibits an organization from collecting any personal information unless the customer specifically authorizes it.

One privacy tool available to consumers is the *Platform for Privacy Preferences* (P3P), a protocol that automatically communicates privacy policies between an electronic commerce Web site and visitors to that site. P3P enables visitors to determine the types of personal data that can be extracted by the sites they visit. It also allows visitors to compare a site's privacy policy

TABLE 6.2   Privacy Policy Guidelines: A Sampler

Data Collection

Data should be collected on individuals only for the purpose of accomplishing a legitimate business objective.

Data should be adequate, relevant, and not excessive in relation to the business objective.

Individuals must give their consent before data pertaining to them can be gathered. Such consent may be implied from the individual's actions (e.g., applications for credit, insurance, or employment).

Data Accuracy

Sensitive data gathered on individuals should be verified before they are entered into the database.

Data should be kept current, where and when necessary.

The file should be made available so that the individual can ensure that the data are correct.

In any disagreement about the accuracy of the data, the individual's version should be noted and included with any disclosure of the file.

Data Confidentiality

Computer security procedures should be implemented to ensure against unauthorized disclosure of data. These procedures should include physical, technical, and administrative security measures.

Third parties should not be given access to data without the individual's knowledge or permission, except as required by law.

Disclosures of data, other than the most routine, should be noted and maintained for as long as the data are maintained.

Data should not be disclosed for reasons incompatible with the business objective for which they are collected.

to the visitors' preferences or to other standards, such as the Federal Trade Commission's (FTC) Fair Information Practices Standard or the European Directive on Data Protection.

Table 6.2 provides a sampling of privacy policy guidelines. The last section, "Data Confidentiality," refers to security, which we consider in Chapter 7. All of the good privacy intentions in the world are useless unless they are supported and enforced by effective security measures.

Despite privacy codes and policies, and despite opt-out and opt-in models, guarding whatever is left of your privacy is becoming increasingly difficult. This problem is illustrated in chapter closing case 1.

International Aspects of Privacy

As the number of online users has increased globally, governments throughout the world have enacted a large number of inconsistent privacy and security laws. This highly complex global legal framework is creating regulatory problems for companies. Approximately 50 countries have some form of data protection laws. Many of these laws conflict with those of other countries, or they require specific security measures. Other countries have no privacy laws at all.

The absence of consistent or uniform standards for privacy and security obstructs the flow of information among countries (*transborder data flows*). The European Union (EU), for one, has taken steps to overcome this problem. In 1998 the European Community Commission (ECC) issued guidelines to all of its member countries regarding the rights of individuals to access information about themselves. The EU data protection laws are stricter than the U.S. laws and therefore could create problems for the U.S.-based multinational corporations, which could face lawsuits for privacy violations.

The transfer of data into and out of a nation without the knowledge of either the authorities or the individuals involved raises a number of privacy issues. Whose laws have jurisdiction when records are stored in a different country for reprocessing or retransmission purposes? For example, if data are transmitted by a Polish company through a U.S. satellite to a British corporation, which country's privacy laws control the data, and at what points in the transmission? Questions like these will become more complicated and frequent as time goes on. Governments must make an effort to develop laws and standards to cope with rapidly changing information technologies to solve some of these privacy issues.

The United States and the European Union share the goal of privacy protection for their citizens, but the United States takes a different approach. To bridge the different privacy approaches, the U.S. Department of Commerce, in consultation with the European Union, developed a "safe harbor" framework to regulate the way that the U.S. companies export and handle the personal data (e.g., names and addresses) of European citizens. See www.export .gov/safeharbor and http://ec.europa.eu/justice_home/fsj/privacy/index_en.htm.

Before you go on...

1. Describe the issue of privacy as it is affected by IT.
2. Discuss how privacy issues can impact transborder data flows.

Apply the Concept 6.2

LEARNING OBJECTIVE 6.2 Discuss at least one potential threat to the privacy of the data stored in each of three places that store personal data.

STEP 1: Background

Section 6.2 has defined privacy as the right to be left alone and to be free of unreasonable personal intrusions. Information privacy is the right to determine when, and to what extent, information about you can be gathered and/or communicated to others. And, where our data are concerned, we are in control, right? If so, then why do people always seem to fear that "Big Brother" is spying on us and violating our privacy? Going further, the law generally assigns a higher priority to society's right to access information than to an individual's right to privacy.

The 2002 movie *Minority Report* presented a future where a special police unit could predict when and where crimes were going to occur before they actually did. This unit could arrest "criminals" before they committed the crime. Along these same lines, a 2008 movie titled *Eagle Eye* focused on a highly intelligent

computer system that chose to abide by the Constitution even if it meant having the president of the United States assassinated.

STEP 2: Activity

Movie night! If you have not seen these two films, then schedule a movie night, and watch them from the perspective of privacy and information security. Discuss the movies with your friends, and obtain their thoughts on these issues. If you don't have time to watch the movies, then visit http://www.wiley.com/go/rainer/MIS4e/applytheconcept to read a synopsis of both films on IMDB .com.

STEP 3: Deliverable

After considering the plots in these movies, prepare a paper identifying three places where you store personal data. For each location, discuss at least one potential threat to your personal privacy that arises from storing your information there. Make them major threats . . . on the scale of the movies. Consider just how far your seemingly innocent decisions can take you! Present your paper to the class and submit it to your instructor.

What's in IT for me?

ACCT For the Accounting Major

Public companies, their accountants, and their auditors have significant ethical responsibilities. Accountants now are being held professionally and personally responsible for increasing the transparency of transactions and assuring compliance with Generally Accepted Accounting Principles (GAAP). In fact, regulatory agencies such as the SEC and the Public Company Accounting Oversight Board (PCAOB) require accounting departments to adhere to strict ethical principles.

FIN For the Finance Major

As a result of global regulatory requirements and the passage of Sarbanes-Oxley, financial managers must follow strict ethical guidelines. They are responsible for full, fair, accurate, timely, and understandable disclosure in all financial reports and documents that their companies submit to the Securities and Exchange Commission (SEC) and in all other public financial reports. Furthermore, financial managers are responsible for compliance with all applicable governmental laws, rules, and regulations.

MKT For the Marketing Major

Marketing professionals have new opportunities to collect data on their customers, for example, through business-to-consumer electronic commerce (discussed in Chapter 9). Business ethics clearly mandate that these data should be used only within the company and should not be sold to anyone else. Marketers do not want to be sued for invasion of privacy over data collected for the marketing database.

Customers expect their data to be properly secured. However, profit-motivated criminals want that data. Therefore, marketing managers must analyze the risks of their operations. Failure to protect corporate and customer data will cause significant public relations problems and outrage customers. Customer relationship management (discussed in Chapter 12) operations and tracking customers' online buying habits can expose unencrypted data to misuse or result in privacy violations.

POM For the Production/Operations Management Major

POM professionals decide whether to outsource (or offshore) manufacturing operations. In some cases, these operations are sent overseas to countries that do not have strict labor laws. This situation raises serious ethical questions. For example: Is it ethical to hire employees in countries with poor working conditions in order to reduce labor costs?

HRM For the Human Resource Management Major

Ethics is critically important to HR managers. HR policies explain the appropriate use of information technologies in the workplace. Questions such as the following can arise: Can employees use the Internet, e-mail, or chat systems for personal purposes while at work? Is it ethical to monitor employees? If so, how? How much? How often? HR managers must formulate and enforce such policies while at the same time maintaining trusting relationships between employees and management.

MIS For the MIS Major

Ethics might be more important for MIS personnel than for anyone else in the organization, because these individuals have control of the information assets. They also have control over a huge amount of the employees' personal information. As a result, the MIS function must be held to the highest ethical standards.

Summary

1. Describe ethics, its three fundamental tenets, and the four categories of ethical issues related to information technology.

Ethics refers to the principles of right and wrong that individuals use to make choices that guide their behavior.

Fundamental tenets of ethics include responsibility, accountability, and liability. Responsibility means that you accept the consequences of your decisions and actions. Accountability refers to determining who is responsible for actions that were taken. Liability is a legal concept that gives individuals the right to recover the damages done to them by other individuals, organizations, or systems.

The major ethical issues related to IT are privacy, accuracy, property (including intellectual property), and access to information. Privacy may be violated when data are held in databases or transmitted over networks.

Privacy policies that address issues of data collection, data accuracy, and data confidentiality can help organizations avoid legal problems.

2. Discuss at least one potential threat to the privacy of the data stored in each of three places that store personal data.

Privacy is the right to be left alone and to be free of unreasonable personal intrusions. Threats to privacy include advances in information technologies, electronic surveillance, personal information in databases, Internet bulletin boards, newsgroups, and social networking sites. The privacy threat in Internet bulletin boards, newsgroups, and social networking sites is that you might post too much personal information that many unknown people can see.

Chapter Glossary

accountability A tenet of ethics that refers to determining who is responsible for actions that were taken.

code of ethics A collection of principles intended to guide decision making by members of an organization.

digital dossier An electronic description of an individual and his or her habits.

electronic surveillance Tracking people's activities with the aid of computers.

ethics The principles of right and wrong that individuals use to make choices to guide their behaviors.

information privacy The right to determine when, and to what extent, personal information can be gathered by and/or communicated to others.

liability A legal concept that gives individuals the right to recover the damages done to them by other individuals, organizations, or systems.

opt-in model A model of informed consent in which a business is prohibited from collecting any personal information unless the customer specifically authorizes it.

opt-out model A model of informed consent that permits a company to collect personal information until the customer specifically requests that the data not be collected.

privacy The right to be left alone and to be free of unreasonable personal intrusions.

privacy codes See privacy policies.

privacy policies (also known as privacy codes) An organization's guidelines for protecting the privacy of customers, clients, and employees.

profiling The process of forming a digital dossier.

responsibility A tenet of ethics in which you accept the consequences of your decisions and actions.

Discussion Questions

1. In 2008, the Massachusetts Bay Transportation Authority (MBTA) obtained a temporary restraining order barring three Massachusetts Institute of Technology (MIT) students from publicly displaying what they claimed to be a way to get "free subway rides for life." Specifically, the 10-day injunction prohibited the students from revealing vulnerabilities of the MBTA's fare card. The students were scheduled to present their findings in Las Vegas at the DEFCON computer hacking conference. Were the students' actions legal? Were their actions ethical? Discuss your answer from the students' perspective and then from the perspective of the MBTA.

2. Frank Abagnale, the criminal played by Leonardo DiCaprio in the motion picture *Catch Me If You Can*, ended up in prison. After he left prison, however, he worked as a consultant to many companies on matters of fraud.

   a. Why do these companies hire the perpetrators (if caught) as consultants? Is this a good idea?

   b. You are the CEO of a company. Discuss the ethical implications of hiring Frank Abagnale as a consultant.

3. Access various search engines to find information relating to the use of drones (unmanned aerial vehicles (UAVs)) for electronic surveillance purposes in the United States.

   a. Take the position favoring the use of drones for electronic surveillance.

   b. Take the position against the use of drones for electronic surveillance.

Problem-Solving Activities

1. An information security manager routinely monitored Web surfing among her company's employees. She discovered that many employees were visiting the "sinful six" Web sites. (*Note:* The "sinful six" are Web sites with material related to pornography, gambling, hate, illegal activities, tastelessness, and violence.) She then prepared a list of the employees and their surfing histories and gave the list to management. Some managers punished their employees. Some employees, in turn, objected to the monitoring, claiming that they should have a right to privacy.

   a. Is monitoring of Web surfing by managers ethical? (It is legal.) Support your answer.

   b. Is employee Web surfing on the "sinful six" ethical? Support your answer.

   c. Is the security manager's submission of the list of abusers to management ethical? Why or why not?

   d. Is punishing the abusers ethical? Why or why not? If yes, then what types of punishment are acceptable?

   e. What should the company do in this situation? (*Note:* There are a variety of possibilities here.)

2. Access the Computer Ethics Institute's Web site at www.cpsr.org/issues/ethics/cei. The site offers the "Ten Commandments of Computer Ethics." Study these rules and decide whether any others should be added.

3. Access the Association for Computing Machinery's code of ethics for its members (see www.acm.org/constitution/code.html). Discuss the major points of this code. Is this code complete? Why or why not? Support your answer.

4. Access www.eightmaps.com. Is the use of data on this Web site illegal? Unethical? Support your answer.

5. The Electronic Frontier Foundation (www.eff.org) has a mission of protecting rights and promoting freedom in the "electronic frontier." Review the organization's suggestions about how to protect your online privacy, and summarize what you can do to protect yourself.

6. Access your university's guidelines for ethical computer and Internet use. Are there limitations as to the types of Web sites that you can visit and the types of material you can view? Are you allowed to change the programs on the lab computers? Are you allowed to download software from the lab computers for your personal use? Are there rules governing the personal use of computers and e-mail?

7. Access http://www.albion.com/netiquette/corerules.html. What do you think of this code of ethics? Should it be expanded? Is it too general?

8. Access www.cookiecentral.com and www.epubliceye.com. Do these sites provide information that helps you protect your privacy? If so, then explain how.

9. Do you believe that a university should be allowed to monitor e-mail sent and received on university computers? Why or why not? Support your answer.

Closing Case 1

The Ashley Madison Breach

The Problem

Launched in 2001, Ashley Madison (www.ashleymadison.com) is an online dating and social network service based in Canada. Unlike most dating services, Ashley Madison marketed specifically to people who are married or in a committed relationship but are seeking an outside relationship. In mid-2015, the site claimed 39 million members in 53 countries, and it generated an estimated $115 million in annual revenue.

Significantly, Ashley Madison purportedly allowed users to hide their account profiles for free. Users who wanted to delete their accounts had to pay a $19 fee. Ashley Madison assured its users that its "full delete option" removed all relevant data from the site: user profiles, all messages sent and received, site usage history, personally identifiable information, and photos.

On July 15, 2015, Ashley Madison was hacked by a group called "The Impact Team." The hackers claimed to have stolen personal information about the site's users, and it threatened to release names, addresses, search histories, and credit card numbers if the site did not immediately cease operations. The Impact Team claimed their demand was caused by Ashley Madison's failure to delete users' personal information following their invoiced requests to do so.

When Ashley Madison ignored the demand, The Impact Team launched its first data release on August 18, followed by a second release three days later. The second batch of data included Ashley Madison CEO Noel Biderman's personal e-mails.

The data, which initially appeared on the Dark Web, were copied and made public on the open Web. The Dark Web is the World Wide Web content that exists on networks that require encryption, specific software, or authorization to access. The Dark Web is not indexed by search engines, and it can be accessed only through a browser called Tor (www.torproject.org). The Dark Web is used today for a wide range of anonymous activities including communication by dissidents in authoritarian countries who wish to access the Internet. It has also emerged as a platform for illegal activities such as cybercrime, child pornography, and drug trafficking.

Ashley Madison's Attempts at a Solution

Immediately following The Impact Team's announcement, CEO Biderman confirmed the hack and asserted that the company was "working diligently and feverishly" to try and stop the spread of the leaked data. Ashley Madison released the following statement: "We are actively monitoring and investigating this situation to determine the validity of any information posted online . . . We will continue to put forth substantial efforts into removing any information unlawfully released to the public, as well as continuing to operate our business." In addition, the company issued copyright takedown notices under the 1998 Digital Millennium Copyright Act (DMCA) to multiple sites, claiming that "intellectual property in the data" was being infringed upon. Many of the sites complied with these requests.

Ashley Madison subsequently announced that it had secured its site. It labeled the hack an act of "cyberterrorism," and it apologized to its users. The company offered $500,000 (Canadian) to anyone with information that leads to the identification of the hackers. Finally, the site announced that in the future it would delete user information free of charge, thus eliminating the $19 fee.

The Results

By late August 2015, more than $1 billion in lawsuits had been filed against Ashley Madison. On August 28, CEO Biderman stepped down. According to the official press release, the senior management team currently in place will continue to lead the company.

Meanwhile, both the site and its users experienced further fallout from the breach. For example, spammers quickly began to extort people whose information was made public. One group, for example, sent e-mails to Ashley Madison users demanding one bitcoin (approximately $225) to prevent their information from being shared. The group gave the users seven days before it exposed them. In addition to extortion, victims of the breach risk identity theft as well. Meanwhile, in 2015, Ashley Madison had announced that it hoped to raise $200 million in an initial public offering in London after it had failed in a previous IPO attempt in Canada. Those plans are now in jeopardy. In fact, as of late 2015, Ashley Madison's very survival is questionable.

While the moral and ethical outrage surrounding the Ashley Madison hack has received most of the headlines, industry analysts maintain that the real issues are the assault on consumer privacy and the inability of businesses to protect their customers' data. Analysts further predict that in the future businesses will likely be held far more accountable for data security than they have been in the past.

From a different perspective, private investigation startup Trustify (www.trustify.info) capitalized on the Ashley Madison breach by launching a service just after the attack that let anyone search the data dump from the hackers. Trustify advertised its services to suspicious partners who were concerned by a name that they found on the list.

Sources: Compiled from R. Hackett, "CEO of Ashley Madison Parent Company Stepping Down," *Fortune*, August 28, 2015; L. Loeb, "Ashley Madison Fallout: Investigations, Lawsuits, Lessons," *InformationWeek*, August 26, 2015; R. King, "IBM Advises Companies to Keep Networks Free from Dark Web," *The Wall Street Journal*, August 26, 2015; B. Krebs, "Who Hacked Ashley Madison?" *Krebs on Security*, August 26, 2015; M. Slater-Robins, "Here's What Ashley Madison's $19 'Full Delete' Feature Actually Removes," *Business Insider*, August 26, 2015; J. Greenberg, "Private Investigator Startup Exploits Ashley Madison Hack," *Wired*, August 25, 2015; A. Blake, "Ashley Madison Hack Could Cost Dating Site More than $1 Billion as Lawsuits Mount," *The Washington Times*, August 25, 2015; W. Ashford, "Avid Life Media Offers Reward for Information on Ashley Madison Hack as Writs Loom," *Computer Weekly*, August 25, 2015; D. George-Cosh, "Canadian Police Call Ashley Madison Hack Criminal," *The Wall Street Journal*, August 24, 2015; "The Ashley Madison Hack... in 2 Minutes," *CNN Money*, August 24, 2015; "Ashley Madison Users Now Facing Extortion," *CNN Money*, August 21, 2015; B. Cole, "Will Data Privacy Finally Come to the Fore, Post Ashley Madison Hack?" *TechTarget*, August 21, 2015; "Ashley Madison Tries to Stop the Spread of Its Leaked Data," *CNN Money*, August 21, 2015; C. Welch, "Ashley Madison's $19 'Full Delete' Option Made the Company Millions," *The Verge*, August 19, 2015; "Ashley Madison Probes Veracity of Data Leaked by Hackers," *CNBC*, August 19, 2015; "Hackers Expose First Ashley Madison Users," *CBS News*, July 22, 2015; Q. Fottrell, "Ashley Madison May Have to Kiss Its IPO Goodbye," *Market Watch*, July 21, 2015; B. Krebs, "Online Cheating Site Ashley Madison Hacked," *Krebs on Security*, July 19, 2015; www.ashleymadison.com, accessed August 29, 2015.

Questions

1. Discuss the legality and the ethicality of the Ashley Madison Web site.

2. Discuss the legality and the ethicality of the actions of the hackers who attacked the Ashley Madison Web site.

3. Discuss the legality and ethicality of the actions of people who copied the Ashley Madison data from the Dark Web and then made the data available on the open Web.

4. Discuss the legality and ethicality of the reporters who used hacked (stolen) information in their stories.

5. Discuss the legality and ethicality of the actions of Trustify.

6. Are there differences in your answers to the first five questions? If so, then describe them. How do you account for them?

7. What are the implications of the Ashley Madison breach for general privacy concerns regarding digital data?

Closing Case 2

The Facebook Experiments

The Problem

Facebook (www.facebook.com) has long conducted digital experiments on various aspects of its Web site. For example, just before the 2012 election, the company conducted an experiment on the News Feeds of nearly two million users so that they would see more "hard news" shared by their friends. In the experiment, news articles that Facebook users' friends had posted appeared higher in their News feeds. Facebook claimed that the news stories being shared were general in nature and not political. The stories originated from a list of 100 top media outlets from *The New York Times* to Fox News. Industry analysts claim that the change may have boosted voter turnout by as much as 3 percent.

Next, Facebook decided to conduct a different kind of experiment that analyzed human emotions. The social network has observed that people's friends often produce more News Feed content than they can read. As a result, Facebook filters that content with algorithms to show users the most relevant and engaging content. For one week in 2012, Facebook changed the algorithms it uses to determine which status updates appeared in the News Feed of 689,000 randomly selected users (about 1 of every 2,500 Facebook users). In this experiment, the algorithm filtered content based on its emotional content. Specifically, it identified a post as "positive" or "negative" if it used at least one word previously identified by Facebook as positive or negative. In essence, Facebook altered the regular news feeds of those users, showing one set of users happy, positive posts while displaying dreary, negative posts to another set.

Previous studies had found that the largely positive content that Facebook tends to feature has made users feel bitter and resentful. The rationale for this finding is that users become jealous over the success of other people, and they feel they are not "keeping up." Those studies, therefore, predicted that reducing the positive content in users' feeds might actually make users less unhappy. Clearly, Facebook would want to determine what types of feeds will make users spend more time on its site rather than leave the site in disgust or despair. Consequently, Facebook designed its experiment to investigate the theory that seeing friends' positive content makes users sad.

The researchers—one from Facebook and two from academia—conducted two experiments, with a total of four groups of users. In the first experiment, they reduced the positive content of News Feeds; in the second experiment, they reduced the negative content. In both experiments, these treatment conditions were compared with control groups in which News Feeds were randomly filtered without regard to positive or negative content.

The results were interesting. When users received more positive content in their News Feed, a slightly larger percentage of words in their status updates were positive, and a smaller percentage were negative. When positivity was reduced, the opposite pattern occurred. The researchers concluded that the emotions expressed by friends, via online social networks, elicited similar emotions from users. Interestingly, the results of this experiment did *not* support the hypothesis that seeing friends' positive content made users sad.

Significantly, Facebook had not explicitly informed the participants that they were being studied. In fact, few users were aware of this fact until the study was published in a paper titled "Experimental evidence of massive-scale emotional contagion through social networks" in the prominent scientific journal *Proceedings of the National Academy of Sciences*. At that point, many people became upset that Facebook had secretly performed a digital experiment on its users. The only warning that Facebook had issued was buried in the social network's one-click user agreement. Facebook's Data Use Policy states that Facebook "may use the information we receive about you . . . for internal operations, including troubleshooting, data analysis, testing, research, and service improvement." This policy led to charges that the experiment violated laws designed to protect human research subjects.

Some lawyers urged legal action against Facebook over its experiment. While acknowledging the potential benefits of digital research, they asserted that online research such as the Facebook experiment should be held to some of the same standards required of government-sponsored clinical trials. What makes the Facebook experiment unethical, in their opinion, was that the company did not explicitly seek subjects' approval at the time of the study.

Some industry analysts challenged this contention, arguing that clinical research requirements should not be imposed on Facebook. They placed Facebook's experiment in the context of manipulative advertising—on the Web and elsewhere—and news outlets that select stories and write headlines in a way that is designed to exploit emotional responses by their readers.

On July 3, 2014, the privacy group Electronic Privacy Information Center (EPIC; www.epic.org) filed a formal complaint with the Federal Trade Commission (FTC; www.ftc.gov) claiming that Facebook had broken the law when it conducted the experiment without the participants' knowledge or consent. EPIC alleged that Facebook had deceived its users by secretly conducting a psychological experiment on their emotions.

Facebook's Response

Facebook Chief Operating Officer Sheryl Sandburg defended the experiment on the grounds that it was a part of ongoing research that companies perform to test different products. She conceded, however, that the experiment had been poorly communicated, and she formally apologized. In addition, the lead author of the Facebook experiment stated, "I can understand why some people have concerns about it (the study), and my coauthors and I are very sorry for the way the (academic) paper described the research and any anxiety it caused."

For its part, Facebook conceded that the experiment should have been "done differently," and it announced a new set of guidelines for how the social network will approach future research studies. Specifically, research that relates to content that "may be considered deeply personal" will go through an enhanced review process before it can begin.

The Results

At Facebook, the experiments continue. In May 2015, the social network launched an experiment called Instant Articles in partnership with nine major international newspapers. This new feature allowed Facebook to host articles from various news publications directly on its platform, an option that the social network claims will generate a richer multimedia experience and faster page-loading times.

The following month Facebook experimented with its Trending sidebar, which groups news and hashtags into five categories among which users can toggle: all news, politics, science and technology, sports, and entertainment. Facebook maintained that the objective is to help users discover which topics they may be interested in. This experiment could be part of Facebook's new effort to become a one-stop news distributor, an approach that would encourage users to remain on the site for as long as possible.

Sources: Compiled from J. Matias, "Were All Those Rainbow Profile Photos Another Facebook Study?" *The Atlantic*, June 28, 2015; J. Vaughn,

"Facebook Experiment Points to Data Ethics Hurdles in Digital Research," *SearchDataManagement*, November 14, 2014; G. Smith, "Facebook Conducted Another Secret Experiment on Users," *The Huffington Post*, November 3, 2014; D. Rushe, "Facebook Sorry – Almost – for Secret Psychological Experiment on Users," *The Guardian*, October 2, 2014; J. O'Toole, "Facebook: We're Still Experimenting on Users, But Now It's Less Creepy," *CNN Money*, October 2, 2014; R. Meyer, "Facebook's Mood Manipulation Experiment Might Have Been Illegal," *The Atlantic*, September 24, 2014; "The Facebook Experiment: What It Means for You," *Forbes*, August 4, 2014; R. Albergotti, "Furor Erupts over Facebook's Experiment on Users," *The Wall Street Journal*, June 30, 2014; "Facebook Emotion Experiment Sparks Criticism," *BBC News*, June 30, 2014; A. Ma, "Facebook Is Experimenting with How You Read the News," *The Huffington Post*, June 30, 2014; M. Meyer, "Everything You Need to Know about Facebook's Controversial Emotion Experiment," *Wired*, June 30, 2014; V. Goel, "Facebook Tinkers with Users' Emotions in News Feed Experiment, Stirring Outcry," *The New York Times*, June 29, 2014; C. Miller, "Why Facebook's News Experiment Matters to Readers," *The New York Times*, May 14, 2014; Z. Corbyn, "Facebook Experiment Boosts U.S. Voter Turnout," *Nature*, September 12, 2012; www.facebook.com, accessed September 3, 2015.

Questions

1. Discuss the ethicality and legality of Facebook's experiment with human emotions.

2. Was Facebook's response to criticism concerning that experiment adequate? Why or why not?

3. Consider the experiments that Facebook conducted in May and June 2015. Is there a difference between these two experiments and Facebook's experiment with human emotions? Why or why not?

4. Should the law require companies to inform their users every time they conduct experiments? Why or why not?

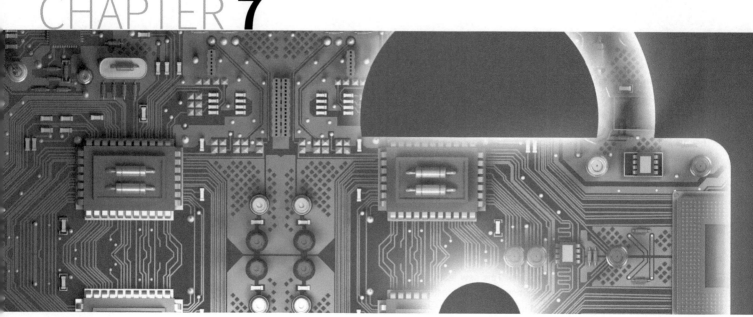

CHAPTER 7

Henrik5000/iStockphoto

Information Security

CHAPTER OUTLINE

7.1 Introduction to Information Security

7.2 Unintentional Threats to Information Systems

7.3 Deliberate Threats to Information Systems

7.4 What Organizations Are Doing to Protect Information Resources

7.5 Information Security Controls

LEARNING OBJECTIVES

7.1. Identify the five factors that contribute to the increasing vulnerability of information resources and specific examples of each factor.

7.2 Compare and contrast human mistakes and social engineering, along with specific examples of each one.

7.3. Discuss the 10 types of deliberate attacks.

7.4. Describe the three risk mitigation strategies and examples of each one in the context of owning a home.

7.5. Identify the three major types of controls that organizations can use to protect their information resources along with an example of each one.

Opening Case

 The St. Louis Cardinals Investigated for Hacking the Houston Astros

From 1994 to 2012, two professional baseball teams, the Houston Astros (http://houston.astros.mlb.com) and the St. Louis Cardinals (http://stlouis.cardinals.mlb.com), were divisional rivals in Major League Baseball's National League. For part of that time, Jeff Luhnow was a Cardinals executive whose primary responsibilities were scouting and player development. He was credited with developing professional baseball's best minor league system, and he drafted several players who were instrumental to the Cardinals victory in the 2011 World Series.

While Luhnow was working for the Cardinals, the team developed a computer system called Redbird. The system managed the team's baseball operations information. This valuable, highly secret information included scouting reports and player information.

Then, in December 2011, the Astros hired Luhnow away from the Cardinals to be their general manager. When Luhnow joined the Astros, some of the Cardinals front-office personnel went with him. The Astros promptly developed a computer system called Ground Control. Similar to Redbird, Ground Control managed the team's baseball operations information. Specifically, the system analyzed a group of variables and weighted them according to the values determined by the team's statisticians, physicians, scouts, and coaches.

In 2014, some of the information from the Astros' information system was anonymously posted online. Details included trade discussions that the Astros had conducted with other teams. Believing that the Astros' network had been compromised, Major League Baseball notified the FBI.

The FBI began investigating the Cardinals' front-office personnel, whom they accused of hacking into an internal network of the Astros to steal proprietary information about players. Investigators uncovered evidence that Cardinals' employees illegally accessed an Astros database containing information concerning internal discussions about trades, proprietary player statistics, and scouting reports. Subpoenas have been served on the Cardinals and Major League Baseball for electronic correspondence.

Law enforcement officials believe that Cardinals' front-office employees hacked the Astros' database to damage Luhnow's work. Specifically, they claim that Cardinals' personnel were concerned that Luhnow had taken both their idea (Redbird) and proprietary baseball information to the Astros. Investigators further contend that they examined a list of passwords used by Luhnow and the other Astros officials when they worked for the Cardinals. The Cardinals' employees are believed to have used those passwords to gain access to the Astros'

network, suggesting that they thought that perhaps Luhnow used the same passwords while working for the Astros that he used while working with the Cardinals.

In July 2015, the Cardinals terminated the contract of their scouting director, who admitted hacking into the Astros' system. He maintained, however, that his sole objective was to determine whether the Astros had stolen proprietary data from the Cardinals.

If the charges against the Cardinals are confirmed, then this attack would represent the first known case of corporate espionage in which a professional sports team hacked the network of another team. Somewhat humorously, when Luhnow was asked how the breach affected the way he deals with other teams, he responded that he now uses a pencil and paper.

Sources: Compiled from D. Brown, "Cardinals Fire Scouting Director, Possibly Linked to Hacking Scandal," *CBS Sports*, July 2, 2015; B. Reiter, "Exclusive: Astros GM Jeff Luhnow Speaks Out about Hacking Scandal," *SI.com*, June 18, 2015; I. Crouch, "Baseball's Data Breaches," *The New Yorker*, June 17, 2015; "FBI Investigates Cardinals for Hacking into Astros' Database," *ESPN.com*, June 17, 2015; D. Wilber and M. Levinson, "FBI Investigating St. Louis Cardinals for Hacking Houston Astros," *Bloomberg BusinessWeek*, June 16, 2015; J. Green, "My Time with the Architect of the Astros' 'Ground Control' Database," *Bloomberg BusinessWeek*, June 16, 2015; M. Schmidt, "Cardinals Investigated for Hacking into Astros' Database," *The New York Times*, June 16, 2015; J. Green, "Extreme Moneyball: The Houston Astros Go All in on Data Analysis," *Bloomberg BusinessWeek*, August 28, 2014; http://houston.astros.mlb.com, http://stlouis.cardinals.mlb.com), accessed July 31, 2015.

Questions

1. Describe how the Cardinals apparently were able to gain access to the Astros' computer system.

2. What lessons should the Astros learn from this security breach?

Introduction

The cases in this chapter provide several lessons. First, it is difficult, if not impossible, for organizations to provide perfect security for their data. Second, there is a growing danger that countries are engaging in economic cyberwarfare among themselves. Third, it appears that it is impossible to secure the Internet. The answer to this question impacts each and every one of us. In essence, our personally identifiable, private data is not secure.

The answers to these issues and others are not clear. As you learn about information security in the context of information technology, you will acquire a better understanding of these issues, their importance, their relationships, and their trade-offs. Keep in mind that the issues involved in information security impact individuals and small organizations as well as large companies.

Information security is especially important to small businesses. Large organizations that experience an information security problem have greater resources to bring to both resolve and survive the problem. In contrast, small businesses have fewer resources and therefore can be destroyed by a data breach.

When properly used, information technologies can have enormous benefits for individuals, organizations, and entire societies. In Chapters 1 and 2, you read about diverse ways in which IT has made businesses more productive, efficient, and responsive to consumers. You also explored fields such as medicine and philanthropy in which IT has improved people's health and well-being. Unfortunately, information technologies can also be misused, often with devastating consequences. Consider the following scenarios:

- Individuals can have their identities stolen.

- Organizations can have customer information stolen, leading to financial losses, erosion of customer confidence, and legal action.

- Countries face the threats of *cyberterrorism* and *cyberwarfare*, terms for Internet-based attacks. Cyberwarfare is a critical problem for the U.S. government. In fact, President Obama signed a cyberwarfare directive in October 2012. In that directive, the White House, for the first time, laid out specific ground rules for how and when the U.S. military can carry out offensive and defensive cyber operations against foreign threats. The directive emphasizes the Obama administration's focus on cybersecurity as a top priority.

Clearly, the misuse of information technologies has come to the forefront of any discussion of IT. Studies have revealed that each security breach costs an organization millions of dollars. For example, consider the Sony and Office of Personnel Management breaches described in this chapter's closing cases. The direct costs of a data breach include hiring forensic experts, notifying customers, setting up telephone hotlines to field queries from concerned or affected customers, offering free credit monitoring, and providing discounts for future products and services. The more intangible costs of a breach include the loss of business from increased customer turnover—called *customer churn*—and decreases in customer trust.

In fact, a study by the Ponemon Institute (www.ponemon.org) revealed that for large companies around the world, the average cost of a data breach was almost $4 million in 2015. In addition, the annual global cost of cybercrime is estimated to be approximately $400 billion. Finally, the two industries with the highest per-record cost of a data breach are healthcare ($359 per record) and education ($294 per record).

Unfortunately, employee negligence caused many of the data breaches, meaning that organizational employees are a weak link in information security. It is therefore very important for you to learn about information security so that you will be better prepared when you enter the workforce.

7.1 | Introduction to Information Security

Security can be defined as the degree of protection against criminal activity, danger, damage, and/or loss. Following this broad definition, **information security** refers to all of the processes and policies designed to protect an organization's information and information systems (IS) from unauthorized access, use, disclosure, disruption, modification, or destruction. You have seen that information and information systems can be compromised by deliberate criminal actions and by anything that can impair the proper functioning of an organization's information systems.

Before continuing, let's consider these key concepts. Organizations collect huge amounts of information and employ numerous information systems that are subject to myriad threats. A **threat** to an information resource is any danger to which a system may be exposed. The **exposure** of an information resource is the harm, loss, or damage that can result if a threat compromises that resource. An information resource's **vulnerability** is the possibility that the system will be harmed by a threat.

Today, five key factors are contributing to the increasing vulnerability of organizational information resources, making it much more difficult to secure them:

1. Today's interconnected, interdependent, wirelessly networked business environment
2. Smaller, faster, cheaper computers and storage devices
3. Decreasing skills necessary to be a computer hacker
4. International organized crime taking over cybercrime
5. Lack of management support

The first factor is the evolution of the IT resource from mainframe-only to today's highly complex, interconnected, interdependent, wirelessly networked business environment. The Internet now enables millions of computers and computer networks to communicate freely and seamlessly with one another. Organizations and individuals are exposed to a world of untrusted networks and potential attackers. In general, a *trusted network*, is any network within your organization and an *untrusted network* is any network external to your organization. In addition, wireless technologies enable employees to compute, communicate, and access the Internet anywhere and anytime. Significantly, wireless is an inherently unsecure broadcast communications medium.

The second factor reflects the fact that modern computers and storage devices (e.g., thumb drives or flash drives) continue to become smaller, faster, cheaper, and more portable, with greater storage capacity. These characteristics make it much easier to steal or lose a computer or storage device that contains huge amounts of sensitive information. Also, far more people are able to afford powerful computers and connect inexpensively to the Internet, thus raising the potential of an attack on information assets.

The third factor is that the computing skills necessary to be a hacker are *decreasing*. The reason is that the Internet contains information and computer programs called *scripts* that users with few skills can download and use to attack any information system connected to the Internet. (Security experts can also use these scripts for legitimate purposes, such as testing the security of various systems.)

The fourth factor is that international organized crime is taking over cybercrime. Cybercrime refers to illegal activities conducted over computer networks, particularly the Internet. iDefense (http://labs.idefense.com), a company that specializes in providing security information to governments and Fortune 500 companies, maintains that groups of well-organized criminal organizations have taken control of a global billion-dollar crime network. The network, powered by skillful hackers, targets known software security weaknesses. These crimes are typically nonviolent, but quite lucrative. Consider, for example, that losses from armed robberies average hundreds of dollars, and those from white-collar crimes average tens of thousands of dollars. In contrast, losses from computer crimes average hundreds of thousands of dollars. Also, computer crimes can be committed from anywhere in the world, at any time, effectively providing an international safe haven for cybercriminals. Computer-based crimes cause billions of dollars in damages to businesses each year, including the costs of repairing information systems and of lost business.

The fifth, and final, factor is lack of management support. For the entire organization to take security policies and procedures seriously, senior managers must set the tone. Unfortunately, senior managers often do not do so. Ultimately, however, lower-level managers may be even more important. These managers are in close contact with employees every day and thus are in a better position to determine whether employees are following security procedures.

Before you go on...

1. Define information security.
2. Differentiate among a threat, an exposure, and a vulnerability.
3. Why are the skills needed to be a hacker decreasing?

Apply the Concept 7.1

LEARNING OBJECTIVE 7.1 Identify the five factors that contribute to the increasing vulnerability of information resources and specific examples of each factor.

STEP 1: Background (Here is what you are learning.)

Section 7.1 has taught you about the importance of information security, particularly when you are conducting business over the Web. It is important to note that a chain is only as strong as its weakest link. Therefore, although you may have been careful to maintain security across your network, if your business partners

have not done so as well, then as your information passes over their networks it will be at risk.

STEP 2: Activity (Here is what you are doing.)

Visit http://www.wiley.com/go/rainer/MIS4e/applytheconcept, and click on the link to VeriSign's Web site. As you read this page, keep in mind that VeriSign is in the business of protecting Web sites and Web users, which is something we all appreciate. In fact, it is likely that you feel some level of comfort when you see the VeriSign symbol on an e-commerce site.

7.2 | Unintentional Threats to Information Systems

Information systems are vulnerable to many potential hazards and threats, as you can see in Figure 7.1. The two major categories of threats are unintentional threats and deliberate threats. This section discusses unintentional threats, and the next section addresses deliberate threats.

FIGURE 7.1 Security threats.

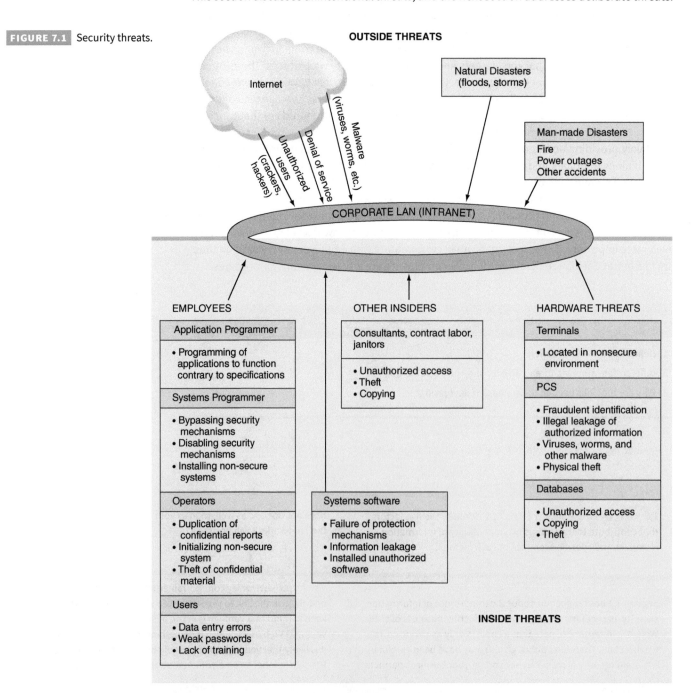

Unintentional threats are acts performed without malicious intent that nevertheless represent a serious threat to information security. A major category of unintentional threats is human error.

Human Errors

Organizational employees span the breadth and depth of the organization, from mail clerks to the CEO, and across all functional areas. There are two important points to be made about employees. First, the higher the level of employee, the greater the threat he or she poses to information security. This is true because higher-level employees typically have greater access to corporate data, and they enjoy greater privileges on organizational information systems. Second, employees in two areas of the organization pose especially significant threats to information security: human resources and information systems (IS). Human resources employees generally have access to sensitive personal information about all employees. Likewise, IS employees not only have access to sensitive organizational data, but also often control the means to create, store, transmit, and modify those data.

Other employees include contract labor, consultants, and janitors and guards. Contract labor, such as temporary hires, may be overlooked in information security arrangements. However, these employees often have access to the company's network, information systems, and information assets. Consultants, although technically not employees, perform work for the company. Depending on the nature of their work, they may also have access to the company's network, information systems, and information assets.

Finally, janitors and guards are the most frequently ignored people in information security systems. Companies frequently outsource their security and janitorial services. As with contractors, then, these individuals work for the company although they technically are not employees. Moreover, they are usually present when most—if not all—other employees have gone home. They typically have keys to every office, and nobody questions their presence in even the most sensitive parts of the building. In fact, an article from *2600: The Hacker Quarterly* described how to get a job as a janitor for the purpose of gaining physical access to an organization.

Human errors or mistakes by employees pose a serious problem. These errors are typically the result of laziness, carelessness, or a lack of awareness concerning information security. This lack of awareness arises from poor education and training efforts by the organization. Human mistakes manifest themselves in many different ways, as illustrated in Table 7.1.

TABLE 7.1   Human Mistakes

Human Mistake	Description and Examples
Carelessness with laptops	Losing or misplacing laptops, leaving them in taxis, and so on.
Carelessness with computing devices	Losing or misplacing these devices, or using them carelessly so that malware is introduced into an organization's network.
Opening questionable e-mails	Opening e-mails from someone unknown, or clicking on links embedded in e-mails (see *phishing attack* in Table 7.2).
Careless Internet surfing	Accessing questionable Web sites; can result in malware and/or alien software being introduced into the organization's network.
Poor password selection and use	Choosing and using weak passwords (see *strong passwords* in the "Authentication" section later in this chapter).
Carelessness with one's office	Leaving desks and filing cabinets unlocked when employees go home at night; not logging off the company network when leaving the office for any extended period of time.
Carelessness using unmanaged devices	Unmanaged devices are those outside the control of an organization's IT department and company security procedures. These devices include computers belonging to customers and business partners, computers in the business centers of hotels, and so on.
Carelessness with discarded equipment	Discarding old computer hardware and devices without completely wiping the memory; includes computers, smartphones, BlackBerry® units, and digital copiers and printers.
Careless monitoring of environmental hazards	These hazards, which include dirt, dust, humidity, and static electricity, are harmful to the operation of computing equipment.

The human errors you have just studied, although unintentional, are committed entirely by employees. However, employees also can make unintentional mistakes in response to actions by an attacker. Attackers often employ social engineering to induce individuals to make unintentional mistakes and disclose sensitive information.

Social Engineering

Social engineering is an attack in which the perpetrator uses social skills to trick or manipulate legitimate employees into providing confidential company information such as passwords. The most common example of social engineering occurs when the attacker impersonates someone else on the telephone, such as a company manager or an information systems employee. The attacker claims he forgot his password and asks the legitimate employee to give him a password to use. Other common ploys include posing as an exterminator, an air-conditioning technician, or a fire marshal. Examples of social engineering abound.

In one company, a perpetrator entered a company building wearing a company ID card that looked legitimate. He walked around and put up signs on bulletin boards reading "The help desk telephone number has been changed. The new number is 555-1234." He then exited the building and began receiving calls from legitimate employees thinking they were calling the company help desk. Naturally, the first thing the perpetrator asked for was username and password. He now had the information necessary to access the company's information systems.

Two other social engineering techniques are tailgating and shoulder surfing. *Tailgating* is a technique designed to allow the perpetrator to enter restricted areas that are controlled with locks or card entry. The perpetrator follows closely behind a legitimate employee and, when the employee gains entry, the attacker asks him or her to "hold the door." *Shoulder surfing* occurs when a perpetrator watches an employee's computer screen over the employee's shoulder. This technique is particularly successful in public areas such as in airports and on commuter trains and airplanes.

Before you go on…

1. What is an unintentional threat to an information system?

2. Provide examples of social engineering attacks other than the ones just discussed.

Apply the Concept 7.2

LEARNING OBJECTIVE 7.2 Compare and contrast human mistakes and social engineering, along with specific examples of each one.

STEP 1: Background

Sensitive information is generally stored in a safe location, both physically and digitally. However, as you have just read, this information is often vulnerable to unintentional threats that result from careless mistakes. As one example, employees frequently use USB (flash) drives to take information home. Although these actions are perfectly legal, the USB drive makes it easy to lose the information or to copy it onto unauthorized machines. In fact, any device that stores information can become a threat to information security—backup drives, CDs, DVDs, and even printers!

Printers?! Because people can "copy" information? Not quite. Continue the activity to find out more.

STEP 2: Activity

Go to http://www.wiley.com/go/rainer/MIS4e/applytheconcept, and click on the link provided for Apply the Concept 7.2. You will find an article about how the hard drive in a printer sometimes stores images of all of the documents that have been copied. In the past, when these printers were discarded their hard drives were not erased, leaving medical records, police reports, and other private information in a vulnerable state.

STEP 3: Deliverable

Compare and contrast human mistakes and social engineering using the example above. How might someone make a mistake with a printer? How might someone use social engineering to access or create copies of personal information? Put your thoughts into a report and submit it to your instructor.

7.3 | Deliberate Threats to Information Systems

There are many types of deliberate threats to information systems. We provide a list of 10 common types for your convenience:

1. Espionage or trespass
2. Information extortion
3. Sabotage or vandalism
4. Theft of equipment or information
5. Identity theft
6. Compromises to intellectual property
7. Software attacks
8. Alien software
9. Supervisory control and data acquisition (SCADA) attacks
10. Cyberterrorism and cyberwarfare

Espionage or Trespass

Espionage or trespass occurs when an unauthorized individual attempts to gain illegal access to organizational information. It is important to distinguish between competitive intelligence and industrial espionage. Competitive intelligence consists of legal information-gathering techniques, such as studying a company's Web site and press releases, attending trade shows, and similar actions. In contrast, industrial espionage crosses the legal boundary.

Information Extortion

Information extortion occurs when an attacker either threatens to steal, or actually steals, information from a company. The perpetrator demands payment for not stealing the information, for returning stolen information, or for agreeing not to disclose the information.

Sabotage or Vandalism

Sabotage and vandalism are deliberate acts that involve defacing an organization's Web site, potentially damaging the organization's image and causing its customers to lose faith. One form of online vandalism is a hacktivist or cyberactivist operation. These are cases of high-tech civil disobedience to protest the operations, policies, or actions of an organization or government agency. For example, the English Twitter account for the Arabic news network Al Jazeera was subject to hacktivism. The Associated Press reported that supporters of Syrian President Bashar Assad used the account to tweet pro-Assad links and messages.

Theft of Equipment or Information

Computing devices and storage devices are becoming smaller yet more powerful with vastly increased storage (e.g., laptops, personal digital assistants, smartphones, digital cameras, thumb drives, iPods). As a result, these devices are becoming easier to steal and easier for attackers to use to steal information.

Table 7.1 points out that one type of human mistake is carelessness with laptops. In fact, many laptops have been stolen due to such carelessness. The cost of a stolen laptop includes the loss of data, the loss of intellectual property, laptop replacement, legal and regulatory costs, investigation fees, and lost productivity.

One form of theft, known as *dumpster diving*, involves rummaging through commercial or residential trash to find discarded information. Paper files, letters, memos, photographs, IDs, passwords, credit cards, and other forms of information can be found in dumpsters. Unfortunately, many people never consider that the sensitive items they throw in the trash might be recovered. When this information is recovered, it can be used for fraudulent purposes.

Dumpster diving is not necessarily theft, because the legality of this act varies. Because dumpsters are usually located on private premises, dumpster diving is illegal in some parts of the United States. Even in these cases, however, these laws are enforced with varying degrees of rigor.

Identity Theft

Identity theft is the deliberate assumption of another person's identity, usually to gain access to his or her financial information or to frame him or her for a crime. Techniques for illegally obtaining personal information include the following:

- Stealing mail or dumpster diving
- Stealing personal information in computer databases
- Infiltrating organizations that store large amounts of personal information (e.g., data aggregators such as Acxiom) (www.acxiom.com)
- Impersonating a trusted organization in an electronic communication (phishing)

Recovering from identity theft is costly, time consuming, and burdensome. Victims also report problems in obtaining credit and obtaining or holding a job, as well as adverse effects on insurance or credit rates. In addition, victims state that it is often difficult to remove negative information from their records, such as their credit reports.

Your personal information can be compromised in other ways. For example, your identity can be uncovered just by examining your searches in a search engine. The ability to analyze all searches by a single user can enable a criminal to identify who the user is and what he or she is doing. To demonstrate this fact, *The New York Times* tracked down a particular individual based solely on her AOL searches.

Compromises to Intellectual Property

Protecting intellectual property is a vital issue for people who make their livelihood in knowledge fields. Intellectual property is the property created by individuals or corporations that is protected under *trade secret*, *patent*, and *copyright* laws.

A trade secret is an intellectual work, such as a business plan, that is a company secret and is not based on public information. An example is the formula for Coca-Cola. A patent is an official document that grants the holder exclusive rights on an invention or a process for a specified period of time. Copyright is a statutory grant that provides the creators or owners of intellectual property with ownership of the property, also for a designated period. Current U.S. laws award patents for 20 years and copyright protection for the life of the creator plus 70 years. Owners are entitled to collect fees from anyone who wants to copy their creations. It is important to note that these are definitions under U.S. law. There is some international standardization of copyrights and patents, but it is far from total. Therefore, there can be discrepancies between U.S. law and other countries' laws.

The most common intellectual property related to IT deals with software. In 1980, the U.S. Congress amended the Copyright Act to include software. The amendment provides protection for the *source code* and *object code* of computer software, but it does not clearly identify what is eligible for protection. For example, copyright law does not protect fundamental concepts, functions, and general features such as pull-down menus, colors, and icons. However, copying a software program without making payment to the owner—including giving a disc to a friend to install on his or her computer—is a copyright violation. Not surprisingly, this practice, called piracy, is a major problem for software vendors. The BSA (www.bsa.org) Global Software Piracy Study found that the commercial value of software theft totals billions of dollars per year.

Software Attacks

Software attacks have evolved from the early years of the computer era, when attackers used malicious software (called malware) to infect as many computers worldwide as possible, to the profit-driven, Web-based attacks of today. Modern cybercriminals use sophisticated, blended malware attacks, typically via the Web, to make money. Table 7.2 displays a variety of software attacks. These attacks are grouped into three categories: remote attacks requiring user action; remote attacks requiring no user action; and software attacks initiated by programmers during the development of a system. This chapter's opening and closing cases provide excellent examples of software attacks.

Not all cybercriminals are sophisticated, however. For example, a student at a U.S. university was sentenced to one year in prison for using keylogging software (discussed later in this chapter) to steal 750 fellow students' passwords and vote himself and four of his fraternity

TABLE 7.2 Types of Software Attacks

Type	Description
Remote Attacks Requiring User Action	
Virus	Segment of computer code that performs malicious actions by attaching to another computer program
Worm	Segment of computer code that performs malicious actions and will replicate, or spread, by itself (without requiring another computer program)
Phishing attack	Phishing attacks use deception to acquire sensitive personal information by masquerading as official-looking e-mails or instant messages.
Spear phishing	Phishing attacks target large groups of people. In spear phishing attacks, attack the perpetrators find out as much information about an individual as possible to improve their chances that phishing techniques will obtain sensitive, personal information.
Remote Attacks Needing No User Action	
Denial-of-service attack	An attacker sends so many information requests to a target computer system that the target cannot handle them successfully and typically crashes (ceases to function).
Distributed denial-of-service attack	An attacker first takes over many computers, typically by using malicious software. These computers are called *zombies* or *bots*. The attacker uses these bots—which form a *botnet*—to deliver a coordinated stream of information requests to a target computer, causing it to crash.
Attacks by a Programmer Developing a System	
Trojan horse	Software programs that hide in other computer programs and reveal their designed behavior only when they are activated
Back door	Typically a password, known only to the attacker, that allows him or her to access a computer system at will, without having to go through any security procedures (also called a *trap door*).
Logic bomb	A segment of computer code that is embedded within an organization's existing computer programs and is designed to activate and perform a destructive action at a certain time or date.

brothers into the student government's president and four vice president positions. The five positions would have brought the students a combined $36,000 in stipends.

The student was caught when university security personnel noticed strange activity on the campus network. Authorities identified the computer used in the activity from its IP address. On this computer, which belonged to the student in question, authorities found a PowerPoint presentation detailing the scheme. Authorities also found research on his computer, with queries such as "how to rig an election" and "jail time for keylogger."

Once the university caught onto the scheme, the student reportedly turned back to hacking to try to get himself out of trouble. He created new Facebook accounts in the names of actual classmates, going as far as conducting fake conversations between the accounts to try to deflect the blame. Those actions contributed to the one-year prison sentence, which the judge imposed even after the student pleaded guilty and requested probation.

There are many different kinds of software attacks, with more appearing every day. As you see in IT's About Business 7.1, ransomware has become a huge problem very quickly.

IT's About Business 7.1

MIS Ransomware

Mark Stevens, president of a small firm, was notified by one of his employees that her computer was locked. Within hours, the malicious software spread from her computer to the company's servers and backup systems. The malware encrypted the firm's client and financial data. A ransom note appeared on the company's computers: Pay $400 within 72 hours to unlock the data.

Mr. Stevens's initial reaction was to ignore the ransom demand. However, his information technology group informed him that it would take far greater time and money to try to break the encryption than to pay the ransom. Therefore, one of his employees went to the local Walgreens, took a MoneyGram gift card, and had the cashier load the $400 on it. Within 30 minutes, a program unencrypted the data.

In the end, no data were stolen, and no confidentiality breaches occurred. Within 72 hours the company was fully operational.

The malicious software that infected Mr. Stevens's company is called *ransomware*. Simply put, ransomware blocks access to a computer system until the system owner or operator pays a sum of money. Types of ransomware include Cryptolocker, Cryptowall, TeslaCrypt, and CTB Locker. The most current form of ransomware demands payment via the hard-to-trace cryptocurrency Bitcoin, and it uses the anonymizing Tor network (www.torproject.org).

When ransomware first appeared, it was relatively unknown and therefore could infect thousands of computers in a few days. The malware was typically disseminated through established botnets and phishing attacks. Victims were told to pay the ransom in Bitcoin or via MoneyGram to untraceable gift cards in Eastern Europe.

Many ransomware victims reported that the attackers were honoring their promise to remove the encryption if the victim met the terms within the specified time period. This situation encouraged additional victims to pay the ransom instead of pursuing another, generally more costly solution.

There are two possible solutions to the ransomware problem. The first is to hope that if your computer is infected, a third-party supplier will have come up with antivirus software to deal with your ransomware. Several antivirus vendors have provided fixes that victims can download to a USB stick. The victim then plugs the stick into the infected computer. Unfortunately, antivirus companies can't always keep up with the ransomware versions that pop up all the time. Therefore, if you are infected with a new type of ransomware, you may have little choice if you want your system and data back, other than to pay the ransom.

The second possible solution to the ransomware problem is more effective. Essentially, hackers profit from the fact that many people don't back up their valuable information. Therefore, an effective defense against ransomware is to back up your entire system (all of your data, your files, and your operating system) every day onto a hard drive that is separate from your computer.

You can also use a cloud storage company or an online backup service to make copies of your operating system and data. See, for example, iDrive (www.idrive.com), CrashPlan (www.code42.com/crashplan), and SOS Online Backup (www.barracuda.com). This process will save you from the inconvenience of having to back up every day, but it will cost more money.

Sources: Compiled from W. Ashford, "Hacker Tries to Hold Plex Video Streaming Service to Ransom," *Computer Weekly*, July 3, 2015; P. Muncaster, "Over One-Third of Firms Hit by Ransomware Blitz," *InfoSecurity Magazine*, June 26, 2015; C. Stobing, "Ransomware Is the New Hot Threat Everyone Is Talking About; What Do You Need to Know?" *Digital Trends*, June 6, 2015; R. Lemos, "Ransomware Threat Drives Companies to Enforce Better Backup Habits," *eWeek*, May 26, 2015; R. Simon, "'Ransomware' a Growing Threat to Small Businesses," *The Wall Street Journal*, April 15, 2015; F. Donovan, "Firms Hit by Ransomware More Willing to Negotiate for Data," *FierceITSecurity*, April 2, 2015; R. Lemos, "How to Prevent Ransomware: What One Company Learned the Hard Way," *PC World*, March 26, 2015; T. Simonite, "Holding Data Hostage: The Perfect Internet Crime?" *MIT Technology Review*, February 4, 2015; L. Constantin, "Malvertising Campaign Delivers Digitally Signed CryptoWall Ransomware," *PC World*, September 29, 2014; "Your Money or Your Life Files," *KnowBe4.com*, June 2014.

Questions

1. Why is ransomware more than a nuisance?

2. Are your digital files adequately backed up? Why or why not?

Alien Software

Many personal computers have alien software, or *pestware*, running on them that the owners are unaware of. Alien software is clandestine software that is installed on your computer through duplicitous methods. It typically is not as malicious as viruses, worms, or Trojan horses, but it does use up valuable system resources. In addition, it can enable other parties to track your Web surfing habits and other personal behaviors.

The vast majority of pestware is adware—software that causes pop-up advertisements to appear on your screen. Adware is common because it works. According to advertising agencies, for every 100 people who close a pop-up ad, 3 click on it. This "hit rate" is extremely high for Internet advertising.

Spyware is software that collects personal information about users without their consent. Two common types of spyware are keystroke loggers and screen scrapers.

Keystroke loggers, also called *keyloggers*, record both your individual keystrokes and your Internet Web browsing history. The purposes range from criminal—for example, theft of passwords and sensitive personal information such as credit card numbers—to annoying—for example, recording your Internet search history for targeted advertising.

Companies have attempted to counter keyloggers by switching to other forms of identifying users. For example, at some point all of us have been forced to look at wavy, distorted letters and type them correctly into a box. That string of letters is called a *CAPTCHA*, and it is a test. The point of CAPTCHA is that computers cannot (yet) accurately read those distorted letters. Therefore, the fact that you can transcribe them means that you are probably not a software program run by an unauthorized person, such as a spammer. As a result, attackers have turned to *screen scrapers*, or *screen grabbers*. This software records a continuous "movie" of a screen's contents rather than simply recording keystrokes.

Spamware is pestware that uses your computer as a launch pad for spammers. Spam is unsolicited e-mail, usually advertising for products and services. When your computer is infected with spamware, e-mails from spammers are sent to everyone in your e-mail address book, but they appear to come from you.

Not only is spam a nuisance, but it wastes time and money. Spam costs U.S. companies billions of dollars every year. These costs arise from productivity losses, clogged e-mail systems, additional storage, user support, and antispam software. Spam can also carry viruses and worms, making it even more dangerous.

Cookies are small amounts of information that Web sites store on your computer, temporarily or more or less permanently. In many cases, cookies are useful and innocuous. For example, some cookies are passwords and user IDs that you do not want to retype every time you access the Web site that issued the cookie. Cookies are also necessary for online shopping because merchants use them for your shopping carts.

Tracking cookies, however, can be used to track your path through a Web site, the time you spend there, what links you click on, and other details that the company wants to record, usually for marketing purposes. Tracking cookies can also combine this information with your name, purchases, credit card information, and other personal data to develop an intrusive profile of your spending habits.

Most cookies can be read only by the party that created them. However, some companies that manage online banner advertising are, in essence, cookie-sharing rings. These companies can track information such as which pages you load and which ads you click on. They then share this information with their client Web sites, which may number in the thousands.

Supervisory Control and Data Acquisition Attacks

SCADA refers to a large-scale, distributed measurement and control system. SCADA systems are used to monitor or to control chemical, physical, and transport processes such as those used in oil refineries, water and sewage treatment plants, electrical generators, and nuclear power plants. Essentially, SCADA systems provide a link between the physical world and the electronic world.

SCADA systems consist of multiple sensors, a master computer, and communications infrastructure. The sensors connect to physical equipment. They read status data such as the open/closed status of a switch or a valve, as well as measurements such as pressure, flow, voltage, and current. They control the equipment by sending signals to it, such as opening or closing a switch or a valve or setting the speed of a pump.

The sensors are connected in a network, and each sensor typically has an Internet address (Internet Protocol, or IP, address, discussed in Chapter 4). If attackers gain access to the network, they can cause serious damage, such as disrupting the power grid over a large area or upsetting the operations of a large chemical or nuclear plant. Such actions could have catastrophic results.

Cyberterrorism and Cyberwarfare

Cyberterrorism and cyberwarfare refer to malicious acts in which attackers use a target's computer systems, particularly via the Internet, to cause physical, real-world harm or severe disruption, often to carry out a political agenda. Although not definitely proven in early 2016, the U.S. government considers the Sony hack (see chapter closing case 1) to be an example of cyberwarfare committed by North Korea. These actions range from gathering data to attacking critical infrastructure (e.g., via SCADA systems). We treat the two types of attacks as synonymous here, even though cyberterrorism typically is carried out by individuals or groups, whereas cyberwarfare is carried out by nation states or non-state actors such as terrorists.

Before you go on…

1. Why has the theft of computing devices become more serious over time?
2. What are the three types of software attacks?
3. Define alien software and explain why it is a serious problem.
4. What is a SCADA system? Why can attacks against SCADA system have catastrophic consequences

---

Apply the Concept 7.3

LEARNING OBJECTIVE 7.3 Discuss the ten types of deliberate attacks.

STEP 1: Background

Unfortunately there are many people who take advantage of others. Fraud, espionage, information extortion, identity theft, cyberterrorism, spamming, phishing, and many other deliberate acts have created a world where we must always confirm the identity of the people we share information with.

STEP 2: Activity

Go to http://www.wiley.com/go/rainer/MIS4e/applytheconcept, and click on the links provided for Apply the Concept 7.3. The link

will take you to a video about foreign lotteries and a Web site the U.S. Postal Service provides to help people realize when they are being scammed. This type of scam has taken advantage of many people who are not aware that such scams exist. After watching the video, search the Web for other fraudulent activities that involve Craigslist, eBay, and any other sites you find.

STEP 3: Deliverable

Imagine you are the owner of a site such as Craigslist. Draft a memo to your users—both buyers and sellers—explaining your intention to run a "clean" site where all parties are safe. In your memo, discuss the ten types of deliberate attacks that you want your users to be aware of as they conduct business on your site. Submit your memo to your instructor.

7.4 What Organizations Are Doing to Protect Information Resources

Why is stopping cybercriminals such a challenge? Table 7.3 illustrates the many major difficulties involved in protecting information. Because organizing an appropriate defense system is so important to the entire enterprise, it is one of the major responsibilities of any prudent CIO as well as of the functional managers who control information resources. In fact, IT security is the business of *everyone* in an organization.

In addition to the problems listed in Table 7.3, another reason why information resources are difficult to protect is that the online commerce industry is not particularly willing to install safeguards that would make completing transactions more difficult or complicated. As one example, merchants could demand passwords or personal identification numbers for all credit card transactions. However, these requirements might discourage people from shopping online. For credit card companies, it is cheaper to block a stolen credit card and move on than to invest time and money prosecuting cybercriminals.

And the final reason why information resources are difficult to protect is that it is extremely difficult to catch perpetrators. However, IT's About Business 7.2 shows that it is possible to catch attackers, albeit with great effort, time, and expense.

TABLE 7.3 Difficulties in Protecting Information Resources

Hundreds of potential threats exist.
Computing resources may be situated in many locations.
Many individuals control or have access to information assets.
Computer networks can be located outside the organization, making them difficult to protect.
Rapid technological changes make some controls obsolete as soon as they are installed.
Many computer crimes are undetected for a long period of time, so it is difficult to learn from experience.
People tend to violate security procedures because the procedures are inconvenient.
The amount of computer knowledge necessary to commit computer crimes is usually minimal. As a matter of fact, a potential criminal can learn hacking, for free, on the Internet.
The costs of preventing hazards can be very high. Therefore, most organizations simply cannot afford to protect themselves against all possible hazards.
It is difficult to conduct a cost–benefit justification for controls before an attack occurs because it is difficult to assess the impact of a hypothetical attack.

IT's About Business 7.2

MIS Catching a Hacker

To be a hacker, all you really need is a computer and an Internet connection. Aleksandr Panin is a Russian hacker who created SpyEye, one of the most sophisticated and destructive malicious software programs ever developed. According to court documents, Panin launched SpyEye on January 10, 2010, using www.darkode.com, a hacker marketplace. Fellow hackers could buy the basic version of SpyEye for $1,000, or advanced versions for up to $8,500.

SpyEye automates the collection of confidential personal and financial information. The malware can hijack Web browsers and/or present fake bank Web pages that prompt users to enter their login information. SpyEye also scans infected computers for credit card credentials.

The FBI estimates that Panin had sold 150 SpyEye packages. Panin allegedly provided his clients with SpyEye updates and security patches as well as after-sale maintenance, updates, and technical support.

SpyEye systematically infected nearly 1.5 million computers around the world, creating a massive botnet. The malware penetrated computers at multinational corporations, financial institutions, and governments. SpyEye collected data ranging from passwords to credit card and bank account information. The U.S. Justice Department estimates that SpyEye caused $500 million worth of theft and other damage.

The Chase The FBI was after Panin. Agents traveled the world, posing as cybercrooks and becoming hackers themselves. They reviewed millions of lines of computer code and worked, not always with cooperation, with police in Thailand, Bulgaria, and Britain. They had to wait until Panin left Russia before they could arrest him. Let's take a closer look at how Panin was brought to justice.

In February 2011, the FBI targeted a SpyEye server allegedly operated by one of Panin's collaborators. The agency seized this server, located near Atlanta, Georgia, which is a command-and-control server. (*Note:* A command-and-control server is a computer that controls a botnet.) The FBI claims that Hamza Bendelladj, working with Panin, operated the server remotely from his home in Algeria. The server controlled SpyEye-infected computers in the United States, including some linked to more than 250 banks in New York, California, Virginia, and North Carolina.

In the summer of 2011, FBI informants, posing as cybercriminals, paid $8,500 to Panin on www.darkode.com to buy a SpyEye package. Panin instructed them to transfer the payment electronically to a digital account at a Costa Rica-based money processor called Liberty Reserve (which was shut down by federal agents the next year). By December, agents had collected enough evidence—two hard drives and more than 1 terabyte of data—to secure a 23-count indictment against Bendelladj. However, they still did not know the identity of the creator of SpyEye. As a result, a grand jury indicted "John Doe."

Federal agents then sought the assistance of "white-hat hackers." This term refers to ethical computer system hackers who specialize in testing organizational information systems to identify weaknesses and thus improve security. The FBI and the Justice Department worked with TrendMicro (www.trendmicro.com), a Dallas-based computer security firm, that employs 1,200 white-hat hackers who identify and stop malware attacks.

TrendMicro's initial step was to identify the digital characteristics of SpyEye's computer code and map the malware's infrastructure (i.e., IP addresses and the location of command-and-control computers). The company then monitored an online hacking forum frequently visited by Panin and his customers.

Fortunately for the investigators, Panin and a computer programmer he worked with who was known online as "bx1" occasionally demonstrated poor judgment. Specifically, they gave up information about e-mail addresses and instant messenger accounts, which TrendMicro followed to discover actual identities.

For instance, on one SpyEye server, TrendMicro analysts analyzed the computer code. In addition to discovering the name "bx1," one of Panin's collaborators, analysts found an e-mail address and login information for Virtest, a service used by hackers to detect malware. The researchers compared that information with names in the underground forum to link the computer code to one of Panin's collaborators. TrendMicro then gave this information to law enforcement officials.

The case wasn't over yet, though. Because Russia and the United States do not have an extradition treaty, federal officials had to wait until Panin left Russia to arrest him. The indictment against him remained sealed for two years so that he would not get word that he'd been found out.

The Capture It wasn't until January 5, 2013, that the first arrest in the case was made. Bendelladj was travelling from Malaysia to Egypt and was arrested by Thai authorities during a stopover in Bangkok. In May 2013, he was extradited to the United States to face charges, and he pleaded not guilty.

Then, on July 1, 2013, FBI agents arrested Panin when he flew through Hartsfield-Jackson Atlanta International Airport. Panin had been visiting a friend in the Dominican Republic and was flying back to Russia. In January 2014, Panin pleaded guilty to bank and wire fraud. In April 2016, Panin was sentenced to 9 and one-half years in prison.

The capture and conviction of Panin is a textbook case of how the war on cybercrime can be won. But it's often an uphill battle to protect U.S. consumers, banks, retailers, and other victims of cybercrime. Law authorities must dig through layers of encryption and anonymous user names, as well as fight with authorities in foreign countries, to bring hackers to justice. In essence, law enforcement officials must chase digital footprints.

Sources: P. Mishra, "Creators of SpyEye Trojan Alsksandr Panin, Hamza Bendelladj Sentenced," *www.hackread.com*, April 22, 2016; "Russian National To Be Sentenced in SpyEye Malware Case in March 2015," *Russian Legal Information Agency*, November 14, 2014; "SpyEye Hacker Arrested," *Cyberwarzone*, May 24, 2014; "SpyEye-Using Cybercriminal Arrested in Britain," *TrendMicro Blog*, May 22, 2014; K. Eichenwald, "The $500,000,000 Cyber-Heist," *Newsweek*, March 13, 2014; D. Leger and A. Arutunyan, "How the Feds Brought Down a Notorious Russian Hacker," *USA Today*, March 5, 2014; D. Neal, "FBI Bests SpyEye Banking Botnet Coder," *The Inquirer*, January 29, 2014; A. Grossman and D. Yadron, "Island Vacation Costs Russian Hacker Aleksandr Panin," *The Wall Street Journal*, January 28, 2014; "Cyber Criminal Pleads Guilty to Developing and Distributing Nororious SpyEye Malware," *U.S. Department of Justice News*, January 28, 2014; D. Kerr, "SpyEye Malware Inventor Pleads Guilty to Bank Fraud," *CNET News*, January 28, 2014.

Questions

1. Why did the FBI need to "argue with law enforcement officials in various countries"?

2. Describe the difficulties that investigators encounter in bringing cybercriminals to justice. Can you propose any additional strategies they should consider?

Organizations spend a great deal of time and money protecting their information resources. Before doing so, they perform risk management.

A **risk** is the probability that a threat will impact an information resource. The goal of **risk management** is to identify, control, and minimize the impact of threats. In other words, risk management seeks to reduce risk to acceptable levels. Risk management consists of three processes: risk analysis, risk mitigation, and controls evaluation.

Organizations perform risk analyses to ensure that their IS security programs are cost effective. **Risk analysis** involves three steps: (1) assessing the value of each asset being protected, (2) estimating the probability that each asset will be compromised, and (3) comparing the probable costs of the asset's being compromised with the costs of protecting that asset. The organization then considers how to mitigate the risk.

In risk mitigation, the organization takes concrete actions against risks. Risk mitigation has two functions: (1) implementing controls to prevent identified threats from occurring, and (2) developing a means of recovery if the threat becomes a reality. There are several risk mitigation strategies that organizations can adopt. The three most common are risk acceptance, risk limitation, and risk transference:

1. Risk acceptance: Accept the potential risk, continue operating with no controls, and absorb any damages that occur.

2. Risk limitation: Limit the risk by implementing controls that minimize the impact of the threat.

3. Risk transference: Transfer the risk by using other means to compensate for the loss, such as by purchasing insurance.

Finally, in controls evaluation, the organization examines the costs of implementing adequate control measures against the value of those control measures. If the costs of implementing a control are greater than the value of the asset being protected, the control is not cost effective. In the next section, you will study the various controls that organizations use to protect their information resources.

Before you go on…

1. Describe several reasons why it is difficult to protect information resources.

2. Compare and contrast risk management and risk analysis.

Apply the Concept 7.4

LEARNING OBJECTIVE 7.4 Describe the three risk mitigation strategies and examples of each one in the context of owning a home.

STEP 1: Background

Section 7.4 has discussed at length the ways businesses deal with risk. Risk management is so important that companies frequently assign an entire department to oversee risk analysis and mitigation. When companies address risk they have three basic methods to choose from: risk acceptance, risk limitation, and risk transference. Significantly, we do the same thing when it comes to our personal assets.

Like businesses, homeowners face intentional and unintentional threats. To mitigate against these threats, almost all homeowners take certain actions. These actions reflect, among other things,

where your home is located. For example, a home on the beach is much more susceptible to hurricanes than is a home in Nebraska. However, the home in Nebraska is (perhaps) more susceptible to tornadoes than is the home on the beach.

STEP 2: Activity

Imagine that you own your home. What risks do you need to manage? What property do you need to assess? What is the probability that any asset will be compromised? (*Note:* You will need to assess the risk to each asset.) What are the costs associated with each asset being compromised?

STEP 3: Deliverable

In a document, define the three risk management strategies and provide an example of each one in the context of owning a home. Submit your document to your instructor.

7.5 | Information Security Controls

To protect their information assets, organizations implement controls, or defense mechanisms (also called *countermeasures*). These controls are designed to protect all of the components of an information system, including data, software, hardware, and networks. Because there are so many diverse threats, organizations utilize layers of controls, or *defense-in-depth*.

Controls are intended to prevent accidental hazards, deter intentional acts, detect problems as early as possible, enhance damage recovery, and correct problems. Before you study controls in more detail, it is important to emphasize that the single most valuable control is user education and training. Effective and ongoing education makes every member of the organization aware of the vital importance of information security.

In this section, you will learn about three major types of controls: physical controls, access controls, and communications controls. **Figure 7.2** illustrates these controls. In addition to applying controls, organizations plan for business continuity in case of a disaster, and they periodically audit their information resources to detect possible threats. You will study these topics in this section as well.

Physical Controls

Physical controls prevent unauthorized individuals from gaining access to a company's facilities. Common physical controls include walls, doors, fencing, gates, locks, badges, guards, and alarm systems. More sophisticated physical controls include pressure sensors, temperature sensors, and motion detectors. One shortcoming of physical controls is that they can be inconvenient to employees.

Guards deserve special mention because they have very difficult jobs, for at least two reasons. First, their jobs are boring and repetitive and generally do not pay well. Second, if guards perform their jobs thoroughly, the other employees harass them, particularly if they slow up the process of entering the facility.

Organizations also implement physical security measures that limit computer users to acceptable login times and locations. These controls also limit the number of unsuccessful login attempts, and they require all employees to log off their computers when they leave for

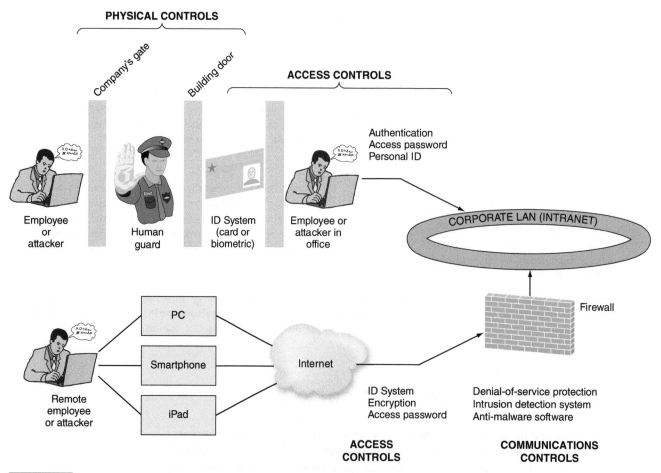

FIGURE 7.2 Where defense mechanisms are located.

the day. In addition, they set the employees' computers to automatically log off the user after a certain period of disuse.

Access Controls

Access controls restrict unauthorized individuals from using information resources. These controls involve two major functions: authentication and authorization. Authentication confirms the identity of the person requiring access. After the person is authenticated (identified), the next step is authorization. Authorization determines which actions, rights, or privileges the person has, based on his or her verified identity. Let's examine these functions more closely.

Authentication. To authenticate (identify) authorized personnel, an organization can use one or more of the following methods: something the user is, something the user has, something the user does, and/or something the user knows.

Something the user is, also known as biometrics, is an authentication method that examines a person's innate physical characteristics. Common biometric applications are fingerprint scans, palm scans, retina scans, iris recognition, and facial recognition. Of these applications, fingerprints, retina scans, and iris recognition provide the most definitive identification. A huge biometric identification project in India provides an example of the power of biometrics.

India has vast numbers of anonymous poor citizens. The Indian government does not officially acknowledge the existence of these citizens because they do not possess birth certificates and other official documentation. Therefore, they cannot access government services to which they are entitled, nor can they open bank accounts.

To address these problems, the nation instituted its Unique Identification Project, also known as *Aadhaar*, which means "the foundation" in several Indian languages. The goal of the project is to issue identification numbers linked to the fingerprints and iris scans of all 1.2 billion Indian citizens. The biometrics and the Aadhaar identification number will serve as a verifiable, portable, and unique national ID. The Aadhaar project should enable millions of poor Indian citizens to access government services that previously were out of reach to them. As of April 2016, Aadhaar had enrolled over one billion million people.

Something the user has is an authentication mechanism that includes regular identification (ID) cards, smart ID cards, and tokens. *Regular ID cards*, or *dumb cards*, typically have the person's picture and often his or her signature. *Smart ID cards* have an embedded chip that stores pertinent information about the user. (Smart ID cards used for identification differ from smart cards used in electronic commerce, which you learn about in Chapter 9. Both types of card have embedded chips, but they are used for different purposes.) *Tokens* have embedded chips and a digital display that presents a login number that the employees use to access the organization's network. The number changes with each login.

Something the user does is an authentication mechanism that includes voice and signature recognition. In *voice recognition*, the user speaks a phrase (e.g., his or her name and department) that has been previously recorded under controlled conditions. The voice recognition system matches the two voice signals. In *signature recognition*, the user signs his or her name, and the system matches this signature with one previously recorded under controlled, monitored conditions. Signature recognition systems also match the speed and the pressure of the signature.

Something the user knows is an authentication mechanism that includes passwords and passphrases. Passwords present a huge information security problem in all organizations. Most of us have to remember numerous passwords for different online services, and we typically must choose complicated strings of characters to make them harder to guess. Passwords must effectively manage the trade-off between convenience and security. For example, if passwords are 50 characters in length and include special symbols, they might keep your computer and its files safe, but they would be impossible to remember.

We have all bought into the idea that a password is sufficient to protect our data, as long as it is sufficiently elaborate. In reality, however, passwords by themselves can no longer protect us, regardless of how unique or complex we make them.

Attackers employ a number of strategies to obtain our passwords, no matter how strong they are. They can guess them, steal them (with phishing or spear phishing attacks), crack them using brute force computation, or obtain them online. Given these problems with passwords, what are users and businesses supposed to do?

To identify authorized users more efficiently and effectively, organizations are implementing more than one type of authentication, a strategy known as *multifactor authentication*. This system is particularly important when users log in from remote locations.

Single-factor authentication, which is notoriously weak, commonly consists simply of a password. Two-factor authentication consists of a password plus one type of biometric identification (e.g., a fingerprint). Three-factor authentication is any combination of three authentication methods. In most cases, the more factors the system utilizes, the more reliable it is. However, stronger authentication is also more expensive, and, as with strong passwords, it can be irritating to users.

Several initiatives are underway to improve the authentication process under the auspices of the Fast Identity Online (FIDO) Alliance (https://fidoalliance.org). FIDO is an industry consortium to address the lack of interoperability among strong authentication devices and the problems that users face in creating and remembering multiple usernames and passwords.

The concept underlying FIDO is that identifiers such as a person's fingerprint, iris scan, and the unique identifier of any USB device or contactless ring will not be sent over the Internet. Rather, they will be checked locally. The only data that will be transferred over the Internet are cryptographic keys that cannot be reverse-engineered to steal a person's identify. Let's consider two types of examples, security systems using biometrics and security systems using physical devices:

- Nok Nok Labs (www.noknok.com) employs tools on user devices, such as a camera, touchscreen, and microphone, to provide voice recognition, facial recognition, and fingerprints.
- The Nymi (www.nymi.com) wristband verifies users' identities by the unique signals generated by their heartbeat.
- Eyelock (www.eyelock.com) manufactures the Myris, a device that scans the iris of users' eyes for authentication.
- Apple (www.apple.com) provides its TouchID feature on certain devices. It analyzes users' fingerprints.
- Hoyos Labs (www.hoyoslabs.com) has developed the 1U, an app and subscription-based service that employs facial recognition.
- The NFC Ring (http://nfcring.com) contains contactless RFID technology that can automatically unlock an NFC-capable phone when a person picks it up. In addition, the ring can operate other RFID devices such as door locks.
- Yubico (www.yubico.com) manufactures the YubiKey, a physical token used in combination with a username and password for two-factor authentication.
- The Google security key (www.google.com) is a physical USB device that users insert into their computers. Users then tap the key when prompted by Chrome.

If you must use passwords, make them *strong passwords*, which are more difficult for hackers to discover. The basic guidelines for creating strong passwords are:

- They should be difficult to guess.
- They should be long rather than short.
- They should have uppercase letters, lowercase letters, numbers, and special characters.
- They should not be recognizable words.
- They should not be the name of anything or anyone familiar, such as family names or names of pets.
- They should not be a recognizable string of numbers, such as a Social Security number or a birthday.

Unfortunately, strong passwords are more difficult to remember than weak ones. Consequently, employees frequently write them down, which defeats their purpose. The ideal solution to this dilemma is to create a strong password that is also easy to remember. To achieve this objective, many people use passphrases.

A *passphrase* is a series of characters that is longer than a password but is still easy to memorize. Examples of passphrases are "maytheforcebewithyoualways" and "goaheadmakemyday." A passphrase can serve as a password itself, or it can help you create a strong password. You can turn a passphrase into a strong password in this manner. Starting with the last passphrase above, take the first letter of each word. You will have "gammd." Then, capitalize every other letter to create "GaMmD." Finally, add special characters and numbers to create "9GaMmD//*." You now have a strong password that you can remember.

One company provides a new type of authentication. IT's About Business 7.3 shows how Trustev analyzes customer behavior to help merchants combat online fraud.

IT's About Business 7.3

 ### Trustev: Helping to Prevent Credit Card Fraud

Many millions of people have been the victim of credit card fraud but with thankfully minimal damage. The reason is that, for the most part, these people are not liable for fraudulent use of their cards.

Industry analysts claim that electronic commerce is unfair to merchants because they assume all of the risk in credit card transactions. Merchants also suffer most, if not all, of the financial damages in fraudulent transactions. The overall effect is that many online retailers fear fraud so much that they limit their business opportunities. In fact, the analysts note that merchants reject approximately 2 percent of legitimate customers. This number is more damaging than it might appear, because merchants suffer hidden costs as well. The cost to acquire an online customer is about $51 per customer. If merchants block a legitimate customer, then they lose the $51. More significantly, they lose the lifetime value of that customer because he or she is not likely to return to the Web site after being denied.

Going further, some merchants block transactions from entire countries. For example, in Europe only 6 percent of online merchants permit electronic transactions from another country. And then there is China, which has a huge demand for high-end merchandise. Since 2010, Chinese citizens have been issued three billion credit cards. Nevertheless, Chinese consumers often cannot shop on foreign retailers' Web sites because few merchants accept payments from China due to fraud concerns.

This problem provides the rationale for startup company, Trustev (www.trustev.com), which enables online retailers to accept more online transactions. The company helps reduce fraud by analyzing customer behavior while they browse and buy online. Using this analysis, Trustev takes roughly two-tenths of a second to decide whether to accept each transaction. In essence, Trustev validates the shoppers themselves, not just their payment method.

When first launching the service, merchants give Trustev access to its systems. Trustev then crafts a profile for a regular online customer by observing transactions for a period of time. It collects data on 80 variables including the customer's device (e.g., desktop, laptop, smartphone), Internet Protocol address, shipping address, physical location, e-mail address, and other relevant data. In essence, Trustev creates a digital picture of the customer at the point in time of a transaction. To protect data security, the company by law must erase all data after 90 days.

Trustev is growing rapidly. One company in the United Kingdom tried out Trustev for four weeks. The company's goal was to stop fraudulent online transactions while letting through real customers who may be accidentally blocked. In just four weeks, the company noted a 5 percent revenue increase from blocking fraudulent transactions and another 6 percent increase from accepting customers who previously would have been blocked. In another example, in September 2014, RadioShack (www.radioshack.com) announced that it would install Trustev in its 4,000 stores in the United States in a multimillion-dollar deal.

And the results? In Trustev's first year of operation, the company was named Europe's Top Technology Startup by the European Union Commission as well as one of *Forbes* Hottest Global Startups.

Sources: Compiled from "Are You Who You Say You Are?" *University of New South Wales Business Think*, April 22, 2015; R. Bradbury, "How 5% of Online Revenues Are Tossed Away," *Trustev Blog*, April 22, 2015; K. Russell, "Trustev Uses Fraud Detection Software to Crack Down on Internet Trolls," *TechCrunch*, December 9, 2014; J. Temperton, "Digital Fingerprinting Could Stop Web Trolls for Good," *Wired*, December 18, 2014; J. Kennedy, "Cork's Trustev in Multimillion-Dollar Security Deal with RadioShack," *Silicon Republic*, September 5, 2014; J. McManus, "Catching Credit Card Cheats from Cork to China," *The Irish Times*, July 11, 2014; "Trustev Taps Datameer Big Data Analytics for E-Commerce ID Verification," *Finextra*, March 5, 2014; www.trustev.com, accessed July 29, 2015.

Questions

1. Describe how Trustev's authentication method differs from other authentication methods.
2. What are potential disadvantages with Trustev's authentication method?

Authorization. After users have been properly authenticated, the rights and privileges to which they are entitled on the organization's systems are established in a process called *authorization*. A privilege is a collection of related computer system operations that a user is authorized to perform. Companies typically base authorization policies on the principle of least privilege, which posits that users be granted the privilege for an activity only if there is a justifiable need for them to perform that activity.

Communications Controls

Communications controls (also called network controls) secure the movement of data across networks. Communications controls consist of firewalls, anti-malware systems, whitelisting and blacklisting, encryption, virtual private networks (VPNs), transport layer security (TLS), and employee monitoring systems.

Firewalls. A firewall is a system that prevents a specific type of information from moving between untrusted networks, such as the Internet, and private networks, such as your company's network. Put simply, firewalls prevent unauthorized Internet users from accessing private networks. All messages entering or leaving your company's network pass through a firewall. The firewall examines each message and blocks those that do not meet specified security rules.

Firewalls range from simple, for home use, to very complex for organizational use. Figure 7.3(a) illustrates a basic firewall for a home computer. In this case, the firewall is implemented as software on the home computer. Figure 7.3(b) shows an organization that has implemented an external firewall, which faces the Internet, and an internal firewall, which faces the company network. Corporate firewalls typically consist of software running on a computer dedicated to the task. A demilitarized zone (DMZ) is located between the two firewalls. Messages from the Internet must first pass through the external firewall. If they conform to the defined security rules, they are then sent to company servers located in the DMZ. These servers typically handle Web page requests and e-mail. Any messages designated for the company's internal network (e.g., its intranet) must pass through the internal firewall, again with its own defined security rules, to gain access to the company's private network.

The danger from viruses and worms is so severe that many organizations are placing firewalls at strategic points *inside* their private networks. In this way, if a virus or worm does get through both the external and internal firewalls, then the internal damage may be contained.

Anti-malware Systems. Anti-malware systems, also called *antivirus*, or *AV*, software, are software packages that attempt to identify and eliminate viruses and worms, and other malicious software. AV software is implemented at the organizational level by the IS department. Hundreds of AV software packages are currently available. Among the best known are Norton AntiVirus (www.symantec.com), McAfee VirusScan (www.mcafee.com), and Trend Micro PC-cillin (www.trendmicro.com).

FIGURE 7.3 (a) Basic firewall for home computer. (b) Organization with two firewalls and a demilitarized zone.

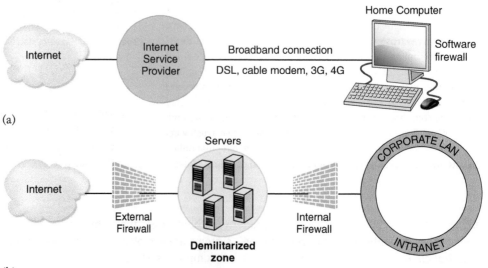

Anti-malware systems are generally reactive. Whereas firewalls filter network traffic according to categories of activities that are likely to cause problems, anti-malware systems filter traffic according to a database of specific problems. These systems create definitions, or signatures, of various types of malware and then update these signatures in their products. The anti-malware software then examines suspicious computer code to determine whether it matches a known signature. If the software identifies a match, then it removes the code. For this reason, organizations regularly update their malware definitions.

Because malware is such a serious problem, the leading vendors are rapidly developing anti-malware systems that function proactively as well as reactively. These systems evaluate behavior rather than relying entirely on signature matching. In theory, therefore, it is possible to catch malware before it can infect systems.

Whitelisting and Blacklisting. A report by the Yankee Group (www.yankeegroup.com), a technology research and consulting firm, stated that 99 percent of organizations had installed anti-malware systems, but 62 percent still suffered malware attacks. As we have seen, anti-malware systems are usually reactive, and malware continues to infect companies.

One solution to this problem is whitelisting. Whitelisting is a process in which a company identifies the software that it will allow to run on its computers. Whitelisting permits acceptable software to run, and it either prevents any other software from running or lets new software run only in a quarantine environment until the company can verify its validity.

Whereas whitelisting allows nothing to run unless it is on the whitelist, blacklisting allows everything to run unless it is on the blacklist. A blacklist, then, includes certain types of software that are not allowed to run in the company environment. For example, a company might blacklist peer-to-peer file sharing on its systems. In addition to software, people, devices, and Web sites can also be whitelisted and blacklisted.

Encryption. Organizations that do not have a secure channel for sending information use encryption to stop unauthorized eavesdroppers. Encryption is the process of converting an original message into a form that cannot be read by anyone except the intended receiver.

All encryption systems use a key, which is the code that scrambles and then decodes the messages. The majority of encryption systems use public-key encryption. Public-key encryption— also known as *asymmetric encryption*—uses two different keys: a public key and a private key (see Figure 7.4). The public key (locking key) and the private key (the unlocking key) are created simul-taneously using the same mathematical formula or algorithm. Because the two keys are mathematically related, the data encrypted with one key can be decrypted by using the other key. The public key is publicly available in a directory that all parties can access. The private key is kept secret, never shared with anyone, and never sent across the Internet. In this system, if Hannah wants to send a message to Harrison, she first obtains Harrison's public key (locking key), which she uses to encrypt her message (put the message in the "two-lock box"). When Harrison receives Hannah's message, he uses his private key to decrypt it (open the box).

Although this arrangement is adequate for personal information, organizations that conduct business over the Internet require a more complex system. In these cases, a third party, called a certificate authority, acts as a trusted intermediary between the companies. The certificate authority issues digital certificates and verifies the integrity of the

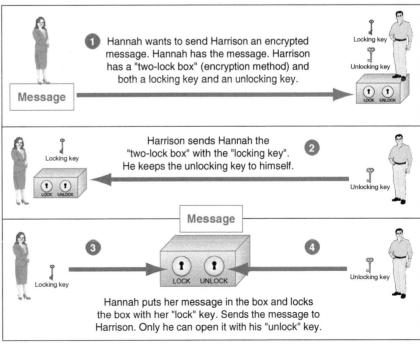

FIGURE 7.4 How public-key encryption works.

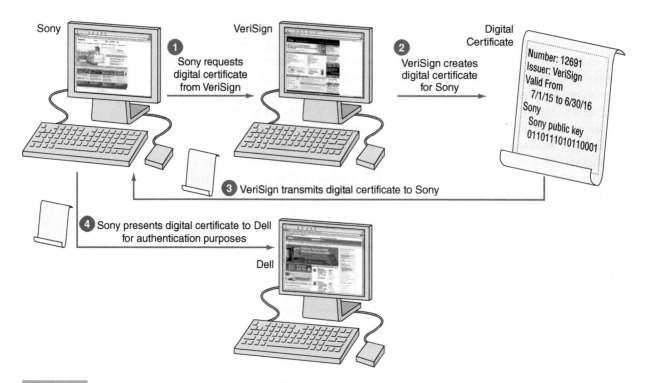

Sony

VeriSign

1 Sony requests digital certificate from VeriSign

2 VeriSign creates digital certificate for Sony

Digital Certificate

Number: 12691
Issuer: VeriSign
Valid From
7/1/15 to 6/30/16
Sony
Sony public key
0110111010110001

3 VeriSign transmits digital certificate to Sony

4 Sony presents digital certificate to Dell for authentication purposes

Dell

FIGURE 7.5   How digital certificates work. Sony and Dell, business partners, use a digital certificate from VeriSign for authentication.

certificates. A **digital certificate** is an electronic document attached to a file that certifies that the file is from the organization it claims to be from and has not been modified from its original format. As you can see in **Figure 7.5**, Sony requests a digital certificate from VeriSign, a certificate authority, and it uses this certificate when it conducts business with Dell. Note that the digital certificate contains an identification number, the issuer, validity dates, and the requester's public key. For examples of certificate authorities, see www.entrust.com, www.verisign.com, www.cybertrust.com, www.secude.com, and www.thawte.com.

Virtual Private Networking. A **virtual private network (VPN)** is a private network that uses a public network (usually the Internet) to connect users. VPNs essentially integrate the global connectivity of the Internet with the security of a private network and thereby extend the reach of the organization's networks. VPNs are called *virtual* because they have no separate physical existence. They use the public Internet as their infrastructure. They are created by using logins, encryption, and other techniques to enhance the user's *privacy*, which we defined in Chapter 6 as the right to be left alone and to be free of unreasonable personal intrusion.

VPNs have several advantages. First, they allow remote users to access the company network. Second, they provide flexibility. That is, mobile users can access the organization's network from properly configured remote devices. Third, organizations can impose their security policies through VPNs. For example, an organization may dictate that only corporate e-mail applications are available to users when they connect from unmanaged devices.

To provide secure transmissions, VPNs use a process called tunneling. **Tunneling** encrypts each data packet to be sent and places each encrypted packet inside another packet. In this manner, the packet can travel across the Internet with confidentiality, authentication, and integrity. **Figure 7.6** illustrates a VPN and tunneling.

Transport Layer Security (TLS). **Transport layer security, formerly called secure socket layer**, is an encryption standard used for secure transactions such as credit card purchases and online banking. TLS encrypts and decrypts data between a Web server and a browser end to end.

TLS is indicated by a URL that begins with "https" rather than "http," and it often displays a small padlock icon in the browser's status bar. Using a padlock icon to indicate a secure connection and placing this icon in a browser's status bar are artifacts of specific browsers. Other

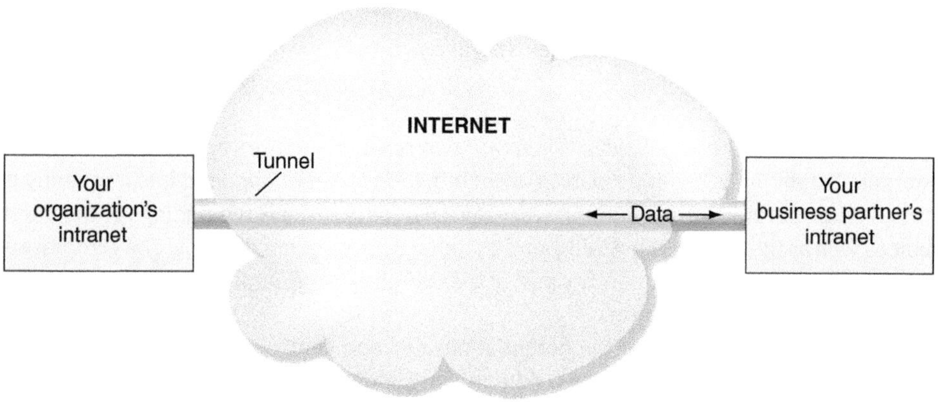

FIGURE 7.6 Virtual private network and tunneling.

INTERNET

Tunnel

Your organization's intranet

← Data →

Your business partner's intranet

browsers use different icons (e.g., a key that is either broken or whole). The important thing to remember is that browsers usually provide visual confirmation of a secure connection.

Employee Monitoring Systems. Many companies are taking a proactive approach to protecting their networks against what they view as one of their major security threats, namely, employee mistakes. These companies are implementing employee monitoring systems, which scrutinize their employees' computers, e-mail activities, and Internet surfing activities. These products are useful to identify employees who spend too much time surfing on the Internet for personal reasons, who visit questionable Web sites, or who download music illegally. Vendors that provide monitoring software include SpectorSoft (www.spectorsoft.com) and Websense (www.websense.com).

Business Continuity Planning

A basic security strategy for organizations is to be prepared for any eventuality. A critical element in any security system is a *business continuity plan*, also known as a *disaster recovery plan*.

Business continuity is the chain of events linking planning to protection and to recovery. The purpose of the business continuity plan is to provide guidance to people who keep the business operating after a disaster occurs. Employees use this plan to prepare for, react to, and recover from events that affect the security of information assets. The objective is to restore the business to normal operations as quickly as possible following an attack. The plan is intended to ensure that critical business functions continue.

In the event of a major disaster, organizations can employ several strategies for business continuity. These strategies include hot sites, warm sites, and cold sites. A *hot site* is a fully configured computer facility with all of the company's services, communications links, and physical plant operations. A hot site duplicates computing resources, peripherals, telephone systems, applications, and workstations. A *warm site* provides many of the same services and options as the hot site. However, it typically does not include the actual applications the company needs. A warm site includes computing equipment such as servers, but it often does not include user workstations. A *cold site* provides only rudimentary services and facilities, such as a building or a room with heating, air conditioning, and humidity control. This type of site provides no computer hardware or user workstations.

Hot sites reduce risk to the greatest extent, but they are the most expensive option. Conversely, cold sites reduce risk the least, but they are the least expensive option.

Information Systems Auditing

Companies implement security controls to ensure that information systems function properly. These controls can be installed in the original system, or they can be added after a system is in operation. Installing controls is necessary but not sufficient to provide adequate security. In addition, people responsible for security need to answer questions such as: Are all controls installed as intended? Are they effective? Has any breach of security occurred? If so, what actions are required to prevent future breaches?

These questions must be answered by independent and unbiased observers. Such observers perform the task of *information systems auditing*. In an IS environment, an **audit** is an examination of information systems, their inputs, outputs, and processing.

Types of Auditors and Audits. There are two types of auditors and audits: internal and external. IS auditing is usually a part of accounting *internal auditing*, and it is frequently performed by corporate internal auditors. An *external auditor* reviews the findings of the internal audit as well as the inputs, processing, and outputs of information systems. The external audit of information systems is frequently a part of the overall external auditing performed by a certified public accounting (CPA) firm.

IS auditing considers all of the potential hazards and controls in information systems. It focuses on issues such as operations, data integrity, software applications, security and privacy, budgets and expenditures, cost control, and productivity. Guidelines are available to assist auditors in their jobs, such as those from the Information Systems Audit and Control Association (www.isaca.org).

How Is Auditing Executed? IS auditing procedures fall into three categories: (1) auditing around the computer, (2) auditing through the computer, and (3) auditing with the computer.

Auditing around the computer means verifying processing by checking for known outputs using specific inputs. This approach is most effective for systems with limited outputs. In *auditing through the computer*, auditors check inputs, outputs, and processing. They review program logic, and they test the data contained within the system. *Auditing with the computer* means using a combination of client data, auditor software, and client and auditor hardware. This approach enables the auditor to perform tasks such as simulating payroll program logic using live data.

Before you go on…

1. What is the single most important information security control for organizations?
2. Differentiate between authentication and authorization. Which of these processes is always performed first?
3. Compare and contrast whitelisting and blacklisting.
4. What is the purpose of a disaster recovery plan?
5. What is information systems auditing?

Apply the Concept 7.5

LEARNING OBJECTIVE 7.5 Identify the three major types of controls that organizations can use to protect their information resources along with an example of each one.

STEP 1: Background

Security controls are designed to protect all components of an information system, including data, software, hardware, and networks. Because there are so many diverse threats, organizations utilize layers of controls. One security feature discussed in this chapter is public key encryption. This feature requires a public key and a private key. The public key is shared and is used to encrypt a message that only the individual's private key can decrypt.

STEP 2: Activity

Visit http://www.wiley.com/go/rainer/MIS4e/applytheconcept, and click on the link provided for Apply the Concept 7.5. The link will take you to an article about the 2004 movie *National Treasure*. Watching the actual film is preferable, but you may not have access to it. For this activity, reading about it will suffice.

In this movie, Ben Gates (played by Nicholas Cage) steals one of our nation's most sacred documents—the Declaration of Independence. In the process, you see how the thief breaches all three of the major types of controls.

STEP 3: Deliverable

Identify the three major types of controls that the National Archives employs—and that Gates ultimately penetrates—and provide examples of them from the movie. Prepare a document with the three types of controls and examples from the movie and submit it to your instructor.

What's in IT for me?

ACCT For the Accounting Major

Public companies, their accountants, and their auditors have significant information security responsibilities. Accountants are now being held professionally responsible for reducing risk, assuring compliance, eliminating fraud, and increasing the transparency of transactions according to Generally Accepted Accounting Principles (GAAP). The SEC and the Public Company Accounting Oversight Board (PCAOB), among other regulatory agencies, require information security, fraud prevention and detection, and internal controls over financial reporting. Forensic accounting, a combination of accounting and information security, is one of the most rapidly growing areas in accounting today.

FIN For the Finance Major

Because information security is essential to the success of organizations today, it is no longer just the concern of the CIO. As a result of global regulatory requirements and the passage of Sarbanes–Oxley Act, responsibility for information security lies with the CEO and CFO. Consequently, all aspects of the security audit, including the security of information and information systems, are a key concern for financial managers.

In addition, CFOs and treasurers are increasingly involved with investments in information technology. They know that a security breach of any kind can have devastating financial effects on a company. Banking and financial institutions are prime targets for computer criminals. A related problem is fraud involving stocks and bonds that are sold over the Internet. Finance personnel must be aware of both the hazards and the available controls associated with these activities.

MKT For the Marketing Major

Marketing professionals have new opportunities to collect data on their customers, for example, through business-to-consumer electronic commerce. Customers expect their data to be properly secured. However, profit-motivated criminals want those data. Therefore, marketing managers must analyze the risk of their operations. Failure to protect corporate and customer data will cause significant public relations problems, make customers very angry, may lead to lawsuits, and may result in losing customers to competitors. CRM operations and tracking customers' online buying habits can expose data to misuse (if they are not encrypted) or result in privacy violations.

POM For the Production/Operations Management Major

Every process in a company's operations—inventory purchasing, receiving, quality control, production, and shipping—can be disrupted by an information technology security breach or an IT security breach at a business partner. Any weak link in supply chain management or enterprise resource management systems puts the entire chain at risk. Companies may be held liable for IT security failures that impact other companies.

HRM For the Human Resource Management Major

HR managers have responsibilities to secure confidential employee data. In addition, they must ensure that all employees explicitly verify that they understand the company's information security policies and procedures.

MIS For the MIS Major

The MIS function provides the security infrastructure that protects the organization's information assets. This function is critical to the success of the organization, even though it is almost invisible until an attack succeeds. All application development, network deployment, and introduction of new information technologies have to be guided by IT security considerations. MIS personnel must customize the risk exposure security model to help the company identify security risks and prepare responses to security incidents and disasters.

Senior executives of publicly held companies look to the MIS function for help in meeting Sarbanes–Oxley Act requirements, particularly in detecting "significant deficiencies" or "material weaknesses" in internal controls and remediating them. Other functional areas also look to the MIS function to help them meet their security responsibilities.

Summary

1. **Identify the five factors that contribute to the increasing vulnerability of information resources, and specific examples of each factor.**

The five factors are the following:

- Today's interconnected, interdependent, wirelessly networked business environment.

  - *Example:* The Internet

- Smaller, faster, cheaper computers and storage devices

  - *Examples:* Netbooks, thumb drives, iPads.

- Decreasing skills necessary to be a computer hacker.

  - *Example:* Information system hacking programs circulating on the Internet

- International organized crime taking over cybercrime.

  - *Example:* Organized crime has formed transnational cybercrime cartels. Because it is difficult to know exactly where cyberattacks originate, these cartels are extremely hard to bring to justice.

- Lack of management support.

  - *Example:* Suppose that your company spent $10 million on information security countermeasures last year, and they did not experience any successful attacks on their information resources. Short-sighted management might conclude that the company could spend less during the next year and obtain the same results. Bad idea.

2. **Compare and contrast human mistakes and social engineering, along with specific examples of each one.**

Human mistakes are unintentional errors. However, employees can also make unintentional mistakes as a result of actions by an attacker, such as social engineering. *Social engineering* is an attack where the perpetrator uses social skills to trick or manipulate a legitimate employee into providing confidential company information.

An example of a human mistake is tailgating. An example of social engineering is when an attacker calls an employee on the phone and impersonates a superior in the company.

3. **Discuss the 10 types of deliberate attacks.**

The 10 types of deliberate attacks are the following:

Espionage or trespass occurs when an unauthorized individual attempts to gain illegal access to organizational information.

Information extortion occurs when an attacker either threatens to steal, or actually steals, information from a company. The perpetrator demands payment for not stealing the information, for returning stolen information, or for agreeing not to disclose the information.

Sabotage and vandalism are deliberate acts that involve defacing an organization's Web site, possibly causing the organization to lose its image and experience a loss of confidence by its customers.

Theft of equipment and information is becoming a larger problem because computing devices and storage devices are becoming smaller yet more powerful with vastly increased storage, making these devices easier and more valuable to steal.

Identity theft is the deliberate assumption of another person's identity, usually to gain access to his or her financial information or to frame him or her for a crime.

Preventing *compromises to intellectual property* is a vital issue for people who make their livelihood in knowledge fields. Protecting intellectual property is particularly difficult when that property is in digital form.

Software attacks occur when malicious software penetrates an organization's computer system. Today, these attacks are typically profit-driven and Web-based.

Alien software is clandestine software that is installed on your computer through duplicitous methods. It typically is not as malicious as viruses, worms, or Trojan horses, but it does use up valuable system resources.

Supervisory control and data acquisition refers to a large-scale, distributed measurement and control system. SCADA systems are used to monitor or control chemical, physical, and transport processes. A *SCADA attack* attempts to compromise such a system in order to cause damage to the real-world processes that the system controls.

With both *cyberterrorism* and *cyberwarfare*, attackers use a target's computer systems, particularly via the Internet, to cause physical, real-world harm or severe disruption, usually to carry out a political agenda.

4. **Describe the three risk mitigation strategies and examples of each one in the context of owning a home.**

The three risk mitigation strategies are the following:

Risk acceptance, where the organization accepts the potential risk, continues operating with no controls, and absorbs any damages that occur. If you own a home, you may decide not to insure it. Thus, you are practicing risk acceptance. Clearly, this is a bad idea.

Risk limitation, where the organization limits the risk by implementing controls that minimize the impact of threats. As a homeowner, you practice risk limitation by putting in an alarm system or cutting down weak trees near your house.

Risk transference, where the organization transfers the risk by using other means to compensate for the loss, such as by purchasing insurance. The vast majority of homeowners practice risk transference by purchasing insurance on their houses and other possessions.

5. **Identify the three major types of controls that organizations can use to protect their information resources along with an example of each one.**

Physical controls prevent unauthorized individuals from gaining access to a company's facilities. Common physical controls include walls, doors, fencing, gates, locks, badges, guards, and alarm systems. More sophisticated physical controls include pressure sensors, temperature sensors, and motion detectors.

Access controls restrict unauthorized individuals from using information resources. These controls involve two major functions: authentication and authorization. Authentication confirms the identity of the person requiring access. An example is biometrics. After the person is authenticated (identified), the next step is authorization. Authorization determines which actions, rights, or privileges the person has, based on his or her verified identity. Authorization is generally based on least privilege.

Communications (network) controls secure the movement of data across networks. Communications controls consist of firewalls, anti-malware systems, whitelisting and blacklisting, encryption, virtual private networking, secure socket layer, and vulnerability management systems.

Chapter Glossary

access controls Controls that restrict unauthorized individuals from using information resources and are concerned with user identification.

adware Alien software designed to help pop-up advertisements appear on your screen.

alien software Clandestine software that is installed on your computer through duplicitous methods.

anti-malware systems (antivirus software) Software packages that attempt to identify and eliminate viruses, worms, and other malicious software.

audit An examination of information systems, their inputs, outputs, and processing.

authentication A process that determines the identity of the person requiring access.

authorization A process that determines which actions, rights, or privileges the person has, based on verified identity.

back door Typically a password, known only to the attacker, that allows the attacker to access the system without having to go through any security procedures.

biometrics The science and technology of authentication (i.e., establishing the identity of an individual) by measuring the subject's physiological or behavioral characteristics.

blacklisting A process in which a company identifies certain types of software that are not allowed to run in the company environment.

bot A computer that has been compromised by, and under the control of, a hacker.

botnet A network of computers that have been compromised by, and under control of, a hacker, who is called the botmaster.

business continuity The chain of events linking planning to protection and to recovery.

certificate authority A third party that acts as a trusted intermediary between computers (and companies) by issuing digital certificates and verifying the worth and integrity of the certificates.

communications controls (also network controls) Controls that deal with the movement of data across networks.

controls Defense mechanisms (also called *countermeasures*).

cookie Small amounts of information that Web sites store on your computer, temporarily or more or less permanently.

copyright A grant that provides the creator of intellectual property with ownership of it for a specified period of time, currently the life of the creator plus 70 years.

cybercrime Illegal activities executed on the Internet.

cyberterrorism Can be defined as a premeditated, politically motivated attack against information, computer systems, computer programs, and data that results in violence against noncombatant targets by subnational groups or clandestine agents.

cyberwarfare War in which a country's information systems could be paralyzed from a massive attack by destructive software.

demilitarized zone (DMZ) A separate organizational local area network that is located between an organization's internal network and an external network, usually the Internet.

denial-of-service attack A cyberattack in which an attacker sends a flood of data packets to the target computer, with the aim of overloading its resources.

digital certificate An electronic document attached to a file certifying that this file is from the organization it claims to be from and has not been modified from its original format or content.

distributed denial-of-service (DDoS) attack A denial-of-service attack that sends a flood of data packets from many compromised computers simultaneously.

employee monitoring systems Systems that monitor employees' computers, e-mail activities, and Internet surfing activities.

encryption The process of converting an original message into a form that cannot be read by anyone except the intended receiver.

exposure The harm, loss, or damage that can result if a threat compromises an information resource.

firewall A system (either hardware, software, or a combination of both) that prevents a specific type of information from moving between untrusted networks, such as the Internet, and private networks, such as your company's network.

identity theft Crime in which someone uses the personal information of others to create a false identity and then uses it for some fraud.

information security Protecting an organization's information and information systems from unauthorized access, use, disclosure, disruption, modification, or destruction.

intellectual property The intangible property created by individuals or corporations, which is protected under trade secret, patent, and copyright laws.

least privilege A principle that users be granted the privilege for some activity only if there is a justifiable need to grant this authorization.

logic bombs Segments of computer code embedded within an organization's existing computer programs.

malware Malicious software such as viruses and worms.

network controls See communications controls.

password A private combination of characters that only the user should know.

patent A document that grants the holder exclusive rights on an invention or process for a specified period of time, currently 20 years.

phishing attack An attack that uses deception to fraudulently acquire sensitive personal information by masquerading as an official-looking e-mail.

physical controls Controls that restrict unauthorized individuals from gaining access to a company's computer facilities.

piracy Copying a software program (other than freeware, demo software, etc.) without making payment to the owner.

privilege A collection of related computer system operations that can be performed by users of the system.

public-key encryption (also called *asymmetric encryption*) A type of encryption that uses two different keys, a public key and a private key.

risk The likelihood that a threat will occur.

risk acceptance A strategy in which the organization accepts the potential risk, continues to operate with no controls, and absorbs any damages that occur.

risk analysis The process by which an organization assesses the value of each asset being protected, estimates the probability that each asset might be compromised, and compares the probable costs of each being compromised with the costs of protecting it.

risk limitation A strategy in which the organization limits its risk by implementing controls that minimize the impact of a threat.

risk management A process that identifies, controls, and minimizes the impact of threats, in an effort to reduce risk to manageable levels.

risk mitigation A process whereby the organization takes concrete actions against risks, such as implementing controls and developing a disaster recovery plan.

risk transference A process in which the organization transfers the risk by using other means to compensate for a loss, such as by purchasing insurance.

secure socket layer (SSL) (also known as transport layer security) An encryption standard used for secure transactions such as credit card purchases and online banking.

security The degree of protection against criminal activity, danger, damage, and/or loss.

social engineering Getting around security systems by tricking computer users inside a company into revealing sensitive information or gaining unauthorized access privileges.

spam Unsolicited e-mail.

spamware Alien software that uses your computer as a launch platform for spammers.

spyware Alien software that can record your keystrokes and/or capture your passwords.

threat Any danger to which an information resource may be exposed.

trade secret Intellectual work, such as a business plan, that is a company secret and is not based on public information.

transport layer security (TLS) See secure socket layer.

trap doors See back door.

Trojan horse A software program containing a hidden function that presents a security risk.

tunneling A process that encrypts each data packet to be sent and places each encrypted packet inside another packet.

virtual private network (VPN) A private network that uses a public network (usually the Internet) to securely connect users by using encryption.

viruses Malicious software that can attach itself to (or "infect") other computer programs without the owner of the program being aware of the infection.

vulnerability The possibility that an information resource will be harmed by a threat.

whitelisting A process in which a company identifies acceptable software and permits it to run, and either prevents anything else from running or lets new software run in a quarantine environment until the company can verify its validity.

worms Destructive programs that replicate themselves without requiring another program to provide a safe environment for replication.

zombie computer See bot.

Discussion Questions

1. Why are computer systems so vulnerable?

2. Why should information security be a prime concern to management?

3. Is security a technical issue? A business issue? Both? Support your answer.

4. Compare information security in an organization with insuring a house.

5. Why are authentication and authorization important to e-commerce?

6. Why is cross-border cybercrime expanding rapidly? Discuss possible solutions.

7. Discuss why the Sarbanes–Oxley Act is having an impact on information security.

8. What types of user authentication are used at your university and/or place of work? Do these measures seem to be effective? What if a higher level of authentication were implemented? Would it be worth it, or would it decrease productivity?

9. Why are federal authorities so worried about SCADA attacks?

Problem-Solving Activities

1. A critical problem is assessing how far a company is legally obligated to go in order to secure personal data. Because there is no such thing as perfect security (i.e., there is always more that you can do), resolving this question can significantly affect cost.

    a. When are security measures that a company implements sufficient to comply with its obligations?

    b. Is there any way for a company to know if its security measures are sufficient? Can you devise a method for any organization to determine if its security measures are sufficient?

2. Assume that the daily probability of a major earthquake in Los Angeles is 0.07 percent. The chance that your computer center will be damaged during such a quake is 5 percent. If the center is damaged, the estimated damage to the computer center will be $4.0 million.

    a. Calculate the expected loss in dollars.

    b. An insurance agent is willing to insure your facility for an annual fee of $25,000. Analyze the offer, and discuss whether to accept it.

3. Enter www.scambusters.org. Find out what the organization does. Learn about e-mail scams and Web site scams. Report your findings.

4. Visit www.dhs.gov/dhspublic (Department of Homeland Security). Search the site for "National Strategy to Secure Cyberspace" and write a report on their agenda and accomplishments to date.

5. Enter www.alltrustnetworks.com and other vendors of biometrics. Find the devices they make that can be used to control access into information systems. Prepare a list of products and major capabilities of each vendor.

6. Software piracy is a global problem. Access the following Web sites: www.bsa.org and www.microsoft.com/piracy/. What can organizations do to mitigate this problem? Are some organizations dealing with the problem better than others?

7. Investigate the Sony PlayStation Network hack that occurred in April 2011.

    a. What type of attack was it?

b. Was the success of the attack due to technology problems at Sony, management problems at Sony, or a combination of both? Provide specific examples to support your answer.

c. Which Sony controls failed?

d. Could the hack have been prevented? If so, how?

e. Discuss Sony's response to the hack.

f. Describe the damages that Sony incurred from the hack.

Closing Case 1

The Sony Pictures Entertainment Hack

MIS   The Problem

On November 24, 2014, a hacker group called the "Guardians of Peace" or GOP successfully attacked Sony Pictures Entertainment (www.sonypictures.com; SPE). The attackers obtained personally identifiable information about 47,000 current and former SPE employees and their dependents. These materials included numerous sensitive e-mails among top SPE executives concerning actors, financial deals, and creative disagreements; executive salaries; and complete copies of unreleased Sony films. The information included names, addresses, social security numbers, driver's license numbers, passport numbers, bank account information, credit card information used for corporate travel and expenses, usernames and passwords, and compensation and other employment-related information. The hackers claimed to have stolen more than 100 terabytes of data from SPE.

The GOP initially released the most damaging information over the Internet. This information consisted of digital copies of SPE films that had been released (e.g., *Fury*) or were yet to be released (e.g., *Annie*). In addition, the attackers announced they would continue to release more interesting SPE information.

Although the specific motives for the attack had not been revealed as of mid-2016, the hack has been linked to the planned release of the SPE film *The Interview*. In this movie, producers of a tabloid television show learn that North Korea's leader, Kim Jong Un, is a big fan of the show, and they set up an interview with him. While the show's team is preparing for the interview, the CIA recruits them to assassinate Kim Jong Un.

Prior to the Sony hack, North Korean officials had expressed concerns about the film to the United Nations. The officials stated that "to allow the production and distribution of such a film on the assassination of an incumbent head of a sovereign state should be regarded as the most undisguised sponsoring of terrorism as well as an act of war."

On December 16, 2014, the GOP mentioned *The Interview* by name, and they threatened to take terrorist actions against the film's New York City premiere at Sunshine Cinema on December 18. The GOP also threatened similar actions on the film's America-wide release date of December 25 (Christmas).

On December 18, two messages allegedly from the GOP appeared. The first claimed that the GOP would not release any further information if SPE agreed not to release *The Interview* and to remove it completely from the Internet. The second stated that SPE had "suffered enough" and it could release the film, but only if Kim Jong Un's death scene was not "too happy."

In the aftermath of the attack, the studio was forced to use fax machines, to communicate through hard-copy posted messages, and to pay its employees with paper checks. Employees worked with pen and paper, and shops located on Sony property accepted only cash.

The Law Enforcement Response

Meanwhile, the FBI launched an investigation into the incident. In 2014, the bureau announced it had connected the North Korean government to the attack. The FBI's statement was based on intelligence gathered during a 2010 U.S. hack of North Korea's networks. In that action, the United States had tracked the internal operations of North Korean computers and networks. North Korea responded to the charges by denying any responsibility for the hack. Although most of the speculation about the attack has focused on North Korea, the authorities are investigating alternative scenarios, including the possibility that an SPE employee or former employee was involved.

The Sony Response

As a result of the attack, SPE shut down its entire network on November 25, 2014, and pulled the theatrical release of *The Interview* on December 17. Two days later, President Obama labeled the attack as "cybervandalism" and not an act of war. He also charged that that Sony's decision to pull the film from release rather than defy the hackers was a mistake because the company appeared to have capitulated to the hackers' demands.

Following initial threats made towards theaters that showed *The Interview*, several cinema chains, including Carmike Cinemas, Bow Tie Cinemas, Regal Entertainment Group, AMC Theaters, and Cinemark Theaters, announced they would not screen the film. On December 23, 2014, SPE authorized 300 largely independent theaters to show the movie on Christmas Day. The following day SPE released *The Interview* to Google Play, Xbox Video, and YouTube.

Sony defended its decision to pull the film by claiming they were a blameless victim. Specifically, because the attackers came from a foreign government, they had far more resources to attack than Sony had to defend. Therefore, the studio concluded that the attack was unstoppable. Significantly, both the FBI and security company FireEye acknowledged that the malicious software used in the Sony hack was "undetectable by industry standard antivirus software."

At the same time, however, Sony apparently failed to employ basic information security countermeasures. For example, the company's e-mail retention policy left up to seven years of old, unencrypted messages on company servers. Sony was using e-mail for long-term storage of business records, contracts, and documents it saved in case of litigation. Also, sensitive information—including user names and passwords for IT administrators—was stored in unencrypted spreadsheets and Word files with names such as "Computer Passwords."

Sony has since implemented its "secure rebuild" information security strategy. The plan's fundamental idea is zero trust. Its objectives are to keep attackers from entering the company's networks, to prevent them from accessing information if they do get in, and to block them from stealing information if they actually manage to access it. Specifically:

- Internet access will be tightly restricted.
- Sony will keep as little information as possible on its active network. The remainder will be stored securely, encrypted, and cut off from the Internet.
- E-mails will be archived after a few weeks. System administrators will have access only to areas required to do their jobs.
- Employees will be able to install only preapproved applications.
- All users must use two-step login (multifactor authentication) procedures.
- Firewalls will be placed on their most restrictive settings.

The Results

Beginning on December 22, 2014, North Korea experienced an Internet failure, for which the government blamed the United States, identifying the disruptions as an attack in retaliation for the SPE hack. The U.S. government denied any role in the disruptions.

Interestingly, North Korea's only Internet connections run through servers in China. Therefore, China could interdict any hacking attempts originating in North Korea. However, China and the United States are embroiled in a dispute over bilateral hacking, so it does not seem likely that China will police North Korean hacking attempts.

The SPE attack had serious repercussions for Sony, for the U.S. government, and for every organization. Consider the damage to SPE. Analysts estimate that the costs of the attack could exceed $150 million. Such costs include business disruption, loss of information and revenue, decreased customer confidence, and many others. However, the damage done to SPE's reputation (via very sensitive e-mails) could be incalculable.

In fact, several former SPE employees are suing the company for failing to adequately protect their personal data. (SPE offered one year of free credit monitoring and fraud protection to current and former employees.) In July 2015, seven cases were consolidated into a proposed class action lawsuit in a Los Angeles federal court.

In October 2015, Sony agreed to pay up to $10,000 to each claimant for identity theft losses and up to $1,000 each to cover the cost of credit-fraud protection services in connection with the cyberattack. The total settlement was expected to cost Sony approximately $8 million.

The U.S. government is faced with a serious problem. By presidential directive, the U.S. military has the responsibility to help protect and defend the nation's critical infrastructure, such as its power grid, banking system, and communications networks. However, U.S. and international entertainment companies are not part of that infrastructure. The question is: If a foreign government is attacking U.S. corporations, what is the federal government's responsibility? A related question is: If the U.S. government had known of an impending cyberattack on SPE, why didn't the government warn SPE?

And the lessons to be learned? SPE's inability to protect its information from hackers serves as a reminder to corporations and individuals that if you are connected to the Internet, your information is simply not safe. Further, no one should commit anything on e-mail that he or she would not want to see on the front page of a newspaper. The likelihood of serious breaches is increasing, as is the damage these breaches can cause. Therefore, the time, effort, and money that organizations spend on information security needs to increase as well.

One final note: In February 2016, cybersecurity companies Kaspersky (www.kaspersky.com) and Alienvault (www.alienvault.com) announced that they had found new evidence linking the SPE attack with ongoing malware attacks directed at South Korea. The security firms did not definitively specify where the attacks originated, but noted only that their evidence pointed to a group operating out of North Korea.

Sources: Compiled from A. Tarantola, "Study Links North Korea to Sony Hack and Malware Campaign," *Engadget*, February 12, 2016; W. Ashford, "Sony $8M Breach Settlement Underlines Need to Secure Personal Data," *Computer Weekly*, October 22, 2015; P. Elkind, "Inside the Hack of the Century," *Fortune*, July 1, 2015; N. Perlroth, "Jolted by Sony Hacking, Hollywood Is Embracing Digital Security," *The New York Times*, March 30, 2015; W. Ashford, "Sony Data Breach Claims First Scalp as Co-Chair Steps Down," *Computer Weekly*, February 6, 2015; A. David, "Security Think Tank: Sony Employee Lawsuit over Data Breach Marks Watershed Moment," *Computer Weekly*, February, 2015; W. Ashford, "U.S. Blamed North Korea for Sony Attack Based on Data from 2010 U.S. Hack," *Computer Weekly*, January 20, 2015; "North Korea Slams 'Hostile' U.S. Sanctions over Sony Cyber Attack," *Computer Weekly*, January 5, 2015; M. Fackler, "North Korea Accuses U.S. of Staging Internet Failure," *The New York Times*, December 27, 2014; "Sony Hack: The Consequences of Mocking Kim Jong Un," *The Week*, December 26, 2014; B. Barnes and M. Cieply, "Sony, in About-Face, Will Screen 'The Interview' in a Small Run," *The New York Times*, December 23, 2014; M. Williams, "Sony Looking for Ways to Distribute 'The Interview' Online," *IDG News Service*, December 21, 2014; B. Tau, "Obama Calls Sony Hack 'Cybervandalism' Not Act of War," *Washington Wire*, December 21, 2014; M. Elgan, "The Sony Pictures Hack Changes Everything," *Baseline Magazine*, December 19, 2014; A. Bacle, "White House Is Treating Sony Hack as 'Serious National Security Matter,'" *Entertainment Weekly*, December 18, 2014; D. Yadron, D. Barrett, and J. Barnes, "U.S. Struggles for Response to Sony Hack," *The Wall Street Journal*, December 18, 2014; E. Weise, "Experts: Sony Hackers 'Have Crossed the Line,'" *USA Today*, December 17, 2014; D. Sanger and N. Perlroth, "U.S. Links North Korea to Sony Hacking," *The New York Times*, December 17, 2014; M. Williams, "Sony Hackers Release More Data, Promise 'Christmas Gift,'" *IDG News Service*, December 14, 2014; B. Child, "Hackers Demand Sony Cancel Release of Kim Jong-un-Baiting Comedy," *The Guardian*, December 9, 2014; W. Ashford, "North Korea Denies Sony Hack That Exposed 47,000 Personal Records," *Computer Weekly*, December 5, 2014; B. Fritz and D. Yadron, "Sony Hack Exposed Personal Data of Hollywood Stars," *The Wall Street Journal*, December 5, 2014; B. Barnes and N. Perlroth, "Sony Pictures and F.B.I. Widen Hack Inquiry," *The New York Times*, December 3, 2014; W. Ashford, "Films Leaked Online After Sony Pictures Hack," *Computer Weekly*, December 1, 2014; "Sony's New Movies Leak Online Following Hack Attack," *Variety*, November 29, 2014; www.sonypictures.com, accessed July 29, 2015.

Questions

1. Was Sony's response to the breach adequate? Why or why not?
2. Should the U.S. government help private organizations that are attacked (or allegedly attacked) by foreign governments? Why or why not?

Closing Case 2

The Office of Personnel Management Breach

MIS   ### The Problem

Despite high-profile security breaches in the past, many U.S. government agencies have not made cybersecurity a priority. In fact, government officials noted that there were 10 times as many security-related incidents at federal agencies in 2014 as there were in 2006. Audits of federal agencies have demonstrated the seriousness of this lack of security. Consider the following cases:

- A January 2015 audit of the Federal Aviation Administration cited "significant security control weaknesses" in the agency's network, placing the operation of the nation's air traffic control system at risk.

- Federal auditors found numerous security problems with the Department of Energy's network, which contains sensitive information on nuclear propulsion and critical nuclear infrastructure. The auditors criticized the Energy Department for poor security controls, lack of encryption, and a failure to repair known vulnerabilities.

- Federal auditors identified 69 security vulnerabilities at the Internal Revenue Service. Then, when IRS officials informed Government Accountability Office auditors that the agency had fixed 24 of the problems, the auditors found that only 14 had been repaired. In May 2015, the IRS conceded that hackers had gained access to the tax returns of 100,000 U.S. citizens.

In June 2015, the U.S. Office of Personnel Management (OPM; www.opm.gov) announced that it had been the target of two data breaches that stole the personal records of approximately 22 million people. U.S. government officials have described the breaches as among the largest thefts of government data in U.S. history.

Evidence of the breaches appears to have been discovered accidentally during a product demonstration by network security company CyTech Services (www.cytechservices.com). CyTech's team was demonstrating the company's product, CyFIR, and the software tool identified the previously unknown malware associated with the breaches.

Information stolen in the OPM breaches affected not only OPM employees, but contractors, applicants, and family members as well. The stolen information included personally identifiable information such as social security numbers, names, dates and places of birth, residency and educational history, and addresses. Also stolen was information about immediate family and other personal and business acquaintances, as well as health, criminal, and financial histories. The attackers also stole detailed security-clearance-related background information that included more than one million fingerprints.

Significantly, the OPM had been warned multiple times of security vulnerabilities. In 2008, the Inspector General's office recommended that OPM eliminate the unnecessary use of social security numbers (SSNs). By 2014, OPM had stopped using SSNs for some systems, but not all. A subsequent 2014 audit of OPM's cloud computing contracts found that OPM did not follow best practices for moving software and data to the cloud. (We discuss cloud computing in Plug IT In 4.) It further discovered that OPM had failed to keep up with required testing and certification to ensure that its systems met security standards. These authorizations must be conducted every three years. In 2014,

11 of 47 major systems due for authorization were operating without it, including systems in human resources, finance, and investigative services. A March 2015 Inspector General report to Congress warned of persistent deficiencies in OPM's security programs.

The IT Solution (?)

To improve the cybersecurity of federal agencies, U.S. Chief Information Officer Tony Scott launched a 30-day "Cybersecurity Sprint." Scott instructed federal agencies to take carefully defined steps to improve cybersecurity:

- Immediately patch critical security vulnerabilities.

- Tighten policies and procedures for privileged users by limiting the number of user accounts.

- Dramatically accelerate the implementation of multifactor authentication, especially for privileged users.

By July 2015, the most advanced defenses had not been fully implemented. In fact, major agencies will not have these defenses until 2017, and smaller agencies could take even longer. Further, legal, political, and bureaucratic roadblocks still make it difficult for cybersecurity officials to act quickly. In particular, bureaucratic obstacles hindered efforts by the Department of Homeland Security to compete in the highly competitive market for cybersecurity specialists. Federal agencies also note that as difficult as it is to hire top cybersecurity talent, government bureaucracy makes it even more difficult to fire underperforming government personnel.

The Results

At some federal agencies, 100 percent of users are, for the first time, logging in with two-factor authentication. Security problems that have existed for years are being patched. Thousands of low-level employees and contractors with access to the nation's most sensitive secrets now have very limited access privileges.

Unfortunately, many federal agencies remain highly vulnerable to sophisticated cybercriminals, who are often sponsored by other countries. The government is still facing obstacles in procuring the most current cybersecurity systems and attracting digital security experts. Further, senior cybersecurity officials maintain that the 30-day Sprint, although helpful, had limited long-range usefulness because federal systems still use out-of-date equipment and security software.

Security experts noted that the breaches have created a significant threat to U.S. national security that will last for decades and cost billions of dollars to monitor. Specifically, the stolen data constitute a counterintelligence threat that could easily last 40 years, or until the youngest members of the federal workforce retire. The security experts further contend that the OPM can do little to reverse the damage that has already been done.

Lawmakers have introduced legislation that would provide affected employees with free lifetime identity protection and $5 million in identity theft insurance. Meanwhile, Katherine Archuleta, the director of the OPM, claimed that her agency suffered from an old technology infrastructure that she was working to improve. Director Archuleta resigned her position in July 2015.

In September 2015, acting OPM Director Beth Cobert announced that the agency had awarded a contract to Identity Theft Guard

Solutions LLC (www.identityguard.com) to provide identity theft and credit protection for those affected by the OPM breach. The contract is valued at approximately $133 million and will provide up to three years of protection for the people affected by the breach, as well as any dependents who were still minors as of July 1, 2015.

The fallout from the OPM breach continued in early February 2016, when OPM's chief information officer, Donna Seymour, also resigned.

Sources: **Compiled from** E. Kelly, "OPM's Cybersecurity Chief Resigns in Wake of Massive Data Breach," *USA Today*, February 22, 2016; M. Heller, "OPM Breach Protection Services on the Way for 21.5M Victims," *TechTarget*, September 3, 2015; C. Bennett, "White House Hands Out 'Cyber Sprint' Grades," *The Hill*, July 31, 2015; M. Shear and N. Perlroth, "U.S. vs. Hackers: Still Lopsided Despite Years of Warnings and a Recent Push," *The New York Times*, July 18, 2015; J. Rogers," Why the OPM Hack Is an Ongoing Cyber Headache," *Fox News*, July 14, 2015; K. Corbin, "How OPM Data Breach Could Have Been Prevented," *CIO*, July 13, 2015; D. Verton, "Impact of OPM Breach Could Last More than 40 Years," *Fedscoop*, July 12, 2015; S. Norton and C. Boulton, "Years of Tech Mismanagement Led to OPM Breach, Resignation of Chief," *CIO Journal*, July 10, 2015; J. Sciutto, "OPM Government Data Breach Impacted 21.5 Million," *CNN*, July 10, 2015; P. Zengerle and M. Cassella, "Millions More Americans Hit by Government Personnel Data Hack," *Reuters*, July 9, 2015; D. Paletta, "Personnel Data Breach a 'Huge Deal'," *The Wall Street Journal*, July 9, 2015; J. Davidson, "New OPM Data Breach Numbers Leave Federal Employees Anguished, Outraged," *The Washington Post*, July 9, 2015; M. Heller, "Stolen Passwords to Blame for OPM Breach; Director May Take the Fall," *TechTarget*, June 25, 2015; S. Vaughan-Nichols, "It Gets Worse: Two Federal OPM Hacks Affected Up to 18 Million," *ZDNet*, June 23, 2015; A. Boyd, "Second OPM Hack Exposed Higly Personal Background Info," *Federal Times*, June 16, 2015; A. Boyd, "Feds on '3-Day Sprint' to Better Cybersecurity," *Federal Times*, June 15, 2015; "Officials: Second Hack Exposed Military and Intel Data," *Associated Press*, June 12, 2015; R. Hackett, "A Product Demo May Have Revealed What Could Be the Biggest Ever Government Data Breach," *Fortune*, June 12, 2015; www.opm.gov, accessed July 31, 2015.

Questions

1. What actions should the OPM have taken to prevent the breaches? Provide specific examples in your answer.

2. Should the U.S. government do anything more for the victims of the breaches? If so, what?

3. Place yourself as a victim in the OPM breaches. What should you do when you are notified that your personal data have been compromised?

4 Does this case really have an IT solution? Why or why not?

Alex Slobodkin/iStockphoto

Social Computing

CHAPTER OUTLINE

CHAPTER 8

LEARNING OBJECTIVES

8.1 Describe six Web 2.0 tools and two major types of Web 2.0 sites.

8.2 Describe the benefits and risks of social commerce to companies.

8.3 Identify the methods used for shopping socially.

8.4 Discuss innovative ways to use social networking sites for advertising and market research.

8.5 Describe how social computing improves customer service.

8.6 Discuss different ways in which human resource managers make use of social computing.

Opening Case

POM **MIS** Social Commerce Company Teespring Plans to Become a Platform

Social commerce company Teespring (http://teespring.com) is one of the leading T-shirt manufacturers and sellers in the United States. In 2014, the company printed more than seven million T-shirts.

Regardless of the T-shirt design, social commerce Web site Teespring either has a design, or it will help independent contractors design and make the T-shirt, sell it, and take a percentage. In fact, hundreds of people made more than $100,000 in 2014 selling tees through the company's Web site and 20 earned more than $1 million. Teespring says that about 60 percent of its sales come through ads on social media, with approximately 20 percent of the people who buy Teespring tees sharing their purchases on Facebook.

Teespring's full-time employees serve as the back-office staff for independent designers, operating their online sales, making and shipping the tees, processing payments, and managing customer service. Teespring charges designers about $9 per shirt, depending on the quality of the cotton and the complexity of the design. The designers set the retail price and earn the difference. Teespring prints shirts only when a customer has placed an online order. As a result, the company and its designers are not left with unsold inventory. This process is an excellent example of mass customization, or make-to-order production.

Independent designers use Facebook extensively because the social network's 1.5 billion users provide such a vast amount of data on what its users like and dislike. In addition, designers use free tools such as Google Trends (www.google.com/trends) and Reddit (www.reddit.com) to identify current trends in specific niches that allows them to identify potential audiences.

For example, one designer noticed hundreds of thousands of shares and social engagement regarding images and sayings related to the U.S. women's soccer team. She then went to Facebook, identified current active groups following the team, and created a large list of people from those groups. She created various designs, uploaded them to Teespring, worked with Teespring designers, and marketed the T-shirts that Teespring produced to this passionate audience.

Teespring's annual revenue exceeds $100 million. In 2014, the firm raised approximately $55 million in venture funding and built a 105,000-square-foot printing factory in Kentucky. The company is planning to contract out as little production as possible to other companies, thereby keeping its production costs to a minimum. Further, Teespring wants to have customer service and production in the same facility. If shoppers have questions about an order, or have a problem with an order, it is more efficient for customer service to be co-located with production.

What's next for Teespring? Its production and payments systems could prove invaluable for many more types of entrepreneurs. One of Teespring's founders noted, "T-shirts are to Teespring what books are to Amazon." The company's next step is to go beyond shirts into hats, stickers, posters, and smartphone cases. Essentially, Teespring plans to become a platform for entrepreneurs to create and sell all types of merchandise online.

Compare a platform with a traditional business model. A traditional business produces one or more closely related products or services, then uses marketing to attract customers. By contrast, businesses using the *platform model* integrate an increasing number of customers and partners into their ecosystems. A *business ecosystem* is a network of organizations—including suppliers, distributors, customers, competitors, government agencies, and others—involved in the delivery of products and services through both competition and cooperation.

Building a powerful platform enables a company's ecosystem to contribute to innovation. The platform enables other businesses to easily connect their businesses to yours, build products and services on top of your products and services, thus co-creating value. Let's look at several examples:

- In 1998, Google was an excellent search engine, but not yet a platform. By adding features such as Gmail, Google Maps, Google Docs, YouTube, and many others, Google has become a very powerful platform.

- By inviting thousands of users to develop apps for its iPhone and iPad, Apple has become a platform and generated billions of dollars in new revenue.

- Facebook began as a social networking Web site for college students. The firm has become a powerful platform by expanding its offerings to include business and marketing sites, community gaming sites, e-mail, instant messaging, groups, blogs, advertising, consumer data mining, and many others.

- Uber developed a mobile app that allows customers with smartphones to submit a trip request that is then sent to Uber drivers who use their own cars. Uber is rapidly becoming a platform as it begins to offer new services such as postal, gift, and grocery delivery, as well as limousine and even medical services.

Consider this example of Teespring becoming a platform. In May 2015, the firm formed a partnership with music merchandise company Manhead Merchandising (www.manheadmerch.com) to deliver custom clothing for its portfolio of music artists. The partnership enables Manhead to leverage Teespring's innovative production and payment system to expand its electronic commerce business. In addition, artists can sell their own merchandise online with no upfront costs or inventory risk.

For example, Manhead artist Fall Out Boy used Teespring to launch a limited-edition T-shirt in a special 24-hour sale. The band promoted this shirt exclusively through its social media channels, generating $40,000 in sales in a single day.

One caveat: Teespring's expenses are increasing at the same time that Facebook ad rates are rising. Further, the company has to deal with a number of legal complaints about tees that use copyrighted images from movies or sports teams, or images that copy existing top sellers. The company says that its staff members review all designs to avoid incurring liability.

Sources: Compiled from S. Perez, "Teespring Eliminates 70 Jobs in Providence as Company Restructures," *TechCrunch*, June 24, 2015; K. Mulvaney, "R.I. Startup Teespring Moving Jobs to Kentucky, San Francisco," *Providence Journal*, June 24, 2015; "Is Teespring and Facebook Marketing Still Viable in 2015?" *CNN News Center*, May 28, 2015; "Teespring & Manhead Merchandising Team Up to Create Social Commerce Opportunities for Musicians," *PRNewswire*, May 12, 2015; A. Satariano, "How Your T-Shirt Can Make You Rich," *Bloomberg BusinessWeek*, April 16, 2015; S. Perez, "Teespring Raises $35 Million Series B from Khosla Ventures as It Prepares to Expand Beyond Apparel," *TechCrunch*, November 18, 2014; A. Konrad, "Teespring Says It's Minting New Millionaires Selling Its T-Shirts, Raises $35 Million of Its Own," *Forbes*, November 18, 2014; A. Taub, "Teespring: Is This Rhode Island Based Startup the Future of Custom Apparel?" *Forbes*, January 3, 2013; http://teespring.com, accessed August 3, 2015.

Questions

1. Discuss the relationship between social computing and Teespring's business model.

2. Explain this statement: "T-shirts are to Teespring what books are to Amazon."

3. What other products and services can Teespring offer to truly become a platform?

Introduction

Humans are social individuals. Therefore, human behavior is innately social. Humans typically orient their behavior around other members of their community. As a result, people are sensitive to the behavior of people around them, and their decisions are generally influenced by their social context.

Traditional information systems support organizational activities and business processes, and they concentrate on cost reductions and productivity increases. A variation of this traditional model, social computing, is a type of IT that combines social behavior and information systems to create value. Social computing is focused on improving collaboration and interaction among people and on encouraging user-generated content, as you see in this chapter's opening case.

Significantly, in social computing, social information is not anonymous. Rather, it is important precisely because it is linked to particular individuals, who in turn are linked to their own networks of individuals.

Social computing makes socially produced information available to everyone. This information may be provided directly, as when users rate a movie (e.g., at Rotten Tomatoes), or indirectly (as with Google's PageRank algorithm, which sequences search results).

In social computing, users, rather than organizations, produce, control, use, and manage content via interactive communications and collaboration. As a result, social computing is transforming power relationships within organizations. Employees and customers are empowered by their ability to use social computing to organize themselves. Thus, social computing can influence people in positions of power to listen to the concerns and issues of "ordinary people." Organizational customers and employees are joining this social computing phenomenon, with serious consequences for most organizations.

Significantly, most governments and companies in modern developed societies are not prepared for the new social power of ordinary people. Today, managers, executives, and government officials can no longer control the conversation around policies, products, and other issues.

In the new world of business and government, organizational leaders will have to demonstrate authenticity, even-handedness, transparency, good faith, and humility. If they do not, then customers and employees may distrust them, to potentially disastrous effects. For example, customers who do not like a product or service can quickly broadcast their disapproval. Another example is that prospective employees do not have to take their employers at their word for what life is like at their companies—they can find out from people who already work there. A final example is that employees now have many more options to start their own companies, which could compete with their former employers.

As you see from these examples, the world is becoming more democratic and reflective of the will of ordinary people, enabled by the power of social computing. On the one hand, social power can help keep a company vital and can enable customers and employee activists to become a source of creativity, innovation, and new ideas that will move a company forward. On the other hand, companies that show insensitivity toward customers or employees quickly find themselves on a downward slide.

For instance, Kenneth Cole came under fire for suggesting on Twitter that news of its spring collection led to riots in Egypt, and American Apparel was blasted online for offering a Hurricane Sandy sale. Lesson to be learned: If companies want to win the favor and loyalty of customers, they should refrain from making comments that may suggest that they were trying to profit from other people's misery.

Social computing is exploding worldwide, with China having the world's most active social media population. In one McKinsey survey, 91 percent of Chinese respondents reported that they had visited a social media site in the previous six months, compared with 70 percent in South Korea, 67 percent in the United States, and 30 percent in Japan. Interestingly, the survey found that social media has a greater influence on purchasing decisions for Chinese consumers than for consumers anywhere else in the world.

Social computing is also increasing dramatically in Africa. Facebook, YouTube, and Instagram are the leading social networks in African countries. However, Facebook does have rivals in Africa, one of which is Mxit (www.mxit.com). Although Mxit's active users have fallen to about five million, the social network is among the most engaged in Africa, with the average user signing in five times per day and spending 105 minutes per day on the site.

The chapter opening case illustrates how businesses today are using social computing in a variety of innovative ways, including marketing, production, customer relationship management, and human resource management. In fact, so many organizations are competing to use social computing in as many new ways as possible that an inclusive term for the use of social computing in business has emerged: *social commerce*. Because social computing is facilitated by Web 2.0 tools and sites, you begin this chapter by examining these technologies. You then turn your attention to a diverse number of social commerce activities, including shopping, advertising, market research, customer relationship management, and human resource management.

When you complete this chapter, you will have a thorough understanding of social computing and the ways in which modern organizations use this technology. You will be familiar with the advantages and disadvantages of social computing as well as the risks and rewards it can bring to your organization. For example, most of you already have pages on social networking sites, so you are familiar with the positive and negative features of these sites. This chapter will enable you to apply this knowledge to your organization's efforts in the social computing arena. You will be in a position to contribute to your organization's policies on social computing. You will also be able to help your organization create a strategy to utilize social computing. Finally, social computing offers incredible opportunities for entrepreneurs who want to start their own businesses.

8.1 | Web 2.0

The World Wide Web, which you learned about in Chapter 4, first appeared in 1990. Web 1.0 was the first generation of the Web. We did not use this term in Chapter 4 because there was no need to say "Web 1.0" until Web 2.0 emerged.

The key developments of Web 1.0 were the creation of Web sites and the commercialization of the Web. Users typically had minimal interaction with Web 1.0 sites. Rather, they passively received information from those sites.

Web 2.0 is a popular term that has proved difficult to define. According to Tim O'Reilly, a noted blogger, Web 2.0 is a loose collection of information technologies and applications, plus the Web sites that use them. These Web sites enrich the user experience by encouraging user participation, social interaction, and collaboration. Unlike Web 1.0 sites, Web 2.0 sites are not so much online places to visit as Web locations that facilitate information sharing, user-centered design, and collaboration. Web 2.0 sites often harness collective intelligence (e.g., wikis); deliver functionality as services, rather than packaged software (e.g., Web services); and feature remixable applications and data (e.g., mashups).

In the following sections, we discuss five Web 2.0 information technology tools: tagging, Really Simple Syndication, blogs, microblogs, and wikis. We then turn our attention to the two major types of Web 2.0 sites: social networking sites and mashups.

Tagging

A tag is a keyword or term that describes a piece of information, for example, a blog, a picture, an article, or a video clip. Users typically choose tags that are meaningful to them. Tagging allows users to place information in multiple, overlapping associations rather than in rigid categories. For example, a photo of a car might be tagged with "Corvette," "sports car," and "Chevrolet." Tagging is the basis of *folksonomies*, which are user-generated classifications that use tags to categorize and retrieve Web pages, photos, videos, and other Web content.

One specific form of tagging, known as *geotagging*, refers to tagging information on maps. For example, Google Maps allows users to add pictures and information, such as restaurant or hotel ratings, to maps. Therefore, when users access Google Maps, their experience is enriched because they can see pictures of attractions, reviews, and things to do, posted by everyone, and all related to the map location they are viewing.

Really Simple Syndication

Really Simple Syndication (RSS) is a Web 2.0 feature that allows you to receive the information you want (customized information), when you want it, without having to surf thousands of Web sites. RSS allows anyone to syndicate (publish) his or her blog, or any other content, to anyone who has an interest in subscribing to it. When changes to the content are made, subscribers receive a notification of the changes and an idea of what the new content contains. Subscribers can then click on a link that will take them to the full text of the new content.

For example, CNN.com provides RSS feeds for each of its main topic areas, such as world news, sports news, technology news, and entertainment news. NBC uses RSS feeds to allow viewers to download the most current version of shows such as *Meet the Press* and *NBC Nightly News*. Figure 8.1 illustrates how to search an RSS and locate RSS feeds.

To use RSS, you can utilize a special newsreader that displays RSS content feeds from the Web sites you select. Many such readers are available, several of them for free (see Feedspot; www.feedspot.com). In addition, most browsers have built-in RSS readers. For an excellent RSS tutorial, visit www.mnot.net/rss/tutorial.

Blogs

A **weblog** (**blog** for short) is a personal Web site, open to the public, in which the site creator expresses his or her feelings or opinions via a series of chronological entries. *Bloggers*—people who create and maintain blogs—write stories, convey news, and provide links to other articles

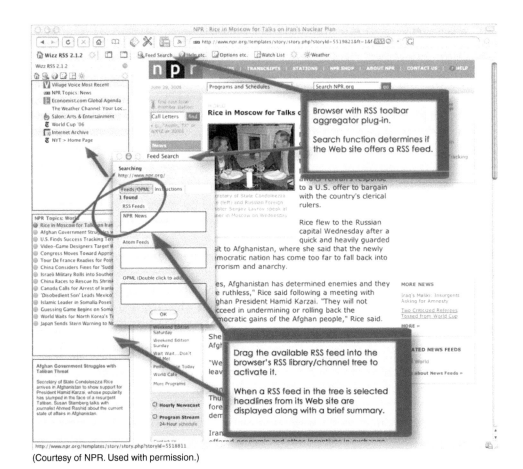

FIGURE 8.1 The Web site of National Public Radio (NPR) with RSS toolbar aggregator and search function.

(Courtesy of NPR. Used with permission.)

and Web sites that are of interest to them. The simplest method of creating a blog is to sign up with a blogging service provider, such as www.blogger.com (now owned by Google), www.xanga.com, and www.sixapart.com. The **blogosphere** is the term for the millions of blogs on the Web.

MIS

Many companies listen to consumers in the blogosphere who express their views on the companies' products. Marketers refer to these views as *consumer-generated media*. For example, Nielsen (www.nielsen-online.com) "mines" the blogosphere to provide information for its clients in several areas. Nielsen helps clients find ways to serve potential markets, ranging from broad-based to niche markets. The company also helps clients detect false rumors before these rumors appear in the mainstream media, and it gauges the potency of a marketing push or the popularity of a new product.

Blogs often provide incredibly useful information, often before the information becomes available in traditional media outlets (e.g., television, newspapers). Although blogs can be very useful, they also have shortcomings. Perhaps the primary value of blogs is their ability to bring current, breaking news to the public in the fastest time possible. Unfortunately, in doing so, bloggers sometimes cut corners, and their blogs can be inaccurate. Regardless of their various problems, however, blogs have transformed the ways in which people gather and consume information.

Microblogging

Microblogging is a form of blogging that allows users to write short messages (or capture an image or embedded video) and publish them. These messages can be submitted via text messaging from mobile phones, instant messaging, e-mail, or simply over the Web. The content of a microblog differs from that of a blog because of the limited space per message (usually up to 140 characters). A popular microblogging service is Twitter.

Twitter is a free microblogging service that allows its users to send messages and read other users' messages and updates, known as **tweets**. Tweets are displayed on the user's profile page and delivered to other users who have signed up to receive them.

MKT

Twitter is becoming a very useful business tool. It allows companies to quickly share information with people interested in their products, thereby creating deeper relationships with their customers. Businesses also use Twitter to gather real-time market intelligence and customer feedback. As an individual user, you can use Twitter to inform companies about your experiences with their business, offer product ideas, and learn about great offers.

Microblogging is very popular in China, with Weibo (www.weibo.com) being the most popular microblogging service in that country. Weibo has over 200 million monthly active members.

Wikis

A **wiki** is a Web site made up entirely of content posted by users. Wikis have an "edit" link on each page that allows any user to add, change, or delete material, thus fostering easy collaboration.

Wikis take advantage of the combined input of many individuals. Consider Wikipedia (www.wikipedia.org), an online encyclopedia that is the largest existing wiki. Wikipedia contains almost five million articles in English (as of mid-2015), which attract some 500 million views every day. Wikipedia relies on volunteer administrators who enforce a neutral point of view, and it encourages users to delete copy that displays a clear bias. Nevertheless, there are still major debates over the reliability of Wikipedia articles. Many educators will not allow students to cite references from Wikipedia because Wikipedia content is of uncertain origin. Moreover, Wikipedia does not provide any quality assessment or fact checking by experts. Therefore, academics and other professionals have major concerns about the accuracy of user-provided content.

POM

MKT

Organizations use wikis in several ways. In project management, for example, wikis provide a central repository for capturing constantly updated product features and specifications, tracking issues, resolving problems, and maintaining project histories. In addition, wikis enable companies to collaborate with customers, suppliers, and other business partners on projects. Wikis are also valuable in knowledge management. For example, companies use wikis to keep enterprisewide documents, such as guidelines and frequently asked questions, accurate and current.

Social Networking Web Sites

A social network is a social structure composed of individuals, groups, or organizations linked by values, visions, ideas, financial exchange, friendship, kinship, conflict, or trade. Social networking refers to activities performed using social software tools (e.g., blogging) or social networking features (e.g., media sharing). Social networking allows convenient connections to those of similar interest.

A social network can be described as a map of all relevant links or connections among the network's members. For each individual member that map is his or her social graph. Mark Zuckerberg of Facebook originally coined this term to refer to the social network of relationships among Facebook users. The idea was that Facebook would take advantage of relationships among individuals to offer a richer online experience.

Social networks can also be used to determine the social capital of individual participants. Social capital refers to the number of connections a person has within and between social networks.

Participants congregate on *social networking Web sites* where they can create their own profile page for free and on which they can write blogs and wikis; post pictures, videos, or music; share ideas; and link to other Web locations they find interesting. Social networkers chat using instant messaging and Twitter, and they tag posted content with their own key words, making content searchable and facilitating interactions and transactions. Social networkers converse, collaborate, and share opinions, experiences, knowledge, insights, and perceptions with one another. They also use these Web sites to find like-minded people online, either to pursue an interest or a goal or just to establish a sense of community among people who may never meet in the real world.

Participants who post on social networking sites tend to reveal a great deal of personal information. As a result, if they are not careful, bad things can happen.

Table 8.1 displays the variety of online social networking platforms. Social networking Web sites allow users to upload their content to the Web in the form of text, voice, images, and videos.

These social networking sites produce a massive amount of information uploaded by their users. As you see in IT's About Business 8.1, startup Banjo has developed software to integrate and analyze all this information.

IT's About Business 8.1

MIS **Banjo Organizes the World's Social Media**

We all encounter "noise" generated by social media. In this context, noise consists of the massive amounts of unstructured data generated from tweets, Facebook updates, images, and full motion video clips, uploaded to various social media Web sites. Within this noise, there are important signals that need to be noted, collected, and analyzed. The problem is clear: How can we make sense of all the noise?

Startup Banjo (http://ban.jo) has developed software that functions as an event-detection engine. The software organizes the world's social signals by location, enabling an unprecedented level of understanding of events that occur anywhere in the world, in real time. As such, Banjo has developed an information-gathering and -disseminating system that works anywhere in the world.

Banjo displays data from geolocated posts uploaded from mobile devices, through a user-friendly Web site. Banjo integrates uploads from more than a dozen social networks, including Twitter (www.twitter.com), Instagram (https://instagram.com), Vine (https://vine.co), Facebook (www.facebook.com), Russia's VKontakte (https://vk.com), and China's Weibo (www.weibo.com), among others.

How Banjo Works. In 2011, Banjo released a consumer news app (called Banjo 1.0), which integrated various social media feeds. According to AppData (www.appdata.com), approximately 7.5 million people downloaded the app. Banjo 1.0 still exists, but the company no longer actively supports it.

The next generation of Banjo, Banjo 2.0, benefits from the fact that users of Banjo 1.0 signed up through a social network. Banjo can access the posts of its 7.5 million users but also those of all their approximately 1.2 billion friends on their social networks. Banjo 2.0 harnesses the power of its reach of 1.2 billion people and their ability to capture images, videos, and text through their mobile devices.

Banjo maps a grid over the whole world, consisting of more than 35 billion squares, each about the size of a football field. Since 2011, Banjo has constantly monitored every square in real time, overlaying every mobile public post onto its grid. The software knows what the usual state is for each square: this square is in a wheat field; this square is in a war zone with smoke and fire; this square is in Disneyland, and so on.

Every minute, Banjo's software analyzes thousands of geo-located mobile posts, examining data on linguistics and location, and classifying photos and videos. When the data indicate an abnormality from the baseline, such as unusual activity in a normally quiet area, Banjo alerts company staff, who investigate the alert and either ignore it or notify users. As Banjo's software accumulates more data and can "learn," staff need to intervene less often.

Banjo's analytics include not only the ability to identify locations and photos, but to "rewind" each social media network. (The rewind function means that users can see what happened before a particular event occurred, for example just before an earthquake.)

Rather than users trying to make sense of their social media feeds via hashtags and keywords, they can have an integrated view of their feeds, from any location on earth. Users enter their location (plus any desired keywords), and the Banjo maps resizes to scale. All the relevant public posts for that location are shown as pins on the map, with links to text, photos, and video. This process occurs in real time.

Traditionally, users have asked, "How do we mine social media?" Banjo integrates social media from the perspective of mobile phones, which are in specific locations in the real world. As a result, Banjo asks, "How can we know what is going on in a specific place at a specific time?"

Naturally, such a treasure trove of data could be a privacy minefield. Banjo has tried to protect users' data by developing a patented method of automatically searching its database and removing any posts that have been made private or deleted by users. When users change their privacy settings, Banjo deletes all information retroactively. The information is no longer in Banjo's system and no longer in Banjo's users' systems, immediately.

Banjo Applications. Banjo's technology has implications for diverse industries, including news and media, financial services, marketing, insurance, public health, and many others.

Banjo isn't just a way to locate an impromptu street party—it can also save lives. It was credited with alerting authorities to a shooting on a Florida campus, thanks to a tweet sent by one of the witnesses. Just after 12:30 AM on November 20, 2014, a single tweet was sent from a location near the Florida State University (FSU; www.fsu.edu) campus in Tallahassee. The tweet contained no hashtag, but Banjo picked up on the words "scared to death," and noted an increase in the number of Twitter and Instagram posts coming from that location. The software noted the deviation in that grid square and alerted Banjo employees, who notified the local CBS affiliate in Tallahassee. That channel investigated and was the first on the scene to report the wounding of three people in a shooting in an FSU library. Media companies, including NBC and ESPN, are among Banjo's longest customers.

Here are more applications of Banjo by media outlets. Sinclair Broadcasting Group (www.sbgi.net), which owns 162 television stations in 79 markets, uses Banjo as a sort of remote reporting team. Banjo alerts its newsrooms to a breaking story. A news director can

travel virtually to the scene, following a real-time stream of all the posts of photos, videos, and commentary from users at that location. The newsroom can then contact the authors of those posts without needing to tweet or email, and get permission to use their content on air, without having to send a reporter to the scene. Sinclair can use Banjo to create a timeline of events leading up a certain activity, such as an album of images and videos that happened just before the Charlie Hebdo attacks in Paris in January 2015. The technology allows Sinclair to syndicate its newscasts to licensees in a cost-effective manner.

Banjo technology is also disrupting the business world. In November 2014, Banjo analyzed images of a fire at a diesel pipeline in Saudi Arabia. Its photo classification algorithms flagged the incident. Customers working in the finance field used the information when trading on oil in under an hour after the photos were flagged. Two hours after the initial Banjo alert, by the time the media picked up on the story, the price of oil futures rose by $2 a barrel. Clearly, traders could make huge amounts of money with the lead times provided by Banjo alerts.

Banjo is quick to point out that its goal is not to gather all the personal information about users and sell it to advertisers. Instead, it generates and sells intelligence from the content that users willingly provide.

In 2014, Banjo Enterprise generated revenue of less than $1 million. However, the company generated the entire amount through word of mouth, with no marketing effort and no sales team.

Social media is not the be-all and end-all source of information; it doesn't provide all the data needed for Banjo's intelligence gathering. Therefore, the startup is adding new data sources, such as weather data from various countries, including the National Weather Service (which has approached Banjo about constructing an alert system) as well as satellite imagery. Further, Banjo notes that in an Internet of Things environment, sensors in physical objects such as vehicles and buildings could also emit data worth collecting.

Sources: Compiled from J. Paduda, "Will Banjo Be the Social Media App that Revolutionizes Insurance?" *joepaduda.com*, June 3, 2015; D. MacMillan, "Banjo Raises $100 Million to Detect World Events in Real Time," *Wall Street Journal Digits*, May 6, 2015; A. Talbert, "How a Social Media Company You've Never Heard Of Is Primed to Revolutionize Customer Service," *Zoho Blogs*, April 27, 2015; W. Schmidt, "What Would You Do If You Had a Crystal Ball?" *Tech.co*, April 22, 2015; H. Clancy, "Why Social Media Startup Banjo Will Strike a Chord with Marketers," *Fortune*, April 2, 2015; W. Bourne, "The Most Important Social Media Company You've Never Heard Of," *Inc*, April, 2015; O. Williams, "Banjo Updates Mobile Apps to Create TiVO for Social Media," *TheNextWeb*, March 8, 2014; D. Etherington, "Banjo Puts News and Live Events Front and Center with Version 4.0 of Its Mobile App," *TechCrunch*, January 16, 2014; M. Butcher, "New Banjo App Aims to Become a True Browser for Location, A Much Bigger Opportunity," *TechCrunch*, November 15, 2012; T. Geron, "Banjo App Connects with the Nearby Social World," *Forbes*, June 22, 2011; http://ban.jo, accessed August 15, 2015.

Questions

1. What are potential disadvantages of Banjo? (*Hint:* What about privacy concerns?)

2. How would marketing managers use Banjo? Provide an example to support your answer.

3. How would insurance companies use Banjo? Provide an example to support your answer.

TABLE 8.1   Categories of Social Networking Web Sites

Socially oriented: Socially focused public sites, open to anyone:

- Facebook (www.facebook.com)
- Google+ (https://plus.google.com)
- Hi5 (www.hi5.com)

Professional networking: Focused on networking for business professionals:

- LinkedIn (www.linkedin.com)

Media sharing:

- *Netcasting* includes podcasting (audio) and videocasting (audio and video). For example, educational institutions use netcasts to provide students with access to lectures, lab demonstrations, and sports events. In 2007, Apple launched iTunes U, which offers free content provided by major U.S. universities such as Stanford and MIT.
- *Web 2.0 media* sites allow people to come together and share user-generated digital media, such as pictures, audio, and video:
  - Video (Amazon Video on Demand, YouTube, Hulu, Facebook)
  - Music (Amazon MP3, Last.fm, Rhapsody, Pandora, Facebook, iTunes)
  - Photographs (Photobucket, Flickr, Shutterfly, Picasa, Facebook)

Communication:

- Blogs: Blogger, LiveJournal, TypePad, WordPress, Vox, Xanga
- Microblogging/Presence applications: Twitter, Tumblr, Yammer

Collaboration: Wikis (Wikimedia, PBworks, Wetpaint)

Social bookmarking (or *social tagging*)**:** Focused on helping users store, organize, search, and manage bookmarks of Web pages on the Internet:

- Delicious (www.delicious.com)
- StumbleUpon (www.stumbleupon.com)
- Google Reader (http://reader.google.com)
- CiteULike (www.citeulike.com)

Social news: Focused on user-posted news stories that are ranked by popularity based on user voting:

- Digg (www.digg.com)
- Chime.in (http://chime.in)
- Reddit (www.reddit.com)

Events: Focused on alerts for relevant events, people you know nearby, etc.:

- Eventful (www.eventful.com)
- Meetup (www.meetup.com)
- Foursquare (www.foursquare.com)

Virtual meeting place: Sites that are essentially three-dimensional worlds, built and owned by the residents (the users):

- Second Life (www.secondlife.com)

Discovery:

- Foursquare (http://foursquare.com) helps its members discover and share information about businesses and attractions around them.

Online marketplaces for microjobs: For example, TaskRabbit (www.taskrabbit.com) and Zaarly (www.zaarly.com) enable people to farm out chores to a growing number of temporary personal assistants. Thousands of unemployed and underemployed workers use these sites. The part-time or full-time tasks are especially popular with stay-at-home moms, retirees, and students. Workers choose their jobs and negotiate their rates.

Enterprise Social Networks

Business-oriented social networks can be public, such as LinkedIn.com. As such, they are owned and managed by an independent company.

MIS

However, an increasing number of companies have created in-house, private social networks for their employees, former employees, business partners, and/or customers. Such networks are "behind the firewall" and are often referred to as *corporate social networks*. Employees utilize these networks to create connections that allow them to establish virtual teams, bring new employees up to speed, improve collaboration, and increase employee retention by creating a sense of community. Employees are able to interact with their coworkers on a level that is typically absent in large organizations or in situations where people work remotely.

Corporate social networks are used for many processes, including:

- Networking and community building, both inside and outside an organization
- *Social collaboration*: Collaborative work and problem solving using wikis, blogs, instant messaging, collaborative office, and other special-purpose Web-based collaboration platforms; for example, see Laboranova (www.laboranova.com)
- *Social publishing*: Employees and others creating, either individually or collaboratively, and posting contents—photos, videos, presentation slides, and documents—into a member's or a community's accessible-content repository such as YouTube, Flickr, SlideShare, and DocStoc
- Social views and feedback
- *Social intelligence and social analytics*: Monitoring, analyzing, and interpreting conversations, interactions, and associations among people, topics, and ideas to gain insights. Social intelligence is useful for examining relationships and work patterns of individuals and groups and for discovering people and expertise.

Mashups

A **mashup** is a Web site that takes different content from a number of other Web sites and mixes them together to create a new kind of content. The launch of Google Maps is credited with providing the start for mashups. A user can take a map from Google, add his or her data, and then display a map mashup on his or her Web site that plots crime scenes, cars for sale, or anything else (see **Figure 8.2**). There are many examples of mashups (for a complete list of mashups, see www.programmableweb.com):

- Craigslist developed a dynamic map of all available apartments in the United States that are listed on their Web site (www.housingmaps.com).

FIGURE 8.2 GoogleMaps (www.googlemaps.com) is a classic example of a mashup. In this case, GoogleMaps is pulling in information from public transportation Web sites to provide the customer with transit directions.

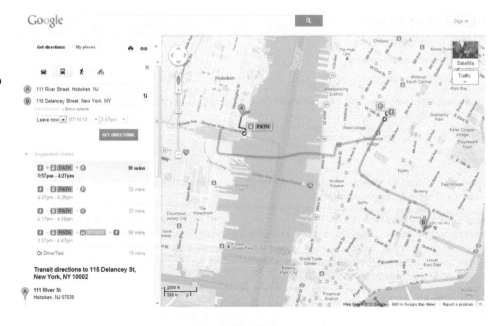

• Everyblock.com is a mashup of Web services that integrates content from newspapers, blogs, and government databases to inform citizens of cities such as Chicago, New York, and Seattle about what is happening in their neighborhoods. This information includes criminal activities, restaurant inspections, and local photos posted on Flickr.

Before you go on...

1. Differentiate between blogs and wikis.

2. Differentiate between social networking Web sites and corporate social networks.

Apply the Concept 8.1

LEARNING OBJECTIVE 8.1 Describe five Web 2.0 tools and the two major types of Web 2.0 sites.

STEP 1: Background (Here is what you are learning.)

This section differentiates Web 1.0, which consists of places to visit, from Web 2.0, where users interact and share information. Whether or not you have thought of these media in these terms, you are familiar with these differences. No doubt you are much more accustomed to Web 2.0, and businesses have begun to integrate information sharing into their public sites.

STEP 2: Activity (Here is what you are doing.)

Visit http://www.wiley.com/go/rainer/MIS4e/applytheconcept, and click on the link for Apply the Concept 8.1. This video provides a valuable overview of Web 2.0 technologies. Take notes of the various features that Web 2.0 makes available, and then click on the second link. This link will take you to a CNN Money Web page that provides a rank-order list of the Fortune 500 companies. Visit the Web sites of the top 10 firms, and identify the Web 2.0 technologies they employ on their site.

STEP 3: Deliverable (Here is what you turn in.)

Create a table similar to the one shown below that displays the following information about 5 of the top 10 companies on the CNN Money rankings:

• The company's name
• The company's rank
• The industry (e.g., retail, consulting services, communications)
• A description of the Web 2.0 technologies/applications that each company uses
• A description of the Web 2.0 tools the company does not use

Name	Rank	Industry	Web 2.0 Used	Web 2.0 Not Used

Submit your table to your professor.

8.2 | Fundamentals of Social Computing in Business

Social computing in business, or *social commerce*, refers to the delivery of electronic commerce activities and transactions through social computing. Social commerce also supports social interactions and user contributions, allowing customers to participate actively in the marketing and selling of products and services in online marketplaces and communities. With social commerce, individuals can collaborate online, obtain advice from trusted individuals, and find and purchase goods and services. A few examples of social commerce include:

• Disney allows people to book tickets on Facebook without leaving the social network.

• PepsiCo provides a live notification when its customers are close to physical stores (grocery, restaurants, gas stations) that sell Pepsi products. The company then uses Foursquare to send them coupons and discount information.

- Mountain Dew attracts video game lovers and sports enthusiasts via Dewmocracy contests. The company also encourages the most dedicated community members to contribute ideas on company products.
- Levi's advertises on Facebook by enabling consumers to populate a "shopping cart" based on what their friends think they would like.

Benefits and Risks of Social Commerce

Social commerce offers numerous benefits to both customers and vendors, as described in Table 8.2.

Despite all of its benefits, social computing does involve risks. It is problematic, for example, to advertise a product, brand, or company on social computing Web sites where content is user generated and is not edited or filtered. Companies that employ this strategy must be willing to accept negative reviews and feedback. Of course, negative feedback can be some of the most valuable information that a company receives, if it utilizes this information properly.

Companies that engage in social computing are always concerned with negative posts. For example, when a company creates a Facebook business page, by default the site allows other members of the Web site—potentially including disgruntled customers or unethical competitors—to post notes on the firm's Facebook Wall and to comment on what the firm has posted.

Going further, if the company turns off the feature that lets other users write on its Wall, people may wonder what the company is afraid of. The company will also be eliminating its opportunity to engage in customer conversations, particularly conversations that could market the firm's products and services better than the company could do itself. Similarly, the company could delete posts. However, that policy only encourages the post author to scream even louder about being censored.

Another risk is the 20–80 rule of thumb, which posits that a minority of individuals (20 percent) contribute most of the content (80 percent) to blogs, wikis, social computing Web sites, and so on. For example, in an analysis of thousands of submissions to the news voting site Digg over a three-week time frame, the *Wall Street Journal* reported that roughly 33 percent of the stories that made it to Digg's homepage were submitted by 30 contributors (out of 900,000 registered members).

TABLE 8.2 Potential Benefits of Social Commerce

Benefits to Customers

- Better and faster vendor responses to complaints, because customers can air their complaints in public (on Twitter, Facebook, YouTube)
- Customers can assist other customers (e.g., in online forums).
- Customers' expectations can be met more fully and quickly.
- Customers can easily search, link, chat, and buy while staying on a social network's page.

Benefits to Businesses

- Can test new products and ideas quickly and inexpensively
- Learn a lot about their customers
- Identify problems quickly and alleviate customer anger
- Learn about customers' experiences via rapid feedback
- Increase sales when customers discuss products positively on social networking sites
- Create more effective marketing campaigns and brand awareness
- Use low-cost user-generated content, for example, in marketing campaigns
- Obtain free advertising through viral marketing
- Identify and reward influential brand advocates

Other risks of social computing include:

- Information security concerns
- Invasion of privacy
- Violation of intellectual property and copyright
- Employees' reluctance to participate
- Data leakage of personal information or corporate strategic information
- Poor or biased quality of users' generated content
- Cyberbullying/cyberstalking and employee harassment

Consider Rosetta Stone (www.rosettastone.com), which produces software for language translation. To obtain the maximum possible mileage out of social computing and limit the firm's risks on social media, Rosetta Stone implemented a strategy to control its customer interaction on Facebook. The strategy involves both human intervention and software to help monitor the firm's Facebook presence. Specifically, the software helps to monitor Wall posts and respond to them constructively.

Fans of facebook.com/RosettaStone who post questions on its Wall are likely to receive a prompt answer because the Facebook page is integrated with customer service software from Parature (www.parature.com). The software scans Wall posts and flags those posts that require a company response, as opposed to those in which fans of the company are talking among themselves. Rosetta Stone customer service representatives are also able to post responses to the Wall that are logged in the Parature issue-tracking database.

A new business model has emerged, enabled by social computing and environmental concerns. This business model is called *collaborative consumption.*

Collaborative Consumption

Collaborative consumption is an economic model based on sharing, swapping, trading, or renting products and services, enabling access over ownership. The premise of collaborative consumption is that having access to goods and services is more important than owning them. This new model is transforming social, economic, and environmental practices.

Collaborative consumption is a broad term that includes many collaborative practices, such as collaborative production, crowdfunding, peer-to-peer lending, and others. In collaborative production, users sell the extra power generated from their solar panels back to the utility company's grid to help power someone else's home. Crowdfunding is the practice of funding a project by raising money from a large number of people, typically via the Internet. Peer-to-peer lending is the practice of lending money to unrelated individuals without using a traditional financial institution such as a bank.

Collaborative consumption is a very old concept. We have been bartering and cooperating throughout human history. If we did not have money, we traded time, meals, favors, or personal belongings, and many cultures today do the same. On the Web, the peer-to-peer model started with eBay (www.ebay.com) in 1995. Then Craigslist (www.craigslist.com) began in the late 1990s, followed by Zipcar (www.zipcar.com) in 2000 and Airbnb (www.airbnb.com) in 2007.

Trust is the greatest concern of this new economic model. Sharing works well only when the participants' reputations are involved. Most sharing platforms try to address this issue by creating a self-policing community. Almost all platforms require profiles of both parties, and they feature community rating systems.

Startups such as TrustCloud (http://trustcloud.com) are trying to become the portable reputation system of this new economy. The company has developed an algorithm that collects (if you choose to opt in) your online "data exhaust"—the trail you leave as you engage with others on Facebook, LinkedIn, Twitter, commentary-filled sites like TripAdvisor, and others. It then calculates your reliability, consistency, and responsiveness. The result is a contextual badge that you carry to any Web site, a trust rating similar to the credit rating you have in the "offline" world.

Collaborative consumption does have advantages. Participants cite advantages that include self-management, variety, and the flexibility that comes from being able to set their own schedules. The model can be beneficial for part-time workers, young people such as students, the unemployed, stay-at-home parents, and retired persons. The model allows people to share their underused assets and earn income.

For example, over half of Airbnb hosts in San Francisco said that the service helps them pay their rent and the average RelayRides member makes an extra $250 per month. *Forbes* magazine estimated that through collaborative consumption, people will earn more than $3.5 billion in 2015, a growth rate of 25 percent.

Collaborative consumption has positive environmental impacts. As our population grows, we are using valuable resources—water, food, oil—in a way that is not sustainable. The new model helps us to utilize our natural resources more wisely, by sharing, not owning.

On the other hand, collaborative consumption does have disadvantages. The law and regulatory agencies are trying to keep abreast of the rapidly growing companies in this economy. Consider these examples:

- Without a permit, residents in San Francisco are prohibited from renting for under 30 days (although the practice still occurs).
- New York City passed an "illegal hotel law" in 2010 that prevents people from subletting apartments for less than 29 days, which is preventing Airbnb from expanding its market in the city.
- Uber and Lyft often function as taxi companies, but do not have to follow worker regulations or laws that apply to existing taxi companies because, the services consider their employees to be independent contractors rather than employees.

People working for collaborative consumption services often work seven-day weeks, performing a series of one-off tasks. They have little recourse when the services for which they work change their business models or pay rates. To reduce the risks, workers typically sign up for multiple services. Another disadvantage is that the pay may be less than expected when participants factor in the time spent, expenses, insurance costs, and taxes on self-employment earnings.

Participants have no basic employee benefits or protections. As independent contractors, they do not qualify for employee benefits such as health insurance, disability insurance, payroll deductions for Social Security, retirement savings plans, or unemployment benefits. They do not have the right to organize into a union, meaning that they do not have access to union-based collective bargaining processes. They also do not have the right to due process should a services remove them from its platform. For example, in June 2015, the California labor commission ruled that an Uber driver was an employee and entitled to expenses. Interestingly, the same commission had ruled in 2012 that another Uber driver was an independent contractor.

There are numerous, diverse companies in the collaborative consumption market including:

- Uber (www.uber.com) operates the Uber mobile app, which allows consumers with smartphones to submit a trip request that is sent to Uber drivers who use their own cars.
- Airbnb (www.airbnb.com) is a Web site for people to list, find, and rent lodgings.
- Zipcar (www.zipcar.com) and RelayRides (http://relayrides.com) are car-sharing services.
- Yerdle (https://yerdle.com) is a smartphone app that helps people give and get things for free. They gain credits by giving things away and spend those credits on whatever they need (e.g., clothes, kitchen appliances and tools).
- Skillshare (www.skillshare.com) provides access to top-class tutors very cheaply.
- Tradesy (www.tradesy.com) lets users sell and buy used clothes from well-known brands. The service takes 9 percent of profits.
- JustPark (www.justpark.com) is a London startup that allows users to charge people to use their driveways as a safe, secure parking spot.

- Bla Bla Car (www.blablacar.com) lets you rent out extra seats in your car when you go on a trip.
- Leftover Swap (http://leftoverswap.com) is an app where users can find leftover food to share. This service is important in the United States, where we waste some 30 percent of our food.
- Streetbank (www.streetbank.com) allows users to lend things to your neighbors or borrow things you need to use for a set amount of time.
- Feastly (https://eatfeastly.com) gives users a way to share any type of meal with people in their area.
- Cookening (www.cookening.com), a service available throughout Europe and in New York City, allows travelers to pay to eat with a local person or family to make your trip more authentic.
- Marriott International (www.marriott.com) offers meeting spaces on LiquidSpace (https://liquidspace.com). LiquidSpace is an online marketplace that allows people to rent office space by the hour or the day. Hundreds of Marriott hotels now list meeting spaces, and the program has expanded the company's reach by attracting local businesspeople from surrounding areas.
- FLOOW2 (www.floow2.com), based in the Netherlands, calls itself a "business-to-business sharing marketplace where companies and institutions can share equipment, as well as the skills and knowledge of personnel." The company lists more than 25,000 types of equipment and services in industries such as construction, agriculture, transportation, real estate, and healthcare.

The economic model of collaborative consumption is growing around the world. IT's About Business 8.2 discusses Tujia, the leading vacation-rental Web site in China.

IT's About Business 8.2

MIS Is Tujia the Airbnb of China?

Vacation-rental Web sites are growing in popularity among travelers around the world as they look for cheaper alternatives to hotels, while property owners gain a new source of income. In recent years, tourism has increased rapidly in China, driven by rising personal incomes. To accommodate this trend, Tujia (www.tujia.com) is a Chinese online holiday rentals Web site. There are more than 50 million vacant properties in China, due in part to a growing economy, rapid urbanization, and low borrowing costs. This situation makes China a prime market for Tujia's business model.

Tujia, founded in 2010, lists almost 300,000 properties in 250 locations in China. The startup manages approximately 10,000 properties themselves, with third-party property managers handling the remainder. For example, in Beijing, one Tujia property manager looks after about two dozen apartments in the Central Business District. If someone applies to Tujia to list their property in that area, then the company has its local manager inspect the property, take photos, and then Tujia lists that property. When a customer books a property, Tujia receives a percentage of the rental income.

The company is expanding globally, with approximately 15,000 properties overseas in more than 100 destinations. It simply follows Chinese tourists to their favorite destinations. The most popular overseas destinations for Chinese tourists are Thailand, Indonesia, Taiwan, Hong Kong, Korea, and Japan. As a result, Tujia concentrates on these areas first.

Airbnb (www.airbnb.com) and Tujia have similar business models, connecting home owners with travelers looking for a place to stay. However, there are differences between the two companies. Specifically, the Chinese consumer, and to a larger extent the Asian consumer, is different from Western consumers. For example, Asian consumers tend to think much longer before staying in a stranger's house. Further, Airbnb targets foreigners traveling to China, where Tujia focuses on Chinese travelers traveling within China or out of the country. Another difference is that Tujia works directly with home owners, cleaning and inspecting their properties, and helps real estate developers rent out their surplus inventory.

Tujia has picked up on key differences between Chinese and other Asian travelers and Western travelers. The first is the trust issue. Trust is critical for Chinese and Asian travelers, as the vacation-rental market is in its infancy relative to the United States and other countries.

Virtually no two Tujia vacation properties are the same, unlike hotels, which have a certain amount of standardization that regular guests can trust. To manage the trust issue, Tujia has local teams handling check-in and check-out, as well as inspecting the properties. The teams ensure that all photos of a property are current and accurate. Tujia also reassures its users that when they reserve a property, it will indeed be available. If a property is not available for any reason, Tujia will find other accommodation for that guest.

The second is the expectation on the level of service provided. When Asians travel, they like to be served. Therefore, Tujia tailors its services to Chinese guests.

To compete with hotels, almost all Tujia properties have certain services, such as cleaning. Some properties, such as villas in Qiandao Hu, close to Shanghai that rent for $1,000 per night, offer services rivaling five-star hotels, such as a dedicated butler in each villa.

Tujia lists other properties in tourist locales, such as one property close to Tai Hu, a famous lake in Suzhou. Chinese visit there on vacation, so Tujia offers them bicycles and tours. Many of Tujia's customers travel with families, so the company lists larger properties such as villas that have activities for children. In addition, many Chinese love to cook, so Tujia lists properties with kitchens.

Tujia follows very specific criteria that determine the kind of properties that are listed. In addition to personal inspections, Tujia monitors customer comments very closely and operates an around-the-clock call center for any complaints. Tujia encourages its customers to provide feedback.

The company takes an especially close look at reviews with three stars or less (out of five stars) and at reviews where the customer said "I'm not going to recommend Tujia to my friends" or "I'm not coming back again." In these cases, Tujia tries to follow up with customers, but the company definitely follows up with property owners and managers. Sometimes, Tujia delists such properties or moves them down in the Tujia rankings system. The company tells these owners and managers that if they correct the problems, then their ranking will improve.

Competitor Web sites such as Maiyi and Xiaozhu list less expensive properties, while Tujia focuses on mid- to high-end properties.

Tujia works with Ctrip (http://english.ctrip.com), China's largest online travel agency. If customers access the Chinese version of Ctrip, there is a tab that drives traffic to Tujia's Web site. In addition, Tujia offers car rentals to its customers via Ctrip.

From its founding, Tujia has had to cooperate closely with the Chinese government. In fact, the company has signed agreements with over 160 local governments across the country. For example, Tujia created the vacation rental association in Sanya by working with the government. Therefore, Tujia help set standards for vacation rental properties in the region. In addition, Tujia is hoping that the wish of Chinese Prime Minister Li Keqiang, who said that China should ease restrictions on e-commerce, will come true.

In another round of funding, Tujia raised $300 million in August 2015, bringing its value to approximately $1.3 billion.

Sources: Compiled from N. Mahajan, "How Tujia, 'China's Airbnb', Is Different from Airbnb," *CKGSB Knowledge*, August 12, 2015; L. Davidson, "Cracking China Just Got Harder for Airbnb as Rival Tujia Lands $300M Funding," *The Telegraph*, August 3, 2015; S. Millward, "China's Airbnb-esque Tujia Is a New Startup Unicorn after $300M Funding," *Techinasia*, August 3, 2015; A. Tsiang, "Chinese Property-Rental Site Tujia Raises $300 Million," *The New York Times*, August 3, 2015; L. Chen and E. Chan, "China's Airbnb Valued at More than $1 Billion after Funding," *Bloomberg Business*, August 2, 2015; J. Osawa, "'China's Airbnb' Rests Easy over $1.3 Billion Valuation," *AsiaOne Business News*, July 30, 2015; "Tujia.com, The Chinese Airbnb, Seeks International Growth," *Hospitality*, April 8, 2015; S. Cheung, "China's Answer to Airbnb, Tujia.com, Raises $100M," *Venture Capital Dispatch*, June 18, 2014; www.tujia.com, accessed August 13, 2015.

Questions

1. Visit Airbnb's Web site and learn about the company's services. Now, describe the differences in the services provided by Airbnb and Tujia.

2. As Airbnb attempts to expand in China and Tujia attempts to expand internationally, describe which company might be more successful and why.

Companies are engaged in many types of social commerce activities, including shopping, advertising, market research, customer relationship management, and human resource management. In the next sections of this chapter, you will learn about each social commerce activity.

Before you go on...

1. Briefly describe the benefits of social commerce to customers.

2. Briefly describe the risks of social commerce to businesses.

3. What are the benefits of collaborative consumption to customers?

4. What are the benefits and risks of collaborative consumption to participants (i.e., workers)?

Apply the Concept 8.2

LEARNING OBJECTIVE 8.2 Describe the benefits and risks of social commerce to companies.

STEP 1: Background

Collaborative consumption has been fueled by social networks because it allows owners to share their goods with those who

would rather rent something than permanently own it. Sharing also makes it cheaper to own because the cost of ownership is spread across many users.

Uber (www.uber.com) allows vehicle owners to share their vehicles with others. In the beginning, Uber involved giving someone a ride for a fee, but today Uber is also delivering goods using their UberRUSH service.

STEP 2: Activity

Visit http://www.wiley.com/go/rainer/MIS4e/applytheconcept and read over Uber's information about the UberRUSH delivery service. There is an introductory video on their homepage. If it is unavailable, you can find it on YouTube at http://www.wiley.com/go/rainer/MIS4e/applytheconcept. Watch the video about the service and take note of the applications they present in the video.

STEP 3: Deliverable

At the time of this writing, UberRUSH is available only San Francisco, Chicago, and New York. Why do you think they started in such heavily populated areas? What advantages would a collaborative consumption business model have in a heavily populated area? What disadvantages would they face? In what ways might a college campus be a prime location to introduce users to collaborative consumption services such as Uber or UberRUSH? Create a table that compares the advantages and disadvantages of collaborative consumption for delivery services. Submit your table to your instructor.

8.3 | Social Computing in Business: Shopping

Social shopping is a method of electronic commerce that takes all of the key aspects of social networks—friends, groups, voting, comments, discussions, reviews, and others—and focuses them on shopping. Social shopping helps shoppers connect with one another based on tastes, location, age, gender, and other selected attributes.

The nature of shopping is changing, especially shopping for brand-name clothes and related items. For example, popular brands such as Gap, Shopbop, InStyle, and Lisa Klein are joining communities on Stylehive (www.stylehive.com) to help promote the season's latest fashion collections. Shoppers are using sites like ThisNext (www.thisnext.com) to create profiles and blogs about their favorite products in social communities. Shoppers can tag each item, so that all items become searchable. Moreover, searching within these Web sites can yield results targeted specifically to individual customers.

There are several methods to shop socially. You will learn about each of them in the next section.

Ratings, Reviews, and Recommendations

Prior to making a purchase, customers typically collect information such as what brand to buy, from which vendor, and at what price. Online customers obtain this information via shopping aids such as comparison agents and Web sites such as Epinions (www.epinions.com). Today, customers also use social networking to guide their purchase decisions. They are increasingly utilizing ratings, reviews, and recommendations from friends, fans, followers, and experienced customers.

Ratings, *reviews*, and *recommendations* are usually available in social shopping. In addition to seeing what is already posted, shoppers have an opportunity to contribute their own ratings and reviews and to discuss ratings and reviews posted by other shoppers (see Figure 8.3). The ratings and reviews come from the following sources:

- *Customer ratings and reviews:* Integrated into the vendor's Web page, a social network page, a customer review site, or in customer feeds (e.g., Amazon, iTunes, Buzzillions, Epinions).
- *Expert ratings and reviews:* Views from an independent authority (e.g., Metacritic).
- *Sponsored reviews:* Paid-for reviews (e.g., SponsoredReviews, PayPerPost).
- *Conversational marketing:* Individuals converse via e-mail, blog, live chat, discussion groups, and tweets. Monitoring these conversations yields rich data for market research and customer service.

As one example, Maui Jim (www.mauijim.com), the sunglass company, employed favorable word-of-mouth marketing as a key sales driver. The company uses Bazaarvoice's Ratings &

MKT

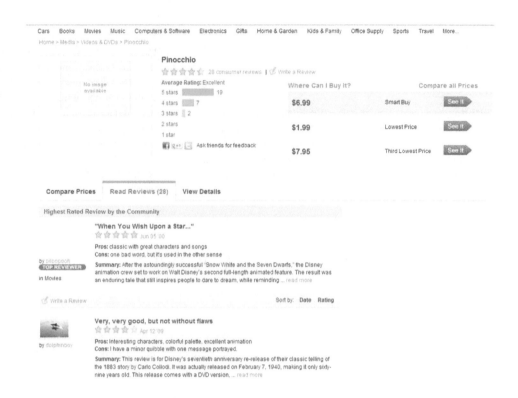

Reviews to allow customers to contribute five-point ratings and authentic product reviews on the company's entire line of sunglasses and accessories. In effect, Maui Jim extended customers' word-of-mouth reviews across the Web.

Maui Jim encourages its customers to share their candid opinions on the style, fit, and performance of all of its sunglass models. To accomplish this goal, the company integrates customer reviews into its Web site search function to ensure that shoppers who are interested in a particular product will see that product's rating in the search results. Customer response to this rating system has been overwhelmingly positive.

Social recommendation Web sites such as ShopSocially (www.shopsocially.com), Blippy (www.blippy.com), and Swipely (www.swipely.com) encourage conversations about purchases. The product recommendations are submitted by users' friends and acquaintances and arguably are more trustworthy than reviews posted by strangers.

ThisNext (www.thisnext.com) is a Web site where people recommend their favorite products to others. The site blends two powerful elements of real-world shopping: word-of-mouth recommendations from trusted sources and the ability to browse products in a way that naturally leads to discovery.

Regarding recommendations, a *filter bubble* is a result of a search in which a Web site algorithm guesses what a user would like to see based on information about that user, such as location and past searches. As a result, users see information that reinforces their viewpoints. For example, one user who searched Google for "BP" received investment news for British Petroleum. Another user searched for that exact term and received information about the Deepwater Horizon oil spill.

We must be careful when our search results begin to reflect only our thinking on a subject. For example, if you search Amazon for only best-selling books in science fiction, you may miss out on best-selling books in many other genres.

Group Shopping

Group shopping Web sites such as Groupon (www.groupon.com) and LivingSocial (www.living-social.com, see **Figure 8.4**) offer major discounts or special deals during a short time frame. Group buying is closely associated with special deals (flash sales).

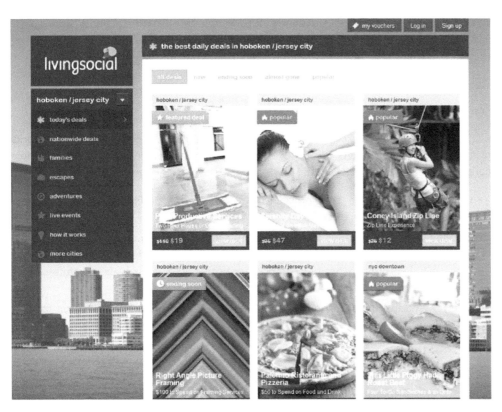

FIGURE 8.4 LivingSocial (www
.livingsocial.com) is a popular example of a group shopping web site.

People who sign up with LivingSocial receive e-mails that offer deals at, for example, a
restaurant, a spa, or an event in a given city. They can click on either "Today's Deal" or "Past
Deal" (some past deals can still be active). They can also click on an icon and receive the deal
the next day. Customers who purchase a deal receive a unique link to share with their friends. If
a customer convinces three or more people to buy that specific deal using his or her link, then
the customer's deal is free.

Individuals can also shop together virtually in real time. In this process, shoppers log on to
a Web site and then contact their friends and family. Everyone then shops online at the same
time. Some real-time shopping providers, such as DoTogether (www.dotogether.com) and Wet
Seal (www.wetseal.com), have integrated their shopping service directly into Facebook. Customers log in to Facebook, install the firm's app, and then invite their friends to join them on a
virtual retail shopping experience.

Shopping Communities and Clubs

Shopping clubs host sales for their members that last just a few days and usually feature luxury
brands at heavily discounted prices. Club organizers host three to seven sales per day, usually
via e-mail messages that entice club members to shop at more than 70 percent off retail—but
quickly, before supplies run out.

Luxury brands effectively partner with online shopping clubs to dispose of special-run,
sample, overstock, or liquidation goods. These clubs are rather exclusive, which prevents the
brands' images from being diminished. Examples are Beyond the Rack (www.beyondtherack.
com), Gilt Groupe (www.gilt.com), Rue La La (www.ruelala.com), and One King's Lane (www
.onekingslane.com).

Kaboodle (www.kaboodle.com) is another example of a shopping community. Kaboodle
is a free service that lets users collect information from the Web and store it on a Kaboodle list
that they can share with other shoppers. Kaboodle simplifies shopping by making it easier for
people to find items they want in a catalog and by allowing users to share recommendations

with one another using Kaboodle lists and groups. People can also use Kaboodle lists for planning vacations, sharing research for work and school, sharing favorite bands with friends, and basically everything else they might want to collect and share information about.

Social Marketplaces and Direct Sales

Social marketplaces act as online intermediaries that harness the power of social networks for introducing, buying, and selling products and services. A social marketplace helps members market their own creations (see Etsy in **Figure 8.5**). Other examples are as follows:

- Craigslist (www.craigslist.com) provides online classifieds in addition to supporting social activities such as meetings and events.
- Fotolia (www.fotolia.com) is a social marketplace for the community of creative people who enjoy sharing, learning, and expressing themselves through images, forums, and blogs; members provide royalty-free stock images that other individuals and professionals can legally buy and share.
- Flipsy (www.flipsy.com) can be used by anyone to list, buy, and sell books, music, movies, and games.

Before you go on...

1. Prior to making a purchase, customers typically Why are ratings, reviews, and recommendations so important to potential customers?
2. Define collaborative consumption, and describe how collaborative consumption is a "green" phenomenon.

FIGURE 8.5 Etsy (www.etsy.com) is a social marketplace for all handmade or vintage items.

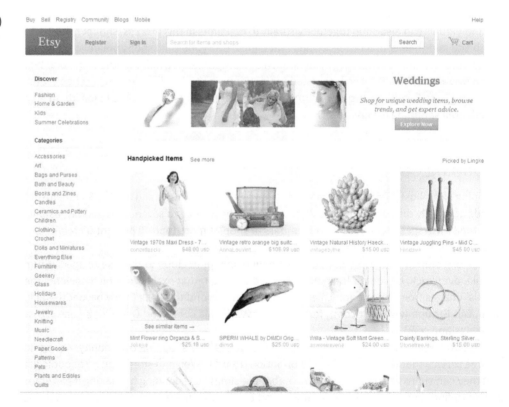

Apply the Concept 8.3

LEARNING OBJECTIVE 8.3 Identify the methods used for shopping socially.

STEP 1: Background

Section 8.3 defines shopping socially as taking the key aspects of social networks (e.g., groups, reviews, discussions) and applying them to shopping. This phenomenon is not new. People have shopped socially for years, through general conversation.

Today, most consumers conduct a lot of research before they make a purchase by reading reviews posted by other customers. Recently, however, the validity of these reviews has been questioned. As you learn about social shopping, you should also become aware of the potential fraud that takes place online.

STEP 2: Activity

Go to http://www.wiley.com/go/rainer/MIS4e/applytheconcept, and click on the link for Apply the Concept 8.3. This link will take you to an article from the *New York Times* and one from the *Denver Post*. Both articles deal with the issue of falsified recommendations and ratings.

Talk to some of your classmates about this topic, and record their feedback. How did they respond to the fact that product ratings may not be legitimate? Ask them the following questions:

- What star rating do you rely on when you are considering a product?
- Do you read reviews or simply notice the number of stars?
- If you read reviews, do you read only the good ones, only the bad ones, or a mixture of both?
- Do you rely on reviews more than a third-party company such as *Consumer Reports*?

STEP 3: Deliverable

Considering the material you have read and your conversations with your classmates, identify various methods of shopping socially and discuss the role that trust plays in each method. Prepare a paper or presentation for your professor documenting what you have learned.

8.4 Social Computing in Business: Marketing

Marketing can be defined as the process of building profitable customer relationships by creating value for customers and capturing value in return. There are many components to a marketing campaign, including (1) define your target audience; (2) develop your message (i.e., how you will solve their problem); (3) decide on how you will deliver your message (e.g., e-mail, snail mail, Web advertising, social networks); and (4) follow up. Social computing is particularly useful for two marketing processes: advertising and market research.

MKT

Advertising

Social advertising refers to advertising formats that make use of the social context of the user viewing the ad. Social advertising is the first form of advertising to leverage forms of social influence such as peer pressure and friend recommendations and likes.

Many experts believe advertising is the solution to the challenge of making money from social networking sites and social commerce sites. Advertisers have long noted the large number of visitors on social networks and the amount of time they spend there. As a result, they are willing to pay to place ads and run promotions on social networks. Advertisers now post ads on all major social networking Web sites.

Most ads in social commerce consist of branded content paid for by advertisers. These ads belong to two major categories: *social advertisements* (or *social ads*) and *social apps*. Social advertisements are ads placed in paid-for media space on social media networks. Social apps are branded online applications that support social interactions and user contributions (e.g., Nike+).

Viral marketing—that is, word-of-mouth advertising—lends itself especially well to social networking. For example, Stormhoek Vineyards (www.stormhoek.com) initiated a marketing campaign by offering bloggers a free bottle of wine. Within six months, roughly 100 of these bloggers had posted voluntary comments—the majority of them positive—about the wine on their blogs. In turn these comments were read by other bloggers.

There are other innovative methods to advertise in social media. Consider the following:

- Use a company Facebook page, including a store that attracts fans and lets them "meet" other customers. Then, advertise in your Facebook store.
- Tweet business success stories to your customers.
- Integrate ads into YouTube videos.
- Use native advertising. *Native advertising* is a sales pitch that fits into the flow of the information being shown. Many publishers view native advertising as risky because it has the potential to erode the public's trust. (See Closing Case 2).

Market Research

MKT

Traditionally, marketing professionals used demographics compiled by market research firms as one of their primary tools to identify and target potential customers. Obtaining this information was time-consuming and costly, because marketing professionals had to ask potential customers to provide it. Today, however, members of social networks provide this information voluntarily on their pages! (Think about all the information that you provide on your favorite social networking Web sites.) Because of the open nature of social networking, merchants can easily find their customers, see what they do online, and learn who their friends are.

This information provides a new opportunity to assess markets in near real time. Word-of-mouth has always been one of the most powerful marketing methods—more often than not, people use products that their friends like and recommend. Social media sites can provide this type of data for numerous products and services.

Companies are utilizing social computing tools to obtain feedback from customers. This trend is referred to as *conversational marketing*. These tools enable customers to supply feedback via blogs, wikis, online forums, and social networking sites. Again, customers are providing much of this feedback to companies voluntarily and for free.

Social computing not only generates faster and cheaper results than traditional focus groups but also fosters closer customer relationships. For example, Dell Computer operates a feedback Web site called IdeaStorm that allows customers to suggest and vote on improvements in its offerings (see Figure 8.6).

FIGURE 8.6 Customers share their ideas and feedback with Dell via IdeaStorm (www.ideastorm .com).

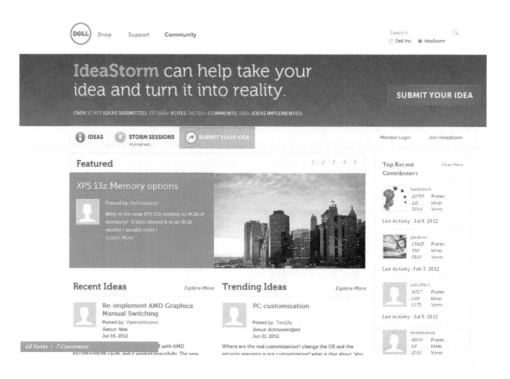

Retailers are aware that customers, especially younger ones, not only want to be heard but also want to know whether other customers agree with them. Consequently, retailers are increasingly opening up their Web sites to customers, allowing them to post product reviews, ratings, and, in some cases, photos and videos.

As a result of this strategy, customer reviews are emerging as prime locations for online shoppers to visit. Approximately one-half of consumers consult reviews before making an online purchase, and almost two-thirds are more likely to purchase from a site that offers ratings and reviews.

Using social computing for market research is not restricted to businesses. Customers also enjoy the capabilities that social computing offers when they are shopping.

Conducting Market Research Using Social Networks

Customer sentiment expressed on Twitter, Facebook, and similar sites represents an incredibly valuable source of information for companies. Customer activities on social networking sites generate huge amounts of data that must be analyzed, so that management can conduct better marketing campaigns and improve their product design and their service offerings. The monitoring, collection, and analysis of socially generated data, and the resultant strategic decisions are combined in a process known as social intelligence.

MKT

An example of social intelligence is Wendy's International (www.wendys.com), which uses software to sift through the more than 500,000 customer messages the fast-food chain collects each year. Using Clarabridge (www.clarabridge.com) text analytics software, Wendy's analyzes comments from its online notes, e-mails, receipt-based surveys, and social media. Prior to adopting this software, the company used a combination of spreadsheets and keyword searches to review comments in what it describes as a slow and expensive manual approach. In contrast, the new software enables Wendy's to track customer experiences at the store level within minutes.

MIS

Social networks provide excellent sources of valuable information for market research. In this section you will see illustrative examples of how to use Facebook, Twitter, and LinkedIn for market research.

Using Facebook for Market Research. There are several ways to use Facebook for market research. Consider the following examples:

- Obtain feedback from your Facebook fans (and their friends if possible) on advertising campaigns, market research, and so on. It is the equivalent of holding a free focus group.

- Test-market your messages. Provide two or three options, and ask fans which one they prefer and why.

- Use Facebook for survey invitations (i.e., to recruit participants). Essentially, turn Facebook into a giant panel, and ask users to participate in a survey. Facebook offers a self-service model for displaying ads, which can function as invitations to take a survey. Facebook also allows you to target your audience very specifically based on traditional demographic criteria such as age and gender.

Using Twitter for Market Research. Your customers, your prospects, and industry thought leaders all use Twitter, making it a rich source of instantly updated information. Consider the following examples:

- Visit Twitter Search (www.twitter.com/search). Enter a company's Twitter name. Not only can you follow what the company is saying, you can also follow what everyone is saying to them. Monitoring replies to your competitors and their employees will help you develop your own Twitter strategy by enabling you to observe (a) what your competitors are doing and, more importantly, (b) what people think about them. You can also follow the company's response to this feedback.

- Take advantage of the tools that enable you to find people in the industries in which they operate. Use search.twitter.com to monitor industry-specific keywords. Check out Twellow (www.twellow.com). This site automatically categorizes a Twitter user into one to three industries based on that person's bio and tweets.

- Do you want to know what topic is on most people's minds today? If so, then review the chart on TweetStats (www.tweetstats.com). It will show you the most frequently used words in all of Tweetdom, so you can be a part of those conversations.
- An increasing number of companies are utilizing Twitter to solicit information from customers and to interact with them. Examples are Dell (connecting with customers), JetBlue (learning about customers), Teusner Wines (gathering feedback, sharing information), and Pepsi (rapid response time in dealing with complaints).

Using LinkedIn for Market Research. Post a question (e.g., solicit advice) regarding the topic or issue you are interested in. You may obtain a better result if you go to a specific LinkedIn group.

Before you go on…

1. Is social advertising more effective than advertising without a social component? Why or why not?
2. Describe how marketing professionals use social networks to perform marketing research.

Apply the Concept 8.4

LEARNING OBJECTIVE 8.4 Discuss innovative ways to use social networking sites for advertising and market research.

STEP 1: Background

Section 8.4 presented the major uses of social computing in advertising and market research. Social advertising is simply a way of presenting information to potential customers via a social platform. Social market research makes use of these same social platforms to examine the ongoing communication between the company and its customer community for information that the company can use to improve products or services.

STEP 2: Activity

Visit http://www.wiley.com/go/rainer/MIS4e/applytheconcept and find the two links. First, read the article about "20 Companies You

Should Be Following on Social Media." Some of these companies are not specifically related to advertising or market research, but you will still enjoy learning about them. Next, read the article on Digimind.com about the innovative ways people are using social media as a rich pool of information.

STEP 3: Deliverable

After reviewing the examples in the articles linked in Step 2, prepare a discussion of the top three innovative ways that these companies are using social networking for advertising and the top three innovative ways that companies are using the information available on social networks as a mechanism for learning about their customers. Submit your discussion to your instructor.

8.5 | Social Computing in Business: Customer Relationship Management

The customer service profession has undergone a significant transformation, both in the ways that customer service professionals conduct business and in the ways that customers adapt to interacting with companies in a newly connected environment. Social computing has vastly altered both the expectations of customers and the capabilities of corporations in the area of customer relationship management. (We discuss customer relationship management in detail in Chapter 12.)

Customers are now incredibly empowered. Companies are closely monitoring social computing not only because they are mindful of the negative comments posted by social network members but also because they perceive an opportunity to involve customers proactively to reduce problems through improved customer service.

Empowered customers know how to use the wisdom and power of crowds and communities to their benefit. These customers choose how they interact with companies and brands, and they have elevated expectations concerning their experiences with a company. They are actively involved with businesses, not just as purchasers but also as advocates and influencers. As a result, businesses must respond to customers quickly and appropriately. Fortunately, social computing provides many opportunities for businesses to do just that, thereby offering businesses the opportunity to turn disgruntled customers into champions for the firm.

Consider this example: Papa John's Pizza fired a cashier at one of its New York restaurants and apologized to an Asian-American customer for a receipt that identified her as "lady chinky eyes." Minhee Cho, a communications manager at the nonprofit investigative journalism group ProPublica, posted a photo of the receipt on her Twitter account, and it was viewed almost 200,000 times in a single day. John Schnatter, chairman and CEO of Papa John's, immediately posted an apology on Facebook. In his apology, he asserted that he had apologized personally to Ms. Cho as well.

An interesting way to empower customers is occurring in the publishing industry. IT's About Business 8.3 shows how Wattpad enables readers to actually participate in the development of a work of fiction.

IT's About Business 8.3

MIS Wattpad Empowers Readers

Today's authors have many options to publish their work. Two of the most common are traditional publishing and self-publishing.

In traditional publishing, authors complete their manuscripts and submit proposal letters to publishing houses (or have a literary agent do this for them, if they can obtain the services of an agent.) An editor reads the manuscript and decides to either reject it, leaving the author free to offer it to another publisher), or to publish it. If the decision is to publish the manuscript, the house buys the rights from the author and puts up the money to edit, design, and market the book. The publishing house pays authors royalties on the number of books sold.

The Internet then enabled authors to publish their own books. One of the most common ways to self-publish is through Amazon, through its self-publishing platform, Kindle Direct. Authors upload their books digitally to Amazon's Web site. The Amazon team, analyzing the company's massive customer databases, designs e-mail and Kindle marketing campaigns and selects key words for Amazon's search engine. In most cases, Amazon handles distribution and payment processing. Amazon sells the majority of its books as e-books through Kindle, but also prints paperback books on demand.

Typically, self-published authors upload their books for free to the Amazon site. Authors receive a percentage of the sale price of each book, which is usually 70 percent.

Now, technology is enabling a new way to write and market works of fiction. Serialized fiction is a work published in sequential installments. Serialized fiction is writing repurposed for a mobile world, where readers' attention is fragmentary. Storytelling app Wattpad (www.wattpad.com), the leader in this new

storytelling environment, has more than two million authors who create an average of 100,000 items per day for 20 million readers.

Wattpad is a social reading platform and writing community in which authors post articles, stories, fiction, and poems, either online or through the mobile app. This process enables authors to make their creative works available to a larger number of readers. Readers are able to comment and like stories. Wattpad is free to readers and does not pay its authors.

The primary goal for Wattpad authors is to gain a fan base. After that, the writer must keep them coming back for more. The writers accomplish this goal by regularly uploading new work and by communicating directly with readers. Having many fans is critical because traditional publishers look more favorably on an author with a manuscript and 15,000 fans, than on an author with only a manuscript. Wattpad has caught the attention of the traditional publishing industry, which is looking for the next J. K. Rowling in its midst. Publishers are also picking up tips from Wattpad on how to boost engagement with readers.

Sometimes the fans help shape the story. Readers can send a private message to the author, become an official fan, vote in favor of a work, or suggest actors to play the roles of certain characters if the story were turned into a movie.

Another way in which Wattpad differs from the traditional publishing industry is that the stories are often first drafts, not having been smoothed with rewriting or editing. There are practical reasons for this process. For one thing, the prose is written as spontaneously as possible, to take advantage of the immediacy of the electronic medium. For another thing, English is a second language for much of Wattpad's international audience, so the spontaneous prose is more direct and therefore easier to understand.

There are few Hemingways among Wattpad authors, who admit they do not make sacrifices for their art or spend hours coming up with just the right word or phrase. Young women are the target audience for the most popular categories of works, which include romance, vampire fiction, and mysteries. Wattpad writers are not paid for their work.

Two examples show the value of Wattpad to its authors. Basically, if authors are successful enough on Wattpad, they might be considered by traditional publishing houses. Consider Wattpad author, Anna Todd. Several times a week, she uses Wattpad to publish a new installment of "After," the story of Tessa and Harry. Within seconds of posting, readers are already commenting on the new episode. By the next day, there are usually some 10,000 comments. One of the ways that Wattpad can make money is by representing popular authors as their agent. Wattpad is shopping for book and movie deals for "After" on behalf of Ms. Todd.

Another Wattpad author, Ali Novak, has published four novels on the app. She was so overwhelmed with fan support that she's had to cut back on engaging with readers. Ms. Novak hit the self-publishing jackpot in 2015 when a traditional publisher, Sourcebooks, published her most popular novel, "My Life with the Walter Boys," whose heroine moves in with a family with 12 boys, in paperback.

Wattpad generates a little revenue, mostly from advertising, although it has received $46 million in venture capital funding.

Sources: Compiled from N. Shapiro, "The Perks, Pitfalls, and Paradoxes of Amazon Publishing," *Seattle Weekly News*, November 4, 2014; D. Jacobs, "How to Self-Publish Your Book Through Amazon," *Forbes*, April 25, 2014; J. Koetsier, "Social Reading Platform Wattpad Announces Massive $46M Financing Round," *Venturebeat*, April 8, 2014; D. Streitfeld, "Web Fiction, Serialized and Social," *The New York Times*, March 23, 2014; G. Bello, "PW Select December 2012: Wattpad Revolutionizes Online Storytelling," P*ublishers Weekly*, December 21, 2012; P. Sansevieri, "Understanding How the Traditional Publishing Model Works," *The Huffington Post*, July 5, 2011; www.wattpad.com, accessed August 12, 2015.

Questions

1. Describe the social computing aspects of Wattpad.
2. What are other ways that Wattpad might generate revenue?
3. What are possible disadvantages for Wattpad authors?

Before you go on…

1. Discuss why social computing is so important in customer relationship management.
2. Describe how social computing improves customer service.

Apply the Concept 8.5

LEARNING OBJECTIVE 8.5 Describe how social computing improves customer service.

STEP 1: Background

Social customer relationship management involves using social networks to maintain customer loyalty. One company that employs this strategy quite skillfully is ZAGG (Zealous About Great Gadgets; www.zagg.com). ZAGG makes and sells accessories for mobile devices such as smartphones and tablets. To help sell its products, the company has developed one of the best social customer relationship management plans around.

When ZAGG develops a new product, it not only posts notes about the product on its social networking page, but it also involves customers in the process. For example, when ZAGG was releasing its ZAGGFolio for the iPad, the company allowed fans to vote on the colors of the new product.

ZAGG is also proficient at monitoring the social network for product-related issues. It is not uncommon for a customer to complain and then receive feedback from a ZAGG employee. Not only does the company retain that individual customer, but it also develops a sense of trust with all of its customers, who are confident they would receive the same treatment.

STEP 2: Activity

Go to http://www.wiley.com/go/rainer/MIS4e/applytheconcept, and click on the link to ZAGG's Web site. At the bottom of the page you will find a link to all of the company's social networks. Visit their Facebook page and review their timeline. Search for customer complaints and for how the company deals with them. Did you find a customer representative present on the social networking site? Does the site offer any competitions? Polls? Giveaways? Can you reverse-engineer the company's social customer relationship management methodology?

STEP 3: Deliverable

Imagine that you are a marketing manager, and you have been selected to present a report to the president to describe how social computing improves customer service. Create the outline that you would use to make your points and present it to the class and to your instructor.

8.6 | Social Computing in Business: Human Resource Management

Human resource (HR) departments in many organizations use social computing applications outside their organizations (recruiting) and inside their organizations (employee development). For example, Deloitte Touche Tohmatsu (www.deloitte.com) created a social network to assist its HR managers in downsizing and regrouping teams.

`HRM`

Recruiting

Both recruiters and job seekers are moving to online social networks as recruiting platforms. Enterprise recruiters are scanning online social networks, blogs, and other social resources to identify and find information about potential employees. If job seekers are online and active, there is a good chance that they will be seen by recruiters. In addition, on social networks there are many passive job seekers—people who are employed but would take a better job if one appeared. So, it is important that both active and passive job seekers maintain online profiles that accurately reflect their background and skills. Closing Case 1 takes a look at the rewards and the difficulties inherent in the online recruiting process. It also provides some tips to assist you in a job search.

In another example, one HR director uses the HR social media management software Bullhorn Reach (www.bullhornreach.com), which allows her to post jobs to eight different social networks simultaneously. Bullhorn Reach also enables her to analyze metrics that measure the effectiveness of her social recruiting efforts.

Onboarding

Onboarding is how new employees acquire the necessary knowledge, skills, and behaviors to become effective members of the organization. Through the use of social media, new hires can learn what to expect in their first few days on the job and find answers to common questions. Because they are available inside the company's firewall, these social communities can provide detailed information about corporate policies, as well as giving employees the opportunity to complete necessary forms online. These communities also provide introductory training, such as workplace safety information and how to use enterprise applications.

Employee Development

Human resource managers know that the best strategy to enable, encourage, and promote employee development is to build relationships with employees. To this end, a number of HR professionals are using enterprise social tools such as Chatter (www.salesforce.com/chatter), Yammer (www.yammer.com), and Tibbr (www.tibbr.com) to tap into the wisdom of every employee. These tools help connect employees to work efficiently across organizations and to collaborate on sales opportunities, campaigns, and projects. They help companies simplify workflows and capture new ideas. They enable HR managers to find subject matter experts within the organization, recommending relevant people for every project team, sales team, and other functions.

As HR managers learn more about employees' skills, expertise, and passions through such tools, they can better motivate them, thereby helping them become more engaged and excited about their work. Employees can then be better rewarded for their expertise.

Another area of employee development is training. A large percentage of the time and expense of employee education and learning management can be minimized by utilizing e-learning and interactive social learning tools. These tools help create connections among learners, instructors, and information. Companies find that these tools facilitate knowledge transfer within departments and across teams. Examples of these tools are Moodle (http://moodle.com), Joomia (www.joomia.org), and Bloomfire (www.bloomfire.com).

In 2015, LinkedIn acquired Lynda.com (www.lynda.com), an online education company offering thousands of video courses in software, creative, and business skills. The company produces video tutorials taught by industry experts. Members of Lynda have unlimited access to watch the videos.

With this acquisition, LinkedIn plans to incorporate job certifications and training into its offerings. One LinkedIn executive noted that a LinkedIn user could be looking for a job, immediately see the skills necessary for that job, and then be prompted to take the relevant and accredited course on Lynda that will help him or her acquire those skills and land the job.

Finding a Job

The other side of organizational recruiting are those people looking for jobs. Let's say you want to find a job. Like the majority of job hunters, you will probably conduct at least part of your search online because the vast majority of entry-level positions in the United States are now listed only online. Job sites are the fastest, least expensive, and most efficient method to connect employers with potential employees.

Today, job searchers use traditional job sites and social networks such as LinkedIn. Applicants like you have helped LinkedIn raise its market share in job searches from 4.7 percent in 2010 to more than 12 percent by early 2015.

To find a job, your best bet is to begin with LinkedIn (www.linkedin.com), which has roughly 165 million members. You should definitely have a profile on LinkedIn, which, by the way, is free. (See the bulleted list that follows for mistakes to avoid on your LinkedIn profile.)

LinkedIn's success comes from its ability to accurately identify its market segment. The company's automated approach does not lend itself well to the upper tier of the job market—for example, CEO searches—where traditional face-to-face searches continue to be the preferred strategy. At the other end of the spectrum—that is, low-paying, low-skill jobs such as cashiers and truck drivers—job boards provide faster results. LinkedIn targets the vast sweet spot between these two extremes, helping to fill high-skill jobs that pay anywhere from $50,000 to $250,000 or more per year. This is the spot you will likely occupy when you graduate.

A number of job-search companies are competing with LinkedIn. These companies are trying to create better-targeted matching systems that leverage social networking functionality. These companies include Monster (www.monster.com), Simply Hired (www.simplyhired.com), Career Builder (www.careerbuilder.com), Indeed (www.indeed.com), Jobvite (http://recruiting.jobvite.com), Dice Open Web (www.dice.com/openweb), and many others.

The most important secret to making online job search sites work for you is to use them carefully. Job coaches advise you to spend 80 percent of your day networking and directly contacting the people in charge of jobs you want. Devote another 10 percent to headhunters. Spend only the remaining 10 percent of your time online.

Here is how to make your time online count. To start with, as you saw above, you should have a profile on LinkedIn. The following list shows you the mistakes NOT to make on your LinkedIn profile.

- Do have a current, professional picture. (No dogs, no spouses, no babies, etc.)
- Do make certain your LinkedIn Status is correct and current.
- Do join groups related to your field of study or even to your personal interests.
- Do list an accurate skill set. Do not embellish.
- Do not use the standard connection request. Do some research on that person and tailor your connection request to that person.
- Do not neglect LinkedIn's privacy settings. When you have a job and are looking for another one, you will want to be discreet. You can set your privacy settings so that your boss does not see that you are looking for opportunities.
- Do not skip the Summary. The Summary is a concise way of selling yourself. Write it in the first person.

- Do not eliminate past jobs or volunteer work.
- Do not say you have worked with someone when you have not.

Next, access the job sites such as those listed above. These sites list millions of jobs and they make it easy to narrow your search using filters. These filters include title, company name, location, and many others. Indeed allows you to search within a specific salary range. SimplyHired lets you sort for friendly, socially responsible, and even dog-friendly workplaces.

These sites have advanced search options. Try plugging in the name of a company you might want to work for or an advanced degree that qualifies you for specialized work. For example, you could enter "CFA" if you are a certified financial analyst or "LEED" if you are a building engineer with expertise in environmental efficiency.

SimplyHired has a useful tool called "Who do I know." If you have a LinkedIn profile, then this tool will instantly display your LinkedIn contacts with connections to various job listings. "Who do I know" also syncs with Facebook.

One more trick to using the aggregators: Configure them to deliver listings to your inbox. Set up an e-mail alert that delivers new job postings to you every day.

You should also search for niche sites that are specific to your field. For technology-related jobs, for instance, Dice (www.dice.com) has a strong reputation. For nonprofit jobs, try Idealist (www.idealist.org). For government jobs, the U.S. government's site is an excellent resource: www.usajobs.gov.

One more great online resource is Craigslist (www.craigslist.com). It is one site the aggregators do not tap. Craigslist focuses on local listings, and it is especially useful for entry-level jobs and internships.

Beyond locating listings for specific jobs, career coaches contend that job sites can be a resource for keywords and phrases that you can pull from job descriptions and include in your résumé, cover letters, and e-mails. Use the language from a job description in your cover letter.

Web sites like Vault (www.vault.com), Monster, and CareerBuilder provide some helpful career tips. Vault, in particular, offers very useful career guides.

The bottom line: It is critical to extend most of your efforts *beyond* an online search.

Before you go on...

1. Explain why LinkedIn has become so important in the recruiting process.
2. If you are looking for a job, what is the major problem with restricting your search to social networks?

Apply the Concept 8.6

LEARNING OBJECTIVE 8.6 Discuss different ways in which human resource managers make use of social computing.

STEP 1: Background

Social human resource management is redefining the ways we search and apply for jobs and make hiring decisions. Going digital was a natural step, but it was also an awkward one. When position announcements went from the bulletin board and local newspaper to Monster.com, the number of positions and applicants exploded. We are so connected today, that it is impossible to go back. After you graduate, you will no doubt use social networks to find and apply for jobs.

STEP 2: Activity

Visit http://www.wiley.com/go/rainer/MIS4e/applytheconcept, and click on the first link for Apply the Concept 8.6. This link will

take you to LinkedIn, a professional social network. Create a profile that includes the college you currently attend. Connect to your classmates as they also complete this activity. You never know when you will need to call on one of these individuals.

Next, search the Web for "Job Search Websites," and see which ones will allow you to connect with your LinkedIn profile. As you connect with these professional sites, consider the differences between a professional and a personal social network.

STEP 3: Deliverable

In a paper, discuss the various ways in which human resources managers can make use of social computing and how you can best present yourself online. Present your paper to your instructor.

What's in IT for me?

ACCT For the Accounting Major

Audit teams use social networking technologies internally to stay in touch with team members who are working on multiple projects. These technologies serve as a common channel of communications. For example, an audit team manager can create a group, include his or her team members as subscribers, and then push information regarding projects to all members at once. Externally, these technologies are useful in interfacing with clients and other third parties for whom the firm and its staff provide services.

FIN For the Finance Major

Many of the popular social networking sites have users who subscribe to finance-oriented subgroups. Among these groups are finance professionals who collaborate and share knowledge as well as nonfinancial professionals who are potential clients.

MKT For the Marketing Major

Social computing tools and applications enable marketing professionals to become closer to their customers in a variety of ways, including blogs, wikis, ratings, and recommendations. Marketing professionals now receive almost real-time feedback on products.

POM For the Production/Operations Management Major

Social computing tools and applications allow production personnel to "enlist" business partners and customers in product development activities.

HRM For the Human Resource Management Major

Social networks offer tremendous benefits to human resource professionals. HR personnel can perform a great deal of their recruiting activities by accessing such sites as LinkedIn. They can also check out potential new hires by accessing a large number of social networking sites. Internally, HR personnel can utilize private, internal social networks for employee expertise and experience in order to find the best person for a position or project team.

MIS For the MIS Major

The MIS department is responsible for two aspects of social computing usage: (1) monitoring employee usage of social computing applications while at work, both time and content, and (2) developing private, internal social networks for company employees and then monitoring the content of these networks.

Summary

1. Describe five Web 2.0 tools and two major types of Web 2.0 sites.

A *tag* is a keyword or term that describes a piece of information (e.g., a blog, a picture, an article, or a video clip).

Really Simple Syndication allows you to receive the information you want (customized information), when you want it, without having to surf thousands of Web sites.

A *weblog* (*blog* for short) is a personal Web site, open to the public, in which the site creator expresses his or her feelings or opinions with a series of chronological entries.

Microblogging is a form of blogging that allows users to write short messages (or capture an image or embedded video) and publish them.

A *wiki* is a Web site on which anyone can post material and make changes to already posted material. Wikis foster easy collaboration and they harness the collective intelligence of Internet users.

Social networking Web sites allow users to upload their content to the Web in the form of text (e.g., blogs), voice (e.g., podcasts), images, and videos (e.g., videocasts).

A *mashup* is a Web site that takes different content from a number of other Web sites and mixes them together to create a new kind of content.

2. Describe the benefits and risks of social commerce to companies.

Social commerce refers to the delivery of electronic commerce activities and transactions through social computing.

Benefits of social commerce to customers include the following: better and faster vendors' response to complaints; customers can assist other customers; customers' expectations can be met more fully and quickly; customers can easily search, link, chat, and buy while staying in the social network's page.

Benefits of social commerce to vendors include the following: can test new products and ideas quickly and inexpensively; learn much about their customers; identify problems quickly and alleviate anger; learn from customers' experiences with rapid feedback; increase sales when customers discuss products positively on social networking site; create better marketing campaigns and brand awareness; use low-cost user-generated content, for example, in marketing campaigns; get free advertising through viral marketing; identify influential brand advocates and reward them.

Risks of social computing include information security concerns; invasion of privacy; violation of intellectual property and copyright; employees' reluctance to participate; data leakage of personal information or corporate strategic information; poor or biased quality of users' generated content; cyberbullying/cyberstalking and employee harassment.

3. Identify the methods used for shopping socially.

Social shopping is a method of electronic commerce that takes all of the key aspects of social networks—friends, groups, voting, comments, discussions, reviews, and others—and focuses them on shopping.

Methods for shopping socially include what other shoppers say; group shopping; shopping communities and clubs; social marketplaces and direct sales; and peer-to-peer shopping.

4. Discuss innovative ways to use social networking sites for advertising and market research.

Social advertising represents advertising formats that employ the social context of the user viewing the ad.

Innovative ways to advertise in social media include the following: create a company Facebook page; tweet business success stories to your customers; integrate ads into YouTube videos; add a Facebook "Like" button with its sponsored story to your product; use sponsored stories.

- *Using Facebook for market research:* Get feedback from your Facebook fans (and their friends if possible) on advertising campaigns, market research, etc.; test-market your messages; use Facebook for survey invitations.
- *Using Twitter for market research:* Use Twitter Search; use Twellow; look at the chart on TweetStats.
- *Using LinkedIn for market research:* Post a question (e.g., solicit advice) regarding the topic or issue you are interested in.

5. Describe how social computing improves customer service.

Customers are now incredibly empowered. Companies are closely monitoring social computing not only because they are mindful of the negative comments posted by social network members but also because they see an opportunity to involve customers proactively to reduce problems by improved customer service.

Empowered customers know how to use the wisdom and power of crowds and communities to their benefit. These customers choose how they interact with companies and brands, and they have elevated expectations. They are actively involved with businesses, not just as purchasers but also as advocates and influencers. As a result, businesses must respond to customers quickly and accurately. Fortunately, social computing provides many opportunities for businesses to do just that, thereby giving businesses the opportunity to turn disgruntled customers into champions for the firm.

6. Discuss different ways in which human resource managers make use of social computing.

- *Recruiting:* Both recruiters and job seekers are moving to online social networks as new recruiting platforms. Enterprise recruiters are scanning online social networks, blogs, and other social resources to identify and find information about potential employees. If job seekers are online and active, there is a good chance that they will be seen by recruiters. In addition, on social networks there are many passive job seekers—people who are employed but would take a better job if it appeared. So, it is important that both active and passive job seekers maintain profiles online that truly reflect them.
- *Employee development:* HR managers are using social tools to build relationships with employees. As HR managers learn more about employees, they can help them become more engaged and excited about their work.

Chapter Glossary

blog (weblog) A personal Web site, open to the public, in which the site creator expresses his or her feelings or opinions with a series of chronological entries

blogosphere The term for the millions of blogs on the Web

collaborative consumption An economic model based on sharing, swapping, trading, or renting products and services, enabling access over ownership

microblogging A form of blogging that allows users to write short messages (or capture an image or embedded video) and publish them

Really Simple Syndication A technology that allows users to receive the information they want, when they want it, without having to surf thousands of Web sites

social advertising Advertising formats that make use of the social context of the user viewing the ad

social capital The number of connections a person has within and between social networks

social commerce The delivery of electronic commerce activities and transactions through social computing

social computing A type of information technology that combines social behavior and information systems to create value

social graph A map of all relevant links or connections for one member of a social network

social intelligence The monitoring, collection, and analysis of socially generated data and the resultant strategic decisions

social marketplaces These act as online intermediaries that harness the power of social networks for introducing, buying, and selling products and services

social network A social structure composed of individuals, groups, or organizations linked by values, visions, ideas, financial exchange, friendship, kinship, conflict, or trade social networking Activities performed using social software tools (e.g., blogging) or social networking features (e.g., media sharing)

social shopping A method of electronic commerce that takes all of the key aspects of social networks (friends, groups, voting, comments, discussions, reviews, etc.) and focuses them on shopping

tag A keyword or term that describes a piece of information

tweet Messages and updates posted by users on Twitter

Twitter A free microblogging service that allows its users to send messages and read other users' messages and updates

Web 2.0 A loose collection of information technologies and applications, plus the Web sites that use them

Web 2.0 media Any Web site that provides user-generated media content and promotes tagging, rating, commenting, and other interactions among users and their media contributions

weblog (see blog)

wiki A Web site on which anyone can post material and make changes to other material

Discussion Questions

1. How would you describe Web 2.0 to someone who has not taken a course in information systems?

2. If you were the CEO of a company, would you pay attention to blogs about your company? Why or why not? If yes, would you consider some blogs to be more important or more reliable than are others? If so, which ones? How would you find blogs relating to your company?

3. Do you have a page on a social networking Web site? If yes, why? If no, what is keeping you from creating one? Is there any content that you definitely would *not* post on such a page?

4. How can an organization best employ social computing technologies and applications to benefit its business processes?

5. What factors might cause an individual, an employee, or a company to be cautious in the use of social networks?

6. Why are advertisers so interested in social networks?

7. What sorts of restrictions or guidelines should firms place on the use of social networks by employees? Are social computing sites a threat to security? Can they tarnish a firm's reputation? If so, how? Can they enhance a firm's reputation? If so, how?

8. Why are marketers so interested in social networks?

9. Why are human resource managers so interested in social networks?

Problem-Solving Activities

1. Enter www.programmableweb.com and study the various services that the Web site offers. Learn how to create mashups and then propose a mashup of your own. Present your mashup to the class.

2. Go to Amazon's Mechanical Turk Web site (www.mturk .com). View the available Human Intelligence Tasks (HITs). Are there any HITs that you would be interested in to make some extra money? Why or why not?

3. Access Pandora (www.pandora.com). Why is Pandora a social network- ing site?

4. Access ChatRoulette (www.chatroulette.com). What is interesting about this social networking site?

5. Using a search engine, look up the following:

   - *Most popular or most visited blogs*. Pick two and follow some of the posts. Why do you think these blogs are popular?

   - *Best blogs* (try www.bloggerschoiceawards.com). Pick two and con- sider why they might be the "best blogs."

6. Research how to be a successful blogger. What does it take to be a suc- cessful blogger? What time commitment might be needed? How fre- quently do successful bloggers post?

Closing Case 1

Pinterest's Business Model for Generating Revenue

The Problem

Founded in 2010, social computing Web site Pinterest (www.pinter- est.com) is a visual discovery social network where people create and share image collections of anything that interests them on their smart- phones, tablets, and computers. Pinterest is particularly popular with women, who make up more than 80 percent of its users. Interestingly, Pinterest doubled the number of active male users in 2014.

Pinterest users upload, save, sort, and manage images using visual bookmarks—known as *pins*—from anywhere on the Web to the- matically organized *boards*, using the "Pin It" button. Users can have several boards for various themes or topics. Users can also browse the content of others and *repin*, meaning that they can pin another user's pin to their own board. The most popular categories on Pinterest are food and drink, do-it-yourself and crafts, fashion, home décor, and travel.

In 2014, Pinterest's user base increased to over 70 million users in the United States, and the company opened offices in London, Paris, Berlin, and Tokyo during that year. International users make up nearly one-half of new sign-ups. By August 2015, Pinterest users had created more than 750 million boards made up of more than 30 billion individ- ual pins, with 54 million new pins added each day.

In 2014, Pinterest decided to monetize their impressive usage sta- tistics. The problem was: How best to accomplish this goal?

The IT Solution

MKT Pinterest presents an interesting opportunity for marketing managers regarding how users interact with the app. Let's compare Pinterest to Facebook and Twitter along the time dimension. Facebook users volunteer a vast amount of historical information such as birthplace, alma mater, vacations, connections, events, and memo- ries, which the company uses to precisely target its ad offerings. In con- trast, Twitter collects current information that is limited to 140 characters per tweet. Therefore, Twitter cannot offer Facebook's level of detail, which is why its revenue per user is only half that of Facebook's.

Therefore, if Facebook collects data on its users' *past* and Twitter on its users' *present*, then Pinterest collects data on its users' *future*. That is, Pinterest collects data about what its users want to do in the future, which is exactly what marketers want to know. When a user pins an image of a wedding dress or a coffee table to one of her boards, she is sending a signal to merchandisers who want to sell her that wedding dress or that coffee table. In essence, there is intent around a pin.

Now let's compare Pinterest to Google along the discovery dimension. Pinterest executives state that, in the e-commerce arena, Google is useful only if users already know what they are looking for. On the other hand, Pinterest exposes people to possibilities that they never would have known existed.

As a result, Pinterest introduced two programs to help businesses leverage the forward-looking nature of user information on Pinterest. The advertising program is called Promoted Pins and the e-commerce program is called Buyable Pins.

The Advertising Program. Promoted Pins are a form of paid advertising. They are native advertisements, meaning that they show up in users' Pinterest boards just like any other pin. That is, like Facebook's Sponsored Posts and Twitter's Promoted Tweets, Promoted Pins take the same form as the user-generated content around it. Businesses can target Promoted Pins at specific users in various demographic, geographic, and other behavior- and interest-based groups.

Let's compare native advertising on Pinterest with native advertising on Facebook. Facebook may know that you are a fan of your university and that you wear a size L (large). However, when you see an ad for a university T-shirt in your News Feed, it can be an interruption, because you probably did not go on Facebook looking to buy your university's T-shirt. On the other hand, Pinterest users are in the mode of planning how to spend their money. If a user is browsing for European vacation ideas, then an Expedia pin showing vacation ideas for Prague or Paris is not an intrusion. On the contrary, the pin is just more information.

Pinterest conducts workshops for the partners in its Promoted Pins program (i.e., its advertising clients). After a workshop, participants typically see the interaction rate on their pins increase by 25 percent. It is important for these advertising clients to see this increase because they are paying $30 to $40 per thousand impressions. This rate is several times higher than the rate that Facebook advertisers pay. (The *cost per thousand impressions* refers to the expense incurred for every thousand potential customers who view an advertisement.)

Instead of choosing to pay for views or click on their Promoted Pins, advertisers can choose to pay with a "cost-per-engagement" (CPE) model or a "cost-per-action" model (CPA). With the CPE model, advertisers will only pay when users engage with their Pins, such as repining. With the CPA model, advertisers will only pay when users download their app or actually click through to their Web site and make a purchase.

Pinterest provides a suite of tools to help retailers quantify the return on their time and dollars and is collaborating with them to develop new ones tailored to their needs. After implementing Promoted Pins, retailers have reported increases in Web traffic, number of new users, audience reach, and audience engagement. One analysis of data from 25,000 retailers showed that users driven to e-commerce sites from Pinterest are 10 percent likelier to buy something than those coming from other social sites.

MIS *The E-Commerce Program.* Pinterest has advantages in e-commerce, as industry analysts find that its users are more likely to share product links and make big purchases than users of other social platforms. In June 2015, Pinterest added Buyable Pins to its app. (At this time, both Facebook and Twitter are conducting tests of "Buy" buttons for frictionless shopping.)

Buyable Pins allow Pinterest to enter the e-commerce business, rather than just driving traffic to retailer's Web sites. They provide a method for merchants to sell products through Pinterest. These pins make it possible for users to purchase a product directly from the pin. Unlike Promoted Pins, Buyable Pins are free to use. That is, Pinterest does not charge merchants or users a fee when they buy through a Buyable Pin.

Buyable Pins are blue "Buy It" buttons that appear next to the site's familiar red "Pin It" buttons. After viewing the Pin and tapping the Buy It button, Pinterest users securely check out using Apple Pay or their credit card, without ever leaving the Pinterest app.

Pinterest is not the merchant of record in transactions that occur through its app. That is, users will not see a charge from Pinterest on credit card statements. The charge will come from the retailer, even though users will not have visited the retailer's Web site or mobile app in the process of making a purchase on Pinterest.

The reason is that Pinterest is using Braintree (www.braintree-payments.com) and Stripe (https://stripe.com) to vault, or securely store, cards. That process means that Pinterest does not have to store card numbers, but it can still keep credit card information for future purchases. In addition, Pinterest users do not have to remember their card numbers every time they click the Buy It button.

The Results

In 2014, Pinterest generated its first revenue, when the company began charging advertisers to promote their products and services. Analysts estimate that ads on the site could generate as much as $500 million in 2016. Many industry analysts believe that, on the basis of average revenue per users, it is only a matter of time before Pinterest exceeds Facebook.

Before 2013, Pinterest accounted for approximately 2 percent of global social-mediated sales. By 2014, the site accounted for some 23 percent of such sales. During the 2014 holiday season, Pinterest accounted for almost one quarter of all social sharing activity. Among social networks, only Facebook, with its 1.5 billion users, drives more traffic to Web publishers.

In May 2015, *Fortune* magazine listed Pinterest in eighth position on its Unicorn List, which ranks startup companies that have a market valuation exceeding $1 billion. By August 2015, Pinterest had a market valuation of approximately $11 billion.

Sources: Compiled from O. Thomas, "Who's Making Money with Pinterest's Buyable Pins?" *ReadWrite*, June 11, 2015; J. Guynn, "Pinterest to Launch 'Buy' Buttons," *USA Today*, June 2, 2015; T. Simonite, "Pinterest's Bid to Reinvent Online Shopping," *MIT Technology Review*, June 1, 2015; E. Baig, "Pinterest's Silbermann: We Are Not a Social Network," *USA Today*, May 28, 2015; J. D'Onfro, "Why $11 Billion Pinterest Thinks It Has the 'Best Kind of Business Model'," *Business Insider*, May 19, 2015; E. Griffith, "The Unicorn List," *Fortune*, May 15, 2015; J. Boorstin, "Pinterest's Big Plan to 'Pin' Profits," *CNBC*, February 17, 2015; J. Bercovici, "Social Media's New Mad Men," *Forbes*, November 3, 2014; J. Bercovici, "Inside Pinterest: The Coming Ad Colossus that Could Dwarf Twitter and Facebook," *Forbes*, October 15, 2014; J. Brandon, "Pinterest Links Up with Salesforce, Others to Monetize Data," *Business Cloud News*, May 21, 2014; J. Marshall, "Pinterest Opens Up Data Firehose for Marketers," *The Wall Street Journal*, May 20, 2014; D. MacMillan, "Pinterest CEO Lays Out Growth Plan, Sees Revenue in 2014," *The Wall Street Journal*, January 21, 2014; www.pinterest.com, accessed August 9, 2015.

Questions

1. Discuss why Pinterest's model of user engagement might be more valuable to marketers than Google's model, Facebook's model, or Twitter's model.

2. Describe the social computing aspects of Pinterest's model of user engagement.

Closing Case 2

POM   The General Motors Recall and Its Aftermath

MKT   The Problem

MIS   On February 7, 2014, General Motors (GM; www.gm.com) began a series of recalls of its small cars due to faulty ignition switches, totaling (in August 2015) 2.6 million Chevrolet Cobalts and other small cars. The switches could shut off the engine during driving, causing the car to stall and preventing the airbags from inflating. GM had known about the ignition switch fault for at least ten years.

The parts needed to repair the ignition switches were scheduled to become available on April 7, 2014, with repairs to begin the same day. However, as of June 2014, the replacement switches had only been delivered intermittently to dealerships as demand far exceeded the supply.

As of July 2015, GM's faulty ignition switches were responsible for at least 124 deaths and 266 injuries, according to a fund set up to compensate victims. The fund, run by attorney Kenneth Feinberg, had finished processing the 4,342 claims it had received.

The Multipart Solution

Although there is no "solution" to the deaths and injuries caused by the faulty ignition switches, we feel that it is instructive to study the various ways in which General Motors attempted to address the disaster.

The Personal Approach.   First, Mary Barra, CEO of GM, gave a speech to the company's employees. She apologized for the defect-and-recall disaster and announced the firing of 15 employees, some of them executives. She also said that GM would compensate consumers rather than fight pending lawsuits. Further, in testimony before the U.S. Congress, Barra apologized to GM customers and promised to make safety the number one issue at the automaker. She also said, "Today's GM will do the right thing."

The Repair Approach.   By the end of 2014, GM had repaired over 1.3 million of the cars with defective ignition switches. The automaker said that it had contacted an additional 2.4 million owners of recalled cars who had not had their cars repaired. GM efforts to contact these owners included:

- Contacting every identified owner at least six times by letter or phone call in English and in Spanish.
- Sending 5.3 million letters to known current and former owners of the recalled vehicles informing them of the GM Ignition Switch Compensation Fund.
- Creating a national call center staffed by 72 people.

The Information Technology approach.   As noted above, GM is primarily using conventional methods, such as letters to customers, blogs, a call center, and the news media to get its recall messages to the public. But social media has also become an important tool for the company to show its commitment to making things right, even as it tries to show off its newest models and build enthusiasm among customers who were unaffected by the recall. The automaker does face problems on social media, where a customer's perceptions of a brand are shaped by both what the company does and what other people say about it.

GM has a team of about 20 people based in Detroit that manages its social media presence. Team members monitor about 100 independent automobile forums and respond to inquiries and complaints seven days per week.

One challenge has been to tell customers that the cars are safe to drive while they wait for repairs. Despite assurances, many customers have requested loaner cars or free rentals. GM did provide more than 6,000 loaner vehicles, and in some cases paid for non-GM vehicles provided by rental car companies.

Consider the Facebook page of General Motors, which promotes jobs and features new cars. However, the page also contains comments from disgruntled GM customers who feel strongly that GM knowingly sold them unsafe automobiles. On the other hand, there are numerous messages from GM representatives to those commenting, trying to answer their questions about the recall and engage them in private messages to clear up individual problems.

Let's look at a specific example of how social media is helping GM deal with the recall disaster. One GM customer in Alaska turned to Twitter after spending an hour on the phone with GM trying to get help with her 2006 Saturn Ion. Those Ions, along with five other models, were recalled because of a defective ignition switch that, if bumped or weighed down by a heavy key ring, could turn off, shutting down the engine and disabling the air bags.

The customer publicly tweeted, "@GM your agents keep telling me to take my car to a GM dealer for the recall, after I've explained I live on an island in Alaska! Help!!!" After a series of private messages with a member of GM's Twitter team, the company agreed to pay the $600 cost of a round-trip ferry to ship her car to the nearest dealer, about 300 miles away in Juneau, and pay for a rental car for the time she is without the Saturn.

Despite the number of headlines about federal investigations into GM's decade-long failure to issue the recall, the overall sentiment about GM and its brands on Twitter remained the same during the crisis. Rather than tweeting about the recalls, many car owners are using social media to trade tips and put public pressure on the company on issues such as giving affected customers loaner cars until their vehicles could be fixed.

In a refinement of its social media strategy, GM is now analyzing social media and blogs to spot potential problems with its cars. In that way, the automaker can catch problems much earlier, perhaps when they affect as few as 10 cars.

The Results

In September 2015, GM agreed to pay $900 million to settle criminal charges related to its recall. Prosecutors had charged GM with wire fraud and scheming to conceal material facts from a U.S. regulator. GM admitted to failing to disclose a potentially lethal safety defect with the switches that kept some air bags from deploying. The automaker also admitted to misleading consumers about the safety of affected vehicles. GM's $900 million payment will be treated as a penalty, and the company cannot treat it as a deductible expense.

Sources: Compiled from J. White, J. Stempel, and N. Raymond, "Recall Settlement Frees GM CEO to Confront New Challenges," *Reuters*, September 17, 2015; D. Durbin, "GM Ignition Switch Deaths Total 124 as Fund Nears Completion," *CBS News*, July 13, 2015; A. Bourque, "How Social Data Helped Jaguar and GM Navigate Troubling Brand Sentiment," *Social Media Today*, June 26, 2015; A. Sharman, "GM Uses Tiny Recalls to Head Off Bigger Problems over Car Faults," *Financial Times*, May 31,

2015; "GM Ignition Switches Now Linked to 90 Deaths, 163 Total Injuries," *Autoblog*, April 29, 2015; G. Gardner, "GM Outreach Extensive, But Doesn't Reach All Owners," *Detroit Free Press*, November 15, 2014; J. Twentyman, "Using Social Media to Drive Change at General Motors," *Diginomica*, October 17, 2014; P. Valdes-Dapena, "GM: Steps to a Recall Nightmare," *CNN Money*, June 30, 2014; R. Cook, "General Motors Announces 30th Recall of Year," *CBS News/Associated Press*, May 23, 2014; T. Lachapelle, "GM Investors Unshaken as Recall Cuts $3 Billion in Value," *Bloomberg BusinessWeek*, April 6, 2014; K. Naughton, "GM Dealers Turn Therapists for Anxious Recall Customers," *Bloomberg News*, April 4, 2014; T. Spangler, "Families Put Human Face on Massive GM Recall," *USA Today*, April 1, 2014; V. Goel, "G.M. Uses Social Media to Manage Customers and Its Reputation," *The New York Times*, March 24, 2014; J. McDermott, "Why GM Is Bringing Its Social Media In-House," *Digiday*, March 13, 2014; V. Bond, "GM Uses Social Media to Respond to Customer Gripes," *Automotive News*, March 10, 2014; www.gm.com, accessed August 12, 2015.

Questions

1. What else could GM do, in general, to manage its recall crisis? Provide specific examples to support your answer.

2. What else could GM do with social media to help manage its recall crisis? Provide specific examples to support your answer.

3. Refer to Chapter 2. Would GM's use of social media be a strategic information system for the automaker? Why or why not?

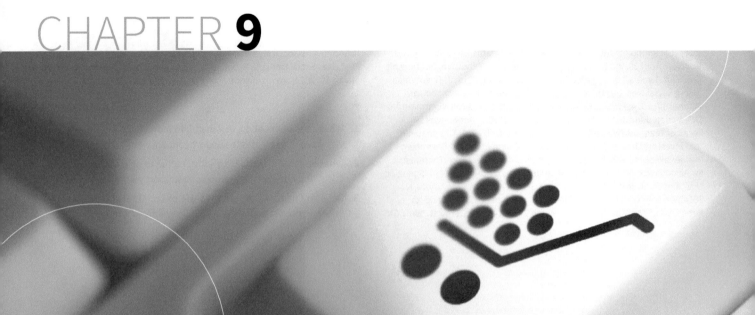

CHAPTER 9

Tom Nulens/iStockphoto

E-Business and E-Commerce

LEARNING OBJECTIVES

9.1 Describe the six common types of electronic commerce.

9.2 Describe the various online services of business-to-consumer (B2C) commerce, along with specific examples of each.

9.3 Describe the three business models for business-to-business electronic commerce.

9.4 Discuss the ethical and legal issues related to electronic commerce, along with examples.

Opening Case

 Thumbtack

MKT Sometimes finding a nearby professional to do a job for you can be challenging. Think of plumbers, moving services, painters, personal trainers, chefs, caterers, cleaning and domestic services, photographers, construction workers, among others. These professionals all belong to a very large industry called local commerce or local services. This industry is difficult to define; however, estimates of its size

range from $400 billion to $800 billion per year. Despite its large size, local commerce remains an inefficient market that depends on phone calls, the Yellow Pages, and, when things go wrong, small claims court.

It is difficult not only for customers to find local professionals but also for local professionals to find customers. In fact, every year professionals spend approximately $65 billion on local ads to generate business leads. Now, a company called Thumbtack is striving to create efficiencies in the local commerce marketplace.

Founded in 2009, Thumbtack (www.thumbtack.com) is a marketplace that connects customers with local service professionals.

On Thumbtack, the providers bid on the customer. Customers fill out an extensive questionnaire, and Thumbtack's software forwards the request to relevant and nearby professionals, who respond with a price for, and description of, their services. The average job request on Thumbtack is $600, and businesses are charged a small fee for the leads. Thumbtack divides its jobs into four categories:

1. Home improvement and repair (e.g., plumbing and painting services);
2. Event services (e.g., wedding photographers and catering services);
3. Instruction (e.g., tutoring and music lessons);
4. Wellness (e.g., personal training and chiropractors)

When Thumbtack entered this marketplace, it faced two major problems. First, the company had to list enough suppliers (local professionals) on its Web site to attract demand (customers). Significantly, Thumbtack did not cold-call anyone. Rather, they analyzed billions of Web pages to create a database of information on local professionals. This process helped them learn where service providers searched online for new business. The company bought targeted Web ads on those pages—specifically Google, Facebook, and Bing—to attract professionals to sign up for Thumbtack. As of mid-2016, Thumbtack still did not employ a dedicated sales team to attract new business.

Thumbtack's second problem was how to get paid. The company's initial policy was to charge fees after projects were completed. However, that process relied on the participating businesses self-reporting based on the honor system. This policy ultimately was unsuccessful. Thumbtack next implemented a subscription model in which professionals would pay a set price for an unlimited number of introductions. Unfortunately, that process led to customers being spammed. Not surprisingly, this system did not provide a positive customer experience. Finally, Thumbtack decided on a pay-per-lead business model, which helped to ensure that professionals would bid only on projects they could complete. This model generated a 500 percent increase in revenue in 2014; the company now makes about $30 million per year.

Consider the case of a photographer in Colorado. She tried different online ads to attract customers, but she received few responses because there were so many photographers in her area. She then turned to Thumbtack, where she pays about $4.50 per lead. Now, roughly one in five ads results in a job, which average about $250. She estimated that she formerly spent $75 per month on Google ads to achieve the same result.

Thumbtack is competing in the local commerce arena with Yelp (www.yelp.com), Angie's List (www.angieslist.com), Zaarly (www.zaarly.com), TaskRabbit (www.taskrabbit.com), HomeAdvisor (www.homeadvisor.com), eBay (with eBay Hire), and Amazon (with Amazon Home Services; www.amazon.com/services). Let's take a closer look at Yelp and Angie's List, as well as Amazon.

- Yelp and Angie's List address different questions and problems than Thumbtack. Specifically, Yelp and Angie's List allow customers to go to almost any local professional for services (haircuts, Chinese food, etc.). By contrast, Thumbtack enables local professionals to come to the customer. Yelp and Angie's List might be considered as directories, where Thumbtack goes a step further and actually matches customers and local professionals.

- Amazon announced in 2015 that it was entering the local services business, initially launching its home services to customers in 15 metropolitan areas including Chicago, Houston, and Miami. The Internet giant maintains it thoroughly screens service providers and individual contractors. It further claims that fewer than 3 percent of applicants survive the vetting process. Amazon charges a 10 to 20 percent referral fee to contractors, and it provides customer support and refunds to dissatisfied customers.

Some professionals have set up anti-Thumbtack groups on Facebook, complaining that unqualified professionals are using the site to challenge them for business. In fact, Thumbtack does not have ratings and reviews, which both customers and professionals rely on to make informed decisions. As a result, the company is building upon its 485-person quality control team to verify the credentials of the service professionals who advertise on their site. The firm is also experimenting with displaying average pricing data on their site so customers can see how much a job should cost in their area.

With more than 75,000 unique paying professionals and 3 million successful job leads in 700 job categories per year, Thumbtack sends some $2 billion of business to local firms in the United States. The company has raised $150 million in venture capital funding, and industry analysts estimate their valuation to exceed $800 million.

Sources: Compiled from S. Mitra, "Angie's List Faces Tougher Competition," *sramanamitra.com*, July 29, 2015; "Amazon Expands Local Services Marketplace in U.S. Cities," *Reuters*, July 22, 2015; H. Stout, "Buying a Faucet from Amazon? Add a Handyman," *The New York Times*, April 13, 2015; C. Pritchard, "Google Inc, Amazon.com Enter Home Services Market," *Business Finance News*, April 13, 2015; H. Stout, "Amazon, Google, and More Are Drawn to Home Services Market," *The New York Times*, April 12, 2015; D. Evans, "Why eBay and Amazon Will Redefine Local Commerce," *Clickz*, April 8, 2015; T. Lee, "Can Amazon Make Hiring a Plumber As Easy As Buying an iPad?" *Vox*, March 30, 2015; S. Loeb, "How Does Thumbtack Make Money?" *VatorNews*, March 27, 2015; R. Mac, "Where Belly Dancers Bid for You," *Forbes*, September 8, 2014; C. Taylor, "12 Questions with the CEO of Thumbtack, Google Capital's New $100 Million Bet," *TechCrunch*, August 20, 2014; R. Mac, "Amazon Chases Local Services, the New E-commerce Battleground," *Forbes*, June 10, 2014; www.thumbtack.com, accessed August 19, 2015.

Questions

1. Consider the highly competitive nature of the local services marketplace. Which of the companies discussed in this case has the best chance of "winning" in this marketplace? Support your answer.

2. What competitive advantages does Thumbtack have in the local services marketplace? Provide examples to support your answer.

3. What competitive advantages does Amazon have in the local services marketplace? Provide examples to support your answer.

Introduction

One of the most profound changes in the modern world of business is the emergence of electronic commerce. **Electronic commerce** (**EC** or **e-commerce**) describes the process of buying, selling, transferring, or exchanging products, services, or information via computer networks, including the Internet. E-commerce is transforming all of the business functional areas we discussed in Chapter 1 as well as their fundamental tasks, from advertising to paying bills. Its impact is so pervasive that it is affecting almost every modern organization. Regardless of where you land a job, your organization likely will be practicing electronic commerce.

Electronic commerce influences organizations in many significant ways. First, it increases an organization's *reach*, defined as the number of potential customers to whom the company can market its products. In fact, e-commerce provides unparalleled opportunities for companies to expand worldwide at a small cost, to increase market share, and to reduce costs. By utilizing electronic commerce, many small businesses can now operate and compete in market spaces that formerly were dominated by larger companies.

Another major impact of electronic commerce has been to remove many of the barriers that previously impeded entrepreneurs seeking to start their own businesses. E-commerce offers amazing opportunities for you to open your own business by developing an e-commerce Web site.

As illustrated in the opening case, electronic commerce is also fundamentally transforming the nature of competition through the development of new online companies, new business models, and the diversity of EC-related products and services. Recall your study of competitive strategies in Chapter 2, particularly the impact of the Internet on Porter's five forces. You learned that the Internet can both endanger and enhance a company's position in a given industry.

It is important for you to have a working knowledge of electronic commerce because your organization almost certainly will be employing e-commerce applications that will affect its strategy and business model. This knowledge will make you more valuable to your organization, and it will enable you to quickly contribute to the e-commerce applications employed in your functional area. As you read What's in IT for Me? at the end of the chapter, envision yourself performing the activities discussed in your functional area.

Going further, you may decide to become an entrepreneur and start your own business, as illustrated in the chapter opening case. If you start your own business, it is even more essential for you to understand electronic commerce, because e-commerce, with its broad reach, will more than likely be critical for your business to survive and thrive. On the other hand, giant, well-known electronic commerce companies utilize the Internet to compete all over the world, as you see in IT's About Business 9.1.

IT's About Business 9.1

Japan's Largest E-Commerce Company, Rakuten, Competes Globally

Rakuten (www.rakuten.com) is a Japanese electronic commerce company. (The Japanese word *rakuten* means *optimism*.) Since it began in 1997, the company has moved into sports, banking, insurance, and even wedding planning. Rakuten is so pervasive in Japan that one in four online purchases in the country occurs on the company's B2C and B2B e-commerce platform, Ichiba. Further, the company's loyalty program has 90 million members. (Japan's population in mid-2016 was approximately 127 million.) The diversified company owns:

- A professional baseball team and a professional soccer team;
- The Rakuten Bank;
- Rakuten Broadband Service;
- Rakuten Beauty, a chain of beauty salons;
- A vehicle inspection service;
- Rakuten Insurance;
- Rakuten Wedding, where couples plan their weddings; and

- The Rakuten smartphone app BeautyC Navigator, which helps couples predict the best time to try to conceive a child.

Despite its national prominence, Rakuten is not as successful outside Japan. The company is not well known in the United States and Europe, and Alibaba controls the majority of e-commerce in China. Rakuten's limited global presence is a barrier to growth given Japan's decreasing population and its poorly performing economy. As a result, the e-commerce giant is expanding overseas, purchasing several foreign companies and investing in others.

In just a little over a year, Rakuten spent $2.6 billion on international deals. Company CEO Hiroshi Mikitani has stated that his firm cannot operate exclusively in Japan. Rather, it simply needs to defend its market position there. Among the firm's major foreign activities are the following:

- In early 2014, Rakuten purchased the Cyprus-based messaging app Viber (www.viber.com) for $905 million.
- In September 2014, Rakuten bought Ebates (www.ebates.com), an online coupon service based in San Francisco, for $3 billion. Rakuten customers who sign up for Ebates can use Rakuten's Web portal to browse the selections of other e-commerce sites,

including Amazon, and earn cash back on their purchases. In 2014, this discount service had $5 billion in transactions and generated about $20 million in operating profit.

- In March 2015, Rakuten purchased OverDrive (www.overdrive .com), a major e-book distributor based in Cleveland, Ohio.

- In March 2015, Rakuten led a $530 million round of funding for Lyft (www.lyft.com/drive), spending $300 million of its own money for 12 percent of the car-service app.

- Rakuten acquired Fits.Me (https://fits.me), a London-based startup that creates virtual fitting rooms. The firm's technology enables online buyers to virtually view how clothing looks on them without visiting a physical store.

- Rakuten has purchased a stake in Pinterest (www.pinterest .com).

- Rakuten acquired French e-commerce portal PriceMinister (www.priceminister.com).

- The Rakuten Institute of Technology opened locations in New York, Tokyo, Paris, Boston, and Singapore. The institute's mission is to support both the company's research and development and its global expansion.

- Rakuten expanded its financial services into the United States, offering a credit card through a subsidiary of First National Bank of Omaha.

Not all of Rakuten's acquisitions have been successful. As one example, the electronic bookstore Kobo (www.kobo.com), which Rakuten purchased in 2011 for $315 million, had not generated a profit as of August 2015. Nevertheless, by the end of 2014, the bookstore boosted its users by 25 percent, with 23 million customers. Further, Kobo helped stem the tide of red ink by concentrating on its mobile app to sell e-books.

One key element of Rakuten's strategy of global diversification has been to encourage its employees to become fluent in English. And they succeeded. The average employee scored 802.6 points out of 990 on the Test of English for International Communication (TOEIC) in 2015. According to TOEIC, a score above 800 indicates advanced proficiency.

Rakuten now has an English-only policy, which it calls "Englishnization." CEO Mikitani made Englishnization a key platform in Rakuten's global expansion. Virtually all company communication and interaction—from meetings to internal e-mails—is conducted in English.

As of mid-2016, Rakuten's attempts to expand its business globally were still in their early stages, and there are risks to that strategy. Specifically, Rakuten may not have the financial resources to compete with Amazon and Alibaba. For example, Rakuten reported $5.66 billion in revenue for 2015. By contrast, Alibaba reported $12.3 billion, and Amazon reported $107 billion.

Sources: Compiled from J. Russell, "Rakuten Launches Its Own Security-Enhanced Android App Store in Japan," *TechCrunch*, August 19, 2015; "Rakuten's Research Centers Focused on Mobile," *PYMNTS. com*, July 30, 2015; C. Shu, "Rakuten Opens New Research Centers in Boston and Singapore," *TechCrunch*, July 29, 2015; E. Brooke, "Amazon Competitor Rakuten Acquires Virtual Try-On Service Fits. Me," *Fashionista*, July 13, 2015; I. Lunden and N. Lomas, "Rakuten Buys Virtual Fitting Room Startup Fits.Me in a Fashion Commerce Play," *TechCrunch*, July 12, 2015; D. Loo, "Rakuten to Raise $1.5 Billion in Japan, Overseas Share Sale," *BloombergBusiness*, June 3, 2015; "Rakuten Forges Ahead in English," *The Japan Times*, May 23, 2015; S. Buhr, "Rakuten Is Looking to Acquire PopSugar for $580 Million," *TechCrunch*, April 13, 2015; B. Einhorn, "Japan's Amazon Has Bigger Dreams," *BloombergBusiness*, April 9, 2015; www.rakuten.com, accessed August 21, 2015.

Questions

1. Discuss the reasons why founder and CEO Mikitani feels it is imperative for Rakuten to expand beyond the boundaries of Japan. Provide examples to support your answer.

2. How should Amazon and Alibaba combat the global expansion of Rakuten? Provide examples to support your answer.

3. Describe any competitive advantages that Rakuten has in its competition with Amazon and Alibaba.

In this chapter, you will discover the major applications of e-business, and you will be able to identify the services necessary for its support. You will then study the major types of electronic commerce: business-to-consumer (B2C), business-to-business (B2B), consumer-to-consumer (C2C), business-to-employee (B2E), and government-to-citizen (G2C). You will conclude by examining several legal and ethical issues that have arisen as a result of the rapid growth of e-commerce.

9.1 | Overview of E-Business and E-Commerce

Any entrepreneur or company that decides to practice electronic commerce must develop a strategy to do so effectively. The first step is to determine exactly *why* you want to do business over the Internet using a Web site. There are several reasons for employing Web sites, including:

- To sell goods and services
- To induce people to visit a physical location
- To reduce operational and transaction costs
- To enhance your reputation

A Web site can accomplish any of these goals. Unless a company (or you) has substantial resources, it is difficult to accomplish all of them at the same time. The appropriate Web site for achieving each goal will be somewhat different. As you set up your Web site, you must consider how the site will generate and retain traffic, as well as a host of other issues. The point here is that when you are studying the various aspects of electronic commerce, you should keep in mind the strategy of the organization or entrepreneur. This will help you determine the type of Web site to use.

This section examines the basics of e-business and e-commerce. First, we define these two concepts. You then become familiar with pure and partial electronic commerce. You then examine the various types of electronic commerce. Next, you focus on e-commerce mechanisms, which are the ways that businesses and people buy and sell over the Internet. You conclude this section by considering the benefits and limitations of e-commerce.

Definitions and Concepts

Recall that electronic commerce describes the process of buying, selling, transferring, or exchanging products, services, or information via computer networks, including the Internet. **Electronic business (e-business)** is a somewhat broader concept. In addition to the buying and selling of goods and services, e-business refers to servicing customers, collaborating with business partners, and performing electronic transactions within an organization.

Electronic commerce can take several forms depending on the degree of digitization involved. The *degree of digitization* is the extent to which the commerce has been transformed from physical to digital. This concept can relate to both the product or service being sold and the delivery agent or intermediary. In other words, the product can be either physical or digital, and the delivery agent can also be either physical or digital.

In traditional commerce, both dimensions are physical. Purely physical organizations are referred to as **brick-and-mortar organizations**. (You may also see the term *bricks-and-mortar*.) In contrast, in *pure EC* all dimensions are digital. Companies engaged only in EC are considered **virtual** (or **pure-play**) **organizations**. All other combinations that include a mix of digital and physical dimensions are considered *partial* EC (but not pure EC). **Clicks-and-mortar organizations** conduct some e-commerce activities, yet their primary business is carried out in the physical world. A common alternative to the term *clicks-and-mortar* is *clicks-and-bricks*. You will encounter both terms. Clicks- and-mortar organizations are examples of partial EC. E-commerce is now so well established that people generally expect companies to offer this service in some form.

Purchasing a shirt at Walmart Online or a book from Amazon.com is an example of partial EC because the merchandise, although bought and paid for digitally, is physically delivered by FedEx or UPS. In contrast, buying an e-book from Amazon.com or a software product from Buy.com constitutes pure EC because the product itself as well as its delivery, payment, and transfer are entirely digital. We use the term *electronic commerce* to denote both pure and partial EC.

Types of E-Commerce

E-commerce can be conducted between and among various parties. In this section, you will identify the six common types of e-commerce, and you will learn about three of them—C2C, B2E, and e-government—in detail. We discuss B2C and B2B in separate sections because they are very complex. We discuss mobile commerce in detail in Chapter 10.

- *Business-to-consumer electronic commerce (B2C):* In B2C, the sellers are organizations, and the buyers are individuals. You will learn about B2C electronic commerce in Section 9.2.
- *Business-to-business electronic commerce (B2B):* In B2B transactions, both the sellers and the buyers are business organizations. B2B comprises the vast majority of EC volume. You will learn more about B2B electronic commerce in Section 9.3. Look back to Figure 1.5 for an illustration of B2B electronic commerce.

- *Consumer-to-consumer electronic commerce (C2C):* In C2C (also called customer-to-customer), an individual sells products or services to other individuals. The major strategies for conducting C2C on the Internet are auctions and classified ads.

In dozens of countries, the volume of C2C selling and buying on auction sites is exploding. Most auctions are conducted by intermediaries such as eBay (www.ebay.com). Consumers can also select general sites such as www.auctionanything.com, a company that sells software and services that help individuals and organizations conduct their own auctions. In addition, many individuals are conducting their own auctions.

The major categories of online classified ads are similar to those found in print ads: vehicles, real estate, employment, pets, tickets, and travel. Classified ads are available through most Internet service providers (AOL, MSN, etc.), at some portals (Yahoo!, etc.), and from Internet directories and online newspapers. Many of these sites contain search engines that help shoppers narrow their searches. Craigslist (www.craigslist.org) is the largest online classified ad provider.

Internet-based classified ads have one major advantage over traditional types of classified ads: They provide access to an international, rather than a local, audience. This wider audience greatly increases both the supply of goods and services and the number of potential buyers. It is important to note that the value of expanded geographical reach depends greatly on what is being bought or sold. For example, you might buy software from a company located 1,000 miles from you, but you would not buy firewood from someone at such a distance.

- *Business-to-employee (B2E):* In B2E, an organization uses EC internally to provide information and services to its employees. For example, companies allow employees to manage their benefits and to take training classes electronically. In addition, employees can buy discounted insurance, travel packages, and tickets to events on the corporate intranet. They can also order supplies and materials electronically. Finally, many companies have electronic corporate stores that sell the company's products to its employees, usually at a discount.

- *E-government:* E-government is the use of Internet technology in general and e-commerce in particular to deliver information and public services to citizens (called government-to-citizen or G2C EC) and to business partners and suppliers (called government-to-business or G2B EC). G2B EC is much like B2B EC, usually with an overlay of government procurement regulations. That is, G2B EC and B2B EC are similar conceptually. However, the functions of G2C EC are conceptually different from anything that exists in the private sector (e.g., B2C EC).

  E-government is also an efficient way of conducting business transactions with citizens and businesses and within the governments themselves. E-government makes government more efficient and effective, especially in the delivery of public services. An example of G2C electronic commerce is electronic benefits transfer, in which governments transfer benefits, such as Social Security and pension payments, directly to recipients' bank accounts.

- *Mobile commerce (m-commerce):* The term *m-commerce* refers to e-commerce that is conducted entirely in a wireless environment. An example is using cell phones to shop over the Internet. You will learn about m-commerce in Chapter 10.

Each type of EC is executed in one or more business models. A business model is the method by which a company generates revenue to sustain itself. Table 9.1 summarizes the major EC business models.

Major E-Commerce Mechanisms

Businesses and customers can buy and sell on the Internet through a number of mechanisms. The most widely used mechanisms are as follows:

- Electronic catalogs
- Electronic auctions

- E-storefronts
- E-malls
- E-marketplaces

Let's look at each one more closely.

Catalogs have been printed on paper for generations. Today, however, they are available over the Internet. Electronic catalogs consist of a product database, a directory and search capabilities, and a presentation function. They are the backbone of most e-commerce sites.

An **auction** is a competitive buying and selling process in which prices are determined dynamically by competitive bidding. Electronic auctions (e-auctions) generally increase revenues for sellers by broadening the customer base and shortening the cycle time of the auction. Buyers generally benefit from e-auctions because they can bargain for lower prices. In addition, they do not have to travel to an auction at a physical location.

The Internet provides an efficient infrastructure for conducting auctions at lower administrative costs and with a greater number of involved sellers and buyers. Both individual consumers and corporations can participate in auctions.

There are two major types of auctions: forward and reverse. In **forward auctions**, sellers solicit bids from many potential buyers. Usually, sellers place items at sites for auction, and buyers bid continuously for them. The highest bidder wins the items. Both sellers and buyers

TABLE 9.1 E-Commerce Business Models

Online direct marketing	Manufacturers or retailers sell directly to customers. Very efficient for digital products and services. Can allow for product or service customization (www.dell.com)
Electronic tendering system	Businesses request quotes from suppliers. Uses B2B with a reverse auction mechanism
Name-your-own-price	Customers decide how much they are willing to pay. An intermediary tries to match a provider (www.priceline.com)
Find-the-best-price	Customers specify a need; an intermediary compares providers and shows the lowest price. Customers must accept the offer in a short time, or they may lose the deal (www.hotwire.com)
Affiliate marketing	Vendors ask partners to place logos (or banners) on partner's site. If customers click on logo, go to vendor's site, and make a purchase, then the vendor pays commissions to the partners
Viral marketing	Recipients of your marketing notices send information about your product to their friends
Group purchasing (e-coops)	Small buyers aggregate demand to create a large volume; the group then conducts tendering or negotiates a low price
Online auctions	Companies run auctions of various types on the Internet. Very popular in C2C, but gaining ground in other types of EC as well (www.ebay.com)
Product customization	Customers use the Internet to self-configure products or services. Sellers then price them and fulfill them quickly (*build-to-order*) (www.jaguar.com)
Electronic marketplaces and exchanges	Transactions are conducted efficiently (more information to buyers and sellers, lower transaction costs) in electronic marketplaces (private or public)
Bartering online	Intermediary administers online exchange of surplus products and/or company receives "points" for its contribution, which it can use to purchase other needed items (www.bbu.com)
Deep discounters	Company offers deep price discounts. Appeals to customers who consider only price in their purchasing decisions (www.half.com)
Membership	Only members can use the services provided, including access to certain information, conducting trades, etc. (www.egreetings.com)

can be either individuals or businesses. The popular auction site eBay.com is a forward auction.

In reverse auctions, one buyer, usually an organization, wants to purchase a product or a service. The buyer posts a request for quotation (RFQ) on its Web site or on a third-party site. The RFQ provides detailed information on the desired purchase. Interested suppliers study the RFQ and then submit bids electronically. Everything else being equal, the lowest-price bidder wins the auction. The reverse auction is the most common auction model for large purchases (in terms of either quantities or price). Governments and large corporations frequently use this approach, which may provide considerable savings for the buyer.

Auctions can be conducted from the seller's site, the buyer's site, or a third party's site. For example, eBay, the best-known third-party site, offers hundreds of thousands of different items in several types of auctions. Overall, more than 300 major companies, including Amazon.com and Dellauction.com, sponsor online auctions.

An *electronic storefront* is a Web site that represents a single store. An *electronic mall*, also known as a *cybermall* or an *e-mall*, is a collection of individual shops consolidated under one Internet address. Electronic storefronts and electronic malls are closely associated with B2C electronic commerce. You will study each one in more detail in Section 9.2.

An *electronic marketplace* (*e-marketplace*) is a central, virtual market space on the Web where many buyers and many sellers can conduct e-commerce and e-business activities. Electronic marketplaces are associated with B2B electronic commerce. You will learn about electronic marketplaces in Section 9.3.

Electronic Payment Mechanisms

Implementing EC typically requires electronic payments. Electronic payment mechanisms enable buyers to pay for goods and services electronically, rather than writing a check or using cash. Payments are an integral part of doing business, whether in the traditional manner or online. Traditional payment systems have typically involved cash and/or checks.

In most cases, traditional payment systems are not effective for EC, especially for B2B. Cash cannot be used because there is no face-to-face contact between buyer and seller. Not everyone accepts credit cards or checks, and some buyers do not have credit cards or checking accounts. Finally, contrary to what many people believe, it may be *less* secure for the buyer to use the telephone or mail to arrange or send payments, especially from another country, than to complete a secured transaction on a computer. For all of these reasons, a better method is needed to pay for goods and services in cyberspace. This method is electronic payment systems. Let's take a closer look at three types of electronic payment: electronic checks, electronic cards, and digital wallets.

Electronic Checks. *Electronic checks* (*e-checks*), which are used primarily in B2B, are similar to regular paper checks. A customer who wishes to use e-checks must first establish a checking account with a bank. Then, when the customer buys a product or a service, he or she e-mails an encrypted electronic check to the seller. The seller deposits the check in a bank account, and the funds are transferred from the buyer's account into the seller's account.

Like regular checks, e-checks carry a signature (in digital form) that can be verified (see www.authorize.net). Properly signed and endorsed e-checks are exchanged between financial institutions through electronic clearinghouses. (For example, see www.eccho.org for details.)

Electronic Cards. There are a variety of electronic cards, and they are used for different purposes. The most common types are electronic credit cards, purchasing cards, stored-value money cards, and smart cards.

Electronic credit cards allow customers to charge online payments to their credit card account. These cards are used primarily in B2C and in shopping by small-to-medium enterprises (SMEs). Here is how e-credit cards work (see Figure 9.1).

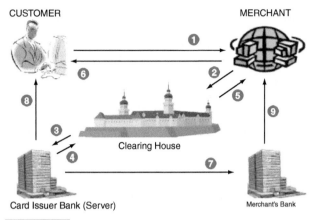

CUSTOMER   MERCHANT

Clearing House

Card Issuer Bank (Server)   Merchant's Bank

FIGURE 9.1 How e-credit cards work. (The numbers 1–9 indicate the sequence of activities.)

1. When you purchase a book from Amazon, for example, your credit card information and purchase amount are encrypted in your browser. This procedure ensures the information is safe while it is "traveling" on the Internet to Amazon.

2. When your information arrives at Amazon, it is not opened. Rather, it is transferred automatically (in encrypted form) to a *clearinghouse*, where it is decrypted for verification and authorization.

3. The clearinghouse asks the bank that issued you your credit card (the card issuer bank) to verify your credit card information.

4. Your card issuer bank verifies your credit card information and reports this to the clearinghouse.

5. The clearinghouse reports the result of the verification of your credit card to Amazon.

6. Amazon reports a successful purchase and amount to you.

7. Your card issuer bank sends funds in the amount of the purchase to Amazon's bank.

8. Your card issuer bank notifies you (either electronically or in your monthly statement) of the debit on your credit card.

9. Amazon's bank notifies Amazon of the funds credited to its account.

Purchasing cards are the B2B equivalent of electronic credit cards (see **Figure 9.2**). In some countries, purchasing cards are the primary form of payment between companies. Unlike credit cards, where credit is provided for 30–60 days (for free) before payment is made to the merchant, payments made with purchasing cards are settled within a week.

Stored-value money cards allow you to store a fixed amount of prepaid money and then spend it as necessary. These cards are used to pay for photocopies in your library, for transportation, and for telephone calls. Each time you use the card, the amount is reduced by the amount you spent. **Figure 9.3** illustrates a New York City Metro (subway and bus) card.

Finally, **smart cards** contain a chip that can store a large amount of information (see **Figure 9.4**). Smart cards are frequently multipurpose—that is, you can use them as a credit card, a debit card, a stored-value money card, or a loyalty card. Smart cards are ideal for *micropayments*, which are small payments of a few dollars or less.

Digital Wallets. A **digital wallet** is an application (app) used for making financial transactions. These apps can be on users' desktops or on their smartphones. When the app is on a smartphone, it becomes a mobile payment system. Digital wallets replace the need to carry physical credit and debit cards, gift cards, and loyalty cards, as well as boarding passes and other forms of identification. Digital wallets may also store insurance and loyalty cards, drivers' licenses, ID cards, Web site passwords, and login information. Further, digital wallets eliminate having to enter shipping, billing, and credit card data each time you make a purchase at a Web site. The data are encrypted in the user's machine, and the wallet contains a digital certificate that identifies the authorized cardholder. Because smartphones know their current location, nearby stores can send offers to users, and the wallet ensures the appropriate discounts are taken if a purchase is made.

A digital wallet allows the user to pay for merchandise in a store by tapping the phone on the merchant's terminal or by scanning a QR code. Security is provided by the phone's fingerprint reader or by entering a PIN. The wallet transmits user data to the terminal using Bluetooth or near field communication (NFC).

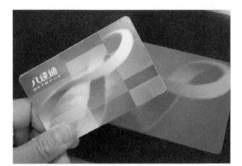

Mike Clarke/AFP/Getty Images/NewsCom

FIGURE 9.2 Example of purchasing card.

© Clarence Holmes Photography/Alamy Limited

FIGURE 9.3 The New York City Metro Card.

© MARKA/Alamy Limited

FIGURE 9.4 Smart cards are frequently multipurpose.

Examples of digital wallets include PayPal (www.paypal.com), Google Wallet (https://www.google.com/wallet), and Apple Pay (www.apple.com). The competition in this field is intense.

For example, the adoption of Apple Pay has been slowed by the Merchant Customer Exchange (MCX; www.mcx.com). MCX is a company created by a consortium of U.S. retail companies to develop a merchant-owned mobile payment system, which will be called "CurrentC." The company is led by merchants such as 7-Eleven, Alon Brands, Best Buy, CVS Health, Darden Restaurants, HMSHost, Hy-Vee, Lowe's, Michaels, Publix, Sears Holdings, Shell Oil Products US, Sunoco, Target Corporation, and Walmart. MCX's flagship product is CurrentC, a digital wallet. CurrentC is designed primarily to prevent merchants from paying credit card transaction fees. Shortly after CurrentC was launched in early 2015, Best Buy and Walmart explicitly stated that they would not accept Apple Pay, while in October 2014, CVS Pharmacy and Rite-Aid disabled all NFC payment systems. On the other hand, Walt Disney World began accepting Apple Pay beginning December 24, 2014.

On February 23, 2015, Google acquired the Softcard digital wallet's intellectual property and integrated it into Google Wallet. The Softcard digital wallet was a joint venture between AT&T (www.att.com), T-Mobile (www.t-mobile.com), and Verizon (www.verizon.com).

Bitcoin. *Bitcoin* is a type of digital currency in which encryption techniques are used to regulate the generation of units of currency and verify the transfer of funds, operating independently of any central bank. Bitcoin can be used to buy things electronically. In that sense, it resembles conventional dollars, euros, or yen, which are also traded digitally. However, bitcoin's most important characteristic, which makes it different from conventional money, is that it is decentralized. No single institution controls the bitcoin network.

Benefits and Limitations of E-Commerce

Few innovations in human history have provided as many benefits to organizations, individuals, and society as e-commerce has. E-commerce benefits organizations by making national and international markets more accessible and by lowering the costs of processing, distributing, and retrieving information. Customers benefit by being able to access a vast number of products and services, around the clock. The major benefit to society is the ability to easily and conveniently deliver information, services, and products to people in cities, rural areas, and developing countries.

Despite all these benefits, EC has some limitations, both technological and nontechnological, that have restricted its growth and acceptance. One major technological limitation is the lack of universally accepted security standards. Also, in less-developed countries, telecommunications bandwidth often is insufficient, and accessing the Web is expensive. Nontechnological limitations include the perceptions that EC is insecure, has unresolved legal issues, and lacks a critical mass of sellers and buyers. As time passes, these limitations, especially the technological ones, will diminish or be overcome.

Before you go on...

1. Define e-commerce and distinguish it from e-business.
2. Differentiate among B2C, B2B, C2C, and B2E electronic commerce.
3. Define e-government.
4. Discuss forward and reverse auctions.
5. Discuss the various online payment mechanisms.
6. Identify some benefits and limitations of e-commerce.

Apply the Concept 9.1

LEARNING OBJECTIVE 9.1 Describe the six common types of electronic commerce.

STEP 1: Background (Here is what you are learning.)

Today there are many companies that specialize in making e-commerce a reality for small businesses. Amazon, Yahoo!, PayPal, and other entities offer services that provide everything a small business needs to sell products and accept payment over the Internet. In fact, many consumers prefer for their transactions to go through these larger global companies because they trust these companies' security.

STEP 2: Activity (Here is what you are doing.)

Visit http://www.wiley.com/go/rainer/MIS4e/applytheconcept and click on the link provided for Apply the Concept 9.1. This link will take you to PayPal's Web site. Click on the business link at the top of the page. You will find that PayPal offers easy solutions for both businesses and customers.

STEP 3: Deliverable (Here is what you turn in.)

Create and submit a table that lists and describes the six common types of e-commerce. Which ones are supported by PayPal and which are not? For the second group, can you explain why they are not supported? Should PayPal move into these areas of e-commerce as well?

9.2 Business-to-Consumer (B2C) Electronic Commerce

B2B EC is much larger than B2C EC by volume, but B2C EC is more complex. The reason is that B2C involves a large number of buyers making millions of diverse transactions per day from a relatively small number of sellers. As an illustration, consider Amazon, an online retailer that offers thousands of products to its customers. Each customer purchase is relatively small, but Amazon must manage every transaction as if that customer were its most important one. The company needs to process each order quickly and efficiently, and ship the products to the customer in a timely manner. In addition, it has to manage returns. Multiply this simple example by millions, and you get an idea of how complex B2C EC can be. Overall, B2B complexities tend to be more business related, whereas B2C complexities tend to be more technical and volume related. IT's About Business 9.2 illustrates how Swipely helps businesses better understand their customers. That is, Swipely is an example of B2C commerce.

IT's About Business 9.2

MKT Swipely

MIS Founded in 2009, Swipely (www.swipely.com) is a service that processes credit card transactions for merchants. The online software works with point-of-sale systems and terminals used by independent businesses, including restaurants, salons, boutiques, and grocers, without the need for additional hardware. Merchants in the Swipely network use the product to integrate customer spending, social media, and other data to obtain valuable insights into customer behavior.

Swipely's competitive advantage lies in giving vendors a clearer picture of their customers' buying habits. As its name implies, Swipely's cloud servers (we describe cloud computing in detail in Plug IT In 4) analyze information left by card swipes. To protect customer information, Swipely deletes personally identifying data, and then presents the data to merchants in the form of customer dashboards that reveal which goods each card number purchased and when. The dashboards are capable of performing very finely tuned analyses, such as how a certain weather condition on a certain day affects sales. Swipely also works with vendors' social media accounts so stores and restaurants can track the success of things like Facebook promotions or Yelp reviews.

Swipely becomes even more effective if customers provide merchants with their name and e-mail address, which 20 percent are willing to do. In this way, Swipely's dashboards can display customer responses to e-mail or coupon offers—a service that often costs hundreds of dollars a month, which Swipely provides for free.

Swipely competes with numerous payment-processing services including Square (www.squareup.com), Heartland Payment Systems (www.heartlandpaymentsystems.com), and Chase Paymentech (www.chasepaymentech.com). Many companies are competing in this arena because consumer spending information is extremely valuable. Square (www.squareup.com), for example, is competing for the same customers as Swipely. One of these customers—the Blue Bottle Coffee Company (www.bluebottlecoffee .com), which has more than a dozen locations in Oakland, San

Francisco, and New York—recently moved from Swipely to Square at its registers. It would not take much for Square to expand its services to offer customer analytics as well.

Swipely's competitive advantage over Square, for now, is price. Swipely takes an average of 2.65 percent of its merchants' customer transactions, whereas Square's average charge is 2.75 percent. Furthermore, chances are good that merchants will not have to purchase additional equipment, as long as their registers are one of more than 50 systems that are compatible with the Swipely cloud-based service.

So, how is Swipely doing? In November 2014, Swipely announced that it was processing more than $4 billion of customer transactions annually with its participating merchants.

In May 2015, Swipely CEO Angus David announced an unspecified number of layoffs for "organizational reasons." However, he added that Swipely had tripled its number of customers to 3,000 and also had tripled its recurring revenue.

By August 2015, Swipely had raised $40.5 million in venture capital.

Sources: Compiled from K. Bramson, "CEO Says Swipely Layoffs Due to Sales Shift, But Company Is Still Growing," *Providence Journal*,

May 6, 2015; T. Nesi, "Providence Tech Startup Swipely Lays Off Workers," *WPRI.com*, May 5, 2015; M. Seekamp, "A Better Way to Approach Brand-Level Sales Reporting," *Swipely*, January 6, 2015; "Swipely Announces Managing $4B in Annual Sales," QSR Magazine, November 21, 2014; E. Ducoff, "Swipely Reveals How Menu and Server Performance Impact Sales," *Swipely,* February 11, 2014; "Swipely Release Helps Operators Track Behavior," *QSR Magazine*, January 24, 2014; A. Wilhelm, "Now Processing $1B Annually, Swipely Announces a Partner Network to Support Growth," *TechCrunch*, September 24, 2013; E. Carlyle, "Plastic Insights," *Forbes*, May 27, 2013; O. Thomas, "When Hurricane Sandy Struck, This Company Changed Its Entire Sales Plan—In Minutes," *Business Insider*, January 19, 2013; L. Baverman, "Swipely Brings Big Data to Small Biz," *Upstart Business Journal*, November 8, 2012; T. Geron, "Swipely Expands Credit Card-Based Loyalty Service," *Forbes*, December 15, 2011; L. Gannes, "Swipely Aims to (Politely) Turn Purchases into Conversations," *GigaOM*, May 10, 2010; www.swipely.com, accessed August 20, 2015.

Questions

1. Describe the advantages that Swipely offers merchants that help it maintain a competitive advantage in the marketplace.

2. Refer back to Chapter 2. Does Swipely function as a strategic information system for a merchant? Why or why not?

This section addresses the primary issues in B2C EC. We begin by studying the two basic mechanisms that customers utilize to access companies on the Web: electronic storefronts and electronic malls. In addition to purchasing products over the Web, customers also access online services. Therefore, the next section covers several online services, such as banking, securities trading, job searching, and travel. The complexity of B2C EC creates two major challenges for sellers: channel conflict and order fulfillment. We examine these two topics in detail. Finally, companies engaged in B2C EC must "get the word out" to prospective customers. This section concludes with a look at online advertising.

Electronic Storefronts and Malls

For several generations, home shopping from catalogs, and later from television shopping channels, has attracted millions of customers. Today, shopping online offers an alternative to catalog and television shopping. Electronic retailing (e-tailing) is the direct sale of products and services through electronic storefronts or electronic malls, usually designed around an electronic catalog format and/or auctions.

Like any mail-order shopping experience, e-commerce enables you to buy from home and to do so 24 hours a day, 7 days a week. Compared with mail order, however, EC offers a wider variety of products and services, including the most unique items, often at lower prices. Furthermore, within seconds, shoppers can access very detailed supplementary product information. In addition, they can easily locate and compare competitors' products and prices. Finally, buyers can find hundreds of thousands of sellers. Two popular online shopping mechanisms are electronic storefronts and electronic malls.

Electronic Storefronts. As we saw earlier in the chapter, an electronic storefront is a Web site that represents a single store. Today, Internet shoppers can access hundreds of thousands of electronic storefronts. Each storefront has a unique uniform resource locator (URL), or Internet address, at which buyers can place orders. Some electronic storefronts are extensions of physical stores such as Hermes, The Sharper Image, and Walmart. Others are new businesses started by entrepreneurs who discovered a niche on the Web (e.g., Restaurant.com and Alloy .com). Manufacturers (e.g., www.dell.com) and retailers (e.g., www.officedepot.com) also use storefronts.

Electronic Malls. Whereas an electronic storefront represents a single store, an **electronic mall**, also known as a *cybermall* or an *e-mall*, is a collection of individual shops grouped under a single Internet address. The basic idea of an electronic mall is the same as that of a regular shopping mall: to provide a one-stop shopping place that offers a wide range of products and services. A cybermall may include thousands of vendors. For example, Microsoft Shopping (now Bing shopping, www.bing.com/shopping) includes tens of thousands of products from thousands of vendors.

There are two types of cybermalls. In the first type, known as *referral malls* (e.g., www .hawaii.com), you cannot buy anything. Instead, you are transferred from the mall to a participating storefront. In the second type of mall (e.g., http://shopping.google.com), you can actually make a purchase. At this type of mall, you might shop from several stores, but you make only one purchase transaction at the end. You use an *electronic shopping cart* to gather items from various vendors and then pay for all of them in a single transaction. The mall organizer, such as Google, takes a commission from the sellers for this service.

Online Service Industries

In addition to purchasing products, customers can also access needed services via the Web. Selling books, toys, computers, and most other products on the Internet can reduce vendors' selling costs by 20–40 percent. Further reduction is difficult to achieve because the products must be delivered physically. Only a few products, such as software and music, can be digitized and then delivered online for additional savings. In contrast, services, such as buying an airline ticket and purchasing stocks or insurance, can be delivered entirely through e-commerce, often with considerable cost reduction. Not surprisingly, then, online delivery of services is growing very rapidly, with millions of new customers being added each year.

One of the most pressing EC issues relating to online services (as well as in marketing tangible products) is **disintermediation**. Intermediaries, also known as middlemen, have two functions: (1) they provide information, and (2) they perform value-added services such as consulting. The first function can be fully automated and most likely will be assumed by e-marketplaces and portals that provide information for free. When this development occurs, the intermediaries who perform only (or primarily) this function are likely to be eliminated. The process whereby intermediaries are eliminated is called disintermediation.

In contrast to simply providing information, performing value-added services requires expertise. Unlike the information function, then, this function can be only partially automated. Thus, intermediaries who provide value-added services not only are likely to survive but they may also actually prosper. The Web helps these employees in two situations: (1) when the number of participants is enormous, as with job searches, and (2) when the information that must be exchanged is complex.

In this section, you will examine some leading online service industries: banking, trading of securities (stocks, bonds), job matching, travel services, and advertising.

FIN   **Cyberbanking.** *Electronic banking*, also known as cyberbanking, involves conducting various banking activities from home, at a place of business, or on the road instead of at a physical bank location. Electronic banking has capabilities ranging from paying bills to applying for a loan. For customers, it saves time and is convenient. For banks, it offers an inexpensive alternative to branch banking—for example, about 2 cents cost per transaction versus $1.07 at a physical branch. Cyberbanking also enables banks to attract remote customers. In addition to regular banks with added online services, *Internet-only banks*, which are dedicated solely to Internet transactions, are emerging.

International banking and the ability to handle trading in multiple currencies are critical for international trade. Transfers of electronic funds and electronic letters of credit are vital services in international banking. An example of support for EC global trade is provided by TradeCard, in conjunction with MasterCard. TradeCard is an international company that provides a secure method for buyers and sellers to make digital payments anywhere on the globe (see the demo at www.tradecard.com). In another example, banks and companies such as Oanda (www.oanda.com) provide conversions of more than 160 currencies.

Online Securities Trading. Millions of Americans use computers to trade stocks, bonds, and other financial instruments. In fact, several well-known securities companies, including E'Trade, Ameritrade, and Charles Schwab, offer only online trading. In Korea, more than half of stock traders are already using the Internet for that purpose. Why? Because it is cheaper than a full-service or discount broker. On the Web, investors can find a considerable amount of information regarding specific companies or mutual funds in which to invest (e.g., http://money.cnn.com and www.bloomberg.com).

Let's say, for example, that you have an account with Scottrade. You access Scottrade's Web site (www.scottrade.com) from your personal computer or your Internet-enabled mobile device, enter your account number and password to access your personalized Web page, and then click on "stock trading." Using a menu, you enter the details of your order—buy or sell, margin or cash, price limit, market order, and so on. The computer informs you of the current "ask" and "bid" prices, much as a broker would do over the telephone. You can then approve or reject the transaction.

The Online Job Market. The Internet offers a promising new environment for job seekers and for companies searching for hard-to-find employees. Thousands of companies and government agencies advertise available positions, accept resumes, and take applications via the Internet.

Job seekers use the online job market to reply online to employment ads, to place resumes on various sites, and to use recruiting firms (e.g., www.monster.com, www.simplyhired.com, www.linkedin.com, and www.truecareers.com). Companies that have jobs to offer advertise these openings on their Web sites, and they search the bulletin boards of recruiting firms. In many countries (including the United States), governments must advertise job openings on the Internet.

Travel Services. The Internet is an ideal place to plan, explore, and arrange almost any trip economically. Online travel services allow you to purchase airline tickets, reserve hotel rooms, and rent cars. Most sites also offer a fare-tracker feature that sends you e-mail messages about low-cost flights. Examples of comprehensive online travel services are Expedia.com, Travelocity.com, and Orbitz.com. Online services are also provided by all major airline vacation services, large conventional travel agencies, car rental agencies, hotels (e.g., www.hotels.com), and tour companies. In a variation of this process, Priceline.com allows you to set a price you are willing to pay for an airline ticket or hotel accommodations. It then attempts to find a vendor that will match your price.

One costly problem that e-commerce can cause is "mistake fares" in the airline industry. For example, on August 6, 2012, El Al (www.elal.com), Israel's national airline, offered flights to Israel worth up to $1,600 for as little as some $300. This price was incorrect; the actual price was higher. By the time El Al noticed the mistake and pulled the fare, however, several tickets had been sold, thanks in part to online travel discussion groups.

Online Advertising. *Advertising* is the practice of disseminating information in an attempt to influence a buyer–seller transaction. Traditional advertising on TV or in newspapers involves impersonal, one-way mass communication. In contrast, direct response marketing, or telemarketing, contacts individuals by direct mail or telephone and requires them to respond in order to make a purchase. The direct response approach personalizes advertising and marketing. At the same time, however, it can be expensive, slow, and ineffective. It can also be extremely annoying to the consumer.

Internet advertising redefines the advertising process, making it media rich, dynamic, and interactive. It improves on traditional forms of advertising in a number of ways. First, Internet ads can be updated any time at minimal cost and therefore can be kept current. In addition, these ads can reach very large numbers of potential buyers all over the world. Furthermore, they are generally cheaper than radio, television, and print ads. Finally, Internet ads can be interactive and targeted to specific interest groups and/or individuals.

Online Advertising Methods. The most common online advertising methods are banners, pop-ups, and e-mail. Banners are simply electronic billboards. Typically, a banner contains a short text or a graphical message to promote a product or a vendor. It may even contain video clips and sound. When customers click on a banner, they are transferred to the advertiser's home page. Banner advertising is the most commonly used form of advertising on the Internet.

A major advantage of banners is that they can be customized to the target audience. If the computer system knows who you are or what your profile is, it might send you a banner that is specifically intended to match your interests. A major disadvantage of banners is that they can convey only limited information because of their small size. Another drawback is that many viewers simply ignore them.

Pop-up and pop-under ads are contained in a new browser window that is automatically launched when you enter or exit a Web site. A **pop-up ad** appears in front of the current browser window. A **pop-under ad** appears underneath the active window; when users close the active window, they see the ad. Many users strongly object to these ads, which they consider intrusive. Modern browsers let users block pop-up ads, but this feature must be used with caution because some Web sites depend on pop-up capabilities to present content other than advertising.

E-mail is emerging as an Internet advertising and marketing channel. It is generally cost-effective to implement, and it provides a better and quicker response rate than other advertising channels. Marketers develop or purchase a list of e-mail addresses, place them in a customer database, and then send advertisements via e-mail. A list of e-mail addresses can be a very powerful tool because the marketer can target a group of people or even individuals.

As you have probably concluded by now, there is a potential for misuse of e-mail advertising. In fact, some consumers receive a flood of unsolicited e-mail, or *spam*. **Spamming** is the indiscriminate distribution of electronic ads without the permission of the receiver. Unfortunately, spamming is becoming worse over time.

Two important responses to spamming are permission marketing and viral marketing. **Permission marketing** asks consumers to give their permission to voluntarily accept online advertising and e-mail. Typically, consumers are asked to complete an electronic form that asks what they are interested in and requests permission to send related marketing information. Sometimes, consumers are offered incentives to receive advertising.

Permission marketing is the basis of many Internet marketing strategies. For example, millions of users periodically receive e-mails from airlines such as American and Southwest. Users of this marketing service can ask to be notified of low fares from their hometown or to their favorite destinations. Significantly, they can easily unsubscribe at any time. Permission marketing is also extremely important for market research (e.g., search for "Media Metrix" at www.comscore.com).

Viral marketing refers to online word-of-mouth marketing. The strategy behind viral marketing is to have people forward messages to friends, family members, and other acquaintances suggesting they "check this out." For example, a marketer can distribute a small game program embedded with a sponsor's e-mail that is easy to forward. The marketer releases only a few thousand copies, with the expectation that the recipients in turn will forward the program to many more thousands of potential customers. In this way, viral marketing enables companies to build brand awareness at a minimal cost without having to spam millions of uninterested users.

Issues in E-Tailing

Despite e-tailing's increasing popularity, many e-tailers continue to face serious issues that can restrict their growth. Perhaps the two most significant issues are channel conflict and order fulfillment.

Clicks-and-mortar companies may face a conflict with their regular distributors when they sell directly to customers online. This situation, known as **channel conflict**, can alienate the distributors. Channel conflict has forced some companies to avoid direct online sales. For example, Walmart, Lowe's, and Home Depot would rather have customers come to their stores. Therefore, although all three companies maintain e-commerce Web sites, their sites place more emphasis on providing information—products, prices, specials, and store locations—than on online sales.

Channel conflict can arise in areas such as pricing and resource allocation—for example, how much money to spend on advertising. Another potential source of conflict involves the logistics services provided by the offline activities to the online activities. For example, how should a company handle returns of items purchased online? Some companies have completely separated the "clicks" (the online portion of the organization) from the "mortar" or "bricks" (the traditional bricks-and-mortar part of the organization). However, this approach can increase expenses, reduce the synergy between the two organizational channels, and alienate customers. As a result, many companies are integrating their online and offline channels, a process known as multichanneling. In fact, many companies are calling this process omni-channeling, as you see in IT's About Business 9.3.

IT's About Business 9.3

MKT The Omni-Channel Customer Experience

POM In recent years, the traditional bricks-and-mortar strategy for large retailers, with its accompanying high overhead costs, has become a barrier to competitiveness. Amazon (www.amazon.com), which does not maintain any physical stores, has achieved major market share—and has evolved into the world's largest Internet retailer—through a combination of lower prices and huge selection. But traditional retailers with stores have the upper hand over e-commerce for shoppers who want to try in person before they buy.

To compete with Amazon, the world's largest retailers are adopting an omni-channel strategy that enables customers to seamlessly combine their experience of online shopping on any device with in-store shopping. This strategy is becoming increasingly important as Amazon builds its own fulfillment centers closer to customers.

Big-box retailers are rethinking their distribution systems, which are often based on centralized warehouses. Many of them are now filling online orders from the store nearest the customer instead of hundreds of miles away. Staff pluck items from the sales floor, box them up, and send them on their way via FedEx and UPS.

This new order fulfillment model, called *ship-from-store*, benefits customers by speeding up delivery. It benefits the retailers by reducing shipping costs and cutting down on sales-floor overstocks that result in big markdowns. Most importantly, it helps retailers go head to head with Amazon.

Let's consider four retailers: Gap (www.gap.com), Walmart (www.walmart.com), and Best Buy (www.bestbuy.com) in the United States and John Lewis (www.johnlewis.com) in Great Britain.

Gap stores were the first to implement ship-from-store, and the retailer has added this service to the e-commerce systems of two Gap-owned chains, Banana Republic and Athleta. Not coincidentally, Gap's annual revenue increased by $500 million in 2013.

Nearly 70 percent of Americans live within five miles of a Walmart. Therefore, the company is using its stores to fulfill online orders, along with its storage warehouses and specific fulfillment centers. By late 2015, roughly 10 percent of the items ordered on Walmart.com were shipped from 35 stores. Most of those orders were delivered within two days. Walmart charges a $10 fee for same-day delivery service. In some cases, the company uses third-party carriers to ship items from its stores. In addition, Walmart employees sometimes deliver products by car. This ship-from-store strategy exceeded expectations, and Walmart was planning to expand the service to hundreds of its stores.

Best Buy, the biggest U.S. consumer electronics retailer, has deployed ship-from-store in about 50 stores. About one billion visits are made to the Best Buy Web site each year, but up to 4 percent of visitors cannot complete their transaction because the company's online distribution system is out of stock. But 8 times out of 10, the product is available in a Best Buy store, so the company wants to expand its ship-from-store system to more locations.

John Lewis (www.johnlewis.com), a chain of 43 department stores that operates throughout England, Scotland, and Wales, has implemented a different version of the omni-channel strategy with its click-and-collect process. Click-and-collect is similar to ship-from-store, except online customers have to pick up their packages themselves at a John Lewis store—they are not shipped from the store. John Lewis charges two British pounds for click-and-collect orders valued at less than 30 pounds.

Click-and-collect has been a tremendous success for John Lewis. In fact, for the 2014 holiday season, click-and-collect sales surpassed home deliveries. In addition, online sales increased by 19 percent, accounting for more than 30 percent of the retailer's gross revenue. Further, more than half the firm's online orders were of the click-and-collect type.

Sources: Compiled from C. Tode, "Traditional Retailers Crush Ecommerce Giants in Omnichannel Shopping," *Mobile Commerce Daily*, July 1, 2015; D. Schutz, "Top 100 Retailers 2015," *National Retail Federation*, July 1, 2015; R. Smithers, "John Lewis to Charge for 'Click and Collect'," *The Guardian*, July 1, 2015; "Department Store Boosts IT Investment to Create Seamless Omni-Channel Experience," *Computer Weekly*, May 2-8, 2015; T. Team, "Why Is Omni-Channel Retailing So Important for Bed Bath & Beyond?" *Forbes*, February 12, 2015; "The Omni-Channel Opportunity for Retailers: What's the Story?" *The Guardian*, January 14, 2015; J. Popovec, "Nordstrom, Walgreens Praised for Omni-Channel Strategies," *National Real Estate Investor*, October 9, 2014; D. Newman, "The Omni-Channel Experience: Marketing Meets Ubiquity," *Forbes*, July 22, 2014; J. Green, "Why and How Brands Must Go Omni-Channel in 2014, *Marketing Land*, January 27, 2014; A. Barr, "Retail Stores Become Shipping Hubs to Battle Amazon," *USA Today*, October 6, 2013.H. Wallop, "Click and Collect – The New Way to Go Shopping," *The Telegraph*, January 8, 2013.

Questions

1. Why is an "omni-channel" strategy such an important component of retailers' missions today?

2. Describe the problems retailers face in implementing a ship-from-store strategy.

3. Identify some strategies that Amazon could employ to counter the ship-from-store strategy from traditional bricks-and-mortar retailers.

4. Discuss the differences between the ship-from-store and click-and-collect processes.

Multichanneling has created the opportunity for showrooming. *Showrooming* occurs when shoppers visit a brick-and-mortar store to examine a product in person. They then conduct research about the product on their smartphones. Often, they purchase the product from the Web site of a competitor of the store they are visiting. Showrooming is causing problems for brick-and-mortar retailers, such as Target, Best Buy, and others. At the same time, showrooming benefits Amazon, eBay, and other online retailers.

POM

The second major issue confronting e-commerce is order fulfillment, which can create problems for e-tailers. Any time a company sells directly to customers, it is involved in various order-fulfillment activities. It must perform the following activities: quickly find the products to be shipped; pack them; arrange for the packages to be delivered speedily to the customer's door; collect the money from every customer, either in advance, by COD, or by individual bill; and handle the return of unwanted or defective products.

It is very difficult to accomplish these activities both effectively and efficiently in B2C, because a company has to ship small packages to many customers and do it quickly. For this reason, companies involved in B2C activities often experience difficulties in their supply chains.

In addition to providing customers with the products they ordered and doing it on time, order fulfillment provides all related customer services. For example, the customer must receive assembly and operation instructions for a new appliance. In addition, if the customer is unhappy with a product, the company must arrange an exchange or a return.

In the late 1990s, e-tailers faced continuous problems in order fulfillment, especially during the holiday season. These problems included late deliveries, delivering wrong items, high delivery costs, and compensation to unsatisfied customers. For e-tailers, taking orders over the Internet is the easy part of B2C e-commerce. Delivering orders to customers' doors is the hard part. In contrast, order fulfillment is less complicated in B2B. These transactions are much larger, but they are fewer in number. In addition, these companies have had order fulfillment mechanisms in place for many years.

Before you go on…

1. Describe electronic storefronts and malls.
2. Discuss various types of online services, such as cyberbanking, securities trading, job searches, travel services, and so on.
3. Discuss online advertising, its methods, and its benefits.
4. Identify the major issues related to e-tailing.
5. What are spamming, permission marketing, and viral marketing?

Apply the Concept 9.2

LEARNING OBJECTIVE 9.2 Describe the various online services of business-to-consumer (B2C) commerce, along with specific examples of each.

STEP 1: Background

At this point in your "buying" career, you have probably purchased something online, visited an auction site (and possibly won a bid), and engaged in some form of online banking. Your generation is very comfortable with the retail side of e-commerce. While you were engaging in B2C e-commerce, you probably created an account with a few vendors and received some e-mail advertisements. No doubt you have also received some pop-up ads promoting products during your Internet searches.

Another aspect of modern business that has changed is that companies now want you to do their advertising for them. The text refers to this development as viral marketing.

STEP 2: Activity

Imagine that you and some friends decide to start a new online thrift store. To become a member, an individual has to donate to the thrift. For every ten items a person donates, he or she is awarded a two-month membership. However, you have no IT platform for e-commerce. After some research, you determine that Shopify is your best provider. Shopify is an e-commerce platform that enables individuals and businesses to create online stores.

Visit http://www.wiley.com/go/rainer/MIS4e/applytheconcept, and click on the link provided for Apply the Concept 9.2. This link will take you to Shopify's Web site. Near the top of the page you will see a link to "Examples" of other providers. Look through the examples to identify ideas you would like to incorporate into your store.

STEP 3: Deliverable

After reviewing the Shopify site, prepare a presentation or a document that describes the various online services of B2C commerce provided by Shopify. Provide specific examples of services that attracted your attention and discuss how you would apply these services to your store.

9.3 | Business-to-Business (B2B) Electronic Commerce

In *business to business* (*B2B*) e-commerce, the buyers and sellers are business organizations. B2B comprises about 85 percent of EC volume. It covers a broad spectrum of applications that enable an enterprise to form electronic relationships with its distributors, resellers, suppliers, customers, and other partners. Organizations can use B2B to restructure their supply chains and their partner relationships.

B2B applications utilize any of several business models. The major models are sell-side marketplaces, buy-side marketplaces, and electronic exchanges.

Sell-Side Marketplaces

In the sell-side marketplace model, organizations attempt to sell their products or services to other organizations electronically from their own private e-marketplace Web site and/or from a third-party Web site. This model is similar to the B2C model in which the buyer is expected to come to the seller's site, view catalogs, and place an order. In the B2B sell-side marketplace, however, the buyer is an organization.

The key mechanisms in the sell-side model are forward auctions and electronic catalogs that can be customized for each large buyer. Sellers such as Dell Computer (www.dellauction .com) use auctions extensively. In addition to conducting auctions from their own Web sites, organizations can use third-party auction sites, such as eBay, to liquidate items. Companies such as Ariba (www.ariba.com) are helping organizations to auction old assets and inventories.

The sell-side model is used by hundreds of thousands of companies. It is especially powerful for companies with superb reputations. The seller can be either a manufacturer (e.g., Dell or IBM), a distributor (e.g., www.avnet.com), or a retailer (e.g., www.bigboxx.com). The seller uses EC to increase sales, reduce selling and advertising expenditures, increase delivery speed, and lower administrative costs. The sell-side model is especially suitable to customization. Many companies allow their customers to configure their orders online. For example, at Dell (www.dell.com), you can determine the exact type of computer that you want. You can choose the type of chip, the size of the hard drive, the type of monitor, and so on. Similarly, the Jaguar Web site (www.jaguar.com) allows you to customize the Jaguar you want. Self-customization greatly reduces any misunderstandings concerning what customers want, and it encourages businesses to fill orders more quickly.

Buy-Side Marketplaces

Procurement is the overarching function that describes the activities and processes to acquire goods and services. Distinct from purchasing, procurement involves the activities necessary to establish requirements, sourcing activities such as market research and vendor evaluation, and negotiation of contracts. *Purchasing* refers to the process of ordering and receiving goods and services. It is a subset of the procurement process.

The buy-side marketplace is a model in which organizations attempt to procure needed products or services from other organizations electronically. A major method of procuring goods and services in the buy-side model is the reverse auction.

The buy-side model uses EC technology to streamline the procurement process. The goal is to reduce both the costs of items procured and the administrative expenses involved in procuring them. In addition, EC technology can shorten the procurement cycle time.

Procurement by using electronic support is referred to as e-procurement. E-procurement uses reverse auctions, particularly group purchasing. In group purchasing, multiple buyers combine their orders so that they constitute a large volume and therefore attract more seller attention. In addition, when buyers place their combined orders on a reverse auction, they can negotiate a volume discount. Typically, the orders of small buyers are aggregated by a third-party vendor, such as the United Sourcing Alliance (www.usa-llc.com).

Electronic Exchanges

Private exchanges have one buyer and many sellers. Electronic marketplaces (e-marketplaces), called public exchanges or just exchanges, are independently owned by a third party, and they connect many sellers with many buyers. Public exchanges are open to all business organizations. They are frequently owned and operated by a third party. Public exchange managers provide all of the necessary information systems to the participants. Thus, buyers and sellers merely have to "plug in" in order to trade. B2B public exchanges are often the initial point of contacts between business partners. Once the partners make contact, they may move to a private exchange or to private trading rooms provided by many public exchanges to conduct their subsequent trading activities.

Electronic exchanges deal in both direct and indirect materials. *Direct materials* are inputs to the manufacturing process, such as safety glass used in automobile windshields and windows. *Indirect materials* are those items, such as office supplies, that are needed for maintenance, operations, and repairs (MRO).

There are three basic types of public exchanges: vertical, horizontal, and functional. All three types offer diversified support services, ranging from payments to logistics.

Vertical exchanges connect buyers and sellers in a given industry. Examples of vertical exchanges are www.plasticsnet.com in the plastics industry and www.papersite.com in the paper industry. The vertical e-marketplaces offer services that are particularly suited to the community they serve. Vertical exchanges are frequently owned and managed by a *consortium*, a term for a group of major players in an industry. For example, Marriott and Hyatt own a procurement consortium for the hotel industry, and Chevron owns an energy e-marketplace.

Horizontal exchanges connect buyers and sellers across many industries. They are used primarily for MRO materials. Examples of horizontal exchanges are TradersCity (www.traderscity.com), Globalsources (www.globalsources.com), and Alibaba (www.alibaba.com).

Finally, in *functional exchanges*, needed services such as temporary help or extra office space are traded on an "as-needed" basis. For example, Employease (www.employease.com) can find temporary labor by searching employers in its Employease Network.

We have looked closely at B2B electronic commerce in this section. IT's About Business 9.4 shows how Amazon has entered the B2B marketplace.

IT's About Business 9.4

POM **Amazon Moves into the B2B Marketplace**

MKT Amazon Business (www.amazon.com/business) is Amazon's e-commerce Web site that targets the wholesale and distribution business-to-business (B2B) marketplace. Amazon Business does for business customers what Amazon.com does for individual shoppers (B2C).

Amazon's B2B efforts began with AmazonSupply, which launched in 2012 with 500,000 items for sale. By 2014, the product list had expanded to more than 2.25 million items, including tools, home improvement goods, janitorial supplies, steel pipes, and a host of other products.

In 2015, Amazon created Amazon Business and folded AmazonSupply into it. Amazon Business uses a hybrid business model, selling both products directly from its own warehouses, as well as those from third-party vendors. The outside vendors, which still have to compete with Amazon products, receive a commission of between 6 and 15 percent for their items sold, based on the product category and order size.

Amazon Business customers, who will be approved to buy and sell based on their tax ID, will be able to access hundreds of millions of business-only products, obtain bulk discounts, set up a corporate credit line, and receive free two-day shipping on orders over $49. Clients can also chat with manufacturer representatives about product specifications. This process is crucial when dealing with complex technical products.

Amazon Business offers several useful features for sellers. For example:

- The site lists products, along with any accompanying quality credentials such as ISO 9000 certifications.

- Amazon Business account holders can qualify for special offers not available to consumers on the Amazon.com site. This helps vendors meet requirements not to sell products that are forbidden to be sold directly to consumers, such as high-tech healthcare equipment.

- Customers can search for products by both manufacturer and distributor part numbers.

- The site has the ability to demonstrate products in Web videos and to post downloadable computer-aided design (CAD) drawings.

Amazon Business also offers useful features for buyers. For example:

- Both single and multiple buyers can create business accounts, and groups of buyers can share payment methods and shipping addresses.

- Multiple offers from sellers are displayed on a single product page, making it easier to compare pricing and seller ratings issued by Amazon.

- Buyers can view other buyers' product reviews.

- Amazon Business is integrated with buyers' procurement software, enabling buyers to include Amazon on their list of authorized sellers within their procurement system.

Wholesalers are taking Amazon's threat seriously. The wholesale industry in the United States is almost twice the size of the retail industry. In 2014, wholesale sales totaled $7.2 trillion, compared with more than $4 trillion for retail sales. America's 35,000 distributors are largely regional, family-run companies with annual sales of $50 million or less. Only 160 of these businesses report annual sales exceeding $1 billion. In contrast, Amazon reported more than $89 billion in revenues in 2014, selling goods in both the B2C and B2B marketplaces. The average wholesaler offers approximately 50,000 products online, compared to Amazon Business's hundreds of millions of products.

Amazon Business is competitive even in niche markets. Take scientific equipment as an example. Items such as centrifuges and Bunsen burners are usually only available from specialty distributors. But you can get one at the click of a mouse through Amazon Business. Few specialty distributors can compete with Amazon's huge inventory, its easy-to-navigate Web site, two-day delivery, physical infrastructure (fulfillment centers in the United States), and information technology infrastructure (e.g., Amazon Web Services).

To acquire and maintain competitive advantage, Amazon Business keeps inventory that will not necessarily sell quickly, in order to avoid stockouts that plague other distributors of specialty items. Industry analysts estimate that Amazon stocks more than 50 percent of what it offers on the Web site at any given time.

B2B has very small margins, typically 2 to 4 percent. Amazon's scale allows it to make money through high volumes. And it achieves these high volumes through—what else—beating competitors' prices by about 25 percent on common items, according to a Boston Consulting Group (www.bcg.com) study.

Despite its success, Amazon Business does have competition. Consider W.W. Grainger (www.grainger.com), in business since 1927, which controls about 6 percent of the entire U.S. B2B market. The company, which sells tools for maintenance and repair, now operates more than 700 regional sales branches and 33 distribution centers. The company recorded $10 billion in revenue in 2014, most of which it still generated offline. Nevertheless, in 2014, it had more than $3 billion in online sales.

One area that Amazon Business may not be able to penetrate is the close partnerships that some distributors have with institutional clients. For example, medical supplier Cardinal Health (www.cardinalhealth.com) has taken over the entire supply chain at the Nebraska Medical Center. Cardinal handles everything from truck to patient. It orders products from suppliers, tracks product distribution, handles loading dock workers, and deals with supplier invoicing.

The challenge confronting the nation's 35,000 wholesalers and distributors is to compete with Amazon Business. Industry analysts identify two possibilities:

1. Provide value-added, personalized services to customers. For example, Valin Corporation (www.valinonline.com) has focused on the oil and gas sector, dispatching engineers to oil fields to help deploy the company's products that manage output at surface oil wells.

2. Go into areas Amazon may fear to tread. Amazon may not want to meet every customer's needs in a complex, highly segmented business environment. For instance, will Amazon want to sell oxygen tanks or soda pumps? Further, Amazon might not want to manage products that are dangerous or exotic, such as dentists' chairs, or that require specialists.

Sources: Compiled from E. Smith, "Can Amazon 'Uber' Distributors?" *Modern Distribution Management*, June 17, 2015; E. Smith, "Recommended Reading: Amazon Business Open to Distributors," *Modern Distribution Management*, June 9, 2015; D. Buss, "New Amazon Business Marketplace Goes after B2B Dollars," *Brand Channel*, May 1, 2015; E. Smith, "Amazon Reinvents B2B Model," *Modern Distribution Management*, April 29, 2015; S. Soper, "Amazon Business Aims for $1 Trillion Corporate-Spending Market," *BloombergBusiness*, April 28, 2015; P. Demery, "Say Hello To Amazon Business, Good-Bye to AmazonSupply," *Internet Retailer*, April 28, 2015; C. O'Connor, "Amazon Launches Amazon Business Marketplace, Will Close AmazonSupply," *Forbes*, April 28, 2015; C. O'Connor, "Amazon's Wholesale Slaughter: Jeff Bezos' $8 Trillion B2B Bet," *Forbes*, May 7, 2014; J. Hans, "Q&A: How Amazon Could Change 'B2B'," *Manufacturing.net*, February 3, 2014; www.amazon.com/business, accessed August 18, 2015.

Questions

1. Consider Tulsa Community College (www.tulsacc.edu), which is using Amazon Business to order test tubes, basketballs, office supplies, and other goods instead of having employees buy them from local retailers or specialty sellers. The daily needs of the college's 15,000 students translate into about $10,000 of orders per month.

   What is the impact of Amazon Business on local wholesalers and retailers in Tulsa?

   How could local businesses in Tulsa compete with Amazon Business?

2. Provide other methods for wholesalers to compete with Amazon Business.

Apply the Concept 9.3

LEARNING OBJECTIVE 9.3 Describe the three business models for business-to-business electronic commerce.

STEP 1: Background

Section 9.3 describes forward auctions, reverse auctions, and exchanges. Forward auctions are used when a seller is trying to reach several buyers, and reverse auctions are used when a buyer is soliciting from several sellers. In an exchange, both buyers and sellers come to a central Web site to quickly and easily establish a B2B relationship. Some of these Web sites or exchanges are for materials involved in manufacturing a product; others involve materials that help run the business.

STEP 2: Activity

Visit http://www.wiley.com/go/rainer/MIS4e/applytheconcept, and click on the link provided for Apply the Concept 9.3. This link will take you to one of the horizontal exchanges (an exchange for many buyers and sellers across industries) listed in the section. As you examine the available products, you should get a better understanding of the breadth of a horizontal exchange.

STEP 3: Deliverable

Describe the three business models for B2B e-commerce by comparing and contrasting them to Globalsource. Submit your description to your professor.

9.4 Ethical and Legal Issues in E-Business

Technological innovation often forces a society to reexamine and modify its ethical standards. In many cases, the new standards are incorporated into law. In this section, you will learn about two important ethical considerations—privacy and job loss—as well as various legal issues arising from the practice of e-business.

Ethical Issues

Many of the ethical and global issues related to IT also apply to e-business. Here you will learn about two basic issues: privacy and job loss.

By making it easier to store and transfer personal information, e-business presents some threats to privacy. To begin with, most electronic payment systems know who the buyers are. It may be necessary, then, to protect the buyers' identities. Businesses frequently use encryption to provide this protection.

Another major privacy issue is tracking. For example, individuals' activities on the Internet can be tracked by cookies (discussed in Chapter 7). Cookies store your tracking history on your personal computer's hard drive, and any time you revisit a certain Web site, the server recognizes the cookie. In response, antivirus software packages routinely search for potentially harmful cookies.

In addition to compromising individual privacy, the use of EC may eliminate the need for some of a company's employees, as well as brokers and agents. The manner in which these unneeded workers, especially employees, are treated can raise ethical issues: How should the company handle the layoffs? Should companies be required to retrain employees for new positions? If not, how should the company compensate or otherwise assist the displaced workers?

Legal and Ethical Issues Specific to E-Commerce

Many legal issues are related specifically to e-commerce. A business environment in which buyers and sellers do not know one another and cannot even see one another creates opportunities for dishonest people to commit fraud and other crimes. During the first few years of EC, the public witnessed many such crimes. These illegal actions ranged from creating a virtual bank that disappeared along with the investors' deposits to manipulating stock prices on the Internet. Unfortunately, fraudulent activities on the Internet are increasing. In the following section, you explore some of the major legal issues that are specific to e-commerce.

Fraud on the Internet. Internet fraud has grown even faster than Internet use itself. In one case, stock promoters falsely spread positive rumors about the prospects of the companies they touted in order to boost the stock price. In other cases, the information provided might have been true, but the promoters did not disclose that they were paid to talk up the companies. Stock promoters specifically target small investors who are lured by the promise of fast profits.

Stocks are only one of many areas where swindlers are active. Auctions are especially conducive to fraud, by both sellers and buyers. Other types of fraud include selling bogus investments and setting up phantom business opportunities. Because of the growing use of e-mail, financial criminals now have access to many more potential victims. The U.S. Federal Trade Commission (FTC) (www.ftc.gov) regularly publishes examples of scams that are most likely to be spread via e-mail or to be found on the Web. Later in this section, you will see some ways in which consumers and sellers can protect themselves from online fraud.

Domain Names. Another legal issue is competition over domain names. Domain names are assigned by central nonprofit organizations that check for conflicts and possible infringement of trademarks. Obviously, companies that sell goods and services over the Internet want customers to be able to find them easily. In general, the closer the domain name matches the company's name, the easier the company is to locate.

A domain name is considered legal when the person or business who owns the name has operated a legitimate business under that name for some time. Companies such as Christian Dior, Nike, Deutsche Bank, and even Microsoft have had to fight or pay to acquire the domain name that corresponds to their company's name. Consider the case of Delta Air Lines. Delta originally could not obtain the Internet domain name delta.com because Delta Faucet had already purchased it. Delta Faucet had been in business under that name since 1954, so it had a legitimate business interest in using the domain name. Delta Air Lines had to settle for delta-airlines.com until it bought the domain name from Delta Faucet. Delta Faucet is now at deltafaucet.com. Several cases of disputed domain names are currently in court.

Cybersquatting. Cybersquatting refers to the practice of registering or using domain names for the purpose of profiting from the goodwill or the trademark that belongs to someone else. The Anti-Cybersquatting Consumer Protection Act (1999) permits trademark owners in the United States to sue for damages in such cases.

However, some practices that could be considered cybersquatting are not illegal, although they may well be unethical. Perhaps the more common of these practices is "domain tasting." Domain tasting lets registrars profit from the complex money trail of pay-per-click advertising. The practice can be traced back to the policies of the organization responsible for regulating Web names, the Internet Corporation for Assigned Names and Numbers (ICANN) (www.icann .org). In 2000, ICANN established the "create grace period, " a five-day period during which a company or person can claim a domain name and then return it for a full refund of the $6 registry fee. ICANN implemented this policy to allow someone who mistyped a domain to return it without cost. In some cases, companies engage in cybersquatting by registering domain names that are very similar to their competitors' domain names in order to generate traffic from people who misspell Web addresses.

Domain tasters exploit this policy by claiming Internet domains for five days at no cost. These domain names frequently resemble those of prominent companies and organizations. The tasters then jam these domains full of advertisements that come from Yahoo! and Google. Because this process involves zero risk and 100 percent profit margins, domain tasters register millions of domain names every day—some of them over and over again. Experts estimate that registrants ultimately purchase less than 2 percent of the sites they sample. In the vast majority of cases, they use the domain names for only a few days to generate quick profits.

Taxes and Other Fees. In offline sales, most states and localities tax business transactions that are conducted within their jurisdiction. The most obvious example is sales taxes. Federal, state, and local authorities are now scrambling to create some type of taxation policy for e-business. This problem is particularly complex for interstate and international e-commerce. For example, some people claim that the state in which the *seller* is located deserves the entire sales tax (in some countries, it is a value-added tax (VAT)). Others contend that the state in which the *server* is located should also receive some of the tax revenues.

In addition to the sales tax, there is a question about where—and in some cases, whether—electronic sellers should pay business license taxes, franchise fees, gross receipts taxes, excise taxes, privilege taxes, and utility taxes. Furthermore, how should tax collection be controlled? Legislative efforts to impose taxes on e-commerce are opposed by an organization named the Internet Freedom Fighters.

In December 2013, the U.S. Supreme Court declined to get involved in state efforts to force Web retailers such as Amazon to collect sales tax from customers even in places where the companies do not have a physical presence. The court's decision to stay out of the issue may put pressure on Congress to come up with a national solution, as both online and traditional retailers complain about a patchwork of state laws and conflicting lower court decisions. As of mid-2016, all but five states impose sales taxes on online purchases, and an increasing number have passed legislation to force online retailers to begin collecting those taxes from customers.

Even before electronic commerce over the Internet emerged, the basic law was that as long as a retailer did not have a physical presence in the state where the consumer was shopping, that retailer did not have to collect a sales tax. Shoppers are supposed to track such purchases and then pay the taxes owed in their annual tax filings. Few people, however, do this or are even aware of it.

The result is that online retailers have been able to undercut the prices of their non-Internet (e.g., brick-and-mortar stores) competitors for years. As state and local governments have increasingly experienced large cash shortcomings since the recession, they have fought back. As of mid-2016, some 25 states required Amazon to collect sales taxes.

Copyright. Recall from Chapter 6 that intellectual property is protected by copyright laws and cannot be used freely. This point is significant because many people mistakenly believe that once they purchase a piece of software, they have the right to share it with others. In fact, what they have bought is the right to *use* the software, not the right to *distribute* it. That right remains with the copyright holder. Similarly, copying material from Web sites without permission is a violation of copyright laws. Protecting intellectual property rights in e-commerce is extremely difficult, however, because it involves hundreds of millions of people in 200 countries with differing copyright laws who have access to billions of Web pages.

Before you go on...

1. List and explain some ethical issues in EC.
2. Discuss the major legal issues associated with EC.
3. Describe buyer protection and seller protection in EC.

Apply the Concept 9.4

LEARNING OBJECTIVE 9.4 Discuss the ethical and legal issues related to electronic commerce, along with examples.

STEP 1: Background

Amazon.com is the world's largest online retailer. In fact, it is one of a kind in many ways. It competes with Apple, Google, Microsoft, and Walmart, some of the biggest names in the tech and retail universe (online and in-store).

However, there is a huge controversy surrounding Amazon. Specifically, the retailer does not collect sales tax in all states. No big deal, right? Not exactly. A quick Web search for "Amazon Sales Tax" will quickly bring you up to speed on this issue. Of course,

Amazon considers their tax-free status to be their competitive advantage. Not surprisingly, the retailer has used its considerable power to discourage state governments from revising their tax policies to alter this status.

From the opposite perspective, if you purchase something online and do not pay sales tax, you are supposed to include this purchase on your income tax statement and pay the taxes at that time. But, do you? Do you think anybody does?

STEP 2: Activity

Search the Web to find out if Amazon collects sales tax in your state. If it doesn't, then it is likely that the issue has been raised.

Imagine that Amazon has fulfillment centers in your state, meaning it operates in your state and therefore should collect sales tax. How would you feel if the retailer charges you tax but doesn't charge consumers in other states? Next, suppose a business in your state uses Amazon's fulfillment services and does not collect sales tax. Should Amazon's partnership with that company require it to collect tax on every purchase in your state?

STEP 3: Deliverable

Take a little time to consider this controversy. Then, create a list of arguments for and against requiring Amazon.com to collect sales tax in *all* states. Make certain your argument identifies both the ethical and legal aspects of this issue.

What's in IT for me?

ACCT For the Accounting Major

Accounting personnel are involved in several EC activities. Designing the ordering system and its relationship with inventory management requires accounting attention. Billing and payments are also accounting activities, as are determining cost and profit allocation. Replacing paper documents with electronic means will affect many of the accountant's tasks, especially the auditing of EC activities and systems. Finally, building a cost-benefit and cost-justification system to determine which products/services to take online and creating a chargeback system are critical to the success of EC.

FIN For the Finance Major

The worlds of banking, securities and commodities markets, and other financial services are being reengineered because of EC. Online securities trading and its supporting infrastructure are growing more rapidly than any other EC activity. Many innovations already in place are changing the rules of economic and financial incentives for financial analysts and managers. Online banking, for example, does not recognize state boundaries, and it may create a new framework for financing global trades. Public financial information is now accessible in seconds. These innovations will dramatically change the manner in which finance personnel operate.

MKT For the Marketing Major

A major revolution in marketing and sales is taking place because of EC. Perhaps its most obvious feature is the transition from a physical to a virtual marketplace. Equally important, however, is the radical transformation to one-on-one advertising and sales and to customized and interactive marketing. Marketing channels are being combined, eliminated, or recreated. The EC revolution is creating new products and markets and significantly altering existing ones. Digitization of products and services also has implications for marketing and sales. The direct producer-to-consumer channel is expanding rapidly and is fundamentally changing the nature of customer service. As the battle for customers intensifies, marketing and sales personnel are becoming the most critical success factor in many organizations. Online marketing can be a blessing to one company and a curse to another.

POM For the Production/Operations Management Major

EC is changing the manufacturing system from product-push mass production to order-pull mass customization. This change requires a robust supply chain, information support, and reengineering of processes that involve suppliers and other business partners. Suppliers can use extranets to monitor and replenish inventories without the need for constant reorders. In addition, the Internet and intranets help reduce cycle times. Many production/operations problems that have persisted for years, such as complex scheduling and excess inventories, are being solved rapidly with the use of Web technologies. Companies can now use external and internal networks to find and manage manufacturing operations in other countries much more easily. Also, the Web is reengineering procurement by helping companies conduct electronic bids for parts and subassemblies, thus reducing cost. All in all, the job of the progressive production/operations manager is closely tied in with e-commerce.

HRM For the Human Resource Management Major

HR majors need to understand the new labor markets and the impacts of EC on old labor markets. Also, the HR department may use EC tools for such functions as procuring office supplies. Moreover, becoming knowledgeable about new government online initiatives and online training is critical. In addition, HR personnel must be familiar with the major legal issues related to EC and employment.

MIS For the MIS Major

The MIS function is responsible for providing the information technology infrastructure necessary for electronic commerce to function. In particular, this infrastructure includes the company's networks, intranets, and extranets. The MIS function is also responsible for ensuring that electronic commerce transactions are secure.

Summary

1. Describe the six common types of electronic commerce.

In *business-to-consumer* (B2C) electronic commerce, the sellers are organizations and the buyers are individuals.

In *business-to-business* (B2B) electronic commerce, the sellers and the buyers are businesses.

In *consumer-to-consumer* (C2C) electronic commerce, an individual sells products or services to other individuals.

In *business-to-employee* (B2E) electronic commerce, an organization uses EC internally to provide information and services to its employees.

E-government is the use of Internet technology in general and e-commerce in particular to deliver information and public services to citizens (called government-to-citizen or G2C EC) and business partners and suppliers (called government-to-business or G2B EC).

Mobile commerce refers to e-commerce that is conducted entirely in a wireless environment.

We leave the examples of each type to you.

2. Describe the various online services of business-to-consumer (B2C) commerce, along with specific examples of each.

Electronic banking, also known as cyberbanking, involves conducting various banking activities from home, at a place of business, or on the road instead of at a physical bank location.

Online securities trading involves buying and selling securities over the Web.

Online job matching over the Web offers a promising environment for job seekers and for companies searching for hard-to-find employees. Thousands of companies and government agencies advertise available positions, accept resumes, and take applications via the Internet.

Online travel services allow you to purchase airline tickets, reserve hotel rooms, and rent cars. Most sites also offer a fare-tracker feature that sends you e-mail messages about low-cost flights. The Internet is an ideal place to plan, explore, and arrange almost any trip economically.

Online advertising over the Web makes the advertising process media-rich, dynamic, and interactive.

We leave the examples to you.

3. Describe the three business models for business-to-business electronic commerce.

In the *sell-side marketplace* model, organizations attempt to sell their products or services to other organizations electronically from their own private e-marketplace Web site and/or from a third-party Web site. Sellers such as Dell Computer (www.dellauction.com) use sell-side auctions extensively. In addition to auctions from their own Web sites, organizations can use third-party auction sites, such as eBay, to liquidate items.

The *buy-side marketplace* is a model in which organizations attempt to buy needed products or services from other organizations electronically.

E-marketplaces, in which there are many sellers and many buyers, are called *public exchanges,* or just exchanges. Public exchanges are open to all business organizations. They are frequently owned and operated by a third party. There are three basic types of public exchanges: vertical, horizontal, and functional. *Vertical exchanges* connect buyers and sellers in a given industry. *Horizontal exchanges* connect buyers and sellers across many industries. In *functional exchanges,* needed services such as temporary help or extra office space are traded on an "as-needed" basis.

4. Discuss the ethical and legal issues related to electronic commerce, along with examples.

E-business presents some threats to privacy. First, most electronic payment systems know who the buyers are. It may be necessary, then, to protect the buyers' identities with encryption. Another major privacy issue is tracking, where individuals' activities on the Internet can be tracked by cookies.

The use of EC may eliminate the need for some of a company's employees, as well as brokers and agents. The manner in which these unneeded workers, especially employees, are treated can raise ethical issues: How should the company handle the layoffs? Should companies be required to retrain employees for new positions? If not, how should the company compensate or otherwise assist the displaced workers?

We leave the examples to you.

Chapter Glossary

auction A competitive process in which either a seller solicits consecutive bids from buyers or a buyer solicits bids from sellers, and prices are determined dynamically by competitive bidding.

banner Electronic billboards, which typically contain a short text or graphical message to promote a product or a vendor.

brick-and-mortar organizations Organizations in which the product, the process, and the delivery agent are all physical.

business model The method by which a company generates revenue to sustain itself.

business-to-business electronic commerce (B2B) Electronic commerce in which both the sellers and the buyers are business organizations.

business-to-consumer electronic commerce (B2C) Electronic commerce in which the sellers are organizations and the buyers are individuals; also known as e-tailing.

business-to-employee electronic commerce (B2E) An organization using electronic commerce internally to provide information and services to its employees.

buy-side marketplace B2B model in which organizations buy needed products or services from other organizations electronically, often through a reverse auction.

channel conflict The alienation of existing distributors when a company decides to sell to customers directly online.

clicks-and-mortar organizations Organizations that do business in both the physical and digital dimensions.

consumer-to-consumer electronic commerce (C2C) Electronic commerce in which both the buyer and the seller are individuals (not businesses).

cyberbanking Various banking activities conducted electronically from home, a business, or on the road instead of at a physical bank location; also known as *electronic banking*.

cybersquatting Registering domain names in the hope of selling them later at a higher price.

disintermediation Elimination of intermediaries in electronic commerce.

e-government The use of electronic commerce to deliver information and public services to citizens, business partners, and suppliers of government entities, and those working in the public sector.

electronic business (e-business) A broader definition of electronic commerce, including buying and selling of goods and services, and servicing customers, collaborating with business partners, conducting e-learning, and conducting electronic transactions within an organization.

electronic commerce (EC or e-commerce) The process of buying, selling, transferring, or exchanging products, services, or information via computer networks, including the Internet.

electronic mall A collection of individual shops under one Internet address; also known as a *cybermall* or an *e-mall*.

electronic marketplace A virtual market space on the Web where many buyers and many sellers conduct electronic business activities.

electronic payment mechanisms Computer-based systems that allow customers to pay for goods and services electronically, rather than writing a check or using cash.

electronic retailing (e-tailing) The direct sale of products and services through storefronts or electronic malls, usually designed around an electronic catalog format and/or auctions.

electronic storefront The Web site of a single company, with its own Internet address, at which orders can be placed.

e-procurement Purchasing by using electronic support.

exchanges (see public exchanges)

forward auctions Auctions that sellers use as a selling channel to many potential buyers; the highest bidder wins the items.

group purchasing The aggregation of purchasing orders from many buyers so that a volume discount can be obtained.

mobile commerce (m-commerce) Electronic commerce conducted in a wireless environment.

multichanneling A process in which a company integrates its online and offline channels.

permission marketing Method of marketing that asks consumers to give their permission to voluntarily accept online advertising and e-mail.

person-to-person payments A form of electronic cash that enables the transfer of funds between two individuals, or between an individual and a business, without the use of a credit card.

pop-under ad An advertisement that is automatically launched by some trigger and appears underneath the active window.

pop-up ad An advertisement that is automatically launched by some trigger and appears in front of the active window.

public exchanges (or exchanges) Electronic marketplaces in which there are many sellers and many buyers, and entry is open to all; frequently owned and operated by a third party.

reverse auctions Auctions in which one buyer, usually an organization, seeks to buy a product or a service, and suppliers submit bids; the lowest bidder wins.

sell-side marketplace B2B model in which organizations sell to other organizations from their own private e-marketplace and/or from a third-party site.

smart cards Cards that contain a microprocessor (chip) that enables the card to store a considerable amount of information (including stored funds) and to conduct processing.

spamming Indiscriminate distribution of e-mail without the receiver's permission.

stored-value money cards A form of electronic cash on which a fixed amount of prepaid money is stored; the amount is reduced each time the card is used.

viral marketing Online word-of-mouth marketing.

virtual (or pure play) organizations Organizations in which the product, the process, and the delivery agent are all digital.

Discussion Questions

1. Discuss the major limitations of e-commerce. Which of these limitations are likely to disappear? Why?

2. Discuss the reasons for having multiple EC business models.

3. Distinguish between business-to-business forward auctions and buyers' bids for RFQs.

4. Discuss the benefits to sellers and buyers of a B2B exchange.

5. What are the major benefits of G2C electronic commerce?

6. Discuss the various ways to pay online in B2C. Which method(s) would you prefer and why?

7. Why is order fulfillment in B2C considered difficult?

8. Discuss the reasons for EC failures.

9. Should Mr. Coffee sell coffeemakers online? *Hint:* Take a look at the discussion of channel conflict in this chapter.

10. In some cases, individuals engage in cybersquatting so that they can sell the domain names to companies expensively. In other cases, companies engage in cybersquatting by registering domain names that are very similar to their competitors' domain names in order to generate traffic from people who misspell Web addresses. Discuss each practice in terms of its ethical nature and legality. Is there a difference between the two practices? Support your answer.

11. Do you think information technology has made it easier to do business? Or has *it* only raised the bar on what is required to be able to do business in the 21st century? Support your answer with specific examples.

12. With the rise of electronic commerce, what do you think will happen to those without computer skills, Internet access, computers, smartphones, and so on? Will they be able to survive and advance by hard work?

Problem-Solving Activities

1. Assume you are interested in buying a car. You can find information about cars at numerous Web sites. Access five Web sites for information about new and used cars, financing, and insurance. Decide which car you want to buy. Configure your car by going to the car manufacturer's Web site. Finally, try to find the car from www.autobytel .com. What information is most supportive of your decision-making process? Write a report about your experience.

2. Compare the various electronic payment methods. Specifically, collect information from the vendors cited in this chapter and find additional vendors using Google.com. Pay attention to security level, speed, cost, and convenience.

3. Conduct a study on selling diamonds and gems online. Access such sites as www.bluenile.com, www.diamond.com, www.thaigem.com, www.tiffany.com, and www.jewelryexchange.com.

   a. What features do these sites use to educate buyers about gemstones?

   b. How do these sites attract buyers?

   c. How do these sites increase customers' trust in online purchasing?

   d. What customer service features do these sites provide?

4. Access www.nacha.org. What is NACHA? What is its role? What is the ACH? Who are the key participants in an ACH e-payment? Describe the "pilot" projects currently underway at ACH.

5. Access www.espn.com. Identify at least five different ways the site generates revenue.

6. Access www.queendom.com. Examine its offerings and try some of them. What type of electronic commerce is this? How does this Web site generate revenue?

7. Access www.ediets.com. Prepare a list of all the services the company provides. Identify its revenue model.

8. Access www.theknot.com. Identify the site's revenue sources.

9. Access www.mint.com. Identify the site's revenue model. What are the risks of giving this Web site your credit and debit card numbers, as well as your bank account number?

10. Research the case of www.nissan.com. Is Uzi Nissan cybersquatting? Why or why not? Support your answer. How is Nissan (the car company) reacting to the www.nissan.com Web site?

11. Enter www.alibaba.com. Identify the site's capabilities. Look at the site's private trading room. Write a report. How can such a site help a person who is making a purchase?

12. Enter www.grubhub.com. Explore the site. Why is the site so successful? Could you start a competing site? Why or why not?

13. Enter www.dell.com, go to "Desktops," and configure a system. Register to "My Cart" (no obligation). What calculators are used there? What are the advantages of this process as compared with buying a computer in a physical store? What are the disadvantages?

14. Enter www.checkfree.com and www.lmlpayment.com to identify their services. Prepare a report.

15. Access various travel sites such as www.travelocity.com, www.orbitz .com, www.expedia.com, www.kayak.com, and www.pinpoint.com. Compare these Web sites for ease of use and usefulness. Note differences among the sites. If you ask each site for the itinerary, which one gives you the best information and the best deals?

16. Access www.outofservice.com, and answer the musical taste and personality survey. When you have finished, click on "Results" and see what your musical tastes say about your personality. How accurate are the findings about you?

17. Tips for safe electronic shopping:

    · Look for reliable brand names at sites such as Walmart Online, Disney Online, and Amazon. Before purchasing, make sure that the site is authentic by entering the site directly and not from an unverified link.

    · Search any unfamiliar selling site for the company's address and phone and fax numbers. Call up and quiz the employees about the seller.

    · Check out the vendor with the local Chamber of Commerce or Better Business Bureau (www.bbbonline.org). Look for seals of authenticity such as TRUSTe.

    · Investigate how secure the seller's site is by examining the security procedures and by reading the posted privacy policy.

    · Examine the money-back guarantees, warranties, and service agreements.

    · Compare prices with those in regular stores. Too low prices are too good to be true and some catch is probably involved.

    · Ask friends what they know. Find testimonials and endorsements on community Web sites and well-known bulletin boards.

    · Find out what your rights are in case of a dispute. Consult consumer protection agencies and the National Consumer League's Fraud Center (www.fraud.org).

    · Check Consumerworld (www.consumerworld.org) for a collection of useful resources.

    · For many types of products, www.resellerratings.com is a useful resource.

Closing Case 1

MKT   The Alibaba Group

The Problem

Chinese consumers traditionally have shopped at stores close to their homes, with merchants they knew, and they paid in cash. This process limited their selection of goods and services. If they wanted to find a wider selection, then they had to travel to China's larger cities.

As China's citizens have become increasingly affluent, their demand for a greater variety of goods and services has increased accordingly. However, Chinese citizens still had to travel to larger cities to satisfy their needs. Given China's huge population, there was a massive, untouched market for goods and services. The problem was how to provide Chinese shoppers with variety and convenience. Enter Jack Ma.

The Solution

In 1998, Ma and 17 colleagues started the Alibaba Group (http://alibabagroup.com), an e-commerce company that provides consumer-to-consumer, business-to-consumer, and business-to-business services via Web portals. The company links its Web portals via its third-party payment platform, Alipay.

Consumer-to-Consumer. Taobao (www.taobao.com) opened in 2003 as Alibaba's response to eBay. Taobao's rapid growth was the consequence of offering free registration and commission-free transactions using a free third-party payment platform. By adopting this strategy, Taobao undercut eBay's standard 15 percent fees. The startup collected money only when sellers chose to advertise their products with banner ads and search ads and when they used Alibaba's payment tools. These strategies succeeded, and Taobao became Alibaba's largest business.

Taobao offers a vast selection of products, ranging from clothes, furniture, and packaged foods to bamboo birdcages and rental "boyfriends" to accompany you to a social event. Although most transactions on Taobao connect buyers and sellers within China, the site reaches international customers as well.

Business-to-Consumer. Alibaba opened Tmall (www.tmall.com), a virtual shopping center, in 2008. Tmall provides international companies with access to Chinese buyers, in exchange for 5 percent of all sales. For example, the online shoe retailer Sneakerhead.com spent 13 years trying to increase its annual revenue beyond $20 million. In 2014, the company accomplished its goal when it doubled its revenues by opening a store on Tmall. This process enabled Sneakerhead to avoid having to use the conventional brokers who were traditionally required to import goods into China. In another example, Premium Australia Foods, a startup company headquartered in Melbourne, sells delicacies such as macadamia nuts, olive oil, honey, and raisins to Chinese shoppers using Tmall, without establishing physical operations in mainland China. In both cases, Alibaba disintermediated the retail process, enabling Sneakerhead and Premium Australia Foods to retain a larger portion of their sales revenues. Combined daily sales on Tmall and Taobao can total more than $7.5 billion.

Business-to-Business. Alibaba.com (www.alibaba.com), the company's original marketplace, connects Chinese manufacturers with small businesses around the world. The portal manages sales between importers and exporters from more than 240 countries and regions. Alibaba.com developed the Chinese portal 1688.com for domestic B2B commerce.

As one example, the cosmetics retailer 100% Pure uses Alibaba.com to source key ingredients and packaging materials from wholesalers that list their products on the site. Before Alibaba, Pure managers would have to travel to China and Taiwan several times per year to meet with suppliers and negotiate contracts. With Alibaba, if one supplier is not reliable, then Pure managers can pick another supplier and shop competitively for prices.

Alibaba.com also provides a retail Web site, AliExpress.com, that consists primarily of small Chinese businesses that offer products to international online buyers. AliExpress has become the most visited e-commerce Web site in Russia.

FIN   *Alipay.* Alibaba's various Web sites are linked via Alipay (http://global.alipay.com), an online third-party payment processor that does not charge transaction fees. Alipay serves as an escrow service, and it guarantees every transaction. Alipay creates trust in a country where people historically have not conducted business with someone they did not know personally.

Alibaba has placed links to its Alipay service on the Web sites of large retailers that work with ShopRunner (www.shoprunner.com), a logistics company in which Alibaba owns a 40 percent stake. ShopRunner has formed ties with thousands of Western retail brands such as Neiman Marcus, Tommy Hilfiger, and Toys "R" Us to enable two-day shipping for an annual fee, a service that resembles Amazon Prime. The Alibaba links, visible only to Chinese shoppers, will allow these shoppers to receive expedited shipments from U.S. retailers.

The Results

Analysts envision Alibaba's future as one in which consumers everywhere can make purchases from retailers everywhere. Alibaba does have advantages as a global enterprise over Amazon and eBay because it facilitates such a large volume of sales into and out of China.

Alibaba does face international challenges, however. Most Western shoppers are not familiar with Alibaba's brand, where they already have relationships with retail Web sites in their home countries.

Alibaba also faces intense competition from Chinese companies. For example, while Tmall controls approximately 50 percent of Chinese e-commerce, JD (http://en.jd.com) has 17 percent, according to iResearch (www.iresearchchina.com). Further, whereas Alibaba's e-commerce is performed primarily on desktops, JD may have an advantage in mobile commerce in a country that now has more than 500 million mobile phone users. JD stocks its own goods, and it employs a highly sophisticated delivery system. This arrangement is in contrast to Alibaba, which facilitates direct sales by other enterprises and then contracts out the delivery.

Tencent (www.tencent.com), another large Chinese e-commerce company, provides the popular communications platform called WeChat as well as a competing online-payments platform called Tenpay that is popular on smartphones. In 2014, Tencent purchased a 15 percent stake in JD, and the two companies formed a strategic partnership. They will provide a formidable competitive challenge to Alibaba in electronic commerce.

Despite the competition, by mid-2015 approximately 80 percent of all Chinese online shopping sales were flowing through Alibaba's various Web portals. In 2014, the company facilitated the delivery of 5 billion packages from transactions on its retail Web sites. More than half of that total was sent by delivery companies in China, according to Alibaba's registration documents with the U.S. Securities and Exchange Commission (SEC). By comparison, UPS (www.ups.com) sent about 4.3 billion packages and documents that same year.

Alibaba's overall strategic direction appears to be expansion in the West, because U.S. consumers spend more money online than anyone else in the world. Ma has invested in many U.S. companies, including the ride-sharing service Lyft (www.lyft.com); Kabam, a maker of online strategy games (www.kabam.com); mobile search engine Quixey.com (www.quixey.com); and mobile messaging app Tango (www.tango.me).

In 2014, Alibaba's initial public offering in the United States raised $25 billion, making it the largest IPO on record in the world. Further, Alibaba's financial reports for its fiscal year ending in March 2016 revealed that the company's revenue was approximately $15.7 billion.

Sources: Compiled from K. Chu and G. Wong, "Alibaba Feels Heat from New Rivals," *The Wall Street Journal*, August 17, 2015; M. Reeves, M. Zeng, and A. Venjara, "The Self-Tuning Enterprise," *Harvard Business Review*, June, 2015; "Alibaba Group Announces March Quarter 2015 and Full Fiscal Year 2015 Results," *Business Wire*, May 7, 2015; C. Larson, "Alipay Leads a

Digital Finance Revolution in China," *MIT Technology Review*, January 26, 2015; R. Mac, "Bezos vs. Ma, Holiday Edition," *Forbes*, December 15, 2014; L. Chen, R. Mac, and B. Solomon, "Alibaba Claims Title for Largest Global IPO Ever with Extra Share Sales," *Forbes*, September 22, 2014; C. Larson, "In China, It's Meet Me at Tmall," *Bloomberg BusinessWeek*, September 15-21, 2014; B. Stone, "The Alibaba Invasion," *Bloomberg BusinessWeek*, August 11-24, 2014; "Alibaba Continues Quest to Own the Chinese Internet," *CNN Money*, June 11, 2014; R. Mac, "Alibaba Launches 11 Main to Grow U.S. Presence Before Its Record American IPO," *Forbes*, June 11, 2014; D. Talbot, "Alibaba's Big Rivals May Have a Mobile Edge," *MIT Technology Review*, May 12, 2014; A. Lee, "How Did Alibaba Capture 80% of Chinese E-Commerce?" *Forbes*, May 8, 2014; www.alibabagroup.com, accessed August 20, 2015.

Questions

1. Discuss the reasons why Chinese consumers have been so eager to embrace electronic commerce.

2. Discuss Alibaba's entry into the business-to-consumer, consumer-to-consumer, and business-to-business e-commerce marketplaces.

3. Why is Alipay so important to the Alibaba Group?

Closing Case 2

 FIN Personalized Pricing (also known as Dynamic Pricing)

MKT The Problem

Today, consumers are accustomed to *standardized pricing*, which means that when a product is sold via multiple channels, the cost should not vary by more than the difference in shipping, taxation, and distribution costs. If the price is higher for a product at a certain retailer, then customers can easily use the Internet to compare prices and features among a huge number of retailers to purchase that product from another retailer.

In theory, charging all consumers the same price is ineffective for merchants, because some customers would have been willing to pay more, and others who opted not to buy would have bought at a lower price. Economic theory states that *personalized pricing*—also called *dynamic pricing*—can save companies this lost revenue.

Personalized pricing is the practice of pricing items at a point determined by a particular customer's perceived ability to pay. This practice has been in existence as long as commerce itself. Consider shopkeepers in the past, who were experts on evaluating prospective customers based on a wide variety of signals—how they spoke, how they dressed, how they acted (e.g., did they look the shopkeeper straight in the eyes), how courteous they were, how much of a hurry they were in, and many other variables. In that way, the shopkeeper could quickly decide on a price *for that customer at that time*.

The optimal outcome of personalized pricing *for the merchant* is maximizing the price that each customer will pay. This situation is difficult to achieve because the means of determining the maximum amount a customer will pay has not yet been developed. Or has it?

The Solution (for the Merchant)

Some online retailers (e-tailers) are attempting to return to the strategies of yesterday's shopkeeper. They are analyzing the data (see

Chapter 3) that all consumers generate with online activities and transactions to set different prices for different customers.

E-tailers can now virtually assess each customer who visits their Web site. Specifically, when a customer accesses an e-tailer's site, the merchant may know where the customer is located based on his or her Internet Protocol address. Merchants also may know the customer's ZIP code. In that case they can determine the customer's socioeconomic status based on data from the most recent federal census.

When merchants combine these data with cookies (see Chapter 7), they can learn a significant amount about individual customers, including some of the Web sites the customers have visited, how regularly they have visited them, how long they stayed on those sites, and which products they inspected and purchased. Further, cookies store information that customers volunteer in online forms – for example, shipping addresses and other profile data. Based on these data, merchants can predict the products a customer is interested in purchasing, when he or she is likely to purchase them, and, critically, the price he or she would be willing to pay. By analyzing customer data, a merchant can estimate customers' *reservation price*—the maximum amount they would be willing to pay for a specific product, before they had "reservations" about buying it—and then charge them that amount.

Currently, many retailers use these data to target individual shoppers with personalized offers and promotions. The analyses that enable retailers to send customized offers to customers also enable them to determine personalized pricing. In addition, with e-commerce, merchants can easily adjust prices for different customers simply by changing them in the system in real time. They therefore avoid the hassle of physically changing the prices on thousands of products.

Let's review some prominent examples of personalized pricing.

- According to *The Wall Street Journal*, Orbitz (www.orbitz.com) used its knowledge of its customers' demographics to charge certain customers more for hotels. Orbitz discovered that users who browsed on Apple Mac computers were willing to pay up to 30 percent more for a hotel than Windows users.

- Delta Airlines (www.delta.com) uses personalized pricing to charge frequent flyers more than they charge infrequent travelers. The reason was that people who travel often are probably doing so out of necessity, most likely for business purposes. They therefore are willing (however begrudgingly) to pay more to get where they need to be.

- Safeway, the grocery chain, sends offers to select customers who have exhibited certain purchasing patterns. For example, one woman received an offer for discounted eggs because the data revealed that her household purchased quantities of high-protein items. With personalized pricing, Safeway can afford to sell the eggs to this customer at a lower price because the store will charge less health-conscious customers more for the same product.

- In 2000, Amazon (www.amazon.com) was found to be charging its regular customers higher prices for some products, after one shopper deleted the cookies on his computer that identified him as a regular Amazon customer and noted that the price of a DVD dropped. Amazon, which attributed the differences in price to a random price test, refunded customers who had paid higher prices. In addition, Amazon CEO Jeff Bezos asserted the company "never will test prices based on customer demographics."

- Staples (www.staples.com) shows customers different prices based on "a range of characteristics that could be discovered about the user." For instance, one customer saw a lower price for a computer on the company's Web site than another customer who lived a few miles further from the store. Staples' reasoning was that if someone is already close to the store, then he or she may be enticed to make a quick drive to purchase the "discounted" item.

- The National Football League (NFL; www.nfl.com) is allowing teams to use personalized pricing for tickets. The Seattle Seahawks (www.seahawks.com) became the first team to employ the practice. The team worked out a deal with ticket brokers to "redistribute" 4,000 season tickets. Half of the tickets were sold as individual tickets to fans on the Blue Pride wait list. The remaining tickets are subject to personalized pricing – the higher the demand at the moment of purchase, the higher the ticket price.

- Liftopia (www.liftopia.com) uses personalized pricing in the ski business. In the past, a day on the slopes cost the same regardless of when it was purchased. Liftopia works with ski resorts to crunch data on historical and real-time supply and demand to vary pricing. Customers who buy tickets early receive discounts. Liftopia raises prices as the ticket's date approaches. The company's pricing appeals to skiers who might not visit a resort based on the rising cost of lift tickets. At Mammoth Mountain Ski Area in California, for example, Liftopia's personalized pricing contributed to a 15 percent increase in advance lift ticket sales during the 2014-2015 ski season.

Companies such as Wiser (www.wiser.com), Dunnhumby (www.dunnhumby.com), and Blue Yonder (www.blue-yonder.com) offer software and data solutions to retailers that employ personalized pricing, where prices change over time in response to variables such as inventory, demand, and/or the prices offered by competitors. Blue Yonder claims it can optimize prices not only according to the region but also to the channel in which the customer is interacting with the retailer.

The Results

Most companies remain hesitant to utilize personalized pricing because it remains to be seen whether consumers will accept the practice. Typically, when consumers hear about the practice, they react negatively, and companies employing the practice experience customer dissatisfaction. It is not easy for consumers to detect when they are being targeted with personalized prices.

For luxury brands in particular, personalized pricing could be damaging because it raises questions concerning the intrinsic value of their products. For example, brands such as Louis Vuitton do not discount their products so as not to undermine the consumer perception of their value. Consumers of luxury goods frequently associate higher prices with higher quality, and vice versa.

Sources: Compiled from S. Soper and L. Rupp, "Stores Try Fixed Prices That Aren't So Fixed," *Bloomberg BusinessWeek*, July 27 – August 2, 2015; A. Leviton, "Delta Causes More Headaches with Skymiles Changes," *USA Today*, July 16, 2015; N. Payton, "Why Do Dynamic Pricing Programs Flop?" *OPower*, July 2, 2015; D. Horne, "Seahawks Announce 'Dynamic Pricing' Ticket Policy," *KIRO TV*, June 29, 2015; S. Lipsey, "How Airlines Might Gouge You in the Future: Personalized Pricing," *Yahoo! News*, June 16, 2015; R. Thomaselli, "Democrats Take On Airline 'Personalized Pricing'," *Travel Pulse*, April 28, 2015; G. Petro, "Dynamic Pricing: Which Customers Are Worth the Most? Amazon, Delta Airlines, and Staples Weigh In," *Forbes*, April 17, 2015; A. Valentine, "How Dynamic Pricing Is Disrupting Online Retail in 2015," *Ecommerce*, April 10, 2015; E. Deprez, "Skiing Gets Online, and Lift Tickets Get Cheaper," *Bloomberg BusinessWeek*, March 9-15, 2015; K. Abnett, "Will Personalized Pricing Take E-Commerce Back to the Bazaar?" *The Business of Fashion*, March 20, 2015; B. Snyder, "Report Analyzes Amazon's Dynamic Pricing Strategy," *CIO*, January 16, 2015; A. Farnham, "Prices Now Pegged to Your Buying History at Some Markets," *ABC News*, December 2, 2013; D. Mattioli, "On Orbitz, Mac Users Steered to Pricier Hotels," *The Wall Street Journal*, August 23, 2012.

Questions

1. How would you feel if you knew that you were being subjected to personalized pricing?

2. Describe the advantages of personalized pricing for merchants.

3. Does personalized pricing provide any advantages for customers? Provide examples to support your answer.

4. Discuss the contributions of information technology to the practices of personalized pricing.

CHAPTER 10

Floresco Productions/Getty Images, Inc.

Wireless, Mobile Computing, and Mobile Commerce

LEARNING OBJECTIVES

10.1 Identify advantages and disadvantages of each of the four main types of wireless transmission media.

10.2 Explain how businesses can use short-range, medium-range, and long-range wireless networks.

10.3 Provide a specific example of how each of the five major m-commerce applications can benefit a business.

10.4 Describe the Internet of Things, along with examples of how organizations can utilize the Internet of Things.

Opening Case

 Google's Project Fi

In April 2015, Google announced its new wireless service, Project Fi (http://fi.google.com), a prepaid phone service that provides users with mobile data service on two mobile networks, Sprint (www.sprint .com) and T-Mobile (www.tmobile.com), as well as on Wi-Fi networks. Project Fi automatically and seamlessly routes customers' data between available Wi-Fi networks and the 4G LTE networks of Sprint

and T-Mobile, depending on which network provides the strongest signal in the user's location. Project Fi utilizes approximately one million free, open Wi-Fi hotspots that Google has verified as fast and reliable. In an effort to protect passwords and personal data, Project Fi encrypts data when a customer uses public Wi-Fi.

Project Fi provides many features. Customers can call, text, and check voicemail on their Web and Android devices, using Google Hangouts. They can also access the history of calls, messages, and voicemail. Project Fi is a prepaid service that allows customers to pay only for the amount of data they actually use each month. This process is the opposite of traditional carriers, which bill customers *after* they use the service. In addition, Project Fi does not require an annual contract. Rather, the service charges $20 per month for unlimited calls, texts, Wi-Fi tethering, and coverage in 120 countries (although customers have to pay 20 cents per minute for calls outside the United States). In addition, it charges $10 per gigabyte of data.

Customers have access to a dashboard where they can change the size of their data plans whenever they want. Further, once a month, customers can decide to put their service on pause. They then lose the ability to forward calls with their Google Voice numbers, and they cannot access mobile data, make calls, or send text messages. However, they receive a credit to their accounts for each day that they keep the service deactivated. They also receive a credit for the cost of the data they purchased but did not use over the course of the month.

As of September 2015, Project Fi operated only on Google's Nexus 6 smartphones. Customers can set up their phones as a mobile Wi-Fi router and allow their laptops or tablets to surf the Internet on their phone's data connection, at no extra charge. This process is called *wireless tethering*. Once customers have activated tethering, any device with a wireless connection can connect to the Internet via their smartphone's connection unless they set up password protection. If they select this option, then only people with access to the password can connect to their smartphones.

Project Fi puts pressure on wireless carriers to do away with lucrative "breakage." Breakage is a term used in the telecommunications industry to indicate unused data at the end of a month. Many traditional wireless plans require subscribers to pay for certain amounts of data that expire at the end of each month. A study by Validas (www.validas .com), a company that analyzes consumers' bills to help them choose the most appropriate wireless plan, noted that smartphone users typically waste $28 each month on unused data. The $28 represents breakage.

The practice of breakage is coming under pressure from other companies as well. Startups such as Republic Wireless (www .republicwireless.com) and Scratch Wireless (www.scratchwireless .com) offer usage-based models. Further, major carriers such as T-Mobile and AT&T (www.att.com) allow subscribers to roll over data.

Google's pricing strategy for its Project Fi service could also put pressure on the industry's prevailing pricing model, which is to purchase expensive wireless spectrum and then sell expensive wireless Internet service. (All wireless communications signals travel over the air via radio frequencies, which are known as *spectrum*.) In fact, Google's entry into the wireless market has the potential to disrupt the wireless industry in much the same way that Google Fiber (http://fiber.google.com) transformed the cable and broadband industries.

Sources: Compiled from D. Orf, "My Time with Google's Cellular Service Was Mostly a Disaster," *Gizmodo*, August 21, 2015; D. Bohn, "Google's Project Fi Cell Phone Service Is Simple, Until It's Not," *The Verge*, August 8, 2015; A. Pressman, "Google's Project Fi a New Option for Cheap Phone Plans," *Yahoo! Finance*, August 5, 2015; A. Martonik, "What Is Project Fi, How Does It Work, and Why Do I Want It?" *Android Central*, July 9, 2015; B. Fung, "Project Fi Review: The Most Remarkable Feature of Google's New Cell Service," *The Washington Post*, July 8, 2015; "5 Things to Know about Google's Project Fi," *CBS News*, May 4, 2015; "Google's Project Fi Aims to Speed Up Mobile Communications by Tapping into Free WiFi Hotspots," *Kurzweilai.net*, April 23, 2015; M. Aguilar, "Project Fi: Google's Plan to Fix Your Wireless Service Is Here," *Gizmodo*, April 22, 2015; R. Metz, "Google's New Wireless Service Should Make Verizon and AT&T Squirm," *MIT Technology Review*, April 22, 2015; R. Knutson and A. Barr, "Google Set to Unveil Wireless Service, *The Wall Street Journal*, April 22, 2015; http://fi.google.com, accessed September 14, 2015.

Questions

1. Describe how Google's Project Fi works.

2. Assume that you are the CEO of Verizon Wireless (www.verizonwireless .com). How would you compete with Project Fi?

Introduction

The traditional working environment that required users to come to a wired computer is ineffective and inefficient. The solution was to build computers that are small enough to carry or wear and that can communicate via wireless networks. The ability to communicate anytime and anywhere provides organizations with a strategic advantage by increasing productivity and speed and improving customer service. The term **wireless** is used to describe telecommunications in which electromagnetic waves, rather than some form of wire or cable, carry the signal between communicating devices such as computers, smartphones, and iPads.

Before you continue, it is important to distinguish between the terms *wireless* and *mobile*— they can mean different things. The term *wireless* means exactly what it says: without wires. In contrast, *mobile* refers to something that changes its location over time. Some wireless networks, such as MiFi (discussed later in this chapter), are also mobile. Others, however, are fixed. For example, microwave towers form fixed wireless networks.

Wireless technologies enable individuals and organizations to conduct mobile computing, mobile commerce, and the Internet of Things. We define these terms here, and then we discuss each one in detail later in the chapter.

Mobile computing refers to a real-time, wireless connection between a mobile device and other computing environments, such as the Internet or an intranet. *Mobile commerce*—also known as *m-commerce*—refers to e-commerce (EC) transactions (see Chapter 9) conducted with a mobile device. The *Internet of Things* means that virtually every object has processing power with either wireless or wired connections to a global network.

Wireless technologies and mobile commerce are spreading rapidly, replacing or supplementing wired computing. Cisco (www.cisco.com) predicts that the volume of mobile Web traffic will continue to increase rapidly over the next decade.

Almost all (if not all) organizations utilize wireless computing. Therefore, when you begin your career, you likely will be assigned a company smartphone and a wirelessly enabled computer. Clearly, then, it is important for you to learn about wireless computing not only because you will be using wireless applications but also because wireless computing will be important to your organization. In your job, you will be involved with customers who conduct wireless transactions, with analyzing and developing mobile commerce applications, and with wireless security. And the list goes on.

Simply put, an understanding of wireless technology and mobile commerce applications will make you more valuable to your organization. When you look at "What's in IT for Me?" at the end of the chapter, envision yourself performing the activities discussed in your functional area. In addition, for those of you who are entrepreneurally inclined, an understanding of wireless technology can help you start and grow your own business.

The wireless infrastructure upon which mobile computing is built may reshape the entire IT field. The technologies, applications, and limitations of mobile computing and mobile commerce are the focus of this chapter. You begin the chapter by learning about wireless devices, wireless transmission media, and wireless security. You continue by examining wireless computer networks and wireless Internet access. You then look at mobile computing and mobile commerce, which are made possible by wireless technologies. Next, you turn your attention to the Internet of Things. You conclude by familiarizing yourself with a critical component of the wireless environment—namely, wireless security.

10.1 | Wireless Technologies

Wireless technologies include both wireless devices, such as smartphones, and wireless transmission media, such as microwave, satellite, and radio. These technologies are fundamentally changing the ways organizations operate.

Individuals are finding wireless devices convenient and productive to use, for several reasons. First, people can make productive use of time that was formerly wasted—for example, while commuting to work on public transportation. Second, because people can take these devices with them, their work locations are becoming much more flexible. Third, wireless technology enables people to schedule their working time around personal and professional obligations.

Wireless Devices

Wireless devices provide three major advantages to users:

1. They are small enough to easily carry or wear.
2. They have sufficient computing power to perform productive tasks.
3. They can communicate wirelessly with the Internet and other devices.

Modern smartphones exhibit a process called *dematerialization*. Essentially, dematerialization occurs when the functions of many physical devices are included in one other physical device. Consider that your smartphone includes the functions of digital cameras for images and video, radios, televisions, Internet access via Web browsers, recording studios, editing suites, movie theaters, GPS navigators, word processors, spreadsheets, stereos, flashlights, board games, card games, video games, an entire range of medical devices, maps, atlases, encyclopedias, dictionaries, translators, textbooks, watches, alarm clocks, books, calculators, address books, credit card swipers, magnifying glasses, money and credit cards, car keys, hotel keys, cellular telephony, Wi-Fi, e-mail access, text messaging, a full QWERTY keyboard, and many, many others. **Figure 10.1** illustrates the process of dematerialization with smartphones.

DEMATERIALIZATION

FIGURE 10.1 Dematerialization with smartphones.

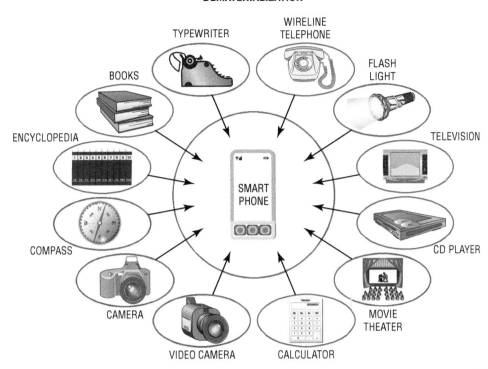

Our smartphones have come a long, long way in a short period of time. Consider these smartphone capabilities (as of mid-2016):

- In the United States alone, Verizon (www.verizon.com) and AT&T (www.att.com) offer 4G LTE to over 300 million people. (4G LTE can reach speeds of 50 Mbps.) Therefore, modern smartphones are about 500 times faster than the first iPhone which was released in 2007.

- Many high-end smartphones can take video in ultra-high definition 4K. 4K resolution refers to a display device having horizontal resolution on the order of 4,000 pixels. Pixels are the dots that make up on-screen images. The more pixels there are, the sharper and more realistic that images and video look.

- Smartphones can function as mobile (digital) wallets.

- Some smartphones can be charged without plugging them in. For example, Google's Nexus 4, 5, 6, and 7 and Samsung's Galaxy 6 all include built-in wireless charging.

- While not all smartphones have wireless charging built-in yet, many of them have fast charging. Motorola (www.motorola.com) says that its Moto X Pure Edition can obtain 8 hours of battery life from a 15-minute charge.

- Smartphones are employing biometrics (discussed in Chapter 7). Apple has fingerprint scanners on its devices with its Touch ID feature. Google has facial recognition on its Android smartphones in the form of its Face Unlock feature. The Android "Smart Lock" feature can use other methods to recognize you and keep you from having to re-authenticate constantly. You can activate "on-body detection" which knows if you have your phone in your hand or in your pocket, "trusted voice" which enables voice recognition, and "trusted devices" which can use Bluetooth to authenticate you when connected to your smartwatch or your car.

- The Nextbit Robin (http://nextbit.com) uses an intelligent method of cloud storage (discussed in Plug IT In 4) to give its Android smartphone virtually unlimited storage. Essentially, the service takes the content that you do not use often and automatically stores it in the cloud, and then silently re-downloads it in the background when you use the content again.

One downside of smartphones is that people can use them to copy and pass on confidential information. For example, if you were an executive at Intel, would you want workers snapping pictures of their colleagues with your secret new technology in the background? After all, one of the functions of a smartphone is that of a digital camera that can transmit wirelessly. New jamming devices are being developed to counter the threat. Some companies, such as Samsung (www.samsung.com), have recognized the danger and have banned these devices from their premises altogether. Regardless of any disadvantages, however, cell phones, and particularly smartphones, have had a far greater impact on human society than most of us realize.

Consider Africa, for example. One in six of Africa's one billion inhabitants now use a cell phone. These phones are transforming healthcare across the continent in many ways:

- Medical personnel are obtaining high-quality data that can inform them of who is dying and from what causes, who is sick, and where clusters of disease are occurring.
- Cell phones are now making it possible for parents to register the birth of a child very easily and for governments to more accurately plan healthcare interventions, such as vaccination schedules.
- Cell phones are improving vaccine supply chains, preventing unnecessary stockouts, and ensuring that vaccines are available when children are brought into clinics to be immunized.
- Healthcare workers in the field can access health records and schedule appointments with patients.

Smartphones are also instrumental in other ways. IT's About Business 10.1 illustrates how they are driving the growth of electronic commerce in Vietnam.

IT's About Business 10.1

 Smartphones Drive Growth of Electronic Commerce in Vietnam

Historically, the Vietnamese economy has been based on cash. The norm has been to borrow money informally from a trusted circle of family and friends. Most merchants do not offer any other option than to pay in cash. At the same time, however, the majority of merchants believe that they would benefit from mobile payments because they could handle less cash and avoid possible counterfeit bills. Meanwhile, Vietnamese consumers are interested in using mobile "wallets" to deposit, withdraw, and save money for safety reasons and to pay for goods and services for convenience. Enter wireless communications and devices.

Wireless communication has had a significant impact in Vietnam. In a country where few people have a landline phone, millions of Vietnamese are moving directly into wireless technologies. In the past, e-commerce companies were not successful in Vietnam because few people had a landline to be able to access the Internet, particularly in outlying areas.

Telecommunications companies such as Viettel Mobile (http://vietteltelecom.vn), which has Vietnam's largest number of subscribers, and Mobiphone (www.mobiphone.vn), owned by Vietnam Mobile Telecom Services Company (http://vnpt.vn), have deployed wireless communications throughout much of the country. Even though data is typically expensive in developing countries, data prices in Vietnam are among the lowest in the world, at just over $3 per gigabyte. In just 10 years, the number of people with an Internet connection went from 12 percent in 2005 to 44 percent in 2015. This growth has been largely thanks to smartphones, which have helped drive a rapid increase in electronic commerce.

In just one year, the number of active mobile social media accounts in Vietnam rose 41 percent by January 2015, a faster increase than in China, India, or Brazil. E-commerce is being buoyed by social networks, which are used by consumers and businesses alike. Nearly one-quarter of Vietnamese firms state that they conduct business via social networks. Facebook is one of the most popular, with 30 million active Vietnamese users in the first quarter of 2015, up from 8.5 million in 2012. Vietnam is one of Facebook's fastest-growing markets.

Electronic commerce in Vietnam generated revenue of $4 billion in 2015, compared with $700 million in 2012. Much of this commerce will be mobile commerce. Popular products for Vietnamese online shoppers include furniture, electronics, fashion, cosmetics, appliances, and books. Nearly 70 percent of these online shoppers pay in cash, with the remainder paying with electronic wallets.

In 2015, Lazada (www.lazada.vn), one of Vietnam's largest online retailers, had approximately 500,000 customers. The company continues to boost the number of products and to improve its delivery. For example, motorcycle riders in Lazada uniforms deliver all types of goods to Lazada customers. Lazada sales in January 2015 were seven times higher than in the same period just one year earlier.

Short video clips are especially popular among Vietnam's mobile users, who like to share clips easily. Yan.vn, an MTV-style music and entertainment organization, is capitalizing on that trend. Yan.vn is using the Web to popularize its television shows, which are carried over cable networks to approximately five million households as well as to many of Ho Chi Minh City's cafés and bars. The company is also posting unedited excerpts of celebrity interviews online before the complete interviews are approved by government censors for television. The company has also launched a free soap opera on YouTube.

Just like in the West, the mobile Web in Vietnam is helping some people achieve celebrity status. For example, farmer Nguyen Duc Hau shot to fame as a TV actor after his off-key renditions of Vietnamese love ballads became a YouTube sensation. Similarly, comedian JVevermind has more than 1.5 million subscribers to his channel on YouTube, building his audience by sharing clips via social media sites such as Facebook, Twitter, Google+, and Instagram.

Even state-owned media outlets, such as the newspaper *Tuoi Tre* (*Youth*), have launched Web sites as content providers vie to become Vietnam's most popular social and entertainment site. There is much at stake. Media Partners Asia, a research and consulting firm, projected that advertising in Vietnam would total $1.2 billion by 2017, nearly double the amount in 2014.

Sources: Compiled from "Mobile Commerce Grows Fast in Vietnam," *VietnamNet NEW*, July 23, 2015; "Mobile Commerce Growing Fast in Asia Pacific with Half of Smartphone Users Now Shopping on Their Device," *The Engagement Bureau*, June 17, 2015; J. Campbell,

"E-Commerce and Retail in Vietnam: Growing Momentum vs Restrictions," *LinkedIn.com*, Mary 26, 2015; N. Ngoc, "Lazada, Sendo Top Vietnam's E-Commerce Market in 2014," *DealStreetAsia*, February 25, 2015; J. Hookway, "Vietnam's Mobile Revolution Catapults Millions Into the Digital Age," *The Wall Street Journal*, June 15, 2015; "Vietnam E-Commerce Report 2014," *Ministry of Industry and Trade of the Socialist Republic of Vietnam*, May 7, 2015; N. Uy, "Surge in Smartphones Spurs Likely M-Commerce Boom in Vietnam," *HKTDC Research*, September 19, 2014; "Mobile Commerce in Emerging Asia," *Ericsson*, August 2014; J. Dung, "Vietnam E-Commerce Overview and Market Size," *eCommerce MILO*, April 9, 2014; www.lazada.vn, accessed September 15, 2015.

Questions

1. Discuss the impact of wireless communications technologies on the growth of electronic commerce in Vietnam.

2. Describe the advantages of wireless connections over landline connections.

3. Discuss the implications of Vietnam "skipping" wireline communications by moving directly to wireless communications.

Wireless Transmission Media

Wireless media, or broadcast media, transmit signals without wires. The major types of wireless media are microwave, satellite, and radio. Table 10.1 lists the advantages and disadvantages of each type.

Microwave. Microwave transmission systems transmit data via electromagnetic waves. These systems are used for high-volume, long-distance, line-of-sight communication. *Line-of-sight* means that the transmitter and receiver are in view of each other. This requirement creates problems because the Earth's surface is curved rather than flat. For this reason, microwave towers usually cannot be spaced more than 30 miles apart.

Clearly, then, microwave transmissions offer only a limited solution to data communications needs, especially over very long distances. In addition, microwave transmissions are susceptible to environmental interference during severe weather such as heavy rain and snowstorms. Although long-distance microwave data communications systems are still widely used, they are being replaced by satellite communications systems.

Satellite. Satellite transmission systems make use of communication satellites. Currently, there are three types of satellites circling Earth: geostationary-earth-orbit (GEO), medium-

TABLE 10.1 Advantages and Disadvantages of Wireless Media

Channel	Advantages	Disadvantages
Microwave	High bandwidth	Must have unobstructed line of sight
	Relatively inexpensive	Susceptible to environmental interference
Satellite	High bandwidth	Expensive
	Large coverage area	Must have unobstructed line of sight
		Signals experience propagation delay
		Must use encryption for security
Radio	High bandwidth	Creates electrical interference problems
	Signals pass through walls	Susceptible to snooping unless encrypted
	Inexpensive and easy to install	

TABLE 10.2 Three Basic Types of Telecommunications Satellites

Type	Characteristics	Orbit	Number	Use
GEO	Satellites stationary relative to point on Earth	22, 300 miles	8	TV signal
	Few satellites needed for global coverage			
	Transmission delay (approximately 0.25 second)			
	Most expensive to build and launch			
	Longest orbital life (many years)			
MEO	Satellites move relative to point on Earth	6, 434 miles	10–12	GPS
	Moderate number needed for global coverage			
	Requires medium-powered transmitters			
	Negligible transmission delay			
	Less expensive to build and launch			
	Moderate orbital life (6–12 years)			
LEO	Satellites move rapidly relative to point on Earth	400–700 miles	Many	Telephone
	Large number needed for global coverage			
	Requires only low-power transmitters			
	Negligible transmission delay			
	Least expensive to build and launch			
	Shortest orbital life (as low as 5 years)			

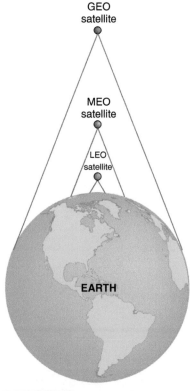

FIGURE 10.2 Comparison of satellite footprints.

earth-orbit (MEO), and low-earth-orbit (LEO). Each type has a different orbit, with GEO being farthest from Earth and LEO the closest. In this section, you examine the three types of satellites and then discuss two major satellite applications: global positioning systems and Internet transmission via satellites. Table 10.2 compares and contrasts the three types of satellites.

As with microwave transmission, satellites must receive and transmit data via line-of-sight. However, the enormous *footprint*—the area of Earth's surface reached by a satellite's transmission—overcomes the limitations of microwave data relay stations. The most basic rule governing footprint size is simple: The higher a satellite orbits, the larger its footprint. Thus, medium-earth-orbit satellites have a smaller footprint than geostationary satellites, and low-earth-orbit satellites have the smallest footprint of all. Figure 10.2 compares the footprints of the three types of satellites.

There are an incredible number of applications of satellites, one of which is commercial images from orbit, using nanosatellites. Very small satellites, called nanosatellites, are built in a standard format known as a CubeSat. CubeSats are 4-inch cubes weighing about 3 pounds. A nanosatellite typically costs between $150,000 and $1 million to develop and launch, compared to $200 million to $1 billion for a full-sized satellite.

Several companies are involved in launching nanosatellites for scientific and commercial purposes. Planet Labs (www.planet.com) take pictures of the Earth more frequently than traditional satellites and at a small fraction of the cost. However, the images from the company's nanosatellites are at a lower resolution.

Spire (http://spire.com) nanosatellites contain sensors and carry out various missions. One of these missions is locating objects. For example, more than 250,000 ships broadcast an automatic identification signal. A fleet of nanosatellites in low earth orbit could pick up these signals and provide frequent updates of the ships' positions without the vessels having to use expensive dedicated satellite communications.

Skybox's (www.skyboximaging.com) small satellites are larger than the other two companies' satellites, weighing about 220 pounds. Skybox satellites are able to capture high-resolution imaging data.

In contrast to line-of-sight transmission with microwave, satellites use *broadcast* transmission, which sends signals to many receivers at one time. So, even though satellites are line-of-sight like microwave, they are high enough for broadcast transmission, thus overcoming the limitations of microwave.

Types of Orbits. *Geostationary-earth-orbit satellites* orbit 22,300 miles directly above the equator. These satellites maintain a fixed position above Earth's surface because, at their altitude, their orbital period matches the 24-hour rotational period of Earth. For this reason, receivers on Earth do not have to track GEO satellites. GEO satellites are excellent for sending television programs to cable operators and for broadcasting directly to homes.

One major limitation of GEO satellites is that their transmissions take a quarter of a second to send and return. This brief pause, one kind of propagation delay, makes two-way telephone conversations difficult. Also, GEO satellites are large and expensive, and they require substantial amounts of power to launch.

Medium-earth-orbit satellites are located about 6,000 miles above Earth's surface. MEO orbits require more satellites to cover Earth than GEO orbits because MEO footprints are smaller. MEO satellites have two advantages over GEO satellites: They are less expensive, and they do not have an appreciable propagation delay. However, because MEO satellites move with respect to a point on Earth's surface, receivers must track these satellites. (Think of a satellite dish slowly turning to remain oriented to a MEO satellite.)

Low-earth-orbit satellites are located 400 to 700 miles above Earth's surface. Because LEO satellites are much closer to Earth, they have little, if any, propagation delay. Like MEO satellites, however, LEO satellites move with respect to a point on Earth's surface and therefore must be tracked by receivers. Tracking LEO satellites is more difficult than tracking MEO satellites because LEO satellites move much more quickly relative to a point on Earth.

Unlike GEO and MEO satellites, LEO satellites can pick up signals from weak transmitters. This feature makes it possible for satellite telephones to operate via LEO satellites, because they can operate with less power using smaller batteries. Another advantage of LEO satellites is that they consume less power and cost less to launch.

At the same time, however, the footprints of LEO satellites are small, which means that many satellites are needed to cover the planet. For this reason, a single organization often produces multiple LEO satellites, known as *LEO constellations*. Two examples are Iridium and Globalstar.

Iridium (www.iridium.com) has placed a LEO constellation in orbit that consists of 66 satellites and 12 in-orbit spare satellites. The company claims it provides complete satellite communications coverage of Earth's surface, including the polar regions. Globalstar (www.globalstar.com) also has a LEO constellation in orbit.

Global Positioning Systems. The global positioning system (GPS) is a wireless system that utilizes satellites to enable users to determine their position anywhere on Earth. GPS is supported by 24 MEO satellites that are shared worldwide. The exact position of each satellite is always known because the satellite continuously broadcasts its position along with a time signal. By using the known speed of the signals and the distance from three satellites (for two-dimensional location) or four satellites (for three-dimensional location), it is possible to find the location of any receiving station or user within a range of 10 feet. GPS software can also convert the user's latitude and longitude to an electronic map.

Most of you are probably familiar with GPS in automobiles, which "talks" to drivers when giving directions. Figure 10.3 illustrates two ways for drivers to obtain GPS information in a car: a dashboard navigation system and a GPS app (in this case, TomTom; www.tomtom.com) on an iPhone.

Jeff Chiu/ASSOCIATED PRESS

FIGURE 10.3 Obtaining GPS information in an automobile.

Commercial use of GPS for activities such as navigating, mapping, and surveying has become widespread, particularly in remote areas. Cell phones in the United States now must have a GPS embedded in them so that the location of a person making an emergency call—for example, 911, known as wireless 911—can be detected immediately.

Three other global positioning systems are either planned or operational. The Russian GPS, *GLONASS*, was completed in 1995. However, the system fell into disrepair with the collapse of the Russian economy. In 2010, however, GLONASS achieved 100 percent coverage of Russian territory. The European Union GPS is called *Galileo*. The first determination of a position relying on Galileo satellites occurred in March 2013. The entire Galileo system is expected to be completed by 2019. China expects to complete its GPS, *Beidou*, by 2020.

GPS technology is used in digital pricing displays. IT's About Business 10.2 shows how many retailers are benefiting from these displays.

IT's About Business 10.2

MKT Digital Pricing Displays

A growing number of U.S. retailers are investing in digital pricing displays, for several reasons. First, these businesses have to accommodate frequent price changes in order to compete with online merchants. Second, their customers are using showrooming tactics in their stores. *Showrooming* occurs when shoppers use their smartphones inside physical stores to scan Amazon, eBay, and other Web sites to compare prices for the same product from several merchants. Third, the rapid growth of online retailing has shortened the shelf life of prices in brick-and-mortar stores. Therefore, rather than setting prices that provide them with desired profit margins, retailers increasingly have to use price-matching to honor the prices of their online competitors. Some retailers are even using software that uses algorithms to beat their competitors' prices and bump up their placement on Web sites that show side-by-side cost comparisons.

Pricer (www.pricer.com), the top provider of in-store digital-pricing displays, notes that this technology is not widely utilized in the United States. This reality might be changing, however. Pricer's U.S. business almost tripled in the first quarter of 2015 from the first quarter of 2014, to $11.6 million. Significantly, equipping a single store with digital displays for a big-box retailer (Walmart, Lowes, etc.) can cost more than $100,000.

Pricer's digital displays not only allow retailers to quickly changes their prices in stores, but the technology can be integrated with smartphone apps and GPS systems to lead customers to particular items. The system allows a customer to trigger the price display to flash as they approach a shelf. Pricer also offers brick-and-mortar retailers so-called "click-and-collect" services, where members of the staff walk through a store to gather items that customers ordered online for in-store pickup.

It's easy to change product prices online, but much more difficult and costly to do it in-store. The digital displays help greatly in this regard. For example, digital displays eliminate the problem of having the price on the shelf not match the price in the register at the checkout, which cuts down on customer complaints and transaction cancellations. Employees no longer have to spend time posting thousands of price changes on the shelves by hand—some large stores can make up to 6,000 price changes every month. The digital displays can change 3,000 prices on the floor every hour. The elimination of manual price changes frees up staff to help customers, especially during busy times.

Consider the case of Nebraska Furniture Mart (www.nfm.com), a chain of four furniture stores. In the past, employees had manually changed prices on the shop floor at each of its stores every morning. This effort enabled the store to offer the lowest prices on televisions, dishwashers, sofas, and flooring. However, it was extremely time consuming. To expedite this process, the store made a major investment in digital-price displays. Now, a single worker in one location can quickly change prices on thousands of products in all of its stores to match or beat those at Home Depot, Sears, and other rivals.

Another retailer, Kohl's (www.kohls.com), has installed Altierre (www.altierre.com) displays in almost 1,200 stores. These displays utilize wireless transmission equipment, sensors, and software to automate thousands of pricing displays on shelves throughout their stores.

Digital pricing displays cannot solve all of the price problems that confront brick-and-mortar establishments. For example, Nebraska Furniture Mart generally only changes the price for any item once a day before the store opens. The reason is that the store does not want the price of an item to change from the time the customer takes the item off the shelf or from the showroom to the time he or she gets to the cash register.

Sources: Compiled from "The Military Has Led Kohl's into Electronic Shelf Labels," *Huntingdon Marketing*, August 12, 2015; S. Soper and L. Rupp, "Stores Try Fixed Prices That Aren't So Fixed," *Bloomberg BusinessWeek*, July 27 – August 2, 2015; J. Renfrow, "Sears, Kohl's, Home Depot Using Digital Price Displays to Combat Showrooming," *FierceRetail*, July 21, 2015; C. Morran,"Retailers Turn to Electronic Price Tags to Combat Amazon," *Consumerist*, July 17, 2015; S. Soper, "Amazon Showrooming Forces Stores to Go Digital on Price Displays," *Bloomberg BusinessWeek*, July 17, 2015; R. Pincus, "Supermarket Ditches Paper Price Tags for Digital Ones," *PSFK*, March 6, 2015; "Sainsbury's Tests Self-Updating E-Ink Price Labels," *Digital Strategy Consulting*, February 20, 2015; R. Stross, "Digital Tags Help Ensure the Price Is Right," *The New York Times*, February 9, 2013; www.pricer.com, www.nfm.com, www.kohls.com, www.altierre.com, accessed September 15, 2015.

Questions

1. Why are brick-and-mortar retailers beginning to implement digital pricing displays?

2. What are possible disadvantages to digital pricing displays?

Internet over Satellite. In many regions of the world, Internet over Satellite (IoS) is the only option available for Internet connections because installing cables is either too expensive or physically impossible. IoS enables users to access the Internet via GEO satellites from a dish mounted on the side of their homes. Although IoS makes the Internet available to many people who otherwise could not access it, it has its drawbacks. Not only do GEO satellite transmissions involve a propagation delay, but they also can be disrupted by environmental influences such as thunderstorms.

Radio. Radio transmission uses radio-wave frequencies to send data directly between transmitters and receivers. Radio transmission has several advantages. First, radio waves travel easily through normal office walls. Second, radio devices are fairly inexpensive and easy to install. Third, radio waves can transmit data at high speeds. For these reasons, radio increasingly is being used to connect computers to both peripheral equipment and local area networks (LANs; discussed in Chapter 6). (Note: Wi-Fi and cellular also use radio frequency waves.)

As with other technologies, however, radio transmission has its drawbacks. First, radio media can create electrical interference problems. Also, radio transmissions are susceptible to snooping by anyone who has similar equipment that operates on the same frequency.

Another problem with radio transmission is that when you travel too far away from the source station, the signal breaks up and fades into static. Most radio signals can travel only 30 to 40 miles from their source. However, satellite radio overcomes this problem. Satellite radio (or *digital radio*) offers uninterrupted, near CD-quality transmission that is beamed to your radio, either at home or in your car, from space. In addition, satellite radio offers a broad spectrum of stations, including many types of music, news, and talk.

XM Satellite Radio and Sirius Satellite Radio were competitors that launched satellite radio services. XM broadcast its signals from GEO satellites, while Sirius used MEO satellites. In July 2008, the two companies merged to form Sirius XM (www.siriusxm.com). Listeners subscribe to the service for a monthly fee.

Wireless Security

Clearly, wireless networks provide numerous benefits for businesses. However, they also present a huge challenge to management—namely, their inherent lack of security. Wireless is a broadcast medium, and transmissions can be intercepted by anyone who is close enough and has access to the appropriate equipment. There are four major threats to wireless networks: rogue access points, war driving, eavesdropping, and radio-frequency jamming.

A *rogue access point* is an unauthorized access point into a wireless network. The rogue could be someone in your organization who sets up an access point meaning no harm but fails to inform the IT department. In more serious cases, the rogue is an "evil twin"—someone who wishes to access a wireless network for malicious purposes.

In an *evil twin attack*, the attacker is in the vicinity with a Wi-Fi-enabled computer and a separate connection to the Internet. Using a *hotspotter*—a device that detects wireless networks and provides information on them (see www.canarywireless.com)—the attacker simulates a wireless access point with the same wireless network name, or SSID, as the one that authorized users expect. If the signal is strong enough, users will connect to the attacker's system instead of the real access point. The attacker can then serve them a Web page asking for them to provide confidential information such as usernames, passwords, and account numbers. In other cases, the attacker simply captures wireless transmissions. These attacks are more effective with public hotspots (e.g., McDonald's and Starbucks) than with corporate networks.

War driving is the act of locating WLANs while driving (or walking) around a city or elsewhere. To war drive or walk, you simply need a Wi-Fi detector and a wirelessly enabled computer. If a WLAN has a range that extends beyond the building in which it is located, then an unauthorized user might be able to intrude into the network. The intruder can then obtain a free Internet connection and possibly gain access to important data and other resources.

Eavesdropping refers to efforts by unauthorized users to access data that are traveling over wireless networks.

Finally, in *radio-frequency (RF) jamming*, a person or a device intentionally or unintentionally interferes with your wireless network transmissions.

Before you go on...

1. Describe the most common types of wireless devices.

2. Describe the various types of transmission media.

3. Describe four threats to the security of wireless transmissions.

Apply the Concept 10.1

LEARNING OBJECTIVE 10.1 Identify advantages and disadvantages of each of the four main types of wireless transmission media.

STEP 1 : Background (Here is what you are learning.)

As stated in this section, mobile communication has changed our world more rapidly and dramatically than any other technology. Although several wireless transmission media are available, rarely will one technology meet all of a business's needs by itself. Vislink is a global technology firm that collects and delivers high-quality video broadcasts. These broadcasts are utilized in sports, news, law enforcement, and other areas. Although Vislink specializes in video, they rely on multiple mobile transmission media to obtain live feeds from multiple locations. Rajant is one of the providers that Vislink has utilized for their wireless media.

STEP 2 : Activity (Here is what you are doing.)

Visit http://www.wiley.com/go/rainer/MIS4e/applytheconcept, and click on the link provided for Apply the Concept 10.1. There are three links. One will take you to Vislink's website, another to Rajant's website, and the last to a YouTube video in which Vislink demonstrates how they can provide live video feed to law enforcement agencies using Rajant's wireless mesh network.

STEP 3 : Deliverable (Here is what you turn in.)

As you watch the video, listen for the wireless transmission media they mention and pay attention to how many of them are discussed in this section of the book. Write and submit a summary of your findings that highlights the advantages and disadvantages of the transmission media types and explains why they were or were not used in the product that Vislink/Rajant demonstrated.

10.2 Wireless Computer Networks and Internet Access

You have learned about various wireless devices and how these devices transmit wireless signals. These devices typically form wireless computer networks, and they provide wireless Internet access. In this section, you will study wireless networks, which we organize by their effective distance: short range, medium range, and wide area.

Short-Range Wireless Networks

Short-range wireless networks simplify the task of connecting one device to another. In addition, they eliminate wires, and they enable users to move around while they use the devices. In general, short-range wireless networks have a range of 100 feet or less. In this section, you consider three basic short-range networks: Bluetooth, ultra-wideband (UWB), and near-field communications (NFC).

Bluetooth. Bluetooth (www.bluetooth.com) is an industry specification used to create small personal area networks. A personal area network is a computer network used for communication among computer devices (e.g., telephones, personal digital assistants, smartphones) located close to one person. Bluetooth 1.0 can link up to eight devices within a 10-meter area (about 30 feet) with a bandwidth of 700 kilobits per second (Kbps) using low-power, radio-based communication. Bluetooth 4.0 can transmit up to approximately 25 megabits per second (Mbps) up to 100 meters (roughly 300 feet). Ericsson, the Scandinavian mobile handset company that developed this standard, called it Bluetooth after the tenth-century Danish King Harald Blatan (*Blatan* means "Bluetooth"). Ericsson selected this name because Blatan unified previously separate islands into the nation of Denmark.

Common applications for Bluetooth are wireless handsets for cell phones and portable music players. Advantages of Bluetooth include low power consumption and the fact that it uses omnidirectional radio waves—that is, waves that are emitted in all directions from a transmitter. For this reason, you do not have to point one Bluetooth device at another to create a connection.

Bluetooth low energy, marketed as *Bluetooth Smart*, enables applications in the healthcare, fitness, security, and home entertainment industries. Compared to "classic" Bluetooth, Bluetooth Smart is less expensive and consumes less power, although it has a similar communication range. Bluetooth Smart is fueling the "wearables" (wearable computer) development and adoption.

Ultra-Wideband. Ultra-wideband is a high-bandwidth wireless technology with transmission speeds in excess of 100 Mbps. This very high speed makes UWB a good choice for applications such as streaming multimedia from, say, a personal computer to a television.

Time Domain (www.timedomain.com), a pioneer in UWB technology, has developed many UWB applications. One interesting application is the PLUS Real-Time Location System (RTLS). An organization can utilize PLUS to locate multiple people and assets simultaneously. Employees, customers, and/or visitors wear the PLUS Badge Tag. PLUS Asset Tags are placed on equipment and products. PLUS is extremely valuable for healthcare environments, where knowing the real-time location of caregivers (e.g., doctors, nurses, technicians) and mobile equipment (e.g., laptops, monitors) is critical.

Near-Field Communications. Near-field communications has the smallest range of any short-range wireless networks. It is designed to be embedded in mobile devices such as cell phones and credit cards. For example, using NFC, you can wave your device or card within a few centimeters of POS terminals to pay for items.

Medium-Range Wireless Networks

Medium-range wireless networks are the familiar wireless local area networks (WLANs). The most common type of medium-range wireless network is Wireless Fidelity, or Wi-Fi. WLANs are useful in a variety of settings, some of which may be challenging.

Wireless Fidelity is a medium-range WLAN, which is a wired LAN but without the cables. In a typical configuration, a transmitter with an antenna, called a wireless access point (see Figure 10.4), connects to a wired LAN or to satellite dishes that provide an Internet connection. A wireless access point provides service to a number of users within a small geographical perimeter (up to approximately 300 feet), known as a hotspot. Multiple wireless access points are needed to support a larger number of users across a larger geographical area. To communicate wirelessly, mobile devices, such as laptop PCs, typically have a built-in wireless network interface capability.

Wi-Fi provides fast and easy Internet or intranet broadband access from public hotspots located at airports, hotels, Internet cafés, universities, conference centers, offices, and homes. Users can access the Internet while walking across a campus, to their office, or through their homes. In addition, users can access Wi-Fi with their laptops, desktops, or PDAs by adding a wireless network card. Most PC and laptop manufacturers incorporate these cards in their products.

The Institute of Electrical and Electronics Engineers (IEEE) has established a set of standards for wireless computer networks. The IEEE standard for Wi-Fi is the 802.11 family. As of mid-2016, there were many standards in this family., including Examples include:

© Roman Samokhin/Shutterstock

FIGURE 10.4 Wireless access point.

- 802.11a: supports wireless bandwidth up to 54 Mbps; high cost; short range; difficulty penetrating walls.

- 802.11b: supports wireless bandwidth up to 11 Mbps; low cost; longer range.

- 802.11g: supports wireless bandwidth up to 54 Mbps; high cost; longer range.

- 802.11n: supports wireless bandwidth exceeding 600 Mbps; higher cost than 802.11g; longer range than 802.11g.

- 802.11ac: will support wireless bandwidth of 1.3 Gbps (1.3 billion bits per second); will provide the ability to fully support a "multimedia home" in which high-definition video can be streamed simultaneously to multiple devices. Essentially, you will be able to wirelessly network your TV, DVR, smartphone, and sound system for complete on-demand access through any Internet-enabled device.

- 802.11 ad: supports wireless bandwidth up to 7 Gbps; targeted to the "wireless office" as opposed to the "wireless home."

The major benefits of Wi-Fi are its low cost and its ability to provide simple Internet access. It is the greatest facilitator of the wireless Internet—that is, the ability to connect to the Internet wirelessly.

 Corporations are integrating Wi-Fi into their strategies. For example, Starbucks, McDonald's, Panera, and Barnes & Noble offer customers Wi-Fi in many of their stores, primarily for Internet access. As you see in IT's About Business 10.3, Bobbejaanland, a family theme park in Belgium, deployed a Wi-Fi network to improve its guest experience.

IT's About Business 10.3

 MKT POM Wi-Fi Network Provides Advantages to a Belgian Theme Park

Founded in 1960, Bobbejaanland Family Park (www.bobbejaanland.be) is one of Belgium's most popular theme parks, boasting a 56-acre campus, 40 rides, and approximately 800,000 visitors per year. To manage all the facilities, the park has various devices installed around the campus, including various computers and point-of-sale (PoS) devices. The management team also wanted its visitors to have free Wi-Fi.

To help accomplish these goals, the park deployed a Wi-Fi network from Fortinet (www.fortinet.com), a California-based provider of network security solutions that consists of 30 hotspots that cover more than 90 percent of the park's area. The wireless network is protected by Fortinet's FortiGate firewall. (We discussed firewalls in Chapter 7.) The park also deployed Fortinet's FortiPresence system, which gathers information from connected devices. Using location information from these devices, FortiPresence can estimate a device's location and place it on a dynamic map of the park.

Gathering data on visitors was valuable to park managers. They utilize the FortiPresence system to map the traffic flow of visitors, to analyze the location and the length of the lines at the park's rides and concession stands, and to develop profiles of new and returning visitors. Managers can learn how visitors come to the park, when and where they eat lunch, which exhibits and rides they visit, how long they remain in specific areas, and which shops they access, to name just a few areas of interest. Basically, park managers wanted to know more about what visitors did in order to increase their enjoyment and to entice them to spend more money. For example, what if the park could attract visitors to specific attractions or specific shops?

To collect visitor information, the park invites guests to register on its Web site via an e-mail address or Facebook. Visitors must accept a disclaimer that clearly explains that their mobile devices will be tracked while they are inside the park. Guests have the option of having their data erased after they leave the park.

At almost no cost, the park's registration system creates a customer database. During the offseason, the park contacts customers on the list with offers and news regarding season passes, upcoming events, and new attractions. With repeat visitors, Bobbejaanland combines location data with analytics to provide increasingly targeted offers to them.

Bobbejaanland doesn't just customize offers to guests before their visit; it targets them while on site through portal access points at certain locations throughout the park. As an example, if a guest accesses the portal near a pizza stand, the portal can display a promotion regarding offers at that stand.

The park tracks visitors' locations not just to send promotional notifications to them, but to alert staff to possible problems before they happen. For instance, a higher number of guests in a particular area could signal the need to refill drinks or vending machines, although the machines themselves send signals over an Internet of Things sensor when they're almost empty. Park staff may also determine that an increase in guests in a certain location requires sending cleaning teams or security guards. Conversely, if the tracking indicates a decrease in guests in an area, then managers can do various things to save money, such as delaying the opening of a ride, operating the ride less often, or closing the ride early.

In implementing its Wi-Fi network, Bobbejaanland had to take data privacy into consideration, because under Belgian law, the park is considered an Internet service provider and therefore it must abide by the country's ISP regulations. That means that it must collect a certain amount of their customers' data as they go through the park in order to investigate potential incidents.

Besides visitors to the park, Fortinet created two other types of profiles for park Wi-Fi users. One is for park office staff and the other is for employees who move throughout the park. All three types of users have distinctive encryption levels and firewalls.

The park notes that the Wi-Fi system paid for itself in only one season. Visitors can download a park app and use the Wi-Fi on site to find their way around, look up prices, and chat with friends. Bobbejaanland was looking into other technologies to help guests, such as Bluetooth low-energy beacons and radio-frequency identification (RFID).

Sources: Compiled from S. Sclafane, "The IoT Revolution: Coming to a Warehouse and a Theme Park Near You," *Carrier Management,* August 17, 2015; X. Mertens, "Wi-Fi Enhances Guest Experience and Profitability for Belgian Theme Park," *Computer Weekly,* July 3, 2015; "Bobbejaanland Selects Fortinet to Deploy Park-Wide Wi-Fi Infrastructure for Visitors and Staff," *www.fortinet.com*, March 25, 2015; D. Mumpower, "6 Huge Ways That Theme Parks Will Change by 2020," *Theme Park Tourist,* April 12, 2015; E. Alton, "What the Internet of Things Might Mean for Theme Parks, Museums, and Other Fun Places," *Entertainment Designer,* January 21, 2015; "Theme Parks Are Trying to Incorporate Tech to Lure You off the Couch," *Mashable,* November 21, 2014; www.bobbejaanland.be, accessed September 22, 2015.

Questions

1. Describe the advantages of the Wi-Fi network to Bobbejaanland Family Park.

2. Describe potential disadvantages of the Wi-Fi network to Bobbejaanland Family Park.

Although Wi-Fi has become extremely popular, the technology does have problems. Three factors are preventing the commercial Wi-Fi market from expanding even further: roaming, security, and cost:

1. At this time, users cannot roam from hotspot to hotspot if the hotspots use different Wi-Fi network services. Unless the service is free, users have to log on to separate accounts and, where required, pay a separate fee for each service. (Some Wi-Fi hotspots offer free service, while others charge a fee.)

2. Security is the second barrier to greater acceptance of Wi-Fi. Because Wi-Fi uses radio waves, it is difficult to shield from intruders.

3. The final limitation to greater Wi-Fi expansion is cost. Even though Wi-Fi services are relatively inexpensive, many experts question whether commercial Wi-Fi services can survive when so many free hotspots are available to users.

Wi-Fi Direct. Until late 2010, Wi-Fi could operate only if the hotspot contained a wireless antenna. Because of this limitation, organizations have typically used Wi-Fi for communications of up to about 800 feet. For shorter, peer-to-peer connections they have used Bluetooth.

This situation changed following the introduction of a new iteration of Wi-Fi known as Wi-Fi Direct. Wi-Fi Direct enables peer-to-peer communications, so devices can connect directly. It allows users to transfer content among devices without having to rely on a wireless antenna. It can connect pairs or groups of devices at Wi-Fi speeds of up to 250 Mbps and at distances of up to 800 feet. Further, devices with Wi-Fi Direct can broadcast their availability to other devices just as Bluetooth devices can. Finally, Wi-Fi Direct is compatible with the more than one billion Wi-Fi devices currently in use.

Wi-Fi Direct will probably challenge the dominance of Bluetooth in the area of device-to-device networking. It offers a similar type of connectivity but with greater range and much faster data transfer.

MiFi. MiFi is a small, portable wireless device that provides users with a permanent Wi-Fi hotspot wherever they go. Thus, users are always connected to the Internet. The range of the MiFi device is about 10 meters (roughly 30 feet). Developed by Novatel, the MiFi device is also called an intelligent mobile hotspot. Accessing Wi-Fi through the MiFi device allows up to five persons to be connected at the same time, sharing the same connection. MiFi also allows users to use voice-over-IP technology (discussed in Chapter 6) to make free (or cheap) calls, both locally and internationally.

MiFi provides broadband Internet connectivity at any location that offers 3G cellular network coverage. One drawback is that MiFi is expensive both to acquire and to use.

Super Wi-Fi. The term *Super Wi-Fi* was coined by the U.S. Federal Communications Commission (FCC) to describe a wireless network proposal that creates long-distance wireless Internet connections. (Despite the name, Super Wi-Fi is *not* based on Wi-Fi technology.) Super Wi-Fi uses the lower-frequency "white spaces" between broadcast TV channels. These frequencies enable the signal to travel further and penetrate walls better than normal Wi-Fi frequencies.

Super Wi-Fi is already in use in Houston, Texas; Wilmington, North Carolina; and the University of West Virginia. The technology threatens cell phone carriers' 3G technology, and it could eventually bring broadband wireless Internet access to rural areas.

Wide-Area Wireless Networks

Wide-area wireless networks connect users to the Internet over a geographically dispersed territory. These networks typically operate over the licensed spectrum—that is, they use portions of the wireless spectrum that are regulated by the government. In contrast, Bluetooth, Wi-Fi, and Super Wi-Fi operate over the unlicensed spectrum and are therefore more prone to interference and security problems. In general, wide-area wireless network technologies fall into two categories: cellular radio and wireless broadband.

Cellular Radio. Cellular telephones (cell phones) provide two-way radio communications over a cellular network of base stations with seamless handoffs. Cellular telephones differ from cordless telephones, which offer telephone service only within a limited range through a single base station attached to a fixed landline—for example, within a home or an office.

The cell phone communicates with radio antennas, or towers, placed within adjacent geographic areas called *cells* (see Figure 10.5). A telephone message is transmitted to the local cell—that is, the antenna—by the cell phone and then is passed from cell to cell until it reaches the cell of its destination. At this final cell, the message either is transmitted to the receiving cell phone or it is transferred to the public switched telephone system to be transmitted to a wireline telephone. This is why you can use a cell phone to call other cell phones as well as standard wireline phones.

Cellular technology is quickly evolving, moving toward higher transmission speeds and richer features. The technology has progressed through a number of stages:

- *First generation* (*1G*) cellular networks used analog signals and had low bandwidth (capacity).

- *Second generation* (*2G*) used digital signals primarily for voice communication; it provided data communication up to 10 Kbps.

- *2.5G* used digital signals and provided voice and data communication up to 144 Kbps.

- *Third generation* (*3G*) uses digital signals and can transmit voice and data up to 384 Kbps when the device is moving at a walking pace, 128 Kbps when it is moving in a car, and up to 2 Mbps when it is in a fixed location. 3G supports video, Web browsing, and instant messaging.

3G does have disadvantages. Perhaps the most fundamental problem is that cellular companies in North America use two separate technologies: Verizon and Sprint use Code Division Multiple Access (CDMA), while AT&T and T-Mobile use Global System for Mobile Communications (GSM). CDMA companies are currently using *Evolution-Data Optimized* (*EV-DO*) technology, which is a wireless broadband cellular radio standard.

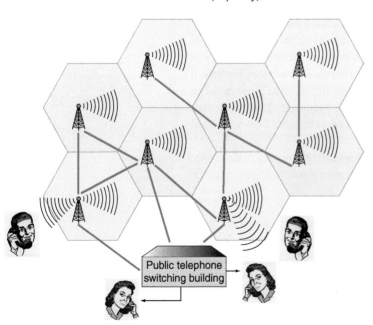

FIGURE 10.5 Smartphone and GPS system. (*Sources:* Image Source; © Engine Images-Fotolia.com; © AP/Wide World Photos)

In addition, 3G is relatively expensive. In fact, most carriers limit how much information you can download and what you can use the service for. For instance, some carriers prohibit you from downloading or streaming audio or video. If you exceed the carriers' limits, they reserve the right to cut off your service.

- *Fourth generation* (*4G*) is not one defined technology or standard. The International Tele-communications Union (ITU) has specified speed requirements for 4G: 100 Mbps (million bits per second) for high-mobility communications such as cars and trains, and 1 Gbps (billion bits per second) for low-mobility communications such as pedestrians. A 4G system is expected to provide a secure all-IP-based mobile broadband system to all types of mobile devices. Many of the current 4G offerings do not meet the ITU specified speeds, but they call their service 4G nonetheless. See "IT's Personal" for more information.

  Long-term evolution (LTE) is a wireless broadband technology designed to support roaming Internet access via smartphones and handheld devices. LTE is approximately 10 times faster than 3G networks.

  XLTE (advanced LTE) is designed to handle network congestion when too many people in one area try to access an LTE network. XLTE is designed to provide all users with no decrease in bandwidth.

- *Fifth generation* (*5G*) is expected to be deployed by 2020. 5G networks are predicted to be faster and more intelligent than previous generations of cellular networks. With 5G, wearable computers (e.g., Fitbit), smartphones, tablets, and other devices with sensors that are location- and context-aware will work together with apps and services that you use.

Wireless Broadband or WiMAX. Worldwide Interoperability for Microwave Access, popularly known as WiMAX, is the name for IEEE Standard 802.16. WiMAX has a wireless access range of up to 31 miles, compared to 300 feet for Wi-Fi. WiMAX also has a data transfer rate of up to 75 Mbps. It is a secure system, and it offers features such as voice and video. WiMAX antennas can transmit broadband Internet connections to antennas on homes and businesses located miles away. For this reason, WiMAX can provide long-distance broadband wireless access to rural areas and other locations that are not currently being served.

Consider this example of the use of WiMAX. On April 1, 2015, a fire broke out in the underground electrical cable ducts in a tunnel under a major highway in London. The fire burned for 36 hours and caused major disruptions to broadband service in the area. With fiber-soptic, broadband access to the Internet not available, businesses turned to WiMAX from Liminet (http://luminet.co.uk). One business owner noted that Luminet helped his company get its main office back online in less than 24 hours. Further, Luminet's broadband service helped the company quickly move its staff back from its disaster recovery site.

It's Personal: Wireless and Mobile

What the GSM3GHSDPA+4GLTE??? This chapter explains the many mobile platforms that are available to you as a consumer. Specifically, it discusses cellular, Bluetooth, Wi-Fi, satellite, and other wireless options. Within the cellular area, however, things get confusing because the telecommunications companies use so many acronyms these days. Have you ever wondered if Verizon 3G was equivalent to AT&T 3G? What about 4G and 4G LTE? Of course, most people assume that 4G is faster than 3G, but by how much?

To appreciate this confusion, consider that when Apple released one update to its mobile operating system (iOS), AT&T suddenly began to display 4G rather than 3G on the iPhone—despite the fact that the phone had not been upgraded! Pretty nice, right? Wrong. In this instance, the "upgrade" simply consisted of a new terminology for the existing technology. The speed of the 3G/4G network had *not* changed. (*Note*: AT&T "4G LTE" is a different technology that does offer significantly higher speeds than AT&T 3G or 4G.)

Actual connection speeds are described in bit rates, meaning how many bits (1s or 0s) a device can transmit in 1 second. For example, a speed listed as 1.5 Mbps translates to 1.5 million bits per second. That sounds like a tremendous rate. Knowing the bits per second, however, is only part of understanding the actual speed. In reality, connection speed is not the same as *throughput*, which is the amount of bandwidth actually available for you to use. Throughput will always be less than the connection speed.

To understand this point, consider how your car operates. It is probably capable of driving more than 100 mph. However, you are "throttled down" by various speed limits, so you never reach this potential speed. Your actual speed varies depending on the route you take, the speed limits imposed along that route, the weather, the amount of traffic, and many other factors. In the same way, even though AT&T, Verizon, Sprint, and other companies boast incredible wireless speeds ("Up to 20 Mbps!"), they will always say "up to" because they know that you will never actually download a file at that rate.

The best method for determining the actual speeds of the various networks is to go to your local wireless store and run a speed test using the demo model they have on display. This test will give you first-hand experience of the actual throughput speed you can expect from their network. The result is much more realistic than terms such as 3G, 4G, and 4G LTE.

Here is how to perform the test: First, make certain the unit is connected only to a cellular network (not Wi-Fi). Then go to http://speedtest.net, and click "Begin Test." I just ran this test from my iPhone 4S on AT&T's 4G (not 4G LTE) network. My download speed was 3.80 Mbps, and my upload speed was 1.71 Mbps. These numbers are more informative than any name they are given (3G, 4G, etc.) because they indicate exactly what I can expect from my wireless connection. Run this test at competing stores (AT&T, Verizon, Sprint, T-Mobile, etc.), and you will have real data to compare. As names change, you can always run a test to find the facts.

Before you go on...

1. What is Bluetooth? What is a WLAN?
2. Describe Wi-Fi, cellular service, and WiMAX.

Apply the Concept 10.2

LEARNING OBJECTIVE 10.2 Explain how businesses can use technology employed by short-range, medium-range, and long-range networks, respectively.

STEP 1: Background

Many cellular phones today contain multiple radios. Both the iPhone 6s (and 6s Plus) and the Galaxy S6 contain three radio transceivers and one radio receiver. The radio transceivers are Cellular (4G LTE, 4G, or 3G depending on your carrier), Bluetooth, and Wi-Fi. GPS is the radio receiver. The Samsung S6 also includes infrared and an NFC chip. With all of these radios embedded in a small mobile device, the possibilities of connectivity are nearly endless because one device can utilize short-range, mid-range, and wide-range connectivity.

STEP 2: Activity

Visit http://www.wiley.com/go/rainer/MIS4e/applytheconcept, and view the video demonstration by Serial IO. There is also a link to their Web site, where you will find several examples of wireless products intended for business use. Although most of these products are short-range devices, you must assume they will be connected to some mid-range and/or wide-range wireless network. In fact, these devices support Windows, Mac, Android, iOS, BlackBerry, and other platforms.

STEP 3: Deliverable

Based on the video and the Serial IO Web site, create and submit a table to explain how businesses can use the technologies employed by short-range, medium-range, and long-range networks to achieve their business purposes.

10.3 Mobile Computing and Mobile Commerce

In the traditional computing environment, users come to a computer, which is connected with wires to other computers and to networks. Because these networks need to be linked by wires, it is difficult or even impossible for people on the move to use them. In particular, salespeople, repair people, service employees, law enforcement agents, and utility workers can be more effective if they can use IT while in the field or in transit. Mobile computing was designed for workers who travel outside the boundaries of their organizations as well as for anyone traveling outside his or her home.

Mobile computing refers to a real-time connection between a mobile device and other computing environments, such as the Internet or an intranet. This innovation is revolutionizing how people use computers. It is spreading at work and at home; in education, healthcare, and entertainment; and in many other areas.

Mobile computing has two major characteristics that differentiate it from other forms of computing: mobility and broad reach. *Mobility* means that users carry a device with them and can initiate a real-time contact with other systems from wherever they happen to be. *Broad reach* refers to the fact that when users carry an open mobile device, they can be reached instantly, even across great distances.

Mobility and broad reach create five value-added attributes that break the barriers of geography and time: ubiquity, convenience, instant connectivity, personalization, and localization of products and services. A mobile device can provide information and communication regardless of the user's location (*ubiquity*). With an Internet-enabled mobile device, users can access the Web, intranets, and other mobile devices quickly and easily, without booting up a PC or placing a call via a modem (*convenience* and *instant connectivity*). A company can customize information and send it to individual consumers as a short message service (SMS) (*customization*). And, knowing a user's physical location helps a company advertise its products and services (*localization*). Mobile computing provides the foundation for mobile commerce (m-commerce).

Mobile Commerce

In addition to affecting our everyday lives, mobile computing is also transforming the way organizations conduct business by allowing businesses and individuals to engage in mobile commerce. As you saw at the beginning of this chapter, mobile commerce (or *m-commerce*) refers to electronic commerce (EC) transactions that are conducted in a wireless environment, especially via the Internet. Like regular EC applications, m-commerce can be transacted via the Internet, private communication lines, smart cards, and other infrastructures. M-commerce creates opportunities for businesses to deliver new services to existing customers and to attract new customers.

The development of m-commerce is driven by the following factors:

- *Widespread availability of mobile devices.* By mid-2016, some six billion cell phones were in use throughout the world. Cell phones are spreading more quickly in the developing world than the developed world. Experts estimate that within a few years about 70 percent of cell phones in developed countries will have Internet access. Mobile Internet access in developing countries will increase rapidly as well. Thus, a mass market has developed for mobile computing and m-commerce.

- *Declining prices.* The price of wireless devices is declining and will continue to decline.

- *Bandwidth improvement.* To properly conduct m-commerce, you need sufficient bandwidth for transmitting text, voice, video, and multimedia. Wi-Fi, 4G cellular technology, and WiMAX all provide the necessary bandwidth.

Mobile computing and m-commerce include many applications, which result from the capabilities of various technologies. You will examine these applications and their impact on business activities in the next section.

Mobile Commerce Applications

Mobile commerce applications are many and varied. The most popular applications include location-based applications, financial services, intrabusiness applications, accessing information, and telemetry. The rest of this section examines these various applications and their effects on the ways people live and do business.

Mobile Wallets.   Instead of swiping a plastic card at the checkout counter, consumers merely wave their phones a few inches above a payment terminal. This process uses a contact-free technology called near-field communications (NFC). This technology, known as the **mobile wallet**, is being employed with millions of phones both in the United States and overseas. There are a number of mobile wallets from which to choose:

- *Softcard* (formerly Isis Mobile Wallet) was a joint venture between AT&T, T-Mobile and Verizon. Softcard uses near-field communications technology to make secure payments with credit and debit card credentials stored on their smartphones. In February 2015, Google acquired Softcard's intellectual property and integrated it into its Google Wallet service.

- *Google Wallet* is a mobile wallet that uses near-field communications to allow its users to store debit cards, credit cards, loyalty cards, and gift cards on their smartphones. Google Wallet provided a tap-to-pay feature where users simply tap their smartphones on supported terminals to pay for items. With Google Wallet, users launch an app, then type in a pin so Google can access their stored card credentials. Google Wallet also provides a peer-to-peer payment system that can send money to a real, physical Google Wallet card. Google says that the Google Wallet will continue as a peer-to-peer payment system.

- *Android Pay* is a digital wallet that also provides a tap-to-pay feature. With Android Pay, users do not need an app and do not have to enter a pin. The wallet's functionality is built into the operating system.

- *MasterCard's Contactless, American Express's ExpressPay,* and *Visa's PayWave* are EMV-compatible, contactless payment features. EMV (which stands for Europay, MasterCard, and Visa, the three companies which originally created the standard) is a technical standard for smart payment cards. EMV cards are smart cards that store their data on chips rather than on magnetic stripes. They can be contact cards that must be physically inserted into a reader, or contactless cards that can be read over a short distance using radio frequency identification technology. EMV cards are also called chip-and-pin cards.

- *Apple Pay* is a mobile wallet that uses near-field communications to enable users to make payments using various Apple devices. Apple Pay does not require Apple-specific contactless payment terminals and will work with Visa's PayWave, Mastercard's PayPass, and American Express's ExpressPay terminals. The wallet is similar to other wallets with the addition of two-factor authentication. To pay at points of sale, users hold their authenticated Apple device to the point-of-sale system. iPhone users authenticate by holding their fingerprint to the phone's Touch ID sensor, where Apple Watch users authenticate by double clicking a button on the device.

The stakes in this competition are enormous because the small fees generated every time consumers swipe their cards add up to tens of billions of dollars annually in the United States alone. The potential for large revenue streams is real because mobile wallets have clear advantages. For example: Which are you more likely to have with you at any given moment—your phone or your physical wallet? Also, keep in mind that if you lose your phone, it can be located on a map and remotely deactivated. Plus, your phone can be password protected. Your physical wallet, however, cannot perform these functions.

Location-Based Applications and Services. M-commerce B2C applications include location-based services and location-based applications. Location-based mobile commerce is called location-based commerce (or L-commerce).

Location-based services provide information that is specific to a given location. For example, a mobile user can (1) request the nearest business or service, such as an ATM or a restaurant; (2) receive alerts, such as a warning of a traffic jam or an accident; and (3) find a friend. Wireless carriers can provide location-based services such as locating taxis, service personnel, doctors, and rental equipment; scheduling fleets; tracking objects such as packages and train boxcars; finding information such as navigation, weather, traffic, and room schedules; targeting advertising; and automating airport check-ins.

Consider, for example, how location-based advertising can make the marketing process more productive. Marketers can use this technology to integrate the current locations and preferences of mobile users. They can then send user-specific advertising messages concerning nearby shops, malls, and restaurants to consumers' wireless devices.

Apple's iBeacon app is an interesting location-based service. The app provides location-aware, contextual information to users. iBeacon uses a collection of beacons, which are Bluetooth Smart transmitters. The iBeacons locate a smartphone's location by broadcasting Bluetooth signals.

The beacons, which can be placed anywhere that contextual information would be valuable, are tiny discs about the size of a quarter. The purpose of iBeacons is to allow advertisers and business partners to deliver information, coupons, and other content relevant to a person's location.

Mobile Advertising. *Mobile advertising* is a form of advertising via cell phones, smartphones, or other mobile devices. Analysts estimate that mobile advertising revenue will reach approximately $7 billion by 2020. IT's About Business 10.4 illustrates the effectiveness of mobile advertising by taking a look at the practice in rural India.

IT's About Business 10.4

MKT Mobile Advertising in Rural India

In the developed world, many businesses market to customers via their Web-connected smartphones. In the developing world, however, many people do not have smartphones. As a result, companies are using mobile campaigns to attract customers who have "basic" cell phones and who live in locations where cable television or even newspapers have limited reach.

For example, in India most people do not live in big cities. Of the 400 million mobile phones used by rural residents, some 90 percent are not "smart." Further complicating this situation, many villages do not have access to traditional media such as television, radio, and print. Some villages have intermittent electricity. Despite these limitations, advertisers in India see some benefits to reaching rural consumers via mobile phones rather than traditional mass media campaigns. For one thing, ads on mobile phones cost less and are more targeted. For another thing, consumer spending among India's rural villagers is increasing at a faster rate than among India's urban centers.

Many advertisers are starting to use mobile as a cost-effective strategy to reach areas with a poor infrastructure. For example, 250,000 rupees ($4,100) buys only a 10-*second* advertisement during the mythological drama *Mahabharat* on India's Star Plus television network, which attracts 6.3 million viewers per week. It would cost advertisers roughly the same amount to reach approximately 21,000 people with a 15-*minute* phone call—a much longer period in which to engage with consumers.

Consider the case of Unilever (www.unilever.com), the world's second-largest consumer company, which markets a range of food, hygiene, and cleansing products including Hellman's mayonnaise, Caress soap, Lipton tea, and Axe deodorant. Unilever wanted to reach India's 833 million rural villagers. The company therefore implemented a marketing campaign that operates as follows: A user places a call using a basic cell phone to a special number that disconnects after two rings so that the consumer does not have to pay. The cell phone user then receives a 15-minute pre-recorded selection of Bollywood music and jokes, interspersed with four ads for various Unilever health and beauty products. All users listen to the same recorded segment, which changes each week. In March 2014, at least two million people subscribed to the free service.

Unilever's mobile campaign in India for its Axe men's deodorant takes a similar approach, using free calls to customers. When a consumer buys Axe, he can enter a code on the package into a drawing to win a ticket to a party on a yacht. After registering, the man regularly receives a call on his cell with a woman's prerecorded voice, urging him to buy more Axe to boost his chances of winning.

Unilever maintains that its mobile ads have gained eight million listeners. Advertising via mobile phones can reach massive numbers of people, measure their response, and constantly engage them, claims the CEO of NetCore (www.netcore.in), the company that manages Unilever's mobile service. Mobile advertising is able to obtain information on each subscriber, which helps to target campaigns.

Several companies, including Cadbury, the chocolate-making subsidiary of Mondelez (www.mondelezinternational.com), have adopted a different strategy in which they offer free mobile air-time credit to customers. In India, 97 percent of mobile users have phones with prepaid SIM cards. Buyers of Cadbury's 5-Star chocolate bar can enter a code on the package to get free airtime credits. Similarly, PepsiCo (www.pepsico.com) offers 15 rupees of free airtime for buying various beverages and snacks. And what can Indian consumers do with their free airtime? They can take advantage of an offer from Marico (www.marico.com), India's largest seller of hair oil, which provides mobile customers with prerecorded calls offering basic English lessons.

An advantage to digital marketing is being able to measure so much consumer data. But it's hard for advertisers to determine whether their mobile advertising campaigns directly result in product sales. In a country with over a billion people, advertising costs in India can rapidly reach unsustainable levels if millions of users opt in to the free services. There are also concerns about the shelf life of such ad campaigns: Consumers could become bored with the same, or similar, ads.

And the bottom line? Companies spent approximately $60 million on mobile advertising in India in 2015 and were projected to spend more than $100 million in 2016.

Sources: Compiled from J. Voight, "For Unilever's CMO, Global Growth and Social Responsibility Are Now Inseparable Goals," *AdWeek*, March 23, 2015; G. Jarboe, "Mobile Marketing Done Right: 2 Masterful Case Studies," *Momentology*, April 23, 2015; L. Gonzalez, "Radio Station Reaches Remote Areas through Cell Phones, *PSFK*, June 24, 2014; N. Mortimer, "Unilever's Indian Mobile Entertainment Channel Reaches 60% of Non-TV Households," *The Drum*, June 3, 2014; A. Narayan, "Pick Up. Your Ad Is Calling," *Bloomberg BusinessWeek*, April 21-27, 2014; "Unilever Woos Indian Villagers with Free Mobile Music," *Digital Strategy Consulting*, April 22, 2014; S. Malviya, "Hindustan Unilever Runs Bihar's Most Popular Radio on Mobile Phones," *The Economic Times*, March 4, 2014; www.unilever.com, accessed September 10, 2015.

Questions

1. Why is it so important to adapt business strategies to existing technologies? Provide examples from this case in your answer.

2. Describe the impacts of wireless technologies on various companies' marketing campaigns in India.

3. Discuss the limitations that "basic" cell phones can place on marketing campaigns.

FIN

Financial Services. Mobile financial applications include banking, wireless payments and micropayments, money transfers, wireless wallets, and bill payment services. The bottom line for mobile financial applications is to make it more convenient for customers to transact business regardless of where they are or what time it is. Harried customers are demanding such convenience.

In many countries, banks increasingly offer mobile access to financial and account information. For example, Citibank (www.citibank.com) alerts customers on their digital cell phones about changes to their account information.

If you took a taxi ride in Frankfurt, Germany, you could use your cell phone to pay the taxi driver. Such very small purchase amounts (generally less than $10) are called *micropayments*.

Web shoppers historically have preferred to pay with credit cards. Because credit card companies sometimes charge fees on transactions, however, credit cards are an inefficient way to make very small purchases. The growth of relatively inexpensive digital content, such as music (e.g., iTunes), ring tones, and downloadable games, is driving the growth of micropayments, as merchants seek to avoid paying credit card fees on small transactions.

Ultimately, however, the success of micropayment applications will depend on the costs of the transactions. Transaction costs will be small only when the volume of transactions is large. One technology that can increase the volume of transactions is wireless mobile wallets (m-wallets). Various companies offer m-wallet technologies that enable cardholders to make purchases with a single click from their mobile devices.

In China, SmartPay allows people to use their mobile phones to pay their phone bills and utility bills, buy lottery tickets and airline tickets, and make other purchases. SmartPay launched 172.com (see www.172.com), a portal that centralizes the company's mobile, telephone, and Internet-based payment services for consumers. The company designed the portal to provide a convenient, centralized source of information for all of these transactions.

Intrabusiness Applications. Although business-to-consumer (B2C) m-commerce receives considerable publicity, most of today's m-commerce applications actually are used *within* organizations. In this section, you will see how companies use mobile computing to support their employees.

POM

Mobile devices increasingly are becoming an integral part of workflow applications. For example, companies can use non-voice mobile services to assist in dispatch functions—that is, to assign jobs to mobile employees, along with detailed information about the job. Target areas for mobile delivery and dispatch services include transportation (delivery of food, oil, newspapers, cargo; courier services; tow trucks; taxis), utilities (gas, electricity, phone, water); field service (computers, office equipment, home repair); healthcare (visiting nurses, doctors, social services); and security (patrols, alarm installation).

Accessing Information. Another vital function of mobile technology is to help users obtain and utilize information. Two types of technologies—mobile portals and voice portals—are designed to aggregate and deliver content in a form that will work within the limited space available on mobile devices. These portals provide information to users anywhere and at any time.

A **mobile portal** aggregates and provides content and services for mobile users. These services include news, sports, and e-mail; entertainment, travel, and restaurant information; community services; and stock trading. The world's best-known mobile portal—i-mode from NTT DoCoMo (www.nttdocomo.com)—has more than 40 million subscribers, primarily in Japan. Major players in Europe are Vodafone, O2, and T-Mobile. Some traditional portals—for example, Yahoo!, AOL, and MSN—have mobile portals as well.

A **voice portal** is a Web site with an audio interface. Voice portals are not Web sites in the normal sense because they can also be accessed through a standard phone or a cell phone. A phone number connects you to a Web site, where you can request information verbally. The system finds the information, translates it into a computer-generated voice reply, and tells you what you want to know. Most airlines utilize voice portals to provide real-time information on flight status.

Another example of a voice portal is the voice-activated 511 travel-information line developed by Tellme.com. This technology enables callers to inquire about weather, local restaurants, current traffic, and other valuable information. In addition to retrieving information, some sites provide true interaction. For example, iPing (www.iping.com) is a reminder and notification service that allows users to enter information via the Web and receive reminder calls. This service can even call a group of people to notify them of a meeting or conference call.

Telemetry Applications. **Telemetry** is the wireless transmission and receipt of data gathered from remote sensors. Telemetry has numerous mobile computing applications. For example, technicians can use telemetry to identify maintenance problems in equipment and doctors can monitor patients and control medical equipment from a distance. Car manufacturers use telemetry applications for remote vehicle diagnosis and preventive maintenance. For instance, drivers of many General Motors cars use its OnStar system (www.onstar.com) in numerous ways.

An interesting telemetry application for individuals is an iPhone app called Find My iPhone. Find My iPhone is a part of the Apple iCloud (www.apple.com/icloud). This app provides several very helpful telemetry functions. If you lose your iPhone, for example, it offers two ways to find its approximate location on a map. First, you can sign into the Apple iCloud from any computer. Second, you can use the Find My iPhone app on another iPhone, iPad, or iPod touch.

If you remember where you left your iPhone, you can write a message and display it on your iPhone's screen. The message might say, "Left my iPhone. Please call me at 301-555-1211." Your message appears on your iPhone, even if the screen is locked. And, if the map indicates that your iPhone is nearby—perhaps in your office under a pile of papers—you can tell Find My iPhone to play a sound that overrides the volume or silent setting.

If you left your iPhone in a public place, you may want to protect its contents. You can remotely set a four-digit passcode lock to prevent people from using your iPhone, accessing your personal information, or tampering with your settings. Going further, you can initiate a remote wipe (erase all contents) to restore your iPhone to its factory settings. If you eventually find your phone, then you can connect it to your computer and use iTunes to restore the data from your most recent backup.

If you have lost your iPhone and you do not have access to a computer, you can download the Find My iPhone app to a friend's iPhone, iPad, or iPod touch and then sign in to access all the Find My iPhone features.

Before you go on...

1. What are the major drivers of mobile computing?
2. Describe mobile portals and voice portals.
3. Describe wireless financial services.
4. Discuss some of the major intrabusiness wireless applications.

Apply the Concept 10.3

LEARNING OBJECTIVE 10.3 Provide a specific example of how each of the five major m-commerce applications can benefit a business.

STEP 1: Background

Section 10.3 introduced you to five of the most popular mobile commerce applications. These applications are location-based applications, financial services, intrabusiness applications, accessing information, and telemetry. Although you may not have had experience with each of these, it is likely that you have experienced some.

STEP 2: Activity

Read (or reread) the section and consider the following questions related to your personal experiences with mobile commerce. Do

you use a mobile wallet? Has using a mobile wallet replaced your traditional wallet? What location-based services do you allow on your mobile device? Do you freely share your location or are you more private? What type of intrabusiness applications do you utilize as an employee or customer of an organization? What type of information do you access on a regular basis? Do you utilize any telemetry information (such as a wireless connection to your vehicle computer to record information on your mobile phone)?

STEP 3: Deliverable

Based on your answers to the questions in Step 2, build a table that provides a brief discussion of how each of the five major m-commerce applications benefit businesses and provide your personal experiences with each.

10.4 | The Internet of Things

The **Internet of Things (IoT)**, also called the *Internet of Everything*, the *Internet of Anything*, the *Industrial Internet,* and *machine-to-machine (M2M) communication*, is a system in which any object, natural or manmade, has a unique identity (i.e., its own IP address) and is able to send and receive information over a network (i.e., the Internet) without human interaction. The adoption of IPv6 (discussed in Chapter 6), which created a vast number of IP addresses, has been an important factor in the development of the IoT. In fact, there are enough IP addresses to uniquely identify every object on the earth.

The IoT can be considered as invisible "everywhere computing" that is embedded in the objects around us. Examples of objects are your clock radio, your kitchen appliances, your thermostat, your clothing, your smartphone, a cardiac patient's heart monitor, a chip in a farm animal, and automobile sensors that alert a driver when tire pressure is low or the gas tank needs to be refilled.

Wireless sensors are an underlying technology of the Internet of Things. A **wireless sensor** is an autonomous device that monitors its own condition, as well as physical and environmental conditions around it, such as temperature, sound, pressure, vibration, and movement. Sensors can also control physical systems; for example, opening and closing a valve and controlling the fuel mixture in your car. Wireless sensors can be as small as a grain of rice.

Wireless sensors collect data from many points over an extended space. A sensor contains processing, storage, and radio-frequency antennas for sending and receiving messages. Each sensor "wakes up" or activates for a fraction of a second when it has data to transmit. It then relays those data to its nearest neighbor. So, rather than every sensor transmitting its data to a remote computer, the data travel from sensor to sensor until they reach a central computer where they are stored and analyzed. An advantage of this process is that if one sensor fails, then another one can pick up the data. This process is efficient, reliable, and extends battery life of the sensor. Also, if the network requires additional bandwidth, then operators can boost performance by placing new sensors when and where they are required.

Wireless sensors provide information that enables a central computer to integrate reports of the same activity from different angles within the network. This system enables the network to determine with much greater accuracy myriad types of information such as the direction in which a person is moving, the weight of a vehicle, and the amount of rainfall over a field of crops. One type of wireless sensor uses radio-frequency identification (RFID) technology, which we discuss next.

Radio-Frequency Identification

Radio-frequency identification (RFID) technology allows manufacturers to attach tags with antennas and computer chips on goods and then track their movement via radio signals. RFID was developed to replace bar codes.

A typical bar code, known as the *Universal Product Code* (*UPC*), is made up of 12 digits that are batched in various groups. Bar codes have worked well, but they have limitations. First, they require a line-of-sight to the scanning device. This system works well in a store, but it can pose substantial problems in a manufacturing plant or a warehouse or on a shipping/receiving dock. Second, because bar codes are printed on paper, they can be ripped, soiled, or lost. Third, the bar code identifies the manufacturer and product but not the actual item.

Quick response (QR) codes are also used in place of bar codes. A *QR code* is a two-dimensional code, readable by dedicated QR readers and camera phones. **Figure 10.6** illustrates bar codes, QR codes, and an RFID tag. QR codes have several advantages over bar codes:

- QR codes can store much more information.
- Data types stored in QR codes include numbers, text, URLs, and even Japanese characters.
- QR codes are smaller because they store information both horizontally and vertically.
- QR codes can be read from any direction or angle, so they are less likely to be misread.
- QR codes are more resistant to damage.

RFID systems use tags with embedded microchips, which contain data, and antennas to transmit radio signals over a short distance to RFID readers. The readers pass the data over a network to a computer for processing. The chip in the RFID tag is programmed with information that uniquely identifies an item. It also contains information about the item such as its location and where and when it was made. (See **Figure 10.7**.)

There are two basic types of RFID tags: active and passive. *Active RFID tags* use internal batteries for power, and they broadcast radio waves to a reader. Because active tags contain batteries, they are more expensive than passive RFID tags, and they can be read over greater distances. Therefore, they are used primarily for more expensive items. In contrast, *passive RFID tags* rely entirely on readers for their power. They are less expensive than active tags, but they can be read only up to 20 feet. For these reasons, they are generally applied to less expensive merchandise. Problems with RFID include expense and the comparatively large size of the tags.

Examples of the Internet of Things in Use

There are numerous examples of how the Internet of Things is being deployed. We discuss just a few of them here:

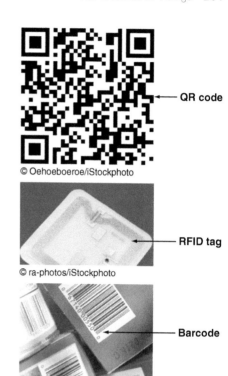

© Oehoeboeroe/iStockphoto

← QR code

© ra-photos/iStockphoto

← RFID tag

Media Bakery

← Barcode

FIGURE 10.6 Bar codes, RFID tags, and QR codes.

FIGURE 10.7 Small RFID reader and RFID tag. (*Source:* © Ecken, Dominique/Keystone Pressedienst/ Zuma Press)

- *The Smart Home*: In a *smart home*, your home computer, television, lighting and heating controls, home security system (including smart window and door locks), thermostats, and appliances have embedded sensors and can communicate with one another via a home network. You control these networked objects through various devices, including your pager, smartphone, television, home computer, and even your automobile. Appropriate service providers and homeowners can access the devices for which they are authorized. Smart home technology can be applied to any building, turning it into a smart building.

  Consider Nest Labs (www.nest.com; now owned by Google), which produces a digital thermostat that combines sensors and Web technology. The thermostat senses not only air temperature, but also the movements of people in a house. It then adjusts room temperatures accordingly to save energy.

- *Healthcare*: Patients with nonlife-threatening conditions can wear sensors, or have them implanted—for example, to monitor blood pressure or glucose levels—that are monitored by medical staff. In many cases, the patients can be shown how to interpret the sensor data themselves. Also, consumer-oriented sensors such as the Fitbit can encourage people to adopt healthier lifestyles.

- *Automotive*: Modern cars have many sensors that monitor functions such as engine operation, tire pressure, fluid levels, and many others. Cars can warn drivers of impending mechanical or other problems and automatically summon roadside assistance or emergency services when necessary. Further, cars can detect vehicles in other lanes to help eliminate blindspots.

POM

- *Supply Chain Management*: The IoT can make a company's supply chain much more transparent. A company can now track, in real time, the movement of raw materials and parts through the manufacturing process to finished products delivered to the customer. Sensors in fleet vehicles (e.g., trucks) can monitor the condition of sensitive consignments (e.g., the temperature of perishable food). In addition, they can trigger automatic security alerts if a container is opened unexpectedly.

- *Environmental Monitoring*: Sensors monitor air and water quality, atmospheric and soil conditions, and the movements of wildlife.

- *Infrastructure Management*: Sensors monitor infrastructures such as bridges, railway tracks, and roads. They can identify and report changes in structural conditions that can compromise safety.

- *Energy Management*: Sensors will be integrated into all forms of energy-consuming devices; for example, switches, power outlets, light bulbs, and televisions. They will be able to communicate directly with utility companies via smart meters to balance power generation and energy usage. Another valuable application of sensors is to use them in smart electrical meters, thereby forming a *smart grid*. Smart meters monitor electricity usage, and they transmit those data in real time to the utility companies. In turn, the utilities can utilize these data to match power demand with production. This process can lead to fewer brownouts and blackouts during periods of peak usage, such as air conditioning during hot summer days.

- *Agriculture*: Sensors monitor, in real time, air temperature, humidity, soil temperature, soil moisture, leaf wetness, atmospheric pressure, solar radiation, trunk/stem/fruit diameter, wind speed and direction, and rainfall. The data from these sensors are used in precision agriculture. (Precision agriculture is a farming technique based on observing, measuring, and responding to inter- and intra-field variability in crops.)

- *Transportation*: Sensors placed on complex transportation machines such as jet engines and locomotives can provide critical information on their operations. Consider General Electric (GE; www.ge.com), which embeds "intelligence" in the form of 250 sensors in each of its giant locomotives. The sensors produce nine million data points every hour. How can these sensors improve the performance of such a huge machine?

  One of the biggest problems on locomotives is faulty bearings. If a bearing fails, then an axle might freeze, leaving a train marooned on the tracks. In remote areas, this situation could be disastrous, not to mention expensive, because other trains would back up for miles behind the stalled one. In this situation, the company would have to send a crane to lift the locomotive off the track and transport it back to a shop.

To avoid this type of scenario, GE embeds one sensor inside each locomotive's gear case that transmits data on oil levels and contaminants. By examining these data, GE can predict the conditions that cause bearings to fail and axles to freeze. GE data analysts claim that sensors that predict part failures before they occur will translate into billions of dollars of savings for GE's rail customers.

GE also uses locomotive sensors to optimize the entire network of U.S. trains. Today, the average velocity of a freight train operating between U.S. cities ranges from 20-25 miles per hour. Why is this number so low? The reason is a combination of factors: congestion in the train yards, breakdowns (see above), and the frequent necessity of letting other trains pass. GE has developed a software tool called Movement Planner that gathers and integrates sensor data on velocity, traffic, and location from many locomotives. This analysis increases the average speed of its customers' trains. One of GE's customers, Norfolk Southern, states that an average speed increase of 1 mile per hour for its trains would be worth $200 million. GE's goal is to increase average train speeds by 4 miles per hour.

IT's About Business 10.5 provides another example, where FedEx implemented its EDEN system to improve the efficiency of its dock operations.

IT's About Business 10.5

POM The Internet of Things Improves FedEx's Dock Operations

A critical part of FedEx's operations is the cooperation among supervisors, forklift drivers, and truck drivers to load and unload items at its freight distribution centers. In the past, dock operations were performed manually, and they were highly inefficient. Supervisors would hand out assignments to dockworkers at their workstations and manually plan workloads and shift schedules, and produce a log of hours actually worked. These and other manualized processes meant that estimated driver arrival times were usually a guess, and supervisors never knew if a dock was occupied unless that dock's computer had been manually updated.

To improve the efficiency and effectiveness of its dock operations, FedEx implemented a scheduling and messaging system that the company calls EDEN (Equipment Detection, Event Notification) Dock/Yard. Employees throughout the FedEx logistics chain have mobile devices and touchscreen displays so the EDEN software can send messages between them, whether they're in a truck, on a forklift, or anywhere in the freight dock. The system also works with handheld devices and computers used by office workers, automating dock assignments and schedules almost in real time.

Perhaps the most impressive automation happens using Internet of Things applications. Even before a truck arrives at the freight distribution center, its every move is tracked and the relevant processes swing into action. Tractor-trailers have sensors that send GPS information to each truck's onboard EDEN-connected computer. Dockworkers use the EDEN information from each truck to know what it's carrying and its location. Each dock door has sensors that tell EDEN which one will be available when the truck arrives. This system ensures that all workers have the same information. Supervisors can get in on the game by assigning a particular dock to a particular truck by clicking on its icon on their EDEN computer.

Millions of actions are made through EDEN each day, and it is intuitive to use. In fact, EDEN is so user-friendly that FedEx was able to roll out the application to 12,000 users in 250 locations in a matter of just a few months. The training for the system involved watching a short video and reading a reference guide.

FedEx expects that EDEN will save more than $9 million a year from improvements in dock and trailer yard planning and management and estimated-time-of-arrival accuracy.

Sources: Compiled from J. Manyika, M. Chui, P. Bisson, J. Woetzel, R. Dobbs, J. Bughin, and D. Aharon, "Unlocking the Potential of the Internet of Things," *McKinsey & Company*, June 2015; B. Franks, "How Disney, FedEx Create Value at the Corner of Customer Experience and the Internet of Things," *Forbes*, March 13, 2015; J. Twentyman, "Internet of Things Is Ready to Deliver," *FT.com*, October 21, 2014; "FedEx Uses Real-Time Messaging and Interconnected Devices to Improve Dock Activities," Datamark Incorporated, May 6, 2014; S. O'Neill, "How FedEx Streamlines Operations at Freight Docks," *InformationWeek*, April 2, 2014; T. Leung, "FedEx Rides the IoT Wave with Near Real-Time Tracking," *Computerworld*, September 10, 2013; www.fedex.com, accessed September 17, 2015.

Questions

1. Describe the problems faced by FedEx that led to the company's decision to implement the EDEN system.

2. Discuss the advantages of the EDEN system.

3. Discuss potential disadvantages of the EDEN system.

Before you go on...

1. Define the Internet of Things and RFID.
2. Provide two examples (other than those mentioned in this section) of how the Internet of Things benefits organizations (public sector, private sector, for-profit, or not-for-profit).
3. Provide two specific business uses of RFID technology.

Apply the Concept 10.4

LEARNING OBJECTIVE 10.4 Describe the Internet of Things, along with examples of how organizations can utilize the Internet of Things.

STEP 1: Background

Section 10.4 has introduced the concept of the Internet of Things (IoT) and provided several examples. There is no doubt that the IoT will continue to grow and shape our lives. Many industries will change from reactive (correcting problems after they happen) to proactive (acting to prevent problems before they happen based on IoT data).

STEP 2: Activity

Visit http://www.wiley.com/go/rainer/MIS4e/applytheconcept and watch the YouTube video link. It describes examples of

personal applications of IoT and professional uses of IoT. After watching the video, let your mind wander into the future to a time when everything is connected via the IoT. Not just the devices mentioned in the video (like your car) but your coffee pot, bed, clothes, closet door, front door, toothbrush, and so much more are all connected to the IoT.

STEP 3: Deliverable

Write a paragraph or two to first describe the IoT, then provide current examples of how it has impacted your life and is currently making a difference for businesses and industries. Finally, provide a few ideas of how the IoT will shape the future.

What's in IT for me?

ACCT For the Accounting Major

Wireless applications help accountants to count and audit inventory. They also expedite the flow of information for cost control. Price management, inventory control, and other accounting-related activities can be improved with the use of wireless technologies.

FIN For the Finance Major

Wireless services can provide banks and other financial institutions with a competitive advantage. For example, wireless electronic payments, including micropayments, are more convenient (anywhere, anytime) than traditional means of payment, and they are less expensive. Electronic bill payment from mobile devices is becoming

more popular, increasing security and accuracy, expediting cycle time, and reducing processing costs.

MKT For the Marketing Major

Imagine a whole new world of marketing, advertising, and selling, with the potential to increase sales dramatically. Such is the promise of mobile computing. Of special interest for marketing are location-based advertising as well as the new opportunities resulting from the Internet of Things and RFID. Finally, wireless technology also provides new opportunities in sales force automation (SFA), enabling faster and better communications with both customers (CRM) and corporate services.

For the Production/Operations Management Major

Wireless technologies offer many opportunities to support mobile employees of all kinds. Wearable computers enable off-site employees and repair personnel working in the field to service customers faster, better, and less expensively. Wireless devices can also increase productivity within factories by enhancing communication and collaboration as well as managerial planning and control. In addition, mobile computing technologies can improve safety by providing quicker warning signs and instant messaging to isolated employees.

For the Human Resource Management Major

Mobile computing can improve HR training and extend it to any place at any time. Payroll notices can be delivered as SMSs. In addition, wireless devices can make it even more convenient for employees to select their own benefits and update their personal data.

For the MIS Major

MIS personnel provide the wireless infrastructure that enables all organizational employees to compute and communicate anytime, anywhere. This convenience provides exciting, creative, new applications for organizations to reduce expenses and improve the efficiency and effectiveness of operations (e.g., to achieve transparency in supply chains). Unfortunately, as you saw earlier, wireless applications are inherently insecure. This lack of security is a serious problem with which MIS personnel must contend.

Summary

1. **Identify advantages and disadvantages of each of the three main types of wireless transmission media.**

Microwave transmission systems are used for high-volume, long-distance, line-of-sight communication. One advantage is the high volume. A disadvantage is that microwave transmissions are susceptible to environmental interference during severe weather such as heavy rain and snowstorms.

Satellite transmission systems make use of communication satellites, and they receive and transmit data via line-of-sight. One advantage is that the enormous footprint—the area of Earth's surface reached by a satellite's transmission—overcomes the limitations of microwave data relay stations. Like microwaves, satellite transmissions are susceptible to environmental interference during severe weather.

Radio transmission systems use radio-wave frequencies to send data directly between transmitters and receivers. An advantage is that radio waves travel easily through normal office walls. A disadvantage is that radio transmissions are susceptible to snooping by anyone who has similar equipment that operates on the same frequency.

2. **Explain how businesses can use short-range, medium-range, and long-range wireless networks, respectively.**

Short-range wireless networks simplify the task of connecting one device to another, eliminating wires, and enabling people to move around while they use the devices. In general, short-range wireless networks have a range of 100 feet or less. Short-range wireless networks include Bluetooth, ultra-wideband, and near-field communications. A business application of ultra-wideband is the PLUS Real-Time Location System from Time Domain. Using PLUS, an organization can locate multiple people and assets simultaneously.

Medium-range wireless networks include Wi-Fi networks. *Wi-Fi* provides fast and easy Internet or intranet broadband access from public hotspots located at airports, hotels, Internet cafés, universities, conference centers, offices, and homes.

Wide-area wireless networks connect users to the Internet over geographically dispersed territory. They include cellular telephones and wireless broadband. *Cellular telephones* provide two-way radio communications over a cellular network of base stations with seamless handoffs. *Wireless broadband* has a wireless access range of up to 31 miles and a data transfer rate of up to 75 Mbps. WiMAX can provide long-distance broadband wireless access to rural areas and remote business locations.

3. **Provide a specific example of how each of the five major m-commerce applications can benefit a business.**

Location-based services provide information specific to a location. For example, a mobile user can (1) request the nearest business or service, such as an ATM or restaurant; (2) receive alerts, such as a warning of a traffic jam or an accident; and (3) find a friend. With *location-based advertising*, marketers can integrate the current locations and preferences of mobile users. They can then send user-specific advertising messages about nearby shops, malls, and restaurants to wireless devices.

Mobile financial applications include banking, wireless payments and micropayments, money transfers, wireless wallets, and bill payment services. The bottom line for mobile financial applications is to make it more convenient for customers to transact business regardless of where they are or what time it is.

Intrabusiness applications consist of m-commerce applications that are used *within* organizations. Companies can use non-voice mobile services to assist in dispatch functions—that is, to assign jobs to mobile employees, along with detailed information about the job.

When it comes to *accessing information*, mobile portals and voice portals are designed to aggregate and deliver content in a form that will work within the limited space available on mobile devices. These portals provide information anywhere and anytime to users.

Telemetry is the wireless transmission and receipt of data gathered from remote sensors. Company technicians can use telemetry to identify maintenance problems in equipment. Car manufacturers use telemetry applications for remote vehicle diagnosis and preventive maintenance.

4. **Describe the Internet of Things along with examples of how various organizations can utilize the Internet of Things.**

The Internet of Things (IoT) is a system where any object, natural or manmade, has a unique identity (using IPv6) and the ability to send and receive information over a network (i.e., the Internet) without human interaction.

We leave the examples of various uses of the IoT to the student.

Chapter Glossary

Bluetooth Chip technology that enables short-range connection (data and voice) between wireless devices.

cellular telephones (cell phones) Phones that provide two way radio communications over a cellular network of base stations with seamless handoffs.

global positioning system (GPS) A wireless system that uses satellites to enable users to determine their position anywhere on Earth.

hotspot A small geographical perimeter within which a wireless access point provides service to a number of users.

Internet of Things (IoT) A scenario in which objects, animals, and people are provided with unique identifiers and the ability to automatically transfer data over a network without requiring human-to-human or human-to-computer interaction.

location-based commerce (L-commerce) Mobile commerce transactions targeted to individuals in specific locations, at specific times.

microwave transmission A wireless system that uses microwaves for high-volume, long-distance, point-to-point communication.

mobile commerce (or m-commerce) Electronic commerce transactions that are conducted with a mobile device.

mobile computing A real-time connection between a mobile device and other computing environments, such as the Internet or an intranet.

mobile portal A portal that aggregates and provides content and services for mobile users.

mobile wallet (m-wallet) A technology that allows users to make purchases with a single click from their mobile devices.

near-field communications (NFC) The smallest of the short range wireless networks that is designed to be embedded in mobile devices such as cell phones and credit cards.

personal area network A computer network used for communication among computer devices close to one person.

propagation delay Any delay in communications from signal transmission time through a physical medium.

radio-frequency identification (RFID) technology A wireless technology that allows manufacturers to attach tags with antennas and computer chips on goods and then track their movement through radio signals.

radio transmission Uses radio-wave frequencies to send data directly between transmitters and receivers.

satellite radio (or digital radio) A wireless system that offers uninterrupted, near CD-quality music that is beamed to your radio from satellites.

satellite transmission A wireless transmission system that uses satellites for broadcast communications.

telemetry The wireless transmission and receipt of data gathered from remote sensors.

ultra-wideband (UWB) A high-bandwidth wireless technology with transmission speeds in excess of 100 Mbps that can be used for applications such as streaming multimedia from, say, a personal computer to a television.

voice portal A Web site with an audio interface.

wireless Telecommunications in which electromagnetic waves carry the signal between communicating devices.

wireless 911 911 emergency calls made with wireless devices.

wireless access point An antenna connecting a mobile device to a wired local area network.

Wireless Fidelity (Wi-Fi) A set of standards for wireless local area networks based on the IEEE 802.11 standard.

wireless local area network (WLAN) A computer network in a limited geographical area that uses wireless transmission for communication.

Discussion Questions

1. Given that you can lose a cell phone as easily as a wallet, which do you feel is a more secure way of carrying your personal data? Support your answer.

2. If mobile computing is the next wave of technology, would you ever feel comfortable with handing a waiter or waitress your cell phone to make a payment at a restaurant the way you currently hand over your credit or debit card? Why or why not?

3. What happens if you lose your NFC-enabled smartphone or it is stolen? How do you protect your personal information?

4. In your opinion, is the mobile (or digital) wallet a good idea? Why or why not?

5. Discuss how m-commerce can expand the reach of e-business.

6. Discuss how mobile computing can solve some of the problems of the digital divide.

7. List three to four major advantages of wireless commerce to consumers and explain what benefits they provide to consumers.

8. Discuss the ways in which Wi-Fi is being used to support mobile computing and m-commerce. Describe the ways in which Wi-Fi is affecting the use of cellular phones for m-commerce.

9. You can use location-based tools to help you find your car or the closest gas station. However, some people see location-based tools as an invasion of privacy. Discuss the pros and cons of location-based tools.

10. Discuss the benefits of telemetry in healthcare for the elderly.

11. Discuss how wireless devices can help people with disabilities.

12. Some experts say that Wi-Fi is winning the battle with 3G cellular service. Others disagree. Discuss both sides of the argument and support each one.

13. Which of the applications of the Internet of Things do you think are likely to gain the greatest market acceptance over the next few years? Why?

Problem-Solving Activities

1. Investigate commercial applications of voice portals. Visit several vendors, for example, Microsoft and Nuance. What capabilities and applications do these vendors offer?

2. Using a search engine, try to determine whether there are any commercial Wi-Fi hotspots in your area.

3. Examine how new data-capture devices such as RFID tags help organizations accurately identify and segment their customers for activities such as targeted marketing. Browse the Web, and develop five potential new applications not listed in this chapter for RFID technology. What issues would arise if a country's laws mandated that such devices be embedded in everyone's body as a national identification system?

4. Investigate commercial uses of GPS. Start with www.neigps.com. Can some of the consumer-oriented products be used in industry? Prepare a report on your findings.

5. Access www.bluetooth.com. Examine the types of products being enhanced with Bluetooth technology. Present two of these products to the class and explain how they are enhanced by Bluetooth technology.

6. Explore www.nokia.com. Prepare a summary of the types of mobile services and applications Nokia currently supports and plans to support in the future.

7. Enter www.ibm.com. Search for "wireless e-business." Research the resulting stories to determine the types of wireless capabilities and applications IBM's software and hardware support. Describe some of the ways these applications have helped specific businesses and industries.

8. Research the status of 3G and 4G cellular service by visiting various links. Prepare a report on the status of 3G and 4G based on your findings.

9. Enter Pitney Bowes Business Insight (www.pbinsight.com). Click on "MapInfo Professional," then click on the "Resources" tab, then on the "Demos" tab. Look for the location-based services demos. Try all the demos. Summarize your findings.

10. Enter www.packetvideo.com. Examine the demos and products and list their capabilities.

11. Enter www.onstar.com. What types of *fleet* services does OnStar provide? Are these any different from the services OnStar provides to individual car owners? (Play the movie.)

12. Access various search engines to find articles about the "Internet of Things." What is the "Internet of Things"? What types of technologies are necessary to support it? Why is it important?

Closing Case 1

How to Find a Parking Place?

POM The Problem

The size of the parking industry in the United States is estimated to be $18 billion, and finding a parking space in cities remains a major challenge. Although many cities have witnessed an increase in the number of residents who are utilizing public transportation, bicycles, or carpools, the number of available parking spaces has not increased. Studies have revealed that motorists can spend as much as 45 minutes searching for an open parking space. Further, parking experts state that as much as 30 percent of traffic in U.S. cities consists of drivers looking for a vacant parking space. As a consequence of inadequate parking, local businesses lose customers and emissions increase significantly.

A Variety of Solutions

Several technologies have emerged in recent years to help alleviate the parking problem. Peer-to-peer parking apps such as MonkeyParking, Parkmodo, and Haystack (www.haystackmobile.com) allow drivers to

sell the rights to parking spaces on streets. Drivers who are about to leave a space use the apps to connect with a client who is willing to pay them to wait and give the client the space. The app company helps set the price, and it takes a commission.

Another app, PocketParker, turns smartphones into passive sensors that track the location and movements of other users who have installed the app. The app integrates parking lot data from OpenStreetMap (www.openstreetmap.org) and data from combined user actions to determine the likelihood that a particular parking lot has an open parking space.

ParkWhiz (www.parkwhiz.com), SpotHero (www.spothero.com), and JustPark (www.justpark.com) are e-parking services that allow users to check the availability of parking spaces in participating parking lots and garages and to book guaranteed spaces before reaching their destination.

Valet companies Zirx (http://zirx.com), Luxe Valet (www.luxe .com), and Caarbon (www.caarbon.com) allow drivers to click on an app so that when they arrive at their destination a valet takes their cars for as long as they need. When drivers are ready for their cars, they simply click on the app again. The three companies view their business model as an entry point to providing a suite of services, such as gas, car washes, and oil changes.

Cities are employing a variety of other methods to address their parking problems. Some cities are attempting to reduce traffic through "consumption pricing" in which they charge everyone entering city limits a flat fee. Other cities are reducing the availability of on-street parking by renting hundreds of city-owned spots to car-sharing services such as Zipcar (www.zipcar.com) and Getaround (www.getaround.com).

Some cities are beginning to charge market rates for all street parking. These rates change according to the time of day and the location of the space. According to economists, such pricing should keep 15 to 20 percent of spaces available at any time, and the money earned would go to the city. Although the public might criticize this practice, cities such as Pasadena, California, won public support for the practice by reinvesting the revenue into street maintenance.

Other cities, including San Francisco and Boston, are installing networks of sensors in parking spaces. The sensors, which cost approximately $225 each, provide motorists with information about available spaces while also providing cities with data to develop pricing that takes demand into account. Installing a limited number of sensors in areas where parking will bring high prices would quickly pay for their installation while reducing traffic. Critics of the plan note that the sensors do not work in parking spaces in residential neighborhoods that have no parking meters.

The Results

In mid-2014, cities including Los Angeles, San Francisco, and Boston banned MonkeyParking, ParkModo, and Haystack. The cities charged that the companies' business model was illegal because they were making money from free public parking. In essence, the apps were selling something they did not own. The cities also approved ordinances making it illegal for any company similar to these three firms to conduct business within city limits.

In March 2015, MonkeyParking (now an app in the Apple iStore) returned to San Francisco with a new business model that complies with the city's laws. Rather than enable users to sell public property, the company is now focused on private property, namely users' driveways. The opportunity for MonkeyParking users is really the space in front of the driveway. (Few city driveways are actually large enough to accommodate a car without blocking the sidewalk.) Drivers who wish to park their cars are matched with driveways or driveway spots in the vicinity. The cost to the driver is a $10 flat fee, and the driveway owner determines how long the car may remain. MonkeyParking takes 20 percent of the flat fee.

Sources: Compiled from D. Streitfeld, "Parking Apps Face Obstacles at Every Turn," *The New York Times*, June 10, 2015; C. Woodward, "The Endless Sage of Haystack, an Illegal App that Tried to Sell Public Parking," *beta Boston*, June 10, 2015; J. Brasuell, "MonkeyParking App Is Back – This Time It's Legal," *Planetizen*, March 24, 2015; J. Eskenazi, "MonkeyParking Is Back and Ready to Disrupt Your Driveway," *San Francisco Magazine*, March 23, 2015; C. Mims, "No 'Free Parking' for an App that Tried," *The Wall Street Journal*, January 25, 2015; "MonkeyParking App Could Soon Be Banned in L.A.," *ABC News*, January 7, 2015; K. Rector, "Canton Resident's Haystack Parking App No Longer Operating," *The Baltimore Sun*, November 24, 2014; A. Vaccaro, "In a Post-Haystack Boston, City Exploring More Parking Technology," *Boston.com*, September 24, 2014; G. Maddaus, "Kicked Out of San Francisco, MonkeyParking App Plans a Fresh Start in Santa Monica," *LA Weekly*, September 24, 2014; C. Garling, "Smartphone Movements Could Reveal Empty Parking Spots," *MIT Technology Review*, September 15, 2014; J. Brustein, "How Much Would You Pay for a Parking Spot?" *Bloomberg BusinessWeek*, August 11-24, 2014; J. Lowensohn, "Parking Spot Startup Vows to Fight San Francisco's Plan to Shut It Down," *The Verge*, June 27, 2014; S. Larson, "San Francisco Tells Parking Apps to Stop Auctioning Spaces," *ReadWrite*, June 23, 2014.

Questions

1. Describe how the e-parking apps use wireless communications.

2. The developers of the e-parking apps argued that they were only selling information about parking places and not the parking places themselves. Was this a valid argument? Why or why not?

3. Were the reactions of San Francisco, Los Angeles, and Boston to the e-parking apps appropriate? Why or why not?

4. Were the cities inhibiting entrepreneurship? Why or why not?

Closing Case 2

Pacific Gas & Electric Turns to Smart Meters

POM The Problem

Peak demand—defined as the hourly period that represents the highest point of customer consumption of electricity—is the major challenge confronting electrical utilities. This period usually occurs around 5:30 PM. It is driven by a combination of office and domestic demand and, at certain times of the year, by the onset of darkness. When peak demand arrives, electric utilities must have the power available to meet it.

One strategy to meet peak demand is to build enough power plants to satisfy every possible supply-and-demand scenario. However, the costs and environmental impacts of this approach would be far too high to make it a realistic solution.

Another strategy is to implement demand-response programs, which are designed to be both fiscally and environmentally responsible. These programs offer incentives (typically in the form of rebates) to businesses that volunteer to temporarily reduce their electricity use at times when demand could outpace supply. These businesses turn off unnecessary lighting and office equipment, raise thermostat settings, and delay using electric appliances until evening hours.

The IT Solution

In addition to implementing demand-response programs, Pacific Gas & Electric (PGE; www.pge.com) was the first California utility and the largest utility in the United States to install smart meters in customers' homes in an effort to meet peak demand. The utility now captures four readings per hour from 9.4 million customers instead of the standard one reading per month.

The smart meters are capable of taking 12 readings per minute. However, even collecting data every 15 minutes has generated concerns among homeowners. For example, demonstrators in Marin County (just north of San Francisco), fearing an invasion of their privacy, blocked PGE installation trucks.

Smart meters capture how much energy is being consumed at each site and then broadcast those data over radio frequency to a PGE neighborhood area network. In turn, each area network reports the data to a central data center. The meters do not have the intelligence to know which types of home devices are consuming energy or how much energy each device is using. They simply collect raw usage data. Even so, PGE can now analyze much more data that it could in the past. Significantly, the company is utilizing those data to upgrade its operations.

The smart meters feed two terabytes of data per month into a PGE data warehouse. PGE replicates the data for each division and makes them available for analysis without any personal identifying information, in order to protect the privacy of its customers.

Using those data, PGE has launched an analytics service, called PG&E Interval Data Analytics, that has helped the utility integrate the functions of energy generation in PGE power plants with energy distribution to customers. These formerly isolated functions—known as *silos*—are now integrated with near-real-time usage data from the smart meters.

The first analysis identified those customers who were using the most electricity. These customers could be two heavy industries in a neighborhood. Alternatively, demand in a residential neighborhood could increase when children get home from school and turn on televisions, computers, and game consoles. In any case, the utility has created a long list of energy-conservation and efficiency incentives that it can offer contributors to peak demand. (One incentive is the utility's demand-response program noted previously.)

For example, on a hot day PGE can utilize the smart meter data to identify which customers are using the most air conditioning, which at one time was causing rolling brownouts in California. Some California homeowners now allow PGE to install a switch on their air conditioners that dials down the air conditioning (increases the thermostat temperature) as peak demand approaches and dials the air conditioning back up (decreases the thermostat temperature) after the demand passes.

The Results

"Shaving peak demand" has been critically important to the utility industry for many years. However, without smart meters and Interval Data Analytics, utility executives lacked the capacity to manage their systems so as to meet customer demand with sufficient precision. The data from smart meters have enabled them to achieve this precision.

PGE now reports usage data directly to consumers over the My Energy section on its Web site. Customers must register to view the data, which includes a graph of each month's energy consumption, with one line comparing similar homes and another line comparing efficient homes.

Further, PGE has added a button to its My Energy page that allows consumers to download the data to their own spreadsheets with a single click. Customers are able to send those data to a third party, such as Opower (www.opower.com). Opower is a software-as-a-service (SaaS; discussed in Plug IT In 4) company that provides cloud-based software to roughly 100 utilities and their customers. Opower's software provides customers with better information about their energy consumption patterns, along with personalized methods to save both energy and money. Customers using Opower have reduced their energy usage by an average of 2.5 percent.

Sources: Compiled from T. Turkel, "Consumers Still Waiting for Smart Meters to Pay Off," *Portland Press Herald*, July 19, 2015; K. Tweed, "Opower Books $90M Contract with PG&E – It Biggest Ever," *Greentech Media*, May 13, 2015; C. Mooney, "Why 50 Million Smart Meters Still Haven't Fixed America's Energy Habits," *Washington Post*, January 29, 2015; "Assessment of Demand Response and Advanced Metering," *Federal Energy Regulatory Commission*, December, 2014; "Smart Meters Lay Foundation for Understanding Energy Costs," *Nationwide Energy Partners*, December 18, 2014; B. Spiller and K. Mohlin, "Smart Meters Need Effective Electricity Pricing to Deliver Their Full Benefits," *Environmental Defense Fund*, December 16, 2014; M. Wald, "Power Savings of Smart Meters Prove Slow to Materialize," *The New York Times*, December 5, 2014; C. Babcock, "PG&E Delivers on Promise of Smart Meters," *InformationWeek*, April 1, 2014; E. Howland, "Smart Meters Are Here. So Why Isn't Dynamic Pricing?" *Utility Dive*, January 8, 2014; Y. Maskrey and E. Ifuku, "Demonstrating Fast Demand Response and Integrating Intermittent Renewable Energy," *Electric Light and Power*, August 22, 2013; C. King, "How Smart Meters Fight Power Outages," *GigaOM*, July 5, 2012; www.pge.com, www.opower.com, accessed September 22, 2015.

Questions

1. What is the role of wireless technologies in smart-metering systems?

2. Describe the potential disadvantages of smart-metering systems.

3. Discuss the advantages of smart meters to utility companies.

4. Discuss the advantages of smart meters to the customers of utility companies.

jsmith/iStockphoto

Information Systems within the Organization

LEARNING OBJECTIVES

11.1 Explain the purpose of transaction processing systems.

11.2 Explain the types of support that information systems can provide for each functional area of the organization.

11.3 Identify advantages and drawbacks to businesses implementing an enterprise resource planning system.

11.4 Describe the three main business processes supported by ERP systems.

Opening Case

The Lion King Continues Its Box Office Dominance

The Lion King opened on Broadway in 1997 to critical acclaim. The play went on to win six Tony Awards, including best musical. Like many Broadway hit shows, *The Lion King* enjoyed increasing ticket sales early on, often grossing $1 million per week. Earnings eventually leveled off, however, as newer musicals such as *The Producers* (2001) became hot attractions. To reverse this trend, Disney actually discounted tickets to *The Lion King* for a period of time.

In 2006, Disney moved *The Lion King* from the New Amsterdam Theater to the slightly smaller Minskoff Theater to make way for its *Mary Poppins* musical. At this time, Disney executives were occupied with opening new musicals such as *The Little Mermaid*. The entertainment giant made the mistake of bundling those shows with *The Lion King* in their ads, even though the target audiences for the two shows were different. Ticket sales for *The Lion King* remained uneven, both before and after the 2008 recession. By March 2009, weekly gross revenues had declined to $813,000.

To reinvigorate ticket sales, in 2011 the show's producers, Disney Theatrical Productions, implemented a proprietary yield management system (YMS)—also known as dynamic pricing—to recommend the highest ticket prices that audiences would be likely to pay for each of the 1,700 seats at every performance at the Minskoff. Although other shows employ YMSs to increase seat prices during tourist-heavy holiday weeks, only Disney has reached the level of yield management sophistication achieved by the airline and hotel industries. Disney uses its system to analyze and set prices based on demand and ticket purchasing patterns.

Yield management systems enable businesses to implement a variable pricing strategy, based on understanding, anticipating, and influencing consumer behavior to maximize revenue from a fixed, perishable resource (e.g., airline seats, hotel rooms, theater seats). YMSs are designed to sell inventory to the right customer at the right time for the right price.

In the case of *The Lion King*, Disney's YMS analyzes historical data for 11.5 million audience members. It then recommends prices for different types of performances—for example, peak dates such as Christmas, off-peak dates such as a weeknight in February, and periods in between. Historical ticket demand for a particular week, for instance, will influence price recommendations for that week in subsequent years.

To help keep audience demand strong, Disney has made a highly unusual choice among Broadway hit shows. The company has factored in an upper ticket price limit of $227 in its YMS. This price is well below the top prices for blockbuster shows such as *The Book of Mormon* ($477), *Kinky Boots* ($349), and *Wicked* ($300). This pricing strategy provides at least three benefits: (1) It makes *The Lion King* relatively affordable for large groups and families; (2) it reduces the chance of buyer's remorse (the sense of regret after having made a purchase), which can generate negative word-of-mouth feedback; and (3) it offers Disney the flexibility to raise prices over the long term.

Based on the results Disney obtained from its YMS, the company abandoned the traditional strategy of charging one price for entire sections of seats. Instead, the producers raise prices for busy weeks by making predictions based on the show's historical data. An interactive seating map accompanies the YMS that allows customers to visually pick their seats. Disney has discovered that customers often choose better, pricier seats when they examine the seating chart.

How successful was Disney's yield management system? In 2013, *The Lion King* stunned Broadway by replacing *Wicked* as the Number 1 earner, a position it had not enjoyed for 10 years. By March 2014, the play was grossing $1.5 million per week. Additionally, consumer demand has grown. In 2013, the show attracted 700,000 theater goers, which was 50,000 more than in 2008. By early 2015, *The Lion King* had become the highest-grossing Broadway play of all time, with $6.2 billion in worldwide ticket sales.

Sources: Compiled from "'The Lion King' Musical Breaks Box Office Record with $6.2 Billion Worldwide," *Associated Press*, September 22, 2014; A. Phadnis, "SpiceJet Revenue Management GM Quits Two Days After Discount Sale," *Business Standard*, April 3, 2014; J. Gereben, "Dynamic Ticket Pricing," *San Francisco Classical Voice*, March 18, 2014; S. Sluis, "Dynamic Pricing Finds a Seat on Broadway," *Destination CRM*, March 17, 2014; P. Healy, "Ticket Pricing Puts 'Lion King' Atop Broadway's Circle of Life," *New York Times*, March 17, 2014; L. Homer, "3 Rules for Pricing Right," *TRG Arts*, October 16, 2013; C. Jones, "How Theater Ticket Prices Are Changing Like Airline Fares," *Chicago Tribune*, October 22, 2012; "Marriott Takes Revenue Management to the Next Level," *Marriott Press Release*, June 4, 2012; P. Healy, "Broadway Hits Make Most of Premium Pricing," *New York Times*, November 24, 2011; www.lionking.com, accessed April 8, 2015.

Questions

1. Why are yield management systems so important to the producers of Broadway shows? (*Hint:* What is the value of an unsold seat once the curtain goes up?)

2. Describe potential disadvantages of Disney's yield management system.

Introduction

The opening case illustrates the integral part that information systems (IS) play in an organization's success. As you noted in the case, Disney employed information systems to increase ticket sales for *The Lion King*. IS are everywhere, and they affect organizations in countless ways. Although IS are frequently discussed within the context of large organizational settings, they also play a critical role in small organizations.

It is important to note that "systems within organizations" do not have to be owned by the organization itself. Instead, organizations can deploy very productive IS that are owned by an external vendor. The key point here is that "systems within an organization" are intended to support internal processes, regardless of who actually owns the systems.

It is important for you to have a working knowledge of IS within your organization for a variety of reasons. First, your job will require you to access corporate data that are supplied primarily by your firm's transaction processing systems and enterprise resource planning systems. Second, you will have a great deal of input into the format and content of the reports that you receive from these systems. Third, you will utilize the information contained in these reports to perform your job more productively.

This chapter will teach you about the various information systems that modern organizations utilize. We begin by considering transaction processing systems, the most fundamental organizational information systems. We continue with the functional area management information systems, and we conclude with enterprise resource planning systems.

11.1 | Transaction Processing Systems

Millions (sometimes billions) of transactions occur in large organizations every day. A **transaction** is any business event that generates data worthy of being captured and stored in a database. Examples of transactions are a product manufactured, a service sold, a person hired, and a payroll check generated. In another example, when you are checking out of Walmart, each time the cashier swipes an item across the bar code reader is one transaction.

A **transaction processing system (TPS)** supports the monitoring, collection, storage, and processing of data from the organization's basic business transactions, each of which generates data. The TPS collects data continuously, typically in *real time*—that is, as soon as the data are generated—and it provides the input data for the corporate databases. The TPSs are critical to the success of any enterprise because they support core operations.

In the modern business world, TPSs are inputs for the functional area information systems and business intelligence systems, as well as business operations such as customer relationship management, knowledge management, and e-commerce. TPSs have to efficiently handle both high volumes of data and large variations in those volumes (e.g., during periods of peak processing). In addition, they must avoid errors and downtime, record results accurately and securely, and maintain privacy and security. Figure 11.1 illustrates how TPSs manage data. Consider these examples of how TPSs handle the complexities of transactional data:

- When more than one person or application program can access the database at the same time, the database has to be protected from errors resulting from overlapping updates. The most common error is losing the results of one of the updates.

MIS

- When processing a transaction involves more than one computer, the database and all users must be protected against inconsistencies arising from a failure of any component at any time. For example, an error that occurs at some point in an ATM withdrawal can enable a customer to receive cash, although the bank's computer indicates that he or she did not. (Conversely, a customer might not receive cash, although the bank's computer indicates that he or she did.)

ACCT

- It must be possible to reverse a transaction in its entirety if it turns out to have been entered in error. It is also necessary to reverse a transaction when a customer returns a purchased item. For example, if you return a sweater that you have purchased, then the store must credit your credit card for the amount of the purchase, refund your cash, or offer you an in-store credit to purchase another item. In addition, the store must update its inventory.

- It is frequently important to preserve an audit trail. In fact, for certain transactions an audit trail may be legally required.

These and similar issues explain why organizations spend millions of dollars on expensive mainframe computers. In today's business environment, firms must have the dependability, reliability, and processing capacity of these computers to handle their transaction processing loads.

FIGURE 11.1 How transaction processing systems manage data.

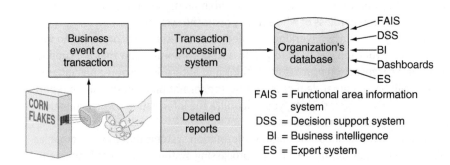

FAIS = Functional area information system
DSS = Decision support system
BI = Business intelligence
ES = Expert system

Regardless of the specific data processed by a TPS, the actual process tends to be standard, whether it occurs in a manufacturing firm, a service firm, or a government organization. As the first step in this procedure, people or sensors collect data, which are entered into the computer via any input device. Generally speaking, organizations try to automate the TPS data entry as much as possible because of the large volume involved, a process called *source data automation* (discussed in Plug IT In 2).

Next, the system processes data in one of two basic ways: batch processing and online processing. In batch processing, the firm collects data from transactions as they occur, placing them in groups or *batches*. The system then prepares and processes the batches periodically (say, every night).

In online transaction processing (OLTP), business transactions are processed online as soon as they occur. For example, when you pay for an item at a store, the system records the sale by reducing the inventory on hand by one unit, increasing sales figures for the item by one unit, and increasing the store's cash position by the amount you paid. The system performs these tasks in real time by means of online technologies.

Before you go on...

1. Define TPS.
2. List the key functions of a TPS.

Apply the Concept 11.1

LEARNING OBJECTIVE 11.1 Explain the purpose of transaction processing systems.

STEP 1: Background

Section 11.1 has explained that transaction processing systems (TPS) capture data and then automatically transmit those data to the various functional area systems. Most TPS are designed based on an organization's existing processes. To better understand how a TPS operates, you should consider the flow of data through the student application process.

STEP 2: Activity

Visit http://www.wiley.com/go/rainer/MIS4e/applytheconcept and click on the link provided for Apply the Concept 11.1.

This link will take you to a Web page that describes the process of creating data flow diagrams (DFDs). The page uses the example of a college student application to demonstrate the flow of data through a university. Review this description, and identify the transactions that take place throughout the process.

STEP 3: Deliverable

Consider your student application process. Are there any pieces of your application that you feel were handled differently than the example described? Prepare a short description of the application process described in the video and discuss the purpose of the TPS for this process.

11.2 | Functional Area Information Systems

Each department or functional area within an organization has its own collection of application programs, or information systems. Each of these functional area information systems (FAIS) supports a particular functional area in the organization by increasing each area's internal efficiency and effectiveness. FAISs often convey information in a variety of reports, which you will see later in this chapter. Examples of FAISs are accounting IS, finance IS, production/operations management (POM) IS, marketing IS, and human resources IS.

As illustrated in Figure 11.1, the FAIS access data from the corporate databases. The following sections discuss the support that FAISs provide for these functional areas.

Information Systems for Accounting and Finance

A primary mission of the accounting and finance functional areas is to manage money flows into, within, and out of organizations. This mission is very broad because money is involved in all organizational functions. Therefore, accounting and finance information systems are very diverse and comprehensive. In this section, you focus on certain selected activities of the accounting/finance functional area.

Financial Planning and Budgeting. Appropriate management of financial assets is a major task in financial planning and budgeting. Managers must plan for both acquiring and utilizing resources, for example:

- *Financial and economic forecasting:* Knowledge about the availability and cost of money is a key ingredient for successful financial planning. Cash flow projections are particularly important because they inform organizations what funds they need, when they need them, and how they will acquire them.

  Funds for operating organizations come from multiple sources, including stockholders' investments, bond sales, bank loans, sales of products and services, and income from investments. Decisions concerning funding for ongoing operations and for capital investment can be supported by decision support systems and business intelligence applications (discussed in Chapter 5), as well as expert systems (discussed in Plug IT In 5). In addition, numerous software packages for conducting economic and financial forecasting are available. Many of these packages can be downloaded from the Internet, some of them for free.

- *Budgeting:* An essential component of the accounting/finance function is the annual budget, which allocates the organization's financial resources among participants and activities. The budget allows management to distribute resources in the way that best supports the organization's mission and goals.

  Several software packages are available to support budget preparation and control and to facilitate communication among participants in the budget process. These packages can reduce the time involved in the budget process. Furthermore, they can automatically monitor exceptions for patterns and trends.

Managing Financial Transactions. Many accounting/finance software packages are integrated with other functional areas. For example, Peachtree by Sage (www.peachtree.com) offers a sales ledger, a purchase ledger, a cash book, sales order processing, invoicing, stock control, a fixed assets register, and more.

Companies involved in electronic commerce need to access customers' financial data (e.g., credit line), inventory levels, and manufacturing databases (to determine available capacity and place orders). For example, Microsoft Dynamics GP (formerly Great Plains Software) offers 50 modules that meet the most common financial, project, distribution, manufacturing, and e-business needs.

Organizations, business processes, and business activities operate with, and manage, financial transactions. Consider these examples:

- *Global stock exchanges:* Financial markets operate in global, 24/7/365, distributed electronic stock exchanges that use the Internet both to buy and sell stocks and to broadcast real-time stock prices.

- *Managing multiple currencies:* Global trade involves financial transactions that are carried out in different currencies. The conversion ratios of these currencies are constantly in flux. Financial and accounting systems utilize financial data from different countries, and they convert the currencies from and to any other currency in seconds. Reports based on these data, which formerly required several days to generate, can now be produced in only seconds. In addition to currency conversions, these systems manage multiple languages as well.

- *Virtual close:* Companies traditionally closed their books (accounting records) quarterly, usually to meet regulatory requirements. Today, many companies want to be able to close their books at any time, on very short notice. Information systems make it possible to close the books quickly in what is called a *virtual close*. This process provides almost real-time information on the organization's financial health.

- *Expense management automation:* Expense management automation (EMA) refers to systems that automate the data entry and processing of travel and entertainment expenses. EMA systems are Web-based applications that enable companies to quickly and consistently collect expense information, enforce company policies and contracts, and reduce unplanned purchases as well as airline and hotel expenses. They also allow companies to reimburse their employees more quickly because expense approvals are not delayed by poor documentation.

Investment Management. Organizations invest large amounts of money in stocks, bonds, real estate, and other assets. Managing these investments is a complex task, for several reasons. First, organizations have literally thousands of investment alternatives dispersed throughout the world to choose from. In addition, these investments are subject to complex regulations and tax laws, which vary from one location to another.

Investment decisions require managers to evaluate financial and economic reports provided by diverse institutions, including federal and state agencies, universities, research institutions, and financial services firms. In addition, thousands of Web sites provide financial data, many of them for free.

To monitor, interpret, and analyze the huge amounts of online financial data, financial analysts employ two major types of IT tools: Internet search engines and business intelligence and decision support software.

Control and Auditing. One major reason why organizations go out of business is their inability to forecast and/or secure a sufficient cash flow. Underestimating expenses, overspending, engaging in fraud, and mismanaging financial statements can lead to disaster. Consequently, it is essential that organizations effectively control their finances and financial statements. Let's examine some of the most common forms of financial control:

- *Budgetary control:* After an organization has finalized its annual budget, it divides those monies into monthly allocations. Managers at various levels monitor departmental expenditures and compare them against the budget and the operational progress of corporate plans.

- *Auditing:* Auditing has two basic purposes: (1) to monitor how the organization's monies are being spent and (2) to assess the organization's financial health. *Internal audits* are performed by the organization's accounting/finance personnel. These employees also prepare for periodic *external audits* by outside CPA firms.

- *Financial ratio analysis:* Another major accounting/finance function is to monitor the company's financial health by assessing a set of financial ratios, including liquidity ratios (the availability of cash to pay debt), activity ratios (how quickly a firm converts noncash assets to cash assets), debt ratios (measure the firm's ability to repay long-term debt), and profitability ratios (measure the firm's use of its assets and control of its expenses to generate an acceptable rate of return).

Information Systems for Marketing

`MKT`

It is impossible to overestimate the importance of customers to any organization. Therefore, any successful organization must understand its customers' needs and wants and then develop its marketing and advertising strategies around them. Information systems provide numerous types of support to the marketing function. Customer-centric organizations are so important that we devote Chapter 12 to this topic.

© paci77/iStockphoto

A "Quality Guarantee" requires data collection and analysis throughout production to maintain standards.

POM Information Systems for Production/Operations Management

The production/operations management (POM} function in an organization is responsible for the processes that transform inputs into useful outputs as well as for the overall operation of the business. The POM function is responsible for managing the organization's supply chain. Because supply chain management is vital to the success of modern organizations, we address this topic in detail in Chapter 13. Because of the breadth and variety of POM functions, we discuss only four here: in-house logistics and materials management, planning production and operation, computer-integrated manufacturing (CIM), and product lifecycle management (PLM).

In-House Logistics and Materials Management. Logistics management deals with ordering, purchasing, inbound logistics (receiving), and outbound logistics (shipping) activities. Related activities include inventory management and quality control.

Inventory Management. As the name suggests, inventory management determines how much inventory an organization should maintain. Both excessive inventory and insufficient inventory create problems. Overstocking can be expensive because of storage costs and the costs of spoilage and obsolescence. However, keeping insufficient inventory is also expensive because of last-minute orders and lost sales.

Operations personnel make two basic decisions: when to order and how much to order. Inventory models, such as the economic order quantity (EOQ) model, support these decisions. A large number of commercial inventory software packages are available that automate the application of these models.

Many large companies allow their suppliers to monitor their inventory levels and ship products as they are needed. This strategy, called *vendor-managed inventory* (VMI), eliminates the need for the company to submit purchasing orders. We discuss VMI in Chapter 13.

Quality Control. Quality control systems used by manufacturing units provide information about the quality of incoming material and parts, as well as the quality of in-process semifinished and finished products. These systems record the results of all inspections and then compare these results with established metrics. They also generate periodic reports that contain information about quality—for example, the percentage of products that contain defects or that need to be reworked. Quality control data, collected by Web-based sensors, can be interpreted in real time. Alternatively, they can be stored in a database for future analysis.

Planning Production and Operations. In many firms, POM planning is supported by IT. POM planning has evolved from material requirements planning (MRP) to manufacturing resource planning (MRP II), to enterprise resource planning (ERP). We briefly discuss MRP and MRP II here, and we examine ERP in detail later in this chapter.

Inventory systems that use an EOQ approach are designed for items for which demand is completely independent—for example, the number of identical personal computers a computer manufacturer will sell. In manufacturing operations, however, the demand for some items is interdependent. Consider, for example, a company that makes three types of chairs, all of which use the same screws and bolts. In this case, the demand for screws and bolts depends on the total demand for all three types of chairs and their shipment schedules. The planning process that integrates production, purchasing, and inventory management of interdependent items is called *material requirements planning* (MRP).

MRP deals only with production scheduling and inventories. More complex planning also involves allocating related resources, such as money and labor. For these cases, more complex, integrated software, called *manufacturing resource planning* (MRP II), is available. MRP II integrates a firm's production, inventory management, purchasing, financing, and labor activities. Thus, MRP II adds functions to a regular MRP system. In fact, MRP II has evolved into *enterprise resource planning* (ERP).

Computer-Integrated Manufacturing. Computer-integrated manufacturing (CIM) (also called *digital manufacturing*) is an approach that integrates various automated factory systems. CIM has three basic goals: (1) to simplify all manufacturing technologies and techniques, (2) to automate as many of the manufacturing processes as possible, and (3) to integrate and coordinate all aspects of design, manufacturing, and related functions via computer systems.

Product Lifecycle Management. Even within a single organization, designing and developing new products can be expensive and time consuming. When multiple organizations are involved, the process can become very complex. *Product lifecycle management* (PLM) is a business strategy that enables manufacturers to share product-related data that support product design and development and supply chain operations. PLM applies Web-based collaborative technologies to product development. By integrating formerly disparate functions, such as a manufacturing process and the logistics that support it, PLM enables these functions to collaborate, essentially forming a single team that manages the product from its inception through its completion.

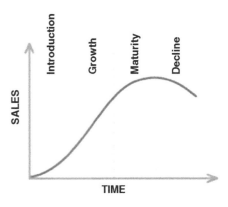

Product lifecycle.

Information Systems for Human Resource Management

HRM

Initial human resource information system (HRIS) applications dealt primarily with transaction processing systems, such as managing benefits and keeping records of vacation days. As organizational systems have moved to intranets and the Web, so have HRIS applications.

Many HRIS applications are delivered via an HR portal. (See our discussion of LinkedIn in Chapter 8.) For example, numerous organizations use their Web portals to advertise job openings and to conduct online hiring and training. In this section, you consider how organizations are using IT to perform some key HR functions: recruitment, HR maintenance and development, and HR planning and management.

Recruitment. Recruitment involves finding potential employees, evaluating them, and deciding which ones to hire. Some companies are flooded with viable applicants; others have difficulty finding the right people. IT can be helpful in both cases. In addition, IT can assist in related activities such as testing and screening job applicants.

With millions of resumes available online (in particular, LinkedIn), it is not surprising that companies are trying to find appropriate candidates on the Web, usually with the help of specialized search engines. Companies also advertise hundreds of thousands of jobs on the Web. Online recruiting can reach more candidates, which may bring in better applicants. In addition, the costs of online recruitment are usually lower than traditional recruiting methods such as advertising in newspapers or in trade journals.

Human Resources Development. After employees are recruited, they become part of the corporate human resources pool, which means they must be evaluated and developed. IT provides support for these activities.

Most employees are periodically evaluated by their immediate supervisors. In addition, in some organizations, peers or subordinates also evaluate other employees. Evaluations are typically digitized, and they are used to support many decisions, ranging from rewards to transfers to layoffs.

IT also plays an important role in training and retraining. Some of the most innovative developments are taking place in the areas of intelligent computer-aided instruction and the application of multimedia support for instructional activities. For example, companies conduct much of their corporate training over their intranet or via the Web.

Human Resources Planning and Management. Managing human resources in large organizations requires extensive planning and detailed strategy. IT support is particularly valuable in the following three areas:

1. *Payroll and employees' records:* The HR department is responsible for payroll preparation. This process is typically automated, meaning that paychecks are printed or money is transferred electronically into employees' bank accounts.

2. *Benefits administration:* In return for their work contributions to their organizations, employees receive wages, bonuses, and various benefits. These benefits include healthcare and dental care, pension contributions (in a decreasing number of organizations), 401K contributions, wellness centers, and child care centers.

    Managing benefits is a complex task because multiple options are available and organizations typically allow employees to choose and trade off their benefits. In many organizations, employees can access the company portal to self-register for specific benefits.

3. *Employee relationship management:* In their efforts to better manage employees, companies are developing *employee relationship management* (ERM) applications, for example, a call center for employees' to discuss problems.

Table 11.1 provides an overview of the activities that the FAIS support. Figure 11.2 shows many of the information systems that support these five functional areas.

TABLE 11.1 Activities Supported by Functional Area Information Systems

Accounting and Finance
Financial planning and cost of money
Budgeting—allocates financial resources among participants and activities
Capital budgeting—financing of asset acquisitions
Managing financial transactions
Handling multiple currencies
Virtual close—the ability to close the books at any time on short notice
Investment management—managing organizational investments in stocks, bonds, real estate, and other investment vehicles
Budgetary control—monitoring expenditures and comparing them against the budget
Auditing—ensuring the accuracy of the organization's financial transactions and assessing the condition of the organization's financial health
Payroll
Marketing and Sales
Customer relations—knowing who customers are and treating them appropriately
Customer profiles and preferences
Salesforce automation—using software to automate the business tasks of sales, thereby improving the productivity of salespeople
Production/Operations and Logistics
Inventory management—when to order new inventory, how much inventory to order, and how much inventory to keep in stock
Quality control—controlling for defects in incoming materials and goods produced
Materials requirements planning—planning process that integrates production, purchasing, and inventory management of interdependent items (MRP)
Manufacturing resource planning—planning process that integrates an enterprise's production, inventory management, purchasing, financing, and labor activities (MRP II)
Just-in-time systems—a principle of production and inventory control in which materials and parts arrive precisely when and where needed for production (JIT)
Computer-integrated manufacturing—a manufacturing approach that integrates several computerized systems, such as computer-assisted design (CAD), computer-assisted manufacturing (CAM), MRP, and JIT
Product lifecycle management—business strategy that enables manufacturers to collaborate on product design and development efforts, using the Web
Human Resource Management
Recruitment—finding employees, testing them, and deciding which ones to hire
Performance evaluation—periodic evaluation by superiors
Training
Employee records
Benefits administration—retirement, disability, unemployment, and so on

Profitability Planning	Financial Planning	Employment Planning, Outsourcing	Product Life Cycle Management	Sales Forecasting, Advertising Planning	**STRATEGIC**
Auditing, Budgeting	Investment Management	Benefits Administration, Performance Evaluation	Quality Control, Inventory Management	Customer Relations, Sales Force Automation	**TACTICAL**
Payroll, Accounts Payable, Accounts Receivable	Manage Cash, Manage Financial Transactions	Maintain Employee Records	Order Fulfillment, Order Processing	Set Pricing, Profile Customers	**OPERATIONAL**
ACCOUNTING	**FINANCE**	**HUMAN RESOURCES**	**PRODUCTION/ OPERATIONS**	**MARKETING**	

FIGURE 11.2 Examples of information systems supporting the functional areas.

Reports

All information systems produce reports: transaction processing systems, functional area information systems, ERP systems, customer relationship management systems, business intelligence systems, and so on. We discuss reports here because they are so closely associated with FAIS and ERP systems. These reports generally fall into three categories: routine, ad hoc (on-demand), and exception.

Routine reports are produced at scheduled intervals. They range from hourly quality control reports to daily reports on absenteeism rates. Although routine reports are extremely valuable to an organization, managers frequently need special information that is not included in these reports. At other times, they need the information that is normally included in routine reports, but at different times ("I need the report today, for the last three days, not for one week").

Such out-of-the routine reports are called ad hoc (on-demand) reports. Ad hoc reports can also include requests for the following types of information:

- Drill-down reports display a greater level of detail. For example, a manager might examine sales by region and decide to "drill down" by focusing specifically on sales by store and then by salesperson.

- Key indicator reports summarize the performance of critical activities. For example, a chief financial officer might want to monitor cash flow and cash on hand.

- Comparative reports compare, for example, the performances of different business units or of a single unit during different times.

Some managers prefer exception reports. Exception reports include only information that falls outside certain threshold standards. To implement *management by exception*, management first establishes performance standards. The company then creates systems to monitor performance (via the incoming data about business transactions such as expenditures), to compare actual performance to the standards, and to identify exceptions to the standards. The system alerts managers to the exceptions via exception reports.

Let's use sales as an example. First, management establishes sales quotas. The company then implements a FAIS that collects and analyzes all of

Monthly sales report.

the sales data. An exception report would identify only those cases where sales fell outside an established threshold—for example, more than 20 percent short of the quota. It would *not* report expenditures that fell *within* the accepted range of standards. By leaving out all "acceptable" performances, exception reports save managers time, thus helping them focus on problem areas.

Before you go on…

1. Define a functional area information system and list its major characteristics.
2. How do information systems benefit the finance and accounting functional area?
3. Explain how POM personnel use information systems to perform their jobs more effectively and efficiently.
4. What are the most important HRIS applications?
5. Compare and contrast the three basic types of reports.

11.3 | Enterprise Resource Planning Systems

Historically, the functional area information systems were developed independent of one another, resulting in *information silos*. These silos did not communicate well with one another, and this lack of communication and integration made organizations less efficient. This inefficiency was particularly evident in business processes that involve more than one functional area, such as procurement and fulfillment.

Enterprise resource planning (ERP) systems are designed to correct a lack of communication among the functional area IS. ERP systems resolve this problem by tightly integrating the functional area IS via a common database. For this reason, experts credit ERP systems with greatly increasing organizational productivity. ERP systems adopt a business process view of the overall organization to integrate the planning, management, and use of all of an organization's resources, employing a common software platform and database.

The major objectives of ERP systems are to tightly integrate the functional areas of the organization and to enable information to flow seamlessly across them. Tight integration means that changes in one functional area are immediately reflected in all other pertinent functional areas. In essence, ERP systems provide the information necessary to control the business processes of the organization.

It is important to understand that ERP systems are an evolution of FAIS. That is, ERP systems have much the same functionality as FAIS, and they produce the same reports. As you see in IT's About Business 11.1, ERP systems simply integrate the functions of the individual FAIS.

IT's About Business 11.1

FIN **ACCT** The Army Transitions from Legacy Systems to Enterprise Resource Planning Tools

Almost every organization that is more than 20 years old has some type of legacy information system—an outdated IT system that was usually developed with a specific focus and designed without considering future needs. In essence, legacy systems were developed as silos. (Silos refer to functional area information systems that do not communicate with other FAIS or organizational information systems.) Further, each legacy system was typically created with its own data in a specific format. Unfortunately, these formats are often incompatible within the same organization. In these scenarios, one legacy system cannot use the data from other systems.

The U.S. Army (www.army.mil) is one of the oldest national organizations in our country. Information technology plays a critical role in all of the Army's processes. It is no surprise that the Army has numerous legacy information systems that, while successfully supporting various operations over the years, nonetheless do not share data efficiently or effectively.

Today, however, the Army must pass audits as part of a federally mandated Department of Defense (www.dod.gov; DOD) financial audit scheduled for 2017. The Army's legacy systems, while proficient within their specific areas, were not able to produce the necessary documentation required by the DOD.

Many organizations, when they retire their separate legacy systems, merge the relevant functions into one enterprise resource planning (ERP) system. The migration to an ERP is very difficult, however, often taking several years and costing large amounts of money. Large organizations such as the Army cannot simply turn off one or more legacy systems until the organization is certain that the new ERP system will work and that employees are trained to utilize the new system.

Other branches of the military have transitioned to ERP systems. Some of the implementations failed, and some succeeded. In 2012, for example, the Air Force cancelled an ERP system implementation (the Expeditionary Combat Support System) after spending more than $1 billion on the project. In that same year, a Navy ERP system was deemed a "qualified" success because it did work, but it cost over 30 percent more than originally estimated, and it took more than two years longer to implement than scheduled.

In 2005, the Army began working with Accenture (www .accenture.com) to develop a SAP-based (www.sap.com) ERP system called the General Fund Enterprise Business System (GFEBS). By 2012 (seven years later!), the Army had begun phasing in the new system. As of late 2015, the Army was still phasing out its legacy systems, some of which are more than 40 years old. The ERP rollout is scheduled to be completed in 2018.

The GFEBS is designed to create accountability and audit trails for the Army's business operations. It is a Web-based tool, meaning it is accessible anywhere with Internet access. The GFEBS standardizes, streamlines, and shares critical data across all Army divisions. This will help decision makers analyze business processes, cost structures, and inventories. It will also provide support for the DOD's greater transparency initiative. As of late 2015, the Army had passed several audits by outside auditing firms. This is a sign that the implementation is moving the right direction.

Sources: Compiled from H. Kenyon, "Army ERP System Enables Financial Transparency," *InformationWeek*, April 15, 2014; D. Perera, "ERP Implementation Continues to Challenge the Military," *fiercegovernmentit.com*, March 31, 2013; H. Kenyon, "DOD Pushes Toward Joint Information Environment," *InformationWeek*, March 26, 2014; D. Perera, "Air Force Cancels ECSS," *fiercegovernmentit.com*, November 29, 2012; D. Perera, "Navy ERP a 'Qualified Success'," *fiercegovernmentit.com*, September 9, 2012; T. Weiss, "Accenture wins $537M Army Financial Services Contract," *Computerworld*, June 28, 2005.

Questions

1. Why do you think the U.S. Army's legacy systems were not as useful today as they were when they were developed?

2. How does this military example parallel large businesses like Sears and Walmart that have had to maintain their own legacy systems?

Although some companies have developed their own ERP systems, most organizations use commercially available ERP software. The leading ERP software vendor is SAP (www.sap.com). Other major vendors include Oracle (www.oracle.com) and PeopleSoft (www.peoplesoft.com), now an Oracle company. (With more than 700 customers, PeopleSoft is the market leader in higher education). For up-to-date information on ERP software, visit http://erp.ittoolbox.com.

ERP II Systems

ERP systems were originally deployed to facilitate business processes associated with manufacturing, such as raw materials management, inventory control, order entry, and distribution. However, these early ERP systems did not extend to other functional areas, such as sales and marketing. They also did not include any customer relationship management (CRM) capabilities that enable organizations to capture customer-specific information. Finally, they did not provide Web-enabled customer service or order fulfillment.

Over time, ERP systems evolved to include administrative, sales, marketing, and human resources processes. Companies now employ an enterprisewide approach to ERP that utilizes the Web and connects all facets of the value chain. (You might want to review our discussion of value chains in Chapter 2.) These systems are called ERP II.

ERP II systems are interorganizational ERP systems that provide Web-enabled links among a company's key business systems—such as inventory and production—and its customers, suppliers, distributors, and other relevant parties. These links integrate internal-facing ERP applications with the external-focused applications of supply chain management and customer relationship management. **Figure 11.3** illustrates the organization and functions of an ERP II system.

The various functions of ERP II systems are now delivered as e-business suites. The major ERP vendors have developed modular, Web-enabled software suites that integrate ERP, customer relationship management, supply chain management, procurement, decision support, enterprise portals, and other business applications and functions. Examples are Oracle's

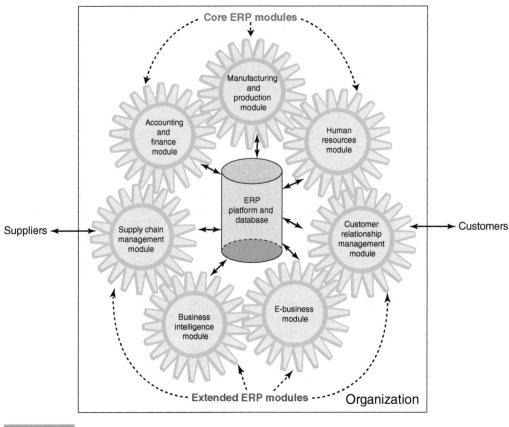

FIGURE 11.3 ERP II system.

e-Business Suite and SAP's mySAP. The goal of these systems is to enable companies to execute most of their business processes using a single Web-enabled system of integrated software rather than a variety of separate e-business applications.

ERP II systems include a variety of modules that are divided into core ERP modules—financial management, operations management, and human resource management—and extended ERP modules—customer relationship management, supply chain management, business intelligence, and e-business. If a system does not have the core ERP modules, then it is not a legitimate ERP system. The extended ERP modules, in contrast, are optional. Table 11.2 describes each of these modules.

Benefits and Limitation of ERP Systems

ERP systems can generate significant business benefits for an organization. The major benefits fall into the following three categories:

1. *Organizational flexibility and agility:* As you have seen, ERP systems break down many former departmental and functional silos of business processes, information systems, and information resources. In this way, they make organizations more flexible, agile, and adaptive. The organizations can therefore respond quickly to changing business conditions and capitalize on new business opportunities.

2. *Decision support:* ERP systems provide essential information on business performance across functional areas. This information significantly improves managers' ability to make better, more timely decisions.

3. *Quality and efficiency:* ERP systems integrate and improve an organization's business processes, generating significant improvements in the quality of production, distribution, and customer service.

TABLE 11.2 ERP Modules

Core ERP Modules

Financial Management. These modules support accounting, financial reporting, performance management, and corporate governance. They manage accounting data and financial processes such as general ledger, accounts payable, accounts receivable, fixed assets, cash management and forecasting, product-cost accounting, cost-center accounting, asset accounting, tax accounting, credit management, budgeting, and asset management.

Operations Management. These modules manage the various aspects of production planning and execution such as demand forecasting, procurement, inventory management, materials purchasing, shipping, production planning, production scheduling, materials requirements planning, quality control, distribution, transportation, and plant and equipment maintenance.

Human Resource Management. These modules support personnel administration (including workforce planning, employee recruitment, assignment tracking, personnel planning and development, and performance management and reviews), time accounting, payroll, compensation, benefits accounting, and regulatory requirements.

Extended ERP Modules

Customer Relationship Management. (Discussed in detail in Chapter 12.) These modules support all aspects of a customer's relationship with the organization. They help the organization to increase customer loyalty and retention, and thus improve its profitability. They also provide an integrated view of customer data and interactions, helping organizations to be more responsive to customer needs.

Supply Chain Management. (Discussed in detail in Chapter 13.) These modules manage the information flows between and among stages in a supply chain to maximize supply chain efficiency and effectiveness. They help organizations plan, schedule, control, and optimize the supply chain from the acquisition of raw materials to the receipt of finished goods by customers.

Business Intelligence. (Discussed in detail in Chapter 5.) These modules collect information used throughout the organization, organize it, and apply analytical tools to assist managers with decision making.

E-Business. (Discussed in detail in Chapter 9.) Customers and suppliers demand access to ERP information including order status, inventory levels, and invoice reconciliation. Furthermore, they want this information in a simplified format that can be accessed via the Web. As a result, these modules provide two channels of access into ERP system information—one channel for customers (B2C) and one for suppliers and partners (B2B).

Despite all of their benefits, however, ERP systems do have drawbacks. The major limitations of ERP implementations include the following:

- The business processes in ERP software are often predefined by the best practices that the ERP vendor has developed. *Best practices* are the most successful solutions or problem-solving methods for achieving a business objective. As a result, companies may need to change their existing business processes to fit the predefined business processes incorporated into the ERP software. For companies with well-established procedures, this requirement can create serious problems, especially if employees do not want to abandon their old ways of working and therefore resist the changes.

- At the same time, however, an ERP implementation can provide an opportunity to improve and in some cases completely redesign inefficient, ineffective, or outdated procedures. In fact, many companies benefit from implementing best practices for their accounting, finance, and human resource processes, as well as other support activities that companies do not consider a source of competitive advantage.

  Recall from Chapter 2, however, that different companies organize their value chains in different configurations to transform inputs into valuable outputs and achieve competitive advantage. Therefore, although the vendor's best practices, by definition, are appropriate for most organizations, they might not be the "best" one for your company if they change those processes that give you competitive advantage.

- ERP systems can be extremely complex, expensive, and time consuming to implement. (We discuss the implementation of ERP systems in detail in the next section.) In fact, the costs and risks of failure in implementing a new ERP system are substantial. Quite a few companies have experienced costly ERP implementation failures. Specifically, they have suffered losses in revenue, profits, and market share when core business processes and information systems failed or did not work properly. In many cases, orders and shipments were lost, inventory changes were not recorded correctly, and unreliable inventory levels caused major stock outs. Companies such as Hershey Foods, Nike, A-DEC, and Connecticut General sustained losses in amounts up to hundreds of millions of dollars. In the case of FoxMeyer Drugs, a $5 billion pharmaceutical wholesaler, the ERP implementation was so poorly executed that the company had to file for bankruptcy protection.

In almost every ERP implementation failure, the company's business managers and IT professionals underestimated the complexity of the planning, development, and training that were required to prepare for a new ERP system that would fundamentally transform their business processes and information systems. The following are the major causes of ERP implementation failure:

- Failure to involve affected employees in the planning and development phases and in change management processes
- Trying to accomplish too much too fast in the conversion process
- Insufficient training in the new work tasks required by the ERP system
- Failure to perform proper data conversion and testing for the new system

Implementing ERP Systems

Companies can implement ERP systems by using either on-premise software or software-as-a-service (SaaS). We differentiate between these two methods in detail in Plug IT In 4.

On-Premise ERP Implementation. Depending on the types of value chain processes managed by the ERP system and a company's specific value chain, there are three strategic approaches to implementing an on-premise ERP system:

1. *The vanilla approach:* In this approach, a company implements a standard ERP package, using the package's built-in configuration options. When the system is implemented in this way, it will deviate only minimally from the package's standardized settings. The vanilla approach can enable the company to perform the implementation more quickly. However, the extent to which the software is adapted to the organization's specific processes is limited. Fortunately, a vanilla implementation provides general functions that can support the firm's common business processes with relative ease, even if they are not a perfect fit for those processes.

2. *The custom approach:* In this approach, a company implements a more customized ERP system by developing new ERP functions designed specifically for that firm. Decisions concerning the ERP's degree of customization are specific to each organization. To utilize the custom approach, the organization must carefully analyze its existing business processes to develop a system that conforms to the organization's particular characteristics and processes. In addition, customization is expensive and risky because computer code must be written and updated every time a new version of the ERP software is released. Going further, if the customization does not perfectly match the organization's needs, then the system can be very difficult to use.

3. *The best-of-breed approach:* This approach combines the benefits of the vanilla and customized systems while avoiding the extensive costs and risks associated with complete customization. Companies that adopt this approach mix and match core ERP modules as well as other extended ERP modules from different software providers to best fit their unique internal processes and value chains. Thus, a company may choose several core ERP modules from an established vendor to take advantage of industry best practices—for example, for financial management and human resource management. At the same time, it may also choose specialized software to support its unique business processes—for

example, for manufacturing, warehousing, and distribution. Sometimes companies arrive at the best of breed approach the hard way. For example, Dell wasted millions of dollars trying to customize an integrated ERP system from a major vendor to match its unique processes before it realized that a smaller, more flexible system that integrated well with other corporate applications was the answer.

Software-as-a-Service ERP Implementation. Companies can acquire ERP systems without having to buy a complete software solution (i.e., on-premise ERP implementation). Many organizations are utilizing software-as-a-service (SaaS) (discussed in Chapter 14 and Plug IT In 4) to acquire cloud-based ERP systems. (We discuss cloud computing in Plug IT In 4).

In this business model, the company rents the software from an ERP vendor who offers its products over the Internet using the SaaS model. The ERP cloud vendor manages software updates and is responsible for the system's security and availability.

Cloud-based ERP systems can be a perfect fit for some companies. For instance, companies that cannot afford to make large investments in IT, yet already have relatively structured business processes that need to be tightly integrated, might benefit from cloud computing.

The relationship between the company and the cloud vendor is regulated by contracts and by service level agreements (SLAs). The SLAs define the characteristics and quality of service; for instance, a guaranteed uptime, or the percentage of time that the system is available. Cloud vendors that fail to meet these conditions can face penalties.

The decision about whether to use on-premise ERP or SaaS ERP is specific to each organization, and it depends on how the organization evaluates a series of advantages and disadvantages. The following are the three major advantages of using a cloud-based ERP system:

1. The system can be used from any location that provides Internet access. Consequently, users can work from any location using online shared and centralized resources (data and databases). Users access the ERP system via a secure virtual private network (VPN) connection (discussed in Chapter 4) with the provider.

2. Companies using cloud-based ERP avoid the initial hardware and software expenses that are typical of on-premise implementations. For instance, to run SAP on-premise, a company must purchase SAP software as well as a license to use SAP. The magnitude of this investment can hinder small- to medium-sized enterprises (SMEs) from adopting ERP.

3. Cloud-based ERP solutions are scalable, meaning it is possible to extend ERP support to new business processes and new business partners (e.g., suppliers) by purchasing new ERP modules.

There are also disadvantages of adopting cloud-based ERP systems that a company must carefully evaluate. The following are the three major disadvantages of using a cloud-based ERP system:

1. It is not clear whether cloud-based ERP systems are more secure than on-premise systems. In fact, a survey conducted by North Bridge Venture Partners indicated that security was the primary reason why organizations did not adopt cloud-based ERP.

2. Companies that adopt cloud-based ERP systems sacrifice their control over a strategic IT resource. For this reason, some companies prefer to implement an on-premise ERP system, utilizing a strong in-house IT department that can directly manage the system.

3. A direct consequence of the lack of control over IT resources occurs when the ERP system experiences problems, for example, some ERP functions are temporarily slow or are not available. In such cases, having an internal IT department that can solve problems immediately rather than dealing with the cloud vendor's system support can speed up the system recovery process.

   This situation is particularly important for technology-intensive companies. In such companies, IT is crucial to conduct any kind of business with customers. Examples are e-commerce companies, banks, and government organizations that manage emergencies or situations that might involve individual and national security (e.g., healthcare organizations, police, homeland security department, antiterrorism units, and others).

Finally, slow or unavailable software from a cloud-based ERP vendor creates business continuity problems for the client. (We discuss business continuity in Chapter 7.) That is, a sudden system problem or failure makes it impossible for the firm to operate. Companies lose money when they lose business continuity because customers cannot be serviced and employees cannot do their jobs. A loss of business continuity also damages the company's reputation because customers lose trust in the firm.

Enterprise Application Integration

For some organizations, integrated ERP systems are not appropriate. This situation is particularly true for companies that find the process of converting from their existing system too difficult or time consuming.

Such companies, however, may still have isolated information systems that need to be connected with one another. To accomplish this task, these companies can use enterprise application integration. An **enterprise application integration (EAI) system** integrates existing systems by providing software, called *middleware*, that connects multiple applications. In essence, the EAI system allows existing applications to communicate and share data, thereby enabling organizations to utilize existing applications while eliminating many of the problems caused by isolated information systems. EAI systems also support implementation of best-of-breed ERP solutions by connecting software modules from different vendors.

Before you go on...

1. Define ERP and describe its functions.
2. What are ERP II systems?
3. Differentiate between core ERP modules and extended ERP modules.
4. List some drawbacks of ERP software.
5. Highlight the differences between ERP configuration, customization, and best-of-breed implementation strategies.

11.4 | ERP Support for Business Processes

ERP systems effectively support a number of standard business processes. In particular, ERP systems manage end-to-end, cross-departmental processes. A **cross-departmental process** is one that (1) originates in one department and ends in a different department or (2) originates and ends in the same department but involves other departments.

The Procurement, Fulfillment, and Production Processes

The following are the three prominent examples of cross-departmental processes:

1. The *procurement process*, which originates in the warehouse department (need to buy) and ends in the accounting department (send payment)
2. The *fulfillment process*, which originates in the sales department (customer request to buy) and ends in the accounting department (receive payment)
3. The *production process*, which originates and ends in the warehouse department (need to produce and reception of finished goods) but involves the production department as well

These three processes are examined in more detail in the following sections, focusing on the steps that are specific to each one.

The Procurement Process. The procurement process originates when a company needs to acquire goods or services from external sources, and it concludes when the company receives and pays for them. Let's consider a procurement process where the company needs to acquire physical goods (see Figure 11.4). This process involves three main departments—Warehouse, Purchasing, and Accounting—and it consists of the following steps:

1. The process originates in the Warehouse department, which generates a purchase requisition to buy the needed products.
2. The Warehouse forwards the requisition to the Purchasing department, which creates a purchase order (PO) and forwards it to a vendor. Generally, companies can choose from a number of vendors, and they select the one that best meets their requirements in terms of convenience, speed, reliability, and/or other characteristics.
3. After the company places the order, it receives the goods in its Warehouse department, where someone physically checks the delivery to make certain that it corresponds to what the company ordered. He or she performs this task by comparing a packing list attached to the shipment against the PO.
4. If the shipment matches the order, then the Warehouse issues a goods receipt document.
5. At the same time or shortly thereafter, the Accounting department receives an invoice from the vendor. Accounting then checks that the PO, the goods receipt document, and the invoice match. This process is called the *three-way-match*.
6. After Accounting verifies the match, it processes the payment and sends it to the vendor.

The Order Fulfillment Process. In contrast to procurement, in which the company purchases goods from a vendor, in the order fulfillment process, also known as the *order-to-cash process*, the company sells goods to a customer. Fulfillment originates when the company receives a customer order, and it concludes when the company receives a payment from the customer.

The fulfillment process can follow two basic strategies: sell-from-stock and configure-to-order. *Sell-from-stock* involves fulfilling customer orders directly using goods that are in the warehouse (stock). These goods are standard, meaning that the company does not customize them for buyers. In contrast, in *configure-to-order*, the company customizes the product in response to a customer request.

A fulfillment process involves three main departments: Sales, Warehouse, and Accounting. This process includes the following steps:

1. The Sales department receives a customer inquiry, which essentially is a request for information concerning the availability and price of a specific good. (We restrict our discussion here to fulfilling a customer order for physical goods rather than services.)
2. After Sales receives the inquiry, it issues a quotation that indicates availability and price.
3. If the customer agrees to the price and terms, then Sales creates a customer purchase order (PO) and a sales order.

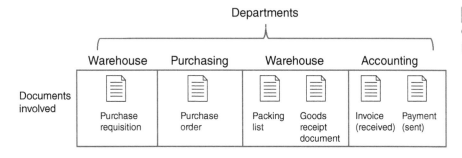

FIGURE 11.4 Departments and documents flow in the procurement process.

4. Sales forwards the sales order to the Warehouse. The sales order is an interdepartmental document that helps the company keep track of the internal processes that are involved in fulfilling a specific customer order. In addition, it provides details of the quantity, price, and other characteristics of the product.

5. The Warehouse prepares the shipment and produces two other internal documents: the picking document, which it uses to remove goods from the Warehouse, and the packing list, which accompanies the shipment and provides details about the delivery.

6. At the same time, Accounting issues an invoice for the customer.

7. The process concludes when Accounting receives a payment that is consistent with the invoice.

Figure 11.5 shows the fulfillment process. Note that it applies to both sell-from-stock and configure-to-order because the basic steps are the same for both strategies.

The Production Process. The production process does not occur in all companies because not all companies produce physical goods. In fact, many businesses limit their activities to buying (procurement) and selling products (e.g., retailers).

The production process can follow two different strategies: make-to-stock and make-to-order. (See the discussion of the pull model and the push model in Chapter 13.) *Make-to-stock* occurs when the company produces goods to create or increase an *inventory*; that is, finished products that are stored in the warehouse and are available for sales. In contrast, *make-to-order* occurs when production is generated by a specific customer order.

Manufacturing companies that produce their own goods manage their interdepartmental production process across the Production and Warehouse departments. The production process involves the following steps:

1. The Warehouse department issues a planned order when the company needs to produce a finished product, either because the Warehouse has insufficient inventory or because the customer placed a specific order for goods that are not currently in stock.

2. Once the planned order reaches Production, the production controller authorizes the order and issues a production order, which is a written authorization to start the production of a certain amount of a specific product.

3. To assemble a finished product, Production requires a number of materials (or parts). To acquire these materials, Production generates a material withdrawal slip, which lists all of the needed parts, and forwards it to the Warehouse.

4. If the parts are available in the Warehouse, then the Warehouse delivers them to Production. If the parts are not available, then the company must purchase them via the procurement process.

5. After Production has created the products, it updates the production order specifying that, as planned, a specific number of units of product can now be shipped to the Warehouse.

6. As soon as the Warehouse receives the finished goods, it issues a goods receipt document that certifies how many units of a product it received that are available for sales.

This overview of the Production process is a highly simplified one. In reality, the process is very complex, and it frequently involves additional steps. In addition, ERP systems collect a number

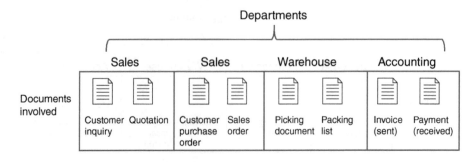

FIGURE 11.5 Departments and documents flow in the fulfillment process.

Departments

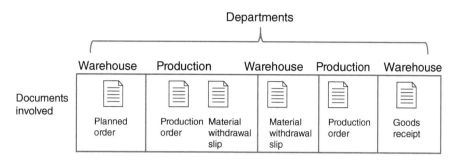

FIGURE 11.6 Departments and documents flow in the production process.

of other documents and pieces of information such as the bill of materials (a list of all materials needed to assemble a finished product), the list of work centers (locations where the production takes place), and the product routing (production steps). All of these topics require an in-depth analysis of the production process and are therefore beyond the scope of our discussion here. Figure 11.6 illustrates the production process.

A number of events can occur that create exceptions or deviations in the procurement, fulfillment, and production processes. Deviations may include the following:

- A delay in the receipt of products
- Issues related to an unsuccessful three-way-match regarding a shipment and its associated invoice (procurement)
- Rejection of a quotation
- A delay in a shipment
- A mistake in preparing the shipment or in invoicing the customer (fulfillment)
- Overproduction of a product
- Reception of parts that cannot be used in the production process
- Unavailability of certain parts from a supplier

Companies use ERP systems to manage procurement, fulfillment, and production because these systems track all of the events that occur within each process. Furthermore, the system stores all of the documents created in each step of each process in a centralized database, where they are available as needed in real time. Therefore, any exceptions or mistakes made during one or more interdepartmental processes are handled right away by simply querying the ERP system and retrieving a specific document or piece of information that needs to be revised or examined more carefully. Therefore, it is important to follow each step in each process and to register the corresponding document into the ERP system.

Figure 11.7 portrays the three cross-functional business processes we just discussed. It specifically highlights the integration of the three processes, which is made possible by ERP systems.

Interorganizational Processes: ERP with SCM and CRM

Although the procurement and the fulfillment processes involve suppliers and customers, they are considered (together with the production process) intraorganizational processes because they originate and conclude within the company. However, ERP systems can also manage processes that originate in one company and conclude in

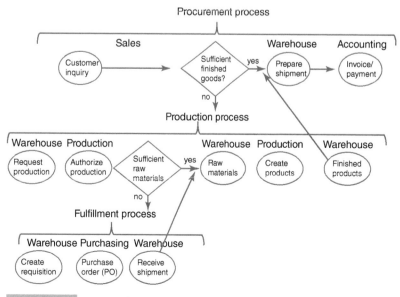

FIGURE 11.7 Integrated processes with ERP systems.

another company. These processes are called *interorganizational processes*, and they typically involve supply chain management (SCM) and customer relationship management (CRM) systems. You can find a more detailed description of CRM (see Chapter 12) and SCM (see Chapter 13). Here, we focus on the integration of these processes within a firm's industry value chain.

SCM and CRM processes help multiple firms in an industry coordinate activities such as the production-to-sale of goods and services. Let's consider a chain of grocery stores whose supply chain must properly manage perishable goods. On the one hand, store managers need to stock only the amount of perishable products that they are reasonably sure they will sell before the products' expiration dates. On the other hand, they do not want to run out of stock of any products that customers need.

ERP SCM systems have the capability to place automatic requests to buy fresh perishable products from suppliers in real time. That is, as each perishable product is purchased, the system captures data on that purchase, adjusts store inventory levels, and transmits these data to the grocery chain's warehouse as well as the products' vendors. The system executes this process by connecting the point-of-sale barcode scanning system with the Warehouse and Accounting departments, as well as with the vendors' systems. In addition, SCM systems utilize historical data to predict when fresh products need to be ordered before the store's supply becomes too low.

ERP CRM systems also benefit businesses by generating forecasting analyses of product consumption based on critical variables such as geographical area, season, day of the week, and type of customer. These analyses help grocery stores coordinate their supply chains to meet customer needs for perishable products. Going further, CRM systems identify particular customer needs and then utilize this information to suggest specific product campaigns. These campaigns can transform a potential demand into sales opportunities, and convert sales opportunities into sales quotations and sales orders. This process is called the *demand-to-order* process.

Before you go on…

1. What are the three main intraorganizational processes that are typically supported by ERP systems?
2. Why is it important that all steps in each process generate a document that is stored in the ERP system?
3. What is the difference between intraorganizational and interorganizational processes?
4. What are the two main ES systems that support interorganizational processes?

What's in IT for me?

ACCT   For the Accounting Major

Understanding the functions and outputs of TPSs effectively is a major concern of any accountant. It is also necessary to understand the various activities of all functional areas and how they are interconnected. Accounting information systems are a central component in any ERP package. In fact, all large CPA firms actively consult with clients on ERP implementations, using thousands of specially trained accounting majors.

FIN   For the Finance Major

IT helps financial analysts and managers perform their tasks better. Of particular importance is analyzing cash flows and securing the financing required for smooth operations. In addition, financial applications can support such activities as risk analysis, investment management, and global transactions involving different currencies and fiscal regulations.

Finance activities and modeling are key components of ERP systems. Flows of funds (payments), at the core of most supply chains, must be executed efficiently and effectively. Financial arrangements are especially important along global supply chains, where currency conventions and financial regulations must be considered.

MKT   For the Marketing Major

Marketing and sales expenses are usually targets in a cost-reduction program. Also, sales force automation improves not only salespeoples' productivity (and thus reduces costs) but also customer service.

POM For the Production/Operations Management Major

Managing production tasks, materials handling, and inventories in short time intervals, at a low cost, and with high quality is critical for competitiveness. These activities can be achieved only if they are properly supported by IT. In addition, IT can greatly enhance interaction with other functional areas, especially sales. Collaboration in design, manufacturing, and logistics requires knowledge of how modern information systems can be connected.

HRM For the Human Resource Management Major

Human resources managers can increase their efficiency and effectiveness by using IT for some of their routine functions. Human resources personnel need to understand how information flows between the HR department and the other functional areas. Finally, the integration of functional areas via ERP systems has a major impact on skill requirements and scarcity of employees, which are related to the tasks performed by the HRM department.

MIS For the MIS Major

The MIS function is responsible for the most fundamental information systems in organizations: the transaction processing systems. The TPSs provide the data for the databases. In turn, all other information systems use these data. MIS personnel develop applications that support all levels of the organization (from clerical to executive) and all functional areas. The applications also enable the firm to do business with its partners.

Summary

1. Explain the purpose of transaction processing systems.

TPSs monitor, store, collect, and process data generated from all business transactions. These data provide the inputs into the organization's database.

2. Explain the types of support that information systems can provide for each functional area of the organization.

The major business functional areas are production/operations management, marketing, accounting/finance, and human resources management. Table 11.1 provides an overview of the many activities in each functional area supported by FAIS.

3. Identify advantages and drawbacks to businesses of implementing an ERP system.

Enterprise resource planning (ERP) systems integrate the planning, management, and use of all of the organization's resources. The major objective of ERP systems is to tightly integrate the functional areas of the organization. This integration enables information to flow seamlessly across the various functional areas.

The following are the major benefits of ERP systems:

- Because ERP systems integrate organizational resources, they make organizations more flexible, agile, and adaptive. The organizations can therefore react quickly to changing business conditions and capitalize on new business opportunities.

- ERP systems provide essential information on business performance across functional areas. This information significantly improves managers' ability to make better, more timely decisions.

- ERP systems integrate organizational resources, resulting in significant improvements in the quality of customer service, production, and distribution.

The following are the major drawbacks of ERP systems:

- The business processes in ERP software are often predefined by the best practices that the ERP vendor has developed. As a result, companies may need to change existing business processes to fit the predefined business processes of the software. For companies with well-established procedures, this requirement can be a huge problem.

- ERP systems can be extremely complex, expensive, and time consuming to implement. In fact, the costs and risks of failure in implementing a new ERP system are substantial.

4. Describe the three main business processes supported by ERP systems.

The *procurement process*, which originates in the warehouse department (need to buy) and ends in the accounting department (send payment).

The *fulfillment process* that originates in the sales department (customer request to buy) and ends in the accounting department (receive payment).

The *production process* that originates and ends in the warehouse department (need to produce and reception of finished goods), but involves the production department as well.

We leave the details of the steps in each of these processes to you.

Chapter Glossary

ad hoc (on-demand) reports Nonroutine reports that often contain special information that is not included in routine reports.

batch processing Transaction processing system (TPS) that processes data in batches at fixed periodic intervals.

comparative reports Reports that compare performances of different business units or times.

computer-integrated manufacturing (CIM) An information system that integrates various automated factory systems; also called *digital manufacturing.*

cross-departmental process A business process that originates in one department and ends in another department, and/or originates and ends in the same department while involving other departments.

drill-down reports Reports that show a greater level of details than is included in routine reports.

enterprise application integration (EAI) system A system that integrates existing systems by providing layers of software that connect applications together.

enterprise resource planning (ERP) systems Information systems that take a business process view of the overall organization to integrate the planning, management, and use of all of an organization's resources, employing a common software platform and database.

ERP II systems Interorganizational ERP systems that provide Web-enabled links among key business systems (e.g., inventory and production) of a company and its customers, suppliers, distributors, and others.

exception reports Reports that include only information that exceeds certain threshold standards.

functional area information systems (FAIS) Systems that provide information to managers (usually midlevel) in the functional areas, in order to support managerial tasks of planning, organizing, and controlling operations.

key indicator reports Reports that summarize the performance of critical activities.

online transaction processing (OLTP) Transaction processing system (TPS) that processes data after transactions occur, frequently in real time.

order fulfillment process A cross-functional business process that originates when the company receives a customer order, and it concludes when it receives a payment from the customer.

procurement process A cross-functional business process that originates when a company needs to acquire goods or services from external sources, and it concludes when the company receives and pays for them.

production process A cross-functional business process in which a company produces physical goods.

routine reports Reports produced at scheduled intervals.

transaction Any business event that generates data worth capturing and storing in a database.

transaction processing system (TPS) Information system that supports the monitoring, collection, storage, and processing of data from the organization's basic business transactions, each of which generates data.

Discussion Questions

1. Why is it logical to organize IT applications by functional areas?

2. Describe the role of a TPS in a service organization.

3. Describe the relationship between TPS and FAIS.

4. Discuss how IT facilitates the budgeting process.

5. How can the Internet support investment decisions?

6. Describe the benefits of integrated accounting software packages.

7. Discuss the role that IT plays in support of auditing.

8. Investigate the role of the Web in human resources management.

9. What is the relationship between information silos and enterprise resource planning?

Problem-Solving Activities

1. Finding a job on the Internet is challenging as there are almost too many places to look. Visit the following sites: www.careerbuilder.com, www.craigslist.org, www.linkedin.com, www.jobcentral.com, and www.monster.com. What does each of these sites provide you as a job seeker?

2. Enter www.sas.com and access *revenue optimization* there. Explain how the software helps in optimizing prices.

3. Enter www.eleapsoftware.com and review the product that helps with online training (training systems). What are the most attractive features of this product?

4. Examine the capabilities of the following (and similar) financial software packages: Financial Analyzer (from Oracle) and CFO Vision (from SAS Institute). Prepare a report comparing the capabilities of the software packages.

5. Surf the Net and find free accounting software. (Try www.cnet.com, www.rkom.com, www.tucows.com, www.passtheshareware.com, and www.freeware-guide.com.) Download the software and try it. Compare the ease of use and usefulness of each software package.

6. Examine the capabilities of the following financial software packages: TekPortal (from www.tekknowledge.com), Financial Analyzer (from www.oracle.com), and Financial Management (from www.sas.com). Prepare a report comparing the capabilities of the software packages.

7. Find Simply Accounting Basic from Sage Software (http://www.sage.com/us/sage-50-accounting). Why is this product recommended for small businesses?

8. Enter www.halogensoftware.com and www.successfactors.com. Examine their software products and compare them.

9. Enter www.iemployee.com and find the support it provides to human resources management activities. View the demos and prepare a report on the capabilities of the products.

Closing Case 1

 National Australian Bank Adapts to Global Performance Measures

The Problem

Bad decisions often have a ripple effect. Really bad decisions are like a tsunami wave that forces people to take action. Such was the case after the global financial crisis of 2007-2009. Financial institutions were subject to increased scrutiny from regulatory agencies. Banks around the world had to adapt to the new regulatory environment, and they were held to more stringent standards. In fact, asset management firms and auditors began requesting updated performance measures. Unfortunately, it became obvious that National Australian Bank (www.nab.com.au; NAB) was not able to comply because their information systems were unable to provide asset management reports that contained newly required information or newly required levels of detail.

NAB maintained several legacy systems that supported asset management. It lacked any mechanism, however, to integrate information from multiple systems in order to create the necessary reports. Rather, creating a report involved extracting data from multiple sources and then manually analyzing the data. NAB needed real-time data and specific calculations. However, the bank's legacy systems could not provide them.

The Technology Solution

In 2011, NAB began searching for a new IT solution to meet the bank's reporting requirements. NAB decided to adopt Eagle Investment Systems' (www.eagleinvsys.com; EIS) Performance Management solution to be able to comply with the new regulatory environment. The EIS solution provided NAB with the tools the bank needed to track its $600 billion (Australian dollars) in assets. The EIS also provided a robust Web portal for its asset management clients. (A portal is a gateway that allows non-employees to access information stored inside the proprietary information system.)

NAB chose an implementation team that represented a cross-section of stakeholders, who included representatives from NAB's performance, risk, and IT functional areas, NAB consultants, Eagle (the solution provider), and IBM (NAB's infrastructure provider). Bringing together this wide variety of team members helped ensure that NAB would be able to appropriately navigate the difficulties of a large system implementation.

The Results

NAB's new Eagle tool required the bank's clients to update their systems to work with Eagle. For example, in mid-2014 NAB provided two clients with access to the new system through the EIS client portal, and these clients were very pleased. The new system not only helped the clients comply with regulations, but it also enabled them to create custom dashboards, generate routine reports, and run complex calculations within the system rather than having to download the data and perform analysis in a different system. Clients were also able to access the asset data necessary to create the reports they needed directly through the client portal. This process reduced NAB's overhead expense because the bank did not have to find their clients' data for them.

The remainder of NAB's clients are scheduled to migrate to the new EIS Performance Management tool by 2016. Ultimately, NAB will continue to work with EIS to develop the system to support dynamic, real-time dashboards and mobile access to further support the integration of this tool into the culture of NAB and NAB's clients.

Sources: Compiled from J. Thomases, "Australia's Largest Custodian Picks Eagle for Performance Management," *waterstechnology.com*, April 29, 2014; A. Rawland, "How NAB Boosted Its Performance Management Capabilities," *InformationWeek*, December 30, 2014; S. Durham, "NAB Deploys New Analytics System," *assetservicingtimes.com*, May 6, 2014; W. Klijn, "NAB Custody Unit Implements New Risk System," *theinstoreport.com*, May 8, 2014; http://www.eagleinvsys.com/solutions/performance-measurement.cfm accessed December 16, 2015.

Questions

1. How did the global financial crisis impact NAB's decision to adopt performance management tools?

2. Why did NAB's choice of a solution create its own ripple effect with their clients?

Closing Case 2

IBM and CVS Partner to Bring Watson to Doctor's Office Visits

 **The Problem**

In today's healthcare system, physicians typically react to, or treat, symptoms that patients present to them. In treating those symptoms, physicians develop treatment plans. Unfortunately, treatment plans are rarely foolproof. The reason is that there are so many variables that impact the way a patient responds to treatment including allergies, existing conditions, genetics, and lifestyle. Further, in many situations, physicians must make decisions based on incomplete information. Either the patient has not divulged all of the necessary information or another physician has not shared patient information. Additionally, insurance plans do not always provide benefits that correspond to the treatment options provided by physicians.

Ideally, proactive (or preventive) healthcare is the best possible solution for our healthcare system. Technology could help enable proactive healthcare if it could be used as a tool to help physicians diagnose patients, develop treatment plans, and encourage patients to stay on the prescribed treatment plan, make positive lifestyle choices, take their medications on schedule, and track their progress.

The IT Solution

Today's technology can help physicians deal with these problems and provide these advantages. For example, physicians can now share a single database to obtain a more complete picture of the patient's health before creating a treatment plan. Imagine if a physician were able to access a patient's entire health history and find patients with similar histories to include their responses to various treatment plans. Medical practice would then become data-driven. Combine data from health-tracking devices—for example, wearable devices such as the Fitbit—that display weight fluctuations, activity levels, blood pressure changes, and blood sugar patterns over time, and physicians would have much better data on which to prescribe treatment.

Despite all of these benefits, there are several problems with this type of data sharing. To begin with, the government enforces HIPAA regulations, which protect patients' privacy. In addition, special interest groups fear the government's involvement from a "Big Brother" perspective, physicians may have concerns about sharing patient data, and individuals have various reasons for not wanting their health histories to be shared. Still, the potential benefits have led IBM (www .ibm.com) and CVS (www.cvs.com) to team up to provide a workable technology solution, at least in part, for healthcare.

In July 2015, the two companies announced that they were working on a predictive analytics project that will bring IBM's Watson into the physician's office. (IBM Watson is an information technology platform that uses natural language processing and machine learning to reveal insights from large amounts of unstructured data. Recall the Watson is the IT system that won Jeopardy! in 2011.) The ultimate goal is to identify markers—such as the combination of increased blood pressure and weight gain that may be related to heart disease—that point to the onset of obesity, heart disease, and hypertension (high blood pressure), because these chronic conditions are the leading causes of death in the United States.

Watson's predictive analytics tools will be available at CVS Minute Clinics to help physician's assistants and nurses make better decisions regardless of whether they have ever seen a particular patient. (CVS Minute Clinics are walk-in clinics at staffed by certified nurse practitioners and physician assistants who provide treatments and health screenings.) Patients will also be able to reduce the number of office visits required for treatment because most of the data captured at physicians' offices would now be recorded on an ongoing basis by wearable technology that automatically shares data with the clinic.

The adoption of this type of automatic data collection would drastically transform the nature of the patient-physician discussion in the physician's office. Rather than spending time asking questions to gather data, the results of the data analysis would be the topic of conversation. Treatment plans would be revised based on data that IBM's Watson had analyzed and compared to other patients with similar symptoms. This process would completely transform the way physicians are able to apply their expertise and would enable them to provide more concrete directions to their patients.

The Results

This partnership is just beginning, so there are no reportable outcomes. However, the potential exists to identify subtle changes in health that could point to the onset of a chronic illness or a life-threatening disease. It is highly likely that predictive analytics will someday change the nature of your visits to your physician.

Annual physicals could become a thing of the past if data are collected and shared with doctors on a daily (perhaps hourly) basis. Doctors could send you an annual report rather than require you to come in for an annual visit. These improvements sound very positive. But, what if the system notices from your meal tracking app that you had three slices of chocolate cake and you are already borderline obese and a candidate for heart disease? What if your insurance drops your coverage because you are not complying with your treatment plan and your personal health tracker sent your data to them?

There are several potential consequences of automatic data sharing, both positive and negative. As with most technological advances, we strive to achieve the positive and navigate the negative. This relationship between CVS and IBM's Watson will be no different.

Sources: Compiled from B. Japsen, "CVS and IBM's Watson Cloud Pursue Ways to Predict Patient Health," *Forbes*, July 30, 2015; G. Laurer, "IBM Hopes CVS Watson Partnership Leads to More Connections in Cloud," *CaliforniaHealthLine.org*, August 6, 2015; Z. Seigel, "IBM's Watson Wants Your Health Data," *TheDailyBeast.com*, August 3, 2015; A. Kaufman, "IBM Watson Is Helping CVS Fight Chronic Disease," *The Huffington Post*, July 30, 2015; J. Calfas, "CVS, IBM Partner for Technology-Based Health Care," *USA Today*, July 30, 2015; D. Reisinger, "IBM's Watson Wants to Make You Healthier with Deal with CVS Health," *CNET.com*, July 30, 2015; S. Buhr, "CVS Health Taps IBM's Watson to Predict Patient Health Decline Before It Happens," *techcrunch.net*, July 30, 2015; A. Cha, "IBM Watson, CVS Deal: How the Smartest Computer on Earth Could Shake Up Health Care for 70 M Pharmacy Customers," *The Washington Post*, July 30, 2015; L. Loeb, "IBM, CVS Partner on WatsonBased Patient Care," *InformationWeek*, July 30, 2015.

Questions

1. What will the impact be of the CVS Minute Clinic obtaining access to this software within their clinical setting? How will their daily operations change?

2. If you were the physician, would you like to adopt and use this type of technology in your practice? Why or why not?

CHAPTER 12

Neustockimages/iStockphoto

Customer Relationship Management

CHAPTER OUTLINE

12.1 Defining Customer Relationship Management

12.2 Operational Customer Relationship Management

12.3 Other Types of Customer Relationship Management Systems

LEARNING OBJECTIVES

12.1 Identify the primary functions of both customer relationship management (CRM) and collaborative CRM strategies.

12.2 Describe how businesses might utilize applications of each of the two major components of operational CRM systems.

12.3 Explain the advantages and disadvantages of mobile CRM systems, on-demand CRM systems, open-source CRM systems, social CRM systems, and real-time CRM systems.

Opening Case

MKT Do Persuasive Technologies Go Too Far?

Persuasive technologies are designed to influence people's behavior and change their attitudes. These technologies, which include apps, Web sites, video games, social media, and others, integrate traditional methods of persuasion—the use of information and incentives, for example—with capabilities of information technology to modify user behavior. Persuasive technologies can be found in mobile downloads and on Web sites where behavior-oriented design persuades consumers to purchase more items (e.g., one-click checkout at Amazon) or to stay logged in longer (e.g., manipulating social media news feeds on Facebook).

Marketing professionals argue that persuasive technologies can benefit consumers, who want better service and more suitable offerings. The marketers note that the best persuasive technologies are those that gently influence people to do something they wish they had been doing anyway.

Today, many companies are using technologies that measure customer behavior in order to design products that are not only persuasive but are specifically intended to create new habits. In addition to the technologies themselves, companies use data generated by these technologies to further refine persuasive and perhaps habit-forming strategies.

Many companies have included habit formation as a business model (for example, casinos, cigarette manufacturers, alcohol producers, fast food establishments, and many others.) Persuasive technologies have provided that option to a broad range of companies. Insights from psychology and behavioral economics concerning how and why people make certain choices, combined with information technologies, have enabled designers of Web sites, apps, and many other products to create sophisticated persuasive technologies.

Persuasive technologies raise many ethical issues, particularly the line between persuasion and manipulation. Manipulation implies persuasion with the intent to fool or control people into doing something, believing something, or buying something that either harms them or provides no benefit to them. The question is: Given the depth of information about consumers that persuasive technologies generate, coupled with companies' increasingly sophisticated attempts to influence consumer behavior, what are the appropriate limits for these technologies, which can be so well designed that they are essentially invisible?

Let's consider several examples of companies that are using persuasive technologies:

- GSN Games (www.gsn.com) designs mobile games such as poker and bingo. The company collects billions of data points each day from its players' smartphones and tablets. These data reveal everything from the time of day that users play, to the type of game they prefer, to how they deal with failure. Insights from these data are so effective that, if two people were to download a game into the same type of smartphone simultaneously, in as little as five minutes their games would begin to diverge, with each game automatically tailored to its user's style of play.

    Significantly, GSN does more than simply track customers' preferences and customize its offerings accordingly. To induce players to play longer and to try more games, the company uses the data to watch for signs that players are tiring. By measuring how frequently and how quickly players press on their screens, GSN can predict when they are likely to lose interest. It then suggests other games before players reach that point. The games are free, but GSN displays ads and sells virtual items that are useful to players. Therefore, the longer the company can persuade someone to play, the more money it makes.

- Rocket Fuel (www.rocketfuel.com) uses artificial intelligence to predict the best ad to present to a given customer who is visiting a particular Web page, taking into account multiple types of information, such as: (a) data gathered from Web sites; (b) the browsing, advertising, and purchase history associated with a given shopper's Internet Protocol address; and (c) insights into what style of ad works best on a particular Web site. The company claims that its targeted ads generate revenue for clients amounting to 2 to 8 times what clients spend on the ads.

- Opower (www.opower.com) is a software company that promotes home energy efficiency. Instead of showing customers the usual power bill, Opower collects data from the home and displays the data in a chart that compares a homeowner's energy use to the average energy use of his or her neighbors.

- Companies have been working for years on strategies to help people remember to take their medicines on time. GlowCaps (www.glowcaps.com) produces a special cap that fits on top of a standard pill bottle. The cap lights up when patients need to take their medicine. The caps are also wirelessly enabled, and they can send reports about how well patients are adhering to their medication schedule.

- In hybrid cars, including the Toyota Prius and Ford Fusion hybrid, display panels inform drivers of how efficiently they are driving at any given moment. The Prius plots this information on a bar graph that indicates current miles per gallon. The Fusion displays a virtual plant growing (or dying) on the dashboard screen as a person's driving efficiently increases or decreases.

- Approximately 1.6 million people in the African country of Mozambique live with the human immunodeficiency virus (HIV). Unfortunately, only 74 percent of patients who begin HIV treatment are still taking their medication one year later. In November 2011, the British-based international children's charity Ark began sending text messages to HIV-positive people in one of Mozambique's provinces to remind them about treatments and appointments. The messages helped urban and recently diagnosed HIV patients continue with their treatment regimens. Results at rural treatment centers were disappointing, possibly due to transportation issues or limited cellular coverage.

Sources: Compiled from E. Tucker, "Can an App Really Persuade Children to Go to Sleep?" *The Guardian*, May 19, 2015; S. Wolf, "A Brief Look at Persuasive Technology," *kachwanya.com*, April 30, 2015; E. Howell, "Using Tech to Persuade Us to Pay Attention, Just a Little Longer," *Herox*, April 21, 2015; P. Newton, "The Persuasive Power of Technology," *IntelligentHQ*, April 11, 2015; K. Majcher, "Persuasive Texting in Mozambique," *MIT Technology Review*, March 23, 2015; N. Byrnes, "Technology and Persuasion," *MIT Technology Review*, March 23, 2015; J. Larson, "The Invisible, Manipulative Power of Persuasive Technology," *Pacific Standard*, May 14, 2014; "Do Persuasive Technologies Persuade?" *Gamification Research Network*, April 8, 2014; T. Fritz, E. Huang, G. Murphy, and T. Zimmerman, "Persuasive Technology in the Real World: A Study of Long-Term Use of Activity Sensing Devices for Fitness," *CHI Conference Proceedings*, Toronto, Canada, 2014; J. Sutter, "Tech Guilt: 5 'Persuasive' Technologies to Help You Be Good," *CNN News*, August 13, 2010; www.gsn.com, www.rocketfuel.com, www.opower.com, www.glowcaps.com, accessed October 23, 2015.

Questions

1. Discuss the advantages and disadvantages of persuasive technologies to companies.

2. Discuss the advantages and disadvantages of persuasive technologies to consumers.

3. Debate the ethical nature of persuasive technologies. (Hint: Refer to Chapter 6 for ethical frameworks.)

4. Do persuasive technologies take customer relationship management too far? Why or why not? Support your answer.

Introduction

Organizations increasingly are emphasizing a customer-centric approach to their business practices because they realize that long-term customer relationships provide sustainable value that extends beyond an individual business transaction. Significantly, **customer relationship**

management (CRM) is not important solely for large enterprises. Rather, it is essential for small organizations as well.

The chapter opening case points out that perhaps an organization's customer relationship management efforts can go too far. With today's sophisticated information technology, organizations must be careful not to breach ethical guidelines in how they manage relationships with their customers.

In Chapter 11, you learned about information systems that supported organizational activities within the organization. In this chapter, you study information systems that support organizational activities that extend outside the organization to customers.

An organization's CRM system includes two major components: operational CRM systems and analytical CRM systems. You learn about operational CRM systems in Section 12.2. We discuss analytical CRM systems very briefly here because we provided an in-depth discussion of business analytics (including analytical CRM systems) in Chapter 5.

Analytical CRM systems provide business intelligence by analyzing customer behavior and perceptions. For example, analytical CRM systems typically provide information concerning customer requests and transactions, as well as customer responses to the organization's marketing, sales, and service initiatives. These systems also create statistical models of customer behavior and the value of customer relationships over time, as well as forecasts about acquiring, retaining, and losing customers.

Important technologies in analytical CRM systems include data warehouses, data mining, decision support, and other business intelligence technologies. After these systems have completed their various analyses, they supply information to the organization in the form of reports and digital dashboards.

Analytical CRM systems analyze customer data for a variety of purposes, including:

- Designing and executing targeted marketing campaigns
- Increasing customer acquisition, cross-selling, and upselling
- Providing input into decisions relating to products and services (e.g., pricing and product development)
- Providing financial forecasting and customer profitability analysis

At this point, you might be asking yourself: Why should *I* learn about CRM? The answer, as you will see in this chapter, is that customers are supremely important to *all* organizations. Regardless of your job, you will have an impact, whether direct or indirect, on managing your firm's customers. When you read the What's in IT for Me? section at the end of the chapter, you will learn about opportunities to make immediate contributions on your job. Therefore, it is essential that you acquire a working knowledge of CRM and CRM systems.

12.1 Defining Customer Relationship Management

Before the supermarket, the mall, and the automobile, people purchased goods at their neighborhood store. The owners and employees recognized customers by name and knew their preferences and wants. For their part, customers remained loyal to the store and made repeated purchases. Over time, however, this personal customer relationship became impersonal as people moved from farms and small towns to cities, consumers became mobile, and supermarkets and department stores achieved economies of scale through mass marketing. Although prices were lower and products were more uniform in quality, the relationship with customers became nameless and impersonal.

The customer relationship has become even more impersonal with the rapid growth of the Internet and the World Wide Web. In today's hypercompetitive marketplace, customers are increasingly powerful; if they are dissatisfied with a product and/or a service from one organization, a competitor is often just one mouse click away. Furthermore, as more and more customers shop on the Web, an enterprise does not even have the opportunity to make a good first impression *in person*.

Customer relationship management returns to personal marketing. That is, rather than market to a mass of people or companies, businesses market to each customer individually. By employing this approach, businesses can use information about each customer—for example, previous purchases, needs, and wants—to create highly individualized offers that customers are more likely to accept. The CRM approach is designed to achieve *customer intimacy*.

Customer relationship management is a customer-focused and customer-driven organizational strategy. That is, organizations concentrate on assessing customers' requirements for products and services and then providing a high-quality, responsive customer experience. CRM is not a process or a technology per se; rather, it is a customer-centric way of thinking and acting. The focus of modern organizations has shifted from conducting business transactions to managing customer relationships. In general, organizations recognize that customers are the core of a successful enterprise, and the success of the enterprise depends on effectively managing relationships with them.

The CRM approach is enabled by information technology in the form of various systems and applications. However, CRM is not only about the software. Sometimes the problem with managing relationships is simply time and information. Old systems may contain the needed information, but this information may take too long to access and may not be usable across a variety of applications. The result is that companies have less time to spend with their customers.

In contrast, modern CRM strategies and systems build sustainable long-term customer relationships that create value for the company as well as for the customer. That is, CRM helps companies acquire new customers and to retain and expand their relationships with profitable existing customers. Retaining customers is particularly important because repeat customers are the largest generator of revenue for an enterprise. Also, organizations have long understood that winning back a customer who has switched to a competitor is vastly more expensive than keeping that customer satisfied in the first place.

Figure 12.1 depicts the CRM process. The process begins with marketing efforts, where the organization solicits prospects from a target population of potential customers. A certain number of these prospects will make a purchase and thus become customers. A certain number of these customers will become repeat customers. The organization then segments its repeat customers into low- and high-value repeat customers. An organization's overall goal is to maximize the *lifetime value* of a customer, which is that customer's potential revenue stream over a number of years.

Over time all organizations inevitably lose a certain percentage of customers, a process called *customer churn*. The optimal result of the organization's CRM efforts is to maximize the number of high-value repeat customers while minimizing customer churn.

CRM is a fundamentally simple concept: Treat different customers differently because their needs differ and their value to the company may also differ. A successful CRM strategy not only improves customer satisfaction but also makes the company's sales and service employees more productive, which in turn generates increased profits. Researchers at the National Quality Research Center at the University of Michigan discovered that a 1 percent increase in customer satisfaction can lead to as much as a 300 percent increase in a company's *market capitalization*, defined as the number of shares of the company's stock outstanding multiplied by the price per share of the stock. Put simply, a minor increase in customer satisfaction can generate a major increase in a company's overall value.

Up to this point, you have been looking at an organization's CRM strategy. It is important to distinguish between a CRM *strategy* and CRM *systems*. Basically, CRM systems are information systems designed to support an organization's CRM strategy. For organizations to pursue excellent relationships with their customers, they need to employ CRM systems that provide the infrastructure needed to support those relationships. Because customer service and support are essential to a successful business, organizations must place a great deal of emphasis on both their CRM strategy and their CRM systems.

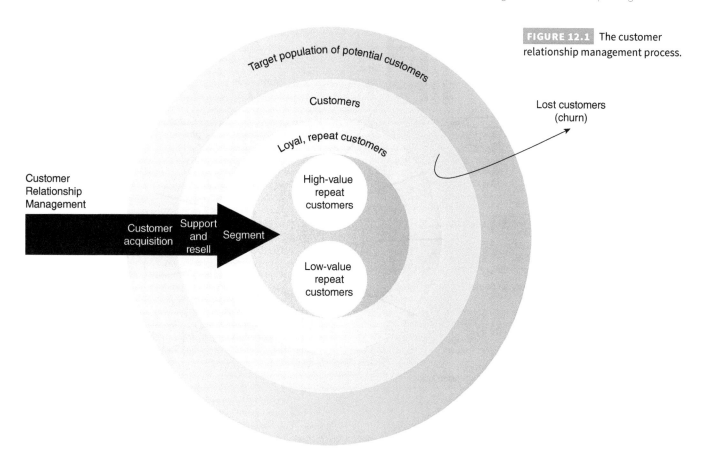

FIGURE 12.1 The customer relationship management process.

Broadly speaking, CRM systems lie along a continuum, from *low-end CRM systems*—designed for enterprises with many small customers—to *high-end CRM systems*—for enterprises with a few large customers. An example of a low-end system is Amazon, which uses its CRM system to recommend products to returning customers. An example of a high-end system is Boeing, which uses its CRM system to coordinate staff activities in a campaign to sell its new 787 aircraft to Delta Airlines. As you study the cases and examples in this chapter, consider where on the continuum a particular CRM system would fall.

Although CRM varies according to circumstances, all successful CRM policies share two basic elements: (1) The company must identify the many types of customer touch points, and (2) it needs to consolidate data about each customer. Let's examine these two elements in more detail.

Customer Touch Points

Organizations must recognize the numerous and diverse interactions they have with their customers. These interactions are referred to as *customer touch points*. Traditional customer touch points include telephone contact, direct mailings, and actual physical interactions with customers during their visits to a store. Organizational CRM systems, however, must manage many additional customer touch points that occur through the use of popular personal technologies. These touch points include e-mail, Web sites, and communications via smartphones (see Figure 12.2).

The business–customer relationship is constantly evolving. As personal technology usage changes, so too must the methods that businesses use to interface with their customers. It is now possible to physically locate customers via their smartphones. As a result, location information can now provide another customer touch point, as you see in IT's About Business 12.1.

FIGURE 12.2 Customer touch points.

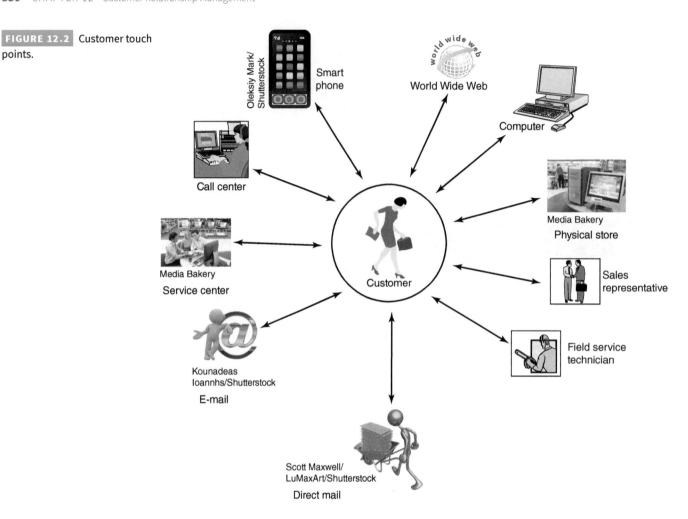

IT's About Business 12.1

MKT **Location-Based Systems in Customer Relationship Management**

The Golden State Warriors (www.nba.com/warriors) won the NBA championship in June 2015. Significantly, technology increased the enjoyment of fans who were on hand to enjoy the victory at Oracle Arena, the team's current home court in Oakland, California.

The arena sends personalized messages to fans' smartphones about merchandise deals at the team store. They can also receive notifications that they can upgrade their seats while at the arena for a game. Warriors fans—called members of Dub Nation—can sign up for an app that detects their location in the arena and alerts them to which entrances are less busy. The technology uses a beacon, a wireless hardware device that pinpoints the app users through the geolocation-based technology.

The idea behind the Warriors' apps is that location is an important way to add value for customers who are essentially a captive audience. Specifically, location-based services (LBS) enable the Warriors to provide better service and to deepen customer loyalty. LBS can target customers where they are in real time, giving them offers they can take advantage of right away.

The Warriors have experienced mixed results from their location-based services. On the positive side, LBS notifications were credited with making it easier for fans to upgrade seats, generating approximately 15 percent of arena seat upgrades. In contrast, fans

largely ignored the LBS notifications about free popcorn with the purchase of a pizza slice.

Even if technology can do something, it doesn't always make practical sense. For example, the Warrior app has the ability to deliver instant replays to fans in the arena. But the organization nixed that idea, figuring the game already moved too fast for replays to be of value. However, the team was considering making instant replays available to fans not attending the game.

The LBS data on its own won't give the Warriors the complete picture of their fans and enable them to provide experiences in context. The team must integrate that data with information from CRM, inventory management, and workforce management applications. Fan behavior also varies whether they are in the arena, on the phone, or online.

There are other interesting examples of location-based services employed in customer relationship management. In Brazil, Nivea, the maker of skin care products, embeds a beacon in magazine ads that parents can tear out and make into a wristband for their children. A smartphone app can track how far the children are from their parents in public places. The app alerts parents when the child strays beyond a certain range. As a result of this CRM tool, Brazilians now perceive Nivea as a brand that cares about its customers' children.

As another example, 313 Somerset, a mall in Singapore, has deployed a beacon-based mobile advertising service. The Tring313 app detects when users who opted in to the service are within a predefined distance from the mall. That triggers the sending of coupons and other offers to their smartphones. Retailers have enjoyed a 46 percent sales conversion rate thanks to the app. (The sales conversion rate is the percentage of prospective customers who actually make a purchase.)

LBS does have downsides. Critics feel that some companies use the brute-force approach, sending so many messages that consumers either ignore them or turn off their phones. Even worse, customers may be so irritated and feel the messages are so irrelevant that they delete the app entirely. For LBS to succeed with empowered customers, companies must offer true value to their customers at the right moment.

Sources: Compiled from L. Horwitz, "Where the Customer Leads," *Business Information*, October, 2015; J. Nyland, "Five Ways to Use Location-Based Marketing Right Now," *MarketingProfs*, June 29, 2015;

M. Rao, "Mobile + Creativity: 8 Innovative Examples of Location-Based Marketing," *YourStory.com*, June 4, 2015; L. Alton, "10 Ways Location-Based Marketing Will Evolve in 2015," *Huffington Post*, January 7, 2015; P. Britt, "Consumers Love Mobile Marketing, Location-Based Services," *Enterprise Apps Today*, November 11, 2014; L. Johnson, "4 Location-Based Marketing Tactics That Are Working," *AdWeek*, August 4, 2014; R. Goodrich, "Location-Based Services: Definition & Examples," *Business News Daily*, October 30, 2013; www.nba.com/warriors, accessed October 27, 2015.

Questions

1. Describe the advantages of location-based services for customers and for businesses.

2. Describe the disadvantages of location-based services for customers and for businesses.

3. What are other location-based services that the Golden State Warriors could provide for their fans?

Data Consolidation

Data consolidation is also critical to an organization's CRM efforts. The organization's CRM systems must manage customer data effectively. In the past, customer data were stored in isolated systems (or silos) located in different functional areas across the business—for example, in separate databases in the finance, sales, logistics, and marketing departments. Consequently, data for individual customers were difficult to share across the various functional areas.

As you saw in Chapter 3, modern interconnected systems built around a data warehouse now make all customer-related data available to every unit of the business. This complete data set on each customer is called a *360° view* of that customer. By accessing this view, a company can enhance its relationship with its customers and ultimately make more productive and profitable decisions.

Data consolidation and the 360° view of the customer enable the organization's functional areas to readily share information about customers. This information sharing leads to collaborative CRM. Collaborative CRM systems provide effective and efficient interactive communication with the customer throughout the entire organization. That is, they integrate communications between the organization and its customers in all aspects of marketing, sales, and customer support. Collaborative CRM systems also enable customers to provide direct feedback to the organization. As you read in Chapter 8, social media applications such as social networks, blogs, microblogs, and Wikis are very important to companies that value customer input into their product and service offerings, as well as into new product development.

Recall that an organization's CRM system contains two major components: operational CRM systems and analytical CRM systems. You will learn about operational CRM systems in the next section. We covered analytical CRM systems in Chapter 5.

Before you go on . . .

1. What is the definition of customer relationship management?

2. Why is CRM so important to any organization?

3. Define and provide examples of customer touch points.

Apply the Concept 12.1

LEARNING OBJECTIVE 12.1 Identify the primary functions of both customer relationship management (CRM) and collaborative CRM strategies.

STEP 1: Background (Here is what you are learning.)

Section 12.1 introduced the concept of a CRM system, and it suggested that it is better to focus on relationships than on transactions. The idea is that relationships create transactions, so if you grow the relationship, you keep the customers (and the transactions)!

STEP 2: Activity (Here is what you are doing.)

Visit http://www.wiley.com/go/rainer/MIS4e/applytheconcept, and click on the link provided for Apply the Concept 12.1. This link will take you to a YouTube video that illustrates how Recreational Equipment Incorporated (REI) uses CRM to service their customers.

STEP 3: Deliverable (Here is what you submit.)

In a report, identify the primary functions of both customer relationship management (CRM) and collaborative CRM strategies. What are REI's approaches to CRM? Can you make any suggestions to help them improve? Submit your report to your professor.

12.2 | Operational Customer Relationship Management Systems

Operational CRM systems support front-office business processes. Front-office processes are those that directly interact with customers; that is, sales, marketing, and service. The two major components of operational CRM systems are customer-facing applications and customer-touching applications (discussed below). Operational CRM systems provide the following benefits:

- Efficient, personalized marketing, sales, and service
- A 360° view of each customer
- The ability of sales and service employees to access a complete history of customer interaction with the organization, regardless of the touch point

An example of an operational CRM system involves Caterpillar, Inc. (www.cat.com), an international manufacturer of industrial equipment. Caterpillar uses its CRM tools to accomplish the following objectives:

- Improve sales and account management by optimizing the information shared by multiple employees and by streamlining existing processes (e.g., taking orders using mobile devices)
- Form individualized relationships with customers, with the aim of improving customer satisfaction and maximizing profits
- Identify the most profitable customers, and provide them with the highest level of service
- Provide employees with the information and processes necessary to know their customers
- Understand and identify customer needs, and effectively build relationships among the company, its customer base, and its distribution partners

Customer-Facing Applications

In **customer-facing CRM applications**, an organization's sales, field service, and customer interaction center representatives interact directly with customers. These applications include customer service and support, salesforce automation, marketing, and campaign management.

Customer Service and Support. Customer service and support refers to systems that automate service requests, complaints, product returns, and requests for information. Today, organizations have implemented **customer interaction centers (CIC)**, where organizational representatives use multiple channels such as the Web, telephone, fax, and face-to-face interactions to communicate with customers. The CIC manages several different types of customer interaction.

One of the best known customer interaction centers is the *call center*, a centralized office set up to receive and transmit a large volume of requests by telephone. Call centers enable companies to respond to a large variety of questions, including product support and complaints.

Organizations also use the CIC to create a call list for the sales team, whose members contact sales prospects. This type of interaction is called *outbound telesales*. In these interactions, the customer and the sales team collaborate in discussing products and services that can satisfy customers' needs and generate sales.

Customers can communicate directly with the CIC to initiate a sales order, inquire about products and services before placing an order, and obtain information about a transaction they have already made. These interactions are referred to as *inbound teleservice*. Teleservice representatives respond to requests either by utilizing service instructions stored in an organizational knowledge base or by noting incidents that can be addressed only by field service technicians.

The CIC also provides the Information Help Desk. The Help Desk assists customers with their questions concerning products or services, and it also processes customer complaints. Complaints generate follow-up activities such as quality control checks, delivery of replacement parts or products, service calls, generation of credit memos, and product returns. New technologies are extending the traditional CIC's functionality to include e-mail and Web interaction. For example, Epicor (www.epicor.com) provides software solutions that combine Web channels, such as automated e-mail reply, with Web knowledge bases. The information the software provides is available to CIC representatives and field service personnel. Another new technology, live chat, allows customers to connect to a company representative and conduct an instant messaging session. The advantage of live chat over a telephone conversation is that live chat enables the participants to share documents and photos (see www.livechatinc.com and www.websitealive.com). Some companies conduct the chat with a computer using natural language processing rather than with a real person. IT's About Business 12.2 provides an example of Priceline.com's new customer call center.

IT's About Business 12.2

MKT
MIS **Priceline.com's New Customer Contact Center**

POM Priceline.com (www.priceline.com) is an American company that helps its customers obtain discounts on travel-related services such as airline tickets and hotel stays. The company is not a direct supplier of these services; rather, it helps its suppliers provide travel services to its customers.

Immediately before the online travel industry's rapid growth, Priceline was using customer management software that it developed in-house. The proprietary applications could not provide 360-degree views of customers. Customer service agents had limited access to transaction histories, which severely limited their knowledge of the customers with whom they were speaking.

As the online travel industry blossomed and pricing became cutthroat, Priceline had to be able to react quickly. It needed to keep its customers informed of fast-moving price changes, new products, and changing travel regulations, no matter which method they used to contact the company. The new contact center had to grow as fast as the firm's customer base was growing while supporting significantly higher levels of interaction with each customer. Agents needed access to a list of frequently asked questions, among other content. To accomplish these goals, Priceline moved the process of information management away from its information

technology staff to the firm's marketing and product management teams so they could update the customer knowledge database and FAQs directly.

Priceline developed its new contact center using KANA Software (www.kana.com), which provides on-premise and cloud computing customer relationship management products. (We discuss on-premise and cloud computing in Plug IT In 4.) The contact center provides customer service agents with the ability to quickly manage high volumes of e-mails. The center also links customer contacts and Priceline's internal systems, which include several Oracle databases. This link enables Priceline agents to respond quickly and consistently by having access to a 360-degree view of each customer. The contact center has predefined business rules that streamline the process of responding to customer requests, ensuring that specific questions are handled by the most appropriate customer service representative.

Visitors to Priceline's Web site can also help themselves to a knowledge base to answer the most common questions. Using the self-service option is often faster for customers, and it reduces the number of calls to customer service agents, who can focus on more complex phone enquiries.

Sources: Compiled from S. Sachs, "Contact Center Automation Takes Flight," *TechTarget* March 2015; B. Stackpole, "Contact Center Strives for Strategic Role in Customer Experience Management," *TechTarget*, October 14, 2015; L. Klie, "5 Hot Customer Service Technologies," *DestinationCRM.com*, December 2014; "Priceline.com," *KANA Case Study*, 2014; P. Greenberg, "The Customer Experience Challenge Met: KANA Responds," *ZDNet*, January 9, 2013; www.priceline.com, www.kana.com, accessed October 27, 2015.

Questions

1. Discuss the reasons why Priceline needed a new customer contact center.

2. Describe the benefits of the KANA solution to customers and to Priceline.

Salesforce Automation. Salesforce automation (SFA) is the component of an operational CRM system that automatically records all of the components in a sales transaction process. SFA systems include a *contact management system*, which tracks all communications between the company and the customer, the purpose of each communication, and any necessary follow-up. This system eliminates duplicated contacts and redundancy, which in turn reduces the risk of irritating customers. SFA also includes a *sales lead tracking system*, which lists potential customers or customers who have purchased related products; that is, products similar to those that the salesperson is trying to sell to the customer.

Other elements of an SFA system can include a *sales forecasting system*, which is a mathematical technique for estimating future sales, and a *product knowledge system*, which is a comprehensive source of information regarding products and services. More-developed SFA systems also have online product-building features, called *configurators*, that enable customers to model the product to meet their specific needs. For example, you can customize your own running shoe at NikeID (http://nikeid.nike.com). Finally, many current SFA systems enable the salesperson in the field to connect remotely with customers and the home office via Web-based interfaces on their smart phones.

MKT

Marketing. Thus far, you have focused primarily on how sales and customer service personnel can benefit from CRM systems. However, CRM systems have many important applications for an organization's marketing department as well. For example, they enable marketers to identify and target their best customers, to manage marketing campaigns, and to generate quality leads for the sales teams. Additionally, CRM marketing applications can sift through volumes of customer data—a process known as data mining (discussed in Chapter 5)—to develop a *purchasing profile*; that is, a snapshot of a consumer's buying habits that may lead to additional sales through cross-selling, upselling, and bundling.

Cross-selling is the marketing of additional related products to customers based on a previous purchase. This sales approach has been used very successfully by banks. For example, if you have a checking and savings account at your bank, then a bank officer will recommend other products for you, such as certificates of deposit (CDs) or other types of investments.

Upselling is a strategy in which the salesperson provides customers with the opportunity to purchase related products or services of greater value in place of, or along with, the consumer's initial product or service selection. For example, if a customer goes into an electronics store to buy a new television, a salesperson may show him a pricey 1080i HD LED television placed next to a less expensive LCD television in the hope of selling the more expensive set (assuming that the customer is willing to pay more for a sharper picture). Other common examples of upselling are warranties on electronics merchandise and the purchase of a carwash after buying gas at the gas station.

Finally, bundling is a form of cross-selling in which a business sells a group of products or services together at a lower price than their combined individual prices. For example, your cable company might bundle cable TV, broadband Internet access, and telephone service at a lower price than you would paid for each service separately.

Campaign Management. Campaign management applications help organizations plan campaigns that send the right messages to the right people through the right channels. Organizations manage their campaigns very carefully to avoid targeting people who have opted out of receiving marketing communications. Furthermore, companies use these applications to personalize individual messages for each particular customer.

Customer-Touching Applications

Corporations have used manual CRM systems for many years. In the mid-1990s, for example, organizations began to utilize the Internet, the Web, and other electronic touch points (e.g., e-mail, point-of-sale terminals) to manage customer relationships. In contrast with customer-facing applications, where customers deal with a company representative, customers who utilize these technologies interact directly with the applications themselves. For this reason, these applications are called customer-touching CRM applications or electronic CRM (e-CRM) applications. Customers typically can use these applications to help themselves. There are many types of e-CRM applications. Let's examine some of the major ones.

Search and Comparison Capabilities. It is often difficult for customers to find what they want from the vast array of products and services available on the Web. To assist customers, many online stores and malls offer search and comparison capabilities, as do independent comparison Web sites (see www.mysimon.com).

Technical and Other Information and Services. Many organizations offer personalized experiences to induce customers to make purchases or to remain loyal. For example, Web sites often allow customers to download product manuals. One example is General Electric's Web site (www.ge.com), which provides detailed technical and maintenance information and sells replacement parts to customers who need to repair outdated home appliances. Another example is Goodyear's Web site (www.goodyear.com), which provides information about tires and their use.

Customized Products and Services. Another customer-touching service that many online vendors use is mass customization, a process in which customers can configure their own products. For example, Dell (www.dell.com) allows customers to configure their own computer systems. The Gap (www.gap.com) enables customers to "mix and match" an entire wardrobe. Web sites such as Hitsquad (www.hitsquad.com) and Apple iTunes (www.apple.com/itunes) allow customers to pick individual music titles from a library and customize a CD, a feature that traditional music stores do not offer.

In addition, customers can now view account balances or check the shipping status of orders at any time from their computers or smartphones. If you order books from Amazon, for example, you can look up the anticipated arrival date. Many other companies, including FedEx and UPS, provide similar services (see www.fedex.com and www.ups.com).

Personalized Web Pages. Many organizations permit their customers to create personalized Web pages. Customers use these pages to record purchases and preferences, as well as problems and requests. For example, American Airlines generates personalized Web pages for each of its registered travel-planning customers.

FAQs. Frequently asked questions (FAQs) are a simple tool for answering repetitive customer queries. Customers may find the information they need by using this tool, thereby eliminating the need to communicate with an actual person.

E-mail and Automated Response. The most popular tool for customer service is e-mail. Inexpensive and fast, companies use e-mail not only to answer customer inquiries but also to disseminate information, send alerts and product information, and conduct correspondence on any topic.

Loyalty Programs. **Loyalty programs** recognize customers who repeatedly use a vendor's products or services. Loyalty programs are appropriate when two conditions are met: a high frequency of repeat purchases, and limited product customization for each customer.

Although loyalty programs are frequently referred to as "rewards programs," their actual purpose is not to reward *past* behavior, but, rather, to influence *future* behavior. Significantly, the most profitable customers are not necessarily those whose behavior can be most easily influenced. As one example, most major U.S. airlines provide some "elite" benefits to anyone who flies 25,000 miles with them and their partners over the course of a year. Customers who fly first class pay much more for a given flight than those who fly in economy.

Nevertheless, these customers reach elite status only 1.5–2 times faster than economy-class passengers. Why is this true? The reason is that, although first-class passengers are far more profitable than discount seekers, they also are less influenced by loyalty programs. Discount flyers respond much more enthusiastically to the benefits of frequent flyer programs. Therefore, airlines award more benefits to discount flyers than to first-class flyers (relative to their spending).

The airlines' frequent flyer programs are probably the best-known loyalty programs. Other popular loyalty programs are casino players' clubs, which reward frequent players, and supermarkets, which reward frequent shoppers. Loyalty programs use a database or data warehouse to maintain a record of the points (or miles) a customer has accrued and the rewards to which he or she is entitled. The programs then use analytical tools to mine the data and learn about customer behavior.

We have now completed our discussion of operational CRM systems. Recall that we briefly looked at analytical CRM systems in the chapter Introduction. **Figure 12.3** illustrates the relationship between operational CRM systems and analytical CRM systems.

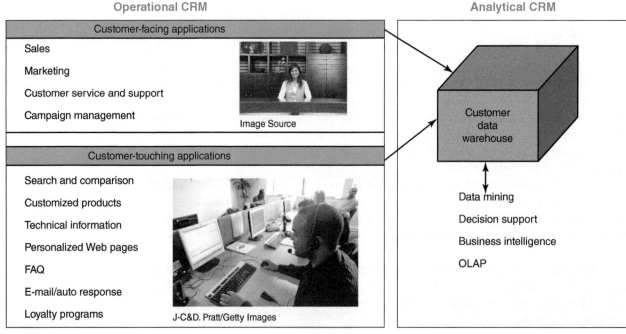

FIGURE 12.3 The relationship between operational CRM and analytical CRM.

Before you go on . . .

1. Differentiate between customer-facing applications and customer-touching applications.
2. Provide examples of cross-selling, upselling, and bundling (other than the examples presented in the text).

Apply the Concept 12.2

LEARNING OBJECTIVE 12.2   Describe how businesses might utilize applications of each of the two major components of operational CRM systems.

STEP 1: Background

Section 12.2 has introduced you to the concept of customer-facing and customer-touching CRM applications, the two major components of operational CRM systems. Many organizations use a combination of both types of systems to establish, develop, and maintain relationships with consumers. This activity will help you to see these systems in action when you do business on a Web site or in a brick-and-mortar business.

STEP 2: Activity

Visit a physical store where you like to shop (or recall a recent visit and discuss it with some friends), and visit the store's Web site.

Make certain to select a company that has both an Internet site and a physical store so you can compare the two channels.

As you walked through the store, did you notice any cues that could tie a customer to a CRM? Did the business have a customer loyalty programs? Are there any significant advantages to joining the program? Is the in-store membership tied to anything online? If so, how? Or, does the store seem to have separate in-store and online memberships?

STEP 3: Deliverable

After considering the points mentioned in Step 2, describe how businesses might utilize both the customer-facing and customer-touching applications of a CRM to integrate the online and traditional shopping experiences. Prepare a report and submit it to your instructor.

12.3 Other Types of Customer Relationship Management Systems

Now that you have examined operational and analytical CRM systems, let's shift our focus to other types of CRM systems. Five exciting developments in this area are on-demand CRM systems, mobile CRM systems, open-source CRM systems, social CRM, and real-time CRM.

On-Demand CRM Systems

Customer relationship management systems may be implemented as either *on-premise* or *on-demand*. Traditionally, organizations utilized on-premise CRM systems, meaning that they purchased the systems from a vendor and then installed them on site. This arrangement was expensive, time consuming, and inflexible. Some organizations, particularly smaller ones, could not justify the costs of these systems.

On-demand CRM systems became a solution for the drawbacks of on-premise CRM systems. An on-demand CRM system is one that is hosted by an external vendor in the vendor's data center. This arrangement spares the organization the costs associated with purchasing the system. In addition, because the vendor creates and maintains the system, the organization's employees need to know only how to access and utilize it. The concept of on-demand is also known as *utility computing* or *software-as-a-service* (SaaS) (see Plug IT In 4).

Salesforce (www.salesforce.com) is the best-known on-demand CRM vendor. The company's goal is to provide a new business model that allows companies to rent the CRM software instead of buying it. The secret to their success appears to be that CRM has common requirements across many customers. Consequently, Salesforce's product meets the demands of its customers without a great deal of customization.

One Salesforce customer is Babson College (www.babson.edu) in Wellesley, Massachusetts. Babson's goal is to deliver the best applicant experience possible. To accomplish this mission, the school decided to use Salesforce to bring together all of the information on prospective students in a single location. All personnel who are involved with admissions have immediate access to candidate contact information, applications, and reports that indicate the status of each applicant within the enrollment process. This system makes it easy for administrators to deliver valuable information to applicants at the right time.

Using the Salesforce platform, Babson built an admissions portal with a fully personalized user experience for prospective students. The portal consolidates all of the information that potential students need. Furthermore, it displays different information to students at different points in the application process.

Despite their benefits, on-demand CRM systems have potential problems. First, the vendor could prove to be unreliable, in which case the client company would have no CRM functionality at all. Second, hosted software is difficult or impossible to modify, and only the vendor can upgrade it. Third, vendor-hosted CRM software may be difficult to integrate with the organization's existing software. Finally, giving strategic customer data to vendors always carries security and privacy risks.

Mobile CRM Systems

A **mobile CRM** system is an interactive system that enables an organization to conduct communications related to sales, marketing, and customer service activities through a mobile medium for the purpose of building and maintaining relationships with its customers. Simply put, mobile CRM systems involve interacting directly with consumers through portable devices such as smartphones. Many forward-thinking companies believe that mobile CRM systems have tremendous potential to create personalized customer relationships that may be accessed anywhere and at any time. In fact, the opportunities offered by mobile marketing appear so rich that many companies have already identified mobile CRM systems as a cornerstone of their future marketing activities.

Open-Source CRM Systems

As explained in Plug IT In 2, the source code for open-source software is available at no cost. **Open-source CRM systems**, therefore, are CRM systems whose source code is available to developers and users.

Open-source CRM systems provide the same features or functions as other CRM software, and they may be implemented either on-premise or on-demand. Leading open-source CRM vendors include SugarCRM (www.sugarcrm.com), Concursive (www.concursive.com), and Vtiger (www.vtiger.com).

The benefits of open-source CRM systems include favorable pricing and a wide variety of applications. In addition, these systems are easy to customize. This is an attractive feature for organizations that need CRM software that is designed for their specific needs. Finally, updates and bug (software error) fixes for open-source CRM systems are rapidly distributed, and extensive support information is available free of charge.

Like all software, however, open-source CRM systems have certain risks. The most serious risk involves quality control. Because open-source CRM systems are created by a large community of unpaid developers, there sometimes is no central authority responsible for overseeing the quality of the product. (We discuss open-source software in Plug IT In 2). Furthermore, for best results, companies must have the same IT platform in place as the one on which the open-source CRM system was developed.

Social CRM

Social CRM is the use of social media technology and services to enable organizations to engage their customers in a collaborative conversation in order to provide mutually beneficial value in a trusted and transparent manner. Social CRM is the company's response to the customers' ownership of this two-way conversation. In social CRM, organizations monitor services such as Facebook, Twitter, and LinkedIn (among many others) for relevant mentions of their products, services, and brand, and they respond accordingly.

Social media are also providing methods that customers are using to obtain faster, better customer service. IT's About Business 12.3 recounts how one customer was pleasantly surprised when Morton's Steakhouse responded to his tweet.

IT's About Business 12.3

MKT Morton's Steakhouse Surprises a Customer

Businessperson Peter Shankman was in meetings all day, and he had to take a later flight home that caused him to miss his dinner. So, he jokingly tweeted Morton's Steakhouse (www.mortons.com) and requested that the restaurant show up with a steak when he landed.

Morton's saw the Tweet, discovered that the tweeter was a frequent customer (and frequent tweeter—Shankman has 100,000 Twitter followers), pulled data on what he typically ordered, identified the flight he was on, and then sent a delivery person to Newark Airport (New Jersey) to serve him his dinner. When Shankman got to the reception lobby at the airport, he noticed a man in a tuxedo holding a card with Shankman's name. The man was also carrying a bag that contained a Porterhouse steak, shrimp, potatoes, bread, two napkins, and silverware.

The nearest Morton's restaurant was 24 miles from the airport, and Shankman's flight took only two hours. This scenario says a lot about both Morton's customer service and the speed of social media. Admittedly, the entire scenario was a publicity stunt that went explosively viral over the Internet. This is not the point, however. The questions that businesses should be asking themselves are: Would your company even consider doing something like this? If not, why not?

Sources: C. Chan, "Morton's Steakhouse Met a Man at the Airport with a Steak After He Asked for One on Twitter," *Gizmodo*, August 19, 2011; M. Flacy, "After a Single Tweet, Air Traveler Gets a Morton's Surprise at Newark Airport," *Digital Trends*, August 18, 2011; "Peter Shankman Tweet Joke Leads to Morton's Surprise Steak Dinner at Newark Airport (TWEETS)," *The Huffington Post*, August 11, 2011; www.mortons.com, accessed March 31, 2015.

Questions

1. Explain how Morton's monitoring of social media illustrates how CRM is reviving personal marketing.

2. Do you see any disadvantages in such close monitoring of social media? Provide specific examples to support your answer.

Real-Time CRM

Organizations are implementing real-time customer relationship management in order to provide a superior level of customer satisfaction for today's always-on, always-connected, more knowledgeable, and less loyal customers. Real-time CRM means that organizations are able to respond to customer product searches, requests, complaints, comments, ratings, reviews, and recommendations in near real-time, 24/7/365. Southwest Airlines provides an excellent example of real-time CRM.

A passenger was in her seat on a Southwest Airlines flight about to take off, when the plane turned back to the gate. A flight attendant asked her to get off the plane. When she checked with the Southwest agent at the desk inside the terminal, he told her that her son was in a coma after suffering a head injury and to call her husband.

Even before she had disembarked, Southwest had rebooked her on the next nonstop flight to her son's city—free of charge. The airline offered her a private waiting area, rerouted her luggage, allowed her to board first, and packed a lunch for her. Moreover, the airline delivered her luggage to where she was going to stay and called her to ask about her son. The woman said that her son was recovering and that she could not be more grateful for the way she was treated.

Southwest Airlines went above and beyond their responsibilities after they learned of the son's accident. Details were not available about how the airline learned of the son's accident, but it is clear that Southwest brought customer relationship management to a new level.

Before you go on . . .

1. Describe on-demand CRM.

2. Describe mobile CRM.

3. Describe open-source CRM.

4. Describe social CRM.

5. Describe real-time CRM.

Apply the Concept 12.3

LEARNING OBJECTIVE 12.3 Explain the advantages and disadvantages of mobile CRM systems, on-demand CRM systems, open-source CRM systems, social CRM systems, and real-time CRM systems.

STEP 1: Background

Section 12.3 has outlined different CRM systems—not operational or analytical—but, instead, the different ways you can actually implement a CRM system. For example, you can run mobile CRM, open-source CRM, on-demand CRM (cloud), and more. You will have most—if not all—of these options with any system you plan to implement!

STEP 2: Activity

Visit http://www.wiley.com/go/rainer/MIS4e/applytheconcept, and click on the links provided for Apply the Concept 12.3.

One link will take you to a YouTube video that describes an on-demand CRM system (Salesforce). Another will take you to a video that highlights an open-source CRM (Sugar CRM). The final link will illustrate a hybrid approach, Sales Cloud (mobile-cloud CRM). Watch these videos, paying special attention to the advantages and disadvantages of each approach. The advantages will be easy to spot (these are promotional videos). The disadvantages of each one will become obvious as you compare the advantages of the others because you may notice particular functions that system one cannot perform but the others can.

STEP 3: Deliverable

Build a table that highlights the advantages and disadvantages of each approach. Do the differences reside in the capabilities of the software or in the user experience? Submit your table to your instructor.

What's in IT for me?

ACCT For the Accounting Major

CRM systems can help companies establish controls for financial reporting related to interactions with customers in order to support compliance with legislation. For example, Sarbanes–Oxley requires companies to establish and maintain an adequate set of controls for accurate financial reporting that can be audited by a third party. Other sections [302 and 401(b)] have implications for customer activities, including the requirements that sales figures reported for the prior year be correct. Section 409 requires companies to report material changes to financial conditions, such as the loss of a strategic customer or significant customer claims about product quality.

CRM systems can track document flow from a sales opportunity to a sales order, to an invoice, to an accounting document, thus enabling finance and accounting managers to monitor the entire flow. CRM systems that track sales quotes and orders can be used to incorporate process controls that identify questionable sales transactions. CRM systems can provide exception-alert capabilities to identify instances outside defined parameters that put companies at risk.

FIN For the Finance Major

CRM systems allow companies to track marketing expenses, collecting appropriate costs for each individual marketing campaign. These costs then can be matched to corporate initiatives and financial objectives, demonstrating the financial impact of the marketing campaign.

Pricing is another key area that impacts financial reporting. For example, what discounts are available? When can a price be overridden? Who approves discounts? CRM systems can put controls into place for these issues.

MKT For the Marketing Major

CRM systems are an integral part of every marketing professional's work activities. CRM systems contain the consolidated customer data that provides the foundation for making informed marketing decisions. Using these data, marketers develop well-timed and targeted sales campaigns with customized product mixes and established price points that enhance potential sales opportunities and therefore increase revenue. CRM systems also support the development of forecasting models for future sales to existing clients through the use of historical data captured from previous transactions.

POM For the Production/Operations Management Major

Production is heavily involved in the acquisition of raw materials, conversion, and distribution of finished goods. However, all of these activities are driven by sales. Increases or decreases in the demand for goods result in a corresponding increase or decrease in a company's need for raw materials. Integral to a company's demand is forecasting future sales, an important part of CRM systems. Sales forecasts are created from the historical data stored in CRM systems.

This information is critically important to a production manager who is placing orders for manufacturing processes. Without an accurate future sales forecast, production managers may face inventory problems (discussed in detail in this chapter). The use of CRM systems for production and operational support is critical to efficiently managing the resources of the company.

HRM For the Human Resources Major

Companies trying to enhance their customer relationships must recognize that employees who interact with customers are critical to the success of CRM strategies. Essentially, the success of CRM is based on the employees' desire and ability to promote the company and its CRM initiatives. In fact, research analysts have found that customer loyalty is based largely on employees' capabilities and their commitment to the company.

As a result, human resource managers know that a company that desires valued customer relationships needs valued relationships with its employees. Therefore, HR managers are implementing programs to increase employee satisfaction and are training employees to execute CRM strategies.

MIS **For the MIS Major**

The IT function in the enterprise is responsible for the corporate databases and data warehouse, as well as the correctness and completeness of the data in them. That is, the IT department provides the data used in a 360° view of the customer. Furthermore, IT personnel provide the technologies underlying the customer interaction center.

Summary

1. Identify the primary functions of both customer relationship management (CRM) and collaborative CRM.

Customer relationship management (CRM) is an organizational strategy that is customer focused and customer driven. That is, organizations concentrate on assessing customers' requirements for products and services and then on providing high-quality, responsive services. CRM functions include acquiring new customers, retaining existing customers, and growing relationships with existing customers.

Collaborative CRM is an organizational CRM strategy where data consolidation and the 360° view of the customer enable the organization's functional areas to readily share information about customers. The functions of collaborative CRM include integrating communications between the organization and its customers in all aspects of marketing, sales, and customer support processes, and enabling customers to provide direct feedback to the organization.

2. Describe how businesses might use applications of each of the two major components of operational CRM systems.

Operational CRM systems support the front-office business processes that interact directly with customers (i.e., sales, marketing, and service). The two major components of operational CRM systems are customer-facing applications and customer-touching applications.

Customer-facing CRM applications include customer service and support, sales force automation, marketing, and campaign management. *Customer-touching applications* include search and comparison capabilities, technical and other information and services, customized products and services, personalized Web pages, FAQs, e-mail and automated response, and loyalty programs.

3. Explain the advantages and disadvantages of mobile CRM systems, on-demand CRM systems, open-source CRM systems, social CRM systems, and real-time CRM systems.

On-demand CRM systems are those hosted by an external vendor in the vendor's data center. Advantages of on-demand CRM systems include lower costs and a need for employees to know only how to access and utilize the software. Drawbacks include possibly unreliable vendors, difficulty in modifying the software, and difficulty in integrating vendor-hosted CRM software with the organization's existing software.

Mobile CRM systems are interactive systems where communications related to sales, marketing, and customer service activities are conducted through a mobile medium for the purpose of building and maintaining customer relationships between an organization and its customers. Advantages of mobile CRM systems include convenience for customers and the chance to build a truly personal relationship with customers. A drawback could be difficulty in maintaining customer expectations; that is, the company must be extremely responsive to customer needs in a mobile, near-real-time environment.

Open-source CRM systems are those whose source code is available to developers and users. The benefits of open-source CRM systems include favorable pricing, a wide variety of applications, easy customization, rapid updates and bug (software error) fixes, and extensive free support information. The major drawback of open-source CRM systems is quality control.

Social CRM is the use of social media technology and services to enable organizations to engage their customers in a collaborative conversation in order to provide mutually beneficial value in a trusted and transparent manner.

Real-time CRM means that organizations are able to respond to customer product searches, requests, complaints, comments, ratings, reviews, and recommendations in near real-time, 24/7/365.

Chapter Glossary

analytical CRM system CRM system that analyzes customer behavior and perceptions in order to provide actionable business intelligence.

bundling A form of cross-selling where an enterprise sells a group of products or services together at a lower price than the combined individual price of the products.

campaign management applications CRM applications that help organizations plan marketing campaigns that send the right messages to the right people through the right channels.

collaborative CRM system A CRM system where communications between the organization and its customers are integrated across all aspects of marketing, sales, and customer support processes.

cross-selling The practice of marketing additional related products to customers based on a previous purchase.

customer-facing CRM applications Areas where customers directly interact with the organization, including customer service and support, sales force automation, marketing, and campaign management.

customer interaction center (CIC) A CRM operation where organizational representatives use multiple communication channels to interact with customers in functions such as inbound teleservice and outbound telesales.

customer relationship management (CRM) A customer focused and customer-driven organizational strategy that concentrates on addressing customers' requirements for products and services, and then providing high-quality, responsive services.

customer-touching CRM applications (also called electronic CRM or e-CRM) Applications and technologies with which customers interact and typically help themselves.

customer touch point Any interaction between a customer and an organization.

electronic CRM (e-CRM) See **customer-touching CRM applications**.

front-office processes Those processes that directly interact with customers; that is, sales, marketing, and service.

interorganizational information system (IOS) An information system that supports information flow among two or more organizations.

loyalty program Programs that offer rewards to customers to influence future behavior.

mobile CRM system An interactive CRM system where communications related to sales, marketing, and customer service activities are conducted through a mobile medium for the purpose of building and maintaining customer relationships between an organization and its customers.

on-demand CRM system A CRM system that is hosted by an external vendor in the vendor's data center.

open-source CRM system CRM software whose source code is available to developers and users.

operational CRM system The component of CRM that supports the front-office business processes that directly interact with customers (i.e., sales, marketing, and service).

real-time CRM system A CRM system enabling organizations to respond to customer product searches, requests, complaints, comments, ratings, reviews, and recommendations in near real-time, 24/7/365.

salesforce automation (SFA) The component of an operational CRM system that automatically records all the aspects in a sales transaction process.

social CRM The use of social media technology and services to enable organizations to engage their customers in a collaborative conversation in order to provide mutually beneficial value in a trusted and transparent manner.

upselling A sales strategy where the organizational representative provides to customers the opportunity to purchase higher-value related products or services in place of, or along with, the consumer's initial product or service selection.

Discussion Questions

1. How do customer relationship management systems help organizations achieve customer intimacy?

2. What is the relationship between data consolidation and CRM systems?

3. Discuss the relationship between CRM and customer privacy.

4. Distinguish between operational CRM systems and analytical CRM systems.

5. Differentiate between customer-facing CRM applications and customer-touching CRM applications.

6. Explain why Web-based customer interaction centers are critical for successful CRM systems.

7. Why are companies so interested in e-CRM applications?

8. Discuss why it is difficult to justify CRM applications.

9. You are the CIO of a small company with a rapidly growing customer base. Which CRM system would you use: an on-premise CRM system, an on-demand CRM system, or an open-source CRM system? Remember that open-source CRM systems may be implemented either on-premise or on-demand. Discuss the pros and cons of each type of CRM system for your business.

Problem-Solving Activities

1. Access www.ups.com and www.fedex.com. Examine some of the IT-supported customer services and tools provided by the two companies. Compare and contrast the customer support provided on the two companies' Web sites.

2. Enter www.anntaylor.com, www.hermes.com, and www.tiffany.com. Compare and contrast the customer service activities offered by these companies on their Web sites. Do you see marked similarities? Differences?

3. Access your university's Web site. Investigate how your university provides for customer relationship management. (*Hint:* First decide who your university's customers are.)

4. Access www.sugarcrm.com, and take the interactive tour. Prepare a report on SugarCRM's functionality to the class.

5. Access www.ups.com and www.fedex.com. Examine some of the IT-supported customer services and tools provided by the two companies. Write a report on how the two companies contribute to supply chain improvements.

Closing Case 1

MKT SugarCRM Is More Than Just a CRM Package

The Problem

The Redglaze Group (www.redglazegroup.com) is an architectural and engineering group with a technology background whose companies provide products and services to the construction industry. The firm consists of eight businesses. Five are in the construction industry and two are in the technology field. The Redglaze Group provides operational business support services to the other companies.

With specialties ranging from branding and marketing to technology and construction, Redglaze Group companies assist architects, designers, and property owners in planning, constructing, and maintaining their commercial buildings. Due to the length of commercial construction projects, the company's customer relationships can last for years.

Redglaze was being limited by its existing customer relationship management software. The firm was trying to use this CRM package for multiple functions throughout its business units, but the software was very rigid. As a result, Redglaze developers had to extensively customize the software. Then, when the vendor upgraded the software, Redglaze had to spend time and money to ensure that all Redglaze customizations were compatible with the newest version.

The overall challenge was to implement an IT solution to achieve consistent customer interactions across all business units, create cost efficiencies, and share data instantly among headquarters and satellite offices. Specifically, the new CRM solution had to integrate the core functions of accounting, marketing, human resources, project management, and information technology to facilitate staff crossover; create a data-sharing platform that securely provides project-specific information to internal staff members; and establish a uniform customer-facing presence throughout all of the Redglaze business units. The objective was to deliver superior customer service and make better use of resources in a highly competitive industry with extremely tight margins.

The IT Solution

Redglaze could have purchased a new software package that might work for some but not all of its companies. Instead, the firm chose to implement Sugar, a product of SugarCRM (www.sugarcrm.com). SugarCRM is a software company that produces an open-source, customer relationship management product called Sugar.

POM The Results

One of Redglaze's companies, RGI Image (www.rgiimage.com), maintains showroom exteriors for approximately 150 automobile dealerships across the United States. RGI project managers supervise maintenance schedules and multiple work crews. They have to know many details about each project, including building height, dealers' preferences regarding cleaning days, equipment placement

restrictions, and many others. Previously they had no effective method to access all of the relevant information regarding dealerships when they planned maintenance crew schedules. Today, project managers can access this information via Sugar dashboards. In addition, they can integrate Google Maps with Sugar dashboards to have an aerial view of each dealership next to their notes about a project.

POM Another of Redglaze's companies, SGH (www.sghinc.com), handles the production and installation of architectural metal products. Prior to Sugar, when SGH project managers were assigned a new project, they would receive information that frequently had no relevance to their projects. Further, the information that they did receive was scattered: Spreadsheets and memos were in Google Docs, photos were in Dropbox, and e-mails were forwarded via Outlook. The process of integrating the relevant information was time-consuming. Today, Sugar enables SGH project managers to have all relevant information at their fingertips.

Sugar also helps SGH project managers resolve field problems. Managers are able to share documents (such as digitally rendered plans) with subcontractors through a Sugar portal developed by Redglaze software engineers. The managers and subcontractors can view the plans together, identify the source of the problem, and resolve issues quickly. In addition, subcontractors can use the portal to upload photos, so SGH project managers remotely receive instant views of job progress or potential problems.

ACCT The Redglaze development team extended Sugar to include the accounting and human resources functions. In accounting, for example, the developers wrote a new invoicing module that stores all of the relevant forms pertaining to each contract. These forms include the industry standard American Institute of Architects documents, lien waivers, insurance certificates, and others. Sugar digitally attaches the necessary forms to each project so that the project can be billed correctly.

HRM The team also implemented a new human resources module. For example, because staff members are shared across business units so frequently, the HR solution continuously updates organizational charts for each project, and it adjusts staff access to internal project data and customer data accordingly. The HR solution also includes a portal for employees who want to request time off or update personal details.

Redglaze's CEO has a customized SugarCRM dashboard that provides him with a high-level view across all of the firm's business units. The dashboard shows him just the information he needs, freeing up his time to pursue new business opportunities. His view includes items such as financials from each business unit, cash on hand, employee count, sales to budget projections, and project tracking.

Redglaze's involvement in a single project often spans years, so building trust with clients and prospects is critical. SugarCRM empowers the company's salespeople, project managers, and engineers by providing the right information to the right people at the right time.

This information includes plan details, photos, case studies, and engineering data on a project or a product.

Photographs are particularly essential in helping staff members in their interactions with current and potential customers. In meetings with current or prospective clients, Redglaze salespeople use Sugar to access photos of the company's previous projects. With a click or a swipe, the salesperson can drill down from the image to identify the building materials, the square footage, the architect or general contractor, as well as other key pieces of information about the job. Salespeople are paid only on what they sell, so having better and quicker information results in better productivity for the salesforce.

Today nearly 75 percent of Redglaze employees rely on direct access to the SugarCRM system to help them do their jobs more efficiently and effectively. The organization notes ongoing gains in staff empowerment, an improved company image, and easily customized SugarCRM modules that make employees' jobs easier.

By consolidating documents in Sugar, Redglaze has reduced server space by 60 percent while continuing to grow its business by 30 percent. Further, because all of the data are stored in a single location and are easily shared, all concerned parties have the necessary information for their clients or contractors.

Sources: Compiled from "SugarCRM Scores 2015 Customer Magazine Product of the Year Award," *SugarCRM Press Release*, October, 2015; "The List: Disruptor 50: SugarCRM," *CNBC News*, May 12, 2015; P. Greenberg, "SugarCon 2015: SugarCRM Continues Its Own Journey," *ZDNet*, May 12, 2015; C. Wood, "The 10 Best Free and Open Source CRM Software Solutions, *Capterra.com*, May 1, 2015; "SugarCRM Honored for CRM Excellence and Innovation by CRM Magazine," *SugarCRM Press Release*, August 18, 2014; "Redglaze Group Deploys SugarCRM to Drive Business Optimization and Deliver a Superior Customer Experience, *Business Wire*, February 25, 2014; "This Is How iCRM: Redglaze Group Aligns the Entire Team to Deliver Customer Success," *SugarCRM Case Study*, 2014; www.redglazegroup.com, www.sugarcrm.com, accessed October 23, 2015.

Questions

1. Discuss the reasons why Redglaze decided to implement SugarCRM rather than an on-premise CRM solution.

2. Describe how Redglaze extended the functionality of SugarCRM beyond customer relationship management.

3. Refer to your answer to Question #2. If you were a SugarCRM marketing manager, how would you market your product?

Closing Case 2

 Eli Lilly Provides a Better CRM System for Its Reps

The Problem

Physicians are arguably the most important component in pharmaceutical sales because they write the prescriptions that determine which drugs their patients will use. Therefore, influencing the physician is the key to success for pharmaceutical sales representatives. Historically, large pharmaceutical salesforces, called drug reps, have been responsible for these marketing efforts. Their strategies have involved physically visiting physicians' offices and providing drug samples.

As of October 2015, there were more than 80,000 drug reps in the United States, marketing to some 830,000 physicians. Drug reps typically try to see a given physician every few weeks. However, the number and persistence of drug reps has placed a burden on physicians' time.

The problem has become so acute that half of all physicians require an appointment before they see a drug rep, and another one-fourth will not see a drug rep at all. In addition, the Pharmaceutical Research and Manufacturers of America (PhRMA; www.phrma.org) provides voluntary ethics guidelines called Interactions with Healthcare Professionals. These guidelines prohibit drug reps from providing restaurant meals to physicians and from giving physicians small gifts and reminder items such as pens and notepads.

Pharmaceutical companies, therefore, have customer-management needs that are more complex than those of other industries. These firms have to deal with tightening restrictions on salespersons' access to physicians and other healthcare decision makers. This changing environment has caused the pharmaceuticals to shift their CRM strategies from frequency-based interactions to technology-supported methods. Let's consider Eli Lilly as an example.

Eli Lilly and Company (Lilly; www.lilly.com) is a global pharmaceutical company based in the United States that maintains offices in 17 other countries plus Puerto Rico. The firm's products are sold in approximately 125 countries. The company employs 16,000 sales representatives, medical liaisons, and account managers who call on healthcare professionals and administrators around the world.

In the past, Lilly's drug reps employed multiple sales force automation products, data management systems, and reporting tools. The old systems required the reps to record call comments at the end of the day rather than during or immediately after a meeting with a physician. This system caused the reps to keep very sparse notes, or none at all. It frustrated and fatigued the reps, and it ultimately led to lost insights concerning the physicians.

Another problem occurred because drug reps in different countries used different CRM systems. This situation made it difficult for Lilly executives to obtain an accurate, integrated view of the entire business. Moreover, staff members had to do a great deal of work each month to manually produce standard, consistent business information at headquarters.

Exacerbating these problems, reps were calling on physicians with personal computers running the Windows XP operating system. (We discuss operating systems in Plug IT In 2.) They had to wait while the machines took several minutes to boot, and they had to rely on less-than-persuasive PowerPoint presentations. In addition, reps required between three and five days of training to learn the system.

The IT Solution

Lilly urgently needed to upgrade its CRM tools. The company therefore turned to Veeva Systems' (www.veeva.com) cloud-based, mobile-friendly CRM product. The firm's reps now use Veeva on their iPads to plan physician calls, record and report on those conversations, present drug information, and analyze trends.

The Veeva system also enables Lilly drug reps to perform eDetailing. Detailing refers to the activity of drug reps when they call on physicians and provide them with "details"—scientific information, benefits, side effects, or adverse events—related to particular drugs.

eDetailing means using interactive, online CRM tools in the drug presentation and sales process. Two examples of eDetailing are:

- Virtual details: Web-based, self-guided information programs with no live communication between drug reps and physicians;
- Video details: online, live, or phone-assisted browsing through virtual sales presentations.

In addition to these examples, Veeva eDetailing enables drug reps to conduct integrated online surveys, market segmentation, and targeting. Because it is becoming increasingly difficult to physically meet with physicians, drug reps depend on eDetailing to deliver the relevant information about their brands and drugs.

The Results

An initial benefit of the Veeva system was that Lilly sales reps could be trained in only half a day. The new system also enables reps to interact with physicians, nurses, and administrators in a customer-centric manner.

Veeva was much easier and faster to deploy than the company's original on-premise CRM software. (We discuss on-premise software in Plug IT In 4.) In fact, the Veeva system saved Lilly millions of dollars per year due to lower IT support costs and improved efficiency.

Lilly's Veeva solution forced the company to standardize its previously separate data stores. Lilly now uses Veeva Network to integrate its customer data from around the world. Field reps can utilize these data to access Lilly's interaction history with customers to tailor their presentations. These presentations can be made either in person or online. Further, the company can identify customers with similar profiles who should receive similar presentations.

The Veeva initiative's success resulted from close partnerships among Lilly's IT group and the company's sales operations team. The data standardization process also provides the potential for Lilly to integrate its data with public data, such as U.S. census data. This process could lead to insights into drug prescription trends and healthcare spending across different demographic groups.

Sources: Compiled from "Veeva Systems Wants to Give Pharma Reps 'Suggestions,'" *Pharmaceutical Commerce*, June 11, 2015; W. Looney, "Capturing the Cloud: A Conversation with Veeva Systems Matt Wallach," *PharmExec.com*, May 20, 2015; L. Wijntjes, "Customer Relationship Management for Pharmaceuticals," *Pharmaceutical Digital Marketing*, May 14, 2015; "Can Veeva Systems' Software Keep Luring Big Pharma?" *Nasdaq.com*, February 17, 2015; T. Staton, "Got a Problem, Doc? In Eli Lilly's Brave New Sales World, That's a Plus," *Fierce Pharma Marketing*, May 28, 2014; M. Endler, "Eli Lilly's Field Reps: Armed with Better Data," *InformationWeek*, April 2, 2014; M. Hammons and L. Trotta, "How CRM Can Improve Efficiencies for Pharma and Life Sciences Firms," *Infinity Information Systems*, February, 2013; www.lilly.com, www.veeva.com, accessed October 25, 2015.

Questions

1. Describe why the Veeva CRM system was critical to Eli Lilly.

2. What are the potential disadvantages of Veeva eDetailing? Provide examples to support your answer.

CHAPTER **13**

© nullplus/iStockphoto

Supply Chain Management

LEARNING OBJECTIVES

13.1 Describe the three components and the three flows of a supply chain.

13.2 Identify popular strategies to solving different challenges of supply chains.

13.3 Explain the utility of each of the three major technologies that support supply chain
management.

Chapter Opening Case

Munchery

POM "What's for dinner?" is a question everyone asks on a daily basis. For people who live and work in large metropolitan areas, the answer might become lost in the rush to and from work, family and personal commitments, and a desire to have something tasty (and perhaps healthy) at the end of the day. But, who has time to prepare the meal?

In 2010, Tri Tran, founder of Munchery (www.munchery.com), noticed that his neighbor had an interesting answer to the "What's for dinner?" question. For $700–$800 a week, a personal chef came to his

neighbor's home to prepare and refrigerate meals that would be ready to warm up on demand and enjoy. Realizing that this model was not financially viable to him or many other people, Tran decided to start a new company. His goal was to provide high-quality, chef-prepared, fresh, almost ready-to-eat meals, delivered right to the customer's door, for $7–$8 per entrée.

Meal delivery is not a new concept. Many companies are in the business of delivering hot, ready-to-eat meals. For example, Dominos (www.dominos.com) delivers more than one million pizzas per day worldwide, and Sprig (www.sprig.com) focuses on healthy, organic meals. However, as hot meals cool, the quality of the meal experience decreases. Hot meals have a very narrow window of time for a quality consumption experience, which puts pressure on the delivery system.

In 1993, this delivery pressure and a desire for quality led Dominos to discontinue their 30-minute delivery promise in lieu of a "Total Satisfaction Guarantee."

Almost ready-to-eat meals are commonly sold at the grocery store, but they require some preparation before they can be consumed. When Munchery entered the meal delivery market, the firm differentiated itself by preparing an entire meal, then chilling the prepared items for a cold delivery. Delivery of the almost ready-to-eat chilled food (with proper warming instructions) decreased the time pressure on the delivery, allowing the delivery team member to carry more meals on an optimized delivery route. This business model fueled Munchery's rapid growth.

Munchery also leveraged its business model to reduce food costs. Whereas a typical restaurant spends one-third of its revenue on food supplies, Munchery spends much less. For example, in San Francisco most restaurants pay $9–$11 per pound for salmon. In contrast, Munchery has successfully negotiated with its suppliers to pay $6. Munchery also employs technology to create very efficient processes in the kitchen.

Information technology is at the heart of Munchery's operation. Customers connect to Munchery through the Web or a mobile app. Because the menu is available only online, Munchery can update it daily. This process allows Munchery to save money by preparing food items from ingredients that are in season (and therefore less expensive). The company is also able to use fresher, healthier foods. In another interesting use of IT, Munchery chefs use programmable, Wi-Fi-enabled smart ovens to prepare meals in bulk while working a traditional 9–5 schedule.

Customers can use the mobile app or the Web to learn more about their current menu options. They can virtually "meet" the chefs who prepare their meals, learn about the origin of the ingredients of their food, place orders, and select a delivery window. Munchery's proprietary software then optimizes the delivery schedule to ensure that customers receive their orders within their desired time window. In addition, customers can track their order through the entire preparation and delivery to their door.

Munchery is disrupting the restaurant industry by using technology in two ways. First, the company offers its customers a novel dining experience. Customers are able to enjoy chef-prepared meals at home, with minimal effort and planning, at a fraction of the cost of visiting a restaurant. Second, Munchery is able to provide a menu that changes daily, thus enabling it to feature fresher, healthier food.

Although Munchery has not reached its target price point of $7–$8 per entrée, the company is moving in that direction thanks to its use of information technology in its operations and along its supply chain. When Munchery launched in 2011, most entrées were priced at $25. By 2016, a combination of increased demand and greater economies of scale had brought prices down to $10–$12 per entre. At this price point, the next time you ask, "What's for dinner?" your answer just might be Munchery—the successful restaurant that delivers cold food to your door.

Sources: Compiled from T. Lien, "Munchery Raises $85 Million in Bid to Make Healthy Meals Accessible to All," *Los Angeles Times*, May 26, 2015; J. Broughton, "Munchery's Recipe for Winning Online Food Delivery," *Inc.*, June 11, 2015; F. Elliot, "New Food Delivery App Munchery Launches Chef-Driven Meals on the Westside Today," *Los Angelos Eater*, May 18, 2015; D. MacMillan, "Munchery Valued at About $300 Million amid Food Fight," *Wall Street Journal, Digits,* May 22, 2015; M. Kosoff, "Food Startup Munchery Has Hired a Bunch of Gourmet Chefs to Answer the Most Popular Question in Your Household," *Business Insider*, April 8, 2015; A. Wilhelm, "Munchery Rebuilds Mobile Apps, Hires 3-Star Chef, and Gets into Booze," *TechCrunch,* October 29, 2013; S. Pishevar, "How Munchery Is Literally Eating the World," www.medium.com, June 8, 2015; www.restaurant.org/News-Research/Research/Operations-Report, accessed October 14, 2015; www.munchery.com; www.sprig.com; www.spoonrocket.com; www.dominos.com, accessed December 14, 2015.

Questions

1. How does Munchery's supply chain benefit from the simple decision to offer chilled rather than hot meals?

2. What role do information systems play in the communication of information from the ingredients to the table?

Introduction

Organizations increasingly are emphasizing a customer-centric approach to their business practices because they realize that long-term customer relationships provide sustainable value that extends beyond an individual business transaction. Significantly, supply chain management (SCM) is vital for organizations to successfully compete in the marketplace.

The chapter opening case about Munchery points out that an organization's supply chain can provide a strategic advantage. In Chapter 11, you learned about information systems that supported organizational activities within the organization. In this chapter, you study information systems that support organizational activities that extend outside the organization to suppliers.

At this point, you might be asking yourself: Why should *I* learn about SCM? The answer, as you will see in this chapter, is that suppliers are supremely important to *all* organizations. Regardless of your job, you will have an impact, whether direct or indirect, on managing your firm's supply chain. When you read the What's in IT for Me? section at the end of the chapter, you will learn about opportunities to make immediate contributions on your first job. Therefore, it is essential that you acquire a working knowledge of SCM and SCM systems.

13.1 | Supply Chains

Modern organizations are increasingly concentrating on their core competencies and on becoming more flexible and agile. To accomplish these objectives, they rely on other companies, rather than on companies they themselves own, to supply the goods and services they need. Organizations recognize that these suppliers can perform these activities more efficiently and effectively than they themselves can. This trend toward relying on an increasing number of suppliers has led to the concept of supply chains. A **supply chain** is the flow of materials, information, money, and services from raw material suppliers, through factories and warehouses, to the end customers. A supply chain also includes the *organizations* and *processes* that create and deliver products, information, and services to the end customers.

Supply chains enhance trust and collaboration among supply chain partners, thus improving supply chain visibility and inventory velocity. **Supply chain visibility** refers to the ability of all organizations within a supply chain to access or view relevant data on purchased materials as these materials move through their suppliers' production processes and transportation networks to their receiving docks. In addition, organizations can access or view relevant data on outbound goods as they are manufactured, assembled, or stored in inventory and then shipped through their transportation networks to their customers' receiving docks. The more quickly a company can deliver products and services after receiving the materials required to make them—that is, the higher the *inventory velocity*—the more satisfied the company's customers will be.

Supply chain information has historically been obtained by manual, labor-based tracking and monitoring, but is now increasingly being generated by sensors, RFID tags, meters, GPS, and other devices and systems. How does this transformation affect supply chain managers? For one thing, they now have real-time information on all products moving through their supply chains. Supply chains will therefore rely less on labor-based tracking and monitoring, because the new technology will allow shipping containers, trucks, products, and parts to report on their own status. The overall result is a vast improvement in supply chain visibility.

Supply chains are a vital component of the overall strategies of many modern organizations. To utilize supply chains efficiently, a business must be tightly integrated with its suppliers, business partners, distributors, and customers. A critical component of this integration is the use of information systems to facilitate the exchange of information among the participants in the supply chain.

The Structure and Components of Supply Chains

The term *supply chain* comes from a picture of how the partnering organizations are linked together. **Figure 13.1** illustrates a typical supply chain. (Recall that Figure 1.5 also illustrated a supply chain, in a slightly different way.) Note that the supply chain involves three segments:

1. *Upstream*, where sourcing or procurement from external suppliers occurs.

   In this segment, supply chain managers select suppliers to deliver the goods and services the company needs to produce its product or service. Furthermore, SC managers develop the pricing, delivery, and payment processes between a company and its suppliers. Included here are processes for managing inventory, receiving and verifying shipments, transferring goods to manufacturing facilities, and authorizing payments to suppliers.

2. *Internal*, where packaging, assembly, or manufacturing takes place.

   SC managers schedule the activities necessary for production, testing, packaging, and preparing goods for delivery. In addition, they monitor quality levels, production output, and worker productivity.

3. *Downstream*, where distribution takes place, frequently by external distributors.

   In this segment, SC managers coordinate the receipt of orders from customers, develop a network of warehouses, select carriers to deliver products to customers, and implement invoicing systems to receive payments from customers.

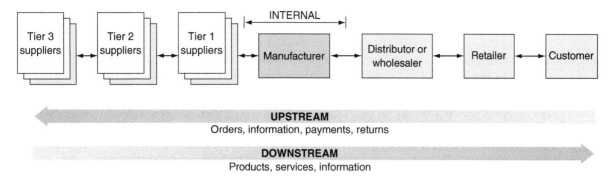

FIGURE 13.1 Generic supply chain.

The flow of information and goods can be bidirectional. For example, damaged or unwanted products can be returned, a process known as *reverse flows* or *reverse logistics*. In the retail clothing industry, for example, reverse logistics involves clothing that customers return, either because the item had defects or because the customer did not like the item.

Tiers of Suppliers. Figure 13.1 shows several tiers of suppliers. As the diagram indicates, a supplier may have one or more subsuppliers, a subsupplier may have its own subsupplier(s), and so on. For an automobile manufacturer, for example, Tier 3 suppliers produce basic products such as glass, plastic, and rubber; Tier 2 suppliers use these inputs to make windshields, tires, and plastic moldings; and Tier 1 suppliers produce integrated components such as dashboards and seat assemblies.

The Flows in the Supply Chain. There are typically three flows in the supply chain: material, information, and financial. *Material flows* are the physical products, raw materials, supplies, and so forth that flow along the chain. Material flows also include the reverse flows discussed above. A supply chain thus involves a *product life cycle* approach, from "dirt to dust."

Information flows consist of data related to demand, shipments, orders, returns, and schedules, as well as changes in any of these data. Finally, *financial flows* involve money transfers, payments, credit card information and authorization, payment schedules, e-payments, and credit-related data.

Significantly, different supply chains have different numbers and types of flows. For instance, in service industries there may be no physical flow of materials, but frequently there is a flow of information, often in the form of documents (physical or electronic copies). For example, the digitization of software, music, and other content can create a supply chain without any physical flow. Notice, however, that in such a case there are two types of information flows: one that replaces materials flow (digitized software), and another that provides the supporting information (orders, billing, and so on). To manage the supply chain, an organization must coordinate all three flows among all of the parties involved in the chain, a topic we turn to next.

Before you go on . . .

1. What is a supply chain?
2. Describe the three segments of a supply chain.
3. Describe the flows in a supply chain.

Apply the Concept 13.1

LEARNING OBJECTIVE 13.1 Describe the three components and the three flows of a supply chain.

STEP 1: Background (Here is what you are learning.)

Section 13.1 has focused on supply chain flows, materials, and "positions" (upstream, internal, and downstream). It is important to understand how products move in the supply chain because data move along with them every step of the way. In fact, the data that travel with materials and products are more important to the efficiency of the operation than the products themselves!

STEP 2: Activity (Here is what you are doing.)

Visit http://www.wiley.com/go/rainer/MIS4e/applytheconcept, and click on the link provided for Apply the Concept 13.1. This link

will take you to a YouTube video titled "Module 1: What Is Supply Chain Management? (ASU-WPC-SCM)" by user "wpcareyschool."

As you watch the video, consider the data that would be transferred with each product movement within the bottled water supply chain. Certain types of data, such as inventory updates, shipment information, quality checks, and supplier information, would deal just with the bottled water itself. In addition, there will be HR information, employee data, and machine data from the internal organization as well as from all of the suppliers!

STEP 3: Deliverable (Here is what you turn in.)

Using the example you learned about in Step 2, describe the three components and the three flows of a water bottle supply chain in a report. Submit your report to your instructor.

13.2 | Supply Chain Management

The function of **supply chain management (SCM)** is to improve the processes a company uses to acquire the raw materials it needs to produce a product or service and then deliver that product or service to its customers. That is, supply chain management is the process of planning, organizing, and optimizing the various activities performed along the supply chain. There are five basic components of SCM:

1. *Plan:* Planning is the strategic component of SCM. Organizations must have a strategy for managing all the resources that are involved in meeting customer demand for their product or service. Planning involves developing a set of metrics (measurable deliverables) to monitor the organization's supply chain to ensure that it is efficient and it delivers high quality and value to customers for the lowest cost.

2. *Source:* In the sourcing component, organizations choose suppliers to deliver the goods and services they need to create their product or service. Supply chain managers develop pricing, delivery, and payment processes with suppliers, and they create metrics to monitor and improve their relationships with their suppliers. They also develop processes for managing their goods and services inventory, including receiving and verifying shipments, transferring the shipped materials to manufacturing facilities, and authorizing supplier payments.

3. *Make:* This is the manufacturing component. Supply chain managers schedule the activities necessary for production, testing, packaging, and preparation for delivery. This component is the most metric-intensive part of the supply chain, where organizations measure quality levels, production output, and worker productivity.

4. *Deliver:* This component, often referred to as logistics, is where organizations coordinate the receipt of customer orders, develop a network of warehouses, select carriers to transport their products to their customers, and create an invoicing system to receive payments.

5. *Return:* Supply chain managers must create a responsive and flexible network for receiving defective, returned, or excess products back from their customers, as well as for supporting customers who have problems with delivered products.

Like other functional areas, SCM utilizes information systems. The goal of SCM systems is to reduce the problems, or friction, along the supply chain. Friction can increase time, costs, and inventories and decrease customer satisfaction. SCM systems, therefore, reduce uncertainty and risks by decreasing inventory levels and cycle time while improving business processes and customer service. These benefits make the organization more profitable and competitive.

Significantly, SCM systems are a type of interorganizational information system. In an **interorganizational information system (IOS)**, information flows among two or more organizations. By connecting the IS of business partners, IOSs enable the partners to perform a number of tasks:

- Reduce the costs of routine business transactions
- Improve the quality of the information flow by reducing or eliminating errors
- Compress the cycle time involved in fulfilling business transactions
- Eliminate paper processing and its associated inefficiencies and costs
- Make the transfer and processing of information easier for users

One of the most important goals of SCM systems is to give an organization visibility into its supply chain. *Supply chain visibility* is the ability of an organization to track products in transit from the manufacturer to their final destination. The goal of SCV is to improve the supply chain by making data readily available to all parties in the supply chain. Supply chain visibility promotes quick responses to problems or changes along the supply chain by enabling companies to shift products to where they are needed. IT's About Business 13.1 illustrates how Apple improved its supply chain visibility.

IT's About Business 13.1

POM Apple Deals with Supply Chain Strain and Faulty Parts

When Apple (www.apple.com) introduced the Apple Watch in April 2015, industry analysts had a hard time predicting how consumers would react. Their estimates ranged from 5 million to 40 million Watches sold in 2015. This huge range in a market forecast creates havoc in planning for a supply chain. In fact, industry experts call it *supply chain strain*.

So, how did Apple's supply chain gear up for such a high degree of sales uncertainty? First, the firm allowed a certain number of Apple Watch preorders. Based on those preorders, Apple could estimate the potential market demand and alter production accordingly. Second, even after releasing the Watch, Apple accepted only online orders for a few months. By controlling the ordering and shipping itself, Apple had accurate data regarding demand. As a result, the company did not have to manage demand by stocking inventory on store shelves.

The plan went off without a hitch, until it stumbled. Apple has multiple partners in its supply chain, and it holds all of them to extremely high standards. For Apple's supply chain to meet the demand for Watches, not to mention consumer expectations of quality, all of its partners had to operate at peak efficiency. With the Watch, one of the suppliers was not up to standards. Production of the Watch was functioning well until the company discovered that one of the key components, produced by a supplier, was faulty. That component was the taptic engine, which imparts forces or vibrations to the wearer to convey information.

The taptic engine supplier was China-based AAC Technologies (AAC; www.aactechnologies.com), maker of several common components in mobile devices. AAC was unable to meet either Apple's demand or its quality standards. The discovery of the faulty parts caused delays and other impacts on Apple's other suppliers as well as its customers. Apple reportedly threw out all of the defective Watches to avoid having to recall them.

Apple then handed over production of the taptic engine to another partner, Nidec Corporation (www.nidec.com) of Japan. Nidec manufactures parts for various industries including automotive, manufacturing, and consumer electronics. It took some time for Nidec to begin making the taptic engines. While Nidec was ramping up production, Apple came under considerable fire over the delayed Watch and extremely long-range shipping times.

Once supply caught up with demand, Apple's supply chain functioned as planned. Apple then lifted its Web-only sales policy and allowed the Watch to be sold in Apple Stores and other retail outlets. This shift is an indication that the firm is better able to manage its demand forecast as well as the Apple Watch supply chain.

Overall, Apple did an excellent job of creating a new product with some completely new components, developing a sales and marketing plan that would go hand-in-hand with its supply chain, recovering from a faulty component from a supply chain partner, and still getting their device to market with great consumer fanfare. Although not everyone will find a use for an Apple Watch, the one thing you do not see is complaints about its quality. That, too, is proof of Apple's ability to maintain ultra-high-quality standards in the face of unknown demand and supply chain strain.

Sources: Compiled from G. Meyers, "Apple—A Supply Chain Model of Excellence," *Supply & Demand Chain Executive*, June 4, 2015; "Apple Watch Shows Value of Strong Supply Chains, and Opportunity in

Disruption," supplychain247.com, May 28, 2015; "Has Supply Chain Strain Become the New Norm?," supplychain247.com, May 1, 2015; R. Bowman, "Can Apple's Supply Chain Handle the Apple Watch?," *Supply Chain Brain*, April 20, 2015; A. Cunningham, "WSJ: Taptic Engine Component Responsible for Limited Apple Watch Supplies," *ArsTechnica,* April 29, 2015; D. Wakabayashi and L. Luk, "Apple Watch: Faulty Taptic Engine Slows Rollout," *Wall Street Journal*, April 29, 2015; www.apple.com; http://www.aactechnologies.com; http://www.nidec.com, accessed October 2, 2015.

Questions

1. Discuss the importance of forecasting demand for supply chain planning.

2. Explain how a defective component can disrupt the flow of materials through a supply chain and the impact that disruption will have on various entities upstream and downstream along the supply chain.

The Push Model Versus the Pull Model

Many SCM systems employ the **push model**. In this model, also known as *make-to-stock*, the production process begins with a forecast, which is simply an educated guess as to customer demand. The forecast must predict which products customers will want and in what quantities. The company then produces the amount of products in the forecast, typically by using mass production, and sells, or "pushes," those products to consumers.

Unfortunately, these forecasts are often incorrect. Consider, for example, an automobile manufacturer that wants to produce a new car. Marketing managers conduct extensive research, including customer surveys and analyses of competitors' cars, and then provide the results to forecasters. If the forecasters' predictions are too high—that is, if they predict that customers will purchase a certain number of these new cars but actual demand falls below this amount—then the automaker has excess cars in inventory and will incur large carrying costs (the costs of storing unsold inventory). Furthermore, the company will probably have to sell the excess cars at a discount.

From the opposite perspective, if the forecasters' predictions are too low—that is, actual customer demand exceeds expectations—then the automaker probably will have to run extra shifts to meet the demand, thereby incurring substantial overtime costs. Furthermore, the company risks losing business to its competitors if the car that customers want is not available. Thus, using the push model in supply chain management can cause problems, as you will see in the next section.

To avoid the uncertainties associated with the push model, many companies now employ the pull model of supply chain management, using Web-enabled information flows. In the **pull model**, also known as *make-to-order*, the production process begins with a customer order. Therefore, companies make only what customers want, a process closely aligned with mass customization (discussed in Chapter 1).

A prominent example of a company that uses the pull model is Dell Computer. Dell's production process begins with a customer order. This order not only specifies the type of computer the customer wants but also alerts each Dell supplier as to the parts of the order for which that supplier is responsible. That way, Dell's suppliers ship only the parts that Dell needs to produce the computer.

Not all companies can use the pull model. Automobiles, for example, are far more complicated and more expensive to manufacture than computers, so automobile companies require longer lead times to produce new models. Automobile companies do use the pull model, but only for specific automobiles that some customers order (e.g., Rolls-Royce, Bentley, and other extremely expensive cars).

Problems Along the Supply Chain

As you saw earlier, friction can develop within a supply chain. One major consequence of friction is poor customer service. In some cases, supply chains do not deliver products or services when and where customers—either individuals or businesses—need them. In other cases, the supply chain provides poor quality products. Other problems associated with supply chain friction are high inventory costs and revenue loss.

The problems along the supply chain arise primarily from two sources: (1) uncertainties, and (2) the need to coordinate multiple activities, internal units, and business partners. A major source of supply chain uncertainties is the *demand forecast*. Demand for a product can be influenced by numerous factors such as competition, price, weather conditions, technological developments, overall economic conditions, and customers' general confidence. Another uncertainty is delivery times, which can be affected by numerous factors ranging from production machine failures to road construction and traffic jams. In addition, quality problems in materials and parts can create production delays, which also generate supply chain problems.

One major challenge that managers face in setting accurate inventory levels throughout the supply chain is known as the bullwhip effect. The bullwhip effect refers to erratic shifts in orders up and down the supply chain (see Figure 13.2). Basically, the variables that affect customer demand can become magnified when they are viewed through the eyes of managers at each link in the supply chain. If each distinct entity that makes ordering and inventory decisions places its interests above those of the chain, then stockpiling can occur at as many as seven or eight locations along the chain. Research has shown that in some cases such hoarding has led to as much as a 100-day supply of inventory that is waiting "just in case," versus the 10- to 20-day supply manufacturers normally keep at hand.

FIGURE 13.2 The bullwhip effect.

Solutions to Supply Chain Problems

Supply chain problems can be very costly. Therefore, organizations are motivated to find innovative solutions. During the oil crises of the 1970s, for example, Ryder Systems, a large trucking company, purchased a refinery to control the upstream part of the supply chain and to ensure it had sufficient gasoline for its trucks. Ryder's decision to purchase a refinery is an example of vertical integration. Vertical integration is a business strategy in which a company purchases its upstream suppliers to ensure that its essential supplies are available as soon as the company needs them. Ryder later sold the refinery because it could not manage a business it did not understand and because oil became more plentiful.

Ryder's decision to vertically integrate was not the best method for managing its supply chain. In the remainder of this section, you will look at some other possible solutions to supply chain problems, many of which are supported by IT.

Using Inventories to Solve Supply Chain Problems. Undoubtedly, the most common solution to supply chain problems is *building inventories* as insurance against supply chain uncertainties. As you have learned, holding either too much or too little inventory can be very costly. Thus, companies make major attempts to optimize and control inventories.

One widely utilized strategy to minimize inventories is the just-in-time (JIT) inventory system. Essentially, JIT systems deliver the precise number of parts, called *work-in-process* inventory, to be assembled into a finished product at precisely the right time.

Although JIT offers many benefits, it has certain drawbacks as well. To begin with, suppliers are expected to respond instantaneously to requests. As a result, they have to carry more inventory than they otherwise would. In this sense, JIT does not *eliminate* excess inventory; rather, it simply *shifts* it from the customer to the supplier. This process can still reduce the overall inventory size if the supplier can spread the increased inventory over several customers. However, that is not always possible.

In addition, JIT replaces a few large supply shipments with a large number of smaller ones. In terms of transportation, then, the process is less efficient.

Information Sharing. Another common approach to solving supply chain problems, and especially to improving demand forecasts, is *sharing information* along the supply chain. Information sharing can be facilitated by electronic data interchange and extranets, topics you will learn about in the next section.

One notable example of information sharing occurs between large manufacturers and retailers. For example, Walmart provides Procter & Gamble with access to daily sales information from every store for every item that P&G makes for Walmart. This access enables P&G to manage the *inventory replenishment* for Walmart's stores. By monitoring inventory levels, P&G knows when inventories fall below the threshold for each product at any Walmart store. These data trigger an immediate shipment.

Information sharing between Walmart and P&G is executed automatically. It is part of a vendor-managed inventory strategy. **Vendor-managed inventory (VMI)** occurs when the supplier, rather than the retailer, manages the entire inventory process for a particular product or group of products. Significantly, P&G has similar agreements with other major retailers. The benefit for P&G is accurate and timely information on consumer demand for its products. Thus, P&G can plan production more accurately, minimizing the bullwhip effect.

Before you go on . . .

1. Differentiate between the push model and the pull model.
2. Describe various problems that can occur along the supply chain.
3. Discuss possible solutions to problems along the supply chain.

Apply the Concept 13.2

LEARNING OBJECTIVE 13.2 Identify popular strategies to solving different challenges of supply chains.

STEP 1: Background

Section 13.2 has explained that managing a supply chain is not a simple task because consumer demand is so uncertain. Although organizations can forecast demand with some accuracy, actual demand almost inevitably will differ from the organizations' predictions. To manage demand fluctuations, organizations are moving toward JIT (just-in-time) inventory models, the amount of data shared along the supply chain increases. These data must be shared in a timely fashion if organizations are to remain flexible and capable of adapting to consumer demand.

STEP 2: Activity

Visit http://www.wiley.com/go/rainer/MIS4e/applytheconcept, and click on the links provided for Apply the Concept 13.2.

The first link will take you to an article that examines how the bullwhip effect wreaks havoc on the supply chain, and the second will take you to an activity where you will manage a supply chain for beer. This latter task might not sound difficult until you consider that there are serious timing issues due to the perishable nature of the product. The simulation begins with your supply chain in equilibrium, but it then suddenly shifts. Your job is to put things back in order!

As you work through the simulation, pay attention to how much information needs to be shared across the supply chain to make the entire operation function smoothly.

STEP 3: Deliverable

Based on your experience, discuss how the popular strategies for dealing with supply chain challenges (building inventory, JIT inventory, vendor-managed inventory) would or would not work for this product. Write a report and submit it to your instructor.

13.3 Information Technology Support for Supply Chain Management

Clearly, SCM systems are essential to the successful operation of many businesses. As you have seen, these systems—and IOSs in general—rely on various forms of IT to resolve problems. Three technologies, in particular, provide support for IOSs and SCM systems: electronic data interchange, extranets, and Web services. You will learn about Web services in Plug IT In 4. In this section, you examine the other two technologies.

Electronic Data Interchange (EDI)

Electronic data interchange (EDI) is a communication standard that enables business partners to exchange routine documents, such as purchasing orders, electronically. EDI formats these documents according to agreed-upon standards (e.g., data formats). It then transmits messages over the Internet using a converter, called *translator*.

EDI provides many benefits that are not available with a manual delivery system. To begin with, it minimizes data entry errors, because each entry is checked by the computer. In addition, the length of the message can be shorter, and the messages are secured. EDI also reduces cycle time, increases productivity, enhances customer service, and minimizes paper usage and storage. Figure 13.3 contrasts the process of fulfilling a purchase order with and without EDI.

EDI does have some disadvantages. Business processes sometimes must be restructured to fit EDI requirements. Also, there are many EDI standards in use today, so one company might have to use several standards in order to communicate with multiple business partners.

In today's world, where every business has a broadband connection to the Internet and where multi-megabyte design files, product photographs, and PDF sales brochures are routinely e-mailed, the value of reducing a structured e-commerce message from a few thousand XML bytes to a few hundred EDI bytes is negligible. As a result, EDI is being replaced by XML-based Web services. (You will learn about XML in Plug IT In 4.)

Extranets

To implement IOSs and SCM systems, a company must connect the intranets of its various business partners to create extranets. Extranets link business partners over the Internet by providing them access to certain areas of each other's corporate intranets (see Figure 13.4).

The primary goal of extranets is to foster collaboration between and among business partners. A business provides extranet access to selected B2B suppliers, customers, and other partners. These individuals access the extranet through the Internet. Extranets enable people located outside a company to collaborate with the company's internal employees. They also allow external business partners to enter the corporate intranet, via the Internet, to access data, place orders, check the status of those orders, communicate, and collaborate. Finally, they make it possible for partners to perform self-service activities such as checking inventory levels.

Extranets use virtual private network (VPN) technology to make communication over the Internet more secure. The major benefits of extranets are faster processes and information flow, improved order entry and customer service, lower costs (e.g., for communications, travel, and administrative overhead), and overall improved business effectiveness.

There are three major types of extranets. The type that a company chooses depends on the business partners involved and the purpose of the supply chain. We present each type below, along with its major business applications.

A Company and Its Dealers, Customers, or Suppliers. This type of extranet centers on a single company. An example is the FedEx extranet, which allows customers to track the status of a delivery. Customers use the Internet to access a database on the FedEx intranet. Enabling customers to monitor deliveries saves FedEx the cost of hiring human operators to perform

FIGURE 13.3 Comparing purchase order (PO) fulfillment with and without EDI.

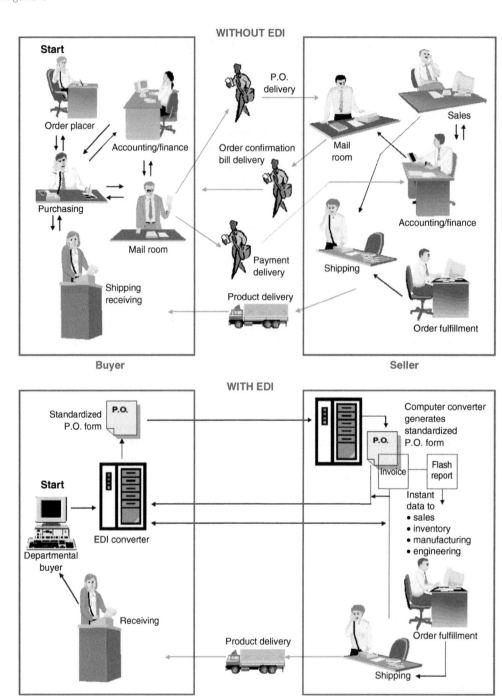

WITHOUT EDI

Start

Order placer

Accounting/finance

Purchasing

Mail room

Shipping receiving

P.O. delivery

Order confirmation bill delivery

Payment delivery

Product delivery

Mail room

Sales

Accounting/finance

Shipping

Order fulfillment

Buyer

Seller

WITH EDI

Standardized P.O. form

P.O.

Start

EDI converter

Departmental buyer

Receiving

Product delivery

Computer converter generates standardized P.O. form

P.O.

Invoice

Flash report

Instant data to
• sales
• inventory
• manufacturing
• engineering

Order fulfillment

Shipping

Buyer

Seller

Drawn by E. Turban.

FIGURE 13.4 The structure of an extranet.

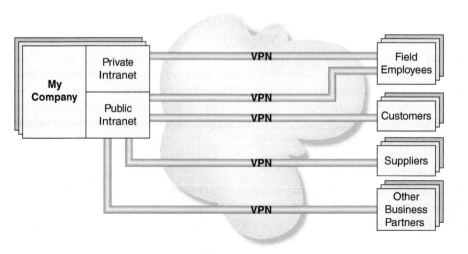

My Company

Private Intranet

Public Intranet

VPN

VPN

VPN

VPN

VPN

Field Employees

Customers

Suppliers

Other Business Partners

that task over the phone. IT's About Business 13.2 illustrates how Caribou Coffee works with its supplier network to provide 100 percent Rainforest Alliance Certified coffee.

An Industry's Extranet. Just as a single company can set up an extranet, the major players in an industry can team up to create an extranet that will benefit all of them. For example, ANXeBusiness (www.anx.com) enables companies to collaborate effectively through a network that provides a secure global medium for B2B information exchange. This network is used for mission-critical business transactions by leading international organizations in aerospace, automotive, chemical, electronics, financial services, healthcare, logistics, manufacturing, transportation, and related industries. It offers customers a reliable extranet as well as VPN services.

Joint Ventures and Other Business Partnerships. In this type of extranet, the partners in a joint venture use the extranet as a vehicle for communication and collaboration. An example is Bank of America's extranet for commercial loans. The partners involved in making these loans include a lender, a loan broker, an escrow company, and a title company. The extranet connects lenders, loan applicants, and the loan organizer, Bank of America. A similar case is Lending Tree (www.lendingtree.com), a company that provides mortgage quotes for homeowners and also sells mortgages online. Lending Tree uses an extranet for its business partners (e.g., the lenders).

IT's About Business 13.2

POM Caribou Coffee Brews A Strong Supply Chain

Food products have complicated supply chains due to the perishable nature of the raw materials. Such is the case for coffee. A typical coffee supply chain includes growers, intermediaries (who buy directly from the growers and resell to other intermediaries, processors, or dealers), processors, government agencies, exporters, brokers, roasters, distributors, and retailers. For a startup coffee-roasting company, managing the beans, seasons, regulations, partners, suppliers, distributors, and online store can be a daunting task. Despite this complexity, many companies begin managing their supply chain with a simple spreadsheet.

Such is the case with Caribou Coffee (www.cariboucoffee.com), a coffee chain based in Minneapolis, Minnesota that has retail outlets as well as a wholesale business. In the early days, Caribou had about 200 independent stockkeeping units (SKUs), which it could track on a spreadsheet. As business increased, that number quickly reached 600 SKUs. At that point Caribou realized that it needed a more sophisticated software.

Part of the reason for this rapid growth was positive reaction from customers to the fact that Caribou Coffee was the first major U.S. coffeehouse to serve 100 percent Rainforest Alliance Certified coffee and espresso. To achieve this certification, farms must follow rigorous environmental, social, and economic standards to achieve long-term sustainability. The goal is to conserve wildlife and ecosystems and protect workers, their families, and local communities.

While having Rainforest Alliance-certified products boosted sales for Caribou, it also meant more work in the procurement process. Caribou does not simply buy beans from a distributor without knowing little to nothing of the source. Instead, Caribou brokers must certify that they are 100 percent Rainforest Alliance Certified.

Caribou was experiencing growing pains with its internal demand forecasting and subsequent downstream supply chain management. Caribou turned to Logility (www.logility.com) to implement Voyager, a cloud-based supply chain management system. The service provides accurate, real-time data that the company uses to improve their forecasting and to provide better customer service to their retailers.

Logility's Voyager was the right solution for Caribou. The company saved time and money by using an off-the-shelf cloud-based system that meant it didn't have to develop in-house expertise or buy expensive technology. Voyager was deployed quickly with little upfront investment. In addition, the solution increased Caribou's ROI.

What were the payoffs for Caribou in ditching its spreadsheet for the Voyager service? It increased the accuracy of its demand forecasts, moved to weekly planning instead of monthly, reduced the spoilage of its perishable inventory, and accelerated its inventory turnover by one-third. (Inventory turnover is the number of times that inventory is sold or used in a particular time period, usually one year. The higher the number, the better.) The implementation of this supply chain management system was a huge success for Caribou Coffee, which can focus on what they do best...provide a nice cup of coffee!

Sources: Compiled from A. Grackin and B. McBeath, "Caribou Coffee's Supply Chain Story," *ChainLink Research*, January 22, 2013; "Coffee – The Supply Chain," *businesscasestudies.co.uk*, accessed October 3, 2015; "Caribou Coffee Shares Its Journey to Supply Chain Success," *Logility*, June 17, 2014; "Logility Announces 2014 Leadership Award Winners," *Logility*, May 1, 2014; www.logility.com, accessed October 3, 2015; www.cariboucoffee.com, accessed October 3, 2015; www.rainforest-alliance.org, accessed October 3, 2015.

Questions

1. Discuss the difficulties involved in the supply chain for any perishable item.

2. Describe the complex issues Caribou Coffee dealt with to ensure their supply chain was not only Rainforest Alliance Certified but also meeting their business needs.

Portals and Exchanges

As you saw in Chapter 4, corporate portals offer a single point of access through a Web browser to critical business information in an organization. In the context of B2B supply chain management, these portals enable companies and their suppliers to collaborate very closely.

There are two basic types of corporate portals: procurement (sourcing) portals for a company's suppliers (upstream in the supply chain), and distribution portals for a company's customers (downstream in the supply chain). **Procurement portals** automate the business processes involved in purchasing or procuring products between a single buyer and multiple suppliers. For example, Boeing has deployed a procurement portal called the Boeing Supplier Portal through which it conducts business with its suppliers. **Distribution portals** automate the business processes involved in selling or distributing products from a single supplier to multiple buyers. For example, Dell services its business customers through its distribution portal at http://premier.dell.com.

Before you go on . . .

1. Define EDI, and list its major benefits and limitations.
2. Define an extranet, and explain its infrastructure.
3. List and briefly define the major types of extranets.
4. Differentiate between procurement portals and distribution portals.

Apply the Concept 13.3

LEARNING OBJECTIVE 13.3 Explain the utility of each of the three major technologies that support supply chain management.

STEP 1: Background

Electronic data interchange (EDI) is defined in this section as a communication standard that enables business partners to exchange routine documents, such as purchasing orders, electronically. You should understand the need for electronic sharing of information if you completed the activity in Apply the Concept 13.2. That activity required you to manage a supply chain on your own. Imagine the challenge of performing this function without being able to share data electronically!

STEP 2: Activity

Visit http://www.wiley.com/go/rainer/MIS4e/applytheconcept, and click on the links provided for Apply the Concept 13.3. The

link will take you to a YouTube video titled "What is EDI" by user "hitekequipment." You will also link to an article that defines EDI and discusses some of its standards.

As you watch the video, pay attention to the important components that are necessary to share information between two organizations. Then, consider the fact that suppliers rarely operate in only a single supply chain. In fact, suppliers typically have multiple customers, which means they are sharing information with many organizations via EDI.

STEP 3: Deliverable

Based on the content of this section and the video you watched in Step 2, explain the utility of each of the three major technologies (EDI, extranets, and corporate portals) that support supply chain management. In other words, how might these technologies interact to enable the participating parties to exchange data? Put your explanation in a report and submit it to your instructor.

What's in IT for me?

ACCT   **For Accounting Majors**

The cost accountant will play an important role in developing and monitoring the financial accounting information associated with inventory and cost of goods sold. In a supply chain, much of the data for these accounting requirements will flow into the organization

from various partners within the chain. It is up to the chief accountant, the comptroller or CFO, to prepare and review these data.

Going further, accounting rules and regulations and the cross-border transfer of data are critical for global trade. IOSs can facilitate such trade. Other issues that are important for accountants are taxation and government reports. In addition, creating information systems that rely on EDI requires the attention of accountants. Finally, fraud detection in global settings (e.g., transfers of funds) can be facilitated by appropriate controls and auditing.

FIN For the Finance Major

In a supply chain, the finance major will be responsible for analyzing the data created and shared among supply chain partners. In many instances, the financial analyst will recommend actions to improve supply chain efficiencies and cash flow. This may benefit all the partners in the chain. These recommendations will be based on financial models that incorporate key assumptions such as supply chain partner agreements for pricing. Through the use of extensive financial modeling, the financial analyst helps to manage liquidity in the supply chain.

Many finance-related issues exist in implementing IOSs. For one thing, establishing EDI and extranet relationships involves structuring payment agreements. Global supply chains may involve complex financial arrangements, which may have legal implications.

MKT For the Marketing Major

A tremendous amount of useful sales information can be derived from supply chain partners through the supporting information systems. For example, many of the customer support activities take place in the downstream portion of the supply chain. For the marketing manager, an understanding of how the downstream activities of the supply chain relate to prior chain operations is critical.

Furthermore, a tremendous amount of data is fed from the supply chain supporting information systems into the CRM systems that are used by marketers. The information and a complete understanding of its genesis are vital for mixed-model marketing programs.

POM For the Production/Operations Management Major

The production/operations management major plays a major role in the supply chain development process. In many organizations, the production/operations management staff may even lead the supply chain integration process because of their extensive knowledge of the manufacturing components of the organization. Because they are in charge of procurement, production, materials control, and logistical handling, a comprehensive understanding of the techniques of SCM is vital for the production/operations staff.

The downstream segment of supply chains is where marketing, distribution channels, and customer service are conducted. An understanding of how downstream activities are related to the other segments is critical. Supply chain problems can reduce customer satisfaction and negate marketing efforts. It is essential, then, that marketing professionals understand the nature of such problems and their solutions. Also, learning about CRM, its options, and its implementation is important for designing effective customer services and advertising.

As competition intensifies globally, finding new global markets becomes critical. Use of IOSs provides an opportunity to improve marketing and sales. Understanding the capabilities of these technologies as well as their implementation issues will enable the marketing department to excel.

HRM For the Human Resources Major

Supply chains require interactions among the employees of partners in the chain. These interactions are the responsibility of the Human Resources Manager. The HR Manager must be able to address supply chain issues that relate to staffing, job descriptions, job rotations, and accountability. All of these areas are complex within a supply chain and require the HR function to understand the relationship among partners as well as the movement of resources.

Preparing and training employees to work with business partners (frequently in foreign countries) requires knowledge about how IOSs operate. Sensitivity to cultural differences and extensive communication and collaboration can be facilitated with IT.

MIS For the MIS Major

The MIS staff will be instrumental in the design and support of information systems—both internal organizational and interorganizational—that will underpin the business processes that are part of the supply chain. In this capacity, the MIS staff must have a concise knowledge of the business, the systems, and the points of intersection between the two.

Summary

1. Describe the three components and the three flows of a supply chain.

A *supply chain* is the flow of materials, information, money, and services from raw material suppliers, through factories and warehouses, to the end customers. A supply chain involves three segments: upstream, where sourcing or procurement from external suppliers occurs; internal, where packaging, assembly, or manufacturing takes place; and downstream, where distribution takes place, frequently by external distributors.

There are three flows in the supply chain: *material flows*, which are the physical products, raw materials, supplies, and so forth; *information flows*, which consist of data related to demand, shipments, orders, returns, and schedules, as well as changes in any of these data; and *financial flows*, which involve money transfers, payments, credit card information and

authorization, payment schedules, e-payments, and credit-related data.

2. Identify popular strategies to solving different challenges of supply chains.

Two major challenges in setting accurate inventory levels throughout a supply chain are the *demand forecast* and the bullwhip effect. Demand for a product can be influenced by numerous factors such as competition, prices, weather conditions, technological developments, economic conditions, and customers' general confidence. The *bullwhip effect* refers to erratic shifts in orders up and down the supply chain.

The most common solution to supply chain problems is *building inventories* as insurance against SC uncertainties. Another solution is the *just-in-time* (JIT) inventory system, which delivers the precise number of parts, called *work-in-process inventory*, to be assembled into a finished product at precisely the right time. The third possible solution is *vendor-managed inventory* (VMI), which occurs when the vendor, rather than the retailer, manages the entire inventory process for a particular product or group of products.

3. **Explain the utility of each of the three major technologies that support supply chain management.**

Electronic data interchange (EDI) is a communication standard that enables the electronic transfer of routine documents, such as purchasing orders, between business partners.

Extranets are networks that link business partners over the Internet by providing them access to certain areas of each other's corporate intranets. The main goal of extranets is to foster collaboration among business partners.

Corporate portals offer a single point of access through a Web browser to critical business information in an organization. In the context of business-to-business supply chain management, these portals enable companies and their suppliers to collaborate very closely.

Chapter Glossary

bullwhip effect Erratic shift s in orders up and down the supply chain.

distribution portals Corporate portals that automate the business processes involved in selling or distributing products from a single supplier to multiple buyers.

electronic data interchange (EDI) A communication standard that enables the electronic transfer of routine documents between business partners.

extranets Networks that link business partners over the Internet by providing them access to certain areas of each other's corporate intranets.

interorganizational information system (IOS) An information system that supports information flow among two or more organizations.

just-in-time (JIT) inventory system A system in which a supplier delivers the precise number of parts to be assembled into a finished product at precisely the right time.

procurement portals Corporate portals that automate the business processes involved in purchasing or procuring products between a single buyer and multiple suppliers.

pull model A business model in which the production process begins with a customer order and companies make only what customers want, a process closely aligned with mass customization.

push model A business model in which the production process begins with a forecast, which predicts the products that customers will want as well as the quantity of each product. The company then produces the amount of products in the forecast, typically by using mass production, and sells, or "pushes," those products to consumers.

supply chain The coordinated movement of *resources* from organizations through *conversion* to the end consumer.

supply chain management (SCM) An activity in which the leadership of an organization provides extensive oversight for the partnerships and processes that compose the supply chain and leverages these relationships to provide an operational advantage.

supply chain visibility The ability of all organizations in a supply chain to access or view relevant data on purchased materials as these materials move through their suppliers' production processes.

vendor-managed inventory (VMI) An inventory strategy where the supplier monitors a vendor's inventory for a product or group of products and replenishes products when needed.

vertical integration Strategy of integrating the upstream part of the supply chain with the internal part, typically by purchasing upstream suppliers, in order to ensure timely availability of supplies.

Discussion Questions

1. List and explain the important components of a supply chain.

2. Explain how a supply chain approach may be part of a company's overall strategy.

3. Explain the important role that information systems play in supporting a supply chain strategy.

4. Would Rolls-Royce Motorcars (www.rolls-roycemotorcars.com) use a push model or a pull model in its supply chain? Support your answer.

5. Why is planning so important in supply chain management?

Problem-Solving Activities

1. Enter www.supply-chain.org, www.cio.com, www.findarticles.com, and www.google.com, and search for recent information on supply chain management.

2. Surf the Web to find a procurement (sourcing) portal, a distribution portal, and an exchange (other than the examples presented in this chapter). List the features they have in common and those features that are unique.

Closing Case 1

 Amazon Deals with the Weather and Its Supply Chain Partners

The Problem

More than 20 years after completing its first sale, Amazon has become an online retailing powerhouse that is competing with bricks-and-mortar global retailers such as Walmart and Target. In addition, it is competing in the digital marketplace (e.g., ebooks, music, movies, and TV shows) with Apple's iTunes store and Google's Google Play.

Amazon's goal is to provide customers with the best selection, price, and availability. Sometimes the best price is not the lowest, but the one that provides the best shipping option. Amazon's Web site and apps offer a simple, consistent, and reliable user experience. Product information, prices, customer reviews, related products, recommended products, shipping information, and more appear in the same location on the page. Amazon's analytics systems use a customer's order and search history to create customized experiences for that customer, and Amazon's order fulfillment process delivers products swiftly and accurately.

Supply chain management is critical to Amazon's success. In 1995, Amazon began with two fulfillment centers. The company has now expanded to more than 165 distribution and fulfillment centers located around the world. Amazon supports this operation with a proprietary, in-house information system that is completely integrated. When the company receives an order, the order-management, inventory-management, and warehouse-management systems locate products around the world and determine the optimal fulfillment plan. *Fulfillment* is the business term that refers to the steps involved in receiving, processing, and delivering orders to the end customer. For Amazon, a global company with many products in many distribution centers, and many orders that require cooperation across centers (meaning the entire order cannot be fulfilled through one distribution center), fulfillment requires a very high level of coordination.

MIS To achieve this coordination, Amazon has to know where every product is located in every distribution center worldwide. For example, when suppliers send products to be "Fulfilled by Amazon" (FBA), their products are immediately scanned into Amazon's inventory-management system. A "stower" then places the goods in any available bin. Items are not organized in any logical manner. However, the product and bin location are recorded by the proprietary information system. When an order is received, a "picker" will walk through the warehouse, guided along an optimal route by a scanner (powered by the proprietary information system) to the proper bins in order to select the items. The pickers then bring the items to an "organizer," who begins preparing them for delivery. Prepared boxes are sent down the "slam line," where the packages are weighed and "slammed" with a shipping label. Finally, labeled packages are sorted to appropriate loading docks based on the shipping company that will handle the delivery.

Despite the effectiveness of Amazon's proprietary information system, several key factors, such as the weather, partner delivery companies, and the competition, remain beyond the company's control. For example, during the 2013 holiday season, several companies, including Amazon, Kohl's, and 1-800-flowers.com, promised last-minute delivery without taking into account the capacity of the parcel-delivery companies, FedEx (www.fedex.com) and UPS (www.ups.com), which

were unable to meet the demand. In addition to the demand overload, inclement weather also strained the delivery system. Under normal conditions, parcel-delivery companies can adjust delivery to account for weather. During the 2013 holiday season, however, these companies were already operating at capacity. As a result they could not make the necessary adjustments to account for inclement weather.

After the 2013 holiday season, Amazon tried to smooth things over with its customers by offering gift cards or credit. More importantly, the retailer determined that it needed to implement certain structural changes to expand its control over its entire supply chain and distribution system.

The IT Solution

Amazon needed to develop a method to increase its control over the delivery of its products. One common strategy to increase efficiencies and control is to reduce the number of steps in a system. Significantly, Amazon adopted the opposite approach, adding more sorting centers to its distribution channel. Sorting centers sort pre-packaged orders by zip code. This process enables Amazon to control delivery along the entire route to the local post office for Sunday delivery (in select markets). In certain markets where Amazon owns a delivery system, the company can now maintain control all the way to the customer's door.

Adding a step in the distribution system required Amazon to update its proprietary information system. Previously, once the system had "slammed" a delivery sticker onto a package, Amazon was basically out of the delivery loop. The retailer might maintain tracking (if offered by the delivery company), but it was not in control of the delivery. After adding the new step, the fulfillment center would maintain the package, and the system would direct the pre-packaged order to the appropriate sorting center. When packages arrived at the center, the information system would sort them by zip code. They were then delivered to the local post office or to another carrier for the "last mile" of delivery. In select cities, Amazon maintains its own delivery service. In other cities, the company has contracted with the U.S. Postal Service (USPS) to deliver on Sundays.

Sunday delivery spreads the delivery service over another day of the week, thereby reducing the workload on the other six days. This shift, coupled with the use of sorting centers, enabled Amazon to expand its operations, increase control, and offload some delivery work to another day of the week.

The Results

The additional step and the enhanced coordination enabled by Amazon's proprietary information system increased the company's control over its supply chain and reduced its dependence on parcel-delivery companies. Having learned from the 2013 holiday delivery debacle, Amazon expanded its operations and achieved a strategic advantage by gaining more control over its supply chain.

Amazon's sorting centers, updated supply chain management system, and agreement with the USPS helped the company achieve a record year in 2015. The retailer shipped to more than 185 countries, added more than 54 million Prime Members. In addition, Amazon reported no major problems with the new delivery system. Finally, the company reported sales revenue of $107 billion.

Amazon's updated system has generated some unintended consequences. For example, the increased demand on Sunday delivery through the USPS has increased the agency's workload and caused some postal workers to complain about 60-hour weeks and working 21 consecutive days. Although this problem is beyond Amazon's control, it does impact the firm's operations because it could lead to delivery delays. Additionally, other retailers have contracted with the USPS to offer Sunday delivery, putting more strain on Amazon's ability to rely on the agency as a delivery option.

Sources: Compiled from S. Soper, "Amazon Snags Sorting From FedEx to Avert Package Pileups," *Bloomberg.com*, December 9, 2014; M. Schlangenstein, L. Patton, and A. Barinka, "UPS Shipping Delays Show Perils of Stores Overpromising," *Bloomberg.com*, December 27, 2013; B. Bacheldor, "From Scratch: Amazon Keeps Supply Chain Close To Home," *Information Week*, March 5, 2004; J. Del Ray, "This Is What It Looks Like Inside an Amazon Warehouse," *All Things Digital*, December 23, 2013; B. Thau, "A Post-Mortem On the Holiday '13 Retail Shipping Debacle and Remedies for '14," *Forbes*, January 28, 2014; J. Greene, "Amazon's New

Sorting Centers Aim to Help with Controlling Deliveries," *The Seattle Times*, July 28, 2014; B. Stone, "Amazon's Grand Plan to Avoid Holiday Delivery Snafus Again," *Bloomberg.com*, September 26, 2014; T. Duryee, "Postal Workers Overwhelmed by Flood of Amazon Sunday Deliveries," *Geek Wire*, December 16, 2014; J. D'Onfro, "Amazon: Here's the Final Tally For All the Insane Shopping Everyone Did This Holiday Season," *Business Insider*, December 26, 2014; "Amazon Global Fulfillment Center Network," http://www.mwpvl.com/html/amazon_com.html, accessed October 21, 2015; www.amazon.com, www.ups.com, www.fedex.com, www.usps.com, accessed October 21, 2015.

Questions

1. Describe the problems that Amazon faced during the 2013 holiday season.
2. Discuss how Amazon solved those problems via its supply chain management system.

Closing Case 2

POM   Sustainability by the Supply Chain

The Problem

Sustainable business practices—including green business, environmental responsibility, minimal impact on global or local environment, and the use of renewable clean energy sources—have become more than just a good idea in many industries. History has taught us that non-sustainable business practices—such as early settlers killing off bison for their hides—lead to the rapid decline of an industry.

Tectona grandis, or teak wood, is a prized—and expensive—material due to its elegance and durability. Teak is a tree native to the tropics in the Southeast Asian nations of Thailand, Burma, Malaysia, and Indonesia. Historically, it has been found only in the homes of wealthy and powerful families. A tree takes about 80 years to reach maturity and be ready to harvest. Even then, only the heart of the tree contains the best wood for building furniture. Given the length of time required to replenish a forest, it is critical for the teak furniture industry to use sustainable practices.

Most teak farms are independently owned, and they operate based on traditional practices rather than current knowledge about how to efficiently manage a forest. Historically, they have not been connected to the global supply chain. As a result, they might not understand the impact of their decisions on the overall industry. This situation, however, is beginning to change. Dipantara (http://www.en.dipantara.co.id), a company engaged in Sustainable Community Forest Enterprise Management, works with the growers to emphasize the importance of maintaining their natural resources. Dipantara is particularly interested in teak.

In addition to the teak farms, several other parties are involved in this industry. First, there are independent, nonprofit organizations such as the Forestry Stewardship Council (http://us.fsc.org; FSC) that promote the responsible management of the world's forests. FSC also provides industry certifications that a farm has pursued sustainable management practices. Second, European, U.S., and Australian timber regulations have been established to prevent companies from doing harm to the forests. Finally, customers want assurance that their purchase is not harming the global environment.

These sustainability issues create challenges along the supply chain from the retailer to the root (quite literally). They require a

coordinated effort to develop and maintain a consistent sustainability effort.

The IT Solution

The Forestry Trust (www.tft-earth.org; TFT) is an NGO that focuses on the entire supply chain ecosystem, where all needs must be considered for the industry as a whole to operate and exist sustainably. TFT identifies transparency as the key to establishing this sustainability. To support this level of communication and transparency, the NGO developed a set of tools called SURE Technology that provide its members with transparency dashboards, supply chain management, and product stories. SURE is designed to help growers and companies throughout the supply chain to plan, understand, and communicate.

TFT members use the SURE Technology system to balance the interests and requirements of several external stakeholders. The only way any company can meet the demands of its external stakeholders is to obtain information about the practices of the suppliers of their raw materials. The SURE supply chain management module maps companies' products all the way to the source to help product manufacturers ensure that their orders are the products of legal, responsible, sustainable harvesting and use of the forest.

The SURE Technology allows raw material providers (such as members of the Dipantara community forests in Java) to identify their social and environmental values and track their progress on adhering to those values through dashboards. This information is available to potential buyers, who require confirmation that the materials are provided in a manner that is consistent with their values.

The Results

Maisons du Monde (www.maisonsdumonde.com; MdM) is an environmentally focused home decoration retailer based in France. As a member of TFT, the firm works with Dipantara community farmers in Java, who supply the teak for some of their furniture. MdM has access to information on the forestry practices of the entire supply chain through its TFT membership and the SURE Technology tools that are part of that membership. The result is that more than 50% of MdM products are labeled with one or more industry certifications affirming that the product is not contributing to deforestation. Further, MdM sells more than 1100 products that carry the FSC logo that confirms that the products were manufactured by responsible sources and can be traced all the way to the tree stump.

How is this possible? The answer is the use of the industry supply chain system provided by TFT. The SURE Technology tools bring together all of the supply chain parties into a single platform to create a more transparent, environmentally friendly use of our natural resources.

Sources: Compiled from J. Clark, "What's So Great about Teak Wood Furniture," *howstuffworks.com*, accessed December 14, 2015; S. Hickman, "Indonesian Teak Farmers Achieve Traceability to the Tree Stump,"

The Guardian, March 18, 2014; www.maisonsdumonde.com; www .onepercentfortheplanet.org, www.tft-earth.org; www.en.dipantara.co.id; www.us.fcs.org; www.tft-earth.org/sure; www.theevergreengroup.com; accessed October 26, 2015.

Questions

1. Describe the role of information technology along the teak wood supply chain.

2. Refer to Chapter 2. Is the SURE system a strategic information system for Maisons du Monde? Why or why not?

3. Refer to Chapter 10. How would the Internet of Things help The Forestry Trust in its mission?

adventtr/iStockphoto

Acquiring Information Systems and Applications

LEARNING OBJECTIVES

14.1 Discuss the different cost–benefit analyses that companies must take into account when formulating an IT strategic plan.

14.2 Discuss the four business decisions that companies must make when they acquire new applications.

14.3 Enumerate the primary tasks and the importance of each of the six processes involved in the systems development life cycle.

14.4 Describe alternative development methods and the tools that augment these methods.

Opening Case

 Peoples State Bank Transforms Its Information Technology

The Business Problem

With 15 full-service retail and commercial locations, Peoples State Bank (PSB; www.psbwi.com) has provided central and northern Wisconsin

residents and locally owned businesses with traditional retail and commercial banking products since 1914. Businesses this old often have information systems that have become outdated and no longer meet their needs. These systems, referred to as *legacy systems,* often hinder modern business operations. This was the case with PSB.

PSB's strategic goals are to provide its customers with a superb experience and its employees with the best possible tools and resources. Unfortunately the bank's legacy systems were impeding its ability to accomplish those goals.

Legacy systems in banking provided the core processing necessary to handle simple account transactions such as deposits, withdrawals, and payments. These systems were expensive to build, because they required on-premise hardware, software, and networking technologies. (We discuss on-premise computing in Plug IT In 4.) In general, legacy systems at banks were developed to support hard copy, paper-based transactions. These legacy systems became ineffective over the years because they did not support different ways for customers to interact with the bank (e.g., online from computers, tablets, and smartphones).

Banks were very slow to respond to online business models because their business processes were built on legacy systems that were not designed to engage customers online. Specifically, PSB employed an excessive number of legacy systems, which did not effectively work together. In addition, the bank's information technology platform did not provide the capabilities required for a PSB customer to access account information via a Web browser or mobile app.

To offer superb customer experiences and modern banking tools, PSB needed a new IT infrastructure that was designed to handle Web and mobile banking and near-real-time customer updates. The challenge was that the bank's in-house IT expertise was able to maintain the legacy systems, but it lacked the capability to design or build new systems. For PSB to move forward with their strategic goals, it had to acquire an IT infrastructure that would include the necessary tools to operate in the modern banking environment.

The Solution

Leif Christianson, PSB's Chief Operating Officer, spearheaded a complete technology overhaul that moved the bank away from their legacy systems. Today, when businesses decide to update their systems, they can consider several options. One option was on-premise computing, in which PSB would develop, own, and operate all parts of its IT function. Alternatively, the bank could outsource the entire system. Both models offered advantages. Ultimately, PSB determined that IT was not one of its core competencies (providing outstanding customer service in banking was). The bank therefore decided that outsourcing would allow enable it to scale its operations for growth more quickly than if it owned and operated the IT infrastructure. To implement this plan, PSB entered into a service agreement with Jack Henry & Associates (JHA; www.jackhenry.com) to gain access to the tools and technology it needed without having to develop the expertise within their organization.

JHA, founded in 1976, is a leading provider of computer systems and ATM/debit card/ACH transaction processing services for financial services organizations. (ACH payments are electronic payments that are created when the customer gives an originating institution the authorization to debit directly from the customer's checking or savings account for the purpose of bill payment.) JHA's technology solutions serve more than 11,000 customers nationwide. PSB transferred all of their banking information system operations to JHA.

The Results

The conversion from PSB's legacy system to the JHA solution was a success. This transition brought new core capabilities to the bank. With JHA, PSB is able to offer online banking, mobile banking, customer payment solutions, and other services that were not available with the legacy systems. As a result, PSB's assets grew from before the 2010 conversion to more than $784 million in 2015. By outsourcing the capital expense and maintenance of on-premise information technology, PSB was able to focus on other priorities such as cross-training employees to help customers in areas where they previously were not able to provide service.

Managing change of this size is often difficult for organizations because employees are frequently resistant. However, PSB convinced its employees of the benefits of the new system. As a result the bank received quick employee buy-in and cooperation. Employees appreciated the fact that they could now deliver services in the ways their customers wanted.

Today, PSB customers are able to check account information, pay bills and transfer funds, view a detailed transaction history, download statements, deposit checks, and perform other activities through their mobile banking experience. These tools have enabled PSB to compete with much larger banks.

Sources: Compiled from D. Verman, "Banks Face Major Pressure to Transform Legacy Payment Systems," *PaymentSoursce.com*, July 27, 2015; K. Flinders, "The Obstacles to Software-as-a-Service Adoption in Banking," *ComputerWeekly.com*, July 15, 2015; P. Schaus, "Legacy Systems Prevent Banks From Delivering on Digital Promises," *BankInnovation.net*, June 1, 2015; K. Burger, "Outsourcing Helps Peoples State Bank Execute Growth Strategy," *Information Week*, December 3, 2014; J. Lankenau, "The Benefits of SaaS," *banktech.com*, October 9, 2014; K. Flinders, "Big Banks' Legacy IT Systems Could Kill Them," *ComputerWeekly.com*, January, 2014; peoplesfinancial.com, jackhenry.com, accessed October 29, 2015.

Questions

1. Discuss the problems with PSB's legacy systems that led to the information technology conversion.

2. Why did PSB decide to outsource their IT rather than developing new systems in-house as they had in the past?

3. What are the potential disadvantages that PSB might encounter from outsourcing its IT function?

Introduction

Competitive organizations move as quickly as they can to acquire new information technologies or modify existing ones when they need to improve efficiencies and gain strategic advantage. As you learned from the chapter opening case, problems and pitfalls can arise from the acquisition process.

Today, acquisition goes beyond building new systems in-house, and IT resources involve far more than software and hardware. As you saw in the chapter opening case, the old model in which firms built their own systems is being replaced with a broader perspective of IT resource acquisition that provides companies with a number of options. Thus, companies now must decide which IT tasks will remain in-house, and even whether the entire IT resource should be provided and managed by outside organizations. Regardless of which approach an organization chooses, however, it must be able to manage IT projects adeptly.

In this chapter, you will learn about the process of acquiring IT resources from a managerial perspective. This means from *your* perspective, because you will be closely involved in all aspects of acquiring information systems and applications in your organization. In fact, when we mention "users" in this chapter, we are talking about you. You will also study the available options for acquiring IT resources and how to evaluate those options. Finally, you will learn how organizations plan and justify the acquisition of new information systems.

14.1 Planning for and Justifying IT Applications

Organizations must analyze the need for applications and then justify each purchase in terms of costs and benefits. The need for information systems is usually related to organizational planning and to the analysis of its performance vis-à-vis its competitors. The cost–benefit justification must consider the wisdom of investing in a specific IT application versus spending the funds on alternative projects. This chapter focuses on the formal processes of large organizations. Smaller organizations employ less formal processes, or no processes at all. It is important to note, however, that even if a small organization does not have a formal process for planning and justifying IT applications, the steps of a formal process exist for a reason, and they have value. At the very least, decision makers in small organizations should consider each step when they are planning changes in their information systems.

When a company examines its needs and performance, it generates a prioritized list of both existing and potential IT applications, called the **application portfolio**. These are the applications that have to be added, or modified if they already exist.

IT Planning

The planning process for new IT applications begins with an analysis of the *organizational strategic plan*, which is illustrated in Figure 14.1. The organization's strategic plan identifies the

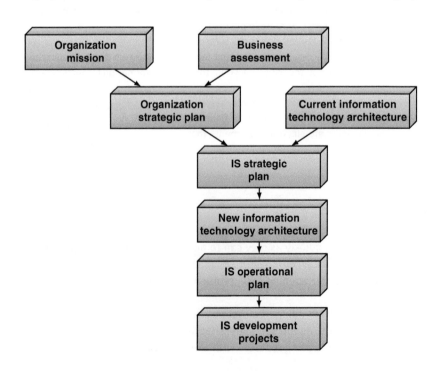

FIGURE 14.1 The information systems planning process.

Organization mission

Business assessment

Organization strategic plan

Current information technology architecture

IS strategic plan

New information technology architecture

IS operational plan

IS development projects

firm's overall mission, the goals that follow from that mission, and the broad steps required to reach these goals. The strategic planning process modifies the organization's objectives and resources to match its changing markets and opportunities.

The organizational strategic plan and the existing IT architecture provide the inputs in developing the IT strategic plan. The *IT architecture* delineates the way an organization should utilize its information resources to accomplish its mission. It encompasses both the technical and the managerial aspects of information resources. The technical aspects include hardware and operating systems, networking, data management systems, and applications software. The managerial aspects specify how the IT department will be managed, how the functional area managers will be involved, and how IT decisions will be made.

The IT strategic plan is a set of long-range goals that describe the IT infrastructure and identify the major IT initiatives needed to achieve the organization's goals. The IT strategic plan must meet three objectives:

1. *It must be aligned with the organization's strategic plan*. This alignment is critical because the organization's information systems must support the organization's strategies. (Recall the discussion of organizational strategies and information systems in Chapter 2.)

   Consider the example of Nordstrom versus Walmart. An application that improves customer service at a small cost would be considered favorably at Nordstrom, but it would be rejected at Walmart. The reason is that the application would fit in favorably (i.e., align) with Nordstrom's service-at-any-cost strategy. However, it would not fit in well with Walmart's low-cost strategy. You see two department stores, same application, same cost and benefits—but different answers to the question "Should we develop the application?"

2. *It must provide for an IT architecture that seamlessly networks users, applications, and databases.*

3. *It must efficiently allocate IS development resources among competing projects so that the projects can be completed on time and within budget and still have the required functionality.*

The existing IT architecture is a necessary input into the IT strategic plan because it acts as a constraint on future development efforts. It is not an absolute constraint, however, because the organization can change to a new IT architecture. Companies prefer to avoid this strategy, however, because it is expensive and time consuming.

Consider this example. You have a Mac (Apple) system, and you need a new software application. You search and find several such packages for both Mac and MS Windows. Unfortunately, the best package runs only on Windows. How much better would this package have to be for you to justify switching from Mac to Windows?

One critical component in developing and implementing the IT strategic plan is the IT steering committee. This committee, comprised of a group of managers and staff who represent the various organizational units, is created to establish IT priorities and to ensure that the MIS function is meeting the organization's needs. The committee's major tasks are to link corporate strategy with IT strategy, to approve the allocation of resources for the MIS function, and to establish performance measures for the MIS function and ensure they are met. The IT steering committee is important to you because it ensures that you get the information systems and applications that you need to do your job.

After a company has agreed on an IT strategic plan, it next develops the IS operational plan. This plan consists of a clear set of projects that the IS department and the functional area managers will execute in support of the IT strategic plan. A typical IS operational plan contains the following elements:

- *Mission:* The mission of the IS function (derived from the IT strategy).
- *IS environment:* A summary of the information needs of the individual functional areas and of the organization as a whole.
- *Objectives of the IS function:* The best current estimate of the goals of the IS function.

- *Constraints on the IS function:* Technological, financial, personnel, and other resource limitations on the IS function.
- *The application portfolio:* A prioritized inventory of present applications and a detailed plan of projects to be developed or continued during the current year.
- *Resource allocation and project management:* A listing of who is going to do what, how, and when.

Evaluating and Justifying IT Investment: Benefits, Costs, and Issues

Developing an IT plan is the first step in the acquisition process. Because all companies have limited resources, they must justify investing resources in some areas, including IT, rather than in others. Essentially, justifying IT investment involves calculating the costs, assessing the benefits (values), and comparing the two. This comparison is frequently referred to as cost–benefit analysis. Cost–benefit analysis is not a simple task.

Assessing the Costs. Calculating the dollar value of IT investments is not as simple as it may seem. One of the major challenges that companies face is to allocate fixed costs among different IT projects. *Fixed costs* are those costs that remain the same regardless of any change in the company's activity level. Fixed IT costs include infrastructure costs and the costs associated with IT services and IT management. For example, the salary of the IT director is fixed, and adding one more application will not change it.

Another complication is that the costs of a system do not end when the system is installed. Rather, costs for maintaining, debugging, and improving the system can accumulate over many years. This is a critical point because organizations sometimes fail to anticipate these costs when they make the investment.

A dramatic example of unanticipated expenses was the Year 2000 (Y2K) reprogramming projects, which cost organizations worldwide billions of dollars. In the 1960s, computer memory was very expensive. To save money, programmers coded the "year" in the date field 19_ _, instead of _ _ _ _. With the "1" and the "9" hard-coded in the computer program, only the last two digits varied, so computer programs needed less memory. However, this process meant that when the year 2000 rolled around, computers would display the year as 1900. This programming technique could have caused serious problems with financial applications, insurance applications, and countless other apps.

The Y2K example illustrates the point that database design choices tend to affect the organization for a long time. As the 21st century approached, no one still used hardware or software from the 1960s (other than a few legacy applications). Database design choices made in the 1960s, however, were often still in effect decades after the companies implemented them.

Assessing the Benefits. Evaluating the benefits of IT projects is typically even more complex than calculating their costs. Benefits may be more difficult to quantify, especially because many of them are intangible (for example, improved customer or partner relations and improved decision making). As an employee, you will probably be asked for input about the intangible benefits that an IS provides for you.

The fact that organizations use IT for multiple purposes further complicates benefit analysis. In addition, to obtain a return from an IT investment, the company must implement the technology successfully. In reality, many systems are not implemented on time, within budget, or with all of the features originally envisioned for them. Also, the proposed system may be "cutting edge." In these cases, there may be no precedent for identifying the types of financial payback the company can expect.

Conducting the Cost-Benefit Analysis. After a company has assessed the costs and benefits of IT investments, it must compare them. You have studied, or will study, cost–benefit analyses in more detail in your finance courses. The point is that real-world business problems do not come in neatly wrapped packages labeled "this is a finance problem" or "this is an IS problem." Rather, business problems span multiple functional areas.

There is no uniform strategy for conducting a cost–benefit analysis. Rather, an organization can perform this task in several ways. Here you see four common approaches: (1) net present value, (2) return on investment, (3) breakeven analysis, and (4) the business case approach:

1. Analysts use the *net present value (NPV)* method to convert future values of benefits to their present-value equivalent by "discounting" them at the organization's cost of funds. They can then compare the present value of the future benefits with the cost required to achieve those benefits to determine whether the benefits exceed the costs.

2. *Return on investment (ROI)* measures management's effectiveness in generating profits with its available assets. ROI is calculated by dividing the net income generated by a project by the average assets invested in the project. ROI is a percentage, and the higher the percentage return, the better.

3. *Breakeven analysis* determines the point at which the cumulative dollar value of the benefits from a project equals the investment made in the project.

4. In the *business case approach*, system developers write a business case to justify funding one or more specific applications or projects. IS professionals will be a major source of input when business cases are developed because these cases describe what you do, how you do it, and how a new system could better support you.

Before you go on . . .

1. What are some problems associated with assessing the costs of IT?
2. Why are the intangible benefits from IT so difficult to evaluate?
3. Describe the NPV, ROI, breakeven analysis, and business case approaches.

Apply the Concept 14.1

LEARNING OBJECTIVE 14.1 Discuss the different cost/benefit analyses that companies must take into account when formulating an IT strategic plan.

STEP 1: Background (Here is what you are learning.)

You may not realize it, but you perform cost-benefit analyses all the time. Imagine that you want to go to the beach for the weekend, but you decide not to because you would have to drive eight hours each way and therefore would not get to spend much time there. In this case, the costs outweigh the benefits. However, if you could extend your stay another day, then the benefits might outweigh the costs. The difficulty in this example is that the benefits are difficult to measure. A cost/benefit analysis is designed to quantify all of the key elements, and sometimes there are subjective benefits for which there are no clear-cut numerical values.

STEP 2: Activity (Here is what you are doing)

Visit http://www.wiley.com/go/rainer/MIS4e/applytheconcept, and click on the links provided for Apply the Concept 14.1.

You will watch three short videos that offer a financial explanation for net present value (NPV), return on investment (ROI), and breakeven analysis. The business case approach is not a financial approach, and it does not require further explanation.

STEP 3: Deliverable (Here is what you turn in.)

Imagine you are creating a Web site to sell promotional items. You have no experience developing a site, so you will have to pay someone to do this for you. You research this service and discover that the site you have in mind will cost $3,500. (For this example, assume there are no monthly hosting fees.) This design will last five years, after which you will need to update it. You anticipate that you can make $500 in year 1, $750 in year 2, $750 in year 3, $1,000 in year 4, and $1,500 in year 5 from the site. Calculate the NPV, ROI, and breakeven analysis for this case, and discuss which metric is most helpful. Also, explain how a business case analysis would be helpful beyond what the numbers provide. Prepare a document with your figures and present it to your instructor.

14.2 Strategies for Acquiring IT Applications

After a company has justified an IT investment, it must then decide how to pursue it. As with cost–benefit analyses, there are several options for acquiring IT applications. To select the best option, companies must make a series of business decisions. The fundamental decisions are the following:

- *How much computer code does the company want to write?* A company can choose to use a totally prewritten application (write no computer code), to customize a prewritten application (write some computer code), or to custom-write an entire application (write all new computer code).
- *How will the company pay for the application?* Once the company has decided how much computer code to write, it must decide how to pay for it. With prewritten applications or customized prewritten applications, companies can buy them or lease them. With totally custom applications, companies use internal funding.
- *Where will the application run?* The next decision is whether to run the application on the company's platform or on someone else's platform. In other words, the company can employ either a software-as-a-service vendor or an application service provider. (You will examine these options later in this chapter.)
- *Where will the application originate?* Prewritten applications can be open-source software or they can come from a vendor. The company may choose to customize prewritten open-source applications or prewritten proprietary applications from vendors. Further, it may customize applications in-house, or it can outsource the customization. Finally, it can write totally custom applications in-house, or it can outsource this process.

In the following sections, you will find more details on the variety of options that companies looking to acquire applications can select from. A good rule of thumb is that an organization should consider all feasible acquisition methods in light of its business requirements. You will learn about the following acquisition methods:

- Purchase a prewritten application.
- Customize a prewritten application.
- Lease the application.
- Use application service providers and software-as-a-service vendors.
- Use open-source software.
- Use outsourcing.
- Employ continuous development.
- Employ custom development.

Purchase a Prewritten Application

Many commercial software packages contain the standard features required by IT applications. Therefore, purchasing an existing package can be a cost-effective and time-saving strategy compared with custom-developing the application in-house. Nevertheless, a company should carefully consider and plan the buy option to ensure that the selected package contains all of the features necessary to address the company's current and future needs. Otherwise, these packages can quickly become obsolete. Before a company can perform this process, it must decide which features a suitable package must include.

In reality, a single software package can rarely satisfy all of an organization's needs. For this reason, a company sometimes must purchase multiple packages to fulfill different needs. It then must integrate these packages with one another as well as with its existing software. Table 14.1 summarizes the advantages and limitations of the buy option.

TABLE 14.1 Advantages and Limitations of the Buy Option

Advantages

Many different types of off-the-shelf software are available.

The company can try out the software before purchasing it.

The company can save much time by buying rather than building.

The company can know what it is getting before it invests in the product.

Purchased software may eliminate the need to hire personnel specifically dedicated to a project.

Disadvantages

Software may not exactly meet the company's needs.

Software may be difficult or impossible to modify, or it may require huge business process changes to implement.

The company will not have control over software improvements and new versions.

Purchased software can be difficult to integrate with existing systems.

Vendors may discontinue a product or go out of business.

Software is controlled by another company with its own priorities and business considerations.

The purchasing company lacks intimate knowledge about how and why the software functions as it does.

Customize a Prewritten Application

Customizing existing software is an especially attractive option if the software vendor allows the company to modify the application to meet its needs. However, this option may not be attractive in cases where customization is the *only* method of providing the necessary flexibility to address the company's needs. It also is not the best strategy when the software is either very expensive or likely to become obsolete in a short time. Further, customizing a prewritten application can be extremely difficult, particularly for large, complex applications.

Lease the Application

Compared with the buy option and the option to develop applications in-house, the lease option can save a company both time and money. Of course, leased packages (like purchased packages) may not exactly fit the company's application requirements. However, as noted, vendor software generally includes the features that are most commonly needed by organizations in a given industry. Again, the company will decide which features are necessary.

Interested companies commonly apply the 80/20 rule when they evaluate vendor software. Put simply, if the software meets 80 percent of the company's needs, then the company should seriously consider modifying its business processes so that it can utilize the remaining 20 percent. Many times this is a better long-term solution than modifying the vendor software. Otherwise, the company will have to customize the software every time the vendor releases an updated version.

Leasing can be especially attractive to small and medium-sized enterprises (SMEs) that cannot afford major investments in IT software. Large companies may also prefer to lease packages to test potential IT solutions before committing to major investments. In addition, a company that does not employ sufficient IT personnel with the appropriate skills for developing custom IT applications may choose to lease instead of developing software in-house. Even those companies that employ in-house experts may not be able to afford the long wait for strategic applications to be developed in-house. Therefore, they lease (or buy) applications from external resources to establish a quicker presence in the market.

Leasing can be executed in one of three ways. The first way is to lease the application from a software developer, install it, and run it on the company's platform. The vendor can assist with the installation and frequently will offer to contract for the support and maintenance of the system. Many conventional applications are leased this way.

The other two options involve leasing an application and running it on the vendor's platform. Organizations can accomplish this process by using an application service provider or a software-as-a-service vendor.

Application Service Providers and Software-as-a-Service Vendors

An **application service provider (ASP)** is an agent or a vendor who assembles the software needed by enterprises and then packages it with services such as development, operations, and maintenance. The customer then accesses these applications via the Internet. **Figure 14.2** illustrates the operation of an ASP. Note that the ASP hosts both an application and a database for each customer.

Software-as-a-service (SaaS) is a method of delivering software in which a vendor hosts the applications and provides them as a service to customers over a network, typically the Internet. Customers do not own the software; rather, they pay for using it. SaaS eliminates the need for customers to install and run the application on their own computers. Therefore, SaaS customers save the expense (money, time, IT staff) of buying, operating, and maintaining the software. For example, Salesforce (www.salesforce.com), a well-known SaaS provider for customer relationship management (CRM) software solutions, provides these advantages for its customers. **Figure 14.3** displays the operation of a SaaS vendor. Note that the vendor hosts an application that multiple customers can use. The vendor also hosts a database that is partitioned for each customer to protect the privacy and security of each customer's data.

FIGURE 14.2 Operation of an application service provider.

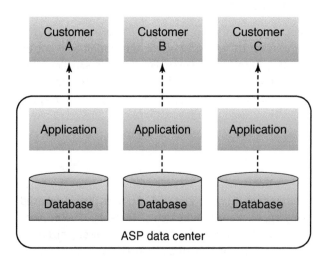

FIGURE 14.3 Operation of a software-as-a-service vendor.

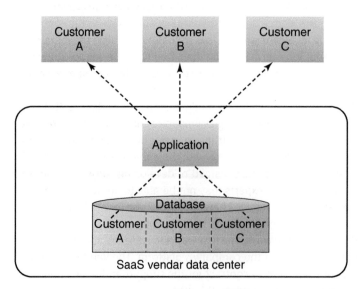

Both ASP and SaaS deliver software packages without requiring an installation on the end user's hardware. However, the method in which they provide the backend might change drastically in the near future. Containers are a method of developing applications that run independently of the base operating system of the server. Containers allow application providers to develop, test, and deploy technology that will always run in practice exactly like it does in testing. This would allow software to be developed more rapidly. See IT's About Business 14.1 for more on this new technology.

IT's About Business 14.1

MIS Containers

Application developers have always been plagued with platform challenges. (A platform is an underlying computer system on which application programs can run. On personal computers, Windows and Mac OS X are examples of platforms.) As one example, if a developer built an application in a Windows environment, then it might not run properly if it were deployed after a Windows update. In addition, it probably would not work in a Linux environment, either. Further, multiple versions of an application need to be developed to run on different environments, and they have to be continuously tested on platform updates.

One solution for this problem is to build and test applications on a virtual machine and then implement them on an identical virtual machine for customers. A *virtual machine* is a self-contained operating environment that behaves as if it were a separate physical computer. Building and testing on a virtual machine ensures that an application developed on one platform will run on a different platform. But, what if you could develop an application that included its own environment and would run as it was developed regardless of the operating system on which it was deployed? That is exactly the idea behind a container.

Containers are not new; in fact, they have been tested since 2005. However, they were not widely embraced by mainstream IT leaders until 2014. The increased popularity of containers is largely due to Docker, an open-source project by Docker, Inc. (https://www.docker.com/). Docker is a Linux-based product that enables applications to be developed and deployed in a container. Docker-created apps will run on any platform.

By late 2015, there were several open-source projects providing this type of container technology available. In addition, in August 2015 Microsoft announced container support in its Windows Server 2016 Technical Preview 3 release.

In response to security concerns, in November 2015 Docker announced an updated set of tools that proactively scan for security vulnerabilities of more than 90 percent of the official Docker repositories on a regular basis. In addition, CoreOS (https://coreos.com), an open-source competitor of Docker, Twistlock (https://www.twistlock.com), a startup tech company that focuses on container security, and Microsoft are all contributing to the development of secure container technology.

Containers are another step in the development of virtual technology. They might, for example, enable SaaS and ASP vendors to deliver products to their clients much more quickly and efficiently.

Sources: Compiled from C. Babcock, "Docker, CoreOS Push Containers to Center Stage," *InformationWeek*, December 29, 2014; P. Yared, "Goodbye SaaS—Hello Containers-as-a-Service," *Venturebeat*, May 9, 2015; P. Rubens, "What Are Containers and Why Do You Need Them?" *CIO.com*, May 20, 2015; A. Froehlich, "Containers 101: 10 Terms To Know" *InformationWeek*, September 2, 2015; M. Schutz, "What's New in Windows Server 2016 and System Center 2016 Technical Preview 3" *blogs.technet.com*, August 19, 2015; C. Babcock, "Containers March into Mainstream with Security, Management Updates," *InformationWeek*, November 20, 2015; F. Lardinois, "Docker Puts Focus on Container Security," *TechCrunch.com*, November 16, 2015; S. Legulalp, "Docker, Twistlock, CoreOS, and the State of Container Security," *InfoWorld Tech Watch*, December 7, 2015; S. Vaughan-Nichols, "Docker 1.8 Adds Serious Container Security," *ZDNet.com*, August 13, 2015; www.docker.com, www.coreos.com, www.twistlock.com, accessed December 14, 2015.

Questions

1. What does the container technology offer developers that traditional deployment methodologies do not?

2. What role do you think large companies like Microsoft and Docker, Inc. play in streamlining application development?

At this point, companies have made the first three decisions and must now decide where to obtain the application. Recall that in general, for prewritten applications, companies can use open-source software or obtain the software from a vendor. For customized prewritten applications, they can customize open-source software or customize vendor software. For totally custom applications, they can write the software in-house, or they can outsource the process.

Use Open-Source Software

Organizations obtain a license to implement an open-source software product and either use it as is, customize it, or develop applications with it. Unless the company is one of the few that want to tinker with their source code, open-source applications are, basically, the same as a proprietary application except for licensing, payment, and support. Open-source software is really an alternative source of applications rather than a conceptually different development option. (We discuss open-source software in Plug IT In 2.)

Outsourcing

Acquiring IT applications from outside contractors or external organizations is called outsourcing. Companies can utilize outsourcing in many situations. For example, they might want to experiment with new IT technologies without making a substantial up-front investment. They also might use outsourcing to obtain access to outside experts. One disadvantage of outsourcing is that companies frequently must place their valuable corporate data under the control of the outsourcing vendor.

Several types of vendors offer services for creating and operating IT systems, including e-commerce applications. Many software companies, from IBM to Oracle, offer a range of outsourcing services for developing, operating, and maintaining IT applications. IT outsourcers, such as EDS, offer a variety of services. Also, the large CPA companies and management consultants—for example, Accenture—offer outsourcing services.

For example, in September 2014, Philip Morris International (the non-U.S. operation of Philip Morris) outsourced its IT infrastructure management to Indian services firm Wipro. The companies concluded a five-year contract where Wipro manages the tobacco company's applications and IT using Wipro's cloud-based management platform. (We discuss cloud computing in Plug IT In 4.) The contract is reported to be worth some $35 million U.S.

Some companies outsource offshore, particularly in India and China. *Offshoring* can save money, but it includes risks as well. The risks depend on which services are being offshored. If a company is offshoring application development, then the major risk is poor communication between users and developers. In response to these risks, some companies are bringing outsourced jobs back in-house, a process called *reverse outsourcing*, or *insourcing*. (See chapter closing case 1.)

Continuous Development

Continuous application development automates and improves the process of software delivery. In essence, a software development project is not viewed as having a defined product, with development stopped when the product is implemented. Rather, a software development project is viewed as constantly changing in response to changing business conditions and in response to user acceptance.

Continuous application development is the process of steadily adding new computer code to a software project when the new computer code is written and tested. Each development team member submits new code when it is finished. Automated testing is performed on the code to ensure that it functions within the software project. Continuous code submission provides developers with immediate feedback from users and status updates for the software on which they are working.

Employ Custom Development

Another option is to custom-build an application. Companies can either perform this operation in-house or outsource the process. Although custom development is usually more time consuming and costly than buying or leasing, it often produces a better fit with the organization's specific requirements.

The development process starts when the IT steering committee (discussed previously in this chapter), having received suggestions for a new system, decides it is worth exploring. These suggestions come from users (who will be you in the near future). Understanding this process will help you obtain the systems that you need. Conversely, not understanding this process will reduce your chances, because other people who understand it better will make suggestions that use up available resources.

As the company goes through the development process, its mind-set changes. In systems investigation (the first stage of the traditional systems development life cycle), the organization is trying to decide whether to build something. Everyone knows it may or may not be built. In the later stages of the development process, the organization is committed to building the application. Although a project can be cancelled at any time, this change in attitude is still important.

The basic, backbone methodology for custom development is the systems development life cycle (SDLC), which you will read about in the next section. Section 14.4 examines the methodologies that complement the SDLC: prototyping, joint application development, integrated computer-assisted systems development tools, and rapid application development. You will also consider four other methodologies: agile development, end-user development, component-based development, and object-oriented development.

Before you go on . . .

1. Describe the four fundamental business decisions that organizations must make when acquiring information systems.

2. Discuss each of the seven development methods in this section with regard to the four business decisions that organizations must make.

Apply the Concept 14.2

LEARNING OBJECTIVE 14.2 Discuss the four business decisions that companies must make when they acquire new applications.

STEP 1: Background

Section 14.2 has discussed the many options available to acquire information systems. One of the more popular methods is software-as-a-service (SaaS). SaaS is popular because it eliminates the need for the company purchasing the software to maintain the hardware that the software will run on. They simply need an Internet connection to access the software from the host company.

STEP 2: Activity

Visit http://www.wiley.com/go/rainer/MIS4e/applytheconcept, and click on the links provided for Apply the Concept 14.2. There

are two videos linked there that illustrate SaaS. As you watch these videos, consider the types of hardware that are required on both sides of the relationship. Also, give some thought to the legal nature of the relationship, given that the data will likely reside with the service provider.

STEP 3: Deliverable

Imagine that a company has decided to use a SaaS model to acquire a new piece of software. Prepare a paper discussing the four business decisions they have made in light of this type of acquisition. Submit your paper to your instructor.

14.3 Traditional Systems Development Life Cycle

The systems development life cycle is the traditional systems development method that organizations use for large-scale IT projects. The SDLC is a structured framework that consists of sequential processes by which information systems are developed. For our purposes (see Figure 14.4), we identify six processes, each of which consists of clearly defined tasks:

1. Systems investigation
2. Systems analysis

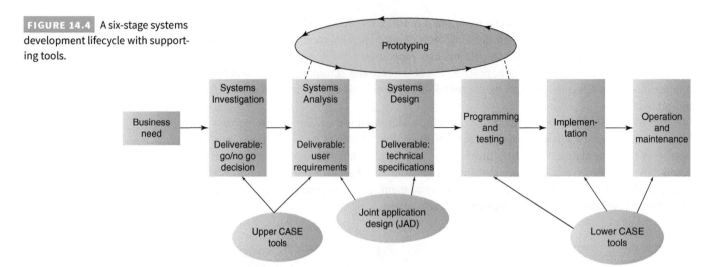

FIGURE 14.4 A six-stage systems development lifecycle with supporting tools.

3. Systems design
4. Programming and testing
5. Implementation
6. Operation and maintenance

Alternative SDLC models contain more or fewer stages. The flow of tasks, however, remains largely the same. When problems occur in any phase of the SDLC, developers often must go back to previous phases.

Systems development projects produce desired results through team efforts. Development teams typically include users, systems analysts, programmers, and technical specialists. *Users* are employees from all functional areas and levels of the organization who interact with the system, either directly or indirectly. **Systems analysts** are IS professionals who specialize in analyzing and designing information systems. **Programmers** are IS professionals who either modify existing computer programs or write new programs to satisfy user requirements. **Technical specialists** are experts on a certain type of technology, such as databases or telecommunications. The **systems stakeholders** include everyone who is affected by changes in a company's information systems—for example, users and managers. All stakeholders are typically involved in systems development at various times and in varying degrees.

Figure 14.5 indicates that users have high involvement in the early stages of the SDLC, lower involvement in the programming and testing stage, and higher involvement in the later stages. **Table 14.2** discusses the advantages and disadvantages of the SDLC.

FIGURE 14.5 Comparison of user and developer involvement over the SDLC.

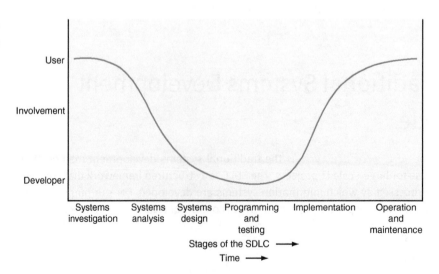

TABLE 14.2 Advantages and Disadvantages of System Acquisition Methods

Traditional Systems Development (SDLC)

Advantages

- Forces staff to systematically go through every step in a structured process.
- Enforces quality by maintaining standards.
- Has lower probability of missing important issues in collecting user requirements.

Disadvantages

- May produce excessive documentation.
- Users may be unwilling or unable to study the approved specifications.
- Takes too long to progress from the original ideas to a working system.
- Users have trouble describing requirements for a proposed system.

Prototyping

Advantages

- Helps clarify user requirements.
- Helps verify the feasibility of the design.
- Promotes genuine user participation.
- Promotes close working relationship between systems developers and users.
- Works well for ill-defined problems.
- May produce part of the final system.

Disadvantages

- May encourage inadequate problem analysis.
- Is not practical with large number of users.
- User may not want to give up the prototype when the system is completed.
- May generate confusion about whether the system is complete and maintainable.
- System may be built quickly, which can result in lower quality.

Joint Application Design

Advantages

- Involves many users in the development process.
- Saves time.
- Generates greater user support for the new system.
- Improves the quality of the new system.
- The new system is easier to implement.
- The new system has lower training costs.

Disadvantages

- It is difficult to get all users to attend the JAD meeting.
- The JAD approach is subject to all of the problems associated with any group meeting.

Integrated Computer-Assisted Software Engineering

Advantages

- Can produce systems with a longer effective operational life.
- Can produce systems that closely meet user requirements.
- Can speed up the development process.
- Can produce systems that are more flexible and adaptable to changing business conditions.
- Can produce excellent documentation.

Disadvantages

- Systems are often more expensive to build and maintain.
- The process requires more extensive and accurate definition of user requirements.
- It is difficult to customize the end product.

(Continued)

Rapid Application Development

Advantages

- Can speed up systems development.
- Users are intensively involved from the start.
- Improves the process of rewriting legacy applications.

Disadvantages

- Produces functional components of final systems, but not the final systems themselves.

End-User Development

Advantages

- Bypasses the IS department and avoids delays.
- User controls the application and can change it as needed.
- Directly meets user requirements.
- Promotes increased user acceptance of new system.
- Frees up IT resources.

Disadvantages

- May eventually require maintenance from IS department.
- Documentation may be inadequate.
- Leads to poor quality control.
- System may not have adequate interfaces to existing systems.
- May create lower-quality systems.

Object-Oriented Development

Advantages

- Objects model real-world entities.
- New systems may be able to reuse some computer code.

Disadvantages

- Works best with systems of more limited scope (i.e., with systems that do not have huge numbers of objects).

Systems Investigation

The initial stage in a traditional SDLC is systems investigation. Systems development professionals agree that the more time they invest in (1) understanding the business problem to be solved, (2) specifying the technical options for the systems, and (3) anticipating the problems they are likely to encounter during development, the greater the chances of success. For these reasons, systems investigation addresses *the business problem* (or business opportunity) by means of the feasibility study.

The primary task in the systems investigation stage is the feasibility study. Organizations have three basic solutions to any business problem relating to an information system: (1) do nothing and continue to use the existing system unchanged, (2) modify or enhance the existing system, and (3) develop a new system. The feasibility study analyzes which of these three solutions best fits the particular business problem. It also provides a rough assessment of the project's technical, economic, and behavioral feasibility, as explained below:

- *Technical feasibility* determines whether the company can develop and/or acquire the hardware, software, and communications components needed to solve the business problem. Technical feasibility also determines whether the organization can use its existing technology to achieve the project's performance objectives.

- *Economic feasibility* determines whether the project is an acceptable financial risk and, if so, whether the organization has the necessary time and money to successfully complete the project. You have already learned about the commonly used methods to determine economic feasibility: NPV, ROI, breakeven analysis, and the business case approach.

- *Behavioral feasibility* addresses the human issues of the systems development project. You will be heavily involved in this aspect of the feasibility study.

After the feasibility analysis is completed, a "go/no-go" decision is reached by the steering committee if there is one or by top management in the absence of a committee. The go/no-go decision does not depend solely on the feasibility analysis. Organizations often have more feasible projects than they can fund. Therefore, the firm must prioritize the feasible projects and pursue those with the highest priority. Unfunded feasible projects may not be presented to the IT department at all. These projects therefore contribute to the *hidden backlog*, which are projects that the IT department is not aware of.

If the decision is no-go, then the project either is put on the shelf until conditions are more favorable or is discarded. If the decision is go, then the project proceeds, and the systems analysis phase begins.

Systems Analysis

Once a development project has the necessary approvals from all participants, the systems analysis stage begins. Systems analysis is the process whereby systems analysts examine the business problem that the organization plans to solve with an information system.

The primary purpose of the systems analysis stage is to gather information about the existing system to determine the requirements for an enhanced system or a new system. The end product of this stage, known as the *deliverable*, is a set of *system requirements*.

Arguably, the most difficult task in systems analysis is to identify the specific requirements that the system must satisfy. These requirements are often called *user requirements*, because users (meaning you) provide them. When the systems developers have accumulated the user requirements for the new system, they proceed to the systems design stage.

Systems Design

Systems design describes how the system will resolve the business problem. The deliverable of the systems design phase is the set of *technical system specifications*, which specify the following:

- System outputs, inputs, and user interfaces
- Hardware, software, databases, telecommunications, personnel, and procedures
- A blueprint of how these components are integrated

When the system specifications are approved by all participants, they are "frozen." That is, they should not be changed. Adding functions after the project has been initiated causes scope creep, in which the time frame and expenses associated with the project expand beyond the agreed-upon limits. Scope creep endangers both the project's budget and its schedule. Because scope creep is expensive, successful project managers place controls on changes requested by users. These controls help to prevent runaway projects.

Programming and Testing

If the organization decides to construct the software in-house, then programming begins. Programming involves translating the design specifications into computer code. This process can be lengthy and time consuming, because writing computer code is as much an art as a science. Large-scale systems development projects can involve hundreds of computer programmers who are charged with creating hundreds of thousands of lines of computer code. These projects employ programming teams. The teams often include functional area users, who help the programmers focus on the business problem.

Thorough and continuous testing occurs throughout the programming stage. Testing is the process that assesses whether the computer code will produce the expected and desired results. It is also intended to detect errors, or bugs, in the computer code.

Implementation

Implementation (or *deployment*) is the process of converting from an old computer system to a new one. The conversion process involves organizational change. Only end users can manage organizational change, not the MIS department. The MIS department typically does not have enough credibility with the business users to manage the change process. Organizations use three major conversion strategies: direct, pilot, and phased.

In a direct conversion, the old system is cut off, and the new system is turned on at a certain point in time. This type of conversion is the least expensive. It is also the most risky because, if the new system does not work as planned, there is no support from the old system. Because of these risks, few systems are implemented using direct conversion.

A pilot conversion introduces the new system in one part of the organization, such as in one plant or one functional area. The new system runs for a period of time and is then assessed. If the assessment confirms that the system is working properly, then the system is implemented in other parts of the organization.

A phased conversion introduces components of the new system, such as individual modules, in stages. Each module is assessed. If it works properly, then other modules are introduced, until the entire new system is operational. Large organizations commonly combine the pilot and phased approaches. That is, they execute a phased conversion using a pilot group for each phase. A fourth strategy is *parallel conversion*, in which the old and new systems operate simultaneously for a time. This strategy is seldom used today. One reason is that parallel conversion is totally impractical when both the old and new systems are online. Imagine that you are completing an order on Amazon, only to be told, "Before your order can be entered here, you must provide all the same information again, in a different form, and on a different set of screens." The results would be disastrous for Amazon. Regardless of the type of implementation process that an organization uses, the new system may not work as advertised. In fact, the new system may cause more problems than the old system that it replaced.

Operation and Maintenance

After the new system is implemented, it will operate for a period of time, until (like the old system it replaced) it no longer meets its objectives. Once the new system's operations are stabilized, the company performs audits to assess the system's capabilities and to determine if it is being utilized correctly.

Systems require several types of maintenance. The first type is *debugging* the program, a process that continues throughout the life of the system. The second type is *updating* the system to accommodate changes in business conditions. An example is adjusting to new governmental regulations, such as changes in tax rates. These corrections and upgrades usually do not add any new functions. Instead, they simply help the system to continue to achieve its objectives. In contrast, the third type of maintenance *adds new functions* to the existing system without disturbing its operation.

Before you go on . . .

1. Describe the feasibility study.
2. What is the difference between systems analysis and systems design?
3. Describe structured programming.
4. What are the four conversion methods?

Apply the Concept 14.3

LEARNING OBJECTIVE 14.3 Enumerate the primary tasks and the importance of each of the six processes involved in the systems development life cycle.

STEP 1: Background

The systems development life cycle uses a very systematic approach in which each stage builds on work completed at an earlier stage. It is an excellent model to follow, assuming that the right decisions are made at each stage of the SDLC and are appropriately communicated to the next stage of the SDLC.

STEP 2: Activity

Visit http://www.wiley.com/go/rainer/MIS4e/applytheconcept, and watch the video titled "Software Development Life Cycle,"

which is linked to Apply the Concept 14.3. The video conveys a realistic (though perhaps a bit pessimistic) view of how poor communication can severely damage the software-development process.

STEP 3: Deliverable

After watching the video, build an outline that specifies the primary tasks and the importance of each of the six processes involved in the SDLC. Make certain to discuss the importance of communication from one step to the next.

14.4 | Alternative Methods and Tools for Systems Development

Alternative methods for systems development include joint application design, rapid application development, agile development, and end-user development.

Joint Application Design

Joint application design (JAD) is a group-based tool for collecting user requirements and creating system designs. It is most often used within the systems analysis and systems design stages of the SDLC. JAD involves a group meeting attended by the analysts and all of the users that can be conducted either in person or via the computer. During this meeting, all users jointly define and agree on the systems requirements. This process saves a tremendous amount of time. Table 14.2 lists the advantages and disadvantages of the JAD process.

Rapid Application Development

Rapid application development (RAD) is a systems development method that can combine JAD, prototyping, and integrated computer-assisted software engineering (ICASE) tools (discussed later in this section) to rapidly produce a high-quality system. In the first RAD stage, developers use JAD sessions to collect system requirements. This strategy ensures that users are intensively involved early on. The development process in RAD is iterative; that is, requirements, designs, and the system itself are developed and then undergo a series, or sequence, of improvements. RAD uses ICASE tools to quickly structure requirements and develop prototypes. As the prototypes are developed and refined, users review them in additional JAD sessions. RAD produces the functional components of a final system, rather than prototypes. To understand how RAD functions and how it differs from SDLC, see Figure 14.6. Table 14.2 highlights the advantages and disadvantages of the RAD process.

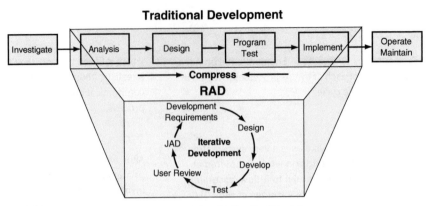

datawarehousetraining.com/Methodologies/rapidapplication-development.

Agile Development

Agile development is a software development methodology that delivers functionality in rapid iterations, which are usually measured in weeks. To be successful, this methodology requires frequent communication, development, testing, and delivery. Agile development focuses on rapid development and frequent user contact to create software that addresses the needs of business users. This software does not have to include every possible feature the user will require. Rather, it must meet only the user's more important and immediate needs. It can be updated later to introduce additional functions as they become necessary. The core tenet of agile development is to do only what you have to do to be successful right now.

One type of agile development uses the *scrum approach*. A key principle of scrum is that during a project users can change their minds about what they want and need. Scrum acknowledges that a development problem cannot be fully understood or defined from the start. Therefore, scrum focuses on maximizing the development team's ability to deliver iterations quickly and to respond effectively to additional user requirements as they emerge.

Scrum contains sets of practices and predefined roles. The primary roles are:

- The *Scrum Master*: Maintains the processes (typically replaces a project manager).
- The *Product Owner*: Represents the business users and any other stakeholders in the project.
- The *Team*: A cross-functional group of about seven people who perform the actual analysis, design, coding, implementation, testing, and so on.

Scrum works this way: During each *sprint*—typically a 2- to 4-week period—the team creates a potentially shippable product increment, such as working and tested software. The set of features that goes into each sprint comes from the product backlog, which is a prioritized set of high-level work requirements to be completed.

The sprint planning meeting determines which backlog items will be addressed during a sprint. During this meeting, the Product Owner informs the team of the items in the product backlog that he or she wants to be completed. The team members then determine how many of these projects they can commit to during the next sprint, and they record this information in the sprint backlog.

During a sprint, no one is allowed to change the sprint backlog, which means that the requirements are frozen for the sprint. Each sprint must end on time. If the requirements are not completed for any reason, then they are left out and returned to the product backlog. After each sprint is completed, the team demonstrates how to use the software.

IT's About Business 14.2 addresses an interesting type of agile development. This methodology is called *Minimum Viable Product* (MVP) development. Applications developed using MVP methodology have just the required amount of functionality to operate successfully. On the other hand, MVP applications do not have so much functionality (i.e., too many features) that the development process took too long and cost too much.

IT's About Business 14.2

MIS SDLC vs. Minimum Viable Product Development

As previously discussed, the SDLC is a traditional approach to software development that aims to produce full-function, feature-rich, user-driven software. The major problem with the SDLC has always been that the time between developing the list of user needs and the actual implementation of the software is too long. Often, the time-consuming nature of the SDLC means that it cannot keep up with the fast-paced business environment.

In 1999, Geoff Wilson founded 352 (http://www.352inc.com), a successful Web design company based in Gainesville, Florida. His company's mission was to bring products to market more quickly for his customers. He did not want to use a lengthy development process such as the SDLC.

Today, 352 provides custom Web projects for customers within weeks using agile development and a minimum viable product (MVP) approach. MVP focuses on developing the basic functions needed to bring a project to completion. After these functions are developed, the client is brought on board, and the product basically designs itself through a series of iterations.

Wilson learned about MVP the hard way. As he was building 352, he noticed several companies developing fantasy games for children. Specifically, Disney's purchase of Club Penguin (http://games.disney.com/club-penguin-app) sparked his interest. Wilson set out to build a fantasy game for children himself.

When Wilson undertook this project, there were only a few competitors in this space. However, after completing an 18-month development process, he noticed that several of his competitors had already gained loyal customers. This situation made

it difficult for Wilson's game to gain traction in the marketplace, even though his fantasy environment was more feature-rich than his competitors' environments. Ultimately, Wilson lost roughly $1 million on his project. In the process he learned the value of rapid development.

Today, development teams at 352 can bring a minimum viable product to customers in 90 days or less. The company's teams are experts at working with clients to fully develop product features. Wilson recommends that developers continuously listen to their user community, remain focused on the long-term goals of the product, and maintain an open mind regarding change.

MVP development won't work for every business in every situation. Nevertheless, it is definitely a concept to keep in mind in relation to the SDLC, because it attempts to create a perfect, complete product in one attempt.

Sources: Compiled from L. Calhoun, "The One Million Dollar Startup Rule Startups Should Never Break," *Inc.*, December 11, 2015; J. Oakhurst, "4 Biggest Custom Software Buying Mistakes," *InformationWeek*, February 18, 2014; G. Wilson, "Moving Beyond MVP: Feedback, Features, and Pricing," www.agilealliance.org, accessed September 30, 2015; http://www.clubpenguin.com/, http://leanstack.com/minimum-viable-product/, https://www.linkedin.com/in/geoffwilson, accessed December 14, 2015.

Questions

1. What lessons did Wilson learn in his attempt to develop a virtual world for children?

2. Compare and contrast the development styles of the SDLC and the agile MVP approach Wilson that promotes.

End-User Development

End-user development is an approach in which the organization's end users develop their own applications with little or no formal assistance from the IT department. Table 14.2 lists the advantages and disadvantages of end-user development. Sometimes this form of IT development and/or acquisition is called Shadow IT (also known as Stealth IT or Rogue IT). While the end-users bypass of the IT Department might make it easier for them to adopt the tools that they want to work with, it also bypasses the security measures that the IT Department is trying to enforce. These shadow IT systems can open systems to vulnerabilities and create avenues for criminals to access private company and customer data. As an employee it is important to carefully consider adopting something that has not been approved by your organization. If your Shadow IT creates a vulnerability that allows a breach, you will probably lose your job!

Tools for Systems Development

Several tools can be used with various systems development methods. These tools include prototyping, integrated computer-assisted software engineering, component-based development, and object-oriented development.

Prototyping. The prototyping approach defines an initial list of user requirements, builds a model of the system, and then refines the system in several iterations based on users' feedback. Developers do not try to obtain a complete set of user specifications for the system at the outset, and they do not plan to develop the system all at once. Instead, they quickly develop a smaller version of the system known as a prototype. A prototype can take two forms. In some cases, it contains only the components of the new system that are of most interest to the users. In other cases, it is a small-scale working model of the entire system.

Users make suggestions for improving the prototype, based on their experiences with it. The developers then review the prototype with the users and utilize their suggestions to refine it. This process continues through several iterations until the users approve the system or it becomes apparent that the system cannot meet the users' needs. If the system is viable, then the developers can use the prototype to build the full system. One typical use of prototyping is to develop screens that a user will see and interact with. Table 14.2 describes the advantages and disadvantages of the prototyping approach.

A practical problem with prototyping is that a prototype usually looks more complete than it is. That is, it may not use the real database, it usually does not have the necessary error checking, and it almost never includes the necessary security features. Users who review a prototype that resembles the finished system may not recognize these problems. Consequently, they might have unrealistic expectations about how close the actual system is to completion.

Integrated Computer-Assisted Software Engineering Tools. Computer-aided software engineering (CASE) refers to a group of tools that automate many of the tasks in the SDLC. The tools that are used to automate the early stages of the SDLC (systems investigation, analysis, and design) are called upper CASE tools. The tools used to automate later stages in the SDLC (programming, testing, operation, and maintenance) are called lower CASE tools. CASE tools that provide links between upper CASE and lower CASE tools are called integrated CASE (ICASE) tools. Table 14.2 lists the advantages and disadvantages of ICASE tools.

Component-Based Development. Component-based development uses standard components to build applications. Components are reusable applications that generally have one specific function, such as a shopping cart, user authentication, or a catalog. Compared with other approaches, component-based development generally involves less programming and more assembly. Component-based development is closely linked with the idea of Web services and service-oriented architectures, which you will study in Plug IT In 4.

Many startup companies are pursuing the idea of component-based application development. One example is Ning (www.ning.com), which allows organizations to create, customize, and share their own social network.

Object-Oriented Development. Object-oriented development is based on a different view of computer systems than the perception that characterizes traditional development approaches. Traditional approaches can produce a system that performs the original task but may not be suited for handling other tasks. This limitation applies even when these other tasks involve the same real-world entities. For example, a billing system will handle billing, but it probably cannot be adapted to handle mailings for the marketing department or to generate leads for the sales force. This is true even though the billing, marketing, and sales functions all use similar data, including customer names, addresses, and purchases. In contrast, an *object-oriented (OO) system* begins not with the task to be performed, but with the aspects of the real world that must be modeled to perform that task. Therefore, in our example, if the firm has a good model of its customers and its interactions with them, then it can use this model equally well for billings, mailings, and sales leads.

The development process for an object-oriented system begins with a feasibility study and an analysis of the existing system. Systems developers identify the *objects* in the new system— the fundamental elements in OO analysis and design. Each object represents a tangible, real-world entity, such as a customer, bank account, student, or course. Objects have *properties*, or *data values*. For example, a customer has an identification number, a name, an address, an account number(s), and so on. Objects also contain the *operations* that can be performed on their properties. For example, operations that can be performed on the customer object may include obtain-account-balance, open-account, withdraw-funds, and so on. Operations are also referred to as *behaviors*.

This approach enables OO analysts to define all the relevant objects needed for the new system, including their properties and operations. The analysts then model how the objects interact to meet the objectives of the new system. In some cases, analysts can reuse existing objects from other applications (or from a library of objects) in the new system. This process saves the analysts the time they otherwise would spend coding these objects. In most cases, however, even with object reuse, some coding will be necessary to customize the objects and their interactions for the new system.

You have studied many methods that can be used to acquire new systems. Table 14.2 provides an overview of the advantages and disadvantages of each of these methods.

Before you go on . . .

1. Describe the tools that augment the traditional SDLC.

2. Describe the alternate methods that can be used for systems development other than the SDLC.

Apply the Concept 14.4

LEARNING OBJECTIVE 14.4 Describe alternative development methods and the tools that augment development methods.

STEP 1: Background

The systems development life cycle is a very thorough method of development. However, it is also very time consuming and expensive. Section 14.4 discusses several alternative methods. Joint application design, rapid application development, and agile development are used in conjunction with several tools for systems development.

STEP 2: Activity

Visit http://www.wiley.com/go/rainer/MIS4e/applytheconcept, and click on the link provided for Apply the Concept 14.4. This link will take you to a Vimeo video about prototyping.

Imagine that you are a developer of iPhone apps. At lunch the other day someone mentioned a very cool idea for a new camera app that would enable users to take pictures simply by opening the app and saying "click" rather than having to push a button.

Describe the idea to a couple of friends to develop a list of user needs and preferences. From this list, draw up a sketch of the app. Then let the same people review your design and make suggestions. Use the second set of suggestions to create your "final" drawings of the app.

STEP 3: Deliverable

Write a short report documenting the alternative development methods you have used and how the tools discussed in this section might help you to actually develop your app. Be sure to mention how you might use different tools at different stages of development.

What's in IT for me?

ACCT For The Accounting Major

Accounting personnel help perform the cost–benefit analyses on proposed projects. They may also monitor ongoing project costs to keep them within budget. Accounting personnel undoubtedly will find themselves involved with systems development at various points throughout their careers.

FIN For the Finance Major

Finance personnel are frequently involved with the financial issues that accompany any large-scale systems development project (e.g., budgeting). They also are involved in cost–benefit and risk analyses. To perform these tasks, they need to stay abreast of the emerging techniques used to determine project costs and ROI. Finally, because they must manage vast amounts of information, finance departments are also common recipients of new systems.

MKT For the Marketing Major

In most organizations, marketing, like finance, involves massive amounts of data and information. Like finance, then, marketing is also a hotbed of systems development. Marketing personnel will increasingly find themselves participating in systems development teams. Such involvement increasingly means helping to develop systems, especially Web-based systems that reach out directly from the organization to its customers.

POM For the Production/Operations Management Major

Participation in development teams is also a common role for production/operations people. Manufacturing is becoming increasingly computerized and integrated with other allied systems, from design to logistics to customer support. Production systems interface frequently with marketing, finance, and human resources. In addition, they may be part of a larger, enterprisewide system. Also, many end users in POM either develop their own systems or collaborate with IT personnel on specific applications.

HRM For the Human Resources Management Major

The human resources department is closely involved with several aspects of the systems acquisitions process. Acquiring new systems may require hiring new employees, changing job descriptions, or terminating employees. Human resources staff performs all of these tasks. Further, if the organization hires consultants for the development project, or outsources it, the human resources department may handle the contracts with these suppliers.

MIS For the Mis Major

Regardless of the approach that the organization adopts for acquiring new systems, the MIS department spearheads it. If the organization chooses either to buy or to lease the application, the MIS department leads in examining the offerings of the various vendors and in negotiating with the vendors. If the organization chooses to develop the application in-house, then the process falls to the MIS department. MIS analysts work closely with users to develop their information requirements. MIS programmers then write the computer code, test it, and implement the new system.

Summary

1. Discuss the different cost–benefit analyses that companies must take into account when formulating an IT strategic plan.

The four common approaches to cost–benefit analysis are the following:

(1) *The net present value* method converts future values of benefits to their present-value equivalent by "discounting" them at the organization's cost of funds. They can then compare the present value of the future benefits with the cost required to achieve those benefits to determine whether the benefits exceed the costs.

(2) *Return on investment* measures management's effectiveness in generating profits with its available assets. ROI is calculated by dividing net income attributable to a project by the average assets invested in the project. ROI is a percentage, and the higher the percentage return, the better.

(3) *Breakeven analysis* determines the point at which the cumulative dollar value of the benefits from a project equals the investment made in the project.

(4) In the *business case approach*, system developers write a business case to justify funding one or more specific applications or projects.

2. Discuss the four business decisions that companies must make when they acquire new applications.

• *How much computer code does the company want to write?* A company can choose to use a totally prewritten application (to write no computer code), to customize a prewritten application (to write some computer code), or to customize an entire application (write all new computer code).

• *How will the company pay for the application?* Once the company has decided how much computer code to write, it must decide how to pay for it. With prewritten applications or customized prewritten applications, companies can buy them or lease them. With totally custom applications, companies use internal funding.

• *Where will the application run?* Companies must now decide where to run the application. The company may run the application on its own platform or run the application on someone else's platform (use either a software-as-a-service vendor or an application service provider).

• *Where will the application originate?* Prewritten applications can be open-source software or come from a vendor. Companies may choose to customize prewritten open-source applications or prewritten proprietary applications from vendors. Companies may customize applications in-house or outsource the customization. They also can write totally custom applications in-house or outsource this process.

3. Enumerate the primary tasks and importance of each of the six processes involved in the systems development life cycle.

The six processes are the following:

(1) *Systems investigation:* Addresses the business problem (or business opportunity) by means of the feasibility study; main task in the systems investigation stage is the feasibility study.

(2) *Systems analysis:* Examines the business problem that the organization plans to solve with an information system; main purpose is to gather information about the existing system in order to determine the requirements for the new system; end product of this stage, known as the "deliverable, " is a set of system requirements.

(3) *Systems design:* Describes how the system will resolve the business problem; deliverable is the set of technical system specifications.

(4) *Programming and testing:* Programming translates the design specifications into computer code; testing checks to see whether the computer code will produce the expected and desired results and detects errors, or bugs, in the computer code; deliverable is the new application.

(5) *Implementation:* The process of converting from the old system to the new system via three major conversion strategies: direct, pilot, and phased; deliverable is properly working application.

(6) *Operation and maintenance:* Types of maintenance include debugging, updating, and adding new functions when needed.

4. **Describe alternative development methods and tools that augment development methods.**

These are the *alternative methods*:

- *Joint application design* is a group-based tool for collecting user requirements and creating system designs.

- *Rapid application development* is a systems development method that can combine JAD, prototyping, and ICASE tools to rapidly produce a high-quality system.

- *Agile development* is a software development methodology that delivers functionality in rapid iterations, which are usually measured in weeks.

- *End-user development* refers to an organization's end users developing their own applications with little or no formal assistance from the IT department.

These are the *tools*:

- The *prototyping* approach defines an initial list of user requirements, builds a model of the system, and then improves the system in several iterations based on users' feedback.

- *Integrated computer-aided software engineering* combines upper CASE tools (automate systems investigation, analysis, and design) and lower CASE tools (programming, testing, operation, and maintenance).

- *Component-based development* uses standard components to build applications. Components are reusable applications that generally have one specific function, such as a shopping cart, user authentication, or a catalog.

- *Object-oriented development* begins with the aspects of the real world that must be modeled to perform that task. Systems developers identify the objects in the new system. Each object represents a tangible, real-world entity, such as a customer, bank account, student, or course. Objects have *properties*, or *data values*. Objects also contain the *operations* that can be performed on their properties.

Table 14.2 shows advantages and disadvantages of alternative methods and tools.

Chapter Glossary

agile development A software development methodology that delivers functionality in rapid iterations, measured in weeks, requiring frequent communication, development, testing, and delivery.

application portfolio The set of recommended applications resulting from the planning and justification process in application development.

application service provider (ASP) An agent or vendor who assembles the software needed by enterprises and packages them with outsourced development, operations, maintenance, and other services.

component-based development A software development methodology that uses standard components to build applications.

computer-aided software engineering (CASE) Development approach that uses specialized tools to automate many of the tasks in the SDLC; upper CASE tools automate the early stages of the SDLC and lower CASE tools automate the later stages.

containers A method of developing applications that run independently of the base operating system of the server.

continuous application development The process of steadily adding new computer code to a software project when the new computer code is written and tested.

direct conversion Implementation process in which the old system is cut off and the new system is turned on at a certain point in time.

end-user development Approach in which the organization's end users develop their own applications with little or no formal assistance from the IT department.

feasibility study Investigation that gauges the probability of success of a proposed project and provides a rough assessment of the project's feasibility.

implementation The process of converting from an old computer system to a new one.

integrated CASE (ICASE) tools CASE tools that provide links between upper CASE and lower CASE tools.

IS operational plan Consists of a clear set of projects that the IS department and the functional area managers will execute in support of the IT strategic plan.

IT steering committee A committee, comprised of a group of managers and staff representing various organizational units, set up to establish IT priorities and to ensure that the MIS function is meeting the needs of the enterprise.

IT strategic plan A set of long-range goals that describe the IT infrastructure and major IT initiatives needed to achieve the goals of the organization.

joint application design (JAD) A group-based tool for collecting user requirements and creating system designs.

lower CASE tools Tools used to automate later stages in the SDLC (programming, testing, operation, and maintenance)

object-oriented development A systems development methodology that begins with aspects of the real world that must be modeled to perform a task.

outsourcing Use of outside contractors or external organizations to acquire IT services.

phased conversion Implementation process that introduces components of the new system in stages, until the entire new system is operational.

pilot conversion Implementation process that introduces the new system in one part of the organization on a trial basis; when the new system is working properly, it is introduced in other parts of the organization.

programmers IS professionals who modify existing computer programs or write new computer programs to satisfy user requirements.

programming The translation of a system's design specifications into computer code.

prototype A small-scale working model of an entire system or a model that contains only the components of the new system that are of most interest to the users.

prototyping An approach that defines an initial list of user requirements, builds a prototype system, and then improves the system in several iterations based on users' feedback.

rapid application development (RAD) A development method that uses special tools and an iterative approach to rapidly produce a high-quality system.

request for proposal (RFP) Document that is sent to potential vendors inviting them to submit a proposal describing their soft - ware package and how it would meet the company's needs.

scope creep Adding functions to an information system after the project has begun.

service-level agreements (SLAs) Formal agreements regarding the division of work between a company and its vendors.

software-as-a-service (SaaS) A method of delivering soft ware in which a vendor hosts the applications and provides them as a service to customers over a network, typically the Internet.

systems analysis The examination of the business problem that the organization plans to solve with an information system.

systems analysts IS professionals who specialize in analyzing and designing information systems.

systems design Describes how the new system will resolve the business problem.

systems development life cycle (SDLC) Traditional structured framework, used for large IT projects, that consists of sequential processes by which information systems are developed.

systems investigation The initial stage in the traditional SDLC that addresses the business problem (or business opportunity) by means of the feasibility study.

systems stakeholders All people who are affected by changes in information systems.

technical specialists Experts on a certain type of technology, such as databases or telecommunications.

upper CASE tools Tools that are used to automate the early stages of the SDLC (systems investigation, analysis, and design).

Discussion Questions

1. Discuss the advantages of a lease option over a buy option.

2. Why is it important for all business managers to understand the issues of IT resource acquisition?

3. Why is it important for everyone in business organizations to have a basic understanding of the systems development process?

4. Should prototyping be used on every systems development project? Why or why not?

5. Discuss the various types of feasibility studies. Why are they all needed?

6. Discuss the issue of assessing intangible benefits and the proposed solutions.

7. Discuss the reasons why end-user-developed information systems can be of poor quality. What can be done to improve this situation?

Problem-Solving Activities

1. Access www.ecommerce-guide.com. Find the product review area. Read reviews of three software payment solutions. Assess them as possible components.

2. Use an Internet search engine to obtain information on CASE and ICASE tools. Select several vendors and compare and contrast their offerings.

3. Access www.ning.com. Observe how the site provides components for you to use to build applications. Build a small application at the site.

4. Enter www-01.ibm.com/software. Find its WebSphere product. Read recent customers' success stories. What makes this software so popular?

5. Enter the Web sites of the Gartner (www.gartner.com), 451 Research (https://451research.com), and CIO (www.cio.com). Search for recent material about ASPs and outsourcing, and prepare a report on your findings.

6. StoreFront (www.storefront.net) is a vendor of e-business software. At its site, the company provides demonstrations illustrating the types of storefronts that it can create for shoppers. The site also provides demonstrations of how the company's software is used to create a store.

   a. Run the StoreFront demonstration to see how this is done.

   b. What features does StoreFront provide?

   c. Does StoreFront support smaller or larger stores?

   d. What other products does StoreFront offer for creating online stores? What types of stores do these products support?

Closing Case 1

Capital One Brings IT Home

`MIS` **The Problem**

Today, when an organization's strategy calls for a technology acquisition, there are several ownership options to consider. The company can build it, buy it, outsource it, or enter into a service agreement with a third party. Each option offers different strategic advantages to the organization. One measure that executives use in decision making is return on investment (ROI). ROI is an accounting measure that helps organizations determine how efficiently their investments will return a financial benefit to the organization.

For technology-related upgrades or purchases, the nature of the improvements often makes it is difficult to calculate an accurate ROI. For example, how do you measure improved employee productivity from a $1,500 investment in a faster desktop computer? Or, how do you measure the ROI for a $15 million investment in mobile banking? For many organizations, the unknown ROI, coupled with the unknown costs of ownership of information systems—continued development, maintenance, and future implementations—lead them to outsource their IT operation either in whole or in part.

Such was the case with Capital One (CO: www.capitalone .com), a major U.S. bank. In fact, at one point the organization had outsourced more than 70 percent of their IT operation. With this arrangement, all service-related issues—software development, requested changes or upgrades, and so on—had to go through the vendor(s). CO was actually limited because they did not have ownership of their IT. The nature of the market had changed, so the former advantage was now a business problem. CO wanted to transform the customer's banking experience into a similar experience to shopping with Amazon or Apple. However, the bank lacked the capability to achieve this goal.

In 2011, CIO Rob Alexander decided it was time for a change. CO needed more control over the IT—both hardware and software—that supported its business processes. They would achieve that only by reversing the outsourcing, a process known as insourcing.

The IT Solution

To insource the 70 percent of IT that was currently outsourced, Capital One had to purchase several technology companies and make a significant investment in human and physical capital. The insourcing approach aimed at improvements in three major areas: finding developers to develop software in-house, developing a culture of agile development methodologies, and purchasing a $150 million data center to quickly test and implement the applications they would be creating.

The first step was to bring software development in-house. Insourcing software development was a challenge because CO needed talent. CO did acquire the human capital of the technology companies it purchased. However, the bank still had to compete with well-known technology companies for the best developers available on the market. To address this problem, CO created partnerships with several colleges to recruit their graduates. Their objective was to acquire a new reputation as a technology company and not just a banking company.

CO understood that without the best developers, it would never be a leading IT company.

Next, CO's in-house development process began to use agile development methodologies in which self-organizing, cross-functional teams analyzed workflow; proposed solutions; and then built, tested, modified, improved, and ultimately implemented technology solutions. Because most of Capital One's newly acquired talent came from other organizations, the company implemented a 24-month training program that helped develop the rapid agile development culture.

Finally, CO bought and operated a data center to support its new development methodologies. Had CO relied on outsourced solutions, it would have taken too long to deploy their solutions to their customers.

The Results

CO has been hard at work developing and improving their new culture. The company has improved their product testing time from 18 days before the insourcing began to less than 5 days. Their ultimate goal is to develop an idea and then test the product that same day. Of course, customers do not care about how fast a company can develop software. Their only concern is that the software works when they need it to work.

In 2011, only 1 percent of CO's software development was conducted in-house and used agile methodologies. By March 2014, CO had trained more than 3,000 software developers and business analysts to work together in the cross-functional environment necessary to implement the agile development method. By that time, 85 percent of new software was developed in-house using agile development. This development process was producing more than 400 new product releases a month, including application updates, Web site improvements, and new features that have taken less than six months to develop. In addition, more than 95 percent of these products met expectations on the first release. These are significant improvements in CO's software development process. In just over three years, CO successfully transitioned from outsourced IT to insourced IT to better support the firm's strategic goals.

Sources: Compiled from K. Burger, "CIO Rob Alexander Helps Execute Capital One's Growth Strategy," *InformationWeek*, September 29, 2011; G. MacSweeney, "Capital One Delivers 85% of Software Through Agile," *InformationWeek*, March 31, 2014; C. Murphy, "Capital One IT Overhaul Powers Digital Strategy," *InformationWeek,* April 2, 2014; J. Buvat and KVJ Subrahmanyam, "Doing Business the Digital Way: How Capital One Fundamentally Disrupted the Financial Services Industry," *capgemini.com*, accessed November 7, 2015; K. Waters, "What Is Agile? (10 Key Principles of Agile)," allaboutagile.com February 2007; S. Stapeles, "Outsourcing vs. Insourcing: You Need Both," *InformationWeek*, September 19, 2013; www .capitalone.com, accessed December 10, 2015.

Questions

1. What were the key factors that drove CO to insource?

2. In what ways did the three major changes discussed in the case complement each other? Would these changes have been successful if Capital One had not changed all of them at the same time?

Closing Case 2

The Federal Aviation Administration's Next Generation Air Transportation System

MIS   The Problem

The U.S. air traffic system has achieved an impressive safety record. Nevertheless, many of the network's features are so antiquated that experts blame them for delays and other inefficiencies that cost billions of dollars each year. The Federal Aviation Administration (FAA; www.faa.gov) estimates that if the increasing congestion in the U.S. air transportation system is not addressed, it will cost the nation's economy $22 billion annually in lost economic activity by 2022. Perhaps more seriously, it will also cause increasing safety issues, potentially endangering the flying public.

The Solution

To resolve these problems, the FAA began to develop the Next Generation Air Transportation System (NextGen; www.faa.gov/nextgen) in 2004. (Development and deployment continue in early 2016.) The purpose of NextGen is to transform America's air traffic control system from a ground-based system to a satellite-based system. NextGen uses global positioning system (GPS) technologies to shorten routes, save time and fuel, reduce traffic delays, increase the number of planes in the air traffic system, and permit controllers to monitor and manage aircraft with greater safety. Planes will be able to fly closer together, take more direct routes, and avoid delays caused when planes remain in holding patterns while they wait for an open runway. To implement NextGen, the FAA will have to transform the nation's entire air transportation system.

The FAA planned for a 20-year, $40 billion project, including upgraded information systems and radar, a new communications network to replace radios, and a satellite-based surveillance system that indicates the locations of nearby planes without relying on air traffic controllers. The goal is to manage planes more precisely and automatically, thereby enabling them to fly closer together and with greater safety. The FAA planned to deploy NextGen across the country in stages between 2012 and 2025.

The FAA estimated that by 2018, NextGen will reduce aviation fuel consumption by 1.4 billion gallons, reduce carbon emissions by 14 million tons, and save billions of dollars in costs. Each mile in the air costs an airline about $0.10 to $0.15 per seat in operating expenses such as flight crew and fuel.

Problem with NextGen's Implementation

Uneven progress, budget overruns, and conflicts among regulators and airlines demonstrate how extremely challenging the task of modernizing the world's most complex air traffic management network really is. The slow pace of NextGen's implementation has drawn harsh criticism. An April 2013 report by the Government Accountability Office (GAO) found that, although the project exhibited some progress, the implementation has been hindered by bureaucracy, delays designing new navigation procedures, and fear of conflicts with airport neighbors and environmentalists. The report further stated that the FAA had failed to set realistic goals, budgets, or expectations for NextGen. The report raised concerns that NextGen's completion could slip to 2035, and its actual costs could be three times as great as its estimated costs.

FAA Administrator Michael Huerta responded that the agency had met 80 percent of its implementation goals since 2008. He asserted

that the FAA will continue to develop NextGen despite government spending cuts.

There were early problems with NextGen. The FAA initially designed new flight paths without much industry input. Airlines, which are responsible for at least $7 billion of NextGen's total cost, have already invested in sophisticated computers and other cockpit equipment to enable pilots to fly more precise paths. Further, various interests have collided frequently. As just one example, simply reworking air routes to and from airports can take years, partly as a result of environmental assessments to address local noise concerns.

Difficulties in NextGen implementation have occurred nearly everywhere, from new landing procedures that were impossible for some planes to execute to aircraft tracking software that misidentified planes. Key initiatives are experiencing delays and are at risk of cost overruns. Further, the FAA lacks "an executable plan" for bringing NextGen fully online, according to the GAO.

Some airline officials, frustrated because they have not seen promised money-saving benefits, assert they want better results before they spend more money to equip planes to use NextGen, a vital step to the system's success. Lawmakers are also frustrated. NextGen has enjoyed broad bipartisan support in Congress. As the government faces increasing pressure to reduce spending, however, supporters fear that the program will not receive the necessary funding to become fully operational. In September 2013, a government–industry advisory committee recommended that, given the likelihood of budget cuts, the FAA should concentrate on just 11 NextGen initiatives that are ready or nearly ready to come online. The committee concluded that the rest of NextGen's 150 initiatives can wait.

Even the use of GPS-based procedures has been slowed by unforeseen problems. Developing each procedure on an airport-by-airport schedule takes several years. At large airports, new procedures are used only sporadically. During busy periods, controllers do not have time to switch back and forth between the new procedures, which most airliners can use, and older procedures that regional airliners and smaller planes still use. Consequently, all flights use the older procedure because all planes can fly them.

The Results so Far (Through 2015)

NextGen—itself years behind schedule—is finally yielding results. Let's examine a few of them:

- Atlanta-Harsfield Jackson Airport (ATL) reported a 20 percent boost in capacity when they implemented NextGen's updated arrival and departure procedures. These new procedures allow for less separation between aircraft based on new research into wake turbulence. Aircraft can now safely take off and land closer to one another, with the help of NextGen. Additionally for fiscal year 2015, Atlanta-Hartsfield reported savings of $6.3 million in fuel, 2.2 million gallons of fuel, and 18.8 thousand metric tons of carbon.

- Phoenix Sky Harbor International Airport (PHX) has implemented a computer-based "point-and-click" method of tracking aircraft to replace the paper strips it had used for years. Although the paper strips functioned well for many years, they also created a level of distraction because air traffic controllers had to physically walk around the tower to gather data and keep the strips updated. In contrast, the current system enables users to share information electronically, remain in one place, and focus their attention on the safety of the aircraft they are responsible for monitoring.

- According to the FAA, the implementation of a surface management (taxi) initiative in Boston saved more than 5,000 gallons of aviation fuel and reduced carbon dioxide emissions by 50 tons during one period of heavy congestion.

- A shared surface surveillance system combined with aircraft monitoring techniques reduced taxi-out time by 7,000 hours per year at New York's JFK airport and by 5,000 hours in Memphis, Tennessee.

- NextGen has also been tested in Memphis with Delta Air Lines and FedEx (www.fedex.com).

- The National Air Traffic Controllers Association conducted a demonstration at Dallas/Fort Worth International Airport of a new surveillance display called the Tower Flight Data Manager system. This system presented surveillance, flight data, weather, airport configuration, and other information critical to controllers.

- Specialized Optimized Profile Descents, also known as Initial Tailored Arrivals, are in operation at airports in San Francisco, Los Angeles, Miami, and Denver.

Through cooperation with the NextGen project, the FAA has initiated a new system called Aviation Safety Information Analysis and Sharing (ASIAS) that leverages data from 185 sources across industry and government, including 45 commercial air carriers and 10 corporate operators. These data include internal FAA datasets, proprietary airline safety data, public data, aircraft manufacturers' data, and more. ASIAS enables users to create a more complete profile for each flight, especially those involved in some type of accident or incident. An accident is defined as anything that happens between the times when a person enters the aircraft and when all persons have exited. In contrast, incidents occur at other times such as when an aircraft is being moved around an airport.

The FAA uses the ASIAS profiles to share information with other aircraft manufacturers and operators to help ensure the safety of the public. The agency has broken these profiles into three categories: airplane life cycle, threat categories, and common themes. The FAA has also utilized this information to develop more than 7,000 performance-based navigation (PBN) procedures that help pilots descend into busy airports using a tighter navigation path in a safer and more efficient manner.

Sources: Compiled from E. Pianin, "Congress Enraged by the FAA's $40B White Elephant," *The Fiscal Times*, November 19, 2014; C. Howard, "NextGen GA Fund Selects Banks to Help Finance General Aviation NextGen Installations, Accelerate FAA's NextGen Implementation," *Avionics Intelligence*, March 14, 2014; W. Bellamy, "NextGen Among Top US Transportation Issues for 2014," *Avionics Today*, December 17, 2013; J. Lowy, "The FAA's Next Big Issue Is Acting on Its NextGen Air Traffic Control Dreams," *Associated Press*, November 1, 2013; J. Lowy, "Air Traffic Control Modernization Hits Turbulence," *Associated Press*, October 31, 2013; S. Carey, "The FAA's $40 Billion Adventure," *The Wall Street Journal*, August 19, 2013; W. Jackson, "What's Keeping FAA's NextGen Air Traffic Control on the Runway?" *GCN.com*, July 22, 2013; S. Carey, "The FAA's $40 Billion Adventure," *The Wall Street Journal*, March 20, 2013; J. Mouawad, "Alaska Airlines, Flying Above an Industry's Troubles," *The New York Times*, March 2, 2013; J. Hoover, "Problems Plague FAA's NextGen Air Traffic Control Upgrade," *InformationWeek*, October 5, 2011; "Fact Sheet – Next Generation Air Transportation System," *FAA News*, May 27, 2010; www.faa.gov/nextgen, www.faa.gov, accessed December 14, 2015.

Questions

1. Describe the many problems that have caused problems with implementing NextGen.

2. In Plug IT In 2, you learned that hardware capabilities double roughly every 18 months (Moore's law). What impact will increases in hardware processing power, with accompanying decreases in size, have on the NextGen system? Support your answer.

3. Recall the discussion of cloud computing in Plug IT In 4. What impact might a cloud computing solution have on the future of the NextGen system? Support your answer.

Business Processes and Business Process Management

LEARNING OBJECTIVES

PI1.1 Discuss ways in which information systems enable cross-functional business processes and business processes for a single functional area.

PI1.2 Differentiate between business process reengineering, business process improvement, and business process management.

PI1.1 | Business Processes

A **business process** is an ongoing collection of related activities that create a product or a service of value to the organization, its business partners, and/or its customers. The process involves three fundamental elements:

- *Inputs:* Materials, services, and information that flow through and are transformed as a result of process activities
- *Resources:* People and equipment that perform process activities
- *Outputs:* The product or a service created by the process

If the process involves a customer, then that customer can be either internal or external to the organization. A manager who is the recipient of an internal reporting process is an example of an internal customer. In contrast, an individual or a business that purchases the organization's products is the external customer of the fulfillment process.

Successful organizations measure their process activities to evaluate how well they are executing these processes. Two fundamental metrics that organizations employ in assessing their processes are efficiency and effectiveness. *Efficiency* focuses on doing things well in the process; for example, progressing from one process activity to another without delay or without wasting money or resources. *Effectiveness* focuses on doing the things that matter; that is, creating outputs of value to the process customer—for example, high-quality products.

Many processes cross functional areas in an organization. For example, product development involves research, design, engineering, manufacturing, marketing, and distribution. Other processes involve only a single functional area. Table PI1.1 identifies the fundamental business processes performed in an organization's functional areas.

TABLE PI1.1   Examples of Business Processes

Accounting Business Processes

- Managing accounts payable
- Managing accounts receivable
- Reconciling bank accounts
- Managing cash receipts

- Managing invoice billings
- Managing petty cash
- Producing month-end close
- Producing virtual close

Finance Business Processes

- Managing account collection
- Managing bank loan applications
- Producing business forecasts
- Applying customer credit approval and credit terms

- Producing property tax assessments
- Managing stock transactions
- Generating financial cash flow reports

Marketing Business Processes

- Managing post-sale customer follow-up
- Collecting sales taxes
- Applying copyrights and trademarks
- Using customer satisfaction surveys
- Managing customer service

- Handling customer complaints
- Handling returned goods from customers
- Producing sales leads
- Entering sales orders
- Training sales personnel

Production/Operations Management Business Processes

- Processing bills of materials
- Processing manufacturing change orders
- Managing master parts list and files
- Managing packing, storage, and distribution
- Processing physical inventory
- Managing purchasing

- Managing quality control for finished goods
- Auditing for quality assurance
- Receiving, inspecting, and stocking parts and materials
- Handling shipping and freight claims
- Handling vendor selection, files, and inspections

Human Resources Business Processes

- Applying disability policies
- Managing employee hiring
- Handling employee orientation
- Managing files and records
- Applying healthcare benefits
- Managing pay and payroll

- Producing performance appraisals and salary adjustments
- Managing resignations and terminations
- Applying training/tuition reimbursement
- Managing travel and entertainment
- Managing workplace rules and guidelines
- Overseeing workplace safety

Management Information Systems Business Processes

- Antivirus control
- Computer security issues incident reporting
- Training computer users
- Computer user/staff training
- Applying disaster recovery procedures

- Applying electronic mail policy
- Generating Internet use policy
- Managing service agreements and emergency services
- Applying user workstation standards
- Managing the use of personal software

Cross-Functional Processes

All of the business processes in Table PI1.1 fall within a single functional area of the company. However, many other business processes, such as procurement and fulfillment, cut across multiple functional areas; that is, they are cross-functional business processes, meaning that no single functional area is responsible for their execution. Rather, multiple functional areas collaborate to perform the process. For a cross-functional process to be successfully completed, each functional area must execute its specific process steps in a coordinated, collaborative way. To clarify this point, let's take a look at the procurement and fulfillment cross-functional processes. We discuss these processes in greater detail in Chapter 10.

The *procurement process* includes all of the tasks involved in acquiring needed materials externally from a vendor. Procurement comprises five steps that are completed in three different functional areas of the firm: warehouse, purchasing, and accounting.

POM

The process begins when the warehouse recognizes the need to procure materials, perhaps due to low inventory levels. The warehouse documents this need with a purchase requisition, which it sends to the purchasing department (step 1). In turn, the purchasing department identifies a suitable vendor, creates a purchase order based on the purchase requisition, and sends the order to the vendor (step 2). When the vendor receives the purchase order, it ships the materials, which are received in the warehouse (step 3). The vendor then sends an invoice, which is received by the accounting department (step 4). Accounting sends payment to the vendor, thereby completing the procurement process (step 5).

The *fulfillment process* is concerned with processing customer orders. Fulfillment is triggered by a customer purchase order that is received by the sales department. Sales then validates the purchase order and creates a sales order. The sales order communicates data related to the order to other functional areas within the organization, and it tracks the progress of the order. The warehouse prepares and sends the shipment to the customer. Once accounting is notified of the shipment, it creates an invoice and sends it to the customer. The customer then makes a payment, which accounting records.

An organization's business processes can create a competitive advantage if they enable the company to innovate or to execute more effectively and efficiently than its competitors. They can also be liabilities, however, if they make the company less responsive and productive. Consider the airline industry. It has become a competitive necessity for all of the airlines to offer electronic ticket purchases via their Web sites. To provide competitive advantage, however, these sites must be highly responsive and they must provide both current and accurate information on flights and prices. An up-to-date, user-friendly site that provides fast answers to user queries will attract customers and increase revenues. In contrast, a site that provides outdated or inaccurate information, or has a slow response time, will hurt rather than improve business.

Clearly, good business processes are vital to organizational success. But how can organizations determine if their business processes are well designed? The first step is to document the process by describing its steps, its inputs and outputs, and its resources. The organization can then analyze the process and, if necessary, modify it to improve its performance.

To understand this point, let's consider the e-ticketing process. E-ticketing consists of four main process activities: searching for flights, reserving a seat, processing payment, and issuing an e-ticket. These activities can be broken down into more detailed process steps. The result may look like the process map in **Figure PI1.1**. Note that different symbols correspond to different types of process steps. For instance, rectangles (steps) are activities that are performed by process resources (reserve seats, issue e-ticket). Diamond-shaped boxes indicate decisions that need to be made (seats available?). Arrows are used as connectors between steps; they indicate the sequence of activities.

These symbols are important in the process flowchart (which is similar to a programming flowchart). Other symbols may be used to provide additional process details. For example, D-shaped boxes are used instead of rectangles when a waiting period is part of a process; ovals can show start and stop points; and process resources can be attached to activities with resource connector lines, or included as an annotation or property for each activity box.

The customers of the process are travelers planning a trip, and the process output is an e-ticket. Travelers provide inputs to the process: the desired travel parameters to begin the search, the frequent flyer miles number, and their credit card information. In addition, a computerized reservation system that stores information for many airlines also provides some of the process inputs—such as the seat availability and prices. The resources used in the process are the airline Web site, the computerized reservation system, and, if the customer calls the airline call center at any time during the process, the call center system and the human travel agents. The process creates customer value by efficiently generating an output that meets

Airline (Web site)

Traveler

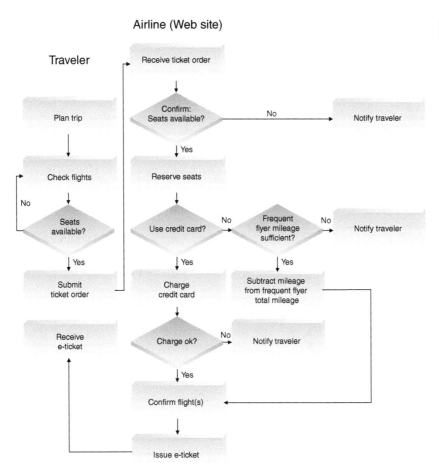

the customer search criteria—dates and prices. The performance of the process depends on efficiency metrics such as the time required to purchase an e-ticket, from the moment the customer initiates the ticket search until he or she receives the e-ticket. Effectiveness metrics include customer satisfaction with the airline Web site. Finally, the performance of the process may be affected if the quality or the timeliness of the inputs is low—for example, if the customer enters the wrong dates—or if the process resources are not available—for example, if the Web site crashes before the purchase is finalized.

Information Systems and Business Processes

An information system (IS) is a critical enabler of an organization's business processes. Information systems facilitate communication and coordination among different functional areas, and allow easy exchange of, and access to, data across processes. Specifically, ISs play a vital role in three areas:

MIS

- Executing the process
- Capturing and storing process data
- Monitoring process performance

In this section, you will learn about each of these roles. In some cases the role is fully automated—that is, it is performed entirely by the IS. In other cases, the IS must rely on the manager's judgment, expertise, and intuition. IT's About Business PI1.1 shows how NASCAR uses information technology to streamline its pre-race process.

IT'S About Business PI1.1

POM NASCAR Uses IT in Its Pre-Race Inspection

The National Association for Stock Car Auto Racing (NASCAR; www.nascar.com) is a family-owned-and-operated business that governs multiple auto racing events. One of NASCAR's key business processes is the pre-race inspection of the cars. The rationale for pre-race inspection is to ensure that all cars are as evenly matched as possible.

Pre-race inspection begins two days before a race. Each car on the entry list for a particular race must pass a thorough inspection to compete. Here is how the process works.

In the first inspection, NASCAR officials assess whether a car meets NASCAR requirements—for example, height off the ground at the front and the back of the car, weight, fuel tank capacity, and many other factors. Cars that meet these requirements are cleared to practice, and they qualify for the race.

If a car does not pass the first inspection, then NASCAR allows that team to fix the problem and undergo a second inspection. However, the team is sent to the end of the line. This process can cause a backup of cars waiting to be cleared before the race. In the past, NASCAR would allow a team with a violation to keep its spot in line while it fixed the problem, essentially cutting in front of teams still waiting to undergo the initial inspection. That situation meant that crew chiefs had little incentive when trying to repair violations. If the repair did not fix the violation, they would simply try again.

After the first inspection, each team has two days before the race to work on their cars. After each team qualifies, NASCAR conducts a second, postqualifying inspection. On race morning, all cars are inspected one final time.

Historically, NASCAR officials performed the pre-race inspection by walking to each inspection station and visually observing each car. Moreover, they recorded their observations on paper forms. These forms contained more than 100 items clustered in categories depending on the type of inspection. The form would remain with each vehicle as it went through the inspection process. Each season, NASCAR used roughly 25,000 sheets of paper for inspections.

In September 2014, NASCAR implemented an app from Microsoft that incorporates everything from the paper-based form, but in a more informative format. Each vehicle is shown on a dashboard that tracks its stages through the inspection process. The dashboard also uses color-coded flags to highlight violations. NASCAR officials can be alerted to any pending issues for each vehicle and they can access the NASCAR rulebook at the press of a digital button. Officials can also add digital notes and photographs to detail any infractions. In addition, the app enables officials to determine whether pre-race inspections are on time. Finally, the race director can use his tablet to monitor each inspection station, identify which cars have been cited for violations, and find out the status of every car.

The Microsoft app has simplified the pre-race inspection process. Consider, for instance, that the paper form needed a NASCAR official's signature on every item. In contrast, the app by default assumes every item's status is good unless otherwise noted by officials.

One interesting benefit of the app is the cumulative value of the collected data. Information on the pre-race inspections of all vehicles is collected and stored in real time. Consequently, NASCAR executives can identify trends and patterns to help maintain a level playing field for all racers.

Sources: Compiled from N. Linhart, "NASCAR App Improves Inspection Efficiency," *Charlotte Sun Times*, February 10, 2015; J. Gluck, "App Improves NASCAR Inspection Process," *USA Today*, February 9, 2015; "Going Through Inspections," *NASCAR.com*, January 5, 2015; "A Day at the Track for a NASCAR Race," *NASCAR.com*, January 5, 2015; J. Richter, "NASCAR Pre-Race Inspection? There's an App for That," *Fox Sports*, October 23, 2014; T. Bradley, "NASCAR Turns to Microsoft and Windows 8 to Streamline Race Operations," *Forbes*, October 21, 2014; J. Hammond, "NASCAR Inspections a Work in Progress," *Fox Sports*, June 6, 2014; www.nascar.com, accessed March 2, 2015.

Questions

1. Describe why pre-race inspection is a business process for NASCAR.
2. Describe the various benefits that the app provides NASCAR.
3. Refer back to Chapter 2. Is the app a strategic information system for NASCAR? Why or why not? Support your answer.

Executing the Process. An IS helps organizations execute processes efficiently and effectively. ISs are typically embedded into the processes, and they play a critical role in executing the processes. In other words, an IS and the processes are usually intertwined. If the IS does not work, the process cannot be executed. IS helps execute processes by informing people when it is time to complete a task, by providing the necessary data to complete the task, and, in some cases, by providing the means to complete the task.

In the procurement process, for example, the IS generates the purchase requisitions and then informs the purchasing department that action on these requisitions is needed. The accountant will be able to view all shipments received to match an invoice that has been received from a supplier and verify that the invoice is accurate. Without the IS, these steps, and therefore the process, cannot be completed. For example, if the IS is not available, how will the warehouse know which orders are ready to pack and ship?

In the fulfillment process, the IS will inform people in the warehouse that orders are ready for shipment. It also provides them with a listing of what materials must be included in the order and where to find those materials in the warehouse.

Capturing and Storing Process Data.

Processes create data such as dates, times, product numbers, quantities, prices, and addresses, as well as who did what, when, and where. IS captures and stores these data, commonly referred to as *process data* or *transaction data*. Some of these data are generated and automatically captured by the IS. These are data related to who completes an activity, when, and where. Other data are generated outside the IS and must be entered into it. This data entry can occur in various ways, ranging from manual entry to automated methods involving data in forms such as bar codes and RFID tags that can be read by machines.

In the fulfillment process, for example, when a customer order is received by mail or over the phone, the person taking the order must enter data such as the customer's name, what the customer ordered, and how much he or she ordered. Significantly, when a customer order is received via the firm's Web site, then all customer details are captured by the IS. Data such as the name of the person entering the data (who), at which location the person is completing the task (where), and the date and time (when) are automatically included by the IS when it creates the order. The data are updated as the process steps are executed. When the order is shipped, the warehouse will provide data about which products were shipped and in what quantities, and the IS will automatically include data related to who, when, and where.

An important advantage of using an IS compared to a manual system or multiple functional area information systems is that the data need to be entered into the system only once. Further, once they are entered, other people in the process can easily access them, and there is no need to reenter them in subsequent steps.

The data captured by the IS can provide immediate feedback. For example, the IS can use the data to create a receipt or to make recommendations for additional or alternative products.

Monitoring Process Performance.

A third contribution of IS is to help monitor the state of the various business processes. That is, the IS indicates how well a process is executing. The IS performs this role by evaluating information about a process. This information can be created either at the *instance level* (i.e., a specific task or activity) or at the *process level* (i.e., the process as a whole).

For example, a company might be interested in the status of a particular customer order. Where is the order within the fulfillment process? Was the complete order shipped? If so, when? If not, then when can we expect it to be shipped? Or, for the procurement process, when was the purchase order sent to the supplier? What will be the cost of acquiring the material? At the process level, the IS can evaluate how well the procurement process is being executed by calculating the lead time, or the time between sending the purchase order to a vendor and receiving the goods, for each order and each vendor over time.

Not only can the IS help monitor a process, but it can also detect problems with the process. The IS performs this role by comparing the information with a standard—that is, what the company expects or desires—to determine if the process is performing within expectations. Management establishes standards based on organizational goals.

If the information provided by the IS indicates that the process is not meeting the standards, then the company assumes that some type of problem exists. Some problems can be routinely and automatically detected by the IS, whereas others require a person to review the information and make judgments. For example, the IS can calculate the expected date that a specific order will be shipped and determine whether this date will meet the established standard. Or, the IS can calculate the average time taken to fill all orders over the last month and compare this information with the standard to determine if the process is working as expected.

Monitoring business processes, then, helps detect problems with these processes. Very often these problems are really symptoms of a more fundamental problem. In such cases, the IS can help diagnose the cause of the symptoms by providing managers with additional, detailed information. For example, if the average time to process a customer order appears to have increased over the previous month, this problem could be a symptom of a more basic problem.

A manager can then drill down into the information to diagnose the underlying problem. To accomplish this task, the manager can request a breakdown of the information by type of product, customer, location, employees, day of the week, time of day, and so on. After reviewing this detailed information, the manager might determine that the warehouse has experienced an exceptionally high employee turnover rate over the last month and that the delays are occurring because new employees are not sufficiently familiar with the process. The manager might conclude that this problem will work itself out over time, in which case there is nothing more to be done. Alternatively, the manager could conclude that the new employees are not being adequately trained and supervised. In this case, the company must take actions to correct the problem. The following section discusses several methodologies that managers can use to take corrective action when process problems are identified.

Before you go on . . .

1. What is a business process?
2. Describe several business processes carried out at your university.
3. Define a cross-functional business process, and provide several examples of such processes.
4. Pick one of the processes described in Question 2 or 3 above, and identify its inputs, outputs, customer(s), and resources. How does the process create value for its customer(s)?

Apply the Concept PII1.1

LEARNING OBJECTIVE PI1.1 Discuss ways in which information systems enable cross-functional business processes and business processes for a single functional area.

STEP 1: Background (This is what you are learning.)

This Plug IT In defines a business process as an ongoing collection of related activities that create a product or a service of value to the organization, its business partners, and/or its customers. Normally, we do not see everything that goes into a process; rather, we observe only the results of the process. For example, when you shop at a grocery store, you see stocked shelves. However, the inventory management processes that operate to keep the shelves stocked— as well as the information systems that support those processes —remain essentially invisible.

STEP 2: Activity (This is what you are doing.)

Visit http://www.wiley.com/go/rainer/MIS4e/applytheconcept, and click on the link provided for Plug IT In 1.1. This link will take you to a YouTube video that focuses on workflow and business process management in a healthcare environment. As you watch the video, look for the ways that information systems enable cross-functional business processes and make the flow of data much easier and quicker for everyone involved.

STEP 3: Deliverable (This is what you turn in.)

Based on the video from Step 2, write a brief description of how information systems enable both cross-functional business processes and business processes for a single functional area. Submit your description to your instructor.

PI1.2 | Business Process Improvement, Business Process Reengineering, and Business Process Management

Excellence in executing business processes is widely recognized as the underlying basis for all significant measures of competitive performance in an organization. Consider the following measures, for example:

- *Customer satisfaction:* The result of optimizing and aligning business processes to fulfill customers' needs, wants, and desires.

- *Cost reduction:* The result of optimizing operations and supplier processes.
- *Cycle and fulfillment time reduction:* The result of optimizing the manufacturing and logistics processes.
- *Quality:* The result of optimizing the design, development, and production processes.
- *Differentiation:* The result of optimizing the marketing and innovation processes.
- *Productivity:* The result of optimizing each individual's work processes.

The question is: How does an organization ensure business process excellence?

In their book *Reengineering the Corporation*, first published in 1993, Michael Hammer and James Champy argued that to become more competitive, American businesses needed to radically redesign their business processes to reduce costs and increase quality. The authors further asserted that information technology is the key enabler of such change. This radical redesign, called **business process reengineering (BPR)**, is a strategy for making an organization's business processes more productive and profitable. The key to BPR is for enterprises to examine their business processes from a "clean sheet" perspective and then determine how they can best reconstruct those processes to improve their business functions. BPR's popularity was propelled by the unique capabilities of information technology, such as automation and standardization of many process steps and error reduction due to improved communication among organizational information silos.

Although some enterprises have successfully implemented BPR, many organizations found this strategy too difficult, too radical, too lengthy, and too comprehensive. The impact on employees, on facilities, on existing investments in information systems, and even on organizational culture was overwhelming. Despite the many failures in BPR implementation, however, businesses increasingly began to organize work around business processes rather than individual tasks. The result was a less radical, less disruptive, and more incremental approach, called business process improvement (BPI).

BPI focuses on reducing variation in the process outputs by searching for root causes of the variation in the process itself (e.g., a broken machine on an assembly line) or among the process inputs (e.g., a decline in the quality of raw materials purchased from a certain supplier). BPI is usually performed by teams of employees that include a process expert—usually the process owner (the individual manager who oversees the process)—as well as other individuals who are involved in the process. These individuals can be involved directly; for example, the workers who actually perform process steps. Alternatively, these individuals can be involved indirectly; for example, customers who purchase the outputs from the process.

Six Sigma is a popular methodology for BPI initiatives. Its goal is to ensure that the process has no more than 3.4 defects per million outputs by using statistical methods to analyze the process. (A defect is defined as a faulty product or an unsatisfactory service.) Six Sigma was developed by Motorola in the 1980s, and it is now used by companies worldwide, thanks in part to promotional efforts by early adopters such as GE. Six Sigma is especially appropriate for manufacturing environments, where product defects can be easily defined and measured. Over the years, the methodology has been modified so that it focuses less on defects and more on customer value. As a result, it can now be applied to services as well as to products. Today, Six Sigma tools are widely used in financial services and healthcare institutions as components of process-improvement initiatives.

Regardless of the specific methodology you use, a successful BPI project generally follows five basic phases: define, measure, analyze, improve, and control (DMAIC).

- In the *define phase*, the BPI team documents the existing "as is" process activities, process resources, and process inputs and outputs, usually as a graphical process map or diagram. The team also documents the customer and the customer's requirements for the process output, together with a description of the problem that needs to be addressed.
- In the *measure phase*, the BPI team identifies relevant process metrics, such as time and cost to generate one output (product or service), and collects data to understand how the metrics evolve over time. Sometimes the data already exist, in which case they can be

extracted from the IS that supports the process, as described in the previous section. Many times, however, the BPI team needs to combine operational process data already stored in the company's IS systems with other data sources, such as customer and employee observations, interviews, and surveys.

- In the *analysis phase*, the BPI team examines the "as is" process map and the collected data to identify problems with the process (e.g., decreasing efficiency or effectiveness) and their root causes. If possible, the team should also benchmark the process; that is, compare its performance with that of similar processes in other companies, or other areas of the organization. The team can employ IT applications such as statistical analysis software or simulation packages in this phase.

It is often valuable to use process simulation software during the analysis phase. Utilizing this software provides two benefits. First, it enables a process manager to quickly simulate a real situation (e.g., with a certain number of people undertaking activities) for a specific amount of time (e.g., a working day, a week, or a month). The manager can then estimate the process performance over time without having to observe the process in practice. Second, it allows the manager to create multiple scenarios; for instance, using a different number of resources in the process and/or using a different configuration for the process steps. In addition, process simulation software can provide a number of outputs regarding a process including the time used by all resources to execute specific activities, the overall cycle time of a process, the identification of resources that are infrequently used, and the bottlenecks in the process. Simulating a process is extremely valuable for process managers because it is a risk-free and inexpensive test of an improvement solution that does not need to be conducted with real resources.

- In the *improve phase*, the BPI team identifies possible solutions for addressing the root causes, maps the resulting "to be" process alternatives, and selects and implements the most appropriate solution. Common ways to improve processes are eliminating process activities that do not add value to the output and rearranging activities in a way that reduces delays or improves resource utilization. The organization must be careful, however, not to eliminate internal *process controls*—those activities that safeguard company resources, guarantee the accuracy of its financial reporting, and ensure adherence to rules and regulations.

- In the *control phase*, the team establishes process metrics and monitors the improved process after the solution has been implemented to ensure the process performance remains stable. An IS system can be very useful for this purpose.

Although BPI initiatives do not deliver the huge performance gains promised by BPR, many organizations prefer them because they are less risky and less costly. BPI focuses on delivering quantifiable results—and if a business case cannot be made, the project is not continued. All employees can be trained to apply BPI techniques in their own work to identify opportunities for improvement. Thus, BPI projects tend to be performed more from the bottom-up, in contrast to BPR projects, which involve top-down change mandates. BPI projects take less time overall, and even if they are unsuccessful, they consume fewer organizational resources than BPR projects. However, if incremental improvements through BPI are no longer possible, or if significant changes occur in the firm's business environment, then the firm should consider BPR projects. One final consideration is that over time, employees can become overstretched or lose interest if the company undertakes too many BPI projects and does not have an effective system to manage and focus the improvement efforts.

To sustain BPI efforts over time, organizations can adopt **business process management (BPM)**, a management system that includes methods and tools to support the design, analysis, implementation, management, and continuous optimization of core business processes throughout the organization. BPM integrates disparate BPI initiatives to ensure consistent strategy execution.

Important components of BPM are process modeling, Web-enabled technologies, and business activity monitoring. BPM begins with *process modeling*, which is a graphical depiction of all of the steps in a process. Process modeling helps employees understand the interactions and dependencies among the people involved in the process, the information systems they rely on, and the information they require to optimally perform their tasks. Process modeling software can support this activity. IT's About Business PI1.2 shows how Chevron has employed BPR, BPI, and BPM.

Web-enabled technologies display and retrieve data via a Web browser. They enable an organization to integrate the necessary people and applications into each process, across functional areas and geographical locations.

Finally, *business activity monitoring* (BAM) is a real-time approach for measuring and managing business processes. Companies use BAM to monitor their business processes, identify failures or exceptions, and address these failures in real time. Further, because BAM tracks process operations and indicates whether they succeed or fail, it creates valuable records of process behaviors that organizations can use to improve their processes.

BPM activities are often supported by *business process management suites* (BPMS). A BPMS is an integrated set of applications that includes a repository of process information, such as process maps and business rules; tools for process modeling, simulation, execution, coordination across functions, and re-configuration in response to changing business needs; as well as process-monitoring capabilities.

BPM is growing in business value. In 2012, Capgemini (www.capgemini.com), an international consulting firm, surveyed more than 1,000 senior business executives. The majority of the respondents indicated that BPM would play a more prominent role in their organizations in 2013 and 2014.

Further, Gartner (www.gartner.com), a leading IT research and advisory firm, stated that companies need to focus on developing and mastering BPM skills throughout the organization. Gartner predicts that by 2016, high-performing companies will use BPM technologies such as real-time process monitoring, visualization, analytics, and intelligent automated decision making—all of them integrated in second-generation BPMS—to support intelligent business operations.

Another promising emerging trend is *social BPM*. This technology enables employees to collaborate, using social media tools on wired and mobile platforms, both internally across functions and externally with stakeholders (such as customers or experts), to exchange process knowledge and improve process execution.

BPM initially helps companies improve profitability by decreasing costs and increasing revenues. Over time, BPM can create a competitive advantage by improving organizational flexibility—making it easy to adapt to changing business conditions and to take advantage of new opportunities. For many companies, BPM can reduce costs, increase customer satisfaction, and ensure compliance with rules and regulations. In all cases, the company's strategy should drive the BPM effort. The following example illustrates these benefits.

Before you go on . . .

1. What is business process reengineering?
2. What is business process improvement?
3. What is business process management?

IT's About Business PI1.2

POM BPR, BPI, and BPM at Chevron

Chevron (www.chevron.com), one of the world's largest oil and gas companies, and its subsidiaries are involved in exploring and producing oil and natural gas, as well as in manufacturing, transporting, and distributing petrochemical products, including gasoline and refined products. In 2013, Chevron employed more than 60,000 people worldwide, produced the equivalent of more than 2.6 million barrels of oil every day, and garnered more than $230 billion in sales. Chevron has initiated several process reengineering and improvement efforts over the years, evolving from BPR to BPI and eventually to BPM, as described below.

In 1995, Chevron's output was less than half of its current amount, producing roughly 1 million barrels of oil per day across six plants. The company had three major departments: Refining, Marketing, and Supply and Distribution (S&D). Management determined that they needed to improve their supply chain (see Chapter 11) to better integrate their multiple internal processes. A key figure in this initiative was Vice President Peter McCrea, who had a strong idea for dramatically improving performance. McCrea was convinced that Chevron had to reengineer the company's core processes from beginning to end: from the acquisition of crude oil to the distribution of final products to Chevron customers.

To accomplish this task, Chevron adopted a holistic approach. The company collaborated with a consulting firm to create a model of the existing processes. The objective was to radically improve these processes to align with Chevron's business goals. In other words, Chevron's strategy was not to concentrate on the existing processes to identify specific areas to improve. Rather, the project identified the desired outputs and then worked backward by examining the supporting processes, utilizing BPR. As an added benefit, this holistic approach led the company to examine the interdependencies among processes used in different business units. This approach ultimately improved the company's overall performance. In a 1996 report, Chevron claimed the BPR project saved the company $50 million.

This complex BPR effort was initially followed by several smaller, employee-driven BPI initiatives. For example, in 1998, six Chevron employees initiated a project to improve water treatment processes at a company plant in California. Operating costs fell by one-third. Their success inspired other employees to initiate BPI projects in Indonesia, Angola, and other locations around the globe by using the Six Sigma improvement methodology. Although some managers were able to demonstrate the benefits of BPI at the local level, it wasn't until 2006 that these efforts achieved companywide recognition and corporate backing. In that year, Lean Six Sigma, which combines statistical process analysis with techniques to eliminate waste and improve process flow, became Chevron's preferred improvement methodology. Since Chevron implemented Lean Six Sigma, company employees have initiated hundreds of BPI projects worldwide, resulting in significant savings. From 2008 to 2010 alone, Chevron reported more than $1 billion in BPI benefits. To support these internal improvement efforts, Chevron got its suppliers on board in BPI initiatives as well.

To coordinate these various BPI efforts, Chevron has adopted a unified BPM approach that involves standardizing processes across the entire company and consolidating process information within a central repository. Chevron estimates that only 20 percent of its processes can be fully automated—the rest involve a combination of manual and automated steps. Thus, process standardization involves not only supporting activities that can be automated but also ensuring that relevant employees are familiar with the standards for manual activities. To familiarize employees with all these processes, Chevron implemented Nimbus (nimbus.tibco.com), a BPMS that acts as a repository of standard, companywide rules, and procedures. In addition, Nimbus can provide employees with detailed work instructions.

Take Chevron's shipping process as an example where the BPMS could shine. Shipping was executed in different ways in locations throughout Asia, Europe, and the United States. To establish uniform company standards, Chevron employed a BPI approach. The company documented its processes as they existed across different geographical locations, identified best practices, and combined these practices into a common process to implement. It then detailed these new policies and procedures, which it distributed to managers through the company's Web-based BPMS.

Chevron has a companywide management system that focuses on operational excellence, and BPM is a key part of that system. All Chevron operating companies and business units must implement continuous improvement, using carefully defined guidelines, metrics, and targets that are reviewed and adapted every year. Chevron's metrics focus on process efficiency, safety, risk, and the environment. The commitment to continuous improvement is part of Chevron's corporate culture. All employees participate in operational excellence activities, and managers receive specific operational excellence training.

Operational excellence is especially crucial when economic times are tough. For example, in the fourth quarter of 2014, Chevron's net income was $3.5 billion, down nearly 30 percent from $4.9 billion for the same period in 2013. This decline resulted primarily from the steep drop in crude oil prices. However, it's likely that results would have been worse without the operational excellence initiatives. Chevron's CEO noted that the lower crude oil prices were partially offset by increased operational efficiency in the company's downstream operations—that is, refining oil products and delivering them to customers. This increased efficiency was a product of the company's ongoing BPR, BPI, and BPM efforts.

Sources: Compiled from "Operational Excellence," *chevron.com*, March 2012; "Chevron—Using Nimbus Control Software to Manage Processes," *Finding FindingPetroleum.com*, September 23, 2010; "Chevron Wins Boston Strategies International's 2010 Award for Lean Six Sigma Implementation in Oil and Gas Operations," *www.boston strategies.com*, September 22, 2010; E. Schmidt, "From the Bottom Up: Grassroots Effort Finds Footing at Chevron," *isixsigma.com*, March 1, 2010; R. Parker, "Business Process Improvement: A Talk with Chevron's Jim Boots," *Ebizq.net*, August 26, 2009; P. Harmon, *Business Process Management*, Elsevier, Burlington, MA, 2007; www.chevron.com, accessed February 22, 2015.

Questions

1. Describe the main advantages of BPR at Chevron.

2. Why did Chevron adopt BPI?

3. How does Chevron apply BPM in its operations today?

Apply the Concept PI1.2

LEARNING OBJECTIVE PI1.2 Compare and contrast business process reengineering and business process management to determine the advantages and disadvantages of each.

STEP 1: Background

One of the most difficult decisions related to business processes is whether they need to be reengineered or simply managed. Reengineering business processes is a "clean slate" approach where you build completely new processes to accomplish current tasks. In contrast, managing these processes involves making current processes more efficient. Put simply, reengineering is radical, whereas management is incremental.

STEP 2: Activity

Consider the many processes involved in getting you (as a student) accepted, enrolled, registered, housed, fed, and,

ultimately, educated. Do you recall the processes you went through to accomplish these tasks? Did any of these processes strike you as inefficient?

STEP 3: Deliverable

Imagine that you are a student representative on a committee whose task is to consider reengineering or modifying (managing) these business processes. Prepare a written statement for the committee that will compare and contrast BPR and BPM to determine the advantages and disadvantages of each strategy. Make a recommendation as to which one your university should follow and present your recommendation to your instructor.

What's in IT for me?

For All Business Majors

All functional areas of any organization are literally composed of a variety of business processes, as we can see from the examples in this chapter. Regardless of your major, you will be involved in a variety of business processes from your first day on the job. Some of these processes you will do by yourself, some will involve only your group, team, or department, while others will involve several (or all) functional areas of your organization.

It is important for you to be able to visualize processes, understand the inputs and outputs of each process, and know the "customer" of each process. If you can do these things, you will contribute to making processes more efficient and effective, which often means incorporating information technology in the process. It is also important for you to know how each process fits into your organization's strategy.

Summary

1. **Discuss ways in which information systems enable cross-functional business processes and processes for a single functional area.**

A business process is an ongoing collection of related activities that produce a product or a service of value to the organization, its business partners, and/or its customers. Examples of business processes in the functional areas include managing accounts payable, managing accounts receivable, managing after-sale customer follow-up, managing bills of materials, managing manufacturing change orders, applying disability policies, employee hiring, computer user/staff training, and applying Internet use policy. The procurement and fulfillment processes are examples of cross-functional business processes.

2. **Compare and contrast business process reengineering and business process management to determine the different advantages and disadvantages of each.**

Business process reengineering (BPR) is a radical redesign of business processes that is intended to improve the efficiency and effectiveness of an organization's business processes. The key to BPR is for enterprises to examine their business processes from a "clean sheet" perspective and then determine how they can best reconstruct those processes to improve their business functions. Because BPR proved difficult to implement, organizations have turned to business process management. Business process management (BPM) is a management technique that includes methods and tools to support the design, analysis, implementation, management, and optimization of business processes.

Chapter Glossary

business process A collection of related activities that create a product or a service of value to the organization, its business partners, and/or its customers.

business process management A management technique that includes methods and tools to support the design, analysis, implementation, management, and optimization of business processes.

business process reengineering A radical redesign of a business process that improves its efficiency and effectiveness, often by beginning with a "clean sheet" (i.e., from scratch).

cross-functional processes No single functional area is responsible for a process's execution.

Discussion Questions

1. Consider the student registration process at your university:

   • Describe the steps necessary for you to register for your classes each semester.

   • Describe how information technology is used (or is not used) in each step of the process.

2. Why is it so difficult for an organization to actually implement business process reengineering?

Hardware and Software

LEARNING OBJECTIVES

PI2.1 Discuss strategic issues that link hardware design to business strategy.

PI2.2 Differentiate between the two major types of software.

Introduction

As you begin this Plug IT In, you might be wondering, why do I have to know anything about hardware and software? There are several reasons why you will benefit from understanding the basics of hardware and software. First, regardless of your major (and future functional area in an organization), you will be using different types of hardware and software throughout your career. Second, you will have input concerning the hardware and software that you will use. In this capacity, you will be required to answer many questions, such as follows:

- Is my hardware performing adequately for my needs? If not, what types of problems am I experiencing?
- Does my software help me do my job?
- Is this software easy to use?
- Do I need more functionality, and if so, what functionality would be most helpful to me?

Third, you will also have input into decisions when your functional area or organization upgrades or replaces its hardware and/or software. In addition, some organizations allocate the hardware and software budget to functional areas or departments. In such cases, you might be responsible for making hardware and software decisions (at least locally) yourself. MIS employees will act as advisors, but you will provide important input into such decisions.

PI2.1 Introduction to Hardware

Recall from Chapter 1 that the term *hardware* refers to the physical equipment used for the input, processing, output, and storage activities of a computer system. Decisions about hardware focus on three interrelated factors: appropriateness for the task, speed, and cost. The incredibly rapid rate of innovation in the computer industry complicates hardware decisions because computer technologies become obsolete more quickly than other organizational technologies.

The overall trends in hardware are that it becomes smaller, faster, cheaper, and more powerful over time. In fact, these trends are so rapid that they make it difficult to know when to purchase (or upgrade) hardware. This difficulty lies in the fact that companies that delay hardware purchases will, more than likely, be able to buy more powerful hardware for the same amount of money in the future. It is important to note that buying more powerful hardware for the same amount of money in the future is a trade-off. An organization that delays purchasing computer hardware gives up the benefits of whatever it could buy today until the future purchase date arrives.

Hardware consists of the following:

- *Central processing unit (CPU):* Manipulates the data and controls the tasks performed by the other components.
- *Primary storage:* Temporarily stores data and program instructions during processing.
- *Secondary storage:* Stores data and programs for future use.
- *Input technologies:* Accept data and instructions and convert them to a form that the computer can understand.
- *Output technologies:* Present data and information in a form people can understand.
- *Communication technologies:* Provide for the flow of data from external computer networks (e.g., the Internet and intranets) to the CPU, and from the CPU to computer networks.

Strategic Hardware Issues

For most businesspeople, the most important issues are what the hardware enables, how it is advancing, and how rapidly it is advancing. In many industries, exploiting computer hardware is a key to achieving competitive advantage. Successful hardware exploitation comes from thoughtful consideration of the following questions:

- How do organizations keep up with the rapid price reductions and performance advancements in hardware? For example, how often should an organization upgrade its computers and storage systems? Will upgrades increase personal and organizational productivity? How can organizations measure such increases?
- How should organizations determine the need for the new hardware infrastructures, such as cloud computing? (We discuss cloud computing in Plug IT In 4.)
- Portable computers and advanced communications technologies have enabled employees to work from home or from anywhere. Will these new work styles benefit employees and the organization? How do organizations manage such new work styles?
- How do organizations manage employees who use their own portable devices (e.g., tablets and smartphones) for both personal and work purposes? That is, how do organizations handle the bring-your-own-device (BYOD) phenomenon?

Computer Hierarchy

The traditional standard for comparing classes of computers is their processing power. This section presents each class of computers, from the most powerful to the least powerful. It describes both the computers and their roles in modern organizations.

Supercomputers. The term supercomputer does not refer to a specific technology. Rather, it indicates the fastest computers available at any given time. At the time of this writing (mid-2015), the fastest supercomputers had speeds exceeding 30 petaflops (1 petaflop is 1,000 trillion floating point operations per second). A floating point operation is an arithmetic operation that involves decimals.

Large organizations use supercomputers to execute computationally demanding tasks involving very large data sets, such as military and scientific applications. In the business environment, for example, large banks use supercomputers to calculate the risks and returns of various investment strategies, and healthcare organizations use them to analyze giant databases of patient data to determine optimal treatments for various diseases.

Mainframe Computers. Mainframes remain popular in large enterprises for extensive computing applications that are accessed by thousands of users at one time. Examples of mainframe applications are airline reservation systems, corporate payroll programs, Web site transaction processing systems (e.g., Amazon and eBay), and student grade calculation and reporting.

Today's mainframes perform at teraflop (trillions of floating point operations per second) speeds and can handle millions of transactions per day. In addition, mainframes provide a secure, robust environment in which to run strategic, mission-critical applications.

Microcomputers. Microcomputers—also called *micros, personal computers*, or *PCs*—are the smallest and least expensive category of general-purpose computers. It is important to point out that people frequently define a PC as a computer that utilizes the Microsoft Windows operating system. In fact, a variety of PCs are available, and many of them do not use Windows. One well-known example is Apple Mac, which uses the Mac OS X operating system (discussed later in this Plug IT In). The major categories of microcomputers are desktops, thin clients, notebooks and laptops, netbooks, and tablets.

Laptop and Notebook Computers. Laptop computers (or notebook computers) are small, easily transportable, lightweight microcomputers that fit comfortably into a briefcase (Figure PI2.1). They also provide users with access to processing power and data outside an office environment.

For example, the Google Chromebook is a thin client laptop that runs Google's Chrome operating system. A thin client is a computer that does not offer the full functionality of a PC. A fat client is a computer that has the ability to perform many functions without a network connection. Thin clients are less complex than fat clients because they do not have locally installed software. When thin clients need to run an application, they access it from a server over a network rather than from a local disk drive.

A thin client would not have Microsoft Office installed on it. Thus, thin clients are easier and less expensive to operate and support than fat clients. The benefits of thin clients include fast application deployment, centralized management, lower cost of ownership, and easier installation, management, maintenance, and support. The main disadvantage of thin clients is that if the network fails, then users can do very little on their computers. In contrast, if users have fat clients and the network fails, they can still perform some functions because they have software, such as Microsoft Office, installed on their computers.

Laptop computer

Tablet Computers. A tablet computer (or tablet) is a complete computer contained entirely in a flat touch screen that users operate via a stylus, digital pen, or fingertip instead of a keyboard or mouse. Examples of tablets are the Apple iPad 3 (www.apple.com/ipad), the HP Slate 10 (www.hp.com), the Microsoft Surface Pro 3 (www.microsoft.com), and many others.

Motorola Xoom tablet

© PhotoEdit/Alamy

Wearable Computers. Wearable computers are miniature computers that people wear under, with, or on top of their clothing. Key features of wearable computers are that there is constant interaction between the computer and the users and that the users can multitask, meaning they do not have to stop what they are doing to utilize the device. Examples of wearable computers are the Apple Watch (www.apple.com/watch/), the Sony SmartWatch 3 (http://www.sonymobile.com/global-en/products/smartwear/smartwatch-3-swr50/), Google Glass (www.google.com/glass/start/), and the Fitbit (www.fitbit.com) activity tracker.

Google Glass is an excellent example of a device that provides augmented reality. Augmented reality is a live, direct or indirect, view of a physical, real-world environment whose elements are augmented, or enhanced, by computer-generated sensory input such as sound, video, graphics, or GPS data. That is, augmented reality enhances the user's perception of reality. Note that, in contrast, virtual reality replaces the real world with a simulated world. As an example of augmented reality with Google Glass, let's say that you are looking for a destination in an unfamiliar city. You ask Google Glass for directions, and the device will overlay your vision with a graphic display of a street map, with the route to your destination highlighted.

© Oleksiy Makymenko/Alamy

Apple iPad tablet

FIGURE PI2.1 Laptop, notebook, and tablet computers.

IT's Personal: Purchasing a Computer

One day you will purchase a computer for yourself or your job. When that day comes, it will be important for you to know what to look for. Buying a computer can be very confusing if you just read the box. This Plug IT In has explained the major hardware components of a computer. There are more things you need to consider, however, when you purchase a computer: what you plan to do with it, where you plan to use it, and how long you need service from it? Let's look at each question more closely.

- What do you plan to do with your computer? Consider that when you buy a vehicle, your plans for using the vehicle determine the type of vehicle you will purchase. The same rules apply to purchasing a computer. You need to consider what you currently do with a computer and what you may do before you replace the one under consideration. Although many people simply buy as much as they can afford, they may overpay because they do not consider what they need the computer for.

- Where do you plan to use your computer? If you only plan to use it at home at your desk, then a desktop model will be fine. In general, you can get more computer for your money in a desktop model as opposed to a laptop (i.e., you pay extra for mobility). However, if you think you may want to take the computer with you, then you will need some type of a laptop or tablet computer. When portability is a requirement, you will want to reconsider what you plan to use the computer for because as computers become more portable (smaller), their functionality changes, and you want to make sure the computer will meet your needs.

- How long do you need service from this computer? Today, we anticipate that most of the devices we purchase will become outdated and need to be replaced in a few years. Therefore, the length of service is really more about warranty and the availability of repair services. In some cases, you should base your purchase decision on these issues rather than speed because they can extend the life of your computer.

Input and Output Technologies

Input technologies allow people and other technologies to enter data into a computer. The two main types of input devices are human data-entry devices and source-data automation devices. As their name implies, *human data-entry* devices require a certain amount of human effort to input data. Examples are keyboard, mouse, pointing stick, trackball, joystick, touchscreen, stylus, and voice recognition.

In contrast, *source-data automation* devices input data with minimal human intervention. These technologies speed up data collection, reduce errors, and gather data at the source of a transaction or other event. Barcode readers are an example of source-data automation. Table PI2.1 describes the various input devices.

TABLE PI2.1 Input Devices

Input Device	Description
Human Data-Entry Devices	
Keyboards	Most common input device (for text and numerical data).
Mouse	Handheld device used to point the cursor at a point on screen, such as an icon; the user clicks a button on the mouse, instructing the computer to take some action.
Optical mouse	The mouse is not connected to computer by a cable; rather, it uses camera chip to take images of surface it passes over, comparing successive images to determine its position.
Trackball	User rotates a ball built into top of device to move the cursor (rather than moving an entire device such as a mouse).
Pointing stick	Small button-like device; the cursor moves in the direction of the pressure the user places on the stick. Located between the keys near the center of the keyboard.
Touchpad	User moves the cursor by sliding a finger across a sensitized pad and then can tap the pad when the cursor is in (also called a trackpad) the desired position to instruct the computer to take action (also called glide-and-tap pad).
Graphics tablet	A device that can be used in place of, or in conjunction with, a mouse or trackball; it has a flat surface for drawing and a pen or stylus that is programmed to work with the tablet.

Joystick	The joystick moves the cursor to the desired place on the screen; commonly used in video games and in workstations that display dynamic graphics.
Touchscreen	Users instruct computer to take some action by touching a particular part of the screen; commonly used in information kiosks such as ATM machines. Touchscreens now have gesture controls for browsing through photographs, moving objects around on a screen, flicking to turn the page of a book, and playing video games. For example, see the Apple iPhone.
Stylus	Pen-style device that allows user either to touch parts of a predetermined menu of options or to handwrite information into the computer (as with some PDAs); works with touch-sensitive screens.
Digital pen	Mobile device that digitally captures everything you write; built-in screen confirms that what you write has been saved; also captures sketches, figures, and so on with on-board flash memory.
Web camera (Webcam)	A real-time video camera whose images can be accessed via the Web or instant messaging.
Voice recognition	Microphone converts analog voice sounds into digital input for a computer; critical technology for physically challenged people who cannot use other input devices.

Gesture-Based Input

Gesture recognition refers to technologies that enable computers to interpret human gestures. These technologies would be the first step in designing computers that can understand human body language. This process creates a richer interaction between machines and humans than has been possible via keyboards, graphical user interfaces, and the mouse. Gesture recognition enables humans to interact naturally with a computer without any intervening mechanical devices. With gesture-based technologies, the user can move the cursor by pointing a finger at a computer screen. These technologies could make conventional input devices (the mouse, keyboards, and touchscreens) redundant. Examples of gesture-based input devices are the Nintendo Wii (www.nintendo.com/wii), the Microsoft Kinect (www.xbox.com/kinect), and the Leap Motion Controller (www.leapmotion.com).

Wii	A video game console produced by Nintendo. A distinguishing feature of the Wii is its wireless controller, which can be used as a handheld pointing device and can detect movement in three dimensions.
Microsoft Kinect	A device that enables users to control and interact with the Xbox 360 through a natural interface using gestures and spoken commands. Kinect eliminates the need for a game controller.
Leap Motion Controller	A motion-sensing, matchbox-sized device placed on a physical desktop. Using two cameras, the device "observes" an area up to a distance of about three feet. It precisely tracks fingers or items such as a pen that cross into the observed area. The Leap can perform tasks such as navigating a Web site, using pinch-to-zoom gestures on maps, performing high-precision drawing, and manipulating complex three-dimensional visualizations. The smaller observation area and higher resolution of the device differentiates it from the Microsoft Kinect, which is more suitable for whole-body tracking in a space the size of a living room.

Source-Data Automation Input Devices

Automated teller machine (ATM)	A device that includes source-data automation input in the form of a magnetic stripe reader; human input via a keyboard; and output via a monitor, printer, and cash dispenser.
Magnetic stripe reader	A device that reads data from a magnetic stripe, usually on the back of a plastic card (e.g., credit and debit cards).
Point-of-sale terminals	Computerized cash registers that also may incorporate touchscreen technology and barcode scanners to input data such as item sold and price.
Barcode scanners	Devices that scan black-and-white barcode lines printed on merchandise labels.
Optical mark reader	Scanner for detecting the presence of dark marks on a predetermined grid, such as multiple-choice test answer sheets.
Magnetic ink character reader	A device that reads magnetic ink printed on checks that identify the bank, checking account, and check number.
Optical character recognition	Software that converts text into digital form for input into computer.

Sensors	Devices that collect data directly from the environment and input data directly into computer; examples are vehicle airbag activation sensors and radio-frequency identification tags.
Cameras	Digital cameras capture images and convert them into digital files.
Radio-frequency identification (RFID)	Uses technology that uses active or passive tags (transmitters) to wirelessly transmit product information to electronic readers. (We discuss RFID in detail in Chapter 8.)

The output generated by a computer can be transmitted to the user via several output devices and media. These devices include monitors, printers, plotters, and voice. Table PI2.2 describes the various output devices.

TABLE PI2.2 Output Devices

Output Device	Description
Monitors	
Cathode ray tubes	Video screens on which an electron beam illuminates pixels on a display screen.
Liquid crystal displays (LCDs)	Flat displays that have liquid crystals between two polarizers to form characters and images on a backlit screen.
Flexible displays	Thin, plastic, bendable computer screens.
Organic light-emitting diodes (OLEDs)	Displays that are brighter, thinner, lighter, cheaper, faster, and take less power to run than LCDs.
Retinal scanning displays	Project image directly onto a viewer's retina; used in medicine, air traffic control, and controlling industrial machines.
Heads-up displays	Any transparent display that presents data without requiring the user to look away from his or her usual viewpoint; for example, see Microvision (www.microvision.com).
Printers	
Laser	Use laser beams to write information on photosensitive drums; produce high-resolution text and graphics.
Inkjet	Shoot fine streams of colored ink onto paper; usually less expensive to buy than laser printers but can be more expensive to operate; can offer resolution quality equal to laser printers.
Thermal	Produce a printed image by selectively heating coated thermal paper; when the paper passes over the thermal print head, the coating turns black in the areas where it is heated, producing an image.
Plotters	Use computer-directed pens for creating high-quality images, blueprints, schematics, drawing of new products, and so on.
Voice output	A speaker/headset that can output sounds of any type; voice output is a software function that uses this equipment.
Electronic book reader	A wireless, portable reading device with access to books, blogs, newspapers, and magazines. Onboard storage holds hundreds of books (e.g., Amazon Kindle, Sony Reader).
Pocket projector	A projector in a handheld device that provides an alternative display method to alleviate the problem of tiny display screens in handheld devices. Pocket projectors will project digital images onto any viewing surface (e.g., see the Pico Projector).

Multimedia technology is the computer-based integration of text, sound, still images, animation, and digitized motion video. It usually consists of a collection of various input and output technologies. Multimedia merges the capabilities of computers with televisions, CD players, DVD players, video and audio recording equipment, and music and gaming technologies.

High-quality multimedia processing requires powerful microprocessors and extensive memory capacity, including both primary and secondary storage.

The Central Processing Unit

The central processing unit performs the actual computation or "number crunching" inside any computer. The CPU is a microprocessor (e.g., Intel's Core i3, i5, and i7 chips with more to come) made up of millions of microscopic transistors embedded in a circuit on a silicon wafer or *chip*. For this reason, microprocessors are commonly referred to as chips.

As shown in Figure PI2.2, the microprocessor has different parts, which perform different functions. The control unit sequentially accesses program instructions, decodes them, and controls the flow of data to and from the arithmetic logic unit, the registers, the caches, primary storage, secondary storage, and various output devices. The arithmetic logic unit (ALU) performs the mathematical calculations and makes logical comparisons. The registers are high-speed storage areas that store very small amounts of data and instructions for short periods.

FIGURE PI2.2 Parts of a microprocessor.

How the CPU Works

In the CPU, inputs enter and are stored until they are needed. At that point, they are retrieved and processed, and the output is stored and then delivered somewhere. Figure PI2.3 illustrates this process, which works as follows:

- The inputs consist of data and brief instructions about what to do with the data. These instructions come into the CPU from random access memory (RAM). Data might be entered by the user through the keyboard, for example, or read from a data file in another part of the computer. The inputs are stored in registers until they are sent to the next step in the processing.

- Data and instructions travel in the chip via electrical pathways called *buses*. The size of the bus—analogous to the width of a highway—determines how much information can flow at any time.

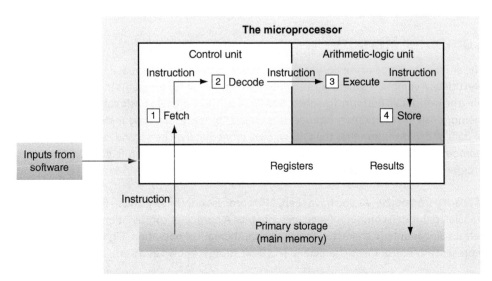

FIGURE PI2.3 How the CPU works.

- The control unit directs the flow of data and instructions within the chip.
- The ALU receives the data and instructions from the registers and makes the desired computation. These data and instructions have been translated into binary form—that is, only 0s and 1s. A "0" or a "1" is called a bit. The CPU can process only binary data. All types of data, such as letters, decimal numbers, photographs, music, and so on, can be converted to a binary representation, which can then be processed by the CPU.
- The data in their original form and the instructions are sent to storage registers and then are sent back to a storage place outside the chip, such as the computer's hard drive. Meanwhile, the transformed data go to another register and then on to other parts of the computer (e.g., to the monitor for display or to storage).

Intel offers excellent demonstrations of how CPUs work: Search the web for "Intel" with "Explore the Curriculum" to find their demos. This cycle of processing, known as a *machine instruction cycle*, occurs billions of times per second.

Advances in Microprocessor Design

Innovations in chip designs are coming at a faster and faster rate, as described by Moore's law. In 1965, Gordon Moore, a cofounder of Intel Corporation, predicted that microprocessor complexity would double approximately every 18 months. His prediction has been amazingly accurate.

The advances predicted from Moore's law arise mainly from the following changes:

- Producing increasingly miniaturized transistors.
- Placing multiple processors on a single chip. Chips with more than one processor are called *multicore* chips. For example, the Cell chip, produced by a consortium of Sony, Toshiba, and IBM, contains nine processors. Intel (www.intel.com) and AMD (www.amd.com) offer multicore chips (e.g., quadcore chips with four CPUs).
- Intel's three-dimensional (3D) chips require less power than Intel's current chips while improving performance. These chips enhance the performance of all computers. However, they are particularly valuable in handheld devices, because they extend the device's battery life.

In addition to increased speeds and performance, Moore's law has had an impact on costs. For example, in 1997, a desktop computer with a Pentium II microprocessor, 64 megabytes of random access memory, a 4-gigabyte hard drive, and a 17-inch monitor cost $4,000. In early 2015, a desktop computer with an Intel i7 quad-core processor, 12 gigabytes of random access memory, a 1-terabyte hard drive plus 32 gigabytes of solid-state storage, and a 24-inch touchscreen cost approximately $1,500.

Computer Memory

The amount and type of memory that a computer possesses has a great deal to do with its general utility. A computer's memory also determines the types of programs that the computer can run, the work it can perform, its speed, and its cost. There are two basic categories of computer memory. The first is *primary storage*. It is called "primary" because it stores small amounts of data and information that the CPU will use immediately. The second category is *secondary storage*, which stores much larger amounts of data and information (e.g., an entire software program) for extended periods.

Memory Capacity. As you have seen, CPUs process only binary units—0s and 1s—which are translated through computer languages into bits. A particular combination of bits represents a certain alphanumeric character or a simple mathematical operation. Eight bits are needed to represent any one of these characters. This 8-bit string is known as a byte. The storage capacity of a computer is measured in bytes. Bits typically are used as units of measure only for telecommunications capacity, as in how many million bits per second can be sent through a particular medium.

The hierarchy of terms used to describe memory capacity is as follows:

- *Kilobyte. Kilo* means "one thousand," so a kilobyte (KB) is approximately 1,000 bytes. Actually, a kilobyte is 1,024 bytes. Computer designers find it convenient to work with powers of 2: 1,024 is 2 to the 10th power, and 1,024 is close enough to 1,000 that for *kilobyte* people use the standard prefix *kilo*, which means exactly 1,000 in familiar units such as the kilogram or kilometer.
- *Megabyte.* Mega means "one million," so a megabyte (MB) is approximately 1 million bytes. Most personal computers have hundreds of megabytes of RAM memory.
- *Gigabyte.* Giga means "one billion," so a gigabyte (GB) is approximately 1 billion bytes.
- *Terabyte.* A terabyte is approximately 1 trillion bytes. The storage capacity of modern personal computers can be several terabytes.
- *Petabyte.* A petabyte is approximately 1,000 terabytes.
- *Exabyte.* An exabyte is approximately 1,000 petabytes.
- *Zettabyte.* A zettabyte is approximately 1,000 exabytes.

To get a feel for these amounts, consider the following example: If your computer has one terabyte of storage capacity on its hard drive (a type of secondary storage), it can store approximately 1 trillion bytes of data. If the average page of text contains about 2,000 bytes, then your hard drive could store approximately 10 percent of all the print collections of the Library of Congress. That same terabyte can store 70 hours of standard-definition compressed video.

Primary Storage. Primary storage, or main memory, as it is sometimes called, stores three types of information for very brief periods of time: (1) data to be processed by the CPU, (2) instructions for the CPU as to how to process the data, and (3) operating system programs that manage various aspects of the computer's operation. Primary storage takes place in chips mounted on the computer's main circuit board, called the *motherboard*. These chips are located as close as physically possible to the CPU chip. As with the CPU, all the data and instructions in primary storage have been translated into binary code.

The four main types of primary storage are (1) register, (2) cache memory, (3) random access memory, and (4) read-only memory (ROM). You learn about each type of primary storage next.

Registers are part of the CPU. They have the least capacity, storing extremely limited amounts of instructions and data only immediately before and after processing.

Cache memory is a type of high-speed memory that enables the computer to temporarily store blocks of data that are used more often and that a processor can access more rapidly than main memory (RAM). Cache memory is physically located closer to the CPU than RAM. Blocks that are used less often remain in RAM until they are transferred to cache; blocks used infrequently remain in secondary storage. Cache memory is faster than RAM because the instructions travel a shorter distance to the CPU.

Random access memory is the part of primary storage that holds a software program and small amounts of data for processing. Compared with the registers, RAM stores more information and is located farther away from the CPU. However, compared with secondary storage, RAM stores less information and is much closer to the CPU.

RAM is temporary and, in most cases, *volatile*—that is, RAM chips lose their contents if the current is lost or turned off, as from a power surge, brownout, or electrical noise generated by lightning or nearby machines.

Most of us have lost data at one time or another due to a computer "crash" or a power failure. What is usually lost is whatever is in RAM, cache, or the registers at the time, because these types of memory are volatile. Therefore, you need greater security when you are storing certain types of critical data or instructions. Cautious computer users frequently save data to nonvolatile memory (secondary storage). In addition, most modern software applications have autosave functions.

Read-only memory is the place—actually, a type of chip—where certain critical instructions are safeguarded. ROM is nonvolatile, so it retains these instructions when the power to the computer is turned off. The read-only designation means that these instructions can only be read by the computer and cannot be changed by the user. An example of ROM is the instructions needed to start or "boot" the computer after it has been shut off.

Secondary Storage. Secondary storage is designed to store very large amounts of data for extended periods. Secondary storage has the following characteristics:

- It is nonvolatile.
- It takes more time to retrieve data from it than from RAM.
- It is cheaper than primary storage (see Figure PI2.4).
- It can utilize a variety of media, each with its own technology.

One secondary storage medium, magnetic tape, is kept on a large open reel or in a smaller cartridge or cassette. Although this is an old technology, it remains popular because it is the cheapest storage medium, and it can handle enormous amounts of data. As a result, many organizations (e.g., the U.S. Government Social Security Administration) use magnetic tape for archival storage. The downside is that it is the slowest method for retrieving data because all the data are placed on the tape sequentially. This process means that the system might have to run through the majority of the tape before it comes to the desired piece of data.

Magnetic disks (or hard drives or fixed disk drives) are the most commonly used mass storage devices because of their low cost, high speed, and large storage capacity. Hard disk drives read from, and write to, stacks of rotating (at up to 15,000 rpm) magnetic disk platters mounted in rigid enclosures and sealed against environmental and atmospheric contamination (see Figure PI2.5). These disks are permanently mounted in a unit that may be internal or external to the computer.

Solid-state drives (SSDs) are data storage devices that serve the same purpose as a hard drive and store data in memory chips. Whereas hard drives have moving parts, SSDs do not. SSDs use the same interface with the computer's CPU as hard drives and are therefore a seamless replacement for hard drives. SSDs offer many advantages over hard drives. They use less power, are silent and faster, and produce about one-third the heat of a hard drive. The major disadvantage of SSDs is that they cost more than hard drives.

Unlike magnetic media, optical storage devices do not store data via magnetism. Rather, a laser reads the surface of a reflective plastic platter. Optical disk drives are slower than magnetic hard drives, but they are less fragile and less susceptible to damage from contamination.

FIGURE PI2.4 Primary memory compared with secondary storage.

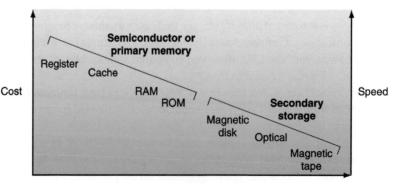

Homiel / iStockphoto

© Krzysztof Krzyscin/iStockphoto

FIGURE PI2.5 Traditional hard drives are less expensive, but solid-state drives are faster and are more reliable.

In addition, optical disks can store a great deal of information, both on a routine basis and when combined into storage systems. Types of optical disks include compact disk read-only memory and digital video disk.

Compact disk read-only memory (*CD-ROM*) storage devices feature high capacity, low cost, and high durability. However, because a CD-ROM is a read-only medium, it cannot be written on. *CD-R* can be written to, but once this is done, what was written on it cannot be changed later. That is, CD-R is writable, which CD-ROM is not, but it is not rewritable, which *CD-RW* (compact disk, rewritable) is. There are applications where not being rewritable is a plus, because it prevents some types of accidental data destruction. CD-RW adds rewritability to the recordable compact disk market.

The digital video disk (*DVD*) is a 5-inch disk with the capacity to store about 135 minutes of digital video. DVDs can also perform as computer storage disks, providing storage capabilities of 17 gigabytes. DVD players can read current CD-ROMs, but current CD-ROM players cannot read DVDs. The access speed of a DVD drive is faster than that of a typical CD-ROM drive.

A dual-layer *Blu-ray disk* can store 50 gigabytes, almost three times the capacity of a dual-layer DVD. Development of Blu-ray technology is ongoing, with three- and four-layered Blu-ray disks available.

Flash memory devices (or *memory cards*) are nonvolatile electronic storage devices that contain no moving parts and use 30 times less battery power than hard drives. Flash devices are also smaller and more durable than hard drives. The trade-offs are that flash devices store less data than hard drives. Flash devices are used with digital cameras, handheld and laptop computers, telephones, music players, and video game consoles.

One popular flash memory device is the thumb drive (also called *memory stick, jump drive*, or *flash drive*). These devices fit into Universal Serial Bus (USB) ports on personal computers and other devices, and they can store many gigabytes. Thumb drives have replaced magnetic floppy disks for portable storage.

Before you go on . . .

1. Decisions about hardware focus on what three factors?

2. What are the overall trends in hardware?

3. Define hardware and list the major hardware components.

4. Describe the different types of computers.

5. Distinguish between human data-input devices and source-data automation.

6. Briefly describe how a microprocessor functions.

7. Distinguish between primary storage and secondary storage.

Apply the Concept PI2.1

LEARNING OBJECTIVE PI2.1 Discuss strategic issues that link hardware design to business strategy.

STEP 1: Background (Here is what you are learning.)

In the modern businesses environment, computer hardware components are inextricably linked to business strategy. Put simply, computers are tools that allow businesses to automate some transactions and make others more efficient. As technology evolves, businesses need to evolve the ways they use that technology to execute their business strategies. The generally accepted rule is that technology should NOT drive business strategy, but business strategy MUST consider how the organization can implement new types of hardware to achieve its goals.

STEP 2: Activity (Here is what you are doing.)

Consider Lowe's (http://www.lowes.com). A large home improvement warehouse store might seem very distant from the use of information technology. However, in 2011 Lowe's made significant improvements to its customer experience by implementing a type of hardware. What hardware is that? The answer is—smartphones.

Visit http://www.wiley.com/go/rainer/MIS4e/applytheconcept, and click on the link provided for Apply the Concept PI2.1. This link will take you to a *U.S. News and World Report* article that discusses how Lowe's implemented smartphone technology for their employees and their customers.

STEP 3: Deliverable (Here is what you will turn in.)

Discuss strategic issues that link hardware design to business strategy, using the Lowe's case to illustrate these links. Put your discussion in a Word document and submit it to your professor.

PI2.2 Introduction to Software

Computer hardware is only as effective as the instructions you give it. Those instructions are contained in software. The importance of computer software cannot be overestimated. The first software applications for computers in business were developed in the early 1950s. At that time, software was less costly. Today, software comprises a much larger percentage of the cost of modern computer systems because the price of hardware has dramatically decreased, while both the complexity and the price of software have dramatically increased.

The ever-increasing complexity of software has also increased the potential for errors, or *bugs*. Large applications today may contain millions of lines of computer code, written by hundreds of people over the course of several years. Thus, the potential for errors is huge, and testing and debugging software is expensive and time consuming.

In spite of these overall trends—increasing complexity, cost, and numbers of defects—software has become an everyday feature of our business and personal lives. Your examination of software begins with definitions of some fundamental concepts. Software consists of computer programs, which are sequences of instructions for the computer. The process of writing or coding programs is called programming. Individuals who perform this task are called *programmers*.

Computer programs include documentation, which is a written description of the program's functions. Documentation helps the user operate the computer system, and it helps other programmers understand what the program does and how it accomplishes its purpose. Documentation is vital to the business organization. Without it, the departure of a key programmer or user could deprive the organization of the knowledge of how the program is designed and functions.

The computer can do nothing until it is instructed by software. Computer hardware, by design, is general purpose. Software enables the user to instruct the hardware to perform specific functions that provide business value. There are two major types of software: systems software and application software. Figure PI2.6 illustrates the relationship among hardware, systems software, and application software.

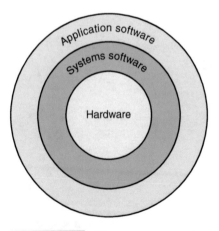

FIGURE PI2.6 Systems software services as intermediary between hardware and functional applications.

Software Issues

The importance of software in computer systems has brought new issues to the forefront for organizational managers. These issues include software defects (bugs), licensing, open systems, and open-source software.

Software Defects. All too often, computer program code is inefficient, poorly designed, and riddled with errors. The Software Engineering Institute (SEI) at Carnegie Mellon University in Pittsburgh defines good software as usable, reliable, defect free, cost effective, and maintainable. As our dependence on computers and networks increases, the risks associated with software defects are becoming more serious.

The SEI maintains that, on average, professional programmers make between 100 and 150 errors in every 1,000 lines of code they write. Fortunately, the software industry recognizes this problem. Unfortunately, however, the problem is enormous, and the industry is taking only initial steps to resolve it. One critical step is better design and planning at the beginning of the development process (discussed in Chapter 13).

Software Licensing. Many people routinely copy proprietary software. However, making copies without the manufacturer's explicit permission—a practice known as *piracy*—is illegal. The Business Software Alliance (BSA; www.bsa.org), a nonprofit trade association dedicated to promoting a safe and legal digital world, collects, investigates, and acts on software piracy tips. The BSA has calculated that piracy costs software vendors around the world billions of dollars annually. Most of the tips the BSA receives come from current and past employees of offending companies.

To protect their investment, software vendors must prevent their products from being copied and distributed by individuals and other software companies. A company can copyright its software, which means that the U.S. Copyright Office grants the company the exclusive legal right to reproduce, publish, and sell that software.

The number of computing devices in organizations continues to grow, and businesses continue to decentralize, so IS managers are finding it increasingly difficult to supervise their software assets. In fact, the majority of chief information officers (CIOs) are not confident that their companies were in compliance with software licensing agreements. For example, one medium-size company was fined $10,000 for unknowingly using Microsoft Exchange mailbox licenses that had not been purchased. Worse, the company was also fined $100,000 for not having the necessary licenses for Autodesk, Inc.'s AutoCAD design software.

To help companies manage their software licenses, new firms have arisen that specialize in tracking software licenses for a fee. For example, Cherwell (https://www.cherwell.com) will track and manage a company's software licenses to ensure they are in compliance with U.S. copyright laws.

Open Systems. The open systems concept refers to a group of computing products that work together. In an open system, the same operating system with compatible software is installed on all computers that interact within an organization. A complementary approach is to employ application software that will run across all computer platforms. Where hardware, operating systems, and application software are all designed as open systems, users can purchase the best software, called *best of breed*, for a job without worrying whether it will run on particular hardware.

Open-Source Software. Organizations today are increasingly selecting open-source software rather than proprietary software. Proprietary software is purchased software that has restrictions on its use, copying, and modification. Companies that develop proprietary software spend money and time developing their products, which they then sell in the marketplace. This software is labeled *proprietary* because the developer keeps the source code—the actual computer instructions—private (just as Coca-Cola does with its formula). Therefore, companies that purchase the software can utilize it in their operations, but they cannot change the source code themselves.

In contrast, the source code for open-source software is available at no cost to both developers and users. This software is distributed with license terms that ensure that its source code will always be available.

Open-source software is produced by worldwide "communities" of developers who write and maintain the code. Inside each community, however, only a small group of developers, called *core developers*, is allowed to modify the code directly. All the other developers must submit their suggested changes to the core developers.

There are advantages to implementing open-source software in an organization. According to OpenSource (www.opensource.org), open-source development produces high-quality, reliable, low-cost software. This software is also flexible, meaning that the code can be changed to meet users' needs. In many cases, open-source software can be more reliable than proprietary software. Because the code is available to many developers, more bugs are discovered early and quickly, and they are fixed immediately. Technical support for open-source software is also available from firms that offer products derived from the software. An example is Red Hat (www.redhat.com), a major Linux vendor that supplies solutions to problems associated with open-source technology. Specifically, Red Hat provides education, training, and technical support, for a fee.

Open-source software, however, also has disadvantages. The major drawback is that companies that use open-source software depend on the continued goodwill of an army of volunteers for enhancements, bug fixes, and so on, even if they have signed a contract that includes support. Some companies will not accept this risk, although as a practical matter the support community for Linux, Apache, and Firefox is not likely to disappear. Further, organizations that do not have in-house technical experts will have to purchase maintenance–support contracts from a third party. In addition, open-source software poses questions concerning ease of use, the time and expense needed to train users, and compatibility with existing systems either within or outside the organization.

There are many examples of open-source software, including the GNU (GNU's Not UNIX) suite of software (www.gnu.org) developed by the Free Software Foundation (www.fsf.org); the Linux operating system (see www.linux.com); Apache Web server (www.apache.org); sendmail SMTP (Send Mail Transport Protocol) e-mail server (www.sendmail.com); the Perl programming language (www.perl.org); and the Firefox browser from Mozilla (www.mozilla.com). In fact, more than 150,000 open-source projects are under way at SourceForge (www.sourceforge.net), the popular open-source hosting site.

Open-source software is moving to the mainstream, as you see by the many major companies that use this type of software. For example, Japan's Shinsei Bank (www.shinseibank.com) uses Linux on its servers; SugarCRM (www.sugarcrm.com) for certain customer relationship management tasks; and MySQL (www.mysql.com) open-source database management software. Further, the *Los Angeles Times* uses Alfresco (www.alfresco.com) to manage some of the images and video for its Web site.

Systems Software

Systems software is a set of instructions that serves primarily as an intermediary between computer hardware and application programs. Systems software performs many functions:

- It controls and supports the computer system and its information-processing activities.
- It enables computer systems to perform self-regulatory functions by loading itself when the computer is first turned on.
- It provides commonly used sets of instructions for all applications.
- It helps users and IT personnel program, test, and debug their own computer programs.
- It supports application software by directing the computer's basic functions.

The major type of systems software with which we are concerned is the operating system. The operating system (OS) is the "director" of your computer system's operations. It supervises the overall operation of the computer by monitoring the computer's status, scheduling operations, and managing input and output processes. Well-known desktop operating systems include Microsoft Windows (www.microsoft.com), Apple Mac OS X (www.apple.com), Linux (www.linux.com), and Google Chrome (www.google.com/chrome). When a new version with new features is released, the developers often give the new version a new designation. For example, in early 2015, the latest version of Windows was Windows 10, and the latest version of OS X was Yosemite.

The operating system also provides an interface between the user and the hardware. This user interface hides the complexity of the hardware from the user. That is, you do not have to know how the hardware actually operates; you simply have to know what the hardware will do and what you need to do to obtain the desired results.

The ease or difficulty of the interaction between the user and the computer is determined to a large extent by the graphical user interface (GUI). The GUI allows users to directly control the hardware by manipulating visible objects (such as icons) and actions that replace complex commands. Microsoft Windows provides a widely recognized GUI.

GUI technology incorporates features such as virtual reality, head-mounted displays, speech input (user commands) and output, pen and gesture recognition, animation, multimedia, artificial intelligence, and cellular/wireless communication capabilities. These new interfaces, called *natural user interfaces* (NUIs), will combine social, haptic, and touch-enabled gesture-control interfaces. (A *haptic interface* provides tactile feedback through the sense of touch by applying forces, vibrations, or motions to the user.)

A social interface guides the user through computer applications by using cartoon-like characters, graphics, animation, and voice commands. The cartoon-like characters can be puppets, narrators, guides, inhabitants, or *avatars* (computer-generated human-like figures). Social interfaces are hard to create without being corny. For example, the assistant "Clippy" was so annoying to users of Microsoft Office 97 that it was eliminated from Office 2003 and all subsequent versions.

Motion control gaming consoles are another type of interface. Three major players currently offer this interface: the Xbox 360 Kinect, the PS3 PlayStation Move, and the Nintendo Wii.

- Kinect tracks your movements without a physical controller, has voice recognition, and accommodates multiple players.

- The PlayStation Move uses a physical controller with motion-sensing electronics, making it the technological "cross" between Kinect and Wii. Move requires each player to use a wand.

- Wii uses a physical controller. Compared with Kinect and Move, Wii has been on the market longer, it has the biggest library of motion-sensing games, and it is the least expensive. On the negative side, Wii has the least accurate motion sensing of the three systems, and, unlike Kinect and Move, it is not available in high definition.

Touch-enabled gesture-control interfaces enable users to browse through photos, "toss" objects around a screen, "flick" to turn the pages of a book, play video games, and watch movies. Examples of this type of interface are Microsoft Surface and the Apple iPhone. Microsoft Surface is used in casinos such as Harrah's iBar in Las Vegas and in some AT&T stores. A very visible use of Surface was the touch wall used by the major television networks during their coverage of various elections.

Application Software

Application software is a set of computer instructions that provides specific functionality to a user. This functionality may be broad, such as general word processing, or narrow, such as an organization's payroll program. Essentially, an application program applies a computer to a certain need. As you will see, modern organizations use many different software applications.

Application software may be developed in-house by the organization's information systems personnel, or it may be commissioned from a software vendor. Alternatively, the software can be purchased, leased, or rented from a vendor that develops applications and sells them to many organizations. This "off-the-shelf" software may be a standard package, or it may be customizable. Special-purpose programs or "packages" can be tailored for a specific purpose, such as inventory control and payroll. A **package**, or **software suite**, is a group of programs with integrated functions that has been developed by a vendor and is available for purchase in a prepackaged form. Microsoft Office is a well-known example of a package, or software suite.

General-purpose, off-the-shelf application programs designed to help individual users increase their productivity are referred to as **personal application software**. Table PI2.3 lists some of the major types of personal application software.

TABLE PI2.3 Personal Application Software

Category of Personal Application Software	Major Functions	Examples
Spreadsheets	Use rows and columns to manipulate primarily numerical data; useful for analyzing financial information and for what–if and goal-seeking analyses	Microsoft Excel Corel Quattro Pro Apple iWork Numbers
Word processing	Allow users to manipulate primarily text with many writing and editing features	Microsoft Word Apple iWork Pages
Desktop publishing	Extend word processing software to allow production of finished, camera-ready documents, which may contain photographs, diagrams, and other images combined with text in different fonts	Microsoft Publisher QuarkXPress
Data management	Allow users to store, retrieve, and manipulate related data	Microsoft Access FileMaker Pro
Presentation	Allow users to create and edit graphically rich information to appear on electronic slides	Microsoft PowerPoint Apple iWork Keynote
Graphics	Allow users to create, store, and display or print charts, graphs, maps, and drawings	Adobe PhotoShop Corel DRAW
Personal information management	Allow users to create and maintain calendars, appointments, to-do lists, and business contacts	IBM Lotus Notes Microsoft Outlook
Personal finance	Allow users to maintain checkbooks, track investments, monitor credit cards, and bank and pay bills electronically	Quicken Microsoft Money
Web authoring	Allow users to design Web sites and publish them on the Web	Microsoft FrontPage Macromedia Dreamweaver
Communications	Allow users to communicate with other people over any distance	Novell Groupwise

Speech-recognition software, also called *voice recognition*, is an input technology, rather than strictly an application, that enables users to provide input to systems software and application software. As the name suggests, this software recognizes and interprets human speech, either one word at a time (*discrete speech*) or in a conversational stream (*continuous speech*). Advances in processing power, new software algorithms, and better microphones have enabled developers to design extremely accurate speech-recognition software. Experts predict that, in the near future, voice recognition systems will be built into almost every device, appliance, and machine that people use. Applications for voice recognition technology abound. Consider these examples:

- Call centers are using this technology. The average call costs $5 if it is handled by an employee, but only 50 cents with a self-service, speech-enabled system.

- Apple's OS X and Microsoft's Windows 10 operating systems come with built-in voice technology.
- Nuance's Dragon NaturallySpeaking (www.nuance.com) enables accurate voice-to-text and e-mail dictation.

Before you go on . . .

1. What does the following statement mean? "Hardware is useless without software."
2. What are the differences between systems software and application software?
3. What is open-source software, and what are its advantages? Can you think of any disadvantages?
4. Describe the functions of the operating system.

Apply the Concept PI2.2

LEARNING OBJECTIVE PI2.2 Differentiate between the two major types of software.

STEP 1: Background

There are two types of software (systems and application), two general ways of obtaining software licenses (proprietary vs. open-source), and two general types of uses (traditional vs. mobile). You should be sufficiently familiar with software to be able to categorize programs that you use.

STEP 2: Activity

Visit http://www.wiley.com/go/rainer/MIS4e/applytheconcept, and click on the link for Apply the Concept PI2.2. This link will take you to CNET's Download.com. At this Web site, you should immediately notice one of the categories mentioned above. At the time of this writing, the site automatically recognized the type of computer operating system on the user's computer.

For example, this author is writing on a Mac, and the system recognized the Mac OS and defaulted to the Mac software page.

Review the available software, and differentiate between the operating systems and the applications. Within applications, differentiate by method of obtaining a license — some you have to pay for, and some are available by open-source or freeware licensing.

STEP 3: Deliverable

Build a table that differentiates between the two major types of software. To complete this task, list 10 applications you reviewed on the Web site mentioned in Step 2. Use the template provided below. Turn your completed table to your instructor.

Application	Operating System	Licensing

What's in IT for me?

Hardware

For All Business Majors

The design of computer hardware has profound impacts for businesspeople. Personal and organizational success can depend on an understanding of hardware design and a commitment to knowing where it is going and what opportunities and challenges hardware innovations will bring. Because these innovations are occurring so rapidly, hardware decisions both at the individual level and at the organizational level are difficult.

At the *individual level*, most people who have a home or office computer system and want to upgrade it, or people who are contemplating their first computer purchase, are faced with the decision of *when* to buy as much as *what* to buy and at what cost. At the *organizational level*, these same issues plague IS professionals. However, they are more complex and more costly. Most organizations have many different computer systems in place at the same time. Innovations may come to different classes of computers at different times or rates. Therefore, managers must decide when old hardware *legacy systems* still have a productive role in the organization and when they should be replaced. A legacy system is an old computer system or application that continues to be used, typically because it still functions for the users' needs, even though newer technology is available.

Software

ACCT For the Accounting Major

Accounting application software performs the organization's accounting functions, which are repetitive and performed in high volumes. Each business transaction (e.g., a person hired, a paycheck produced, an item sold) produces data that must be captured. Accounting applications capture these data and then manipulate them as necessary. Accounting applications adhere to relatively standardized procedures, handle detailed data, and have a historical focus (i.e., what happened in the past).

FIN For the Finance Major

Financial application software provides information about the firm's financial status to persons and groups inside and outside the firm. Financial applications include forecasting, funds management, and control applications. Forecasting applications predict and project the firm's future activity in the economic environment. Funds management applications use cash flow models to analyze expected cash flows. Control applications enable managers to monitor their financial performance, typically by providing information about the budgeting process and performance ratios.

MKT For the Marketing Major

Marketing application software helps management solve problems that involve marketing the firm's products. Marketing software includes marketing research and marketing intelligence applications. Marketing applications provide information about the firm's products and competitors, its distribution system, its advertising and personal selling activities, and its pricing strategies. Overall, marketing applications help managers develop strategies that combine the four major elements of marketing: product, promotion, place, and price.

POM For the Production/Operations Management Major

Managers use production/operations management (POM) application software for production planning and as part of the physical production system. POM applications include production, inventory, quality, and cost software. These applications help management operate manufacturing facilities and logistics. Materials requirements planning (MRP) software also is widely used in manufacturing. This software identifies which materials will be needed, how much will be needed, and the dates on which they will be needed. This information enables managers to be proactive.

HRM For the Human Resources Management Major

Human resources management application software provides information concerning recruiting and hiring, education and training, maintaining the employee database, termination, and administering benefits. HRM applications include workforce planning, recruiting, workforce management, compensation, benefits, and environmental reporting subsystems (e.g., equal employment opportunity records and analysis, union enrollment, toxic substances, and grievances).

MIS For the MIS Major

If your company decides to develop its own software, the MIS function is responsible for managing this activity. If the company decides to buy software, the MIS function deals with software vendors in analyzing their products. The MIS function also is responsible for upgrading software as vendors release new versions.

Summary

1. Discuss the strategic issues that link hardware design to business strategy.

Strategic issues linking hardware design to business strategy include the following: How do organizations keep up with the rapid price/performance advancements in hardware? How often should an organization upgrade its computers and storage systems? How can organizations measure benefits gained from price/performance improvements in hardware?

2. Differentiate between the two major types of software.

Software consists of computer programs (coded instructions) that control the functions of computer hardware. There are two main categories of software: systems software and application software. Systems software manages the hardware resources of the computer system; it functions between the hardware and the application software. The major type of systems software is the operating system. Application software enables users to perform specific tasks and information-processing activities. Application software may be proprietary or off-the-shelf.

Glossary

application software The class of computer instructions that directs a computer system to perform specific processing activities and provide functionality for users.

arithmetic logic unit (ALU) Portion of the CPU that performs the mathematical calculations and makes logical comparisons.

augmented reality A live, direct or indirect, view of a physical, real-world environment whose elements are enhanced by computer-generated sensory input such as sound, video, graphics, or GPS data.

binary form The form in which data and instructions can be read by the CPU—only 0s and 1s.

bit Short for *binary digit* (0s and 1s), the only data that a CPU can process.

byte An 8-bit string of data, needed to represent any one alphanumeric character or simple mathematical operation.

cache memory A type of high-speed memory that enables the computer to temporarily store blocks of data that are used more often and that a processor can access more rapidly than main memory (RAM).

central processing unit (CPU) Hardware that performs the actual computation or "number crunching" inside any computer.

computer programs The sequences of instructions for the computer, which comprise software.

control unit Portion of the CPU that controls the flow of information.

documentation Written description of the functions of a software program.

fat clients Computers that offer full functionality without having to connect to a network.

flash memory devices Nonvolatile electronic storage devices that are compact, are portable, require little power, and contain no moving parts.

gesture recognition An input method that interprets human gestures, in an attempt for computers to begin to understand human body language.

graphical user interface (GUI) Systems software that allows users to have direct control of the hardware by manipulating visible objects (such as icons) and actions, which replace command syntax.

laptop computers (notebook computers) Small, easily transportable, lightweight microcomputers.

magnetic disks (or hard drives or fixed disk drives) A form of secondary storage on a magnetized disk divided into tracks and sectors that provide addresses for various pieces of data.

magnetic tape A secondary storage medium on a large open reel or in a smaller cartridge or cassette.

mainframes Relatively large computers used in large enterprises for extensive computing applications that are accessed by thousands of users.

microcomputers The smallest and least expensive category or general-purpose computers, also called micros, personal computers, or PCs.

microprocessor The CPU, made up of millions of transistors embedded in a circuit on a silicon wafer or chip.

Moore's law Prediction by Gordon Moore, an Intel cofounder, that microprocessor complexity would double approximately every 2 years.

multimedia technology Computer-based integration of text, sound, still images, animation, and digitized full-motion video.

notebook computer See laptop computers.

open-source software Software made available in source-code form at no cost to developers.

open systems Computing products that work together by using the same operating system with compatible software on all the computers that interact in an organization.

operating system (OS) The main system control program, which supervises the overall operations of the computer, allocates CPU time and main memory to programs, and provides an interface between the user and the hardware.

optical storage devices A form of secondary storage in which a laser reads the surface of a reflective plastic platter.

package Common term for an integrated group of computer programs developed by a vendor and available for purchase in prepackaged form.

personal application software General-purpose, off-the-shelf application programs that support general types of processing, rather than being linked to any specific business function.

primary storage (also called main memory) High-speed storage located directly on the motherboard that stores data to be processed by the CPU, instructions telling the CPU how to process the data, and operating system programs.

programming The process of writing or coding programs.

proprietary software Software that has been developed by a company and has restrictions on its use, copying, and modification.

random access memory (RAM) The part of primary storage that holds a software program and small amounts of data when they are brought from secondary storage.

read-only memory (ROM) Type of primary storage where certain critical instructions are safeguarded; the storage is nonvolatile and retains the instructions when the power to the computer is turned off.

registers High-speed storage areas in the CPU that store very small amounts of data and instructions for short periods.

secondary storage Technology that can store very large amounts of data for extended periods.

sequential access Data access in which the computer system must run through data in sequence to locate a particular piece.

server Computers that support networks, enabling users to share files, software, and other network devices.

social interface A user interface that guides the user through computer applications by using cartoon-like characters, graphics, animation, and voice commands.

software A set of computer programs that enable the hardware to process data.

software suite See **package**.

solid-state drives (SSDs) Data storage devices that serve the same purpose as a hard drive and store data in memory chips.

speech-recognition software Software that recognizes and interprets human speech, either one word at a time (discrete speech) or in a stream (continuous speech).

systems software The class of computer instructions that serve primarily as an intermediary between computer hardware and application programs; provides important self-regulatory functions for computer systems.

thin client A computer that does not offer the full functionality of a fat client.

thumb drive Storage device that fits into the USB port of a personal computer and is used for portable storage.

wearable computer A miniature computer worn by a person allowing the users to multitask.

Discussion Questions

1. What factors affect the speed of a microprocessor?

2. If you were the CIO of a firm, what factors would you consider when selecting secondary storage media for your company's records (files)?

3. Given that Moore's law has proved itself over the past two decades, speculate on what chip capabilities will be in 10 years. What might your desktop PC be able to do?

4. If you were the CIO of a firm, how would you explain the workings, benefits, and limitations of using thin clients as opposed to fat clients?

5. Where might you find embedded computers at home, at school, and/or at work?

6. What does this statement mean: "Hardware is useless without software."

7. You are the CIO of your company, and you have to develop an application of strategic importance to your firm. What are the advantages and disadvantages of using open-source software?

Problem-Solving Activities

1. Access the Web sites of the major chip manufacturers—for example, Intel (www.intel.com), Motorola (www.motorola.com), and Advanced Micro Devices (www.amd.com)—and obtain the latest information regarding new and planned chips. Compare performance and costs across these vendors. Be sure to take a close look at the various multi-core chips.

2. Access "The Journey Inside" on Intel's Web site at http://www.intel.com/content/www/us/en/education/k12/the-journey-inside.html. Prepare a presentation of each step in the machine instruction cycle.

3. A great deal of free software is available over the Internet. Go to http://www.pcmag.com/article2/0, 2817, 2381528, 00.asp, and observe all the software available for free. Choose a software program, and download it to your computer. Prepare a brief discussion about the software for your class.

4. Enter the IBM Web site (www.ibm.com), and perform a search on the term "software." Click on the drop box for Products, and notice how many software products IBM produces. Is IBM only a hardware company?

5. Compare the following proprietary software packages with their open-source software counterparts. Prepare your comparison for the class.

Proprietary	Open Source
Microsoft Office	Google Docs, OpenOffice
Adobe Photoshop	Picnik.com, Google Picasa

Fundamentals of Relational Database Operations

LEARNING OBJECTIVES

PI3.1 Understand the process of querying a relational database.

PI3.2 Understand the process of entity–relationship modeling.

PI3.3 Understand the process of normalization and the process of joins.

Introduction

There are many operations possible with relational databases. In this Plug IT In, we discuss three of these operations: query languages, normalization, and joins.

As you saw in Chapter 3, a relational database is a collection of interrelated two-dimensional tables, consisting of rows and columns. Each row represents a record, and each column (or field) represents an attribute (or characteristic) of that record. Every record in the database must contain at least one field that uniquely identifies that record so that it can be retrieved, updated, and sorted. This identifier field, or group of fields, is called the *primary key*. In some cases, locating a particular record requires the use of secondary keys. A *secondary key* is another field that has some identifying information, but typically does not uniquely identify the record. A *foreign key* is a field (or group of fields) in one table that matches the primary key value in a row of another table. A foreign key is used to establish and enforce a link between two tables.

These related tables can be joined when they contain common columns. The uniqueness of the primary key tells the DBMS which records are joined with others in related tables. This feature allows users great flexibility in the variety of queries they can make. Despite these features, however, the relational database model has some disadvantages. Because large-scale databases can be composed of many interrelated tables, the overall design can be complex, leading to slow search and access times.

PI3.1 Query Languages

The most commonly performed database operation is searching for information. Structured query language (SQL) is the most popular query language used for interacting with a database. SQL allows people to perform complicated searches by using relatively simple statements or key words. Typical key words are SELECT (to choose a desired attribute), FROM (to specify the table or tables to be used), and WHERE (to specify conditions to apply in the query).

To understand how SQL works, imagine that a university wants to know the names of students who will graduate cum laude (but not magna or summa cum laude) in May 2014. (Refer to

Figure 3.3 in Chapter 3.) The university IT staff would query the student relational database with an SQL statement such as

> SELECT Student_Name
> FROM Student_Database
> WHERE Grade_Point_Average >= 3.40 and Grade_Point_Average < 3.60;

The SQL query would return John Jones and Juan Rodriguez.

Another way to find information in a database is to use *query by example* (*QBE*). In QBE, the user fills out a grid or template—also known as a *form*—to construct a sample or a description of the data desired. Users can construct a query quickly and easily by using drag-and-drop features in a DBMS such as Microsoft Access. Conducting queries in this manner is simpler than keying in SQL commands.

Before you go on . . .

1. What is structured query language?

2. What is query by example?

Apply the Concept PI3.1

LEARNING OBJECTIVE PI3.1 Understand the process of querying a relational database.

STEP 1: Background (Here is what you are learning.)

Structured query language is a type of computer code that allows you to ask questions of a database, much as you would ask a question in a library. Somewhere in that library is the answer you are seeking. To find it, however, you have to know how to look. Perhaps the correct area, row, call number, or author would help you locate what you are looking for. Working with SQL is much the same. SQL is the key to unlocking many "data doors," and you must learn how to use it.

STEP 2: Activity (Here is what you are doing.)

Imagine that you have access to a database that contains data on the number of traffic accidents in Panama City, FL. There are four

tables in this database: Accidentinfo, Driverinfo, AccidentCauses, and Injuries.

STEP 3: Deliverable (Here is what you will turn in.)

Write the SQL code that will answer the following questions.

- How many accidents were caused by DUI during the summer months (May–August) of 2014?

- How many one-car accidents occurred that involved drivers who were only 16 years old?

To write these SQL queries correctly, you will need to use your imagination as to the data that could be contained in each table. However, you should be able to determine which tables contain the appropriate data. Submit your SQL code to your instructor.

PI3.2 | Entity–Relationship Modeling

Designers plan and create databases through the process of **entity–relationship modeling**, using an **entity–relationship (ER) diagram**. There are many approaches to ER diagramming. You will see one particular approach here, but there are others. The good news is that if you are familiar with one version of ER diagramming, then you will be able to easily adapt to any other version.

ER diagrams consist of entities, attributes, and relationships. To properly identify entities, attributes, and relationships, database designers first identify the business rules for the particular data model. Business rules are precise descriptions of policies, procedures, or principles in any organization that stores and uses data to generate information. Business rules are derived from a description of an organization's operations, and help to create and enforce business processes in that organization. Keep in mind that *you* determine these business rules, not the MIS department.

Entities are pictured in rectangles, and relationships are described on the line between two entities. The attributes for each entity are listed, and the primary key is underlined. The data dictionary provides information on each attribute, such as its name, if it is a key, part of a key, or a non-key attribute, the type of data expected (alphanumeric, numeric, dates, etc.), and valid values. Data dictionaries can also provide information on why the attribute is needed in the database; which business functions, applications, forms, and reports use the attribute; and how often the attribute should be updated.

ER modeling is valuable because it allows database designers to communicate with users throughout the organization to ensure that all entities and the relationships among the entities are represented. This process underscores the importance of taking all users into account when designing organizational databases. Notice that all entities and relationships in our example are labeled in terms that users can understand.

Relationships illustrate an association between entities. The *degree of a relationship* indicates the number of entities associated with a relationship. A unary relationship exists when an association is maintained within a single entity. A binary relationship exists when two entities are associated. A ternary relationship exists when three entities are associated. In this Plug IT In, we discuss only binary relationships because they are the most common. Entity relationships may be classified as one-to-one, one-to-many, or many-to-many. The term, connectivity, describes the relationship classification.

Connectivity and cardinality are established by the business rules of a relationship. Cardinality refers to the maximum number of times an instance of one entity can be associated with an instance in the related entity. Cardinality can be mandatory single, optional single, mandatory many, or optional many. Figure PI3.1 displays the cardinality symbols. Note that we have four possible cardinality symbols: mandatory single, optional single, mandatory many, and optional many.

Let's look at an example from a university. An *entity* is a person, place, or thing that can be identified in the users' work environment. For example, consider student registration at a university. Students register for courses, and they also register their cars for parking permits. In this example, STUDENT, PARKING PERMIT, CLASS, and PROFESSOR are entities. Recall that an instance of an entity represents a particular student, parking permit, class, or professor. Therefore, a particular STUDENT (James Smythe, 8023445) is an instance of the STUDENT entity; a particular parking permit (91778) is an instance of the PARKING PERMIT entity; a particular class (76890) is an instance of the CLASS entity; and a particular professor (Margaret Wilson, 390567) is an instance of the PROFESSOR entity.

Entity instances have *identifiers*, or *primary keys*, which are attributes (attributes and identifiers are synonymous) that are unique to that entity instance. For example, STUDENT instances can be identified with Student Identification Number; PARKING PERMIT instances can be identified with Permit Number; CLASS instances can be identified with Class Number; and PROFESSOR instances can be identified with Professor Identification Number.

Entities have attributes, or properties, that describe the entity's characteristics. In our example, examples of attributes for STUDENT are Student Name and Student Address. Examples of attributes for PARKING PERMIT are Student Identification Number and Car Type. Examples of attributes for CLASS are Class Name, Class Time, and Class Place. Examples of attributes for PROFESSOR are Professor Name and Professor Department. (Note that each course at this university has one professor—no team teaching.)

Why is Student Identification Number an attribute of both the STUDENT and PARKING PERMIT entity classes? That is, why do we need the PARKING PERMIT

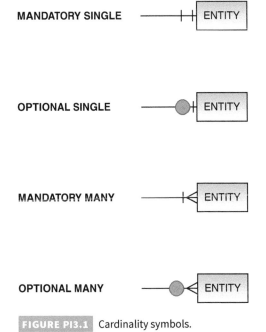

MANDATORY SINGLE

OPTIONAL SINGLE

MANDATORY MANY

OPTIONAL MANY

FIGURE PI3.1 Cardinality symbols.

entity class? If you consider all of the interlinked university systems, the PARKING PERMIT entity class is needed for other applications, such as fee payments, parking tickets, and external links to the state Department of Motor Vehicles.

Let's consider the three types of binary relationships in our example.

In a *one-to-one (1:1)* relationship, a single-entity instance of one type is related to a single-entity instance of another type. In our university example, STUDENT–PARKING PERMIT is a 1:1 relationship. The business rule at this university represented by this relationship is: Students may register only one car at this university. Of course, students do not have to register a car at all. That is, a student can have only one parking permit but does not need to have one.

Note that the relationship line on the PARKING PERMIT side shows a cardinality of optional single. A student can have, but does not have to have, a parking permit. On the STUDENT side of the relationship, only one parking permit can be assigned to one student, resulting in a cardinality of mandatory single. See Figure PI3.2.

The second type of relationship, *one-to-many (1:M)*, is represented by the CLASS–PROFESSOR relationship in Figure PI3.3. The business rule at this university represented by this relationship is: At this university, there is no team teaching. Therefore, each class must have only one professor. On the other hand, professors may teach more than one class. Note that the relationship line on the PROFESSOR side shows a cardinality of mandatory single. In contrast, the relationship line on the CLASS side shows a cardinality of optional many.

The third type of relationship, *many-to-many (M:M)*, is represented by the STUDENT–CLASS relationship. Most database management systems do not support many-to-many relationships. Therefore, we use *junction* (or *bridge*) *tables*, so that we have two one-to-many relationships. The business rule at this university represented by this relationship is: Students can register for one or more classes, and each class can have one or more students (see Figure PI3.4). In this example, we create the REGISTRATION table as our junction table. Note that Student ID and Class ID are foreign keys in the REGISTRATION table.

Let's examine the following relationships:

- The relationship line on the STUDENT side of the STUDENT–REGISTRATION relationship shows a cardinality of optional single.
- The relationship line on the REGISTRATION side of the STUDENT–REGISTRATION relationship shows a cardinality of optional many.
- The relationship line on the CLASS side of the CLASS–REGISTRATION relationship shows a cardinality of optional single.

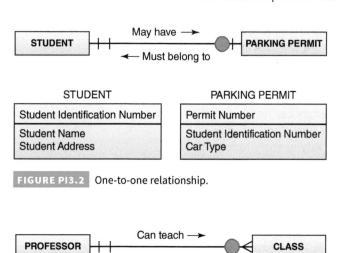

FIGURE PI3.2 One-to-one relationship.

FIGURE PI3.3 One-to-many relationship.

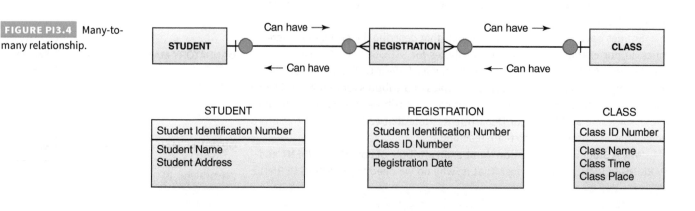

FIGURE PI3.4 Many-to-many relationship.

- The relationship line on the REGISTRATION side of the CLASS–REGISTRATION relationship shows a cardinality of optional many.

Before you go on . . .

1. What is an entity? An attribute? A relationship?

2. Describe one-to-one, one-to-many, and many-to-many relationships.

Apply the Concept PI3.2

LEARNING OBJECTIVE PI3.2 Understand the process of entity–relationship modeling.

STEP 1: Background

It is very important that you understand the connections among entities, attributes, and relationships. This section has defined each of these terms for you. Typically, entities are described by their attributes, and they are related to other entities. For example, if "student name" is the entity, then age, gender, country of origin, marital status, and other demographic data are the attributes (characteristics) of that particular student. That student is also related to other entities such as financial information, major, and course information.

STEP 2: Activity

An entity–relationship model is one of the most challenging aspects of designing a database because you have to (1)

understand the rules that govern how processes work and (2) be able to define and describe these rules in a picture. This section has provided you with the necessary tools to draw a basic ER model.

Imagine the following scenario. You are designing a database for your local police department to keep track of traffic violations. The department has provided you with the following rules:

- Each office can write multiple tickets.
- Each ticket will list only one office.
- Each ticket will list only one driver.
- Drivers can receive multiple tickets.

STEP 3: Deliverable

Using the tools described in this section, demonstrate that you understand the process of ER modeling by drawing and submitting an ER model for the scenario provided in Step 2.

PI3.3 | Normalization and Joins

To use a relational database management system efficiently and effectively, the data must be analyzed to eliminate redundant data elements. Normalization is a method for analyzing and reducing a relational database to its most streamlined form to ensure minimum redundancy, maximum data integrity, and optimal processing performance. Data normalization is a methodology for organizing attributes into tables so that redundancy among the non-key attributes is eliminated. The result of the data normalization process is a properly structured relational database.

Data normalization requires a list of all the attributes that must be incorporated into the database and a list of all of the defining associations, or functional dependencies, among the attributes. Functional dependencies are a means of expressing that the value of one particular attribute is associated with a specific single value of another attribute. For example, for a Student Number 05345 at a university, there is exactly one Student Name, John C. Jones, associated with it. That is, Student Number is referred to as the determinant because its value *determines* the value of the other attribute. We can also say that Student Name is functionally dependent on Student Number.

As an example of normalization, consider a pizza shop. This shop takes orders from customers on a form. Figure PI3.5 shows a table of nonnormalized data gathered by the pizza shop. This table has two records, one for each order being placed. Because there are several

Order Number	Order Date	Customer ID	Customer F Name	Customer L Name	Customer Address	Zip Code	Pizza Code	Pizza Name	Quantity	Price	Total Price
1116	9/1/14	16421	Rob	Penny	123 Main St.	37411	P	Pepperoni	1	$11.00	$41.00
							MF	Meat Feast	1	$12.00	
							V	Vegetarian	2	$9.00	
1117	9/2/14	17221	Beth	Jones	41 Oak St.	29416	HM	Ham and Mushroom	3	$10.00	$56.00
							MF	Meat Feast	1	$12.00	
							TH	The Hawaiian	1	$14.00	

FIGURE PI3.5 Raw data gathered from orders at the pizza shop.

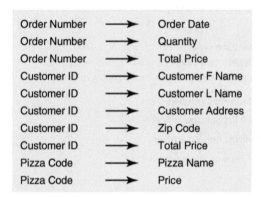

FIGURE PI3.6 Functional dependencies in pizza shop example.

pizzas on each order, the order number and customer information appear in multiple rows. Several attributes of each record have null values. A null value is an attribute with no data in it. For example, Order Number has four null values. Therefore, this table is not in first normal form. The data drawn from that form is shown in Figure PI3.5.

In our example, ORDER, CUSTOMER, and PIZZA are entities. The first step in normalization is to determine the functional dependencies among the attributes. The functional dependencies in our example are shown in Figure PI3.6.

In the normalization process, we will proceed from nonnormalized data, to first normal form, to second normal form, and then to third normal form. (There are additional normal forms, but they are beyond the scope of this book.)

Figure PI3.7 demonstrates the data in *first normal form*. The attributes under consideration are listed in one table and primary keys have been established. Our primary keys are Order Number, Customer ID, and Pizza Code. In first normal form, each ORDER has to repeat the order number, order date, customer first name, customer last name, customer address, and customer zip code. This data file contains repeating groups and describes multiple entities. That is, this relation has data redundancy, a lack of data integrity, and the flat file would be difficult to use in various applications that the pizza shop might need.

Consider the table in Figure PI3.7, and notice the very first column (labeled Order Number). This column contains multiple entries for each order—three rows for Order Number 1116

Order Number	Order Date	Customer ID	Customer F Name	Customer L Name	Customer Address	Zip Code	Pizza Code	Pizza Name	Quantity	Price	Total Price
1116	9/1/14	16421	Rob	Penny	123 Main St.	37411	P	Pepperoni	1	$11.00	$41.00
1116	9/1/14	16421	Rob	Penny	123 Main St.	37411	MF	Meat Feast	1	$12.00	$41.00
1116	9/1/14	16421	Rob	Penny	123 Main St.	37411	V	Vegetarian	2	$9.00	$41.00
1117	9/2/14	17221	Beth	Jones	41 Oak St.	29416	HM	Ham and Mushroom	3	$10.00	$56.00
1117	9/2/14	17221	Beth	Jones	41 Oak St.	29416	MF	Meat Feast	1	$12.00	$56.00
1117	9/2/14	17221	Beth	Jones	41 Oak St.	29416	TH	The Hawaiian	1	$14.00	$56.00

FIGURE PI3.7 First normal form for data from pizza shop.

Order Number	Order Date	Customer ID	Customer F Name	Customer L Name	Customer Address	Zip Code	Total Price
1116	9/1/14	16421	Rob	Penny	123 Main St.	37411	$41.00
1116	9/1/14	16421	Rob	Penny	123 Main St.	37411	$41.00
1116	9/1/14	16421	Rob	Penny	123 Main St.	37411	$41.00
1117	9/2/14	17221	Beth	Jones	41 Oak St.	29416	$56.00
1117	9/2/14	17221	Beth	Jones	41 Oak St.	29416	$56.00
1117	9/2/14	17221	Beth	Jones	41 Oak St.	29416	$56.00

Order Number	Pizza Code	Quantity
1116	P	1
1116	MF	1
1116	V	2
1117	HM	3
1117	MF	1
1117	TH	1

Pizza Code	Pizza Name	Price
P	Pepperoni	$11.00
MF	Meat Feast	$12.00
V	Vegetarian	$9.00
HM	Ham and Mushroom	$10.00
TH	The Hawaiian	$14.00

FIGURE PI3.8 Second normal form for data from pizza shop.

and three rows for Order Number 1117. These multiple rows for an order are called *repeating groups*. The table in Figure PI3.6 also contains multiple entities: ORDER, CUSTOMER, and PIZZA. Therefore, we move on to second normal form.

To produce second normal form, we break the table in Figure PI3.6 into smaller tables to eliminate some of its data redundancy. Second normal form does not allow partial functional dependencies. That is, in a table in second normal form, every non-key attribute must be functionally dependent on the entire primary key of that table. Figure PI3.8 shows the data from the pizza shop in second normal form.

If you examine Figure PI3.8, you will see that second normal form has not eliminated all the data redundancy. For example, each Order Number is duplicated three times, as are all customer data. In *third normal form*, non-key attributes are not allowed to define other non-key attributes. That is, third normal form does not allow transitive dependencies in which one non-key attribute is functionally dependent on another. In our example, customer information depends both on Customer ID and Order Number. Figure PI3.9 shows the data from the pizza shop in third normal form. Third normal form structure has these important points:

- It is completely free of data redundancy.
- All foreign keys appear where needed to link related tables.

Let's look at the primary and foreign keys for the tables in third normal form:

- *The ORDER relation*: The primary key is Order Number and the foreign key is Customer ID.
- *The CUSTOMER relation:* The primary key is Customer ID.
- *The PIZZA relation:* The primary key is Pizza Code.

ORDER

Order Number	Order Date	Customer ID	Total Price
1116	9/1/14	16421	$41.00
1117	9/2/14	17221	$56.00

CUSTOMER

Customer ID	Customer F Name	Customer L Name	Customer Address	Zip Code
16421	Rob	Penny	123 Main St.	37411
17221	Beth	Jones	41 Oak St.	29416

ORDER-PIZZA

Order Number	Pizza Code	Quantity
1116	P	1
1116	MF	1
1116	V	2
1117	HM	3
1117	MF	1
1117	TH	1

PIZZA

Pizza Code	Pizza Name	Price
P	Pepperoni	$11.00
MF	Meat Feast	$12.00
V	Vegetarian	$9.00
HM	Ham and Mushroom	$10.00
TH	The Hawaiian	$14.00

FIGURE PI3.9 Third normal form for data from pizza shop.

- *The ORDER–PIZZA relation:* The primary key is a composite key, consisting of two foreign keys, Order Number and Pizza Code.

Now consider an order at the pizza shop. The tables in third normal form can produce the order in the following manner by using the join operation (see Figure PI3.10). The join operation combines records from two or more tables in a database to obtain information that is located in different tables. In our example, the join operation combines records from the four normalized tables to produce an ORDER. Here is how the join operation works:

- The ORDER relation provides the Order Number (the primary key), Order Date, and Total Price.
- The primary key of the ORDER relation (Order Number) provides a link to the ORDER–PIZZA relation (the link numbered 1 in Figure PI3.10).
- The ORDER–PIZZA relation supplies the Quantity to ORDER.
- The primary key of the ORDER–PIZZA relation is a composite key that consists of Order Number and Pizza Code. Therefore, the Pizza Code component of the primary key provides a link to the PIZZA relation (the link numbered 2 in Figure PI3.10).
- The PIZZA relation supplies the Pizza Name and Price to ORDER.
- The Customer ID in ORDER (a foreign key) provides a link to the CUSTOMER relation (the link numbered 3 in Figure PI3.10).

FIGURE PI3.10 The join process with the tables of third normal form to produce an order.

- The CUSTOMER relation supplies the Customer FName, Customer LName, Customer Address, and Zip Code to ORDER.

At the end of this join process, we have a complete ORDER. Normalization is beneficial when maintaining databases over a period of time. One example is the likelihood of having to change the price of each pizza. If the pizza shop increases the price of the Meat Feast from $12.00 to $12.50, this process is one easy step in Figure PI3.10. The price field is changed to $12.50 and the ORDER is automatically updated with the current value of the price.

Before you go on . . .

1. What is the purpose of normalization?

2. Why do we need the join operation?

Apply the Concept PI3.3

LEARNING OBJECTIVE PI3.3 Understand the process of normalization and the process of joins.

STEP 1: Background

Normalization, as described in this section, breaks a flat data file into multiple tables to eliminate redundancy by creating redundancy in the form of keys that link the tables together. In the example provided in the text, the normalized database allows for a pizza order to contain multiple pizzas without having to repeat the order number and leave blank (null) values.

Joins are very important because they take the data from multiple locations and link them together with relationships. Repeating and relating the order number on the pizza table as a primary key in the order table enables you to maintain a cleaner set of data without null values.

STEP 2: Activity

Normalize the following student table into first, second, and third normal forms.

Student Table (Raw Data)

Student	Student ID	Age	Courses
Juan	11011	19	English (13579)
			History (14876)
			College Algebra (95827)
			Intro to Business (87650)
Anita	12015	18	English (13579)
			Public Speaking (13121)
			French (97869)
			Biology (75675)
Jason	53879	19	History (14876)
			Intro to MIS (24680)
			Intro to Business (87650)
			Communications (12670)

STEP 3: Deliverable

Demonstrate that you understand the normalization process by producing the table provided in Step 2 in first normal form, second normal form, and third normal form.

What's in IT for me?

For all Business Majors

All business majors will have to manage data in their professional work. One way to manage data is through the use of databases and database management systems. First, it is likely that you will need to obtain information from your organization's databases. You will probably use structured query language to obtain this information. Second, as your organization plans and designs its databases, it will most likely use entity–relationship diagrams. You will provide much of the input to these ER diagrams. For example, you will describe the entities that you use in your work, the attributes of those entities, and the relationships among them. You will also help database designers as they normalize database tables, by describing how the normalized tables relate to each other (e.g., through the use of primary and foreign keys). Finally, you will help database designers as they plan their join operations to give you the information that you need when that information is stored in multiple tables.

Summary

1. Understand the process of querying a relational database.

The most commonly performed database operation is requesting information. *Structured query language* is the most popular query language used for this operation. SQL allows people to perform complicated searches by using relatively simple statements or key words. Typical key words are SELECT (to specify a desired attribute), FROM (to specify the table to be used), and WHERE (to specify conditions to apply in the query).

Another way to find information in a database is to use *query by example*. In QBE, the user fills out a grid or template—also known as a *form*—to construct a sample or a description of the data desired. Users can construct a query quickly and easily by using drag-and-drop features in a DBMS such as Microsoft Access. Conducting queries in this manner is simpler than keying in SQL commands.

2. Understand the process of entity–relationship modeling.

Designers plan and create databases through the process of **entity-relationship modeling**, using an **entity-relationship diagram**. ER diagrams consist of entities, attributes, and relationships. Entities are pictured in boxes, and relationships are represented as diamonds. The attributes for each entity are listed, and the primary key is underlined.

ER modeling is valuable because it allows database designers to communicate with users throughout the organization to ensure that all entities and the relationships among the entities are represented. This process underscores the importance of taking all users into account when designing organizational databases. Notice that all entities and relationships in our example are labeled in terms that users can understand.

3. Understand the process of normalization and the process of joins.

Normalization is a method for analyzing and reducing a relational database to its most streamlined form to ensure minimum redundancy, maximum data integrity, and optimal processing performance. When data are *normalized*, attributes in each table depend only on the primary key.

The *join operation* combines records from two or more tables in a database to produce information that is located in different tables.

Glossary

attribute Each characteristic or quality describing a particular entity.

binary relationship A relationship that exists when two entities are associated.

business rules Precise descriptions of policies, procedures, or principles in any organization that stores and uses data to generate information.

connectivity Describes the classification of a relationship: one-to-one, one-to-many, or many-to-many.

data dictionary A collection of definitions of data elements; data characteristics that use the data elements; and the individuals, business functions, applications, and reports that use these data elements.

entity–relationship (ER) diagram Document that shows data entities and attributes and relationships among them.

entity–relationship (ER) modeling The process of designing a database by organizing data entities to be used and identifying the relationships among them.

functional dependency A means of expressing that the value of one particular attribute is associated with, or determines, a specific single value of another attribute.

join operation A database operation that combines records from two or more tables in a database.

normalization A method for analyzing and reducing a relational database to its most streamlined form to ensure minimum redundancy, maximum data integrity, and optimal processing performance.

query by example To obtain information from a relational database, a user fills out a grid or template—also known as a form—to construct a sample or a description of the data desired.

relationships Operators that illustrate an association between two entities.

structured query language The most popular query language for requesting information from a relational database.

ternary relationship A relationship that exists when three entities are associated.

unary relationship A relationship that exists when an association is maintained within a single entity.

Discussion Questions

1. Draw the entity–relationship diagram for a company that has departments and employees. In this company, a department must have at least one employee, and company employees may work in only one department.

2. Draw the entity–relationship diagram for library patrons and the process of checking out books.

3. You are working at a doctor's office. You gather data on the following entities: PATIENT, PHYSICIAN, PATIENT DIAGNOSIS, and TREATMENT. Develop a table for the entity, PATIENT VISIT. Decide on the primary keys and/or foreign keys that you want to use for each entity.

Cloud Computing

LEARNING OBJECTIVES

PI4.1 Describe the problems that modern information technology departments face.

PI4.2 Describe the key characteristics and advantages of cloud computing.

PI4.3 Describe each of the four types of clouds.

PI4.4 Explain the operational model of each of the three types of cloud services.

PI4.5 Identify the key benefits of cloud computing.

PI4.6 Discuss the concerns and risks associated with cloud computing.

PI4.7 Explain the role of Web services in building a firm's IT applications, providing examples.

We devote this Plug IT In to a vital topic: cloud computing. A working knowledge of cloud computing will enhance your appreciation of what technology can and cannot do for a business. In addition, it will enable you to make an immediate contribution by analyzing how your organization manages its IT assets. Going further, you will be using these computing resources in your career, and you will have input into decisions about how your department and organization can best utilize them. Additionally, cloud computing can be extremely valuable if you decide to start your own business.

This Plug IT In defines cloud computing as a type of computing that delivers convenient, on-demand, pay-as-you-go access for multiple customers to a shared pool of configurable computing resources (e.g., servers, networks, storage, applications, and services) that can be rapidly and easily accessed over the Internet. Cloud computing allows customers to acquire resources at any time and then delete them the instant they are no longer needed. We present many examples of how the cloud can be used for business purposes. In addition, the cloud provides you with personal applications. Therefore, this guide can help you plan for your own use of the cloud. For a more detailed discussion of how you can utilize the cloud, see the section titled IT's Personal: "The Cloud."

PI4.1 Introduction

You were introduced to the concept of IT infrastructure in Chapter 1. Recall that an organization's *IT infrastructure* consists of IT components—hardware, software, networks, and databases—and IT services—developing information systems, managing security and risk, and managing data. (It is helpful to review Figure 1.3 of Chapter 1 here.) The organization's IT infrastructure is the foundation for all of the information systems that the organization uses.

Modern IT infrastructure has evolved through several stages since the early 1950s, when firms first began to apply information technology to business applications. These stages are as follows:

- *Stand-alone mainframes:* Organizations initially used mainframe computers in their engineering and accounting departments. The mainframe was typically housed in a secure area, and only MIS personnel had access to it.

- *Mainframe and dumb terminals:* Forcing users to go to wherever the mainframe was located was time consuming and inefficient. As a result, firms began placing so-called "dumb terminals"—essentially electronic typewriters with limited processing power—in user departments. This arrangement enabled users to input computer programs into the mainframe from their departments, a process called *remote job entry.*

- *Stand-alone personal computers:* In the late 1970s, the first personal computers appeared. The IBM PC's debut in 1981 legitimized the entire personal computer market. Users began bringing personal computers to the workplace to improve their productivity—for example, by using spreadsheet and word processing applications. These computers were not initially supported by the firm's MIS department. However, as the number of personal computers increased dramatically, organizations decided to support these devices, and they established policies as to which PCs and software they would support.

- *Local area networks (client/server computing):* When personal computers are networked, individual productivity increases. For this reason, organizations began to connect personal computers to local area networks (LANs) and then connected these LANs to the mainframe, a type of processing known as *client/server computing.*

- *Enterprise computing:* In the early 1990s, organizations began to use networking standards to integrate different kinds of networks throughout the firm, thereby creating enterprise computing. As the Internet became widespread after 1995, organizations began using the TCP/IP networking protocol to integrate different types of networks. All types of hardware were networked, including mainframes, personal computers, smartphones, printers, and many others. Software applications and data now flow seamlessly throughout the enterprise and between organizations.

- *Cloud computing and mobile computing:* Today, organizations and individuals can use the power of cloud computing. As you will see in this Plug IT In, cloud computing provides access to a shared pool of computing resources, including computers, storage, applications, and services, over a network, typically the Internet.

Keep in mind that the computing resources in each stage can be cumulative. For instance, most large firms still use mainframe computers (in addition to all the other types of computing resources) as large servers to manage operations that involve millions of transactions per day.

To appreciate the impacts of cloud computing, you first need to understand traditional IT departments in organizations and the challenges they face. Traditionally, organizations have utilized on-premise computing. That is, they own their IT infrastructure (their software, hardware, networks, and data management) and maintain it in their data centers.

On-premise computing incurs expenses for IT infrastructure, the expert staffs needed to build and maintain complex IT systems, physical facilities, software licenses, hardware, and staff training and salaries. Despite all of this spending, organizations, however, typically do not use their infrastructure to its full capacity. The majority of these expenses are typically applied to maintaining the existing IT infrastructure, with the remainder being allocated to developing new systems. As a result, on-premise computing can actually inhibit an organization's ability to respond quickly and appropriately to today's rapidly changing business environments.

As you will see in the next section, cloud computing can help organizations manage the problems that traditional IT departments face with on-premise computing. The next section defines cloud computing and describes its essential characteristics.

Before you go on . . .

1. Describe the stages in the evolution of today's IT infrastructure.

2. Describe the challenges that traditional IT departments face.

Apply the Concept PI4.1

LEARNING OBJECTIVE PI4.1 Describe the problems that modern information technology departments face.

STEP 1: Background (This is what you are learning.)

This section has discussed the evolution of computer infrastructure over time. Early computing models were called "terminal to host"; today we have "cloud" or "distributed computing" models available. A knowledge of how infrastructure models have changed can help you understand the challenges confronting modern IT departments.

STEP 2: Activity (This is what you are doing.)

Review the evolution of IT infrastructure as presented in this section. It is likely that all businesses today have some form of a local area network (LAN) in the client/server model of computing. Beginning with that stage, consider the problems that modern IT departments face as their systems evolve.

Imagine that your boss has asked your advice on moving from traditional LAN computing, in which each department operates a separate network, toward enterprise or cloud computing. What type of challenges could you help your boss anticipate?

STEP 3: Deliverable (This is what you turn in.)

Write a letter to your boss (your instructor) that describes the problems that modern IT departments must address as they evolve toward enterprise and cloud computing.

PI4.2 | What Is Cloud Computing?

Information technology departments have always been tasked to deliver useful IT applications to business users. For a variety of reasons, today's IT departments are facing increased challenges in delivering useful applications. As you study cloud computing, you will learn how it can help organizations manage the problems that occur in traditional IT departments. You will also discover why so many organizations are utilizing cloud computing.

Cloud Computing Characteristics

The cloud computing phenomenon has several important characteristics. We take a closer look at them in this section.

Cloud Computing Provides On-Demand Self-Service. A customer can access needed computing resources automatically. This characteristic gives customers *elasticity* and *flexibility*. That is, customers can increase (scale up) or decrease (scale down) the amount of computing they need.

Consider retailers. During the Christmas buying season, these firms need much more computational capacity than at other times of the year. Therefore, if they used cloud computing, they would scale up during peak periods of business activity and scale down at other times.

Cloud Computing Encompasses the Characteristics of Grid Computing. Grid computing pools various hardware and software components to create a single IT environment with shared resources. Grid computing shares the processing resources of many geographically dispersed computers across a network.

- Grid computing enables organizations to utilize their computing resources more efficiently.

- Grid computing provides fault tolerance and redundancy, meaning that there is no single point of failure, so the failure of one computer will not stop an application from executing.

- Grid computing makes it easy to *scale up*—that is, to access increased computing resources (i.e., add more servers)—to meet the processing demands of complex applications.
- Grid computing makes it easy to *scale down* (remove computers) if extensive processing is not needed.

Consider Oxford University's (the United Kingdom) Digital Mammogram National Database project. The project aims to improve breast cancer screening and reduce the rate of erroneous diagnoses. The users of the system are radiologists, doctors, and technicians who want to query, retrieve, process, and store patients' breast images and diagnostic reports. These images tend to be large, requiring fast access, high quality, and rigid privacy.

The system utilizes a large distributed database that runs on a grid computing system. The grid is formed in a collaborative way, by sharing resources (CPU cycles and data) among different organizations. The database contains digital mammographies with explanatory notes and comments about each image. Because medical and university sites have different equipment, the images and reports are standardized before they are stored in the database.

The system enables individual medical sites to store, process, and manage mammograms as digital images and to enable their use through data mining and sharing of these mammography archives. Radiologists can collaborate on diagnoses without being in the same physical location.

With this system in place, the institutions involved have improved their collaboration resulting in quicker and more accurate diagnoses. By pooling their resources, each institution gained access to a much larger and more sophisticated set of resources, without increasing their costs proportionately.

Cloud Computing Encompasses the Characteristics of Utility Computing. In **utility computing**, a service provider makes computing resources and infrastructure management available to a customer as needed. The provider then charges the customer for its specific usage rather than a flat rate. Utility computing enables companies to efficiently meet fluctuating demands for computing power by lowering the costs of owning the hardware infrastructure.

Media Bakery

FIGURE PI4.1 A server farm. Notice the ventilation in the racks and ceiling.

Cloud Computing Utilizes Broad Network Access. The cloud provider's computing resources are available over a network, accessed with a Web browser, and they are configured so that they can be used with any computing device.

Cloud Computing Pools Computing Resources. The provider's computing resources are available to serve multiple customers. These resources are dynamically assigned and reassigned according to customer demand.

Cloud Computing Often Occurs on Virtualized Servers. Cloud computing providers have placed hundreds or thousands of networked servers inside massive data centers called server farms (see **Figure PI4.1**). Recall that a *server* is a computer that supports networks, thus enabling users to share files, software, and other network devices. Server farms require massive amounts of electrical power, air-conditioning, backup generators, and security. They also need to be located fairly closely to fiber-optic communications links (**Figure PI4.2**).

Going further, Gartner estimates that typical utilization rates on servers are very low, generally from 5 to 10 percent. That is, most of the time, organizations are utilizing only a small percentage

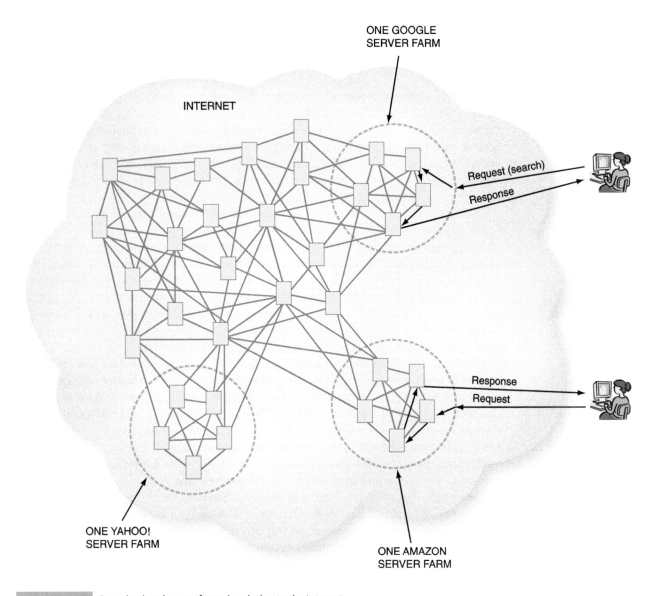

ONE GOOGLE
SERVER FARM

INTERNET

Request (search)

Response

Response

Request

ONE YAHOO!
SERVER FARM

ONE AMAZON
SERVER FARM

FIGURE PI4.2   Organizational server farms in relation to the Internet.

of their total computing capacity. Chief information officers (CIOs) tolerate this inefficiency to make certain that they can supply sufficient computing resources to users in case demand should spike. To alleviate this problem, companies and cloud computing providers are turning to virtualization.

Server virtualization uses software-based partitions to create multiple virtual servers—called *virtual machines*—on a single physical server. The major benefit of this system is that each server no longer has to be dedicated to a particular task. Instead, multiple applications can run on a single physical server, with each application running within its own software environment. As a result, virtualization enables companies to increase server utilization. In addition, companies realize cost savings in two areas. First, they do not have to buy additional servers to meet peak demand. Second, they reduce their utility costs because they are using less energy. The following example illustrates the benefits of virtualization for the city of Yawata in Kyoto, Japan.

The City of Yawata in Kyoto Prefecture, Japan (www.city.yawata.kyoto.jp) is very active in developing its networked city government. Deployed in 2002, the city's information system was designed to support the daily operations of the city. Since that time, the system has functioned as an IT service for city employees and members of the public.

Over a decade later, the city's continuing efforts to develop a more advanced digital community had resulted in an increasing number of physical servers, with accompanying increases in power consumption. The rise in power utilization was a particular problem as the city has a strong commitment to eco-friendliness.

POM

In order to reduce hardware expenses, the city had been running multiple applications on a single physical server, an approach that sometimes caused server availability issues. To make the system more secure and stable, the city wanted to have an individual dedicated server for each application.

The city decided to implement a server virtualization solution and realized a number of benefits. First, the city reduced its number of physical servers from 12 to 4. This reduction led to decreases in power consumption, which has helped the city reduce its environmental impact. Second, each application now runs on a single virtual machine. This benefit means that server availability has increased markedly, each app runs more efficiently, and the entire system is more stable. Third, by virtualizing its data center, the city is able to address future server resource needs, without having to add additional physical servers.

With cloud computing, setting up and maintaining an IT infrastructure need no longer be a challenge for an organization. Businesses do not have to scramble to meet the evolving needs of developing applications. In addition, cloud computing reduces upfront capital expenses and operational costs, and it enables businesses to better utilize their infrastructure and to share it from one project to the next. In general, cloud computing eases the difficult tasks of procuring, configuring, and maintaining hardware and software environments. In addition, it allows enterprises to get their applications up and running faster, with easier manageability and less maintenance. It also enables IT to adjust IT resources (e.g., servers, storage, and networking) more rapidly to meet fluctuating and unpredictable business demand.

Businesses are increasingly employing cloud computing for important and innovative work. Let's take a look at Lionsgate's (www.lionsgate.com) use of Amazon Web Services.

MIS　　Lionsgate is a global entertainment corporation that produces feature films and television shows, which they distribute worldwide. Their products include the television show *Mad Men* and the movie *Hunger Games*. Their productions appear in theaters, on TV, and online. As a successful media and entertainment company, Lionsgate faced IT challenges that included need for additional IT infrastructure capacity, leading to increased costs; increasing enterprise application workloads; and faster time-to-market requirements.

As a result, the company turned to Amazon Web Services (AWS; http://aws.amazon.com) for development and test workloads, production workloads for enterprise applications, and backup, archive, and disaster recovery strategies. Lionsgate's objectives were to reduce costs, increase flexibility, and increase operational efficiency. Lionsgate decided to use Amazon Simple Storage Service and Amazon Elastic Compute Cloud.

Lionsgate has experienced many benefits from using AWS. The firm has reduced the time required to deploy infrastructure from weeks to days or hours. Further, testing and development for its SAP applications also requires less time. AWS has increased the speed of building servers, improved disaster recovery and systems backup, and increased systems availability. The company avoided acquiring additional data center space, saving an estimated $1 million over three years. Overall, Lionsgate believes that moving to AWS saved the company about 50 percent compared to a traditional hosting facility.

These benefits have helped Lionsgate become more agile and more responsive to rapidly changing conditions in the marketplace. AWS has also contributed to helping the company maintain its systems security. Lionsgate is able to use its existing hardware policies and procedures for a secure, seamless, and scalable computing environment that requires few resources to manage.

In the next section, you learn about the various ways in which customers (individuals and organizations) can implement cloud computing. Specifically, you will read about public clouds, private clouds, hybrid clouds, and vertical clouds.

Before you go on . . .

1. Describe the characteristics of cloud computing.
2. Define server virtualization.

PI4.3 | Different Types of Clouds

There are three major types of cloud computing that companies provide to customers or groups of customers: public clouds, private clouds, and hybrid clouds. A fourth type of cloud computing is called vertical clouds (**Figure PI4.3**).

Public Cloud

Public clouds are shared, easily accessible, multicustomer IT infrastructures that are available nonexclusively to any entity in the general public (individuals, groups, and/or organizations). Public cloud vendors provide applications, storage, and other computing resources as services over the Internet. These services may be free or offered on a pay-per-usage model. Samba Tech (www.sambatech.com) provides an example of a young company using the public cloud.

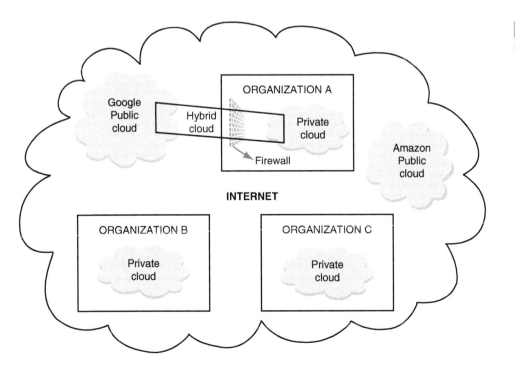

FIGURE PI4.3 Public clouds, private clouds, and hybrid clouds.

`MIS`

International media companies such as Viacom (www.viacom.com), Bloomberg (www .bloomberg.com), and ESPN (www.espn.com) rely on Samba Tech to deliver video content to online viewers across Latin America. As a result of its rapid growth, Samba decided to utilize cloud computing. The firm's chief technology officer noted that buying and managing complex IT (i.e., on-premise computing) was never part of the company's strategy.

Samba turned to Rackspace (www.rackspace.com), a public cloud provider, to help it with its huge IT capacity demands. In 2009, Samba needed Rackspace to host about 1 terabyte of data. In 2015, Rackspace hosts over 100 terabytes of Samba's data. Further, when Samba needs additional processing power—to deliver videos for a new marketing campaign, or to coincide with a large sporting event—Rackspace provides that power quickly and affordably.

Private Cloud

Private clouds (also known as *internal clouds* or *corporate clouds*) are IT infrastructures that can be accessed only by a single entity or by an exclusive group of related entities that share the same purpose and requirements, such as all of the business units within a single organization. Private clouds provide IT activities and applications as a service over an intranet within an enterprise. Enterprises adopt private clouds to ensure system and data security. For this reason these systems are implemented behind the corporate firewall. As an example of a private cloud, let's take a look at the National Security Agency (NSA; www.nsa.gov).

`MIS`

The NSA was running out of storage space for hundreds of different databases that contain information needed to run the agency as well as to produce intelligence on foreign matters. As a result, NSA analysts had to access many different databases to do their jobs. Questions that spanned more than one database had to be manually integrated by the analyst. The agency had to consolidate its databases to make its analysts more efficient and effective.

At first, the NSA decided to simply add more storage capacity. However, this approach actually added to the problem, so the agency decided to implement a private cloud. By putting all its different databases in one private cloud, analysts had to interface with only one system, making their jobs much easier.

The private cloud contains data that the agency acquires and uses for its missions. The cloud has strict security protocols and strong encryption, and has a distributed architecture across multiple geographic areas. In addition, the cloud provides a way to track every instance of every individual accessing data as specific as a single word or name in a file. This tracking includes when the data arrived, who can access them, who did access them, who downloaded them, copied them, printed them, forwarded them, modified them, or deleted them. Further, if the data have legal requirements, such as they must be purged at the five-year point, a notice will automatically tell NSA staff that the data need to be purged. One agency staff member noted that if the NSA had had this ability at the time, it is unlikely that U.S. soldier Bradley Manning would have succeeded in obtaining classified documents in 2010.

After implementation of the private cloud, analysts can perform tasks in minutes that once took days, overall data management costs have decreased, and the security of the data has been greatly enhanced.

Hybrid Cloud

Hybrid clouds are composed of public and private clouds that remain unique entities, but are nevertheless tightly integrated. This arrangement offers users the benefits of multiple deployment models. Hybrid clouds deliver services based on security requirements, the mission-critical nature of the applications, and other company-established policies. For example, customers may need to maintain some of their data in a private cloud for security and privacy reasons while storing other, less-sensitive data in a public cloud because it is less expensive. Let's examine an example of hybrid cloud computing in the city of Asheville, North Carolina.

`POM`

Operating a disaster recovery (DR) facility is expensive, complex, and time consuming because an organization has to set up and maintain an entire backup information technology infrastructure. The new chief information officer of the city of Asheville, North Carolina quickly noticed that Asheville had a DR facility, but it was located only two blocks from the city's main data center. This situation meant that there was not enough geographic dispersal for effective recovery from a disaster.

He turned to cloud computing to help Asheville obtain the necessary geographic dispersal for its DR efforts. He wanted to provide disaster recovery for the city's on-premise applications in the public cloud. As a result, the city used CloudVelox (www.cloudvelox.com), a cloud vendor that offers automated cloud migration and disaster recovery software for deploying organizations' applications and services to the cloud. The city's apps remain in storage in the cloud, ready to be activated if and when they are needed. As the city operates its apps on its private cloud in its main data center, the apps on the public cloud are automatically updated in real time.

Operating the city's DR efforts on the cloud reduced the overall DR cost. Further, the city's financial results improved because the DR efforts are now an operating expenditure rather than a capital expenditure.

Vertical Clouds

It is now possible to build cloud infrastructure and applications for different businesses—the construction, finance, or insurance businesses, for example—thus building vertical clouds (see www.verticalcloud.com).

Before you go on . . .

1. What is a public cloud?
2. What is a private cloud?
3. What is a hybrid cloud?
4. What is a vertical cloud?

Apply the Concept PI4.3

LEARNING OBJECTIVE PI4.3 Identify a use case scenario for each of the four types of clouds.

STEP 1: Background

This section describes four types of clouds: public, private, hybrid, and vertical. The common feature among all four types is that resources are hosted remotely and made available to a wide range of devices over high-speed Internet connections. All four types display the basic features of the cloud that were presented in earlier sections. However, the applications of these features differ for each type.

STEP 2: Activity

Refer to the Boeing example presented in this section. Boeing employs a hybrid cloud. As you have seen, there are many possible strategies for utilizing the cloud. Imagine a use case scenario for Boeing for each type of cloud.

STEP 3: Deliverable

Build a table that identifies a use case scenario for each of the four types of clouds for Boeing.

PI4.4 Cloud Computing Services

Cloud computing services are based on three models: infrastructure-as-a-service (IaaS), platform-as-a-service (PaaS), and software-as-a-service (SaaS). These models represent the three types of computing generally required by consumers: infrastructure to run

FIGURE PI4.4 Comparison of on-premise software, infrastructure-as-a-service, platform-as-a-service, and software-as-a-service.

ON-PREMISE SOFTWARE	INFRASTRUCTURE-AS-A-SERVICE	PLATFORM-AS-A-SERVICE	SOFTWARE-AS-A-SERVICE
CUSTOMER MANAGES: Applications, Data, Operating system, Servers, Virtualization, Storage, Networking	CUSTOMER MANAGES: Applications, Data, Operating system. VENDOR MANAGES: Servers, Virtualization, Storage, Networking	CUSTOMER MANAGES: Applications, Data. VENDOR MANAGES: Operating system, Servers, Virtualization, Storage, Networking	VENDOR MANAGES: Applications, Data, Operating system, Servers, Virtualization, Storage, Networking
Examples	Amazon, IBM, Google, Microsoft, Rackspace	Mircosoft Windows Azure, Google App Engine, Force.com	Salesforce.com, Google Apps, Dropbox, Apple iCloud, Box.net

software and store data (IaaS), platforms to develop applications (PaaS), and software applications to process their data (SaaS). **Figure PI4.4** illustrates the differences among the three models.

As you examine the figure from left to right, note that the customer manages the service less and less, and the vendor manages it more and more.

Although each model has its distinctive features, all three share certain characteristics. First, customers rent them instead of buying them. This arrangement shifts IT from a capital expense to an operating expense. Second, vendors are responsible for maintenance, administration, capacity planning, troubleshooting, and backups. Finally, obtaining additional computing resources—that is, scale from the cloud— is usually fast and easy. Examples are more storage from an IaaS vendor, the ability to handle more PaaS projects, and more users of a SaaS application.

Infrastructure as a Service

With the **infrastructure-as-a-service** model, cloud computing providers offer remotely accessible servers, networks, and storage capacity. They supply these resources on demand from their large resource pools, which are located in their data centers.

IaaS customers are often technology companies with IT expertise. These companies want access to computing power, but they do not want to be responsible for installing or maintaining it. Companies use the infrastructure to run software or simply to store data.

To deploy their applications, IaaS users install their operating system and their application software on the cloud computing provider's computers. They can deploy any software on this infrastructure, including different operating systems, applications, and development platforms. Each user is responsible for maintaining their operating system and application software. Cloud providers typically bill IaaS services on a utility computing basis—that is, the cost reflects the amount of resources the user consumes. In the following example, 3M uses the IaaS capabilities of Microsoft Azure to develop a new app.

The 3M Company (www.3m.com) produces more than 55,000 products for industries, including healthcare, retail, consumer electronics, and construction, hires 88,000 employees, and have customers in more than 200 countries.

In one of its business segments, 3M helps its customers optimize parking operations by automating fee collection and other processes. The company had recently purchased the assets of parking, tolling, and automatic license plate reader businesses, and required better insight into those acquisitions.

3M needed a tracking application that its sales staff could use to obtain real-time information about the type and location of 3M products in parking lots and garages. In order that the solution could be used onsite with potential customers, the app would have to provide access to data anytime, anywhere, and from an array of mobile devices.

Creating an app developed specifically to operate on mobile devices meant that salespeople would be able to work everywhere and at any time. Further, after gathering new information, salespeople would be able to seamlessly synchronize it with existing data in the cloud environment.

To meet these requirements, the 3M development team turned to the Microsoft Azure (http://azure.microsoft.com) infrastructure-as-a-service platform. Using the Azure IT infrastructure, the team was able to develop the app in two days over one weekend.

Salespeople are now using the asset-tracking app to display real-time information about 3M installations. Whenever a salesperson enters new data, the information is immediately available to others through Notification Hubs, which is a "push notification" software tool in Azure. The app also uses the GPS and mapping technologies built into mobile devices to automatically provide visual, location-specific information to the 3M sales force.

Platform as-a-Service

In the **platform-as-a-service** model, customers rent servers, operating systems, storage, a database, software development technologies such as Java and .NET, and network capacity over the Internet. The PaaS model allows the customer both to run existing applications and to develop and test new applications. PaaS offers customers several advantages, which include the following:

- Application developers can develop and run their software solutions on a cloud platform without the cost and complexity of buying and managing the underlying hardware and software layers.
- Underlying computing and storage resources automatically scale to match application demand.
- Operating system features can be upgraded frequently.
- Geographically distributed development teams can work together on software development projects.
- PaaS services can be provided by diverse sources located throughout the world.
- Initial and ongoing costs can be reduced by the use of infrastructure services from a single vendor rather than maintaining multiple hardware facilities that often perform duplicate functions or suffer from incompatibility problems.

As an example of an entity that employed PaaS to improve its performance, consider Novartis International AG (www.novartis.com), a pharmaceutical company based in Basel, Switzerland. The company employs approximately 100,000 people in 140 countries and has core businesses in pharmaceuticals, vaccines and diagnostics, and consumer health.

Novartis needed an alternative to its systems development process. The process was inflexible, expensive, and delivered new functionality much too slowly. These problems meant that the company was limited in the number of new development projects it could undertake. Novartis needed to reduce systems development effort and cost, while delivering systems with required functionality more quickly.

As a result, Novartis turned to Dell Boomi AtomSphere (www.boomi.com) for its platform-as-a-service product. Using this PaaS product, Novartis was able to reduce development efforts, and deliver twice the amount of new functionality in one-sixth the time than was possible earlier.

Software-as-a-Service

With the **software-as-a-service** delivery model, cloud computing vendors provide software that is specific to their customers' requirements. SaaS is the most widely utilized service model, and it provides a broad range of software applications. SaaS providers typically charge their customers a monthly or yearly subscription fee.

SaaS applications reside in the cloud instead of on a user's hard drive or in a data center. The host manages the software and the infrastructure that runs this software and stores the customer's data. The customers do not control either the software, beyond the usual configuration settings, or the infrastructure, beyond changing the resources they use, such as the amount of disk space required for their data. This process eliminates the need to install and run the application on the user's computers, thereby simplifying maintenance and support.

What differentiates SaaS applications from other applications is their ability to scale. As a result, applications can run on as many servers as is necessary to meet changing demands. This process is transparent to the user.

To reduce the risk of an infrastructure outage, SaaS providers regularly back up all of their customers' data. Customers can also back up their data on their storage hardware.

HRM

To understand how SaaS operates, consider Zenefits (www.zenefits.com). Most businesses with fewer than 1,000 employees arrange for various benefit packages (e.g., health insurance plans, 401(k) plans, and many others) not through the companies themselves, but through brokers who collect fees for managing these plans. SMBs (small-to-medium size businesses) save time and money by having brokers negotiate deals with benefits providers.

San Francisco startup Zenefits offers SMBs a software-as-a-service product that simplifies the process of completing forms, collects all the necessary HR data in one interface, and offers preset rates for its lists of available insurers. Further, Zenefits does not charge for its software. The company makes money through fees that benefits providers pay for people signing up for their plans. Since the company's founding in 2013, more than 2,000 SMBs have signed up for its SasS HR software.

For example, on a new worker's first day, she can log in to the Zenefits Web site to register for health plans, 401(k) plans, stock options, flexible spending accounts, and other benefits. She enters her personal information, selects from lists of health and financial plans, and signs documents with a finger on any monitor that acts as a touchscreen. The Zenefits system can also be used to keep track of her vacation days and time sheets. The system can also manage terminations.

IT's Personal: "The Cloud"

This Plug IT In defines the cloud as distributed computing services, and it presents many examples of how the cloud can be used for both personal and business purposes. This IT's Personal is intended to help you differentiate between the business and personal applications of the cloud and to help you plan for your own use of the cloud.

First, you need to understand that there is no single "cloud." Rather, almost all businesses refer to their Internet-based services as "cloud services." Basically, anything you do over the Internet that you used to do on a local computer is a form of cloud computing. When you store files on Dropbox, create a document using Google Docs, use iCloud to store purchases or sync documents, or use OnLive on your iPad, you are using cloud-based services that are intended for personal use.

Infrastructure-as-a-service is an important application of the cloud for personal purposes. Dropbox is one of the most prominent companies in this area. In the past, users had to carry around a USB drive, a CD, an external hard drive, or (way back in the day) floppy

disks to store their personal information. Today, users can employ Dropbox for this purpose. At the time of this writing, a free Dropbox account offered 2 GB of online storage. Not only does Dropbox offer you a place to store your files (eliminating the need for a personal infrastructure of removable storage), but it also provides synchronization across computers and access from mobile devices!

Virtualization is gaining ground. If you have an iPad, you should look up the app called "OnLive" and give it a test run. OnLive allows you to log into a virtual computer that is running Windows 7 or Windows 8. Here, your iPad is simply providing the input/output, and the server is "serving up" a virtual operating system. It is very likely that one day your home computer will be virtual as well.

Software-as-a-service has been a popular option for quite some time. For example, Google Docs offers Internet-based word processing, spreadsheet, presentation, forms, and drawing tools. Recently, Microsoft has moved into the game with their Microsoft Office 365 product. Basically, each of these services allows you to use a computer program without having to install it on your computer or mobile device. You simply access the entire program (and your saved files) over the Internet.

Google has combined a couple of these cloud services with Google Drive, a service that offers the same services as Dropbox in addition to Google Docs' online editing and file-sharing capabilities. This also crosses over with SaaS because of the added benefit of Google Docs. It is very likely that one day Google will merge virtualization, infrastructure, and software into a single cloud-based service. If this technology becomes available, then all you will need as a consumer is an Internet-connected device, and you will be able to store, access, edit, and share your files from the cloud. You will also be able to choose apps to run on your "virtual machine" much the way you currently purchase applications for your mobile devices from a vendor-approved store.

So, what is the point? Simply, cloud-based services are here to stay. The rise of ubiquitous Internet access has engendered a new world of possibilities.

A word of caution, however. Along with its seemingly endless possibilities, cloud computing raises many critical security and privacy issues. Because your files, apps, and editing capability will no longer be stored on a local machine, they are only as safe as the company to which you have entrusted them makes them. So, when you select a cloud provider, make sure you choose wisely!

A subset of SaaS is the *desktop-as-a-service* (DaaS) model, also known as a *cloud desktop* or *desktop in the cloud*. In this model, a SaaS provider hosts a software environment for a desktop personal computer, including productivity and collaboration software—spreadsheets, word processing programs, and so on—such as Google Apps, Microsoft 365, and other products. The DaaS model can be financially advantageous for consumers because they do need to purchase a fully configured personal computer, or fat client. In addition, this model makes the PC environment simpler to deploy and administer.

Before you go on . . .

1. Describe infrastructure-as-a-service.

2. Describe platform-as-a-service.

3. Describe software-as-a-service.

Apply the Concept PI4.4

LEARNING OBJECTIVE PI4.4 Explain the operational model of each of the three types of cloud services.

STEP 1: Background

Infrastructure-as-a-service, platform-as-a-service, and software-as-a-service are relatively new processing models made available by the rise in dependable, high-speed Internet access and powerful "host-computer" processing capabilities. The three cloud models are differentiated by how users employ them and which services providers offer with each one.

STEP 2: Activity

Review the material in this section. For each operational model, consider who owns the infrastructure, the operating systems, and the applications.

STEP 3: Deliverable

In a Word document, explain the operational model for each of the three types of cloud services by highlighting the differences in who is responsible for the infrastructure, the operating systems, and the applications for each model. Submit your document to your instructor.

PI4.5 | The Benefits of Cloud Computing

Cloud computing offers benefits for both individuals and organizations. It allows companies to increase the scale and power of their IT and the speed at which it can be deployed and accessed. It eliminates administrative problems and it operates across locations, devices, and organizational boundaries.

Nearly half of the respondents in a recent CIO Economic Impact survey indicated that they evaluate cloud computing options first—before traditional IT approaches—before making any new IT investments. IBM predicts that the global cloud computing market will grow 22 percent annually to $241 billion by 2020. Next we examine three major benefits that cloud computing provides to individuals and organizations.

Benefit 1: Cloud Computing Has a Positive Impact on Employees

Cloud computing enables companies to provide their employees with access to all the information they need no matter where they are, what device they are using, or with whom they are working. Consider this example.

MIS The attorneys of one multistate law firm needed to access documents and data on a constant basis. Since 2000, the firm's data volume had expanded from 30 gigabytes to more than 40 terabytes. Moreover, all of these data have to be stored and accessed securely. In the past, attorneys often had to manually copy case-relevant data onto external hard drives and USB devices, and then ship these devices back and forth among themselves and the firm's headquarters. These processes were nonsecure, time-consuming, and expensive.

To address these needs, the law firm turned to cloud computing for data storage, offsite disaster recovery, and multisite access within a highly secure public cloud. Rather than maintaining a massive inventory of extra storage as required by its old IT infrastructure, the firm can now increase storage capacity on demand. The cloud provides attorneys with constant access via encrypted communication channels. Furthermore, the cloud facilitates collaboration among distributed teams of attorneys, thereby increasing their overall productivity. The cloud environment has made the firm's attorneys much more efficient and the firm's IT expenses have declined by 60 percent.

Benefit 2: Cloud Computing Can Save Money

Over time, the cost of building and operating an on-premise IT infrastructure will typically be more expensive than implementing the cloud computing. Cloud providers purchase massive amounts of IT infrastructure (e.g., hardware and bandwidth) and gain cost savings by buying in large quantity. As a result, these providers continually take advantage of Moore's law (discussed in Plug IT In 2). For example, the Amazon cloud, known as Amazon Web Services, reduced its prices many times over the last 10 years.

As a result, cloud computing can reduce or eliminate the need to purchase hardware, build and install software, and pay software licensing fees. The organization pays only for the computing resources it needs, and then only when it needs them. This pay-for-use model provides greater flexibility and it eliminates or reduces the need for significant capital expenditures.

MIS Let's consider the United States General Services Administration (GSA; www.gsa.gov). In 2010, the agency began a multiyear strategy to migrate core agency information systems to the cloud. In the first phase of the strategy, the GSA migrated 17,000 employees to Google Apps, making it the first federal agency to move basic e-mail and collaboration services entirely into a cloud environment. The GSA notes that the migration saves the agency approximately $3 million per year.

HRM In the second phase of the strategy, the GSA worked with Salesforce.com (www.salesforce .com) to implement cloud-based software that made it easier for GSA employees to collaborate on projects, share and manage case files, find internal subject-matter experts, and capture new ideas. In one instance, employees used the software to generate 640 ideas in 30 days to streamline GSA business processes, an initiative that eventually saved the agency $5 million per year.

The GSA also established a rapid application development platform (discussed in Chapter 14) in the cloud. Within six months, GSA's IT department developed and delivered more than 100 enterprise applications that replaced more than 1700 legacy applications. The new applications lowered the total cost of ownership by 92 percent.

And the bottom line? The GSA spent $593 million on IT in fiscal year 2014, nearly $100 million less than the previous year.

Benefit 3: Cloud Computing Can Improve Organizational Flexibility and Competitiveness

Cloud computing allows organizations to use only the amount of computing resources they need at a given time. Therefore, companies can efficiently scale their operations up or down as needed to meet rapidly changing business conditions. Cloud computing is also able to deliver computing services faster than the on-premise computing.

Consider PAC2000A (http://www.pac2000a.it/), a large Italian retailer. The company had been using a custom-developed, in-house application to manage shelf prices across more than 1,000 outlets. The pricing application was not able to incorporate consumer demand into its algorithms, whether on a national or a local scale. When the retailer implemented a SaaS-based price optimization system, it gained sophisticated analytical capabilities on very detailed cost and competitors' data. This process led to more precise localized pricing decisions, more accurate forecasts, and a 2.4 percent increase in comparable store sales.

POM

Before you go on . . .

1. Describe how cloud computing can help organizations expand the scope of their business operations.

2. Describe how cloud computing can help organizations respond quickly to market changes.

Apply the Concept PI4.5

LEARNING OBJECTIVE PI4.5 Identify the key benefits of cloud computing.

STEP 1: Background

This section has outlined the benefits that are driving many organizations to transition to cloud computing. Productivity, cost reductions, collaboration, more robust data mining, flexibility, and scope expansion are just the beginning. Cloud computing is a powerful tool that is changing the ways we do business.

STEP 2: Activity

Visit http://www.wiley.com/go/rainer/MIS4e/applytheconcept, and click on the link provided for Apply the Concept PI4.5. This

link will take you to the amazon.com site that describes Amazon's business cloud services. This site contains several customer testimonials. As you watch them, look for common benefits the various customers receive from cloud computing.

STEP 3: Deliverable

Based on the video and the material in this section, identify the key benefits of cloud computing that amazon.com offers its business customers.

PI4.6 | Concerns and Risks with Cloud Computing

Gartner predicts that cloud computing will grow at an annual rate of 19 percent through the year 2015. Even if this prediction is accurate, however, cloud computing will still account for less than 5 percent of total worldwide IT spending that year. Why is this percentage so low? The reason is that there are serious concerns with cloud computing. These concerns fall into six categories: legacy IT systems, reliability, privacy, security, the legal and regulatory environment, and criminal use of cloud computing.

Concern 1: Legacy IT Systems

Historically, organizational IT systems have accumulated a diversity of hardware, operating systems, and applications. When bundled together, these systems are called "legacy spaghetti." These systems cannot easily be transferred to the cloud because they must first be untangled and simplified. Furthermore, many IT professionals have vested interests in various legacy systems, and they resist efforts to exchange these systems for cloud computing.

Concern 2: Reliability

Many skeptics contend that cloud computing is not as reliable as a well-managed, on-premise IT infrastructure. Although cloud providers are improving the redundancy and reliability of their offerings, outages still occur. Consider the examples of Dropbox and Google.

On January 10, 2014, file-sharing service Dropbox (www.dropbox.com) went offline for about two days. Although hackers tried to claim credit for the crash, Dropbox said that the outage was its own fault. According to the company, a programming error caused upgrades its operating system to be applied on actively running machines during routine maintenance. Engineers attempted to restore the systems from backups, but thanks to the sheer size of Dropbox's databases, it took two days to get back to normal. The company maintained that no user data were damaged or compromised.

Then, on March 14, 2014, Dropbox service stopped working for about one hour. Users received errors when attempting to access the Dropbox Web site or mobile apps. The company acknowledged the outage on Twitter, describing it only as a "service issue." Forty minutes after that first tweet, Dropbox said that the issue had been resolved. The company never went into detail about what exactly happened with this outage.

When Gmail, Google Calendar, Google Docs, and Google+ go offline, people notice. On January 24, 2014, these Google services went down for some 25 minutes. Google says a software bug on its end caused the glitch. According to engineers, a system that controls the services sent faulty configurations to a variety of servers, which resulted in widespread errors. Google had everything back up and running for most folks in about 25 minutes, but for some users, it took 30 minutes to an hour for services to get back online.

Then, on March 17, 2014, several Google services went down for about three and one-half hours, including Google Hangouts, Google Voice, and parts of Google Drive. Once again, Google blamed maintenance problems. The company said that routine procedures redirected traffic to the wrong set of servers, causing a cycle of overloaded machines trying to handle more requests than they could manage.

Concern 3: Privacy

Privacy advocates have criticized cloud computing for posing a major threat to privacy because the providers control, and thus lawfully or unlawfully monitor, the data and communication stored between the user and the host company. For example, AT&T and Verizon collaborated with NSA to use cloud computing to record more than 10 million phone calls between American citizens. In addition, providers could accidentally or deliberately alter or even delete some information.

Using a cloud computing, provider also complicates data privacy because of the extent to which cloud processing and cloud storage are used to implement cloud services. The point is that customer data may not remain on the same system or in the same data center. This situation can lead to legal concerns over jurisdiction.

There have been efforts to address this problem by integrating the legal environment. One example is the US-EU Safe Harbor, a streamlined process for U.S. companies to comply with the European Union directive on the protection of personal data.

Concern 4: Security

Critics also question how secure cloud computing really is. Because the characteristics of cloud computing can differ widely from those of traditional IT architectures, providers need to reconsider the effectiveness and efficiency of traditional security mechanisms. Security issues include access to sensitive data, data segregation (among customers), privacy, error exploitation, recovery, accountability, malicious insiders, and account control.

The security of cloud computing services is a contentious issue that may be delaying the adoption of this technology. Security issues arise primarily from the unease of both the private and public sectors with the external management of security-based services. The fact that providers manage these services provides great incentive for them to prioritize building and maintaining strong security services.

Another security issue involves the control over who is able to access and utilize the information stored in the cloud. (Recall our discussion of least privilege in Chapter 7.) Many organizations exercise least-privilege controls effectively with their on-premise IT infrastructures. Some cloud computing environments, in contrast, cannot exercise least-privilege controls effectively. This problem occurs because cloud computing environments were originally designed for individuals or groups, not for hierarchical organizations in which some people have both the right and the responsibility to exercise control over other people's private information. To address this problem, cloud computing vendors are working to incorporate administrative, least-privilege functionality into their products. In fact, many have already done so.

Consider Panama City, Florida as an example. Panama City was one of the first cities in the United States to adopt Google Apps for Government. The city was searching for a way to gain visibility into who was using Google Apps and how users were collaborating both inside and outside the city's IT domain. Further, the city had to have the ability to control and enforce data-sharing policies where necessary. The city decided to adopt CloudLock (www.cloudlock.com).

`MIS`

CloudLock provides a security system to protect its clients' information assets located in public cloud applications such as Google Apps. CloudLock provides key data management issues such as the following:

- *Data inventory:* How many information assets exist and what are their types?
- Which information assets are shared with the public or over the Internet?
- Who has access to what information asset and what information asset is accessible to whom?

Using CloudLock, Panama City was able to notify data owners of policy violations or exposed documents containing potentially sensitive information; change or revoke excessive privilege; and audit permissions changes. Further, the city's IT manager was able to designate department leaders to manage their respective organizational unit's data policies and usage by giving them access to the CloudLock application.

Concern 5: The Regulatory and Legal Environment

There are numerous legal and regulatory barriers to cloud computing, many of which involve data access and transport. For example, the European Union prohibits consumer data from being transferred to nonmember countries without the consumers' prior consent and approval. Companies located outside the European Union can overcome this restriction by demonstrating that they provide a "safe harbor" for the data. Some countries, such as Germany, have enacted even more restrictive data export laws. Cloud computing vendors are aware of these regulations and laws, and they are working to modify their offerings so that they can assure customers and regulators that data entrusted to them are secure enough to meet all of these requirements.

To obtain compliance with regulations such as the Federal Information Security Management Act (FISMA), the Health Insurance Portability and Accountability Act (HIPAA), and the Sarbanes-Oxley Act in the United States, the Data Protection Directive in the European Union,

`FIN`
`ACCT`

and the credit card industry's Payment Card Industry's Data Security Standard (PCI DSS), cloud computing customers may have to adopt hybrid deployment modes that are typically more expensive and may offer restricted benefits. This process is how, for example, Google is able to "manage and meet additional government policy requirements beyond FISMA," and Rackspace (www.rackspace.com) is able to claim PCI compliance. FISMA requires each federal agency to develop, document, and implement a program to provide information security for the information and information systems that support the operations of the agency, including those provided by contractors. PCI DSS is a set of requirements designed to ensure that all companies that process, store, or transmit credit card information maintain a secure environment.

Concern 6: Criminal Use of Cloud Computing

Cloud computing makes available a well-managed, generally reliable, scalable global infrastructure that is, unfortunately, as well suited to illegal computing activities as it is to legitimate business activities. We look at a number of possible illegal activities here.

The huge amount of information stored in the cloud makes it an attractive target for data thieves.

Cloud computing makes immense processing power available to anyone. Criminals using cloud computing have access to encryption technology and anonymous communication channels that make it difficult for authorities to detect their activities. When law enforcement pursues criminals, the wrongdoers can rapidly shut down computing resources in the cloud, thus greatly decreasing the chances that there will be any clues left for forensic analysis. When criminals no longer need a machine and shut it down, other clients of cloud vendors immediately reuse the storage and computational capacity allocated to that machine. Therefore, the criminal information is overwritten by data from legitimate customers. It is nearly impossible to recover any data after the machine has been "de-provisioned."

Criminals are registering for an account (with assumed names and stolen credit cards, of course) with a cloud vendor and "legitimately" using services for illegal purposes. For example, criminals are using Gmail or the text-sharing Web site Pastebin (www.pastebin.com) to plan crimes and share stolen information. Another example is that criminals use cloud computing in brute-force password cracking (see Chapter 7). Although such uses are prohibited by most company's terms-of-service agreements, policing the cloud is expensive and not very rewarding for cloud providers.

Many cloud vendors offer geographical diversity—that is, virtual machines that are located in different physical locations around the world. Criminals can use this feature in transnational attacks. Such attacks place political and technical obstacles in the way of authorities seeking to trace a cyberattack back to its source.

Another weakness exploited by criminals arises from the Web-based applications, or SaaS offerings, provided by cloud vendors. With millions of users commingling on tens of thousands of servers, a criminal can easily mix in among legitimate users.

Even more complicated for authorities and victims, cyberattacks can originate within cloud programs that we use and trust. For instance, researchers at the security firm F-Secure reported that they had detected several phishing sites hosted within Google Docs. What made the attacks possible is a feature within Google's spreadsheet system that lets users create Web-based forms, with titles such as "Webmail Account Upgrade" and "Report a Bug." These forms, located on a Google server, were authenticated with Google's encryption certificate. Significantly, they requested sensitive information such as the user's full name, username, Google password, and so on, according to the F-Secure researchers.

> ### Before you go on . . .
>
> **1.** Discuss the various risks of cloud computing.
>
> **2.** In your opinion, which risk is the greatest? Support your answer.

Apply the Concept PI4.6

LEARNING OBJECTIVE PI4.6 Discuss the concerns and risks associated with cloud computing.

STEP 1: Background

This section has discussed why the risks associated with cloud computing outweigh the benefits for some organizations. The statistics provided early on that cloud computing will remain a small portion of IT spending reflect concerns regarding these risks.

STEP 2: Activity

Visit http://www.wiley.com/go/rainer/MIS4e/applytheconcept, and click on the link provided for Plug IT In 4.6. This link will take you to an article that addresses some of the risks of cloud computing that senior managers need to consider. As you read the article, try to organize the managers' thoughts according to the concerns presented in this section: legacy systems, costs, reliability, security, privacy, and regulatory and legal environment.

Imagine you have just overheard a conversation about how wonderful cloud computing is that mentioned all of the positives and none of the negatives. How would you respond?

STEP 3: Deliverable

Based on the material contained in this section and the information conveyed in the article, write a response to the above scenario that discusses the concerns and risks associated with cloud computing.

PI4.7 | Web Services and Service-Oriented Architecture

Thus far we have explained how cloud computing can deliver a variety of functionality to users in the form of services (think IaaS, PaaS, and SaaS). We conclude by examining Web services and service-oriented architecture.

Web services are applications delivered over the Internet (the cloud) that MIS professionals can select and combine through almost any device, from personal computers to mobile phones. By using a set of shared standards, or protocols, these applications permit different systems to "talk" with one another—that is, to share data and services—without requiring human beings to translate the conversations. Web services have enormous potential because they can be employed in a variety of environments: over the Internet, on an intranet inside a corporate firewall, on an extranet set up by business partners. In addition, they perform a wide variety of tasks, from automating business processes to integrating components of an enterprisewide system to streamlining online buying and selling.

Web services provide numerous benefits for organizations:

- The organization can utilize the existing Internet infrastructure without having to implement any new technologies.
- Organizational personnel can access remote or local data without having to understand the complexities of this process.
- The organization can create new applications quickly and easily.

The collection of Web services that are used to build a firm's IT applications constitutes a service-oriented architecture. Businesses accomplish their processes by executing a series of these services. One of the major benefits of Web services is that they can be reused across an organization in other applications. For example, a Web service that checks a consumer's credit could be used with a service that processes a mortgage application or a credit card application.

Web services are based on four key protocols: XML, SOAP, WSDL, and UDDI. Extensible markup language (XML) is a computer language that makes it easier to exchange data among a variety of applications and to validate and interpret these data. XML is a more powerful and flexible markup language than hypertext markup language (HTML). HTML is a page-description language for specifying how text, graphics, video, and sound are placed on a Web page document. HTML was originally designed to create and link static documents composed primarily

(a) html

```
<!DOCTYPE HTML PUBLIC "-//W3C//DTD XHTML 1.0 Transitional//EN" http://www.wiley.com/college/gisslen/0470179961/video/
video111
<html xmlns="http://www.wiley.com/college/rainer/0470179061/video/video111.html"><head>
<meta http-equiv="content-Type" content="text/html; charset=ISO-8859-1">
<title>CSS Text Wrapper</title>
<link type="text/css" rel="stylesheet" href="css/stylesheet.css">
</head><body id="examples">

<div id="container">
        <div class="wrapper">
                <div class="ex">
                        <script type="text/javascript">shapewrapp
er("15","7.5,141,145|22.5,89,89|37.5,68,69|52.5,46,50|67.5,3
height: 15px; width: 39px;"></div><div style="float: left; clear: left; height: 15px; width: 27px;"></div><div style="float:
15px; width: 4px;"></div><div style="float: left; clear: left; height: 15px; width: 6px;"></div><div style="float:
right; cle
width: 43px;"></div><div style="float: left; clear: left; height: 15px; width: 57px;"></div><div style="float: right; clear:
                        <span style="font-size: 13px;" class=c">
```

(b) XML

```
<feature numbered="no" xml:id="c08-fea-0001">
    <titleGroup>
        <title type="featureName">OPENING CASE</title>
        <title type="main">Tiger Tans and Gifts</title>
    </titleGroup>
    <section xml:id="c08-sec-0002">
        <p>
            <blockFixed onlyChannels="print" type="graphic">
                <mediaResource alt="p0310" copyright="John Wiley &amp; Sons, Inc." eRights="yes"
                    href="urn:x-wiley:9781118443590:media:rainer9781118443590c08:p0310" pRights="yes"/>
            </blockFixed>
            Lisa Keiling owns & tanning salon in Wedowee, Alabama, that does very well from January to May....
        </p>
    </section>
</feature>
```

FIGURE PI4.5 (a) Screenshot of an HTML wrapper. This wrapper gives instructions on how to open a video associated with this book. (b) Example of XML tagging done in Chapter 8 of this book.

of text (Figure PI4.5). Today, however, the Web is much more social and interactive, and many Web pages have multimedia elements, such as images, audio, and video. To integrate these rich media into Web pages, users had to rely on third-party plug-in applications such as Flash, Silverlight, and Java. Unfortunately for users, these add-ons require both additional programming and extensive computer processing.

The next evolution of HTML, called HTML5, solves this problem by enabling users to embed images, audio, and video directly into a document without the add-ons. HTML5 also makes it easier for Web pages to function across different display devices, including mobile devices and desktops. HTML5 also supports offline data storage for apps that run over the Web. Web pages will execute more quickly, and they will resemble smartphone apps. HTML5 is used in a number of Internet platforms, including Apple's Safari browsers, Google Chrome, and Firefox browsers. Google's Gmail and Google Reader also use HTML5. Web sites listed as "iPad ready" are using HTML5 extensively. Examples of such sites are CNN, *The New York Times*, and CBS.

Whereas HTML is limited to describing how data should be presented in the form of Web pages, XML can present, communicate, and store data. For example, in XML a number is not simply a number. The XML tag also specifies whether the number represents a price, a date, or a ZIP code. Consider this example of XML, which identifies the contact information for Jane Smith.

```
<contact-info>
<name>Jane Smith</name>
<company>AT&T</company>
<phone>(212) 555-4567</phone>
</contact-info>
```

Simple object access protocol (*SOAP*) is a set of rules that define how messages can be exchanged among different network systems and applications through the use of XML. These rules essentially establish a common protocol that allows different Web services to interoperate. For example, Visual Basic clients can use SOAP to access a Java server. SOAP runs on all hardware and software systems.

The *Web services description language* (*WSDL*) is used to create the XML document that describes the tasks performed by the various Web services. Tools such as VisualStudio.Net automate the process of accessing the WSDL, reading it, and coding the application to reference the specific Web service.

Universal description, discovery, and integration (*UDDI*) allows MIS professionals to search for needed Web services by creating public or private searchable directories of these services. In other words, UDDI is the registry of descriptions of Web services.

Examples of Web services abound. As one example, the Food and Nutrition Service (FNS) within the U.S. Department of Agriculture (USDA) uses Amazon Web Services successfully. The FNS administers the department's nutrition assistance programs. Its mission is to provide children and needy families with improved access to food and a healthier diet through its food assistance programs and comprehensive nutrition education efforts.

The Supplemental Nutrition Assistance Program, or SNAP, is the cornerstone of the USDA's nutrition assistance mission. More than 47 million people—most of them children—receive SNAP benefits each month. To help recipients, in 2010 the FNS created a Web application called the SNAP Retail Locator. Faced with limited budget and time to implement the solution, the FNS selected Amazon Web Services to host the application. As its name suggests, the SNAP Retail Locator, which receives 30,000 visitors per month, helps SNAP recipients find the closest SNAP-authorized store and also provides driving directions to the store. The application has been available 100 percent of the time since it was launched. In addition, by employing Amazon, the FNS saved 90 percent of the cost it would have incurred had it hosted the application on-premises.

Before you go on . . .

1. What are Web services?
2. What is a service-oriented architecture?

Apply the Concept PI4.7

LEARNING OBJECTIVE PI4.7 Explain the role of Web services in building a firm's IT applications, providing examples.

STEP 1: Background

Web services allow companies to increase functionality with minimal effort by using standard protocols to access and share data. The advantage of using Web services is that it standardizes the Web platform. Using the same Web protocols that allow you to access any Web site makes sharing data much easier.

STEP 2: Activity

Imagine you work for a bank and you want to display some financial data on your intranet to keep your employees up-to-date on major market trends. One option is to gather data, perform an analysis, build and share charts and graphs, and

then keep everything current. This probably sounds like a lot of work. But, suppose someone else had done all of the work for you?

Visit http://www.wiley.com/go/rainer/MIS4e/applytheconcept, and click on the link provided for Apply the Concept PI4.7. This link will take you to a Web site that discusses the available "widgets" (another name for an embeddable Web service) that businesses can select to display on their sites. Review the available information, and consider how it would help you add content to your bank's intranet with minimal effort.

STEP 3: Deliverable

Write a summary that explains the role of Web services in building a firm's IT applications. Include a few examples based on the options you viewed in Step 2.

What's in IT for me?

For all Business Majors

As with hardware (see Plug IT In 2), the design of enterprise IT architectures has profound impacts for businesspeople. Personal and organizational success can depend on an understanding of cloud computing and a commitment to knowing the opportunities and challenges they will bring.

At the organizational level, cloud computing has the potential to make the organization function more efficiently and effectively,

while saving the organization money. Web services and SOA make the organization more flexible when deploying new IT applications.

At the individual level, you might utilize cloud computing yourself if you start your own business. Remember that cloud computing provides startup companies with world-class IT capabilities at a very low cost.

Summary

1. **Describe the problems that modern information technology departments face.**

Traditional IT departments (on-premise computing) face many problems:

*   They spend huge amounts on IT infrastructure and expert staffs to build and maintain complex IT systems. These expenses include software licenses, hardware, and staff training and salaries.

*   They must manage an infrastructure that often is not used to its full capacity.

*   They spend the majority of their budgets on maintaining existing IT infrastructure, with the remainder being spent on developing new systems.

*   They have difficulty capturing, storing, managing, and analyzing all these data.

*   They can actually inhibit an organization's ability to respond quickly and appropriately to rapidly changing dynamic environments.

*   They are expensive.

2. **Describe the key characteristics and advantages of cloud computing.**

Cloud computing is a type of computing that delivers convenient, on-demand, pay-as-you-go access for multiple customers to a shared pool of configurable computing resources (e.g., servers, networks, storage, applications, and services) that can be rapidly and easily accessed over the Internet. The essential *characteristics* of cloud computing include the following:

*   Cloud computing provides on-demand self-service.

*   Cloud computing includes the characteristics of grid computing.

*   Cloud computing includes the characteristics of utility computing.

*   Cloud computing utilizes broad network access.

*   Cloud computing pools computing resources.

*   Cloud computing typically occurs on virtualized servers.

3. **Describe each of the four types of clouds.**

Public clouds are shared, easily accessible, multicustomer IT infrastructures that are available nonexclusively to any entity in the public (individuals,

groups, and/or organizations). *Private clouds* (also known as *internal clouds* or *corporate clouds*) are IT infrastructures that are accessible only by a single entity, or by an exclusive group of related entities that share the same purpose and requirements, such as all the business units within a single organization. *Hybrid clouds* are composed of public and private clouds that remain unique entities but are bound together, offering the benefits of multiple deployment models. *Vertical clouds* serve specific industries.

4. **Explain the operational model of each of the three types of cloud services.**

With the *infrastructure-as-a-service* model, cloud computing providers offer remotely accessible servers, networks, and storage capacity. In the *platform-as-a-service* model, customers rent servers, operating systems, storage, a database, software development technologies such as Java and. NET, and network capacity over the Internet. With the *software-as-a-service* delivery model, cloud computing vendors provide software that is specific to their customers' requirements.

5. **Identify the key benefits of cloud computing.**

The benefits of cloud computing include making individuals more productive; facilitating collaboration; mining insights from data; developing and hosting applications; cost flexibility; business scalability; improved utilization of hardware; market adaptability; and product and service customization.

6. **Discuss the concerns and risks associated with cloud computing.**

Cloud computing does raise concerns and have risks, which include legacy spaghetti, cost, reliability, privacy, security, and the regulatory and legal environment.

7. **Explain the role of Web services in building a firm's IT applications, providing examples.**

Web services are applications delivered over the Internet that MIS professionals can select and combine through almost any device, from personal computers to mobile phones. A service-*oriented architecture* makes it possible for MIS professionals to construct business applications using Web services.

Glossary

cloud computing A technology in which tasks are performed by computers physically removed from the user and accessed over a network, in particular the Internet.

extensible markup language (XML) A computer language that makes it easier to exchange data among a variety of applications and to validate and interpret these data.

grid computing A technology that applies the unused processing resources of many geographically dispersed computers in a network to form a virtual supercomputer.

HTML5 A page-description language that makes it possible to embed images, audio, and video directly into a document without add-ons. Also makes it easier for Web pages to function across different display devices, including mobile devices as well as desktops. Supports the storage of data offline.

hybrid clouds Clouds composed of public and private clouds that remain unique entities but are bound together, offering the benefits of multiple deployment models.

hypertext markup language (HTML) A page-description language for specifying how text, graphics, video, and sound are placed on a Web page document.

infrastructure-as-a-service (IaaS) A model with which cloud computing providers offer remotely accessible servers, networks, and storage capacity.

on-premise computing A model of IT management where companies own their IT infrastructure (their software, hardware, networks, and data management) and maintain it in their data centers.

platform-as-a-service (PaaS) A model with which customers rent servers, operating systems, storage, a database, software

development technologies such as Java and .NET, and network capacity over the Internet.

private clouds (also known as *internal clouds* or *corporate clouds*) IT infrastructures that are accessible only by a single entity or by an exclusive group of related entities that share the same purpose and requirements, such as all the business units within a single organization.

public clouds Shared, easily accessible, multicustomer IT infrastructures that are available nonexclusively to any entity in the general public (individuals, groups, and/or organizations).

server farms Massive data centers, which may contain hundreds of thousands of networked computer servers.

server virtualization A technology that uses software-based partitions to create multiple virtual servers (called *virtual machines*) on a single physical server.

service-oriented architecture An IT architecture that makes it possible to construct business applications using Web services.

software-as-a-service (SaaS) A delivery model with which cloud computing vendors provide software that is specific to their customers' requirements.

utility computing A technology whereby a service provider makes computing resources and infrastructure management available to a customer as needed.

Web services Applications delivered over the Internet that IT developers can select and combine through almost any device, from personal computers to mobile phones.

Discussion Questions

1. What is the value of server farms and virtualization to any large organization?

2. If you were the chief information officer of a firm, how would you explain the workings, benefits, and limitations of cloud computing?

3. What is the value of cloud computing to a small organization?

4. What is the value of cloud computing to an entrepreneur who is starting a business?

Problem-Solving Activities

1. Investigate the status of cloud computing by researching the offerings of the following leading vendors: Dell (www.dell.com), Oracle (www.oracle.com), IBM (www.ibm.com), Amazon (www.amazon.com), Microsoft (www.microsoft.com), and Google (www.google.com). Note any inhibitors to cloud computing.

PLUG IT IN **5**

Artificial Intelligence

LEARNING OBJECTIVES

PI5.1 Explain the potential value and the potential limitations of artificial intelligence.

PI5.2 Provide use case examples of expert systems, machine learning systems, deep learning systems, and neural networks.

PI5.3 Provide use case examples of computer vision, natural language processing, robotics, image recognition, and intelligent agents.

PI5.1 Introduction to Artificial Intelligence

Artificial intelligence (AI) is a subfield of computer science that studies the thought processes of humans and re-creates the effects of those processes via information systems. We define artificial intelligence as the theory and development of information systems able to perform tasks that normally require human intelligence. That is, we define AI in terms of the tasks that humans perform, rather than how humans think.

This definition raises the question, "What is *intelligent behavior*?" The following capabilities are considered to be signs of intelligence: learning or understanding from experience, making sense of ambiguous or contradictory messages, and responding quickly and successfully to new situations.

The ultimate goal of AI is to build machines that mimic human intelligence. A widely used test to determine whether a computer exhibits intelligent behavior was designed by Alan Turing, a British AI pioneer. The *Turing test* proposes a scenario in which a man and a computer both pretend to be women or men, and a human interviewer has to identify which is the real human. Based on this standard, the intelligent systems exemplified in commercial AI products are far from exhibiting any significant intelligence.

We can better understand the potential value of AI by contrasting it with *natural (human) intelligence*. AI has several important commercial advantages over natural intelligence, but it also displays some limitations, as outlined in Table PI5.1.

It is important to distinguish between strong artificial intelligence and weak artificial intelligence. Strong AI is *hypothetical* artificial intelligence that matches or exceeds human intelligence—the intelligence of a machine that could successfully perform any intellectual task that a human being can. Strong AI, therefore, could be considered to have consciousness or sentience. Weak AI (also called narrow AI) performs a useful and specific function that once required human intelligence to perform, and does so at human levels or better (for example, character recognition, speech recognition, machine vision, robotics, data mining, medical informatics, automated investing, and many other functions).

TABLE PI5.1   Comparison of the Capabilities of Natural Versus Artificial Intelligence

Capabilities	Natural Intelligence	Artificial Intelligence
Preservation of knowledge	Perishable from an organizational point of view	Permanent
Duplication and dissemination of knowledge in a computer	Difficult, expensive, takes time	Easy, fast, and inexpensive
Total cost of knowledge	Can be erratic and inconsistent, incomplete at times	Consistent and thorough
Documentability of process and knowledge	Difficult, expensive	Fairly easy, inexpensive
Creativity	Can be very high	Low, uninspired
Use of sensory experiences	Direct and rich in possibilities	Must be interpreted first; limited
Recognizing patterns and relationships	Fast, easy to explain	Machine learning still not as good as people in most cases, but in some cases better than people
Reasoning	Making use of wide context of experiences	Good only in narrow, focused, and stable domains

Today, systems that are labeled "artificial intelligence" are weak AI. Weak AI is already powerful enough to make a dramatic difference in human life. Weak AI applications enhance human endeavors by complementing what people can do. For example, when you call your bank and talk to an automated voice, you are probably talking to a weak AI program. Researchers at universities and companies around the world are building weak AI applications that are rapidly becoming more capable.

Consider chess, which weak AI systems now play better than any human. In 1997, IBM's Deep Blue system beat the world chess champion (Gary Kasparov) for the first time. Since that time, chess playing systems have become significantly more powerful. However, the way these systems play chess has not changed. They search through all possible future moves to find the best move to make next.

Today however, the best players in the world are not machines, but what Garry Kasparov, a grandmaster, calls "centaurs." Centaurs are teams of humans and chess playing programs. In freestyle chess matches, competitors can play unassisted as humans, unassisted as chess playing programs, or as centaurs. In the Freestyle Battle of 2014, pure chess playing AI software won 42 games, while centaurs won 53 games.

Interestingly, the advent of AI did not diminish the performance of purely human chess players. Quite the opposite. Cheap, highly functional chess programs have inspired more people than ever to play chess and the players have become better than ever. In fact, today there are more than twice as many grandmasters as there were when Deep Blue beat Kasparov.

Similar to centaurs, physicians who are supported by AI will have an enhanced ability to spot cancer in medical images; speech recognition algorithms running on smartphones will bring the Internet to many millions of illiterate people in developing countries; digital assistants will suggest promising hypotheses for academic research; and image classification algorithms will allow wearable computers to layer useful digital information onto people's views of the real, physical world.

Weak AI does present challenges. For example, consider the power that AI brings to national security agencies, in both autocracies and democracies. The capacity to monitor billions of conversations and to pick out every citizen from the crowd by his or her voice or face poses serious threats to liberty. Also, many individuals could lose their jobs as a result of advances in AI.

Several technological advancements have led to advancements in artificial intelligence. We take a brief look at each of them here.

- *Advancements in chip technology:* AI systems employ graphics processing units (called GPU chips). These chips were developed to meet the visual and parallel processing demands of video games. In fact, GPU chips facilitate parallel processing in neural networks, which are the primary information architecture of AI software. (We discuss neural networks later in this Plug IT In.)

- *Big Data:* As we discussed in Chapter 3, Big Data consists of diverse, high-volume, high-velocity information assets that require new types of processing to enable enhance decision making, insight discovery, and process optimization. Big Data is now being used to train deep learning software. (We discuss deep learning later in this Plug IT In.)

- *The Internet and cloud computing:* The Internet (discussed in Chapter 4) and cloud computing (discussed in Plug IT In 4) make Big Data available to AI systems, specifically neural networks, and provide the computational capacity needed for AI systems.

- *Improved algorithms:* An **algorithm** is a problem-solving method expressed as a finite sequence of steps. Researchers are rapidly improving the capabilities of AI algorithms. In addition, AI algorithms run much faster on GPU chips.

Before you go on . . .

1. What is artificial intelligence?
2. Differentiate between artificial and human intelligence.
3. Differentiate between strong AI and weak AI.

Apply the Concept PI5.1

LEARNING OBJECTIVE PI5.1 Explain the potential value and the potential limitations of artificial intelligence.

STEP 1: Background (Here is what you are learning.)

This section introduced you to several applications of artificial intelligence. One of these applications was the Google self-driving car. This innovation presents a scenario where technology could potentially greatly enhance the safety of motorists, pedestrians, and passengers. However, there are also significant risks posed by turning over the keys to the computer.

STEP 2: Activity (Here is what you do.)

Visit http://www.wiley.com/go/rainer/MIS4e/applytheconcept, and click on the link provided for Plug IT In 5.1. This link will take you to a YouTube video that introduces the Google self-driving car. Although this innovation is very exciting, it can also be very scary! While you are watching the video, imagine the advantages and disadvantages of this type of intelligent system. Would it function best as a "pilot" or a very helpful "copilot"?

STEP 3: Deliverable (Here is what you turn in.)

Build a table that displays both the potential value (advantages) and the potential limitations (disadvantages) of artificial intelligence for different scenarios illustrated in the example below.

	Advantages	Disadvantages
Tired driver		
Distracted driver (texting)		
Sick/stressed driver		
Ambulance driver		
School bus driver		
Soccer mom, mini van driver		

PI5.2 | Artificial Intelligence Technologies

A variety of technologies have been developed in the field of artificial intelligence. In this section we begin our discussion with expert systems, one of the earliest AI technologies. We continue with two technologies that have relatively recently revolutionized the field of artificial intelligence: machine learning and deep learning. We then discuss neural networks that are essential to machine learning and deep learning.

Expert Systems

Expert systems (ESs) are computer systems that attempt to mimic human experts by applying expertise in a specific domain. Expert systems can either *support* decision makers or completely *replace* them.

Essentially, an ES transfers expertise from a domain expert (or other source) to the system. This knowledge is then stored in the system, which users can call on for specific advice as needed. The system can make inferences and arrive at conclusions. Then, like a human expert, it offers advice or recommendations. In addition, it can explain the logic behind the advice. Because ESs can integrate and manipulate enormous amounts of data, they sometimes perform better than any single human expert can. On the other hand, expert systems do present problems, which include the following:

- Transferring domain expertise from human experts to the expert system can be difficult because humans cannot always explain *how* they know and what they know. Often they are not aware of their complete reasoning process.

- Even if the domain experts can explain their entire reasoning process, automating that process may not be possible. The process might be either too complex or too vague, or it might require too many rules. Essentially, it is very difficult to program all the possible decision paths in an expert system.

- In some contexts, there is a potential liability from the use of expert systems. Humans make errors occasionally, but they are generally "let off the hook" if they took reasonable care and applied generally accepted methods. An organization that uses an expert system, however, may lack this legal protection if problems arise later. The usual example of this issue is medical treatment, but it can also arise if a business decision driven by an expert system harms someone financially.

For example, in the case of medical treatment, consider a physician who consults with a medical expert system when treating a patient. If the patient's care goes poorly, then the question arises, who is liable? The physician? The expert system? The vendor of the expert system?

A large number of expert systems have been developed, such as MYCIN and PROSPECTOR. MYCIN was designed to identify bacteria causing infections and suggest appropriate antibiotics. PROSPECTOR was designed to help geologists in mineral exploration.

New developments in the field of artificial intelligence now largely take place in the areas of machine learning and deep learning. We turn our attention to these two technologies and then discuss how neural networks enable each technology.

Machine Learning

Machine learning develops algorithms that can learn from and make predictions about data. These algorithms operate by building a model from example inputs in order to make data-driven predictions or decisions, rather than following explicit instructions in computer program. Therefore, we can say that *machine learning* is the ability to accurately perform new, unseen tasks, built on known properties learned from training or historic data that are labeled.

Machine learning systems have the ability to improve their performance by exposure to data without the need to follow explicitly programmed instructions. Essentially, machine learning automatically discovers patterns in data. Once discovered, the pattern can be used to make predictions. For instance, presented with data about credit card transactions, including date, time, merchant, merchant location, price, and whether the transaction was legitimate or fraudulent, a machine learning system learns patterns that are predictive of fraud.

The more the transaction data the system processes, the better the predictions expected from them.

MIS

For example, a machine learning system can be trained on e-mail messages to learn to distinguish between spam and nonspam messages. After learning, the system can then be used to classify new e-mail messages into spam and nonspam folders. The following are other examples of machine learning:

FIN

- In banking, automated fraud detection systems use machine learning to identify behavior patterns that could indicate fraudulent payment activity.

- In the life sciences, machine learning systems are used to predict cause-and-effect relationships from biological data and the activities of compounds, helping pharmaceutical companies identify promising drugs.

POM

- In the oil and gas industry, producers use machine learning in many applications, from locating mineral deposits to diagnosing mechanical problems with drilling equipment.

MKT

- Retailers use machine learning to discover attractive cross-sell offers and effective promotions.

- In 2014, Google announced that it had just completed mapping the exact location of every business, every household, and every street number in all of France. The process took Google one hour. How? The company used its street-view database containing hundreds of millions of images. Humans manually examined a few hundred of the images and circled the street numbers in them. Then Google fed those labeled images into a machine-learning algorithm that figured out what was unique about the circled objects. The software then looked for that type of object in the remainder of the images and read the numbers that it found.

Deep Learning

Deep learning is a subset of machine learning where the system discovers new patterns without being exposed to labeled historical or training data. Example applications of deep learning include speech recognition, image recognition, natural language processing, drug discovery and toxicology, and customer relationship management. Let's look at specific examples of deep learning.

- In June 2012, a Google deep learning system that had been shown 10 million images from YouTube videos correctly identified cats, human faces, yellow flowers, and other objects 16 percent of the time. The system identified these discrete objects even though no humans had ever defined or labeled them. The accuracy of the neural network was 70 percent better than any previous method.

MKT

- eBay is using deep learning to categorize products in images posted by sellers. By studying images that have already been tagged, the system can tell the difference, for example, between a pair of flip-flops and a pair of flats. This process is helping eBay's search engine, particularly for products that have not been tagged very accurately.

- Facebook plans to use deep learning to help filter the posts and ads that its users see. Specifically, Facebook will apply deep learning to improve its users' news feeds, the personalized list of recent updates that Facebook calls its "killer app." The company already uses conventional machine learning techniques to manage the 1500 updates that average Facebook users could potentially see down to 30–60 that are judged to be the most likely to be important to them. Facebook needs to become more effective at picking the best updates due to the growing volume of data that its users generate.

- Deep learning has improved voice search on smartphones. Because the multiple layers of neurons in a neural network (discussed next) allow for more precise training on the many variants of a sound, the system can recognize sounds more reliably, especially in noisy environments, such as offices with high levels of background conversations, or subway platforms. Because the system is more likely to understand what the user actually said, it is more likely to return more accurate results.

- At CERN, the world's largest particle physics laboratory, deep learning algorithms are more accurate at identifying subatomic particles than the software written by physicists.

- A team of researchers won a contest sponsored by Merck to identify molecules that could lead to new drugs. The group used deep learning to find molecules that would most likely bind to their targets.

- A major U.S. insurance company is using deep learning to identify fraudulent claims.

Neural Networks

A **neural network** is a set of virtual neurons or central processing units (CPUs), which work in parallel in an attempt to simulate the way the human brain works, although in a greatly simplified form. The neural network assigns numerical values, or weights, to connections between the neurons.

Due to improvements in algorithms and increasingly powerful computer chips and storage, deep learning researchers are able to model many more layers of virtual neurons in neural networks than previously. Current neural networks are able to simulate billions of neurons. Let's look at how neural networks process an image and a sound.

Each layer of the neural network manages a different level of abstraction. To process an image, for example, the first layer is fed with raw images. That layer notes aspects of the images such as the brightness and colors of individual pixels, and how those properties are distributed across the image. The next layer analyzes the first layer's observations into more abstract categories, such as identifying edges, shadows, and so on. The next layer analyzes those edges and shadows, looking for combinations that signify features such as eyes, lips, and ears. The final layer combines these observations into a representation of a face.

To process a sound, the first layer of processors learns the smallest unit of speech sound, called a phoneme. The next layer finds combinations of sound waves that occur more often than they would by chance alone. The next layer looks for combinations of speech sounds such as words, and the final layer can recognize complete segments of speech.

Programmers train neural networks to detect an object or a sound by feeding the network with digitized images containing those objects or sounds containing those phonemes. If the neural network does not accurately recognize a particular object or sound, then an algorithm adjusts the weights or the strength of the connection between processors. The goal of the training is to teach the network to consistently recognize the patterns in sets of images or patterns in speech that humans know as, for instance, image of a dog or the phoneme "d."

For a neural network to learn facial recognition, it will be presented with a "training set" of millions of images. Some will contain faces and some will not. Each image will be labeled by a human, for example, through Amazon's Mechanical Turk. The images act as inputs to the neural network and the labels ("face" or "not face") are the outputs. The network's task is to develop a statistical rule (operationalized through the weights between processors) that correlates inputs with correct outputs.

To accomplish this task, the network will search for those features that are common to the images showing faces. Once these correlations are strong enough (i.e., the weights, or strength of the connections between processors, are high enough) the network will be able to reliably differentiate faces from not-faces in its training set. The next step is to feed the neural network with a fresh set of unlabeled images to see if the facial recognition algorithms that the network has developed actually work with the new data.

Consider this example. In 2015, Matthew Lai created an artificial intelligence system called Giraffe that has taught itself to play chess by evaluating positions much more like humans and in an entirely different way than conventional chess playing programs. Giraffe's level of play is in the top 2 percent of all tournament chess players.

Lai's system uses a neural network that examines each position on the chessboard via three different analyses. The first analysis examines the global state of the game, such as the number and type of pieces on each side, which side is to move next, and other rules of the game. The second analysis examines piece-centric features such as the location of each piece on each side. The third analysis assesses the potential squares that each piece can attack and defend. That is, Giraffe derives its strength not from being able to see far ahead, but from being able to accurately evaluate tricky positions, and understanding complicated positional concepts that are intuitive to humans.

To train his system, Lai randomly chose 5 million positions from a database of computer chess games. He then created greater variety by adding a random legal move to each position before using it to train his neural network. In total, he generated 175 million positions in this manner.

He then had Giraffe play against itself with the goal of improving its prediction of its own future position. In this way, Giraffe learned which positions were strong and which were weak.

Before you go on . . .

1. Define expert systems and describe some problems that expert systems have.
2. Differentiate between machine learning and deep learning.
3. Describe how neural networks function.

Apply the Concept PI5.2

LEARNING OBJECTIVE PI5.2 Provide use case examples of expert systems, machine learning systems, deep learning systems, and neural networks.

STEP 1: Background (Here is what you are learning.)

Throughout much of human history, expertise was transferred from a master to an apprentice through years of training. Only after the apprentice had mastered all of the "tricks of the trade" was he or she considered ready to perform on his or her own. We still employ a similar system for doctors, who must participate in a residency program under the guidance of the resident doctor before they can begin their own practice. This approach is not appropriate, however, for many non-life-threatening situations. In some cases, being able to make an expert decision is simply a matter of having access to the experts' knowledge and experiences. If this knowledge can be captured in a computer-based information system, then it can be distributed for other people to use in similar scenarios. Although this

sounds great, there are many challenges to developing this type of system.

STEP 2: Activity (Here is what you do.)

Visit http://www.wiley.com/go/rainer/MIS4e/applytheconcept, and watch the YouTube video linked for Apply the Concept PI5.2. This video will show you a short demonstration of an expert cooking system. The video mentions that you are responsible for building and testing an expert system, but that is not part of this activity. As you watch the video, pay particular attention to the miscommunication between the cook and the computer. You will find this interaction to be quite comical.

STEP 3: Deliverable (Here is what you turn in.)

Based on the video and material in this section, provide examples of the benefits, applications, and limitations of using artificial intelligence in the world of cooking. Create a Word document to submit to your instructor.

PI5.3 | Artificial Intelligence Applications

The field of artificial intelligence has many applications. Note that these applications use machine learning, deep learning, and neural networks. In this section, we discuss computer vision, natural language processing, robotics, speech recognition, and intelligent agents.

Computer Vision

Computer vision refers to the ability of information systems to identify objects, scenes, and activities in images. Computer vision applications are designed to operate in unconstrained environments. Computer vision has diverse applications:

- Medical imaging to improve prediction, diagnosis, and treatment of diseases:

    To the human eye, an X-ray is an unclear puzzle. But to an AI system, an X-ray—or a CT scan or MRI scan—is a data field that can be assessed down to the pixel level. Images are estimated to make up as much as 90 percent of all medical data today. Image recognition software gathers high-resolution image data from multiple sources—X-rays, MRI scans, ultrasounds, CT scans—and then groups together biological structures that share hard-to-detect similarities. For instance, the software can examine several images of the same breast to measure tissue density. The software then color-codes tissues of similar densities so that humans can observe the pattern as well. The software finds and indexes pixels that share certain properties, even pixels that are far apart in one image or in a different image altogether. This process enables medical personnel to identify hidden features of diffuse structures.

    In 2015, IBM purchased Merge Healthcare (www.merge.com) for $1 billion. Merge specializes in handling all kinds of medical images, and its service is used by more than 7500 hospitals and clinics in the United States, as well as clinical research organizations and pharmaceutical companies. The acquisition is part of an effort to draw on many data sources, including anonymized, text-based medical records, to help physicians make treatment decisions. Merge's data set contains some 30 billion images, which will be used to train the deep learning aspects of IBM Watson.

    IBM Watson is also being used to detect melanoma, a type of skin cancer. Detecting melanoma is difficult due to the variation in the way that it appears in individual patients. By feeding a deep learning system with many images of melanoma, it is possible to teach the system to recognize very subtle but important features associated with the disease.

    Enlitic (www.enlitic.com) is a startup that uses deep learning and image analysis to help physicians make diagnoses and spot abnormalities in medical images. For example, Enlitic software could analyze medical images such as X-rays, MRIs, and CT scans for trends in the data or anomalies in individual images.

- Facial recognition used by Facebook to automatically identify people in photographs and in security and surveillance to spot and identify suspects:

    Specifically, Facebook's Moments app uses facial recognition technology to group the photos on your phone, based on when they were taken and to identify which friends are in the photos.

    In 2014, Facebook unveiled an algorithm called DeepFace that can recognize specific human faces in images about 97 percent of the time, even when those faces are poorly lit or partially hidden. This performance is on par for what humans are able to do.

- Shopping: Consumers now use smartphones to photograph products and be presented with purchase options.

- Self-driving cars: Computer vision systems can now help drive a car down a street and not hit anything or hurt anyone—that is, a high-stake exercise in computer vision that involves many different kinds of data in a constantly changing environment.

- Pinterest is using a computer vision system combined with deep learning to enhance product recommendations by automatically recognizing specific objects contained within the image of a pin.

- Google Photos app uses computer vision combined with deep learning to automatically recognize, classify, and organize a user's photos.

- Google and Microsoft Research are using computer vision combined with deep learning to improve object detection, classification, and labeling. For instance, one computer vision system automatically summarizes a complex scene in a photo and generate captions that accurately describe the scene.

- Microsoft's Traffic Prediction Project uses Bing traffic maps, road cameras, sensors, and other data sources to predict traffic jams.

Natural Language Processing

Natural language processing refers to the ability of information systems to work with text the way that humans do. For instance, these systems can extract the meaning from text and can generate text that is readable, stylistically natural, and grammatically correct.

Because context is critically important, the practical applications of natural language processing typically address relatively narrow areas such as analyzing customer feedback about a particular product or service, automating discovery in civil litigation or government investigations (e-discovery), and automating writing of formulaic stories on topics such as corporate earnings or sports. Two other examples are as follows:

- IBM's Watson uses natural language processing to read and understand the vast amount of medical literature, hypothesis generation techniques to automate diagnosis, and machine learning to improve its accuracy.
- Built into Google's translation app, deep learning technology has the ability to translate printed text such as menus in a live view through your phone's camera. The app can translate among 27 different languages without needing an Internet connection.

Robotics

Integrating computer vision with tiny, high-performance sensors and actuators, a new generation of robots can work alongside people and flexibly perform many different tasks in unpredictable environments. Examples include unmanned aerial vehicles, *cobots* (cooperative robots) that share jobs with humans on the factory floor, robotic vacuum cleaners, and so on. Specifically, recall our discussion of Baxter in Chapter 1.

Speech recognition

Speech recognition focuses on automatically and accurately transcribing human speech. This technology must manage diverse accents, dialects, and background noise. Further, it must distinguish between homophones and work at the speed of natural speech. Applications include medical dictation, hands-free writing, voice control of information systems, and telephone customer service applications.

POM

Duncan Regional Hospital in Oklahoma wanted to improve efficiency in its patient care. Approximately 15 physicians at the hospital are improving their clinical documentation on laptops with Dragon speech recognition software from Nuance Communications.

The hospital also uses a secure, HIPAA-compliant messaging platform from Imprivata (www.imprivata.com). Instead of sending a text message, physicians speak their message rather than having to stop interacting with a patient. Also, nurses use speech recognition software to enter clinical documentation, a critical need as the healthcare industry requires an increasing amount of documentation to meet HIPAA requirements as well as mandates for meaningful use of electronic health records.

Intelligent Agents

According to Gartner, by the end of 2016, two-thirds of consumers in the developed world will regularly use virtual personal assistants in their daily lives. Virtual assistants are the most basic form of AI—the ability of a system to mimic human intelligence through experience and learning. For example, popular voice-based digital assistants, such as Apple Siri, Microsoft Cortana,

Google Now, Amazon Echo, and Facebook M, can understand our words, analyze our questions, and point us in the general direction of the right answer.

An **intelligent agent** is a software program that assists you, or acts on your behalf, in performing repetitive computer-related tasks. You may be familiar with an early type of intelligent agent—the paper clip (Clippy) that popped up in early versions of Microsoft Word. For example, if your document appeared as though it was going to be a business letter—that is, if you typed in a date, name, and address—the animated paper clip would offer helpful suggestions on how to proceed. Users objected so strenuously to this primitive intelligent agent that Microsoft eliminated it from subsequent versions.

Today, there are many intelligent agents (also called *bots*) used for a wide variety of tasks. The following sections examine three types of agents: information agents, monitoring and surveillance agents, and user or personal agents.

Information Agents. **Information agents** search for information and display it to users. The best-known information agents are buyer agents. A **buyer agent**, also called a **shopping bot**, helps customers find the products and services they need on a Web site. There are many examples of information agents. We present here a few illustrative cases.

- Companies in the insurance and financial services sector are using IBM Watson that functions as a customer-facing intelligent advisor. For example, insurance company USAA (www.usaa.com) uses Watson in an application that lets USAA customers who are leaving military service ask question about, for example, college tuition reimbursement or changes to their health benefits. USAA chose the topic of military separation because approximately 150,000 people separate from military service each year. USAA executives say that the goal of the system is to augment employees' expertise, not to replace them. The system offers better insight and information than the original USAA digital portal offered. Watson helps shorten service calls, offers more context to incoming calls, and reduces the amount of paperwork around customer interactions. `MKT`

- Australian bank ANZ deployed IBM's Watson Engagement Advisor. When a customer asks a financial planner about a company or an investment, the planner can relay questions to Watson using natural language, by either speaking or typing. The system then analyzes vast amounts of information—such as annual reports, SEC filings, relevant news stories, and other analysts' views—and produces its own insight on the potential investment. `FIN`

- The information agents for Amazon.com display lists of books and other products that customers might like, based on past purchases. `MKT`

- The Federal Electronic Research and Review Extraction Tool (FERRET) was developed jointly by the Census Bureau and the Bureau of Labor Statistics. You can use FERRET to find information on employment, healthcare, education, race and ethnicity, health insurance, housing, income and poverty, aging, and marriage and the family.

Monitoring and Surveillance Agents. **Monitoring and surveillance agents**, also called **predictive agents**, constantly observe and report on some item of interest. There are many examples of predictive agents. Consider the following:

- Allstate uses monitoring and surveillance agents to manage its large computer networks 24/7/365. Every five seconds, the agent measures 1,200 data points. It can predict a system crash 45 minutes before it happens. The agent also watches to detect electronic attacks early so that they can be prevented.

- Monitoring and surveillance agents can watch your competitors and notify you of price changes and special offers.

- Predictive agents can monitor Internet sites, discussion groups, and mailing lists for stock manipulations, insider trading, and rumors that might affect stock prices.

- These agents can search Web sites for updated information on topics of your choice, such as price changes on desired products (e.g., airline tickets).

User Agents. User agents, also called personal agents, take action on your behalf. Let's look at what these agents can do (or will be able to do shortly).

- Check your e-mail, sort it according to your priority rules, and alert you when high-value e-mails appear in your in-box.
- Automatically fill out forms on the Web for you. They will also store your information for future use.

Before you go on . . .

1. Describe the advantages of computer vision, natural language processing, and speech recognition.

2. What are cobots?

3. Describe how you might use intelligent agents, information agents, monitoring and surveillance agents, and user agents.

Apply the Concept PI5.3

LEARNING OBJECTIVE PI5.3 Provide use case examples of computer vision, natural language processing, robotics, image recognition, and intelligent agents.

STEP 1: Background (Here is what you are learning.)

This section has discussed several applications of technology that apply artificial intelligence to several activities that we take on every day. The applications of artificial intelligence are everywhere. From residential thermostats that automatically adjust temperatures when no one is home to cars that can drive without a human driver, this technology will forever change the world we live in.

STEP 2: Activity (Here is what you do.)

Google is one of the leading developers of a driverless car. Visit http://www.wiley.com/go/rainer/MIS4e/applytheconcept, and

click on the link provided for Apply the Concept PI5.3. This will take you to a Web site with information about Google's Self-Driving Car project. There are so many ramifications of using this technology, both good and bad. But for this activity, we want you to focus on what is possible.

After researching the Google Self-Driving Car (and perhaps watching some of the videos on their site), how many of the artificial intelligence tools discussed in this text do you think would be utilized in a single car ride.

STEP 3: Deliverable (Here is what you turn in.)

Create an outline of a single trip. In this outline, provide examples of how the tools in this section (computer vision, natural language processing, robotics, image recognition, and intelligent agents) would all work together to safely take you to your destination.

What's in IT for me?

ACCT For the Accounting Major

AI systems are used extensively in auditing to uncover irregularities. They are also used to uncover and prevent fraud. Today's CPAs use AI systems for many of their duties, ranging from risk analysis to cost control. Accounting personnel also use intelligent agents for mundane tasks such as managing accounts and monitoring employees' Internet use.

FIN For the Finance Major

People have been using computers for decades to solve financial problems. Innovative AI systems have been developed for activities such as making stock market decisions, refinancing bonds, assessing

debt risks, analyzing financial conditions, predicting business failures, forecasting financial trends, and investing in global markets. Often, AI systems can facilitate the use of spreadsheets and other computerized systems used in finance. Finally, AI systems can help reduce fraud in credit cards, stocks, and other financial services.

MKT For the Marketing Major

Marketing personnel use AI systems in many applications, from allocating advertising budgets to evaluating alternative routings of salespeople. New marketing approaches such as targeted marketing and marketing transaction databases are heavily dependent on IT in general and on AI systems in particular. AI systems are especially useful for mining customer databases and predicting customer behavior. Successful AI applications appear in almost every area of marketing and sales, from analyzing the success of one-to-one advertising to supporting customer help desks. With customer service becoming increasingly important, the use of intelligent agents is critical for providing fast response.

POM For the Production/Operations Management Major

AI systems support complex operations and production decisions, from inventory to production planning. AI systems in the production/operations management field manage tasks ranging from diagnosing machine failures and prescribing repairs to complex production scheduling and inventory control. Some companies, such as DuPont and Kodak, have deployed hundreds of AI systems in the planning, organizing, and control of their operational systems.

HRM For the Human Resources Management Major

Human resources personnel employ AI systems for many applications. For example, recruiters use these systems to find applicants' resumes on the Web and sort them to match needed skills. HR managers also use AI systems to evaluate candidates (tests, interviews). HR personnel use AI systems to train and support employees in managing their fringe benefits and to predict employee job performance and future labor needs.

MIS For the MIS Major

The MIS function develops (or acquires) and maintains the organization's various AI systems, as well as the data and models that these systems use. In addition, MIS staffers often interact with subject area experts to capture the expertise used in AI systems.

Summary

1. **Explain the potential value and the potential limitations of artificial intelligence.**

Table PI5.1 differentiates between artificial and human intelligence on a number of characteristics.

2. **Provide use case examples of expert systems, machine learning systems, deep learning systems, and neural networks.**

Expert systems are computer systems that attempt to mimic human experts by applying expertise in a specific domain.

Machine learning is the ability to accurately perform new, unseen tasks, built on known properties learned from training or historic data that are labeled. Machine learning systems can distinguish between spam and nonspam messages; identify fraudulent banking transactions; help pharmaceutical companies identify promising drugs; and diagnose mechanical problems with drilling equipment.

Deep learning is a subset of machine learning where the system discovers new patterns without being exposed to labeled historical or training data. Example applications of deep learning include speech recognition, image recognition, and natural language processing.

A *neural network* is a system of programs and data structures that simulate the underlying concepts of the human brain. Neural networks are used to detect weapons concealed in personal belongings, in research on various diseases, for financial forecasting, to detect fraud in credit card transactions, to fight crime, and many other applications.

3. **Provide use case examples of computer vision, natural language processing, robotics, and intelligent agents.**

Computer vision refers to the ability of computers to identify objects, scenes, and activities in images. Computer vision has diverse applications, examples of which include medical imaging, facial recognition, and self-driving cars.

Natural language processing refers to the ability of information systems to work with text the way that humans do. Applications of natural language processing include analyzing customer feedback about a particular product or service, automating discovery in civil litigation or government investigations (e-discovery), and automating writing of formulaic stories on topics such as corporate earnings or sports.

Robots integrate computer vision with sensors and actuators. Cooperative robots (called cobots) can work alongside people and flexibly perform many different tasks in unpredictable environments. Examples include unmanned aerial vehicles, "cobots" (cooperative robots) that share jobs with humans on the factory floor, robotic vacuum cleaners, and so on. Specifically, recall our discussion of Baxter in Chapter 1.

Speech recognition focuses on automatically and accurately transcribing human speech. Applications include medical dictation, hands-free writing, voice control of information systems, and telephone customer service applications.

Intelligent agents are software programs that assist you, or act on your behalf, in performing repetitive, computer-related tasks. Intelligent agents are used to display lists of books or other products that customers might like, based on past purchases; to find information; to manage and monitor large computer networks 24/7/365; to detect electronic attacks early so that they can be stopped; to watch competitors and send notices of price changes and special offers; to monitor Internet sites, discussion groups, and mailing lists for stock manipulations, insider trading, and rumors that might impact stock prices; to check e-mail, sort it according to established priority rules, and alert recipients when high-value e-mails appear in their inbox; and to automatically fill out forms on the Web.

Chapter Glossary

algorithm A problem-solving method expressed as a finite sequence of steps.

artificial intelligence (AI) A subfield of computer science that is concerned with studying the thought processes of humans and recreating the effects of those processes via machines, such as computers.

buyer agent (or **shopping bot**) An intelligent agent on a Web site that helps customers find products and services that they need.

computer vision The ability of information systems to identify objects, scenes, and activities in images.

deep learning The ability of information systems to discover new patterns without being exposed to labeled historical or training data.

expert systems (ESs) Information systems that attempt to mimic human experts by applying expertise in a specific domain.

information agent A type of intelligent agent that searches for information and displays it to users.

intelligent agent A software program that assists you, or acts on your behalf, in performing repetitive, computer-related tasks.

machine learning systems The ability of information systems to accurately perform new, unseen tasks, built on known properties learned from training or historic data that are labeled.

monitoring and surveillance agents (or **predictive agents**) Intelligent agents that constantly observe and report on some item of interest.

narrow AI See **weak AI**.

natural language processing The ability of information systems to work with text the way that humans do.

neural network A set of virtual neurons, placed in layers, which work in parallel in an attempt to simulate the way the human brain works, although in a greatly simplified form.

personal agents See **user agents**.

predictive agents See **monitoring and surveillance agents**.

shopping bot See **buyer agent**.

speech recognition The ability of information systems to automatically and accurately transcribe human speech.

strong AI Hypothetical artificial intelligence that matches or exceeds human intelligence and could perform any intellectual task that humans can.

user agents (or **personal agents**) Intelligent agents that take action on your behalf.

weak AI (also called **narrow AI**) Performs a useful and specific function that once required human intelligence to perform, and does so at human levels or better.

Discussion Questions

1. Explain how your university could employ an expert system in its admission process. Could it use a neural network?

   What might happen if a student were denied admission to the university and his parents discovered that an expert system was involved in the admissions process?

2. One difference between a conventional business intelligence system and an expert system is that the former can explain *how* questions, whereas the latter can explain both *how* and *why* questions. Discuss the implications of this statement.

Problem-Solving Activities

1. You have decided to purchase a new "smart" television. To purchase it as inexpensively as possible and still get the features you want, you use a shopping bot. Visit several of the shopping bot Web sites that perform price comparisons for you. Begin with MySimon (www.mysimon.com), BizRate.com (www.bizrate.com), and Google Product Search.

   Compare these shopping bots in terms of ease of use, number of product offerings, speed in obtaining information, thoroughness of information offered about products and sellers, and price selection. Which site or sites would you use, and why? Which television would you select and buy? How helpful were these sites in making your decision?

2. Access the MyMajors Web site (www.mymajors.com). This site contains a rule-based expert system to help students find majors. The expert

   system has more than 300 rules and 15,000 possible conclusions. The site ranks majors according to the likelihood that a student will succeed in them, and it provides 6 possible majors from among 60 alternative majors that a student might consider.

   Take the quiz, and see if you are in the "right major" as defined by the expert system. You must register to take the quiz.

3. Access Exsys (www.exsys.com), and click on the Corvid Expert System demos (www.exsys.com/demomain.html). Provide your e-mail address, and click on the link for "Student—Needed for Class." Try the various demos, and report your results to the class.

Project Management

LEARNING OBJECTIVES

PI6.1 Explain the relationship between the triple constraints on projects.

PI6.2 Describe the five phases of the project management process.

PI6.3 Review how each of the nine processes of the Project Management Body of Knowledge is necessary in order to ensure smooth project deployment.

PI6.1 Project Management for Information Systems Projects

Projects are short-term efforts to create a specific business-related outcome. These outcomes may take the form of products or services. In the context of information systems (IS), many of the resource investments made by organizations are in the form of projects. For example, Home Depot (www.homedepot.com) recently engaged in an IS project to develop an inventory management system. The objectives of the project were to improve inventory turnover, reduce product stockouts, and integrate more tightly with supply chain partners. The outcome was to lower company-wide costs by carrying less physical inventory.

Almost every organization that utilizes information technology to support business processes engages in some form of IS project management. **IS project management** is a directed effort to plan, organize, and manage resources to bring about the successful achievement of specific IS goals. All projects, whether they are IS projects or not, are constrained by the same three factors, known as the **triple constraints of project management**: time, cost, and scope. *Time* refers to the window of opportunity in which a project must be completed to provide a benefit to the organization. *Cost* is the actual amount of resources, including cash and labor, that an organization can commit to completing a project. *Scope* refers to the processes that ensure that the project includes all the work required—and only the work required—to complete the project successfully. For an IS project to be successful, the organization must allow an adequate amount of time, provide an appropriate amount of resources, and carefully define what is and is not included in the project.

The triple constraints are related and involve trade-offs. For example, scope can often be increased by using additional time and incurring increased costs. Cost and/or time can often be saved by reducing scope. For a given scope, time can sometimes be saved by increasing cost. The following example illustrates just how complex projects can be.

Building a Natural Gas Pipeline to Hong Kong

As one of the world's most populous cities, Hong Kong needs energy to supply its 7.1 million residents with electricity. The city relies on a mix of fuels, chosen for reliability, sustainability, and efficiency.

One of these energy sources is natural gas. Since 1996, Hong Kong's Black Point Power Station has drawn natural gas from the reserves of a gas field in Hainan, a nearby Chinese province. However, these reserves had begun to deplete, and it was clear that Hong Kong needed a new plan to maintain a consistent supply of natural gas and to comply with tightened emission caps that will be required by the government of Hong Kong in 2015.

In 2008, the governments of Hong Kong and the People's Republic of China signed a memorandum of understanding on energy cooperation, which identified three new gas sources from which mainland China could supply gas to Hong Kong.

One of the sources was the second West–East Gas Pipeline (WEPII), which is the world's longest natural gas pipeline. Building a natural gas pipeline from the existing WEPII network to Hong Kong is an incredibly complex project, presenting numerous challenges:

Regulations: Because it crossed the border between mainland China and Hong Kong, the project team had to acquire permits from both jurisdictions. The project also had to obtain different statutory approval processes between the jurisdictions.

Communications: The various project team members spoke different languages, and the parties involved had different requirements for documentation and reporting. The teams predominantly used English, Putonghua, and Cantonese. However, they used English and Cantonese for documents and PowerPoint presentations. The project team also had to manage a multitude of stakeholders, including over 30 government departments in both jurisdictions.

Environmental requirements: The project had to fulfill stringent environmental requirements for the two jurisdictions. Project managers instituted a robust monitoring and audit program during the project's execution phase, with intensive water quality monitoring, marine mammal monitoring, and site inspections. Mitigation measures also included the deployment of silt curtains and limitations of working speed during marine dredging operations.

Physical restraints: The actual laying of the pipeline was subject to many physical constraints. The project required a 12-mile undersea pipeline through three shipping channels. There were also challenges involving shallow water with a dredged marine channel, anchorage areas, and an existing subsea pipelines and cables.

Before laying the pipeline, the project team conducted an extensive marine traffic impact assessment. They also coordinated closely with local marine and port control authorities to successfully work around channel traffic, laying the entire 12-mile undersea pipeline in only six to seven months.

To handle a complex project of this magnitude and to finish on time and on budget, the project team needed careful planning. Before project initiation, the team thoroughly planned, scheduled, and engineered the project to ensure that the pipeline would function properly and, more importantly, that it would be safe.

The project had a tight schedule. To meet the deadlines, project managers implemented elements of the waterfall approach, where certain milestones had to be completed before the next tasks could begin. For example, the channel dredging had to be finished before the pipeline could be laid. Proper planning, critical path monitoring, and close coordination between Hong Kong and China helped ensure that the project finished on time.

The project team tightly controlled the scope of the project. Any changes had to go through a rigorous change management process, which kept the project on track.

The team also realized that communication was a key component to successfully completing the pipeline. Project managers made special efforts to build effective teams. They established processes to always engage the right person for the right task and to encourage teamwork. For instance, given the different nationalities involved, all materials and discussions were in multiple languages.

Project managers focused on quality and safety. They performed daily site visits, as well as scheduled and nonscheduled management walkthroughs. There were also third-party inspections done on critical tasks, such as the pipe welding.

As a result of excellent project management, the pipeline was finished on time, and it began supplying Hong Kong with natural gas in 2013. The project also had a minimal impact of heavy marine traffic in the area, especially on the container ships that are vital to that area's economy.

Sources: Compiled from "Hong Kong Natural Gas Pipeline," *Project Management Institute Case Study*, 2014; "Hong Kong Branch of Second West–East Gas Pipeline Completed and Operational," *Penn Energy*, October 21, 2103; J. Cullen, "Second West–East Gas Pipeline Set to Start Hong Kong Supplies This Summer," *South China Morning Post*, June 16, 2013.

Questions

1. What were the drivers of the new natural gas pipeline to Hong Kong?
2. Describe the key factors contributing to the success of the pipeline project.
3. Describe the triple constraints of Hong Kong's pipeline project.

Before you go on . . .

1. What is a project?
2. What is the triple constraint of any project?

Apply the Concept PI6.1

LEARNING OBJECTIVE PI6.1 Explain the relationship between the triple constraints on projects.

STEP 1: Background (This is what you are learning.)

This section describes how companies employ software to support project management. Project management software offers tools such as planning, communication, coordination, measurement, and data collection to help companies navigate the triple constraints on projects: time, cost, and scope.

STEP 2: Activity (This is what you are doing.)

Visit http://www.wiley.com/go/rainer/MIS4e/applytheconcept, and click on the link provided for Plug IT In 6.1. This link will

take you to a Web site that sells project management software. At this site you can click on links that will show you tours, customer success stores, pictures, and demos of the software. As you explore the site, look for the ways different products are marketed to help companies deal with the triple constraints.

STEP 3: Deliverable (This is what you turn in.)

From the site you looked at in Step 2, choose one software package, and explain how it helps companies deal with the relationships among time, cost, and scope of projects. Submit your explanation to your instructor.

PI6.2 | The Project Management Process

The traditional approach to project management divides every project into five distinct phases: initiation, planning, execution, monitoring and control, and completion (see Figure PI6.1). These phases are sequential, and we discuss them in order.

Project Initiation

The first phase in the management of a process is to clearly define the problem that the project is intended to solve and the goals that it is to achieve. In this phase, it is also necessary to

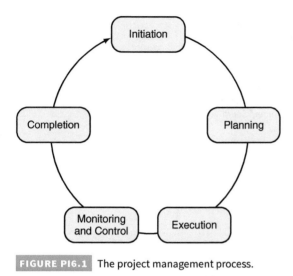

FIGURE P16.1 The project management process.

identify and secure the resources necessary for the project, analyze the costs and benefits of the project, and identify potential risks.

In an IS project, a user's business problem or need typically initiates a project that can solve the problem and meet the need. The user must clearly define the problem so that the IS team can understand it. The user must also define the benefits he or she expects to gain from successful completion of the IS project.

Project Planning As the term *planning* suggests, in this phase, every project objective and every activity associated with that objective must be identified and sequenced. This phase is critically important to avoid scope creep once the project gets underway. **Scope creep** refers to uncontrolled changes in a project's scope. This phenomenon can occur when the scope of a project is not properly defined, documented, or controlled. It is generally considered a negative occurrence that is to be avoided.

In an IS project, users often contribute to scope creep when they ask for additional features or functionality after the project is underway. This situation often leads to the project being overtime and over budget.

Many tools assist developers in sequencing these activities, including dependence diagrams, such as the program evaluation and review technique (PERT), the critical path method (CPM), and a timeline diagram called the Gantt chart. Project managers use these tools to ensure that activities are performed in a logical sequence. As the project progresses, project managers also employ these tools to evaluate whether the project is on schedule and, if not, where the delays are occurring and what the managers must do to correct them.

Project Execution

In this phase, the work defined in the project management plan is performed to accomplish the project's requirements. Execution coordinates people and resources, and it integrates and performs project activities in accordance with the plan.

Users may be involved in project execution. For example, in an IS project, users often evaluate prototypes so that they can provide meaningful feedback to the IS team.

Project Monitoring and Control

The purpose of monitoring and control is to determine whether the project is progressing as planned. This phase consists of three steps: (1) monitoring ongoing project activities (where we are); (2) comparing project variables (cost, effort, time, resources, etc.) with the actual plan (where we should be); and (3) identifying corrective actions (how do we get on track again).

Project Completion

The project is completed when it is formally accepted by the organization. All activities are finalized and all contracts are fulfilled and settled. In addition, all files are archived and all lessons learned are documented.

Project Management Failure

As IT systems have become an important competitive necessity in modern organizations, IT projects are getting larger, involve more parts of the organization, and pose a risk to the company if something goes wrong. Research by McKinsey and the University of Oxford suggest that half of all large IT projects—defined as those with initial price tags exceeding $15 million—go far over their budgets. Their research also shows that, on average, large IT projects run 45 percent over budget and 7 percent over time, while delivering 56 percent less value than predicted.

Such projects are called *runaway projects*, meaning they are so far over budget and past deadline that they must be abandoned, typically with large monetary loss. Even worse, the researchers found that 17 percent of large IT projects are so bad that they threaten the very existence of a company.

The researchers found that four groups of issues caused most IT project failures:

- A lack of focus, including unclear objectives and lack of business focus
- Content issues, such as shifting requirements (e.g., scope creep) and technical complexity
- Skill issues, such as a team not aligned with business objectives and a general lack of skills
- Execution issues, such as an unrealistic schedule and reactive planning (on the fly, as opposed to sufficient planning at the start of a project)

Enabling Project Management Success

The research findings bring up the crucial question: How do companies maximize the chance that their IT projects deliver the expected value on time and within budget? The findings indicated that the key to project management success is in mastering four broad dimensions of project management:

- Focusing on managing strategy and stakeholders instead of exclusively concentrating on budgeting and scheduling
- Mastering technology and project content by securing critical internal and external talent
- Building effective teams by aligning their incentives with the overall goals of projects
- Excelling at core project-management practices, such as short delivery cycles and rigorous quality checks

Let's discuss each of these in turn.

Manage Strategy and Stakeholders. IT projects often pay little attention to strategy and stakeholders and manage projects only according to budget and schedule targets. These problems are illustrated by one bank's IT transformation effort, in which its finance department became involved only a few months before the system was due to become operational. This problem led to several complex changes in the accounting software modules as a result of a recently introduced performance management system. Occurring so late in the project, the changes delayed the launch by more than three months, at a cost of more than $8 million.

Top-performing projects, on the other hand, establish a clear view of the project's strategic value—one that goes beyond technical content. By building a robust, well-understood business case and maintaining focus on business objectives along the entire project timeline, success teams can avoid cost and time overruns.

These teams ensure that the project aligns with the company's business strategy and undertake detailed analyses of stakeholder positions. Team leaders continually engage with all business unit and functional area heads to ensure consistent alignment.

Secure Critical Talent. Drawing on expert help as needed, high-performance teams integrate all technical aspects of the project, including IT architecture and infrastructure, functionality trade-offs, quality assurance, migration and rollout plans, and project scope. The excellent team will understand both business and technical concerns, which is why companies must assign a few high-performing and experienced experts for the length of the project.

One common problem occurs when teams focus too much on technology issues and targets. For instance, a large retailer wanted to create a central data warehouse to overcome inconsistencies that occurred among its business unit financial data, centralized financial data, and risk data. However, the project team focused purely on developing the IT architecture solution for the data warehouse instead of addressing the end goal, which was to manage data inconsistencies. As a result, the project budget increased as the team pursued architectural "perfection," which involved the inclusion of unnecessary data from other systems. The bank finally had to halt the project after 18 months and several million dollars.

Build Effective Teams. Large projects can take a life of their own in an organization. Project teams need a common vision, shared team processes, and a high-performance culture. Members must have a common incentive structure that is aligned with the overall project goal, in contrast with individual goals.

For example, to ensure the smooth start-up of new front-end and core systems that more than 8,000 people would use, one company project team launched a massive, and successful, change management program. This program included a regular newsletter, desktop calendars that highlighted key changes and milestones, and quarterly town hall meetings with the CEO. The team made sure that all business unit leaders were involved during the user acceptance phase of the project.

Excel at Project-Management Practices. To achieve excellent project management, there is no substitute for tested practices. These practices include having a strategic and disciplined project management office and establishing rigorous processes for managing project requirements and change requests.

Before you go on . . .

1. What are the five phases of the project management process?

2. What are the major causes of project failure?

3. Describe how to best ensure the success of projects.

Apply the Concept PI6.2

LEARNING OBJECTIVE PI6.2 Describe the five phases of the project management process.

STEP 1: Background

As you have seen in this section, project management is a complicated task. Multiple people, multiple activities, and multiple opinions about the "right" way to handle the project always make it difficult for the individuals who are actually managing the operation.

STEP 2: Activity

Visit http://www.wiley.com/go/rainer/MIS4e/applytheconcept, and click on the link provided for Plug IT In 6.2. The link will take

you to an article that discusses the difficulties that Hershey's experienced when it implemented a new IT system. In fact, this project cost the company more than $100 million in sales because the ordering system did not function properly.

After reading the article, search the Web for additional information on this story.

STEP 3: Deliverable

Based on what you read in Step 2, describe the five phases of the project management process at Hershey's. Try to determine in which step (or steps) Hershey's made its mistakes. Submit your description to your instructor.

PI6.3 | The Project Management Body of Knowledge

The **Project Management Body of Knowledge (PMBOK)** is a collection of processes and knowledge areas generally accepted as best practice within the project management discipline. As an internationally recognized standard, it provides the fundamentals of project management, regardless of the type of project (e.g., construction, software, engineering, and automotive). The purpose of the PMBOK is to provide and promote a common vocabulary within the project management profession for discussing, writing, and applying project management concepts.

The PMBOK recognizes five basic process groups and nine knowledge areas typical of almost all projects. You learned about the five basic process groups in the previous section:

- Initiation
- Planning
- Execution
- Monitoring and control
- Completion

Processes overlap and interact throughout a project. Processes are described in terms of inputs (documents, plans, designs), tools and techniques, and outputs (documents, products).

The following are the nine knowledge areas of the PMBOK:

- *Project integration management:* Project integration management includes those processes required to ensure that all the project's components are properly coordinated. The project plan development processes, project plan execution processes, and integrated change control processes are all included in this area of knowledge. Each process has expected inputs and outputs and plus the appropriate tools and techniques to support the change of inputs to outputs.

- *Project scope management:* Project scope management defines the processes that limit and control the work included in a project. Scope creep is a serious problem that often causes projects to go over time and over budget. These processes ensure that all the work of the project is included and properly accounted for.

- *Project time management:* Proper sequencing is vital to timely project completion. When the amount of time needed is established, it takes excellent scheduling skills and tools to manage the activities to complete project milestones and the project itself within the allotted time. Different tools are available to assist with this process, such as Gantt charts, milestone charts, and network charts. Each tool helps managers see the big picture and stay in control of the project's progression.

- *Project cost management:* Resource planning and cost estimation are equally vital to time management. These two processes cannot exist independently of each other. Resource cost management is difficult to estimate and even more difficult to manage when unforeseen events take place. Early in a project, managers may project a budget range and then fine-tune it as the project progresses.

- *Project quality management:* Every project needs a set of processes ensuring that project outcomes meet the needs for which the project was executed. Quality planning, assurance, and control are included in this area. There are many quality management models to consider, such as the Deming Prize, TQM, and Six Sigma. All of these aim to help organizations produce quality products the first time they try. There are also many paradigms applicable to this area of knowledge, such as "Zero Defects" and "DTRTRTFT" (Do the right thing right the first time). These paradigms are meant to inspire organizations to operate at higher quality levels.

- *Project human resource management:* People can be the major headache or the major asset of any project. People with differing skill sets are required at various times during a project and their individual skills have to be used effectively for the project to succeed. This area of knowledge includes concepts such as staffing decisions; team management; and organizational culture, style, and structure.

- *Project communications management:* A vast amount of communication is necessary in successful projects. Information must be collected, disseminated, stored, and destroyed at the appropriate time. This area of knowledge contains the processes to perform these functions. Often, organizations investigate personality styles to determine their most effective communicators. Choosing the right person to be a leader can make all the difference in the success of a project.

- *Project risk management:* All projects face risk. With organizational success, jobs, careers, and livelihoods on the line, it is a good idea to minimize the risk of projects as much as feasible. Therefore, risk management must be an integral part of any project because things do not always happen as planned. The risk management process includes identification of risks, quantitative and qualitative analyses, risk response planning, and risk monitoring.

- *Project procurement management:* No matter how good the idea behind a project, without funding it will never be more than a good idea. The accumulated knowledge related to project procurement management encompasses processes of solicitation, selection, contractual agreements, and closeout processes.

Before you go on . . .

1. What is the Project Management Body of Knowledge and why is it important to organizations?

2. What part of the PMBOK do you think is most important? Can a project succeed without all the parts?

Apply the Concept PI6.3

LEARNING OBJECTIVE PI6.3 Review how each of the nine processes of the Project Management Body of Knowledge is necessary in order to ensure smooth project deployment.

STEP 1: Background

Project management is critical to the successful implementation of any new system. As you saw from the Hershey's case in Apply the Concept PI6.2, projects can get out of hand very quickly. (If you did not complete this activity, visit http://www.wiley.com/go/rainer/MIS4e/applytheconcept, and click on the link for Plug IT In 6.2 to read the article). There are many stories you could read that would demonstrate just how quickly projects go awry.

STEP 2: Activity

Visit http://www.wiley.com/go/rainer/MIS4e/applytheconcept, and click on the link provided for Plug IT In 6.3. This link will take you to an article about a failure of the Denver Airport Baggage System. As you review this story, consider the nine processes of the Project Management Body of Knowledge, and try to determine which ones could have helped the project succeed.

STEP 3: Deliverable

Within the context of the Denver Airport Baggage story you read in Step 2, review how each of the nine processes of the Project Management Body of Knowledge is necessary to ensure smooth project deployment.

What's in IT for me?

For all Business Majors

Regardless of the functional area in organizations, each of you will be on project teams beginning very early in your careers. These projects will be critical to your organization's success. Therefore, it is critical that all majors understand the project management process so that you can make immediate contributions to your project teams.

Summary

1. Explain the relationship between the triple constraints on projects.

Projects are short-term efforts to create a specific business-related outcome. *IS project management* is a directed effort to plan, organize, and manage resources to bring about the successful achievement of specific IS goals. All projects, whether they are IS projects or not, are constrained by the same three factors, known as the *triple constraints of project management*: time, cost, and scope. *Time* refers to the window of opportunity in which a project must be completed to provide a benefit to the organization. *Cost* is the actual amount of resources, including cash and labor, that an organization can commit to completing a project. *Scope* refers to the processes that ensure that the project includes all the work required—and only the work required—to complete the project successfully.

2. Describe the five phases of the project management process.

Project initiation clearly defines the problem that the project is intended to solve and the goals that it is to achieve. In *project planning*, every project objective and every activity associated with that objective must be identified and sequenced. In the *project execution* phase, the work defined in the project management plan is performed to accomplish the project's requirements. The purpose of the *monitoring and control phase* is to determine whether the progress is progressing as planned. The *project completion* phase is when the project is formally accepted by the organization.

3. Review how each of the nine processes of the Project Management Body of Knowledge is necessary in order to ensure smooth project deployment.

IS projects do not deliver their potential value for a number of reasons, including lack of sufficient planning at the start of a project; difficulties with technology compatibility (i.e., new technology may not work with existing technology); lack of commitment by management in providing the necessary resources; poorly defined project scope; and lack of sufficient time to complete the project.

Glossary

IS project management A directed effort to plan, organize, and manage resources to bring about the successful achievement of specific IS goals.

project Short-term effort to create a specific business-related outcome.

Project Management Body of Knowledge (PMBOK) A collection of processes and knowledge areas generally accepted as best practice within the project management discipline.

scope creep Uncontrolled changes in a project's scope.

triple constraints of project management Time, cost, and scope.

Discussion Questions

1. You manage the department that will use a system being developed on a large project. After carefully reviewing the requirements definition document, you are positive that there are missing, ambiguous, inaccurate, and unclear requirements. The project manager is pressuring you for your sign-off because he has already received sign-offs from all of your coworkers. If you fail to sign off on the requirements, you are going to put the entire project at risk because the time frame is not negotiable. What should you do? Why? Support your answer.

2. You have been hired as a consultant to build an employee payroll system for a startup restaurant. Before you even have a chance to interview them, the two owners decided to independently come up with a list of their business requirements. When you combine their two lists, you have the following list:

   • All employees must have a unique employee ID.

   • The system must track employee hours worked based on employees' last names.

   • Employees must be scheduled to work a minimum of 8 hours per day.

   • Employee payroll is calculated by multiplying the employees' hours worked by $7.25.

   • Managers must be scheduled to work morning shifts.

   • Employees cannot be scheduled to work more than 8 hours per day.

   • Servers cannot be scheduled to work morning, afternoon, or evening shifts.

   • The system must allow managers to change and delete employees from the system.

   a. Highlight potential issues with the list.

   b. Add requirements that you think should be there but are not.

   c. What do you tell the owners when you derive your new list?

Collaboration Exercise PI6.1

Step 1: Background

One key element of Project Management is dealing with people. In fact, effective interaction skills are listed as one of the nine knowledge areas of the Project Management Body of Knowledge. To help their employees develop these skills, many companies use personality profiles to develop teams that have the best chance of success.

Step 2: Activity

Visit http://www.wiley.com/go/rainer/MIS4e/applytheconcept, and click on the link provided for the Collaboration Exercise for this Plug IT In. This link will take you to a Web site where you can complete a free personality profile. This profile, known as the Jung Typology Test, is based on the Meyers-Briggs personality test that is widely used by HR departments.

Complete this activity as an individual, and print a copy of your results. Then, build a Google Document with your team that includes everyone's results. Determine whether you have a good balance on all four criteria.

Step 3: Deliverable

As a team, determine whether you have a good mix of personalities that would work well together. If there is an area where you do not have good balance, it can pose a problem. Submit your team document that includes both your individual responses and your team's thoughts.

Problem-Solving Activities

1. Apply each of the five project management processes of the PMBOK to the following massive project. Then, discuss each process with regard to that project. Finally, use a search engine to find out where the project stands now. Would this be considered a runaway project? Why or why not?

Established in 1948, the National Health Service (NHS) in the United Kingdom is the largest healthcare organization in Europe. Controlled by the British government, it is also a vast bureaucracy, employing more than 1 million workers and providing a full range of healthcare services to the country's 60 million citizens.

The inspiration to digitize this huge bureaucracy first surfaced in 2001. At that time, much of the NHS was paper based and severely lagging in its use of technology, largely because of years of underinvestment. Hospitals throughout the United Kingdom were dealing with multiple vendors, many of them small to midsize UK software companies. Predictably, the NHS had become a hodgepodge of incompatible systems from different suppliers, with differing levels of functionality. The NHS had created silos of information that were not shared, or even sharable.

In an attempt to resolve these problems, in 2002 the British government initiated the National Program for Information Technology (NPIT), which includes England, Northern Ireland, and Wales (but not Scotland). The overall objective of the NPIT was to build a single, electronic healthcare record for every individual. In effect, this record would be a comprehensive, lifelong history of a patient's healthcare information, regardless of where, when, and by whom he or she was treated. In addition, the NPIT would provide healthcare professionals with access to a national data repository. Finally, it would support the NHS in collecting and analyzing information and monitoring health trends to make the best use of clinical and other resources.

A major obstacle for the NPIT was the sheer size of England's healthcare system. For example, in one year, the system served some 52 million people; it dealt with 325 million consultations in primary care, 13 million outpatient consultations, and 4 million emergency admissions; and it issued 617 million prescriptions.

The NPIT is a 10-year project designed to build new information systems to (1) connect more than 100,000 doctors, 380,000 nurses, and 50,000 other healthcare professionals; (2) allow for the electronic storage and retrieval of patient medical records; (3) permit patients to set up appointments via their computers; and (4) let doctors electronically transmit prescriptions to local pharmacies.

Specifically, the information systems that the NHS is attempting to deliver include the following:

- *The National Spine:* The National Spine is a database at the heart of the NPIT. The Spine encompasses individual electronic NHS lifelong care records for every patient in England, securely accessible by the patients and their health providers. The Spine will enable patients and providers to securely access integrated patient data, prescription ordering, proactive decision support, and best-practice reference data.

- *Choose and Book:* Choose and Book provides convenience for patients in electronically selecting the date, place, and time of their appointments.

- *N3:* The N3 national network is a massive, secure, broadband, virtual private network that provides the IT infrastructure and broadband connectivity for the NHS so that it can share patient information with various organizations. The N3 supports Choose and Book, electronic prescriptions, and electronic transfer of patient information.

The NHS first had McKinsey & Company conduct a study of the UK healthcare system. McKinsey concluded that the project was too large for any one vendor to act as prime contractor for all of it. Consequently, the NHS divided England into five regions—London, Eastern, Northeast, Northwest, and Southern—each with about 12 million people. Each of the five regions would be serviced by a prime IT vendor, known as a Local Service Provider (LSP).

The vendor selection process was conducted with great secrecy. Unfortunately, the secrecy led to most frontline healthcare providers being excluded from the vendor selection process. The NHS offered 10-year service contracts to the LSPs for the five regions, each worth about $2 billion.

The LSPs are responsible for developing and integrating information systems at a local level. The LSPs are also responsible for implementing clinical and administrative applications, which support the delivery of patient care and enable trusts to exchange data with the National Spine. (A trust is a regional healthcare agency that administers England's national healthcare programs). In addition, the LSPs provide the data centers to run all the applications.

Significantly, all of the NHS's contracts with the LSPs stipulated that vendors would not be paid until they delivered working systems. Because the vendors were the prime contractors, this stipulation also meant that the subcontractors would not be paid until they delivered working systems.

Accenture was named LSP for two regions. Computer Sciences Corporation (CSC), British Telecom (BT), and a Fujitsu-led alliance were named LSPs for the other three regions. BT was also given the contract to build both the N3 network and the National Spine. Atos Origin was chosen to provide Choose and Book.

As previously explained, the LSPs were to act as prime contractors for their respective regions, and they were able to choose their own software vendors and subcontractors. BT and the Fujitsu group selected IDX (now part of GE Healthcare), an established healthcare services and software provider, to develop health records software. Accenture and CSC chose iSoft, a UK-based supplier of healthcare software, for that function.

Developing this software presented many challenges. Both iSoft and IDX had to write some of the software from scratch. The difficulty was that the programmers and systems developers did not comprehend some of the terminology used by the British health system and, more important, how the British health system actually operated.

Compounding these problems was the decision by Accenture and CSC to select iSoft as its clinical and administrative software vendor. These companies were depending on iSoft's Lorenzo application suite, which at that time was still in development. However, iSoft seriously underestimated the time and effort necessary to develop the Lorenzo suite. As a result, under the collect-on-implementation contract that the LSPs had signed with the NHS, neither Accenture nor iSoft could generate revenue. In a catch-22 situation, this lack of revenue left iSoft short of the cash it needed to finish developmental work on Lorenzo.

The ongoing delay of Lorenzo left Accenture and CSC in a quandary. Should they continue to wait for Lorenzo, or should they lock into older, existing applications? Accenture opted to wait and use Lorenzo. In contrast, CSC chose to implement iSoft's existing line of products.

While waiting for Lorenzo, Accenture worked with general practitioners, as opposed to CSC, which focused almost entirely on hospitals. Accenture's problem was that the general practitioner implementation was extremely difficult because there are so many of them and the NHS had given them an option called GP Systems of Choice. This option stipulated that the doctors did not have to follow Accenture's lead in selecting a system but could, instead, choose on their own. This choice, in turn, further complicated the transfer of more than 10 years of data from old systems to the Spine-compliant systems being provided by Accenture. Typically, it cost about $9,000 and took six months to transfer the data of each practitioner.

Meanwhile, there were concerns with GE Healthcare's IDX as well. Fujitsu and BT had agreed to develop a Common Solution Program,

meaning that the two LSPs would develop common applications for two of England's regions. Because of time delays at IDX, Fujitsu and BT replaced the firm with Cerner, a U.S. healthcare IT company. This replacement caused additional time delays for the project.

The NPIT was originally budgeted at $12 billion, but that figure has risen to $24 billion as a result of the many problems encountered in developing the NPIT. By mid-2007, the NHS had delivered some of the program's key elements. For example, 1 million patient referrals to specialist care were made through Choose and Book and 97 percent of doctors' offices were connected to the N3 network.

However, many deliverables of the project have been delayed. In addition, the N3 network experienced more than a hundred failures in 2006. One network outage disrupted mission-critical computer services such as patient administration systems for three days.

Another problem was that the project has little support among healthcare workers. This problem stemmed from excluding frontline healthcare professionals in the early phases of the project. Therefore, it fell largely to the vendors and the bureaucrats to create the system. Physicians complained that the system focused too much on administrative needs and not enough on clinicians' concerns. A survey conducted in 2006 showed that only 38 percent of British general practitioners and nurses believed that the project was an important priority for the NHS, and only 13 percent believed that the project represented a good use of NHS resources.

The NHS policy to pay vendors only on delivery of working systems was shortsighted because the policy provided no flexibility to deal with vendors that encountered unexpected problems. In late 2006, Accenture announced that it was walking away from its contract with the NHS. Accenture did not say why it was exiting the project, but the company had set aside some $500 million to cover losses from its work in England.

As of mid-2007, the NHS itself had run short of funding, resulting in huge layoffs, possible closings of hospitals, and reductions in services. These problems were so serious that they prompted the British government to initiate an effort to bring costs under control. Some experts estimate that it will take another $15 billion (over the $24 billion already spent) to get the NPIT initiative fully functional.

The NHS is an incredibly political system. On the one hand, in mid-2014, the NHS continues to operate chronically short of funds. British analysts predict that by 2020, the largest healthcare system in the world will be operating a deficit six times larger than its annual operating budget, forcing the closure of up to 20 percent of Britain's hospitals, which are already inundated with patients.

On the other hand, proponents of the NHS say that it operates efficiently, delivering better health outcomes than the United States at half the cost. In fact, proponents state that NHS physicians, and patients, are more humble about their expectations of what their healthcare system should provide than physicians and patients in the United States.

Protecting Your Information Assets

LEARNING OBJECTIVES

PI7.1 Explain why it is critical that you protect your information assets.

PI7.2 Identify the various behavioral actions you can take to protect your information assets.

PI7.3 Identify the various computer-based actions you can take to protect your information assets.

PI7.1 How to Protect Your Assets: The Basics

We travel on our jobs, we work from home, and we access the Internet from home and from our favorite hot spots for any number of reasons—shopping, ordering products, planning trips, gathering information, and staying in touch with friends and family via e-mail. Unfortunately, every time we use our computers or access the Internet, we risk exposing both professional and personal information to people intent on stealing or exploiting that information. Therefore, we have prepared this Plug IT In to explain how you can protect your information assets when you are computing at home or while you are traveling.

Hopefully, when you are at work or when you access your university's network from home or on the road, you have the advantage of "industrial-strength" information security that your company or university's IS department has implemented. In all other cases, however, you are on your own, so it is *your* responsibility to protect yourself. Maintaining proper security is becoming even more critical because organized crime is increasingly turning its attention to home users. As businesses improve their information security, consumers become the next logical target. According to Symantec (www.symantec.com), which manufactures the Norton Internet security products, if you connected an unprotected personal computer to the Internet in 2003, it would have been attacked within 15 minutes. Today, that same computer will be attacked within seconds.

You can take two types of actions to protect your information assets: behavioral actions and computer-based actions (see Figure PI7.1). Behavioral actions are those actions that do not specifically involve a computer. Computer-based actions relate to safe computing. If you take both types of actions, you will protect your information and greatly reduce your exposure to fraud and identity theft.

Two types of actions can protect your information assets.

Before you go on . . .

1. Why is it so important that you take the responsibility for the security of your information assets?

2. Differentiate between behavioral and computer-based actions taken to protect your information assets.

Apply the Concept PI7.1

LEARNING OBJECTIVE PI7.1 Explain why it is critical that you protect your information assets.

STEP 1: Background (This is what you are learning.)

If you knew all the tricks the thieves would use at a department store, you would know how to fend them off. The same is true online, although it is often much more difficult to know when you have left yourself vulnerable. Sometimes the best strategy to assess your security is a simple tracking activity.

STEP 2: Activity (This is what you are doing.)

Spend one hour online. Keep track of every bit of information you put on the computer: user names, passwords, preferences you

complete, Web sites to which you submit your e-mail address, and so on. If you visit a site that can identify you, make note of that. Visit your junk mail at the end of the hour, and see how many messages have been sent to that folder since you began the activity.

STEP 3: Deliverable (This is what you turn in.)

Review your diary of events, and write a summary to your professor that explains why it is critical that you protect your information assets. Make certain to include specific references to your online activities.

PI7.2 | Behavioral Actions to Protect Your Information Assets

You should take certain behavioral actions to protect your information assets. We discuss these actions in this section.

General Behavioral Actions

You should never provide personal information to anyone in any format—physical, verbal, or electronic. As discussed in Chapter 7, you are vulnerable to social engineering attacks at home as well as at work. Therefore, it is critical to be on your guard at all times. For example, always verify that you are talking to authorized personnel before you provide personal information over the telephone. To accomplish this, you should hang up and call back the person or company, at a number that you obtain independent of the phone call. If the call is fraudulent, then the number the caller gives you will also be fraudulent. Credit card companies usually print their numbers on the back of their cards and/or on every statement. Further, you can find telephone numbers on your credit card company's Web site. Similarly, you should never click on a link received in an e-mail. If your bank e-mails you for an account update, then open your Web browser and go directly to the bank's Web site to complete this activity. If you click through the e-mail, you could fall victim to identity theft by giving your information to someone using a fake Web site.

One critical behavioral action you should take is to protect your Social Security number. Unfortunately, far too many organizations use this number to uniquely identify you. When you are requested to provide this number, ask why you cannot substitute some other combination of nine numbers and letters. If the person asking for your Social Security number—for example, someone at your physician's office—is not responsive, then ask to speak with a supervisor. *Remember:* You have to take the initiative here.

The good news is that the use of Social Security numbers for identification has rapidly decreased. For example, the federal Social Security Number Protection Act of 2007 places restrictions on the use of Social Security numbers for identification purposes. The bad news is that you might have to remember many more identifiers. However, your information will become more secure.

Another critical consideration involves your use of credit cards. Securing your credit cards is important because fraudulent credit card use is so widespread. One security measure you can take is to use credit cards with your picture on them. Although cashiers probably cannot read your signature on the back of your card, they can certainly compare your picture to your face. For example, Bank of America will place your picture on several of its credit cards for free. To access this service, visit www.bankofamerica.com/creditcards, click on "Manage Your Account" on the top menu, and then click on "Protect Your Account." Also, do not sign the back of your credit cards. Instead, write "Photo ID Required" on the back.

You may also want to use virtual credit cards, which offer you the option of shopping online with a disposable credit card number. For no extra charge, you sign up at your credit card provider's Web site and typically download software onto your computer. When you are ready to shop, you receive a randomly generated substitute 16-digit number that you can use at the online store. The number can be used only once or, in some cases, repeatedly, but only at the same store. It can also be used to purchase goods and services over the phone and through the mail, although it cannot be used for in-store purchases that require a traditional plastic card. Several companies offer virtual credit cards, but the major ones are Citibank and Discover. (Recall our discussion of virtual credit cards in Chapter 9.)

Also, pay very close attention to your credit card billing cycles. You should know, to within a day or two, when your credit card bills are due. If a bill does not arrive when expected, call your credit card company immediately. If your credit card is stolen and is being used fraudulently, the first thing the thief does is change the address on the account so that you do not receive the bill. Fortunately, you can view your credit card bills online and on most mobile devices. Further, most credit card issuers offer the option to receive your credit card bills via e-mail. This process eliminates postal mail theft as a problem. In addition, when you write checks to pay any of your accounts, particularly your credit card accounts, do not write your complete card number on the "For" line of your check. Instead, write only the last four digits.

Another important action is to limit your use of debit cards. Debit cards are linked to your bank account, meaning that a person who steals your debit card and personal identification number (PIN) can clean out your bank account. In contrast, your liability with credit cards is usually zero (or a small amount). Instead, your credit card company bears the liability for fraudulent charges, provided that you notify the company within 60 days of the theft.

Do not use a personal mailbox at your home or apartment for anything other than catalogs and magazines. Use a private mailbox or a P.O. (Post Office) box. It is far too easy for thieves to steal mail from home mailboxes when no one is at home for much of the day. Think about the wealth of information that could be stolen from your mailbox: credit card statements, bank statements, investment statements, and so on.

When you discard mail or old records, use a cross-cut, or confetti, shredder to cut them up. Recall our discussion of dumpster diving in Chapter 7. A single-cut shredder is not sufficient because, with enough time, a thief can reassemble the strips.

Another security option is to sign up with a company that provides proactive protection of your personal information. Examples of such companies are LifeLock (www.lifelock.com) and TrustedID (www.trustedid.com).

LifeLock and TrustedID allow customers to lock their credit files so that new lines of credit cannot be opened unless customers first unlock their existing files. When credit files are locked, merchants and banks must have verbal or written permission from the customer before opening new credit in the customer's name. Ordinarily, the locking process involves sending registered mail every 90 days to each of the three major credit agencies: Equifax (www.equifax.com), Experian (www.experian.com), and TransUnion (www.transunion.com). LifeLock and TrustedID perform this service for you and thus proactively monitor your various credit files.

CardCops provides an early warning service that notifies its customers that the company has found their personal information circulating on the Internet. It also collects compromised data on the Internet and makes them available to its customers and to merchants.

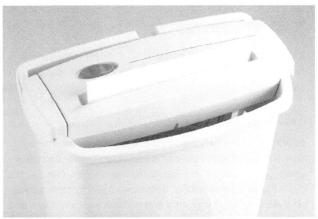

© discpicture/Shutterstock

A paper shredder is a simple, but effective tool to use to protect your identity.

What to Do in the Event of Identity Theft

Identity theft is on the rise, with more than 12.5 million victims reported in the United States in 2012. If you follow the behavioral and computer-based actions recommended in this Plug IT In, you will greatly reduce, but not eliminate, the chances that your identity will be stolen.

The Federal Trade Commission (FTC) provides the following instructions of what to do if your identity is stolen. You can review these instructions at https://www.consumer.ftc.gov /articles/pdf-0009-taking-charge.pdf. The recommended immediate steps are as follows:

1. Place an Initial Fraud Alert by contacting one of the three nationwide credit reporting companies: Equifax, Experian, or TransUnion. Report that you are a victim of identity theft, and request that the company put a fraud alert on your file. Also, make certain the company will contact the other two credit companies. Finally, keep a record of every phone call, letter, e-mail, or other forms of communication for your files.

2. Order your credit reports from each of the three credit reporting companies listed above. Inform them that you have placed an initial fraud alert, and request a free copy of your credit that lists only the last four digits of your Social Security number. Again, keep detailed records of everything you requested and received.

3. Create an Identity Theft Report that includes an Identity Theft Affidavit (you can find examples of this online) and a Police Report.

4. Finally, get in the habit of regularly reviewing your credit report. Pay particular attention to medical benefit explanations from your insurance company, and respond quickly to notices from the Internal Revenue Service (IRS). It is not necessary to obtain legal counsel to report identity theft, but it is a good idea. A lawyer who is experienced in this type of crime will be able to help you get back on your feet more quickly.

Before you go on . . .

1. Describe three behavioral actions you can take to thwart social engineering attacks.
2. Describe the steps you should take if you think your identity is stolen.

Apply the Concept PI7.2

LEARNING OBJECTIVE PI7.2 Identify the various behavioral actions you can take to protect your information assets.

STEP 1: Background

Education is extremely important in being able to determine whether something on the Web is legitimate. This section teaches you how to respond if your identity has been stolen. One way this could happen is via phishing, the process whereby a thief sends an e-mail that looks legitimate and requests your user name and login information so that he or she can update it. Once you send that information, your account—and possibly your identity—is no longer secure. (Recall our discussion of phishing in Chapter 7.)

STEP 2: Activity

Visit http://www.wiley.com/go/rainer/MIS4e/applytheconcept, and click on the link provided for PI7.2. This link will take you to a page on the Chase Web site that provides examples of false e-mails. Read over these e-mails, and develop five clues that suggest these messages may be fraudulent. Also, prepare a statement of best practices to pursue when you receive phishing e-mails.

STEP 3: Deliverable

Based on what you learned by reading this section and reviewing the Chase Web site in Step 2, identify the various behavioral actions you can take to protect your information assets.

PI7.3 | Computer-Based Actions to Protect Your Information Assets

You can take many computer-based actions to increase the security of your information. We first discuss how to determine where persons who use your computer have visited on the Internet. Next, we briefly explain how to access social networking sites safely. We then consider how to determine if your computer is infected with malicious software (malware) and what actions you can take to prevent such infections. Next, we discuss how to protect your portable devices—for example, laptops and flash drives—and the information they contain. We follow with discussions of other valuable computer-based actions, how to protect your privacy when using the Internet and e-mail, how to recover from a disaster, and how to protect yourself when you are computing wirelessly.

Determining Where People Have Visited on the Internet Using Your Computer

At home, you may have a single computer or several computers connected to a network. Although you may practice "safe computing," other people who use your computer might not. For example, you might have roommates who use your computer. Their friends could be using your computer as well. You cannot be certain that these individuals take the same safety precautions that you do. You can, however, identify the Internet sites that anyone who uses your computer has visited. To accomplish this task, check the browser history. It is important to note that all modern browsers have a "private browsing" mode in which the viewing history is not recorded. If someone uses private browsing on your computer, then you will not be able to check that person's browser history. The better practice is to keep your computer password protected so that users must enter the correct password to use it. Also, allow only people you trust to access your computer. If you are paying for the Internet connection, then you are responsible for the actions taken on your computer.

The Dangers of Social Networking Sites

You should never post personal information about yourself or your family in chat rooms or on social networking sites. In fact, you should access these Web sites and review any entries that you have made. Although you may never be able to recover all of your entries because someone could have saved copies of pictures you posted or took screen shots of your posts, you can take positive steps to remove them from the main host. The reason for these precautions is that potential employers are now searching these Web sites for information about you. Well-known social networking sites include MySpace, Friendster, Xanga, YouTube, Facebook, and Flickr. Additionally, several people have been robbed when they posted pictures on social networks that let criminals know they were not home.

The good news is that social networking Web sites have added features to give us more control over our information. The bad news is that the privacy settings are not always easy to find and use. Your first decision is whether to make your profile publicly available or to keep it more private. More than one-third of adult users allow everyone to see their profiles. In contrast, some two-thirds restrict access in some way.

On Facebook the default is a private profile, where users decide what information to make publicly available. To make privacy adjustments on Facebook, follow these steps:

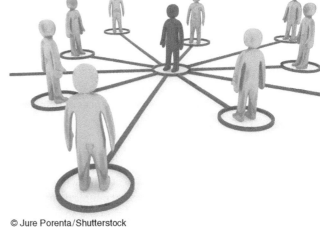

© Jure Porenta/Shutterstock

Social Media operates on openness, but safety is in maintaining some privacy.

- Click on "Settings."
- Click on "Privacy Settings."
- Work with the options you find there.

If you want to keep a low profile on Facebook, it is a good idea to look at the "Applications" section in Privacy Settings. You may have shielded parts of your profile from public access, but that does not mean that you have done the same for Facebook applications that have access to much of the same data by default. For a full explanation of Facebook's privacy settings, see www.facebook.com/privacy/explanation.php.

On LinkedIn, most people want their profiles to be public, and that is the default. The information that LinkedIn users share tends to be professional credentials, not details of their social lives, so there is less need for privacy. If you want additional privacy on LinkedIn, follow these steps:

- Click on "Account & Settings" from your home page.
- Scroll down to adjust your privacy settings.

One company, Reputation Defender (www.reputationdefender.com), will search out all information about you on the Internet and present it to you in the form of a report. Then, at your command, it will "destroy all inaccurate, inappropriate, hurtful, and slanderous information about you."

Determining If Your Computer Is Infected

There are several signs to look for if you think your computer system is infected with malicious software or malware (discussed in Chapter 7), including the following:

- Your computer shuts down unexpectedly by itself.
- Your computer does not start normally.
- Your computer exhibits erratic behavior, displaying some or all of these characteristics:
  - Your system unexpectedly runs out of memory on your computer's hard drive.
  - Your system continually runs out of main memory (RAM).
  - Programs take longer to load than normal.
  - Programs act erratically.
  - Your monitor displays strange graphics or messages.

– Your system displays an unusually high number of error messages.

– Your e-mail program sends messages to all the contacts in your address book without your knowledge or permission.

If you note any or all of these signs, then your computer might be infected with malware. You can then take the computer-based actions discussed later in this chapter to rid your computer of this software. However, taking the actions discussed in the next section will reduce your chances of being infected in the first place.

Computer Actions to Prevent Malware Infections

Many of the actions we discuss in this section are common sense, but surprisingly large numbers of people do not pay attention to them. Taking these steps will help you prevent a malware infection of your computer system. We begin by considering actions that you must *never* take with your computer.

Never open unrequested attachments to e-mail files, even if they are from people you know and trust. Their computers may have been compromised without their knowledge, in which case the e-mail could be a phishing attack. Never open attachments or Web links in e-mails from people you do not know. These attachments can infect your system with a worm or virus. Similarly, these Web links can be a phishing attack that can infect your system with a Trojan horse, turning your computer into a zombie or bot (short for robot). As we saw in Chapter 7, when this occurs your computer is no longer under your control.

Never accept files transferred to you during Internet chat or instant messaging sessions. These files are usually not from people you know, and they can infect your system.

Never download any files or software over the Internet from Web sites that you do not know. Never download files or software that you have not requested.

Test Your System. It is a good idea to test your system. Several Web sites provide free security tests. These tests send different types of messages to your computer to evaluate how well your system is protected from a variety of attacks. Free testing Web sites include Shields Up! (www.grc.com), Symantec Security Check (http://security.norton.com), and McAfee My SecurityStatus (search "McAfee My SecurityStatus" on the Web).

Microsoft provides a valuable scanning tool called the Microsoft Baseline Analyzer. This tool scans Windows-based computers for common security problems and generates individual security reports for each computer that it scans. The Baseline Analyzer can be downloaded for free. You can also run free malware scans on your computer. Several companies, including the following, will scan your computer to identify viruses, worms, and other malware, and offer suggestions about how to clean up your system if it is infected:

- Trend Micro (search the Web for "Trend Micro HouseCall")
- Panda Software (http://www.pandasecurity.com/usa)

Install a Security Suite on Your Computer. Security suites are software packages that contain a variety of security products, such as anti-malware software, spam protection, e-mail fraud protection, spyware detection, intrusion detection, and monitoring software. These suites provide a great deal of functionality in one package. There is a question of whether the individual functions in a security suite can match the combined functions of a group of individual products. Therefore, we discuss individual products in the next sections.

Well-known security suites include the following, but there are many others:

- ZoneAlarm Security Suite (www.zonealarm.com)
- McAfee Internet Security Suite (www.mcafee.com)
- Norton Internet Security (www.symantec.com)
- PC-cillin Internet Security (www.trendmicro.com)

Install an Anti-Malware Product on Your Computer. You should install an anti-malware product on your computer and use it, ideally at least once per week. Remember that every time you scan your computer for malware with your anti-malware product, you must update your malware definitions before you scan. Typically, anti-malware product vendors automatically update your malware definitions over the Web.

There are free anti-malware products and commercial anti-malware products. In general, the free products are adequate, but the commercial products offer more functionality. An excellent resource that offers a great deal of information on free anti-malware products, as well as many other security products, is www.thefreecountry.com. Go to Security > Free Antivirus Software to access their list of anti-malware products.

Well-known commercial anti-malware products include the following, but there are many others:

- Norton Anti-malware (www.symantec.com)
- PC-cillin (www.trendmicro.com)
- VirusScan (www.mcafee.com)

Install a Firewall on Your Computer. A personal firewall is software installed on your home computer that controls communications to and from your computer by permitting or denying communications based on your security settings. A personal firewall usually will protect only the computer on which the software is installed. Nevertheless, firewalls perform essential functions.

Essentially, firewalls should make your computer invisible. This means that your firewall should not respond to Internet requests to ports (i.e., communications links to your computer) that are not used for common Internet use. In effect, your computer operates in stealth mode on the Internet.

Firewalls also should alert you to suspicious behavior. They should tell you when a program or connection is attempting to do something you have not instructed it to do, such as download software or run a program such as ActiveX. ActiveX (by Microsoft), which can execute programs downloaded from Internet Explorer, can be exploited by attackers trying to compromise your computer. It can be managed on all Windows computers. Search the Web to find instructions on managing ActiveX on your particular operating system and Internet browser.

Firewalls should block outbound connections that you do not initiate. Your firewall should not let your computer access the Internet on its own. If your computer tries to access the Internet by itself, this is a sure sign that it is infected with malware.

As with anti-malware programs, firewall products can be either free or commercially produced. Again, the free products are adequate, but the commercial products offer more functionality. For a list of free firewall software, search "about.com free firewalls."

Many companies offer commercial firewall software. These are some of the best-known commercial firewall products:

- ZoneAlarm Security Suite (www.zonealarm.com)
- Norton Internet Security (www.symantec.com)
- PC-cillin Internet Security (www.trendmicro.com)
- McAfee Internet Security (www.mcafee.com)
- F-Secure Internet Security (www.f-secure.com)
- Panda Platinum Internet Security (www.pandasecurity.com)

It is a good idea to test your firewall. However, it is best to use only those test Web sites that are run by actual firewall or security software companies. A good firewall test site is the McAfee HackerWatch site at www.hackerwatch.org/probe. The HackerWatch site allows you to perform a basic probe test on your computer to determine whether your firewall is blocking ports that may be vulnerable.

Install an Antispyware Product on Your Computer. As with anti-malware products and firewalls, free antispyware products are adequate, but commercial antispyware products offer greater functionality. Free antispyware products include the following:

- Ad-Aware SE Personal (www.lavasoft.com)
- Spybot Search&Destroy (www.safer-networking.org)

Well-known commercial antispyware products include the following, but there are many others:

- Spy Sweeper (www.webroot.com)
- SpyCatcher (www.tenebril.com)

In addition, several companies offer free spyware scans:

- Spy Audit (www.webroot.com)
- Zonelabs (www.zonealarm.com)
- Norton (www.symantec.com)

Install Monitoring Software on Your Computer. Monitoring software logs keystrokes, e-mails, applications, windows, Web sites, Internet connections, passwords, chat conversations, Web cams, and even screenshots. Companies that offer monitoring software include the following:

- SpyAgent (www.spytech-Web.com)
- SpyBuddy (www.exploreanywhere.com)
- WinSpy (www.win-spy.com)

Install Content-Filtering Software on Your Computer. Content-filtering software performs many functions. It can block access to undesirable Web sites, and it can record and view all of the Web sites that you or other users have visited. It can also record both sides of chat conversations from AOL Instant Messenger (AIM and AIM Triton), Yahoo! Messenger, and MSN Messenger.

Content-filtering software provides many filter categories, thus enabling you to selectively filter content. Companies that offer this software include the following:

- Cybersitter (www.cybersitter.com)
- NetNanny (www.netnanny.com)
- CyberSpy (www.cyberspyware.com)

Internet Explorer's Content Advisor utility allows you to block access to Web sites that meet specified criteria and to set your own tolerance levels for various types of Internet content. To activate and configure Content Advisor, search the Web for instructions specific to your version of Windows and Internet Explorer.

Install Antispam Software on Your Computer. Antispam software helps you to control spam. Well-known commercial antispam products include the following, but there are many others:

- Cloudmark (www.cloudmark.com)
- MailFrontier Desktop (www.sonicwall.com/)
- SpamKiller (www.mcafee.com)
- Norton Antispam (www.symantec.com)

- SpamGourmet (www.spamgourmet.com)
- SpamAssassin (http://spamassassin.apache.org)

You might also want to set up multiple free e-mail accounts, such as accounts on Hotmail and Gmail. Then, as you surf the Internet and are asked for your e-mail address, you can use one of these accounts rather than your home or business e-mail account. When your free e-mail accounts are full of spam, you can close them and open new accounts.

Manage Patches.   Companies typically release software patches to repair security problems. You should download and install all patches immediately—for example, patches for Windows. If you do not, then your computer will be extremely vulnerable to attack. Both Microsoft and Apple provide automatic downloads for updates and patches. It is recommended that you configure your system to automatically download and install these updates so that your computer is not left vulnerable.

Use a Browser Other Than Internet Explorer.   You might consider using a browser other than Internet Explorer, such as Firefox (www.mozilla.org), Opera (www.opera.com), Safari from Apple (www.apple.com/safari/download), or Google Chrome (www.google.com/chrome). These browsers are not impregnable, but they are less prominent, and hackers, at least so far, have paid less attention to them.

Use an Operating System Other Than Windows.   The two main alternatives to Windows 7 and Windows 8 are Apple's Mac OS X and Linux. These two operating systems are not invulnerable, but they are both based on UNIX, which makes them inherently more secure than any version of Windows. (UNIX is an operating system developed by AT&T in the 1960s and 1970s that usually runs on servers rather than on desktops.) In addition, Linux and Mac OS X have smaller market shares than Windows and thus are less attractive targets for malware.

Protecting Your Portable Devices and Information

Theft or loss of laptops, notebook computers, tablets, thumb drives, and smartphones, as well as the data contained on these devices, is a significant problem. You can take many proactive steps to protect portable devices and their data, including preventing the theft, using two-factor authentication, and encrypting your data. You can also take reactive steps after a theft or loss has occurred. We consider all of these actions in this section.

Before we discuss these steps, there are two commonsense precautions that many people forget. First, keep your laptop in an inconspicuous container. Laptop cases with your company logo simply draw the attention of thieves. Second, do not leave your laptop unattended in plain view—for example, in your car where it can be seen. Instead, lock it in the trunk.

One strategy to prevent the theft of a portable device is to use alarms. Laptop security systems operate by detecting motion, analyzing the motion to determine whether a threat exists, and, if it does, implementing responses. These alarms are battery powered, they are independent of the computer operating system, and they operate whether the laptop is on or off. If a laptop armed with a security system is carried beyond a perimeter specified by the user, then the alarm assumes the laptop is being stolen. In these cases, it can prevent access to the operating system, secure passwords, and encryption keys, and it can sound an audible alarm. One laptop security system is Absolute Software's LoJack for Laptops (www.absolute.com).

Two-factor authentication (discussed in Chapter 7) requires two forms of identification to access your computing device. The first authentication factor uses a token or biometrics. The second factor is your personal password. A token generates a one-time password that you must enter within a specified time limit. This password typically consists of six digits, which appear on the token's LCD screen. Companies offering tokens for two-factor authentication include Authenex (www.authenex.com), Kensington (www.kensington.com), and SecuriKey (www.securikey.com).

Fingerprints are the biometric used for two-factor authentication, by incorporating fingerprint readers into the laptop itself. See IBM (www.ibm.com) and Microsoft (www.microsoft.com). You can also use fingerprint authentication on your thumb drive with the SanDisk Cruzer (www.sandisk.com), the Lexar JumpDrive TouchGuard (www.lexar.com), the Sony MicroVault (www.sony.net), and the Kanguru Bio Slider (www.kanguru.com).

Data encryption provides additional protection by turning data into meaningless symbols that can be deciphered only by an authorized person. You can encrypt some or all of the data on your computer by using built-in encryption, folder-based encryption, or full-disk encryption. If you are not certain how to encrypt files on your particular operating system, search the Web for instructions on how to complete this task. Alternatively, you can purchase a third-party product from firms such as Beachhead Solutions (www.beachheadsolutions.com) and Dell (www.dell.com), which provide applications that allow you to encrypt files and folders.

Another step you can take to improve your security is to encrypt your entire hard drive, including your applications. See TrendMicro (www.trendmicro.com), the Kanguru Wizard (www.kanguru.com), and the PCKey (www.kensington.com).

If your laptop is lost or stolen, then you can use laptop-tracing tools or device reset/remote kill tools. For example, the XTool Computer Tracker (www.computersecurity.com), and PC PhoneHome (www.pcphonehome.com) provide transmitters that secretly send a signal to their respective company control centers via telephone or the Internet. This signal enables the company to track your computer's location, with the help of the local authorities, Internet service providers, and telephone companies.

You can also use device reset/remote kill tools to automatically eliminate specified data on a lost or stolen laptop to prevent it from being compromised or misused. The solution works even when other security software or encryption methods fail. One company providing these solutions is Beachhead Solutions (www.beachheadsolutions.com).

Other Actions That You Can Take on Your Computer

Other actions you can perform on your computer to increase your protection include detecting worms and Trojan horses, turning off peer-to-peer file sharing, searching for new and unusual files, detecting spoofed (fake) Web sites, and adjusting the privacy settings on your computer. Often, Microsoft provides tips on how to handle problems on a Windows computer. Mac computers have built-in software to protect, detect, and remove malware automatically. If you are interested in learning how these features work, look up XProtect, Gatekeeper, and Malware Removal Tool (MRT) for Mac.

How to Detect a Worm. Worms are malicious programs that perform unwanted actions on your computer (see Chapter 7). They exhibit several characteristics you can watch for:

- Your system exhibits unexplained hard disk activity.
- Your system connects to the Internet by itself without any action on your part.
- Your system seems to be short on available memory.
- Your family, friends, or colleagues notify you that they have received an odd e-mail message from you that they are certain you did not send.

Ordinarily, your anti-malware software should detect and remove worms. However, if your Windows-based computer is currently infected with a worm, you may not be able to delete that file. In this case, you will have to reboot (start up) your system from a bootable disk and then delete the worm file from the Command Prompt. Then normally, when you reboot your system, the worm file should no longer be present.

How to Detect a Trojan Horse. Trojan horses are malicious programs disguised as, or embedded within, legitimate software (see Chapter 7). On a Windows computer, you can determine if your computer is infected with a Trojan horse by using a DOS-based utility program called Netstat. The steps to use Netstat will vary depending on the version of Windows you are running. However, it is easy to find instructions online.

© Popovici Ioan/Shutterstock

The Trojan horse virus is named for the Trojan Horse offered to Troy by Greece during the Trojan War. It was part of a plan to destroy the city.

How to Detect Fake Web Sites. A fake Web site is typically created to mimic a well-known, legitimate site with a slightly different or confusing URL. The attacker tries to trick people into going to the spoofed site and providing valuable information by sending out e-mail messages and hoping that some users will not notice the incorrect URL. (We discussed this attack, known as phishing, in Chapter 7.) Products that help detect fake Web sites include the SpoofStick and McAfee's SiteAdvisor. These products are not definitive solutions, but they are helpful.

The SpoofStick (www.spoofstick.com) helps users detect fake Web sites by prominently displaying a new toolbar in your browser that indicates which site you are actually surfing. For example, if you go to Amazon's Web site, the SpoofStick toolbar says, "You're on amazon.com." However, if you go to a fake Web site that pretends to be Amazon, the SpoofStick toolbar displays the actual IP address of the Web site you are surfing; for example, "You're on 137.65.23.117."

Similarly, during a secure communications session with Internet Explorer, you can move your mouse over the padlock to verify that (1) the padlock is genuine and not a fraudulent graphic and (2) the site uses a transport layer security (TLS) certificate (discussed in Chapter 7) that contains the correct information about the company to which you are connected. McAfee's SiteAdvisor (www.siteadvisor.com) sticks a green, yellow, or red safety logo next to search results on Google, Yahoo!, and MSN. It also puts a color-coded button in the Internet Explorer toolbar. Mousing over the button displays details as to why the Web site is good or bad. SiteAdvisor also scores Web sites based on the excessive use of pop-up advertisements, how much spam the Web site will generate if you reveal your e-mail address, and whether the site spreads spyware and adware.

Protecting Your Privacy

In today's hostile Internet environment, you must use strong passwords (discussed in Chapter 7) and adjust the privacy settings on your computer. You may also wish to protect your privacy by surfing the Web and e-mailing anonymously. In this section, we discuss these actions.

Use Strong Passwords. You can use the Secure Password Generator at PCTools to create strong passwords. The Generator lets you select the number and type of characters in your password.

Remembering multiple passwords is difficult. You can use free software such as Password Safe or Roboform (www.roboform.com) to help you remember your passwords and maintain them securely.

How to Adjust Your Privacy Settings on Your Computer. Both Windows and Mac allow you to set personal privacy settings on your computer. Because this process is different for each operating system and space is limited, it is recommended that you visit their respective Web sites for specifics. We do, however, want to make a note about cookies.

Note: A first-party cookie either originates on, or is sent to, the Web site you are currently viewing. These cookies are commonly used to store information, such as your preferences when visiting that site. In contrast, a third-party cookie either originates on, or is sent to, a different Web site from the one you are currently viewing. Third-party Web sites usually provide some content on the Web site you are viewing. For example, many sites rely on advertising from third-party Web sites, which frequently use cookies. A common use for third-party cookies is to track your browsing history for advertising or other marketing purposes.

How to Surf the Web Anonymously. Many users worry that knowledge of their IP addresses is enough for outsiders to connect their online activities to their "real-world" identities. Depending on his or her technical, physical, and legal access, a determined party (such as a government prosecutor) may be able to do so, especially if he or she is assisted by the records of the ISP that has assigned the Internet Protocol (IP) address. To protect their privacy against this type of activity, many people surf the Web and e-mail anonymously.

Surfing the Web anonymously means that you do not make your IP address or any other personally identifiable information available to the Web sites that you are visiting. There are two ways to surf the Web anonymously: You can use an anonymizer Web site as a proxy server, or you can use an anonymizer as a permanent proxy server in your Web browser.

A *proxy server* is a computer to which you connect, which in turn connects to the Web site you wish to visit. You remain anonymous because only the information on the proxy server is visible to outsiders.

Keep in mind that although anonymous surfing is more secure than regular surfing, it is also typically slower. Anonymizers include Anonymize (www.anonymize.net), Anonymizer (www.anonymizer.com), Ultimate Privacy (www.ultimate-anonymity.com), and GhostSurf Platinum. These sites allow you to surf the Web anonymously because the anonymizer acts as a permanent proxy server on your computer.

How to E-Mail Anonymously. The reasons for anonymous e-mail are the same as those for surfing the Web anonymously. Basically, you want to protect your privacy. When you e-mail anonymously, your e-mail messages cannot be tracked back to you personally, to your location, or to your computer. Essentially, your e-mail messages are sent through another server belonging to a company—known as a *re-mailer*—that provides anonymous e-mail services. The recipient of your e-mail sees only the re-mailer's header on your message. In addition, the re-mailer encrypts your messages so that if they are intercepted, they cannot be read. One possible drawback to utilizing a re-mailer is that your intended recipients might not open your e-mail because they will not know it is from you.

Leading commercial re-mailers include CryptoHeaven (www.cryptoheaven.com), Ultimate Privacy (www.ultimate-anonymity.com), and Hushmail (www.hushmail.com). The commercial version of Pretty Good Privacy (PGP) is available at www.symantec.com.

In addition, several free products for anonymous e-mailing and encryption are widely available. For example, the free, open-source version of Pretty Good Privacy, called Open PGP, is available at www.pgpi.org. For a list of these free products and a review of each one, visit http://netsecurity.about.com/. The Outlook e-mail client that comes with Microsoft Office also allows you to encrypt outgoing e-mail messages. This product is based on public key technology (discussed in Chapter 7), so you must download and purchase a digital certificate. The first time you send an encrypted message, Microsoft takes you through the steps necessary to obtain your certificate. Thawte (www.thawte.com) is a company that offers a free personal digital e-mail certificate.

It is a good idea to periodically check the trusted certificate authorities that are configured in your browser and verify that those companies can be trusted. Again, this process will vary depending on the browser you use. Most browsers make these settings easy to review, so you should be able to find instructions through a simple Web search.

Erasing Your Google Search History. If you have signed up for Google's Personalized Search, then you can follow these steps to erase your search history. First you sign in to your Google account at www.google.com/psearch. You can examine the Search History page and choose days on the calendar to see every search you have made since you created your Google account. Click on the Remove Items button. Remember, however, that even after you remove items from your computer, logs and backups will still exist on Google's servers. To prevent Google from collecting this information in the future, select items such as "Web," "Images," and "News" about which you do not want data collected, and then press the "Pause" button.

Preparing for Personal Disasters

Disasters are not limited to businesses. You can experience disasters at home, such as fires and floods. Therefore, you should take certain steps to protect your information assets, whether they are stored on your computer (digital form) or in another form (hard copy). First and foremost, you should have a safety deposit box at your bank for your important papers. You should also have a fireproof safe at home where you can store other important papers. You should make a regular backup of your key files and keep these backups in the safe as well. You might also want to encrypt your backup files if they contain sensitive information.

Both Windows and Mac have fairly easy processes for restoring backup files. Mac computers use a built-in program called Time Machine; in Windows this program is named System Restore. It is important to have a backup of your files in the event that you need to restore them.

Several third-party companies offer external backup drives that include their own backup and restore systems. Before you purchase one, make certain it is compatible with the operating system you are using.

In recent years, the cloud (see Plug IT In 4) has also become a viable backup alternative. You do not necessarily need to back up your entire computer; rather, you might want to save only your important documents. Dropbox.com, Box.com, Google Drive, Apple's iCloud, Microsoft SkyDrive, and many other companies offer substantial cloud storage space where you can back up photos, videos, and other important files.

Wireless Security

Many home users have implemented a wireless local area network (LAN). The security considerations for wireless networks are greater than those for wired networks. The reason for this is simple. If you are wirelessly computing and communicating, then you are broadcasting, and therefore, by definition, you are nonsecure. The most common reason for intruders to connect to a nonsecure wireless network is to gain access to the Internet. Intruders might also connect in order to use your network as a base for spamming or for other unethical or illegal activities. Finally, they may do so to gain access to your sensitive personal information.

Unfortunately, recent studies have indicated that three-fourths of all home wireless users have not activated any security features to protect their information. Unless you take the steps we discuss here, your information assets are extremely vulnerable.

Hide Your Service Set Identifier (SSID). Your wireless router, which connects your home network with your ISP, comes with a default SSID that is the same for thousands or millions of routers made by the manufacturer. Therefore, an attacker can search for wireless networks by looking for a relatively small number of default SSIDs. For this reason, you should (1) change your default SSID to a unique SSID and (2) configure your wireless home network to stop broadcasting the SSID. A step-by-step guide to perform these security measures is available online: Simply search "about.com change default SSID."

Use Encryption. To avoid broadcasting in the clear, you must use encryption with your wireless home network. Wireless equivalent protocol (WEP) is an old protocol that is now very easy to crack and therefore should *not* be used. Instead, you should use Wi-Fi Protected Access (WPA2), which is the second generation of WPA. WPA2 is much stronger than WEP and will protect your encryption against attackers. (*Note:* Your wireless router must support WPA2. Otherwise, use WPA rather than WEP.) In addition, you should use a strong passphrase of at least 20 random characters on your router. (Chapter 7 provides specific instructions for creating strong passphrases.)

Filter Out Media Access Control (MAC) Addresses. Every piece of networking hardware has a unique identification number called a media access control (MAC) address that looks like this: 00-00-00-00-00-00. (This MAC address is only an example.) You should compile the MAC address of all computers on your home wireless network. Then, instruct your router to connect only with those computers, and deny access to all other computers that attempt to connect with your network.

Limit Internet Protocol (IP) Addresses. You should instruct your router to allow only a certain number of IP addresses to connect to your network. Ideally, the number of IP addresses will be the same as the number of computers on your network.

Sniff Out Intruders. A variety of wireless intrusion detection systems will monitor your wireless network for intruders, alert you when intruders are on your network, display their IP addresses and their activity, and even inform them that you know that they are there. Commercial products include the IBM Internet Security Systems (www.ibm.com) wireless scanner and AirSnare which is a free wireless intrusion detection system.

Using a Public Hotspot. When you travel, keep in mind that most public wireless providers and hotspots employ *no security measures at all*. As a result, everything you send and receive is in the clear and is not encrypted. Many intruders go to public hotspots specifically to listen in on the wireless computing and communications taking place there. If you must compute wirelessly at a public hotspot, you should take several precautions before you connect.

- Use virtual private networking (VPN) technology to connect to your organization's network (discussed in Chapter 7).
- Use Remote Desktop to connect to a computer that is running at your home.
- Configure the Windows firewall to be "on with no exceptions."
- Only use Web sites that use secure sockets layer (SSL) for any financial or personal transactions.

Test Your Wireless Network. After you have finished all of the necessary steps to protect your wireless home network, it is a good idea to test the network for vulnerabilities. A free Wi-Fi vulnerability scanner has been created by eEye and is available for download (just search "eEye download" for the link). This tool scans your vicinity looking for wireless devices to test. When you run it, it generates a detailed report that outlines all of the security problems it finds.

Wireless Security Software. For extra security, you can purchase wireless security programs. Trend Micro (www.trendmicro.com) has added Wi-Fi Intrusion Detection to PC-cillin, which also includes a personal firewall, antivirus software, and antispyware software. The software warns you when an unknown user tries to access your wireless network. Zonelabs (www.zonealarm.com) has a product called ZoneAlarm Wireless Security that automatically detects wireless networks and helps secure them.

McAfee (www.mcafee.com) provides a free scan to check the security of the wireless network connection that you are using. The scan works only with Internet Explorer. Go to www.mcafee.com, click the section for home users, and look under Free Services for McAfee Wi-Fi scan.

Mobile Security

In recent years, technology has created a highly mobile computing market that previously was almost unimaginable. Several basic features of modern information technologies made these innovations possible. First, computer processors have become physically smaller and computationally more powerful, thus enabling small devices to operate at amazing speeds. Second, computer memory has become physically smaller while dramatically expanding its capacity. Consequently, small computers can now store and manipulate massive amounts of data. Third, the rise in high-speed Internet access over multiple channels (cellular and Wi-Fi) allows for near ubiquitous connectivity and distributed processing (cloud computing). Finally, input methodologies have migrated to touch screens. As a result, smaller and lighter devices now have larger useful screens. Together, these factors have created the rapidly expanding mobile smartphone/tablet market. Today, that market is dominated by two operating systems: Apple's iOS and Google's Android.

As with all new technologies, issues have arisen concerning how people utilize and secure (or don't secure) their mobile devices. Below we discuss some general principles that apply to securing all mobile devices.

Mobile Best Practices. There are a few habits you should develop no matter what mobile device you are using. First, always use a strong password. Your e-mail, contacts, photos, billing information, and other personal data are stored on your mobile device, and a strong password can help protect your information. A strong password is one that is longer and more difficult to crack than the simple four-digit password that some devices allow. Your settings will allow you to create a password that is much more difficult to figure out. Avoid using common words, names (including your name!), birthdays, and other information that is easy to guess.

In addition, you should keep an encrypted backup all of the information on your device. Most of us use our devices to store pictures, music, videos, contacts, files, e-mails, text messages, calendars, and account information. With so much personal information, it is imperative that you regularly back it up. Fortunately, you have quite a few choices here. If you have an Apple iOS device, your backup will either remain on your personal computer or in iCloud (Apple's proprietary cloud product). Both methods are acceptable, and users have different reasons for choosing one over the other. The local backup keeps a complete copy of your data on your computer, which it can restore to your device. The iCloud backup maintains information about settings and apps, but this information has to be re-downloaded from the app store.

In contrast to iOS, Android devices do not offer a built-in backup system. However, there are several apps on the market that perform this task for you. Various apps will back up your photos, text messages, settings, and other key data. MyBackup Pro (www.rerware.com/Android-Backup/) will keep a complete backup of everything.

Also, make use of the auto-lock feature on your device. We all lay down our devices momentarily, and sometimes they are still on and unlocked. Therefore, you want your device to lock itself as quickly as possible so that an unauthorized user cannot gain access to your information.

Currently, mobile devices allow only one user account. Therefore, a device should be used only by the individual whose account is on the device. Perhaps one day you will be able to create multiple user accounts on mobile devices. Until then, do not share or loan any personal device that contains your personal information. If you have an unused device that you loan, make certain to restore it to factory settings so that none of your personal information is still on the device when the borrower uses it.

Today, most smartphones have a global positioning system (GPS) chip to receive location signals from the GPS satellites. (Recall our discussion of GPS in Chapter 10.) This information was originally intended exclusively for navigation purposes. Today, however, many apps use your position to offer location-based advertising, tags within social apps, and other commercial purposes. To prevent every app you download from sharing your location, access your privacy settings, and select the apps you want to share this information with.

As with your computers, you should keep your operating systems updated. All smartphones have a feature to autodownload and install recent apps and security features. Although you may want to wait a day or two to see if there are problems with the latest update, in general you want to update your mobile device as soon as possible. Many updates offer critical patches to vulnerabilities of the operating systems that hackers could exploit.

Be careful with the apps you download. Both Apple and Google offer virtual stores for you to find and purchase apps, but the clearing procedure is not the same with each system. Apple reviews and clears each app before allowing it to be posted on its store. In contrast, Google's Android system allows users to download apps from any Web site and install them. To be safe, follow these tips:

- Download only from a reputable app store such as Google Play or Amazon Appstore where you can read user reviews. Typically, if people have experienced problems with a particular app, it will be obvious in the ratings.
- Do not download apps that do not have ratings!
- Download only official apps. Unfortunately, it is fairly easy to create a fraudulent app that appears to be from a legitimate company. In addition to using a reputable store and reading reviews, try to determine who developed and owns the app before you download it.
- Use an antivirus program such as Lookout Mobile Security (www.lookout.com), Symantec (www.symantec.com/mobility), or AVG (www.avg.com/us-en/for-mobile).

Before you go on . . .

1. Describe two actions you should take to prevent malware infections.
2. Describe two actions you should take to protect the information on your mobile devices.
3. Describe two actions that you can take to protect your privacy.
4. Describe two mobile best practices for information security.

Apply the Concept PI7.3

LEARNING OBJECTIVE PI7.3

STEP 1: Background

Computer-based actions are vital to computer security. Significantly, all of these actions begin with the decision to protect your information assets. A vast array of tools is available to help you protect your information. Try to become familiar with these tools, many of which are presented in this chapter.

STEP 2: Activity

Visit http://www.wiley.com/go/rainer/MIS4e/applytheconcept, and click on the link provided for PI7.3. This link will take you to a McAfee product Web site called "Site Advisor." Look for the "How

It Works" link at the top of the page. You will see that this simple tool makes it easy for you to be more aware of the security level of the sites you are visiting.

Download and install this tool, and browse the Web for 30 minutes or so. Visit the sites you routinely go to, and write down the security rating McAfee gives each one. Does this activity make you want to change any of your browsing behaviors?

STEP 3: Deliverable

Considering what you learned in Step 2, identify at least five computer-based actions you can take to protect your information assets. Submit those actions to your instructor in a Word document.

Summary

1. **Explain why it is critical that you protect your information assets.**

We live in a digital world. Unfortunately, every time we use our computers or access the Internet, we risk exposing both professional and personal information to people looking to steal or exploit that information. It is your

responsibility to protect yourself in our hostile digital environment. Protecting yourself is becoming even more critical because organized crime is increasingly turning its attention to home users. As businesses improve their information security, consumers become the next logical target.

2. **Identify the various behavioral actions you can take to protect your information assets.**

- Do not provide personal information to strangers in any format (physical, verbal, or electronic).
- Protect your Social Security number.
- Use credit cards with your picture on them.
- Do not sign the back of your credit cards. Instead, write "Photo ID Required."
- Pay very close attention to your credit card billing cycles.
- Limit your use of debit cards.
- Do not use a personal mailbox at your home for anything other than catalogs and magazines.
- Use a cross-cut, or confetti, shredder.
- Sign up with a company that provides proactive protection of your personal information.

3. **Identify the various computer-based actions you can take to protect your information assets.**

- Identify the Internet sites that anyone who used your computer visited.
- Never post personal information about yourself or your family in chat rooms or on social networking sites. Use the privacy features provided by social networking sites to limit public access to your profile.
- Never open unrequested attachments to e-mail files, even from people you know and trust.
- Never open attachments or Web links in e-mails from people you do not know.
- Never accept files transferred to you during Internet chat or instant messaging sessions.
- Never download any files or software over the Internet from Web sites that you do not know.
- Never download files or software that you have not requested.
- Test your system.
- Run free malware scans on your computer.
- Install an anti-malware product on your computer, and use it (ideally at least once per week).
- Install a firewall on your computer.
- Install an antispyware product on your computer.
- Install monitoring software on your computer.
- Install content-filtering software on your computer.
- Install antispam software on your computer.
- Install proactive intrusion detection and prevention software on your computer.

- Manage patches.
- Use a browser other than Internet Explorer.
- Use a laptop security system.
- Use two-factor authentication.
- Use encryption.
- Use laptop-tracing tools or device reset/remote kill tools.
- Look for new and unusual files.
- Detect fake Web sites.
- Use strong passwords.
- Surf the Web anonymously.
- E-mail anonymously.
- Adjust the privacy settings on your computer.
- Erase your Google search history.
- Personal disaster preparation: back up, back up, back up!
- Wireless security
  - Hide your service set identifier (SSID).
  - Use encryption.
  - Filter out media access control (MAC) addresses.
  - Limit IP addresses.
  - Sniff out intruders.
  - Change the default administrator password on your wireless router to something not easily guessed.
  - Use VPN technology to connect to your organization's network.
  - Use Remote Desktop to connect to a computer that is running at your home.
  - Configure Windows firewall to be "on with no exceptions."
  - Visit only those Web sites that use SSL for any financial or personal transactions.
  - Use wireless security programs.
- Mobile security
  - Use a strong password.
  - Keep an encrypted backup.
  - Use your device's auto-lock feature.
  - Do not share your device.
  - Be careful with whom you share your location.
  - Keep your operating system updated.
  - Use caution with the apps you download.

Discussion Questions

1. Why is it so important for you to protect your information assets? Can you assume that your organization's MIS department will do it for you?

2. Discuss the differences between behavioral actions that you should take and computer-based actions that you should take.

Problem-Solving Activities

1. Using one product suggested in this Plug IT In or a product you find, do the following:

   - Test or scan your computer for malware.

   - Test your firewall.

   - Scan your computer for spyware.

2. Follow the steps in this Plug IT In to see if you have a Trojan horse on your computer.

Index